**A
CRITICAL
APPROACH
TO
CHILDREN'S
LITERATURE**

A Critical Approach To Children's Literature

James Steel Smith
Department of English
San Fernando Valley State College

McGraw-Hill Book Company
New York, St. Louis
San Francisco
Toronto
London
Sydney

To my wife Ruth and daughter Martha

PREFACE

*T*his book has grown out of my teaching of college courses in literature and my writing of poetry. Each of these activities involved both children's literature and adult literature, and, together, the writing and teaching forced me to consider the problems peculiar to children's literature and to adult literature and the relationships—the differences and similarities—between them.

As a college teacher of both adult literature (contemporary British literature, the Romantic Age, etc.) and children's literature, I have found my-self looking for the fundamental criteria common to all literature and, at the same time, the special characteristics of form that distinguish children's literature and adult literature from each other. And the literary questions and values of which I gradually became aware as a teacher of literature appeared to be similar to those I encountered as a writer of children's and adult's poems. In two decades of work as a poet "for children" and as a poet "for adults," I have moved toward the realization that in both kinds of poetry I had to cope with essentially the same creative problems but under somewhat different circumstances, in different forms.

My basic assumptions in writing the following book have been that children's literature, like all other literature, is susceptible of serious critical analysis and understanding and that application of relevant critical questions to individual works can assist the adult—parent, teacher, librarian—in his own reading of children's writings and then in his bringing them to children. Such a critical approach need not be ponderous or pretentious. It simply seeks to avoid the inclination either to patronize children's books—to look down on them as poor cousins to adult literature—or to become uncritically indulgent.

As I indicate more fully in Chapter 1, "Thinking about Children's Literature," this book views children's literature primarily as literature, not mainly as psychology or as cultural history or as ethical instruction or as a source of historical, scientific, social or other information. These latter aspects of children's reading are not overlooked here, but they do not provide the central focus. I have, instead, chosen to give more attention than is often devoted to the nature of the literary experience, to concern the reader less with the topical subject matter of children's books than with the special worlds authors have created out of experience. The view in which this approach originates is that children's literature is not just about things—fairies or dogs or locomotives or airplanes or urban twentieth-century homes and neighborhoods or medieval battles—but is, rather, a kind of experience of its own. It grows out of other experiences, of course, but it has its own special values and its own problems of evaluation. These I have tried to describe in A Critical Approach to Children's Literature.

In writing this book I have profited much from the assistance of many teachers, librarians, and students. I owe a special debt of gratitude to a number of my fellow teachers of children's literature who have discussed children's books with me—Professors Henry Van Slooten, Helen Lodge, Robert Oliphant, Gwen Brewer, Prudence Bostwick, Richard Blakeslee, Mitchell Marcus, and Eva Latif—and to my wife Ruth and my daughter Martha, who have done the same and who have, in addition, helped me in finding and keeping track of materials. I should also like to thank Ada Rose, formerly editor of Jack and Jill, whose encouragement of my writing children's poetry helped develop my interest in children's literature.

James Steel Smith

CONTENTS

A
CRITICAL
APPROACH
TO
CHILDREN'S
LITERATURE

CHAPTER 1

THINKING ABOUT CHILDREN'S LITERATURE

*O*ne can think about children's literature in various ways, and these ways, separately or in combination, will determine the shape and coloring of a book or course in children's literature.

Historical Study

One may approach children's literature historically—trying to determine what it used to be, how modern children's literature developed, what its main tendencies have been, and where it is now tending. This would result in chronological study—the study of authors, books, and trends as they came along. A course based on this approach would be much like the traditional college survey course in English or American literature, only it would be confined to children's literature.

The Subject-matter Emphasis

Or one may study children's literature in terms of subject matter, what the books are about—birds and animals, space travel, fairies, trucks, planes, the everyday neighborhood experiences of children, machinery, history, geography, holidays, famous men, technology, exploration. In such study one would list and examine books under their subject classifications, giving little or no consideration to the ways in which they were written and their feeling and tone. One's concern would be merely to find who wrote books, fiction or nonfiction, in each subject field and to determine how accurately the authors covered their facts.

The Types Approach

Another, somewhat less tidy but very common way of thinking about children's literature is to describe it not according to any single system of content but in terms of more or less arbitrary traditional types—folktales, myths, fables, modern imitations of folktales, Mother Goose verses, reading primers, poetry, folk song, modern fantasies, humor, "stories of real life," regional literature, historical fiction, natural-history and science books, animal stories, adventure stories, sports fiction, domestic fiction, adolescent books. Some of these groupings—animal stories and domestic fiction, for instance—are according to subject matter; some are by origin (folktales); some are by genre (poetry); some are by purpose (reading primers); some are mainly by age levels of readers (Mother Goose and adolescent literature). This is really a whole congeries of ways of thinking about children's books and calls for a constant shifting of direction and method. It might be called the zigzag approach.

The Psychological Approach

A more systematic, consistent approach to children's literature is through the psychology of child readers—their needs, both their conscious desires and those needs unrecognized by the children themselves. This kind of thinking about children's literature is founded on the assumptions that children have desires and that they try to fulfill them by, among other things, reading and listening to stories and poetry, and that all children's reading fits into various need categories—the need for security, for knowledge, for social acceptance, for laughter, for play, for beauty, etc.

The Application Emphasis

Many persons, especially where the study of children's literature is closely tied in to teacher-training programs, learn about children's literature largely in terms of its educational applications. This is the vocational or "how to" attack. They think of children's reading for certain situations—bedtime, school or playground or library story hour, mathematics or social science or geography units, verse choirs, quiet time or rest time, Columbus Day or Washington's Birthday or Easter. They also address themselves directly to problems of getting the books and materials, introducing them in class or elsewhere, keeping up with the mass of new publishing. This application study of children's literature is frequently combined with the psychological emphasis; thus the student thinks much about the use of certain reading materials to meet the child's specific psychological needs.

Another Alternative: Literature as Literature

Different from one another though they may seem, these five ways of thinking about children's reading—historical, subject-centered, by types, psychological, and application-oriented, or utilitarian—all have one very important common characteristic: None of them examines and analyzes the children's literature itself with any seriousness and care. They look at the development of children's reading material or at the subject content or at the psychological goals or ends or at types or at particular uses and the conditions of usage. They all focus on something else besides the examining and understanding of the book itself. Courses of study based on them become primarily programs in child psychology, social history or cultural history, librarianship, or day-to-day pedagogy—or some combination of these.

Now, these are all quite useful ways of thinking about children's literature and deserve serious consideration by anyone dealing with children and their reading. But none of them, of and by itself, directly involves the actual critical analysis of children's books—examination of each book as a book, as a creative literary work, a piece of writing and illustrating. Nor do they call for the systematic consideration of the principal questions that arise— or ought to arise—in the sensitive, intelligent reading of children's literature. Such reading really involves examining the nature of literature—and specifically, children's literature—to determine how literature manifests itself, what forms it takes, what things transpire in it, and then, on the basis of this analysis, what questions of judgment and selection are relevant to it.

This is the approach of the present book. The critical analysis of children's literature provides the book's primary focus. In the course of our study of children's literature we shall gradually, inductively, develop a number of central questions that may help us better understand books we have already read and books we will encounter in the future; and through the application of these questions we shall try to develop a useful critical attitude and method, a practical, responsible way of thinking analytically about the books we are likely to encounter as teachers, librarians, or parents.

This way of coming into children's literature should make it easier for us to sidestep certain pitfalls that we well might drop into if we took other approaches. We shall be less likely to forget the literature if we do not hurry directly to the child, less likely to lose our footing in a lot of guessing about the psychology of the child reader (whom we will eventually reach, anyway) or in the idealistic sentimentalizing that so easily besets one who starts out with a vision of "little children reading." We shall also be less inclined to wander off into all the various subject areas in which children's books have been written if we start with the writing rather than with the subjects, which are endless in their variety. Nor shall we be so likely to leap hastily into the questions of use of children's literature—at various age levels, in different classes, and for particular purposes—before we have really thought carefully about the literature we will be using, before we even know whether it is one or many. And finally, the present approach should reduce the risk of our getting lost in a pathless jungle of "just children's books" without any sort of compass.

Primary Aims and General Principles

This book, then, is essentially an exercise in method, and the method we use will be inductive discovery of pertinent, useful questions to ask ourselves in reading children's books critically and practice in the application of these questions. Now this means we shall not be primarily seeking a certain final set of principles or criteria; rather, we shall be trying to set up procedures by which to reach sound, useful ones. However, in touching on significant questions and exploring their implications we will often reach a point where a principle will seem to suggest itself, and by the end of the book we should have a number of broad, flexible criteria—a number of possible positions or values—that we may choose to carry with us into our future reading and use of children's books. The process might be likened to a series of onion peelings. Getting at the important aspects of children's books will involve peeling away false or at least useless conceptions and gradually reaching a number of realizations—awarenesses of tendencies, likelihoods, problems.

Here, in brief synopsis, are the three main principles into which we will move and which will inform our discussions of particular works and kinds of works:

1   The Relativistic Conception of Value in Children's Literature   This is the view that art may do *many* things—cause laughter (of diverse sorts) and evoke feelings of sorrow, instruct or not instruct, lead to or away from reality, calm or excite, be logical or illogical, be wittily comic or slapstick comic, be poetry or prose, be stark and simple or elaborate and intricate, be largely verbal narrative or heavily dependent on visual telling. None of these things makes a children's book superior or inferior. The question of value enters when we ask how well, in comparison to other books of its kind (e.g., slapstick, everyday realistic, delicately fantastic), a particular book does what it is trying to do. Is the fantasy effective fantasy? the realism convincingly real? the beauty movingly beautiful? the grotesque intriguingly grotesque? the nonsense logically nonsensical? The direction of this book is toward values, but values relative to particular, limited literary goals. And we will find that a given story or poem may have, or be, a number of kinds of literary experience. A book—for instance, one of the Pooh books—may have all sorts of language fantasy, a little rather restrained physical fantasy, close observation of human character and experience, and lyric poetry; and within the work these different levels may vary in their effectiveness. And of course, a specific kind of expression, say, wild funniness, may waver in its vigor and tellingness from one part of the book to another; and we will find such variation between one work and another work by the same author. Sensitiveness to such differences in the doing of a certain kind of thing is one of the skills which this book emphasizes and in which it seeks to give—or at least suggest opportunities for——practice. Nowhere will arise the question, "What is *great* children's literature?" or the question, "Is this a *masterpiece* of children's literature?" Rather, questions will emerge in terms of better and poorer, more and less effective, in relation to specific ends. Such questions are more easily answerable than questions about absolute value, and more useful when we have answered them.

2   The Literary Value of Children's Literature   In the present book we will see that children's books can have many values besides literary or aesthetic values——they can have ethical values (they can present moral lessons and approved behavior patterns and can affect behavior), informational values (accurate information about mountains, markets, weather, history, laboratory experiments, musicians and music) and direct "how to" values (how to identify a bird, how to clean one's teeth, how to use the library, how to pass an examination). But these values are not identical with the literary values——the qualities that make a story an impressive imaginative experience, that cause a funny story to be funny or a sad one sad, that make a poem memorable. We will find that a story may create an effectively imagined, imaginable experience without teaching any lesson or giving information one can use, and that a quite moral or informative story may be told in an unimaginative way. We will learn to distinguish between the part of a reading experience that is of value in itself, as an imagined and imaginable experience, and the part of it that has little or no value in itself but may lead to experiences that have value for the reader. In short, we will, it is hoped, refine our distinctions between the literary value of reading and the nonliterary value. This does not mean we will raise one above the other——we will merely try to sharpen our understanding of each and our ability to know which we are working with at any given time. We will, for instance, be aware of the distance between a dog book that is just a story about dogs and a dog book that is an imaginatively conceived, vividly told story about dogs; we will know that the telling makes a world of difference between the two dog stories, that it creates two essentially different kinds of experience.

3   The Nature of Literary Value in Children's Books   We will look at many forms of children's literature and at books with similar forms but wholly different emphases, and in looking at this tremendous variety of children's books, we may at first feel we are fragmenting children's literature and making it impossible for us ever to find any useful common denominators of literary value. But gradually, as we look at many pieces of children's literature in terms of specific questions, we will see that in effective writing for children the language, the other patterns (plotting, character making, illustration, rhythms, etc), and the selection of content all combine to create a sense of wonder, specialness, intensity——call it what one will. The source of this sense of wonder may be in fantasy, in its denial of reality or flight from reality, or it may be in realistic literature, in its intense atmosphere of realness. The only—but not easily met—requirement of the realistic literature is that it be unprosaic, special; the one requirement of the fantasy, also difficult to fulfill, is that it be in its own way logical, unstrained, capable of suspending disbelief for the time being. This creation of a sense of wonder is a broad, flexible criterion, but a useful one; in applying it, we can avoid getting into either the camp which considers literature for children as pure escape or into the opposite camp which places all children's literature in a shadow relationship to everyday experience.

Using this broad criterion, we will find that good children's literature may differ from good adult literature in certain interesting but limited ways. In good children's literature there will be (1) some restriction of the range of experience described by the author to types of experience comprehensible to the young, (2) a less complex combination of language, character, plot, and theme, (3) a lesser range of language, though not less ingenuity and flexibility within that range, (4) a greater reliance on action to do what the author wants, (5) a fuller integration of visual patterns with the verbal patterns. But we will find the similarities of good children's literature and adult literature to be as significant as the differences. We will find that good children's writing, like good adult writing, tends to have a high degree of (1) unity, (2) concreteness, particularity, specificity, (3) appropriateness of the form—organization and language—to the content, (4) a formal pattern that is in itself appealing in some ways, (5) an absence of waste motion or indirectness. (One may note that all but the first of these five characteristics are characteristics of the treatment of content, not of subject matter itself; they are literary criteria.)

But we will find that these characteristics of children's literature—both those peculiar to it and those shared fully with adult literature—need to be considered, not as in themselves good, but rather as contributing to the heightening of the reader's experience, the creation in him of the sense of *wonder* which I have suggested will be an essential criterion.

Yet it bears repeating that our goal here will not be to put together a neat package of criteria for children's literature, but rather to develop a critical approach to children's literature, a way of asking relevant questions about it, a method of search. This "onion peeling" process takes practice and itself needs constant analysis; if it is taken for granted and used more or less mechanically, then it will become a superficial approach.

Focus: The Literature Itself

In describing and practicing critical analysis of children's books, it is hoped we will become acquainted with a usefully large body of children's literature. In some cases our memories will require refurbishing; in others, we will need to enlarge our acquaintance with children's books. Some children's books will be described rather fully in the discussion of critical points; some will be alluded to more briefly in the text; others will be mentioned only in the bibliographies at the end of chapters. One point should be made very clear now: the kind of analysis described in this book calls for constant focus on the works themselves. This means that we need to apply the method to children's books—we need to practice and test the suggested method of analysis. If we read beyond the selections included in the text, we will then have achieved two important ends: we will have explored the suggested methods and concepts, and we will have become better acquainted with the body of children's literature. Constant rambling through the shelves of children's libraries and thumbing of books in children's bookstores are major parts of any study of children's literature, but they are an absolute necessity in a program of study based on the critical reading of children's books themselves. Indeed, a compelling reason for not crowding a group of brief selections into this present book is that the method calls for the individual's own exploration of the works themselves—the stories, novels, poems and collections of poetry, the plays themselves, the reference books themselves.

In looking at children's literature in terms of central critical questions, then, we will not read in survey fashion through the common types of present-day children's books. By the time we have completed our own critical kind of inspection of children's books, we will have encountered numerous examples of all the usual major types of children's writings— fantasies (both traditional folktale and modern), folktales, myths, fables, children's adaptations of classics, ballads, modern narrative poems, non- sense poetry, lyric poetry, commonsense and everyday-life poetry, humor, historical fiction, regional stories, animal stories, sports stories, science fiction, "awareness" books, biographies, science books, children's en- cyclopedias, and also various kinds of adult books often overlooked as children's literature but frequently read by children.

Overview

Now with the foregoing rationale in mind, what specific plan of organization shall we follow in our study of children's literature?

In Chapter 2 I shall raise a fundamental and difficult question (which we will not settle for good and all in that chapter): what is the nature of literary value in children's literature? This will be followed by a historical chapter—a selection of certain historic stages in the literature, not a chronological survey of the whole field. We will begin to see, by the ex- amples from history, that children's literature can be many different things, that it may go in many different directions. Incidentally, we shall see in this backward look some of the major goals that still motivate the makers of children's reading; observing these in historical distance should help us better see what we have under our very noses. In Chapter 4 we shall pursue further this aspect of the diversity of children's literature by looking at the kinds of users of children's books today and at their very different sets of criteria.

Then, in Chapters 5 through 11, we shall scrutinize main critical questions as they may be encountered in certain broad areas of children's literature—books borrowed from adult literature, so-called classics, realistic literature ("supermarket"), fantasy ("superman"), humor, poetry, and various kinds of presentation of factual information. Chapter 12 presents questions concerning the role of illustrations in children's reading.

Chapters 13 and 14 seek to recognize and define certain questions of use that can be realistically considered *on the critical base of understanding* we will have by that time prepared. These questions are concerned with the relation of children's literature to the other aspects of education—purposes, methods, courses, etc.—and to the child's other sources of vicarious experience. In the final chapter we will consider the practical problems of the adult who, presumably now having thought out how he will think about children's reading, needs to know where to find it and how to keep up with it when he finds it. These last three chapters are not so much literary criticism as they are considerations of how to apply in a busy and confusing world the critical principles at which we hope to arrive.

The General Feeling of This Book

Certain broad assumptions and governing attitudes underlie all the various questionings, discussions, and analyses that compose this book.

First, it is assumed that children's literature is neither lower nor higher than adult literature, that it involves aesthetic values and questions of form just as adult literature does. A second and corollary position held here is that children's literature is just as difficult (or as easy) to understand, that is, to be intelligent about and sensitive to, as adult literature.

Thirdly, the following discussions rest on the premise that effective reading of children's literature calls for *an intelligent, perceptive method*—one which causes the reader to ask the right questions of what he is reading. This means that we shall not assume, on the one hand, that the adult experienced with children will necessarily apprehend children's books more fully and clearly than others without such experience, or, on the other hand, that the person widely read and trained in just adult literature and many years removed from his own juvenile reading will have any real advantage; neither one may have thought critically about children's literature, and it is assumed here that such preparation is necessary for the soundly thoughtful reading and use of children's books.

This book is basically motivated by the expectation that through it we will, in a reasonably enjoyable way, further develop our feeling of responsibility in coming as adult readers to children's books. It is to be hoped that we will thus avoid both the common inclination to consider children's reading beneath our serious adult attention and the equally widespread tendency to become undiscriminatingly, rhapsodically, uncritically enthusiastic about all children's reading materials. The adult reader can be a sensitive reader of children's literature if he retains and uses all his grown-up senses.

THE NATURE
OF LITERARY VALUE
IN CHILDREN'S LITERATURE:
How
Good
Can a
Children's Book
Be?

$\mathcal{C}$an standards of literary value be seriously considered in judging children's literature? And, if so, then what are the criteria that should be applied?

These related questions are central and ticklish ones for any parent, teacher, or librarian seriously concerned with children's reading. Either a complete dodging of these matters or a thoughtless jumping to easy conclusions about them has given rise to much of the confusion and superficiality which have plagued the study of children's literature. To deal with the question of literary value in children's books does not require a highly specialized training in literature or in pedagogy or psychology, but it does call for considerable *mental agility*, the ability to dodge clichés and not take things for granted.

Two Common Assumptions

A great many well-read adults make one of two assumptions about the nature of children's literature: (1) that children's literature involves the same elements and hence the same criteria of literary quality as adult literature, and (2) that *no* literary criteria, or at least none meriting the serious attention of responsible, mature adults, can be applied to children's books.

The first view makes it almost impossible for one to deal sensitively and realistically with children's reading. People who share this view pay no attention whatsoever to *the children* who will read the book and so do not consider the various wants that reading may in part meet; they do not look into special conditions shaping the creation of a literature *for children*.

They simply select what they already regard as good adult literature and thereby turn their backs on almost all writings more or less intended for children, for these "juveniles," or children's books, do not normally meet adult criteria of literary excellence, and when measured against adult literary criteria, they make a poor showing.

The second view—that children's books call for no criteria at all, or at least none which merit the serious attention of mature adult minds—is equally disastrous to the wise selection and use of children's books. Feeling that children's books are for incomplete, undeveloped human beings and so do not merit full-minded critical attention, people of this persuasion may refuse to think at all about them or to read more of them than they absolutely have to. They will certainly scorn teaching or writing about children's literature, permanently relegating it to a place of inferiority.

People who have less literary background will often apply to children's books solely nonliterary, nonaesthetic criteria. Instead of aesthetic standards, they will use only criteria of psychological and ethical utility and scientific truth. *Their* questions or criteria will be: What does it teach? Does it disturb or reassure children? Does it cultivate racial tolerance? Can it be used to advantage in a social studies unit? Will it make Mary more understanding of her baby brother? Will it give useful information about nature, social institutions, etc.? Will it instill desirable social attitudes? They will view children's reading almost entirely as an auxiliary service, a feeder for more important activities.

It is significant that many literary people—thoughtful, sophisticated, widely read readers—and persons quite uninformed and unaware in literature should have in common a feeling of carelessness about children's literature *as literature*. The bookish adults do not pay attention to children's books, and the nonbookish do not pay attention to the literary qualities in them. The result in each case is much the same, and at the college level the combined effect of these two views is to create a conception of work in children's literature as padding, snap courses, or vocational courses purely.

Yet the study of children's books *can* be intellectually and aesthetically solid, for the assumption that children's literature is a literary wasteland and the assumption that it involves the same criteria of literary excellence as adult literature are both unsound.

Better and Worse Children's Books

If one is willing to set aside the wasteland assumption temporarily and actually read and use children's books with children, he soon discovers that just as in adult literature, there are qualitative differences—a continuum from excellence to mediocrity by any selected criterion and within any given type. When we set aside foregone conclusions, we look at particular examples of writing for children, and in so doing, we immediately discover that the problem of value is essentially the same as the problem of value we find when we look at adult literature; we discover real differences in value, better and worse children's books of a particular kind.

In children's books about family life, for example, we find some writing to be vigorous, reasonably honest, and close to real people and their living, and we also find some writing (the majority of juvenile domestic novels are of this latter sort) that is both timid and overblown, saccharinely sentimental, dishonest. On the one hand, we have Louisa May Alcott's *Little Women, Little Men, Jo's Boys,* etc., and E. Nesbit's *The Railway Children.* Alcott's and Nesbit's books are all heavily touched with sentiment, but generally they avoid bathos; their characters, somewhat simplified, still react variously and with occasional inconsistency. Within the domestic-story genre there is, on the other hand, Martha Finley's Elsie Dinsmore series and Margaret Sidney's *The Five Little Peppers and How They Grew.* In these latter books the pathos has become bathos; the characters are black and white, wooden type figures; situations and emotions are generally described in unoriginal clichés and generalities; the dialogue is empty, puffed up. Excerpts from the contrasting kinds of writing describing a similar event—the attempt of a family to keep up its spirits after moving into run-down quarters—should make the difference altogether clear.

Here is a passage from Nesbit's *The Railway Children*;* the coming-down-in-the-world family has just arrived at a newly rented house in the middle of the night; they have heard rats scampering behind the door, and have had their candle blown out by the wind.

"What fun!" said Mother, in the dark, feeling for the matches on the table. "How frightened the poor mice were—I don't believe they were rats at all!"

She struck a match and relighted the candle, and everyone looked at each other by its winky, blinky light.

"Well," she said "you've often wanted something to happen and now it has. This is quite an adventure, isn't it? I told Mrs. Viney to get us some bread and butter and meat and things, and to have supper ready. I suppose she's laid it in the dining-room. So let's go and see."

The dining-room opened out of the kitchen. It looked much darker than the kitchen when they went in with the one candle. Because the kitchen was whitewashed, but the dining-room was darkwood from floor to ceiling, and across the ceiling there were heavy black beams. There was a muddled maze of dusty furniture—the breakfast-room furniture from the old home where they had lived all their lives. It seemed a very long time ago, and a very long way off.

There was a table certainly, and there were chairs, but there was no supper.

"Let's look in the other rooms," said Mother; and they looked. And

* Works indicated by asterisks are described in the Sources of Quoted Materials section beginning on page 415.

in each room was the same kind of blundering half-arrangement of furniture, and fire-irons and crockery, and all sorts of odd things on the floor, but there was nothing to eat; even in the pantry there were only a rusty cake-tin and a broken plate with whitening mixed in it.

"What a horrid old woman!" said Mother; "She's just walked off with the money and not got us anything to eat at all."

"Then shan't we have any supper at all?" asked Phyllis, dismayed, stepping back on to a soap-dish that cracked responsively.

"Oh, yes," said Mother, "only it'll mean unpacking one of those big cases that we put in the cellar. Phil, do mind where you're walking to, there's a dear. Peter, hold the light."

The cellar door opened out of the kitchen. There were five wooden steps leading down. It wasn't a proper cellar at all, the children thought, because its ceiling went up as high as the kitchen's. A bacon-rack hung under its ceiling. There was wood in it, and coal. Also the big cases.

When Sidney in her *Five Little Peppers** describes a similar family crisis—trying to carry on against disheartening physical odds and un-certainty about the future—the passage is startlingly different. Here are the first several paragraphs of the book:

The little old kitchen had quieted down from the bustle and con-fusion of midday; and now, with its afternoon manners on, presented a holiday aspect that, as the principal room in the brown house, it was eminently proper it should have. It was just on the edge of twilight; and the little Peppers, all except Ben, the oldest of the flock, were taking a "breathing spell" as their mother called it, which meant some quiet work suitable for the hour. It was all the "breathing spell" they could remember, however, poor things; for times were hard with them now. The father had died when Phronsie was a baby, and since then Mrs. Pepper had had hard work to scrape together money enough to put bread into her children's mouths, and to pay the rent of the Little Brown House.

But she had met life too bravely to be beaten down now. So with a stout heart and a cheery face, she had worked away day after day at making coats, and tailoring and mending of all descriptions; and she had seen with pride that couldn't be concealed, her noisy, happy brood growing up around her, and filling her heart with comfort, and making the Little Brown House fairly ring with jollity and fun.

"Poor things!" she would say to herself, "They haven't had any bringing up; they've just scrambled up!" And then she would set her lips together tightly, and fly at her work faster than ever. "I must get learning for 'em someway, but I don't see how!"

Nesbit and Sidney wrote the same general type of children's fiction, the novel of everyday, pinched family living and of tender, humane feelings; but one writer, as the above comparison makes evident, wrote much better fiction than the other. Nesbit's prose, even in this small excerpt, appears superior to Sidney's in its freshness of observation, its relative freedom from cliché, its concreteness. And a comparison of the entire books would reveal the greater unity and firmer direction of Nesbit's tale telling.

Another comparison: Will James's *Smoky* versus such animal stories as Walter Farley's *Black Stallion*, Warren Garst's *Texas Trail Drive*, and Jack O'Brien's *Silver Chief, Dog of the North* and *The Return of Silver Chief*. Their plots, centered on the close relationship between once-wild animals and their masters, are similar, and they all have something of the same appeal—animal subject matter, exciting events, much suspense. But James's *Smoky* is superior to the others in most respects. Its figures, men and four-footed animals, come alive in a way that theirs do not; the figures in *Smoky* are rounded, have a number of forces at work in them, are not mere puppets at the end of an author's string. The talk of *Smoky* is specially vivid and appropriate to the speakers. Also, *Smoky* seems to develop in a unified way, whereas the others are more obviously cut out to fit a formula or pattern. The others are somewhat mechanical, artificial, and melodramatic; *Smoky* is full of a sense of life.

In short, when we really read and analyze—that is, come to grips with—writing for children, we find ourselves as much concerned with critical problems as we would were we to read and analyze writing for adults. We find ourselves as much involved in the making of critical judgments—discovering that different authors are trying to do the same or different things, that they do the same thing more or less successfully, that they are strong and weak in different ways. The criteria may be different from those we would use in thinking critically about adult literature—but they are still criteria, and we arrive at judgments, just as we would at the levels of adult literature and adult criticism of it. The possibility of arriving at different conclusions clearly indicates the existence of qualitative differences in children's literature, of better and worse, of this way rather than that.

Another comparison, between two lullabies. Here is Eugene Field's "The Rock-a-By Lady"*:

The Rock-a-By Lady from Hushaby street
  Comes stealing; comes creeping;
The poppies they hang from her head to her feet,
And each hath a dream that is tiny and fleet—
She bringeth her poppies to you, my sweet,
  When she findeth you sleeping!

There is one little dream of a beautiful drum—
  "Rub-a-dub!" it goeth;
There is one little dream of a big sugar-plum,

And lo! thick and fast the other dreams come
Of popguns that bang, and tin tops that hum,
  And a trumpet that bloweth!

And dollies peep out of those wee little dreams
  With laughter and singing;
And boats go a-floating on silvery streams,
And the stars peek-a-boo with their own misty gleams,
And up, up, and up, where the Mother Moon beams,
  The fairies go winging!

Would you dream all these dreams that are tiny and fleet?
  They'll come to you sleeping;
So shut the two eyes that are weary, my sweet,
For the Rock-a-By Lady from Hushaby street,
With poppies that hang from her head to her feet,
  Comes stealing; comes creeping.

And here is Alfred Tennyson's "Sweet and Low"*:

Sweet and low, sweet and low,
  Wind of the western sea,
Low, low, breathe and blow,
  Wind of the western sea!
Over the rolling waters go,
Come from the dying moon and blow,
  Blow him again to me;
While my little one, while my pretty one sleeps.

Sleep and rest, sleep and rest,
  Father will come to thee soon;
Rest, rest on mother's breast,
  Father will come to thee soon;
Father will come to his babe in the nest,
Silver sails all out of the west
  Under the silver moon:
Sleep, my little one, sleep, my pretty one, sleep.

Both lullabies are apparently intended to capture or create a sense of dreaming, the soft edge of sleep, and peace, but the result in one case is a self-consciously elaborate showpiece, in the other a deft, expressive lyric, the achieving of the same sense less ostentatiously. In Field's poem the means are too obvious, overused (the long e's in "Comes stealing; comes creeping," the repeated use of -eth, the heavy repetition of "hang from her head to her feet" and dreams that are "tiny and fleet"). Sleep is personified in the abstract form of the rock-a-by lady rather than suggested concretely. The poem is pervaded by a strained sentimentality ("my sweet," stars playing "peek-a-boo with their own misty gleams," "the Mother Moon," "wee little dreams"). The poem's rhythm succeeds in creating a certain languor, and some of the imagery (hanging poppies, banging pop-guns and humming tin tops, a blowing trumpet, misty gleams) does create pictures, but on the whole the poet tried too hard; the resulting poem is overdone, cloying. In "Sweet and Low" the sense of wind and sea and night and safe harbor is created by a few vivid images and two stanzas of suggestive rhythms. The second poem is better done than the first; it is a better work of art by the relevant criteria.

Differences in Criteria for Adult and Children's Literature

But even if we get over that first "it doesn't count" hurdle and become convinced that children's literature calls for serious attention and the exercising of critical judgment, we can still get entangled in the mistaken view that children's literature involves *the same criteria* of literary excellence as adult literature does.

The differences in quality that we will find in children's books *are not identical* with those we may have become accustomed to find in adult literature. And even when we discover some correspondence in the kinds of differences, we will not find these differences to be of equal importance in adult and juvenile literature. In other words, the criteria relevant to adult literature and the criteria relevant to children's literature may differ markedly in important ways.

What are the reasons for these differences?

1   Most children have had *more limited experience*—more limited in both kinds and amount—than most adults. This means that books for children, by the very nature of their readers, must work within a narrow circle of reference or that if they go far beyond childhood's common experience, they need to explain it to a degree not ordinarily needed in writing for adults.

Similarly, young children may not know many small wild animals that are quite familiar to older children, who have been to zoos and may even have seen raccoons, squirrels, and coyotes in their natural surroundings, and who have probably had read to them books on the nature and habits of these wild animals. It is probable that a small child's understanding of the relative ferociousness of animals will be more vague than his older brother's. And it is probable that a child of seven or eight will have a very slight notion of the nature of animals' mating, whereas his twelve- or thirteen-year-old brother and sister may have a fair comprehension of it. So the younger child could easily be puzzled by a full account of a deer's experiences in fighting for a mate or by anything more than the most generalized sort of reference to the deer's mating. Similarly, a four- to six-year-old child will very likely not understand stories that depend heavily on a basic concept of time—of day and night, of seasonal change, of past, present, and future generally. And most children from preschool through the first three or four grades will have difficulty in comprehending tales and poetry which deal in any important way with birth, death, marriage, money, and jobs. These are more central to adult experience than to children's lives. Books about getting and keeping steady jobs do not begin to come within the ken of boys and girls until they get into junior high school, and for most children this does not become a pressing reading interest until high school. John Steinbeck's story, *The Red Pony*—about a boy's caring for a pony, the death of the pony under circumstances that could lead the boy to blame himself for it, the boy's rage against the death, and the horrible but natural circumstances of the death—will very likely only shock and puzzle most children under eleven or twelve and a good many children older than that. Its view of death is adult, and rather mature adult at that.

The writer for children cannot handle adult experiences with complete freedom, or children's experiences seen and interpreted through maturer understanding; if he does refer to these, he must do so partially or with considerable explanation or even with falsification. A Joseph Conrad story, for instance, may contain some physical settings and episodes that suggest to teachers these could be used in the eighth to eleventh grades, but generally its central concerns will be thoroughly grown-up questions of loyalty, the frustration of the social outcast, the quest for allegiance; even in a story like *Youth*, about a boy's adventure, the experience is viewed in retrospect, through the wise eyes of a much older man who *once was* that boy. Lincoln Steffens's boyhood with horses in California is similarly treated from the reminiscing point of view of a grown man, and for this reason is not as comprehensible to children of junior high school age as some librarians and teachers assume it to be. (One reason why teachers and parents so often fail to recognize this gap is that they are so often satisfied with simple, factual answers about what happened, and where and to whom, as proof of the young reader's understanding: "What kinds of information did old Nokomis give the young Hiawatha?" "Give the name of the forest in which Robin Hood and his band hid." "Where are the gray Azores?")

When the subjects a child may understand and be interested in are dealt with fully and frequently enough in a book, the presence of adult matters and adult points of view will not knock the book out of the child's range. Mark Twain's *Huckleberry Finn*, for instance, provides enough of the former and has them distributed evenly enough to attract children. Charles Dickens's *David Copperfield, Great Expectations,* and *A Christmas Carol* are for the same reason highly readable by good readers of twelve to fourteen. The romantic writers of the nineteenth century are a rich source of writing in which youthful attitudes and interests are mingled with more complex adult motivations and concerns—for instance, James Fenimore Cooper's *Last of the Mohicans* and *The Deerslayer* and Sir Walter Scott's novels. The romantic disguising of sex or total avoidance of sexual reference in these nineteenth-century writings has helped make it possible for children to read them without going beyond their own depth of sexual knowledge or interest and without raising the threat of censorship from their elders. It will be noted that for the most part, these are writings which mature adult readers are likely to tire of most quickly and not return to.

Here is a representative sampling of nineteenth-century and early-twentieth-century romantic works originally intended for adults and now probably of greater interest to children and adolescents:

Bacheller, Irving, *Eben Holden*
Barrie, James M., *The Little Minister, Sentimental Tommy*
Blackmore, R. D., *Lorna Doone*
Brontë, Charlotte, *Jane Eyre*
Buchan, John, *The Thirty-nine Steps, Greenmantle, John Macnab, Salute to Adventurers, Prester John*
Bulwer-Lytton, Edward, *The Last Days of Pompeii*
Cather, Willa, *Shadows on the Rock*
Churchill, Winston, *Richard Carvel, The Crisis*
Chute, Marchette, *The Wonderful Winter*
Doyle, Arthur Conan, *The White Company, The Adventures of Sherlock Holmes*
Dumas, Alexandre, *The Count of Monte Cristo, The Three Musketeers*
Eggleston, Edward, *The Hoosier Schoolmaster*
Ferber, Edna, *Show Boat, Cimarron*
Forester, C. S., *The African Queen*
Haggard, Rider, *She*
Harte, Bret, *The Outcasts of Poker Flat and Other Tales*
Hilton, James, *Lost Horizon; Good-bye, Mr. Chips*
Hough, E. M., *The Covered Wagon*
Hudson, W. H., *Green Mansions*
Irving, Washington, *The Legend of Sleepy Hollow, Rip van Winkle*
Jackson, Helen Hunt, *Ramona*
Johnston, Mary, *To Have and to Hold*
Kingsley, Charles, *Westward Ho!*
Kipling, Rudyard, *Captains Courageous, Kim, The Light That Failed, short stories*
Lever, Charles, *Charles O'Malley*
Mitchell, Margaret, *Gone with the Wind*
Mulock, Dinah Craik, *John Halifax, Gentleman*
Sabatini, Rafael, *The Sea Hawk, Captain Blood*
Scott, Sir Walter, *Ivanhoe, The Talisman*
Sienkiewicz, Henryk, *Quo Vadis*
Stevenson, Robert Louis, *The New Arabian Nights*
Tarkington, Booth, *Monsieur Beaucaire*
Verne, Jules, *Around the World in Eighty Days, 20,000 Leagues under the Sea*

Wallace, Lew, *Ben Hur*
Wells, H. G., *The Invisible Man, The Time Machine, The War of the Worlds*
West, Jessamyn, *The Friendly Persuasion*
Weyman, Stanley J., *Under the Red Robe*
Wister, Owen, *The Virginian*
Wren, Percival, *Beau Geste*

A problem related to the child's lack of adult experience and interests is that the child is constantly dealing with, and may be deeply interested in, kinds of experience the adult no longer has and which he may have altogether forgotten, or at least transformed into something seemingly quite different. To the small child it may be very interesting that popcorn can be bought in a theater lobby and that it crackles and bounces, that night follows day, that one has cousins. A small boy may be entranced by the problem of filling a toy dump truck, his sister by the collecting and care of dolls. To a girl in the eighth grade the details of high school routine—homerooms, moving from classroom to classroom, having one's own locker—may be fascinating enough to serve as the basis for a mild piece of fiction.

There is, then, a difference in experiences—not in all kinds but in some—that children and adults can understand and be interested in, and this disparity must be taken into consideration in establishing our criteria for children's books, unless, of course, we subscribe to the critical principle that the critic operates as if a book were to have either no readers or just one ideal reader.

2   Most children, besides having a more limited range of understandable experience, have a more limited range of language experience than most adults. This means that even for the experiences he *has* had the young child probably possesses a more limited terminology than his elders have. He may, for instance, know what happens when something stops or finishes or comes to an end, but he may not know what happens when something terminates, is completed, comes to a dead halt, or gets stymied. Out of the synonyms and near-synonyms *girl, young woman, gal, lassie, lass, twelve-year-old adolescent, miss, maid, maiden,* and *teen-ager,* he may know the one term *girl.* He will very likely know *fewer* synonyms for a thing or event than even a rather poorly educated adult would know.

For children, therefore, the meanings which language can convey about experience through reading—the semantic dimensions of language—are drastically limited. A child who can get meaning from only two out of, say, ten possible terms for an object is seriously handicapped in the variety of ideas he can receive about that object. A writer using the single term *girl* cannot convey as many particular meanings as he might if he could also use *undersized girl* and *adolescent girl.* If his audience's reading vocabulary does not include *tutor* or *professor,* he may not be able to make clear a particular kind of teacher he may have in mind. He may not be able to make clear to his readers (without an illustrator's aid) that a snake he is

talking about is a python, boa constrictor, or coral or garter or grass snake. The child's small vocabulary makes it difficult to be specific in writing to him. And the smallness of his reading vocabulary also makes it hard to convey a variety of abstract ideas to him. The little child probably knows the words *water, milk,* and *orange juice,* but he may not know what *liquid* refers to. He may know the meanings of *elm* and *maple* but not the meaning of *deciduous tree,* of *iron* and *coal* but not of *minerals.* As the writer moves in the direction of either generalization or greater particularity, it becomes harder for children to follow him. A writer's vocabulary for children's reading would appear, then, to be necessarily limited in flexibility and imaginative resources in comparison to that of the writer for adults. Hence it would be unrealistic to apply to children's books exactly the same criteria of style one would use with adult books.

3   Not only is the child reader limited in the amount and kind of experience he can comprehend and the language about it which he can take in, but he is also *limited in his ability to attend* to those experiences over lengths of time. The seven-year-old child simply finds it hard to sit still physically, and mentally he finds it difficult to keep his attention focused on one problem for long or to track one thread through changing situations. As he grows older, his ability to concentrate for appreciable periods of time increases, and he becomes better able, therefore, to follow a longer trail and to keep a destination in mind.

This age difference in attention is reflected in various important ways in children's literature. Because of it most books for young children are quite short; as the child grows older, his books increase in length. The writer for young children may turn to the use of repetition as a way of directing and holding attention. Pictures interspersed throughout a book may serve, too, to keep the child from simply tiring and drifting away from the story. These elements, of course, limit what the children's author can attempt within the bounds of a story.

4   Besides having a shorter attention span than older persons, the child normally *cannot manipulate as many elements at once.* He finds it difficult to attend to more than one or two developing ideas or lines of action at the same time, to trace out relations among numerous persons, places, and events. The writer for children, therefore, is more limited than the adults' writer in the number of balls of meaning he can keep in the air at one time, the number of aspects of any situation he can present, and the degree to which he can use complexity itself as a value. And so the interweaving of lines of events—a source of interest to the mature adult reader—cannot be carried very far with the child reader. Characterization, too, may need to be kept rather broad and simple; it takes a fairly sophisticated, experienced adult to comprehend the possibility of a liar who also tells the truth or a physically brave but morally cowardly man. This, too, is a reason why children's literature does not permit as full and elaborate symbolism as does adult writing; symbolism by its very nature makes *at least* two factors operate at one time—the concrete object or situation and

what it stands for. The number of levels of meaning that the younger reader is likely to reach in a book is limited; thus *Pilgrim's Progress, Gulliver's Travels, Don Quixote, Lord Jim,* and *Les Misérables,* when adapted for children's reading, tend to become exciting tales of adventure and endurance and simultaneously lose much of their metaphysical or ethical or social significance.

The increase in children's ability to juggle many things all at once is not a matter of intelligence. Rather, it connotes development—the collection of more and new kinds of experience, practice in relating points, and the growth of mental habits.

5   Children are *less inclined than older persons to worry over probability,* over the question, "Is this thing likely to happen, or at least to happen in this way?" They are less likely to insist that rationalistic criteria be applied to *all* kinds of events. In their thinking certain expectations and conventional ways of thinking are not yet firmly established; for example, a child may not yet have considered that animals do not talk, that grandmothers do not come out of a wolf's belly unharmed, that mice do not suddenly get transformed into horses drawing a coach. Still, children may—in fact, are very much inclined to—insist on things' being consistent within a certain set of circumstances. Thus a child is apt to question some slight oddness in the daily routine of a fictional family or some unusual detail in a gasoline truck or plane or elephant—*if* the writer has started to give him a picture of something familiar to him. But that child may well be more agile than many adults in moving *among* well-developed frames of reference; that is why he may feel the boy was behaving quite sensibly in peopling a very ordinary street with extraordinary animals in Dr. Seuss's *Mulberry Street.*

There would, then, appear to be a number of important ways in which children and adults read differently and, therefore, important reasons for children's writers and writers for adults writing in different ways. Such considerations make it almost mandatory that we not blithely operate by a single standard but that we go to the trouble of thinking somewhat differently—in certain particulars—about literature for the young and literature for the old.

Differences in Reading for Different Ages

Not only do we find, as already suggested, that the criteria for children's books must in some ways differ from those for adult books, but we also find that the criteria suitable for six-year-old reading may not be the same as those appropriate to twelve-year-old reading. Childhood is not just one generalized state of existence, but is a succession of stages of development with their own levels of reading ability and interest. The young reader changes drastically in a six-year period; the six-year-old understands and likes things different from those his older brothers and sisters comprehend and fancy, and so he imposes different demands on his reading. In the next six years his experience and vocabulary will expand tremendously, and his emotional and intellectual needs also will shift. Therefore, the criteria that can be applied to young-child books are not altogether relevant to books for older children.

1   Between the ages of six and twelve, roughly, everyday familiar matters cease to be the core of children's reading interests and to give way partly, not wholly, to feeling for the significance of fantasy, of the improbable. The reason for this shift is not hard to find. To the preschool child the world of everyday things like cars, canned goods, the house next door, and dogs is not everyday; to him it is new, strange, and wonderful, a fantastic world of cabbages and clicking gates and clanging metal market carts and tremendous chariots called cars. So to him the so-called familiar is the center, or at least a center, of meaning. Hence it does not seem sensible to call for qualities of delicate fantasy, for escape from the ordinary and humdrum; these qualities, which we find in many fairy tales like *Rapunzel* and *The Snow Queen* and in much of the poetry of Rose Fyleman and Walter de la Mare, are not for most young children, and to condemn the "young" stories for lacking these qualities is unrealistic.

But children after six or perhaps seven may begin to find greater satis-faction in a new, created world, a place of fantasy; and so the writer then would need to be able to cause suspension of disbelief, to construct marvels, to invent, at the same time that he is still looking for wonder in normality. The ages of eight to ten, more than any other period, are the time for elaborate fairy tales (*The Frog Prince*, *East of the Sun*, most of the traditional fairy tales, *The Snow Queen*) and for myths and for tales of adventure in far and strange places. But still once more, in early ado-lescense, the child's interest is likely to shift back from this double set of values, the fantastic and the ordinary, to a set of probabilities, a literary world of real places and real people, or at least *possible* ones, a kind of existence that "makes sense" to him. The thirteen- or fourteen-year-old's interests may be considerably closer in kind to those of the six-year-old than to those of the eleven-year-old. He wants to get from his reading a set of heightened impressions that he can easily relate to his junior high school world of classroom routines, lessons, clubs, school contests, games, the problems of growing up, family problems, and jobs. Stories set in actual countries and sometimes involving topical events, such as new inventions and discoveries, may attract children at this stage of develop-ment. And books of undiluted information may come back into their own now.

So without any narrowing of the range of possibilities for creativeness in children's books, it seems wise to grant there are good qualities for young children's books that might *not* be good qualities in books for older children. This is simply an extension of the broad, flexible distinction between criteria for children's literature and criteria for adult literature.

2   The differences in reading vocabulary between children at various age levels are no less dramatic and significant than differences in subject

interest, and the vocabulary differences, being more obvious, are less likely to be overlooked. Parents and teachers become aware of a tremendous expansion in word comprehension and availability between, say, six and eleven. The child's vocabulary increases in total number of concrete and abstract terms, particularly the latter, and the child develops a store of substitutions, or synonyms. This vocabulary development means, of course, that the writer for the younger child needs to *work with less* than does the writer for older children; in this respect his job is more difficult. He needs to create excitement and wonder and understanding with fewer, more limited tools.

Significant Implications, with Some Qualifications

The idea running through the foregoing discussion is that a good book for children, by whatever criteria selected, is not necessarily a good book for adults, and that a good book for some children may not be a good book for younger or older children. Our finding Dickens's *Dombey and Son* or Marquand's *H. M. Pulham, Esquire* or Hemingway's *The Old Man and the Sea* a good book according to certain standards does not mean that it is a superior children's book; by the same token, an Andersen fairy tale that may deservedly delight ten-year-olds may not be a good tale when read to six-year-olds.

But recognition of this fact is *not* to be taken to mean that a meritorious book for adults cannot be a meritorious children's book. The traditional folktales were largely told first to an adult audience, yet many of them are eminently appropriate as children's reading or listening. That *David Copperfield* remains interesting adult reading does not mean that it cannot be interesting reading to thirteen- and fourteen-year-old children. *The Bears' Invasion of Sicily* can be excellent both as an adult satire and as a children's fantasy. Adult tales of sea adventure like Richard Henry Dana's *Two Years before the Mast* and Thor Heyerdahl's *Kon-Tiki* are fine for younger readers, too.

Nor does our distinguishing between children's and adult's literature and seeking appropriate criteria for each mean that a book cannot be a superior book for children and adults *for some of the same reasons.* Ludwig Bemelmans's squat, flat-hatted Madelines are merrily distraught for both children and adults; the reluctance of Kenneth Grahame's reluctant dragon is funny for pretty much the same reason to younger and older readers; both parents and children may find Pooh Bear appealing in his earnest muddleheadedness. Several reasons why children and adult literatures will tend to be different, and so to have different criteria, have been suggested here, but this still leaves room for considerable overlapping of appeal.

An important thing for us to keep in mind is that a book may be superior or inferior in *different ways* for children and adults. A particular book may possess in outstanding degree a quality specially appropriate for children's literature and have other qualities appropriate to adult reading. In Hans Christian Andersen's *The Princess and the Pea,* the satire against social snobbery is sharpest in its jab for adults, while the merry whimsy comes through to the child; the child may become intrigued by the wonders of *Alice in Wonderland* without perceiving the references to human behavior that help to make the book amusing to adults.

The general view suggested in this chapter is a *relativistic* approach to literary, aesthetic values in children's literature. It holds that questions of literary value *do* apply to children's writing but that they need not be identical—indeed, are not likely to be—with criteria one may find applicable to literature for adults. And it has been suggested that such an approach is more helpful in both understanding and using children's reading materials than the assumption that only adult literary criteria—or no significant criteria at all—can apply to writing for children.

This general view brings with it a less cavalier or bored attitude toward children's literature. It means that to judge and select children's books, one must have thought seriously about basic premises of literary value and not just have learned a set of them in literature classes. It means that one must have thought about children, because what children read is connected directly with children. It means that to deal with children's reading, one must *know children's literature well,* must be up on the actual materials in the field. One should know adult literature well, too, for this view does not presume that things written for adults *cannot* contain elements that make them children's literature.

In short, the philosophy of children's literature here proposed calls for careful critical analysis and for knowing the vast field. Neither of these is easy. On the other hand, here the harder way is likely to be the more practical way. It works.

SUGGESTED SOURCES

Some Suggested Literary Comparisons

Here are groupings of children's books similar in subject but significantly different in style—the ways in which the authors have treated their subjects. The basic assumption behind this bibliography is that in each grouping the books on the left and the books on the right have roughly the same raw materials—subjects and themes—but differ in important ways because of the writer's different styles. One side is not necessarily superior to the other. The purpose of this list is to provide practice in determining such differences. You may, however, consider whether in the course of several comparisons it becomes easier to see certain patterns or elements in those books you may wish to call superior among their kind.

Alcott, Louisa: *Little Women,* ill. by Barbara Cooney, Crowell, 1955.	**Farquharson, Martha (pseud. for Martha Finley):** *Elsie Dinsmore,* Grosset & Dunlap, 1896.

Estes, Eleanor: *The Moffats,* ill. by Louis Slobodkin, Harcourt, Brace & World, 1941.
Nesbit, E. (pseud. for Edith Bland): *The Railway Children,* ill. by Lynton Lamb, Benn, 1957.

Sidney, Margaret (pseud. for Harriet M. Lothrop): *The Five Little Peppers and How They Grew,* ill. by William Sharp, Grosset & Dunlap, 1948.

Haywood, Carolyn: *Little Eddie,* ill. by author, Morrow, 1947.

Haywood, Carolyn: *"B" Is for Betsy,* ill. by author, Harcourt, Brace, 1939. Or other Betsy books.

Lipkind, William, and Nicolas Mordvinoff: *Even Steven,* Harcourt, Brace & World, 1952.
Renick, Marion: *Pete's Home Run,* ill. by Pru Herric, Scribner, 1952. Or *Nicky's Football Team,* ill. by Marian Honigman, Scribner, 1951.

Wilson, Hazel: *Herbert,* ill. by John Barron, Knopf, 1950.
Cleary, Beverly: *Henry Huggins,* ill. by Louis Darling, Morrow, 1950. Or other Henry books.

Coatsworth, Elizabeth: *Away Goes Sally,* ill. by Helen Sewell, Macmillan, 1934. Also *The Fair American.*
Forbes, Esther: *Johnny Tremain,* ill. by Lynd Ward, Houghton Mifflin, 1943.
Gray, Elizabeth: *Beppy Marlowe of Charleston,* ill. by Loren Barton, Viking, 1936.
O'Dell, Scott: *Island of the Blue Dolphins,* Houghton Mifflin, 1960.

Childhood of Famous Americans series, Bobbs-Merrill. Fictionalized biographies.
Kent, Louise: *He Went with Christopher Columbus,* ill. by Paul Quinn, Houghton Mifflin, 1940.

Meader, Stephen W.: *Who Rides in the Dark?,* ill. by James MacDonald, Harcourt, Brace, 1937.

Altsheler, Joseph A.: *The Guns of Bull Run: A Story of the Civil War's Eve,* Appleton, 1914.

A book from a popular series like Sue Barton, the Rover Boys, Tom Swift, Nancy Drew, the Hardy Boys, Tarzan, or Chip Hilton.

Clark, Ann Nolan: *Secret of the Andes,* ill. by Jean Charlot, Viking, 1952.
MacGregor, Ellen: *Miss Pickerell Goes to Mars,* Whittlesey, 1951.
Heinlein, Robert A.: *Have Space Suit—Will Travel,* Scribner, 1958. Or *Rocket Ship Galileo,* ill. by Thomas Voter, Scribner, 1947.

Grahame, Kenneth: *The Reluctant Dragon*, ill. by Ernest H. Shepard, Holiday, 1953.
————: *The Wind in the Willows*, ill. by Ernest H. Shepard, Scribner, 1933.

Brooks, Walter: The Freddy series, Knopf.

Slobodkin, Louis: *The Amiable Giant*, ill. by author, Macmillan, 1955.
Thurber, James: *Many Moons*, ill. by Louis Slobodkin, Harcourt, Brace & World, 1943.
————: *The Great Quillow*, ill. by Doris Lee, Harcourt, Brace & World, 1944.
White, E. B.: *Charlotte's Web*, ill. by Garth Williams, Harper & Row, 1952.

Andersen, Hans Christian: *The Snow Queen*, *The Wild Swans*, and other such fantasies.
Boston, L. M.: *The Children of Green Knowe*, Harcourt, Brace & World, 1954.
Lewis, C. S.: *The Lion, the Witch, and the Wardrobe*, ill. by Pauline Baynes, Macmillan, 1950.
Tolkien, John R. R.: *The Hobbit*, ill. by author, Houghton Mifflin, 1938.

Potter, Beatrix: *The Tale of Peter Rabbit*, ill. by author, Warne.

Henry, Marguerite: *King of the Wind*, ill. by Wesley Dennis, Rand McNally, 1948. Also *Misty of Chincoteague*.

Bright, Robert: *Richard Brown and the Dragon*, Doubleday, 1952.

Milne, A. A.: *The World of Pooh*, ill. by Ernest H. Shepard, Dutton, 1957.

Duvoisin, Roger: Petunia series, Knopf.
Embry, Margaret: *The Blue-nosed Witch*, ill. by Carl Rose, Holiday, 1956.
Kahl, Virginia: *The Duchess Bakes a Cake*, ill. by author, Scribner, 1955. Also *Away Went Wolfgang!* and *The Baron's Booty*.

Baum, L. Frank: *The New Wizard of Oz*, illustrations by Evelyn Copelman, adapted from the illustrations of W. W. Denslow, Grosset & Dunlap, 1944. And many other Oz stories.

Most primers.

O'Brien, John S.: *Silver Chief, Dog of the North*, ill. by Kurt Wiese, Holt, 1933. Also *The Return of Silver Chief*.

Knight, Eric: *Lassie Come Home,* ill. by Marguerite Kirmse, Holt, 1940.

James, Will: *Smoky, the Cowhorse,* ill. by author, Scribner, 1926.

Sewell, Anna: *Black Beauty,* ill. by Wesley Dennis, World (Rainbow Classics), 1946.

Farley, Walter: The Black Stallion series, e.g., *The Black Stallion Challenged,* ill. by Angie Draper, Random House, 1964.

Field, Eugene: *Poems of Childhood,* ill. by Maxfield Parrish, Scribner, 1904.

De la Mare, Walter: *Peacock Pie,* ill. by Barbara Cooney, Knopf, 1961.

Frost, Robert: *You Come, Too,* ill. by Thomas W. Nason, Holt, 1959.

Stevenson, Robert Louis: *A Child's Garden of Verses.*

Riley, James Whitcomb: *Rhymes of Childhood,* Bowen-Merrill, 1894.

Wynne, Annette: *For Days and Days,* Stokes, 1919.

A Dr. Seuss limited-vocabularly book.

A non-limited-vocabulary book by Dr. Seuss.

Twain, Mark (pseud. for Samuel Clemens): *The Adventures of Huckleberry Finn,* Heritage, 1952.

Twain, Mark: *The Adventures of Tom Sawyer,* Heritage, 1952.

CHAPTER 3

A
VERY
SHORT
HISTORY
OF
CHILDREN'S
LITERATURE

*T*his chapter will be not about children's literature itself but about the history of children's literature. Some knowledge of where children's literature has been may help us see a little more clearly where it is—may provide a certain perspective, a context, for whatever we settle on as being children's literature for children today.

For several good reasons this history, despite its seeming sweep and inclusiveness, will be a short one. First, literature specifically for children is a fairly recent development; it is a product of the past three hundred years, and it is only during the past century that children's books have become an important element in the publishing trade. Secondly, if one wants to know the interesting historical details of major developments in children's literature, he can consult quite full works like Percy Muir's *English Children's Books, 1600 to 1900*, F. J. Harvey Darton's *Children's Books in England: Five Centuries of Social Life*, Monica Kiefer's *American Children through Their Books, 1700–1835*, Cornelia Meigs et al., *A Critical History of Children's Literature*, and M. F. Thwaite's *From Primer to Pleasure*. And thirdly and most importantly, this book is not primarily a historical survey of children's literature; rather, it is a critical analysis of those aspects of it which seem most relevant to the wise, informed use of books with children. We need, therefore, concern ourselves with only those historical trends and developments that will clarify the present state of writing for children and throw light on the problems of parents and teachers in the use of this body of literature.

Not for Children

A startling fact about the history of children's literature is the almost total *absence* of a literature specifically designed for children until the late seventeenth century. Books for children today are so common it is difficult to conceive of a time when children's books did not spill from shelves and tables in public, school, and home libraries. But such a time there was.

We need to make a careful distinction here. Prior to the seventeenth century in Europe there was scarcely any writing *for* children, but this does not mean that children did not have literature to read or to listen to. Indeed, many of the folktales, ballads, myths, and fables now an important part of the body of juvenile literature were already in circulation. But they had not been invented for children; in intention they were adult literature.

Perhaps we can understand the situation in which pre-eighteenth-century children found themselves if we can imagine a little twentieth-century boy who, for one reason or another, does not get sent to school. He is being taught the essentials of reading at home, but he does not have children's books or magazines bought or borrowed for him by his mother or father. Nor does he watch children's television programs. All this does not mean the boy absorbs no stories, poems, or true accounts at home. After all, he may sit with his parents and look at "grown-up programs"—soap operas, guessing contests, old western movies, or whatever they like to watch— and he may look at the pictures in their books and magazines. When he can read, he may nibble at the stories in them and scan the front-page headlines of the local newspaper, and, of course, the comics in it. And he may listen in on his parents' gossip and the stories that are passed around when company comes to the house. This little boy finds few things composed just for little boys, but this does not mean he goes without the nourishment of facts and imagination. He borrows and adapts to his own uses whatever he can find. Just so did the child of the centuries before authors, illustrators, and publishers began to collaborate in devising material solely for his amusement and instruction.

Folktales

Most of us know folktales which could easily have originated in a mother's or nurse's efforts to amuse, placate, correct, or send to sleep small children—folktales which seem to have accumulated details by momentary inspiration, like *Henny-Penny.* You may recall how Henny-Penny, hit on the head by something unknown, sets off to tell the king the sky is falling and, along the way, meets and persuades other animals (Cocky-Locky, Ducky-Daddles) to do the same. Meeting Foxy-Loxy, they are gulled into taking a shortcut through his cave, where he snaps off their heads, all except Henny-Penny's—she runs off home. Nor is it difficult to imagine mothers or nursemaids or older sisters working up such similar tales as

The Pancake or *The Gingerbread Boy* or developing such adventure yarns as *The Three Little Pigs.*

But that the nursery is one likely place for folktales to be told should not obscure the fact that the great mass of folktales has been created by adults *for adults.* Most folktales have embodied the feelings and experiences of, and have appealed to the minds of, grown men and women. The English or German or Spanish child of, say, the sixteenth century did not form a special audience for tale-tellers; rather, he was likely to be on the fringe of the yarner's adult audience, or might eventually get a much-amended version of the adults' tale.

That they do not know the adult-audience origin of most folktales is one reason why rather squeamish twentieth-century parents are puzzled and sometimes shocked by about two-thirds of the German folktales in Jacob and Wilhelm Grimm's collection—the tale of *Faithful John,* with its theme of absolute loyalty of servant to master (not easily comprehended today by adults *or* children) and its incidents of a man's turning to stone and the beheading of two children; *The Goosegirl,* crowded with symbols of evil and culminating in the death of a naked woman by being rolled in a barrel lined with spikes; *The Frog Prince,* touched with a solemn awareness of the closeness of ugliness to beauty; *The Snakes' Three Leaves,* a tale of how a king permitted himself to be entombed with his dead queen and through three magic leaves brought her to life, how she repaid him with unfaithfulness, and how on discovering this, he had her and her paramour set adrift in a leaking ship; and *The Fisherman and His Wife,* the droll, shrewd account of how a man and wife lived in a chamber pot, how through magic they obtained first a cottage and then a castle, and how they went full circle back to their chamber pot. Adults who have assumed folktales to be primarily juvenile fare may be startled by American Indian tales, in which cruelties are described in a matter-of-fact way, or by such beast-into-man tales as *East of the Sun, West of the Moon,* in which ancient legends of beast-man relationships may linger. Whether or not we consider primitive or advanced the cultures in which such stories originated, it must be admitted that the lore in many respects reflects adult thinking about adult concerns.

These stories were in the oral tradition of the child's society, and he might overhear them from adults' talk, much as all children today over-hear a certain amount of adult gossip and jesting not intended for their ears, or he might hear versions of them directly from a nurse or mother or old man seeking to amuse or lull or frighten or, perhaps, edify. In any case, the tales would not have been invented primarily for him. Yet they possessed a number of qualities that could make them eventually his— strange, wonderful happenings, exciting violence, suspense, easily accepted contrasts of good and evil, the eventual conquest of evil by good, the simplifying of existence, swift action, the aesthetic appeal of repetition of sounds and ideas.

Let us take for an example the tale *Toads and Diamonds,** found in Charles Perrault's collection, *Fairy Tales.* It begins:

There was once a widow who had two daughters. The elder was so like her mother in temper and face that to have seen the one was to have seen the other. They were both so disagreeable and proud, that it was impossible to live with them. The younger, who was the exact portrait of her father in her kindly and polite ways, was as beautiful a girl as one could see. As we are naturally fond of those who resemble us, the mother doted on her elder daugter, while for the younger she had a most violent aversion and made her take her meals in the kitchen and work hard all day. Among other things that she was obliged to do, this poor child was forced to go twice a day to fetch water from a place a mile or more from the house and carry back a large jug filled to the brim.

In this opening section bold, general strokes give us the two essential elements of the story: (1) the neglected condition of the kind daughter (which sets the ground for her later reward) versus the pampering of the unkind daughter (which establishes the story condition for her punishment later through loss of her favored situation), and (2) the kindness of one daughter versus unkindness of the other. As in most folktales, there is little preliminary palaver to establish a sense of special locality or time, and obviously we are not going to be given the opportunity of probing the psychological intricacies of our characters; they are simply very kind and polite or very unkind and impolite. This is the sort of quick generalizing, the swift getting to the heart of a story situation, that helps to make the adult folktale so adaptable to children. Still, this generalness does not mean that the tale shies away from real life; indeed, the first few sentences of this particular folkstory make it clear that its world contains ugliness and meanness (just as Hansel and Gretel soon introduce us to the poverty in the woodsman's family and to disguised evil in the witch's gingerbread house in the dark wood).

As she was standing one day by this spring, a poor woman came up to her and asked the girl to give her some water to drink.

"Certainly, my good woman," she replied, and the beautiful girl at once stooped and rinsed out the jug; and then, filling it with water from the clearest part of the spring, she held it up to the woman, continuing to support the jug, that she might drink with great comfort.

Having drunk, the woman said to her, "You are so beautiful, so good and kind, that I cannot refrain from conferring a gift upon you," for she was really a fairy, who had taken the form of a poor village woman, in order to see how far the girl's kind-heartedness would go. "This gift I make you," continued the fairy, "that with every word you speak, either a flower or a precious stone will fall from your mouth."

Because the girl's character has already been established as entirely kind, no explanation, no supporting details, are needed to support her unhesitating act of kindness. And no greater need is felt to explain the fairy nature of the poor woman by the well. Magic is accepted as a fact of everyday life and is presented in an altogether matter-of-fact way, with no effort to make it seem unusual or amazing. This wonderfulness, without any feeling of a need to explain or justify it, characterizes many folktales and is one of the sources of their appeal to children. Having a good fairy give a good gift is as normal to the teller of the tale—and to a child—as having a kind girl offer water to a tired-looking woman; the abnormal thing would be to have a good fairy give a bad gift or take something away, or to have a kind girl not offer a drink of water. And the latter sort of thing the folktale, pervaded by a fundamental, matured sense of reality, seldom does.

The girl had no sooner reached home than her mother began scolding her for being back so late. "I am sorry, mother," said she, "to have been out so long," and as she spoke, there fell from her mouth six roses, two pearls, and two large diamonds.

The mother gazed at her in astonishment.

"What do I see!" she exclaimed. "Pearls and diamonds seem to be dropping from her mouth! How is this, my daughter?"—It was the first time she had called her daughter. The poor child related in all simplicity what had happened, letting fall quantities of diamonds in the course of her narrative. "I must certainly send my other daughter there," said the mother. "Look, Fanchon, see what falls from your sister's mouth when she speaks! Would you not be glad to receive a similar gift? All you have to do is go and fetch water from the spring and if an old woman asks you for some to drink, to give it to her nicely and politely."

"I should like to see myself going to the spring," answered the rude, cross girl.

"I insist on you going," rejoined the mother, "and that at once."

We are told, of course, that the mother is astonished, but she apparently soon gets over that. The important thing in a world of magic is not that magical things happen, but how people act consistently with their own natures in a sphere that contains possibilities of magic. And the storyteller immediately focuses the remainder of the story on how the mother and daughter *react in character* to the wonderful event. Moreover, in the oral-storytelling manner of most folktales, the teller balances the first part— the kind girl's going to the well—with the second girl's going. This orderliness, which has an aesthetic appeal as well as giving an aid to the memory of teller and listener, is a further element that makes the folktale particularly adaptable to children's use.

> *The elder girl went off, still grumbling; with her she took the handsomest silver bottle she could find in the house.*
>
> *She had no sooner arrived at the spring, than she saw a lady magnificently dressed walking towards her from the wood, who approached and asked for some water to drink. It was the same fairy who had appeared to the sister, but she had now put on the airs and apparel of a princess, as she wished to see how far this girl's rudeness would go.*
>
> *"Do you think I came here just to draw water for you?" answered the arrogant and unmannerly girl; "I have, of course, brought this silver bottle on purpose for you to drink from, and all I have to say is—drink from it if you like!"*
>
> *"You are scarcely polite," said the fairy, without losing her temper; "however, as you are so disobliging, I confer this gift upon you, that with every word you speak a snake or a toad shall fall from your mouth."*

Here the earlier action and remarks of the fairy are repeated, but with the neatly ironic reversal that characterizes much adult folk—and non-folk—literature.

> *Directly her mother caught sight of her, she called out, "Well, my daughter!"*
>
> *"Well, my mother!" replied the ill-tempered girl, throwing out as she spoke two vipers and a toad.*

Although magic is the immediate cause, what is now happening is altogether consistent with the daughter's character, just as the dropping of roses, pearls, and diamonds from the other girl's mouth was consistent with hers.

> *"Alack!" cried the mother, "what do I see? This is her sister's doing, but I will pay her out for it," and so saying, she ran towards the younger with intent to beat her. The unhappy girl fled from the house, and went and hid herself in a neighboring forest. The King's son, who was returning from hunting, met her, and seeing how beautiful she was, asked her what she was doing there all alone, and why she was crying.*
>
> *"Alas! sir, my mother has driven me from home."*

A matter of chance, one might say of the prince's happening to be there in the forest. Perhaps. But the teller thinks his being there to hunt is enough of an explanation, and anyhow the incident is surrounded by two predictable actions——her being driven away by her bad-tempered mother and her speaking and dropping pearls and diamonds from her mouth.

The King's son, seeing five or six pearls and as many diamonds falling from her mouth as she spoke, asked her to explain how this was, and she told him all her tale. The King's son fell in love with her; and thinking that such a gift as she possessed was worth more than any ordinary dower brought by another, he carried her off to his father's palace, and there married her.

As for her sister, she made herself so hated that her own mother drove her from the house. The miserable girl, having gone about in vain trying to find someone who would take her in, crept away into a corner of a wood and there died.

Thus the story is concluded very swiftly, without explanatory detail, for the important thing has already happened——the kind girl and the unkind girl have been visited by the appropriate wonders——and the ending simply has to indicate, almost casually, the appropriate rewards and punishment. The folktale generally has goodness triumph, but not until one has been made fully aware of evil, its strength and omnipresence. And it seldom seeks to sweeten the picture by having evil forgiven or converted; it is permitted to remain what it was. Also, the punishment, though mentioned, is not described in detail; we need only know in *outline* what happened so that we will have the complete story circle. The folktale teller is seldom interested in exploiting dangerous or ugly or horrifying or cruel situations for their shock value; he simply mentions them in order to make clear the cycle of events. This is one reason why the adult matter of folktales is, in spite of the worries of some adults today, no great problem for the child reader. The emotional possibilities of events are not exploited.

Myths

Myths, like the great majority of folktales, were not originally created for children, but in the minds of many people today they are associated almost solely with children and their reading. The large number of myth collections designed expressly for children in selection, manner of telling, vocabulary, size of print, format, and illustrations may be partly responsible for this common linking. Most of us, either as children or as adults, encounter myths in children's books, and so we come to think of Zeus, Orpheus, Clytie, Perseus, and their adventures mainly in terms of Helen Sewell's or Olivia Coolidge's or Ingri and Edgar Parin d'Aulaire's tellings for children. And that this view should get wide acceptance is assured by the seeming naïveté of mythological explanations of natural phenomena. To a modern reader the explanation of thunder and lightning as manifestations of a god's manlike anger suggests the make-believe of little children; the reduction of the dichotomy of good and evil to Pandora's box or of winter and spring to the coming and going of Persephone between the upper and lower worlds seems a childlike simplifying of a complex fact. But the present-day adult reader who jumps to this conclusion is overlooking two important characteristics of mythology. First, the myths were efforts of mature minds to explain life phenomena without the aid of a fully developed method of scientific investigation, a modern advantage that can make a mediocre modern mind seem, at a superficial glance, superior to a brilliant mind of an early, prescientific culture. Secondly, it would seem that most mythology, even if it was not so considered at first, soon came to be considered as a metaphorical, imaginative explanation rather than as a literal explanation of reality. This can be made plain merely by noting how many of the myths can be rejected as literal truths and yet retain their validity as at least an arguable philosophical position on a basic question. For instance, although we view as fiction the story of how Pandora's curiosity teased her into opening the box and thus letting out all the afflictions that have beset mankind, intelligent and well-informed modern men may still seriously argue the question of whether man's desire for knowledge—his curiosity about unknown facts in a million boxes—is boon or curse. And the fall of Icarus into the sea when he dared to fly too close to the sun with his wings of feathers and wax remains a statement of one debatable view of human pride. And although we reject the relationship of the earth goddess Demeter and her daughter Persephone as a literal explanation of winter's unfruitfulness and spring's fruitfulness, it may still impress us as a vivid statement of the orderly interchange of birth and death in nature. Dismissal of myths as evidence of a culture's naïveté is really evidence of a considerable degree of naïveté in modern men who do so.

Recognizing myths as serious, grown-up thinking about problems and phenomena of lasting significance, one can better understand why he constantly encounters ideas and attitudes of a quite unchildlike short (except where the myths have been so washed and strained of all adult impurities as to bear scarcely any relation to true myth telling). Violence, fear and courage, birth and death, sex, faithfulness and infidelity in many forms, loss and sacrifice, jealousy and suspicion, the pettiness and magnanimity of men and women—these adult themes are interwoven throughout the myths of Greece and Rome, northern Europe, the Near East, China and Japan, and the America of the Indians. In the tragic myth of Oedipus— his exposure on the hills as a baby, his survival, wanderings, and unknowing marriage to his own mother, the eventual discovery of his own sin, and his self-blinding—there is a magnificent groping into the complex mysteries of man's fate. In this myth the Greek mind courageously faced and stated the conundrum of the good man committing an offense against the nature of the universe, an offense that must be avenged by his destruction. Again, the puzzle of destiny, of man's seeming fatedness, is presented in the tale of Meleager, who is from birth destined for death whenever his mother, Althea, throws a certain brand into the fire. Adult

concern with sexual beauty and love and the wonders of birth are integral elements of many Greek myths—Zeus, in the form of a beautiful bull, raping the maiden Europa; the visiting of Danaë by Zeus in
a shower of gold, with the resulting conception of Perseus; the marriage
of the maiden Psyche to the unseen "monster," her being forbidden to see
him, her disobedience and discovery that he is the beautiful Cupid, and
her subsequent loss of him and their eventual reunion after Psyche's loyal
performance of many difficult tasks; and Medea's murderous hatred when
she is deserted by Jason. The adult wondering recognition of the eternal
cycle of life and death recurs again and again—in such myths as that of
Demeter and her annual reunion with Persephone, in the Indian tale of
Little Burntface's reunion with the great invisible god of the rain and his
healing of her many burns.

None of this is kid stuff, either in its specific, concrete situations or in
its pervasive conceptions or themes. Still, as with the Grimm and other
folktales, the myths have great natural riches for children—they can satisfy
children with the atmosphere of nobility that runs through most of them,
intrigue with their strangeness and magic, and stir with their idealized,
valiant action enacted on a plane of godlike humanity. Whether or not the
adults of myth-imbued cultures considered their myths an important part
of children's upbringing (and many, like the ancient Greeks, did), the
myths would be taken up by children and made a part of their literature
whenever they had the chance to share their elders' hearing or reading.

Heroic Legend

The accounts of legendary heroes—the folk heroes around whom gathered
the stories of Jason, Achilles, Ulysses, Aeneas, Beowulf, Roland, King Arthur and his Knights of the Round Table, Robin Hood, and Davy Crockett—
likewise were adult rememberings and imaginings; they embodied the
values, fears, desires, and assurances of the peoples who gradually invented them. They were stories of common knowledge and concern, an
integral part of the cultural context, and as such were often referred to
allusively, in bits and pieces. They were part of adult knowledge and so
filtered down, through both the informal educational channels of over-
hearing and casual informing and the more formal educational channels
of school books and recitations. Unlike the folktales, however, most of
these hero legends underwent a further transformation into sophisticated,
conventionalized, lengthy art forms—the epics. This made them less immediately and directly accessible to children but meant a fuller, more
formal exposure at a later age.

Fables

Fables have become an integral part of children's literature, but they
originated in the folk wisdom—an eminently adult interchange of ethical
warnings and commendations—of India, the Near East, and Europe. They

were a pleasant and colorful means of explaining and giving body to the old sayings and adages passed on from generation to generation.

The most obvious stylistic characteristics of fables reveal not only their source in adult thinking but also their originally mainly adult listeners. Next to the folk sayings themselves, they are the most abstract of all forms of literature; in "The Crow and the Fox," the two protagonists are not so much a particular crow and a certain fox as they are the abstracted characteristics of vanity and cunning. And they are unapologetically moral-pointing and make few concessions to color and vivid excitement. Too, they are essentially satirical; it is significant that La Fontaine, a witty, sophisticated intellectual of the sophisticated French society of the seventeenth century, should choose the old fables or the Aesop and Bidpai collections as the medium for his satirical attacks on the frauds, hypocrisies, and follies of contemporary society.

Some adults, aware of these elements of grown-upness in the fables, use them sparingly with children. Yet it cannot be denied that children can find strong, uncomplicated fun in, say, the situation of the mice who plan to bell the cat before thinking of who will do it; they find in the fables the simple wonder of animals (not real ones, though) talking like human beings; they like the quick, dramatic action of "The Wolf in Sheep's Clothing" or "The Crow and the Pitcher" or "The Lion and the Mouse." The fables, though devised by adults to embody their own values, have elements for listening or reading children.

Folk Songs

During the past two decades folk songs have made an impressive invasion of the preschoolroom and the schoolroom, and many of them are already running the risk of becoming altogether identified with children's tastes and activities—the fate long ago met by folktales.

Some kinds of folk songs—lullabies, game songs, and some nonsense songs like "Froggie Went a-Courtin' "—clearly were created for children; but the great majority of folk songs—ballads like "Edward" or "The Lowlands Low" or "Little Mattie Groves," love plaints like "Careless Love" or "Down in the Valley," work songs like "John Henry"—were brought into being for listeners with adult concerns and attitudes. Like the folktale's, the folk song's directness and concreteness can at first impress us as childlike, but most of the ballads deal with situations of a kind more comprehensible to adults—torn loyalties, desperate courage, infidelity, revenge, death and loss. Any random sampling of folk ballads will make this clear— "Frankie and Johnnie" (a girl shoots her faithless lover), "The Wife of Usher's Well" (a mother is visited by the ghosts of her dead sons), "Bonnie George Campbell" (Bonnie George Campbell's horse returns to his castle without his master), "Casey Jones" (a brave engineer rides his train to destruction), "The Little Mohee" (an Englishman falls in love with "a fair Indian lass," leaves her to return to a girl back home, finds the English girl had not waited for him, and so he comes back to claim his Mohee),

"Jesse James" (an outlaw hero is betrayed), "Robin Hood" (another outlaw fights it out with the authorities), "Old Smokey" (a lover abandoned by his sweetheart wanders and drinks on the hilltop), "Red River Valley" (two lovers part), "Young Cowboy of Laredo" (mortally wounded cowboy recounts his life of gambling, drinking, and fighting), "The Lowlands Low" (a cabin boy heroically bores a hole in the enemy ship and then is left by his captain to sink), "The Boll Weevil Song" (the tenant farmer desperately tries to destroy the boll weevil but in the end loses his farm and all his few possessions to the beetle). Folk songs, filled with a very mature awareness of tragedy and pathos in human existence, frequently describe with disarming realism the ironic mixtures of love and hatred in human character.

This kind of song children overheard in their homes and away from them for many centuries, long before the advent of such folk-song collections as Beatrice Landeck's *Songs to Grow On*, Margaret Bradford Boni's *Fireside Book of Folksongs*, or Ruth Seeger's *American Folk Songs for Children*. These songs were not concert songs, but knocked about the streets and alleys and fields; that is, they permeated the world of the child, though in many respects they were not akin to the child's mental world. And, like the folktales and myths, they had for him things he could use—tales of derring-do, a quick and unwearying pace, strange and romantic places and events and people, occasional rowdy slapstick fun, and the aesthetic joys of rhythm and sound linkings. Hence, it could not be said that a child was without a literature if he grew up in the sixteenth-century world that sang "The Ballad of Chevy Chase" and "Sir Patrick Spens" or in the nineteenth-century world that sang "Sweet Betsy from Pike" and "The E-ri-e Canal" and "The Buffalo Hunters." He had, indeed, a remarkably rich imaginative literature at his disposal, and, to his great advantage, it was available to him almost entirely in oral form, coupled with music.

Popular Rhyme

And, of course, in the centuries before the era of children's books there were miscellaneous rhymes—snatches of doggerel, little jests, rhymed folk wisdom, nonsense rhymes, bitter political jabs and campaign slogans, charms—all of which a child might hear from adults in the streets, in shops and workshops, and by the fireside, and some of which became the core of the greatly diverse editions of *Mother Goose*.

Mother Goose is merely a name that, a couple of hundred years ago when the era of literature *for* children was young, got attached to almost any collection designed for children from the mass of traditional verses, most of which had *not* been created for children. Quite a number of these traditional rhymes and snatches had become the property of the nursery by the time the eighteenth-century editors collected them and put them into children's books, but this does not mean they started out that way, with that audience in mind. It means merely that the common process of appropriation of adult imaginings by imaginative children had been going on. According to Iona and Peter Opie, in the introduction to their *Oxford Dictionary of Nursery Rhymes**:

It can be safely stated that the overwhelming majority of nursery rhymes were not in the first place composed for children; in fact many are survivals of an adult code of joviality, and in their original wording were, by present standards, strikingly unsuitable for those of tender years. They are fragments of ballads or of folk songs ("One misty moisty morning" and "Old woman, old woman, shall we go a-shearing?"). They are remnants of ancient custom and ritual ("Ladybird, ladybird," and "We'll go to the wood"), and may hold the last echoes of long-forgotten evil (Where have you been all day?" and "London Bridge"). Some are memories of street cry and mummers' play ("Young lambs to sell! young lambs to sell!" and "On Christmas night I turned the spit"). One at least ("Jack Sprat") has long been proverbial. Others ("If wishes were horses," and "A man of words") are based on proverbs. One ("Matthew, Mark, Luke, and John") is a prayer of Popish days, another ("Go to bed, Tom") was a barrack room refrain. They have come out of taverns and mug houses. ("Nose, nose, jolly red nose" still flaunts the nature of its early environment.) They are the legacy of war and rebellion ("At the siege of Belle Isle" and "What is the rhyme for porringer?"). They have poked fun at religious practices ("Good morning, Father Francis") and laughed at the rulers of the day ("William and Mary, George and Anne"). They were the diversions of the scholarly, the erudite, and the wits (as Dr. Wallis on a "Twister," Dr. Johnson on a "Turnip seller," and Tom Brown on "Dr. Fell"). They were first made popular on the stage (Jack Cussans's "Robinson Crusoe") or in London streets (Jacob Beuler's "If I had a donkey"). They were rude jests (like "Little Robin Redbreast sat upon a rail"), or romantic lyrics of a decidedly free nature (as "Where are you going to, my pretty maid?"), which were carefully rewritten to suit the new discrimination at the turn of the last century. We can say almost without hesitation that, of those pieces which date from before 1800, the only true nursery rhymes (i.e. rhymes composed especially for the nursery) are the rhyming alphabets, the infant amusements (verses which accompany a game), and the lullabies. Even the riddles were in the first place designed for adult perplexity.

Although the adult origins of many children's rhymes may often be obscure, it should be perfectly clear why children *would* take over these rhymes and gradually appropriate them to their own needs and uses. They had all the things that little children could possibly want—merry nonsense of both situation and language, broad, vigorous humor, swift action, and sturdy rhythms and much experimentation with word sounds. Memory of their origin had only to die out for them to become altogether suitable material for little children to hear, say, and alter.

Assimilation

For thousands of years no one apparently gave much consistent, regular attention to the literary needs of children; it is, then, not unnatural that the children should have taken matters into their own hands and *borrowed* adult literature, using those things in it that they could understand, enjoy, and learn from and altering the parts that could not be used as they stood.

The appetite of children for experience and for the idealization of experience has always been vast. When they could not get especially fashioned literary foods, they took their elders' fare and gulped it down. The history of children's listening and reading prior to our own time would suggest that maybe we can worry too much over a child's not having books correctly designed for him. It is very easy to overlook the ability of children to assimilate the most unlikely materials into their intellectual and emotional matrices.

One way to remind oneself of this ability is to listen to children play-reading to themselves—improvising and filling in and changing the story before them or, out on the playground, shaping new songs, rhymes, and stories from advertisements, tag ends of television programs, Disney movies. Another way is to list, in a free-association manner, *all* the reading you *remember* doing as a child and then to note the surprising titles, the reading a child of that age might not be expected to make much of—the great mélange of your childhood reading. Trash with great literature? Children's stories with adult stories? Fiction with nonfiction? One may find, if he is honest, such nonchildren's reading as the telephone book, the encyclopedia (and not necessarily a children's), the newspaper's first page and sport pages, a mail-order catalog, *The National Geographic* and *Woman's Home Companion*, picture books of world wars and other modern history, monthly-book-club books that his parents maybe didn't get to but he did (like *Gone with The Wind* or *The Age of Jackson*), his father's medical books or garage handbooks, brochures from various adult organizations. And along with approved classics like *The Child's Garden* and *Tom Sawyer* he may find *The Bobbsey Twins,* Nancy Drew or other "mystery" series or *The Hardy Boys,* comic strips or comic books *(Superman, Batman), The Five Little Peppers, Tom Swift,* Zane Grey's westerns, and *Tarzan.*

This is no argument, though, for a scarcity of literature fashioned for children. That children can adapt unpromising materials to their uses certainly does not mean that they cannot profit by a richer, more specialized sort of diet.

A Fundamental Change

Such a diet came into being about three hundred years ago. The grown-up world, becoming more aware of children, and of children as children, at last realized that children listened and read and that what they listened to and read might have some influence on what they became. This growing awareness happened, fortunately, to correspond with the increasing availability of reading materials; printing made it more possible to distribute new reading to young readers.

This new concern with children's reading and with the providing of appropriate books appears to have resulted from a complex of causes. Just what each of these was and what its effect on children's reading may have been is impossible to determine, but many shifts in attitude were occurring that could easily turn men's minds to the task of providing special materials for the young. The Renaissance, with its quick curiosity and renewed interest in education, had sharpened the desire to shape children's minds. There was the Protestants' intense worry for the evil-tainted soul of the young child; this would easily turn adults to any promising avenue of education, and the printed page was an obvious one. European thinking was beginning to be colored by a materialistic, empirical philosophy that elevated the senses—experience—as the primary source of knowledge; clearly, this made the early exposure of the mind critically important in determining adult character, and since reading and listening to tales and rhymes comprised a type of exposure feasible with children, they deserved close attention. And the spreading democratic concept of education as the need and prerogative of all persons meant a greater concern with all the varied educational instruments, since pedagogues would no longer be concerned with a limited and relatively homogenous group of well-born children and must pull and tug and cajole in every possible way.

Whatever the particular components of this complex of causes, the seventeenth, eighteenth, and nineteenth centuries witnessed a rediscovery of the child and a new view of the child's relationship to the adult he would become. These new orientations in turn meant a greater concentration on the discovery and use of all possible educative influences. Tales and poems for children were quickly seized upon as means for filling and changing the child.

As a consequence, for the first two hundred years of children's literature, the books written for them were strongly and frankly didactic in purpose and tone. Of the classical twin aims of literature—pleasure and instruction—the latter was most intensely adhered to. Pleasure, when attended to at all, generally remained primarily a means to that more vital end instruction, the early shaping of behavior.

Puritan Purpose in Children's Literature

The first main wave of books directly intended for children's consumption was Puritan, a kind of children's literature that has persisted, though in greatly lessened degree, up to the present day despite the decline of Puritan tenets and modes of behavior.

The seventeenth-century English or the American colonial Puritan was intensely and constantly aware of sin—sin in himself and sin in others. Evil was real, and man was touched with evil. By humiliating the flesh, men might hope to be among the few elect who would be saved; all others were damned to eternal suffering for their sins. Man's span of life was not for pleasure; it was for the rigorous enslavement of worldly desires. Indeed fortunate the rare person who, still pure, departed from this valley of temptation as a child. But children were not regarded as necessarily less corrupt than adults; if anything, they were felt to be weaker vessels, requiring hardening, disciplining. They must be imbued quite early with a sense of their own weakness and a willingness to obey the moral directors of their society. And coupled with this awareness of enemies within and without the individual personality, there had to be a certain prudence in all things, in calculations about human as well as divine intercourse. Puritans, predominantly middle class, reflected the high values placed on the middle-class virtues of caution, propriety, thrift, and planning.

Puritan society tried to convey these views and precepts to its children through a variety of instructional media—hornbooks, primers, catechisms, moral story lessons, or *exempla*, prayers, and hymns. In all these media— from the little page of advice slipped beneath the shell of the hornbook of the younger child to the stories for older children—the method of exposition was most often bluntly admonitory, with only the slightest effort to clothe the ethical or theological idea in action and character.

Typical of much of the direct homiletic warning to youth about virtue's reward and sin's punishment is Benjamin Keach's *War with the Devil, or the Young Man's Conflict with the Powers of Darkness, in a Dialogue Discovering the Corruption and Vanity of Youth, the Horrible Nature of Sin, and the Deplorable Condition of Fallen Man**; and typical of this particular work of unvarnished didacticism is this excerpt:

Let all backsliders of me warning take,
Before they fall into the Stygian Lake;
Yea, and return and make with God their peace
Before the Days of Grace and Mercy cease;
For mine are past forever, Oh! condole
My sad Estate and miserable Soul.
My Days will quickly end, and I must lie
Broyling in Flames to all Eternity.

Like this example, many less hortatory warnings were couched in verse, a kind of sugaring for the bitter pill of life, as in Isaac Watts' "The All-seeing Eye"*:

There's not a sin that we commit,
Nor wicked word we say,
But in thy dreadful book 'tis writ
Against the judgment day.

Lord, at thy foot ashamed I lie,
Upwards I dare not look;

Pardon my sins before I die,
And blot them from thy book.

New England children learned through the "Shorter Catechism of the Assembly of Divines" in their *New England Primer* the central doctrines of the Calvinist faith. And the child was counseled in methods of applying to daily behavior the fundamental beliefs of his faith by such exhortations as those of Eleazer Moodey in *The School of Good Manners** (Boston, 1772):

1. *Let thy Thoughts be Divine, Awful, and Godly.*
2. *Let thy Talk be Little, Honest, and True.*
3. *Let thy Works be Profitable, Holy and Charitable.*
4. *Let thy Manners be Grave, Courteous, and Chearful.*
5. *Let thy Diet be Temperate, Convenient, and Frugal.*
6. *Let thy Apparel be Sober, Neat, and Comely.*
7. *Let thy Will be Compliant, Obedient, and Ready.*
8. *Let thy Sleep be Moderate, Quiet, and Seasonable.*
9. *Let thy Prayers be Devout, Often and Fervent.*
10. *Let thy Recreations be Lawful, Brief, and Seldom.*
11. *Let thy Meditations be of Death, Judgment, and Eternity.*

But the child growing up in a Puritan culture was not limited to edification in the form of such abstract and generalized preachment; the Calvinist views of heaven and hell and earth and of the human lot were made explicit by brief, dramatic story illustrations. One very popular form of juvenile didactic story was the history of good or bad children. Histories of good children usually gave accounts of how pious children met early deaths happily. Janeway introduced his *Token for Children: Being an Exact Account of the Conversion, Holy and Exemplary Lives and Joyful Deaths of Several Young Children,** the most famous of these efforts, with this description of purpose and method:

You may now hear (my dear Lambs) what other good Children have done, and remember how they wept and prayed by themselves; how earnestly they cried out for an interest in the Lord Jesus Christ. . . . Would you be in the same condition as naughty Children? O Hell is a terrible place, that is a thousand times worse than Whipping. God's Anger is worse than your Father's Anger.

To most adults in the mid-twentieth century it may seem fantastic that adults should ever have conceived such lugubrious, sorry fare for child readers and even more bizarre that young readers should apparently have read it not altogether unwillingly. But it may really not be so much the threatening, scolding method and tone that upsets them as it is the stern lessons offered. The majority of present-day parents and teachers do not accept the hellfire-and-damnation message of these little moralities, and so these books seem more remote from them than they really are. For great numbers of teachers and parents find nothing particularly upsetting in the Munro Leaf books *Manners Can Be Fun, Grammar Can Be Fun,* etc. Yet Leaf uses just about the same techniques as the Puritans did—the threat to the bad child, the direct explanation, the exhortation, the praise of the good child—and his books have the same tone of adult condescension. Leaf's text, accompanied by strenuously primitive drawings, first tells what polite children do. "If we want something we say PLEASE. We say THANK YOU if you help us or give us something or do things for us." "Before we leave the table we ask if we may be excused, and say THANK YOU if we are told we may." He then contrasts their behavior with "some people we don't like to play with." These include the Pigs, (who "have all sorts of toys but they never let anyone else play with them. They just squeal THAT'S MINE"), the Whineys, (who "whine if they can't have things they should not"), the Noiseys, the Me Firsts. The slap-bang cartooning, of course, may amuse children; but so did the woodcuts in the *New England Primer,* quite probably. The distance between the didactic children's books of the seventeenth and eighteenth centuries and this Fun series is quite short.

Gelett Burgess's Goops in *New Goops and How to Know Them,* * dreadful embodiments of all forms of naughty behavior, are cousins to the awful examples of the 18th-century children's writer:

I cannot caution you too much
Not to take others' things, or touch.
For even if you do not take them
By handling them you often break them.
And then, in spite of all you say
They'll call you Goop—why shouldn't they?

or

A gentleman or lady may
Be recognized by what they say;
They are polite, and so they don't
Exclaim, Shut up! Me first! I won't!
They use instead such words as these:
Excuse me. Thank you. If you please.

And Burgess's balloon-headed cartoon figures add an old-time touch of grimness to the scolding verses.

The recently published *Phantom Tolbooth,* written by Norton Juster and illustrated by Jules Feiffer, which received considerable critical praise, is a thinly disguised allegory about language and numbers in Dictionopolis and Digitopolis. And the parents and grandparents of Leaf users had their Elsie Dinsmore series—fearful, cautious, preachy, condescending—and before these there were the Peter Parley books crammed with information and good counsel for young readers of early-nineteenth-century America.

The preachment, in both its direct, heavy method and its general attitude to humanity, has never wholly disappeared from the children's library shelf.

The Enlightenment and Children's Books

The Puritan warning to the young, though never altogether extinguished, was replaced as the dominant trend in children's literature by the late-eighteenth-century social reformers' earnest admonition to youth.

This was the Age of Enlightenment—the time of Voltaire, Diderot, Rousseau, Hume, Tom Paine, Helvetius, William Godwin, Mary Wollstonecraft. It was a time in which traditional beliefs and behavior were coming in for heavy criticism. Philosophers, political thinkers, economists, educators, and scientists wrote earnest attacks upon the way things were and made eager prophecies of what society might become if only men permitted reason to have its way against the weight of custom and tradition. Although many people, perhaps the majority, were unmoved by the new ideas (or even unaware of them), the educated upper middle classes and the aristocracy talked and wrote about these views and in various ways even acted on them. What were these ideas?

They were based pretty much on a few assumptions about the nature of man. Man, unlike the Puritan's "mankind," did not come with a burden of original sin upon his back. Rather, he was part and product of a fundamentally rational universe under a reasonable, somewhat remote God or principle of divine rightness, and man himself was capable of taking any sort of impression from his new environment. He had unlimited capabilities; he was a sheet of white paper on which anything could be written. A corollary of this view was the refusal to accept existing institutions and traditional ways of doing things as sacred and inevitable. Hence all that man had inherited from the past was inspected closely and without reverence—and in fact antiquity came to be looked on not as a hallowing characteristic, but as reason for suspicion. Another corollary was a belief—indeed, it tended to become a mystical faith—in the superiority of natural, unspoiled, simple societies and physical nature. Simplicity of speech, dress, and physical needs became an ideal. And running through much Enlightenment thinking was a general tendency to look quizzically at established conceptions of human class and rank. This leveling, of course, took different forms; these liberal thinkers certainly did not entirely agree among themselves. One important view was that men, though not all equal in natural endowments, were equal before God in their rights as human beings—in their right to freedom of worship, belief, and speech, their right to some part in determining their political and economic fate. This blended into a more extreme view, one that became increasingly important as the eighteenth century waned—the view that all men were equal not only in rights but in ability. A conception of universal brotherhood became an important force in European thought—the leveling of classes, nations, races. Tolerance became a virtue—tolerance of differing religions, political views, customs. And a rising humanitarian feeling expressed itself in diverse ways—in sentiment against warfare, against slavery, against exploitation of women and children in the rising industries, against cruelty to animals, and in favor of all sorts of philanthropy and good works, in favor of gentleness and kindness to children.

These were the ideas that in varying degree many children's authors of the late eighteenth century sought to promulgate in their writings, and they are ideas that may seem very different from those that preceded them. Yet the methods were not markedly different. The situations in the tales were obviously contrived to point up a lesson—usually to make a comparison between right and wrong conduct. The new authors put lessons and philosophical arguments into the mouths of protagonists, just as the Puritan writers gave their heroes sermons to preach. The tone remained didactic and condescending. The verses were as pedestrian and directly moralizing as ever, though they might express a greater worry about the poor bird in the tree than about a little boy's immortal soul.

The new writers' aim, like that of the Puritans, was to sugarcoat instruction—in the poetry by rhythm and rhyme, in the fiction by the use of children (usually young in years only) as central characters, realistic settings (villages, farms, schools), melodramatic situations, excitement, and a rather heavy sprinkling of sentiment in the form of tears and faintings.

The following passage from Thomas Day's *History of Sandford and Merton,* * one of the most popular children's books at the turn of the century, is typical in content and method of much of this new wave of didactic juvenile writing:

Harry and Tommy then agreed to go early the next morning to buy some clothes for the poor children. They accordingly set out before breakfast, and had proceeded nearly half way, when they heard the noise of a pack of hounds that seemed to be running full cry at some distance. Tommy then asked Harry if he knew what they were about. "Yes," said Harry, "I know well enough what they are about; it is squire Chase and his dogs worrying a poor hare. But I wonder they are not ashamed to meddle with such a poor inoffensive creature, that cannot defend itself: if they have a mind to hunt, why don't they hunt lions, and tigers, and such fierce mischievous creatures, as I have read they do in other countries?" "Oh! dear," said Tommy, "how is that? it must surely be very dangerous."—"Why, you know," said Harry, "the men are accustomed in some places to go almost naked; and that makes them so prodigiously nimble, that they can run like a deer. . . .

After Harry's vivid account of a lion hunt, the boys notice the fleeing hare that occasioned the lecture:

Presently, up came the dogs, who had now lost all scent of their game, and a gentleman mounted upon a fine horse, who asked Harry, if he had seen the Hare? Harry made no answer; but, upon the gentleman's repeating the question in a louder tone of voice, he answered that he had. "And which way is she gone?" said the gentleman. "Sir, I don't choose to tell you," answered Harry, after some hesitation. "Not choose!" said the gentleman, leaping off his horse, "but I'll make you choose in an instant"; and coming up to Harry, who neved moved from the place where he had been standing, began to lash him in a most unmerciful manner with his whip, continually repeating, "Now, you little rascal, do you choose to tell me now?" To which Harry made no other answer than this: "If I would not tell you before, I won't now, though you should kill me." But this fortitude of Harry, and the tears of Tommy, who cried in the bitterest manner to see the distress of his friend, made no impression on this barbarian, who continued his brutality till another gentleman rode up full speed, and said, "For God's sake, squire, what are you about? You will kill the child, if you do not take care."—"And the little dog deserves it," said the other; "he has seen the hare, and will not tell me which way she is gone." "Take care," replied the gentleman, in a low voice, "you don't involve yourself in a disagreeable affair; I know the other to be the son of a gentleman of great fortune in the neighbourhood": and then, turning to Harry, he said, "Why, my dear, would you not tell the gentleman which way the hare had gone, if you saw her?" "Because," answered Harry, as soon as he had recovered breath enough to speak, "I don't choose to betray the unfortunate." "This boy," said the gentleman, "is a prodigy; and it is a happy thing for you, Squire, that his age is not equal to his spirit. But you are always passionate—." At this moment the hounds recovered the scent, and bursting into a full cry, the Squire mounted his horse, and galloped away, attended by all his companions.

When they were gone, Tommy came up to Harry in the most affectionate manner, and asked him how he did?—"A little sore," said Harry; "but that does not signify."—Tommy. I wish I had a pistol or a sword!—Harry. Why, what would you have done with it?—T. I would have killed that good-for-nothing man who treated you so cruelly.—H. That would have been wrong, Tommy; for I am sure he did not want to kill me. Indeed, if I had been a man, he should not have used me so; but it is all over now, and we ought to forgive our enemies, as Mr. Barlow tells us Christ did; and then perhaps they may come to love us, and be sorry for what they have done.—T. But how could you bear to be so severely whipped, without crying out?—H. Why, crying out would have done me no good at all, would it? and this is nothing to what many little boys have suffered without ever flinching, or bemoaning themselves.—T. Well, I should have thought a great deal.—H. Oh! it's nothing to what the young Spartans used to suffer.—T. Who are they?

And of course Harry accepts the invitation to inform the extremely ignorant and benighted Tommy.

The tutor Mr. Barlow bears most of the responsibility for noting significant events, telling stories to point out their significance or offering learned discourses to make their implications inescapable. Typical of Day's use of the tutor—and of many other authors' uses of instructors and instructresses—is the following dialogue which begins when the gentleman's son Tommy proudly tells Mr. Barlow that he has planted a garden of his own:

He could not help telling Mr. Barlow what he had done, and asking him, whether he was not a very good boy, for working so hard to raise corn? "That," said Mr. Barlow, "depends upon the use you intend to make of it, when you have raised it: what is it you intend doing with it?" "Why, sir," said Tommy, "I intend to send it to the mill that we saw and have it ground into flour; and then I will get you to show me how to make bread of it; and then I will eat it, that I may tell my father that I have eaten bread out of corn of my own sowing." "That will be very well done," said Mr. Barlow, "but where will be the great goodness that you sow corn for your own eating? That is no more than all the people round continually do; and if they did not do it, they would be obliged to fast." "But then," said Tommy, "they are not gentlemen, as I am."

"What then," answered Mr. Barlow, "must not gentlemen eat as well as others, and therefore is it not for their interest to know how to procure food as well as other people?" "Yes, sir," answered Tommy, "but they can have other people to raise it for them, so that they are not obliged to work for themselves." "How does that happen," said Mr. Barlow.—Tommy. Why sir, they pay other people to work for them, or buy bread when it is made, as much as they want. Mr. B. Then they pay for it with money?—T. Yes, sir.—Mr. B. Then they must have money before they can buy corn?—T. Certainly, sir. —Mr. B. But have all gentlemen money?—Tommy hesitated some time at his question; at last he said, "I believe not always, sir."— Mr. B. Why then, if they have not money, they will find it difficult to procure corn, unless they raise it for themselves.—"Indeed," said Tommy, "I believe they will; for perhaps they may not find any body good-natured enough to give it them." "But," said Mr. Barlow, "as we are talking upon this subject, I will tell you a story that I read a little time past, if you choose to hear it." Tommy said he should be very glad if Mr. Barlow would take the trouble of telling it to him, and Mr. Barlow told him the following history of The Two Brothers.

Whatever our evaluation of these eighteenth-century liberal-minded writers, most of us find this sort of writing for children amazing, unbelievable—in short, silly or ridiculous. Our first impulse is to conclude that we have come a long way since then, that the children's books of our time bear no resemblance whatever to these strange volumes. But again, we may be letting surface differences in belief obscure essential similarities in both belief and method. The day of the enlightened, liberal tale for children is not over. There are, for instance, many books about a child's finding out how to use and enjoy the library or his discovering how enjoyable school really is or how much like him a child of a different class, nation, or race may really be, and these tales are frequently quite as given to strong contrasts, obvious moralizing, artificial plotting, and quivery sentimentality as their eighteenth-century predecessors were.

Such writing is not necessarily silly and worthless just because it is like writings of a past generation that in retrospect appear silly. But also, past writings that look silly today should not simply be ignored. Time is hard on products of the human brain, and maybe not altogether just, for the passage of time frequently tends to show up the odd mannerisms and the excesses and thereby to obscure those central ideas to which, rightly or wrongly, we ourselves still subscribe. The Puritan hornbook lessons in rhyme seem odd to us today, and maybe Leaf's moralizings or Joan Walsh Anglund's counsels in *Love Is a Special Way of Feeling* do not. Day's *Sandford and Merton* appears hilarious to us today in its unctuous naïveté, and perhaps John Tunis's books about good sportsmanship do not. And yet these books are not altogether unalike in their pressing for certain moral codes. If, then, we find books of this sort not altogether objectionable and unacceptable today, are we perhaps at last in a position to understand a little more fully why Puritan and liberal-minded adults could give their children such a seemingly strange diet and why children took it?

One can go to the past for two different things: for giggles and for instruction. If he goes for giggles, he can find them mainly in the differences between then and now—"those funny dresses," etc. If one goes for understanding, he may find it mostly in the similarities—in the things done then that help us see freshly and more realistically the things we are now doing.

The Big Shift

There is a popular notion that children were somehow rediscovered in the nineteenth century, and there is another current, related opinion that children's literature began then, too—about a hundred years ago. Neither is quite true. Rather, both are distortions of important truths.

If there may be said to have been a rediscovery of the child, it had occurred long before the nineteenth century. Not that the child had ever been wholly forgotten—the medieval nobleman was much concerned that his son be properly tutored in the arts of war, and the church saw to it that the young received indoctrination in religious matters. But a real breakthrough occurred in the Renaissance, with men's revived curiosity about themselves and their reawakened awareness of the possibilities of shaping their children, of the importance of education. The Puritans, as we have seen, made books of instruction for their children, and the liberal-minded intellectuals of the eighteenth century made books of instruction for *their* children. By mid-nineteenth century there was a long tradition of children's literature.

But in the nineteenth century a major change began to occur in people's feelings about children and in their view of literature for the young, and, with occasional slowings down and erratic dips, the progress of new views that emerged then has continued into our day. The child *had* been attended to. Now he began to be attended to somewhat differently.

Gradually the older conception of the child as a passive vessel to be filled with correct ideas and useful information gave way, at least in some quarters, to a picture of the child as an already existing personality with a will and needs of its own. The new child was dynamic, wanting things in the sense of *wishing* as well as in the sense of *needing.* The child was a human being and therefore desirous of being happy. This changed view of the child brought a change in the notion of children's reading.

Always the pleasure part of the instruction-through-pleasure idea of literature had been considered instrumental, a means, quite secondary and not to be worried over too much. But now, with more concern for the happiness of the child, the pleasure aspect came out of its secondary position and became of equal importance and in some types of reading eventually all but supplanted the former. The aesthetic pleasure was no longer just a sugarcoating to a pill. It was the pill. The child reader became a *selective* reader to be entertained; through the reading he *might* be made a better-informed, better-behaved child, but this latter goal was no longer the primary purpose of his reading. In short, the instructional motive became less prominent than it had long been in children's literature, and the literature was now free to develop into a tremendous fair of kinds of juvenile entertainment—ranging all the way from *Little Women* and *Little Lord Fauntleroy* and *The Moffats* to *Treasure Island* and *Who Rides in the Dark?* and *Dog of the North,* from the old Christmas Annuals to *Fun Fun Fun,* from George MacDonald's *At the Back of the North Wind* to James Thurber's *Many Moons* and Dr. Seuss.

Before the big change, of course, there had been signs of things to come—John Newbery's *Mother Goose* and Perrault's *Tales of Mother Goose* in the early eighteenth century, various editions of *Mother Goose Rhymes* in England and America, and some rather jolly children's miscellanies in the early 1800s. But it was in the 1840s, 1850s, and 1860s that it became evident a major shift had occurred. In these mid-nineteenth-century years Andersen, Alcott, Charles Kingsley, and dozens of other talented authors were writing for children, and in their writings are evident most of the sorts of writing for children now being done a hundred years later. And with this change in kind of book came a tremendous increase in the amount of writing, adapting, and editing done *specifically for children*. It was the beginning of the deluge.

Glancing quickly over titles of books for children published from about 1846, the date of Andersen's *Fairy Tales*, to the first decade of the twentieth century, one is bound to be startled by the number of contemporary types of children's literature that were established in those years and by the number of outstanding books written within those developing categories.

Fantasies? Andersen's tales, of course—*The Snow Queen, The Steadfast Tin Soldier, The Fir Tree*, etc.—and John Ruskin's *King of the Golden River*, Charles Kingsley's *Water-babies*, Lewis Carroll's *Alice in Wonderland* and *Through the Looking Glass*, Howard Pyle's *The Wonder Clock*, Oscar Wilde's *The Happy Prince*, James Barrie's *Peter Pan*, George MacDonald's *At the Back of the North Wind* and *The Princess and the Goblin*, L. Frank Baum's *The Wizard of Oz*, Rudyard Kipling's *Just So Stories*, Helen Bannerman's *Little Black Sambo*, Kenneth Grahame's *The Wind in the Willows*.

Adaptations of folktales and myths with children especially in mind? Nathaniel Hawthorne's *Twice-told Tales* and *Tanglewood Tales*, Kipling's *Just So Stories*, Joel Chandler Harris's *Uncle Remus Stories*.

Adaptations of famous adult literature? Charles and Mary Lamb's *Tales from Shakespeare*, Sidney Lanier's *The Boy's King Arthur*, Howard Pyle's *Story of King Arthur and His Knights*.

Historical fiction? Mary Mapes Dodge's *Hans Brinker; or, the Silver Skates*, D. Weir Mitchell's *Hugh Wynne, Free Quaker*, Charles Kingsley's *Westward Ho!*

Other fiction of adventure? Robert Louis Stevenson's *Treasure Island* and *Kidnapped*, Johann David Wyss's *Swiss Family Robinson*, Frederick Marryat's *Masterman Ready* and *Mr. Midshipman Easy*, Kipling's *Kim* and *Captains Courageous*, Jules Verne's *20,000 Leagues under the Sea* and *The Mysterious Island* and *Around the World in Eighty Days*.

Stories about other boys? Thomas Bailey Aldrich's *Story of a Bad Boy*, Mark Twain's *Tom Sawyer* and *Huckleberry Finn*, Thomas Hughes's *Tom Brown's School Days*.

Nonsense tales and verse? Edward Lear's *Book of Nonsense*, Lewis Carroll's verse, Lucretia Peabody Hale's *Peterkin Papers*, L. Leslie Brooke's *Johnny Crow's Garden*, Laura Richards's verses.

More or less realistic stories of domestic life? Louisa May Alcott's *Little Women* and *Little Men* and *Jo's Boys*, Johanna Spyri's *Heidi*, Kate Douglas Wiggins's *Rebecca of Sunnybrook Farm*, Margaret Sidney's *Five Little Peppers and How They Grew*, E. Nesbit's *The Railway Children* and *The Bastable Children*, Frances Hodgson Burnett's *Sara Crewe*.

Animal stories? Anna Sewell's *Black Beauty*, Louise de la Ramée's *Dog of Flanders*, and Beatrix Potter's *Tale of Peter Rabbit* and her many others.

Poetry for children? Kate Greenway's *Under the Window*, Christina Rossetti's *Sing-song*, Stevenson's *Child's Garden of Verses*.

And, of course, each of these lists could be greatly lengthened. Wherever one dips into the children's literature of the last half of the nineteenth century, he must remark both the flood of all varieties of writing for children and the remarkably high level of achievement in them.

Modern Children's Literature

Now, in this hundred-year spate of books for children there are many currents, some of them confusingly contradictory or opposed—sophistication and innocence, pollyannaism and bold realism, fantasy and stolid, pedestrian reporting, the extraordinary and the ordinary, pathos and avoidance of sorrow at all costs, delicacy and coarseness, language play and an almost total absence of language. There has been something for everybody— a range that makes modern children's literature (that is, children's literature in the past hundred years) an exceedingly difficult body of writing to generalize about. It is interesting to conjecture whether this multiplicity of appeal in our children's books may be one symptom of the individualism—the expression of it and the attempt to satisfy it—that has marked *all* Western literature of the past hundred years and, possibly, the whole society. Perhaps it is but a reflection of a democratic society or of the democratic elements in our society.

Despite this appearance of fragmentation and variety, however, modern writing for children would seem to have taken two main directions, to have made two different kinds of appeal to child readers: (1) the appeal of the familiar and ordinary, and (2) the appeal of the unfamiliar and extraordinary. This distinction is sufficiently important and useful in thinking about children's books that we will consider it in some detail in Chapters 7 and 8. Suffice it here to note the general nature of the split.

On the one hand, there is the tale or poem which brings to the reader situations and experiences with which he is familiar, or at least enough of these to give him familiar ground from which to venture into less familiar territory. The reader's reaction is, "I know this," or "I could know this"— and in this knowingness lies the major attraction of the work. This familiarity may be expressed in a wide variety of ways—domestic family situations, characters who are recognizable types of people or who may even be actual persons, the picturing of familiar physical objects and scenes. Lois Lenski's small chronicles of the Small family, Aldrich's *Story of a Bad Boy*, Alcott's domestic stories, and the picture books about market, street, school, and gas station—these offer more of the familiar than of the unfamiliar.

On the other hand, there is the children's book which provides mainly an escape into the realms of the unfamiliar, the strange and fantastic. Such adventure tales as Verne's *Mysterious Island,* such fantasies as *Alice in Wonderland* and *Pinocchio,* MacDonald's *At the Back of the North Wind,* J. R. Tolkien's *The Hobbit,* and Maurice Dolbier's *Torten's Christmas Secret,* such fairy lore as de la Mare's and Eleanor Farjeon's, such nonsense verse as Lear's and Laura Richards's writings—all these make their primary appeal in terms of the unusual, the unfamiliar. Of course, in modern children's literature these two appeals have been combined. In *Heidi*, for instance, a familiar domestic situation and recognizable kinds of people are combined with a faraway land, and in *Alice in Wonderland* we find familiar kinds of thinking and behavior in a wonderland. Indeed, it would be hard to find a child's book that does not make both appeals in some way and to some degree, but it would be just about as difficult to find books that do not move strongly in one direction or the other.

The primary purpose of both kinds of modern children's literature, however, is *the pleasing of the child*. Other purposes may be there, but they are pretty much incidental to the contributing to the child's happiness, the satisfying of his wantings. This basic development is not a matter of just the past few decades; it was clearly in evidence in the early years of Queen Victoria's reign in England and decades before the Civil War in this country. There have been no fundamental shifts in direction in children's literature since then; the purposes, themes, and methods then established have continued to dominate children's books. There has been tremendous variety in the work for children since the early 1800s, but it has been a constant variation on the basic patterns then established. The focus remains the child reader or listener, the major purpose to please the child.

Other Significant Developments in the Past Century

This central tendency in children's literature has been accompanied and indeed reinforced by a number of developments which have made present-day children's literature different from what it was two centuries ago.

1   Graphic illustration has assumed a tremendously more important role in children's books than it had in the days of the little black-and-white woodcut; in fact, at times it has appeared to some easily alarmed critics to have taken over children's literature and thus to have made the word account an auxiliary or complement to the visual account. This would seem to be an unrealistic view of what has happened; except in books for the prereader, the verbal pattern is still essential. The important change is that visual pattern has come to be thought of in close relation to the verbal, except in books for older children, say, over twelve.

Much has happened during the past century in the field of children's book illustration. The amount of illustration in each book has increased, and the individual illustrations have tended to grow bigger. Greater care has been shown in their use in the book, so that, instead of being sprinkled lightly throughout the text, they are integrated with it, moving in and out among the words and illuminating and being illuminated by them. The increased use of color has done much to change the general appearance of children's books; although costs have acted as a brake on this trend toward color, color has become almost an identifying characteristic of children's books. And with the opening of the children's book—illustration field to all media and approaches, there has been no dearth of talent available for the job. A great number of artists have become almost entirely identified with the illustrating of children's books—Kate Greenaway, Randolph Caldecott, Howard Pyle, Walter Crane, Leonard Weisgard, Ernest Shepard, Roger Duvoisin, Leslie Brooke, Maurice Sendak, Leo Politi. Many artists who have done their major work outside books—John Tenniel, Jean Charlot, Lynd Ward, Peggy Bacon, Doris Lee—have happily given their talents occasionally to children's book illustration. And in recent years photographers have been called on to illustrate juvenile tales and books of information.

The importance of the visual experience in children's reading today is suggested by the fact that one of the two major annual American awards in the children's book field is given for outstanding illustrating.

2   It was quite natural that in an era of greater attention to the pleasing of children there should arise a publishing business concerned primarily with children's books. A hundred years ago children's books were an occasional and peripheral venture for publishers almost totally concerned with guessing and meeting adult reading needs. Today most publishing firms have special juvenile departments, and there are dozens of large organizations that publish nothing but books or magazines for children.

3   The increase in both mass and variety of children's literature has been accompanied by two highly significant developments in the *distribution* of reading materials for children—the rise of public libraries and school libraries and the development of the ubiquitous cheap book for children. These two phenomena have helped to increase and hold the number of child readers.

The rise of an interlocking system of public and school libraries has made books available to millions of children who in earlier years would not have had the chance to use them. Availability is a particularly important factor in children's reading, for children are not generally as free as adults are to go seeking and finding their own materials; children cannot travel as far and as independently as adults, nor do they normally have their own money to spend on reading material. So the rise and expansion of interlocking systems of public and school libraries have been necessary to assure the wide use of the new children's books. Of course, such exposure of children to books often is limited by the behavior of their elders. The community can pinch the library budget or put the library in uncomfortable or inaccessible quarters; forbidding personnel can discourage children's use of the library; certain books or classes of books may be withdrawn from circulation or put on a special shelf; library reading rules and borrowing procedures may be made so strict or complex as to repel potential users. Such restrictive measures, however, have not prevented the rise of the children's library as a major factor in American culture.

The race between rising costs and mass production and distribution has been reflected in the adult field by the spread of the pocket book, or paperback, and in the children's field by cheaply bound, mass-produced, and mass-distributed juvenile books like Golden Books. Children's books, with their bright covers, have gone beyond the bounds of the bookstore and the library and may be found in drugstores and supermarkets and on magazine stands. The motivation may be quite different from that behind the development of public and school libraries, but the phenomena have one result in common—the wider availability of reading materials for children.

4   Alongside and supplementing this expansion in the publishing and distribution of children's reading materials, there have come into existence literary media other than books or magazines—movies, filmstrips, radio, television, records. Through these new visual and auditory means children now can obtain new literary experiences or experiences which supplement or reinforce their reading. It is now possible for a child to be bombarded with an idea or a plot or an image from half a dozen directions. For instance, he may read *Sleeping Beauty*, may hear it told by the "story-telling lady" down at the library, may see or even participate in a dramatization of it at school, may hear it read or dramatized over the radio, may see an elaborate presentation of it on the family's television set, may see a movie of it, or may even find it retold in a comic book. The child may encounter the old tale in any one of these forms or, more likely, in a number of them. Such is the tremendous change modern technology has brought about from three hundred years ago, when he would have just listened in on whatever scrap of song or story for adults he could manage to catch as it fell.

5   With all this proliferation and increasing use of children's literature has almost inevitably come the quick rise of an elaborate professional corps concerned with producing and selecting this material—thousands of writers who write just for children (not writers like Dickens or Kipling or Stevenson who may do an occasional work for children), children's editors and children's reviewers, and even writers of books about children's literature and teachers of courses in its use.

Summary

Sometimes all this structure may seem to become top-heavy and to threaten to crush the freshness and creativity out of children's reading. It may seem to bury a basic appeal under an elaborate technical structure. Or even if it does none of these, it just simply and undeniably makes it difficult to think clearly and freshly about our children's reading. It is a case of embarrassment of riches.

There is no denying, though, that we, or rather, our children, *are* richer. Although, as I have pointed out, it is possible to overstate the lack of literary diet before the modern era of children's publishing, at no time have the opportunities of the individual child for pleasure through literature— and for instruction through literary pleasures—been greater or more varied than they are today. And for this very reason the problems of the parent, teacher, and librarian in relation to the child's literature have ceased to be those of scarcity—making and finding materials for the child to hear and read—and have become those of plenty—judgment and selection and illumination.

SUGGESTED SOURCES

Histories of Children's Literature

Darton, F. J. Harvey: *Children's Books in England: Five Centuries of Social Life,* 2d ed., Cambridge, 1960.

————: "Children's Books," in *Cambridge History of English Literature* (15 vols.), Putnam, 1914, vol. XI, chap. XVI, pp. 407–430.

Green, Roger Lancelyn: *Tellers of Tales: British Authors of Children's Books from 1800 to 1964,* Watts, 1965.

Halsey, R. V.: *Forgotten Books of the American Nursery,* Goodspeed, Boston, 1911.

Jordan, Alice: *From Rollo to Tom Sawyer and Other Papers,* Horn Book, 1948.

Kiefer, Monica: *American Children through Their Books, 1700–1835,* University of Pennsylvania Press, 1948.

Meigs, Cornelia, et al.: *A Critical History of Children's Literature,* Macmillan, 1953.

Muir, Percy: *English Children's Books, 1600 to 1900,* Frederick A. Praeger, 1954.

Rosenbach, Abraham S. W.: *Early American Children's Books with Bibliographical Descriptions of the Books in His Private Collection,* Southworth Press, 1933.

Sloane, William: *Children's Books in England and America in the Seventeenth Century: A History and a Checklist, Together with the Young Christian's Library, the First Printed Catalogue of Books for Children,* King's Crown, 1955.

Smith, Dora V.: *Fifty Years of Children's Books, 1910–1960: Trends, Backgrounds, Influences,* National Council of Teachers of English, 1963.

Smith, Elva S.: *The History of Children's Literature: A Syllabus with Selected Bibliographies,* American Library Association, 1937.

Targ, William: *Bibliophile in the Nursery: A Bookman's Treasury of Collectors' Lore on Old and Rare Children's Books,* World, 1957.

Tassin, Algeron: "Books for Children," in *Cambridge History of American Literature* (3 vols.), Macmillan, 1933, vol. II, ch. VII, pp. 396–409.

Thwaite, M. F.: *From Primer to Pleasure: An Introduction to the History of Children's Books in England, from the Invention of Printing to 1900,* Library Association, London, 1963.

Tuer, Andrew W. (compiler): *Pages and Pictures from Forgotten Children's Books*, Leadenhall Press, 1898.

Seventeenth- and Eighteenth-Century Children's Reading

Aiken, John, and Anna Letitia Barbauld: *Evenings at Home* (6 vols.), 1792–1796.

Ashton, John: *Chap Books of the Eighteenth Century*, Chatto, 1882.

Barbauld, Anna Letitia Aikin: *Hymns in Prose*, 1781.

————: *Lessons for Children, from Two to Four Years Old*, B. F. Bache, Philadelphia, 1788.

Berquin, Arnaud: *The Looking-glass for the Mind*, 1787.

Comenius, John Amos: *Orbis Sensualium Pictus . . . Visible World. Or, a Picture and Nomenclature of All the Chief Things That Are in the World; and of Mens Employment Therein . . .*, tr. by Charles Hoole, J. Kirton, London, 1659.

Day, Thomas: *The History of Sandford and Merton, a Work Intended for the Use of Children* (3 vols.), J. Stockdale, London, 1783–1789.

Edgeworth, Richard L.: *Practical Education: Or, the History of Harry and Lucy*, J. Johnson, 1780.

Flowers of Delight: An Agreeable Garland of Prose and Poetry 1765–1830, sel. by Leonard de Vries from Osborne Collection, Pantheon, 1965.

Foxe, John: *Foxe's Book of Martyres*, ed. by W. Grinton Berry, Abingdon, 1932.

History of Little Goody Two-shoes, ed. by Charles Welsh, Heath, 1930. First published by John Newbery in 1765.

Janeway, James: *A Token for Children: Being an Exact Account of the Conversion, Holy and Exemplary Lives and Joyful Deaths of Several Young Children to Which Is Added: A Token for the Children of New England*, N. Boone, Boston, 1700.

Keach, Benjamin: *War with the Devil, or the Young Man's Conflict with the Powers of Darkness*, William Bradford, New York, 1707.

A Little Pretty Pocket-book, Intended for the Instruction and Amusement of Little Master Tommy and Pretty Miss Polly, Newbery and Carnan, London, 1770.

New England Primer, ed. by Paul Leicester Ford, Dodd, 1897; reissued, Teachers College (Classics in Education series, no. 13), 1962.

Perrault, Charles: *Tales of Mother Goose*, tr. by Charles Welsh, ill. by D. J. Munro after Gustave Doré, Heath, 1901. Collected in 1696.

Royal Primer; or, an Easy and Pleasant Guide to the Art of Reading, J. Newbery and B. Collins, London, 1751.

Trimmer, Sarah Kirby: *The History of Robins* (1786), ed. by E. E. Hale, Heath, 1901.

Watts, Isaac: *Divine and Moral Songs for Children*, James Nisbet, 1866.

Wollstonecraft, Mary: *Original Stories from Real Life; with Conversations Calculated to Regulate the Affections, and Form the Mind to Truth and Goodness* (1788), London, 1906.

Early-nineteenth-century Books for Children

Abbott, Jacob: *Franconia Stories*, ed. by Margaret Armstrong, Putnam, 1923.

————: *The Rollo Books*, e.g., *The Little Scholar Learning to Talk: A Picture Book for Rollo*, John Allen, 1835.

Edgeworth, Maria: *Early Lessons* (4 vols.), 1801–1815.

————: *Parent's Assistant, or Stories for Children*, ill. by Chris Hammond, Macmillan, 1897.

————: *Simple Susan, and Other Tales*, ill. by C. M. Burd, Macmillan, 1929.

Goodrich, Samuel: *Tales of Peter Parley about America*, S. G. Goodrich, 1827. History, science, travel; also *Peter Parley's Tales about Europe*.

Lamb, Charles and Mary: *Tales from Shakespear Designed for the Use of Young Persons* (2 vols.), T. Hodgkins, 1807.

More, Hannah: *The Shepherd of Salisbury Plain*.

Roscoe, William: *The Butterfly's Ball, and The Grasshopper's Feast*, J. Harris, 1807.

Taylor, Ann and Jane: *Original Poems for Infant Minds*, Stokes, 1904.

Folktales: General Collections

Aardema, Verna: *Tales from the Story Hat*, ill. by Elton Fox, Coward-McCann, 1960. Nine stories.

The Aesop for Children, ill. by Milo Winter, Rand McNally, 1955. First printed in 1919; large, realistic illustrations.

Aesop's Fables, ill. by Fritz Kredel, Grosset & Dunlap (Illustrated Junior Library), 1947.

Arbuthnot, May Hill (ed.): *Time for Fary Tales, Old and New*, ill. by John Averill and others, Scott, 1961.

Baker, Augusta (ed.): *The Golden Lynx and Other Tales*, ill. by Johannes Troyer, Lippincott, 1960. From Scandinavia, India, Italy, Poland, and Scotland.

Deutsch, Babette, and Avrahm Yarmolinsky (ed.): *Tales of Faraway Folk,* ill. by Irena Lorentowicz, Harper & Row, 1953. Baltic, Russian, and Asian tales.

————: *More Tales of Faraway Folk,* ill. by Janina Domanska, Harper & Row, 1963.

Huber, Miriam Blanton: *Story and Verse for Children,* ill. by Lynd Ward, Macmillan, 1955.

Hutchinson, Veronica (ed.): *Chimney Corner Stories,* ill. by Lois Lenski, Putnam, 1925.

————: *Fireside Stories,* ill. by Lois Lenski, Putnam, 1927.

Johnson, Edna, et al.: *Anthology of Children's Literature,* Houghton Mifflin, 1959.

Lang, Andrew (ed.): *Blue Fairy Book,* ill. by Ben Kutcher, McKay, 1948.

————: *Green Fairy Book,* ill. by Dorothy Lake Gregory, McKay, 1948; reprinted, 1962.

————: *Red Fairy Book,* ill. by Marc Simont, McKay, 1948.

————: *Yellow Fairy Book,* ill. by Janice Holland, McKay, 1948.

Rojankovsky, Feodor: *The Tall Book of Nursery Tales,* Harper & Row, 1944.

Rugoff, Milton (ed.): *A Harvest of World Folk Tales,* Viking, 1955.

Sawyer, Ruth: *The Long Christmas,* ill. by Valenti Angelo, Viking, 1960. Mixture of old stories and carols.

United Nations Women's Guild: *Ride with the Sun,* ed. by Harold Courlander, ill. by Roger Duvoisin, Whittlesey, 1955. Stories from the countries in the United Nations.

Folktales: Collections of Stories from Various Areas

Africa

Arnott, Kathleen: *African Myths and Legends,* ill. by Jean Kiddell-Monroe, Walck, 1963.

Courlander, Harold: *The King's Drum and Other Stories,* ill. by Enrico Arno, Harcourt, Brace & World, 1962. Thirty African stories.

———— **and George Herzog:** *The Cow-tail Switch and Other West African Stories,* ill. by Mayde Lee Chastain, Holt, 1947.

Gilstrap, Robert, and Irene Estabrook: *The Sultan's Fool and Other North African Tales,* ill. by Robert Greco, Holt, 1958.

The Americas

Barbeau, Marius: *The Golden Phoenix and Other French-Canadian Fairy Tales,* retold by Michael Hornyansky, ill. by Arthur Price, Oxford University Press, 1958.

Bell, Corydon: *John Rattling-gourd of Big Cave: A Collection of Cherokee Indian Legends,* ill. by author, Macmillan, 1955.

Belting, Natalia M.: *The Long Tailed Bear and Other Indian Legends,* ill. by Louis F. Cary, Bobbs-Merrill, 1961. Legends of twenty-two tribes.

Botkin, Ben, and Carl Withers: *The Illustrated Book of American Folklore,* ill. by Irv Docktor, Grosset & Dunlap, 1958.

Carlson, Natalie Savage: *The Talking Cat and Other Stories of French Canada,* ill. by Roger Duvoisin, Harper & Row, 1952.

Chase, Richard (ed.): *Grandfather Tales,* ill. by Berkeley Williams, Jr., Houghton Mifflin, 1948. Twenty-five tales.

————: *The Jack Tales,* ill. by Berkeley Williams, Jr., Houghton Mifflin, 1943.

Cothran, Jean (ed.): *With a Wig, with a Wag, and Other American Folk Tales,* ill. by Clifford N. Geary, McKay, 1954.

Credle, Ellis: *Tall Tales from the High Hills,* ill. by author, Nelson, 1957. Blue Ridge stories.

Felton, Harold W.: *John Henry and His Hammer,* ill. by Aldren A. Watson, Knopf, 1950.

Finger, Charles J.: *Tales from Silver Lands,* Doubleday, 1924. South American tales; Newbery Medal.

Fisher, Anne B.: *Stories California Indians Told,* ill. by Ruth Robbins, Parnassus Press, Berkeley, Calif., 1957.

Gillham, Charles Edward: *Beyond the Clapping Mountains: Eskimo Stories from Alaska,* ill. by Chanimum, Macmillan, 1943.

Grinnell, George Bird: *Blackfoot Lodge Tales,* University of Nebraska Press, 1962.

Harris, Joel Chandler: *The Complete Tales of Uncle Remus,* comp. by Richard Chase, ill. by Arthur Burdette Frost and others, Houghton Mifflin, 1955.

Jagendorf, M. A., and R. S. Boggs: *The King of the Mountains: A Treasury of Latin American Folk Stories,* ill. by Carybé, Vanguard, 1960.

Jagendorf, Moritz: *New England Bean Pot: American Folk Stories to Read and to Tell,* ill. by Donald McKay, Vanguard, 1948.

Jodan, Philip D.: *The Burro Benedicto and Other Folktales and Legends of Mexico,* ill, by R. M. Powers, Coward-McCann, 1960. Fine black-and-white, abstract illustrations.

Macmillan, Cyrus: *Glooskap's Country, and Other Indian Tales,* ill. by John A. Hall, Walck, 1956. First published 1918 as *Canadian Wonder Tales.*

Malcolmsen, Anne: *Yankee Doodle's Cousins,* ill. by Robert McCloskey, Houghton Mifflin, 1941.

Martin, Fran: *Nine Tales of Coyote,* ill. by Dorothy McEntee, Harper & Row, 1950. Northwest Indian tales.

————: *Nine Tales of Raven*, ill. by Dorothy McEntee, Harper & Row, 1951. Northwest Indian tales.

Nusbaum, Aileen: *Zuni Indian Tales*, ill. by Margaret Finnan, Putnam, 1926.

Shannon, Monica: *California Fairy Tales*, ill. by C. E. Millard, Stephen Daye Press, 1926; reprinted, 1957.

Sherlock, Philip M. (told by): *Anansi the Spider Man: Jamaican Folk Tales*, ill. by Marcia Brown, Crowell, 1954.

Czechoslovakia

Fillmore, Parker: *Czechoslovak Fairy Tales*, ill. by Jan Matulka, Harcourt, Brace, 1919.

England, Scotland, Wales, and Ireland

Haviland, Virgina (ed.): *Favorite Fairy Tales Told in Ireland*, ill. by Arthur Marokvia, Little, Brown, 1961.

Jacobs, Joseph (ed.): *Celtic Fairy Tales*, ill. by John D. Batten, Putnam, 1892.

————: *English Fairy Tales*, 3d ed., rev., ill. by John D. Batten, Putnam, 1892.

————: *More Celtic Fairy Tales*, ill. by John D. Batten, Putnam, 1895.

Jones, Gwyn: *Welsh Legends and Folk Tales*, ill. by Joan Kiddell-Monroe, Walck, 1955.

Leodhas, Sorche Nic: *Thistle and Thyme: Tales and Legends from Scotland*, ill. by Evaline Ness, Holt, 1962. Useful explanatory introduction; interesting black-and-white drawings.

MacManus, Seumas: *The Bold Heroes of Hungry Hill and Other Irish Folk Tales*, ill. by Jay Chollick, Ariel Books, 1951.

Sheppard-Jones, Elisabeth: *Scottish Legendary Tales*, ill. by Paul Hogarth, Nelson, 1962.

Steel, Flora Annie: *English Fairy Tales*, ill. by Arthur Rackham, Macmillan, 1962.

Thomas, W. Jenkyn: *The Welsh Fairy Book*, ill. by Willy Pogány, Stokes.

Wilson, Barbara Ker: *Scottish Folk-tales and Legends*, ill. by Joan Kiddell-Monroe, Walck (Oxford Myths and Legends), 1954.

France

Douglas, Barbara (compiler): *Favourite French Fairy Tales; Retold from the French of Perrault, Madame d'Aulnoy, and Madame Leprince de Beaumont*, ill. by R. Cramer, Dodd, Mead, 1952.

Folk Tales of France, adapted by Polly Curren, Bobbs-Merrill, 1963. In series, Folk Tales around the World.

Perrault, Charles: *All the French Fairy Tales*, retold, with a foreword by Louis Untermeyer, ill. by Gustave Doré, Didier, 1946.

Picard, Barbara Leonie: *French Legends, Tales and Fairy Stories*, ill. by Joan Kiddell-Monroe, Walck, 1955.

Robinson, W. Heath: *Perrault's Complete Fairy Tales*, ill. by W. Heath Robinson, Dodd, Mead, 1961.

Germany

Grimm, Jacob and Wilhelm: *Grimm's Fairy Tales*, complete ed., ill. by Josef Schnarl, Pantheon, 1944.

————: *Grimm's Fairy Tales*, trans. by Mrs. E. V. Lucas and others, ill. by Fritz Kredel, Grosset & Dunlap, 1945.

————: *Grimm's Fairy Tales*, ill. by Arnold Roth, Macmillan, 1963.

————: *Tales from Grimm*, freely trans. and ill. by Wanda Gág, Coward-McCann, 1936. Also *More Tales from Grimm*, Coward-McCann, 1947.

Picard, Barbara Leonie: *German Hero-sagas and Folk-tales*, ill. by Joan Kiddell-Monroe, Walck, 1958.

Italy

Jagendorf, M. A.: *The Priceless Cats and Other Italian Folk Stories*, ill. by Kathryn L. Fligg, McKay, 1958.

The Orient

Carpenter, Frances: *The Elephant's Bathtub: Wonder Tales from the Far East*, ill. by Hans Guggenheim, Doubleday, 1962. Stories from sixteen Eastern countries.

————: *Tales of a Chinese Grandmother*, ill. by Malthé Hasselriis, Doubleday, 1937.

Colum, Padraic (ed.): *The Arabian Nights: Tales of Wonder and Magnificence*, ill. by Lynd Ward, Macmillan (New Children's Classics), 1953.

Courlander, Harold, and George Herzog: *Kantchil's Lime Pit and Other Stories from Indonesia*, ill. by Robert W. Kane, Harcourt, Brace & World, 1950.

Gray, John E. B.: *India's Tales and Legends*, ill. by Joan Kiddell-Monroe, Walck, 1961.

Housman, Laurence (retold by): *Stories from the Arabian Nights*, ill. by Edmund Dulac, Hodder, 1911. Only six stories; elaborate color illustrations.

Jacobs, Joseph (ed.): *Indian Fairy Tales*, ill. by J. D. Batten, Putnam, 1892.

Jewett, Eleanore M.: *Which Was Witch? Tales of Ghosts and Magic from Korea*, ill. by Taro Yashima, Viking, 1959.

Lang, Andrew (ed.): *Arabian Nights*, ill. by Vera Bock, Longmans, 1951.

Lim, Sian-Tek: *Folk Tales from China*, ill. by William Arthur Smith, John Day, 1944.

————: *More Folk Tales from China*, ill. by William Arthur Smith, John Day, 1948.

McAlpine, Helen and William (compilers): *Japanese Tales and Legends*, ill. by Joan Kiddell-Monroe, Walck, 1959.

Sechrist, Elizabeth H.: *Once in the First Times: Folk Tales from the Philippines*, ill. by John Sheppard, Macrae Smith, 1949.

Turnbull, E. Lucia: *Fairy Tales of India*, ill. by Hazel Cook, Criterion, 1960.

Uchida, Yoshiko: *The Dancing Kettle and Other Japanese Folk Tales*, ill. by Richard C. Jones, Harcourt, Brace & World, 1949.

————: *The Magic Listening Cap: More Folk Tales from Japan*, ill. by author, Harcourt, Brace & World, 1955.

Russia and Eastern Europe

Downing, Charles: *Russian Tales and Legends*, ill. by Joan Kiddell-Monroe, Oxford University Press, 1957.

Ransome, Arthur: *Old Peter's Russian Tales*, ill. by Dmitri Mitrokhin, Nelson, 1917.

Wheeler Post: *Russian Wonder Tales*, new ed., ill. by Bilibin, Thomas Yoseloff, 1957.

Scandinavia

Asbjörnsen, Peter C., and Jörgen Moe: *East o' the Sun and West o' the Moon*, ill. by Kay Nielsen, Doubleday, 1922. Fifteen stories.

————: *Norwegian Folk Tales*, trans. by Pat Shaw Iversen and Carl Norman, ill. by Erick Werenskiold and Theodor Kittelson, Viking, 1961.

Bowman, James Cloyd, and Margery Bianco: *Tales from a Finnish Tupa*, from a trans. by Aili Kolehmainen, ill. by Laura Bannon, Whitman, 1936.

Fillmore, Parker (retold by): *The Shepherd's Nosegay: Stories from Finland and Czechoslovakia*, ed. by Katherine Love, ill. by Enrico Arno, Harcourt, Brace & World, 1958.

Jones, Gwyn: *Scandinavian Legends and Folk Tales*, ill. by Joan Kiddell-Monroe, Walck (Oxford Myths and Legends), 1956.

Thorne-Thomsen, Gudrun: *East o' the Sun and West o' the Moon*, rev. ed., ill. by Frederick Richardson, Harper & Row, 1946.

Spain

Boggs, Ralph Steele, and Mary Gould Davis: *Three Golden Oranges and Other Spanish Folk Tales,* ill. by Emma Brock, McKay, 1936.

Sawyer, Ruth: *Picture Tales from Spain,* ill. by Carlos Sanchez, Lippincott, 1936.

Switzerland

Müller-Guggenbühl, Fritz: *Swiss-Alpine Folk-tales,* trans. by Katharine Potts, ill. by Joan Kiddell-Monroe, Walck (Oxford, Myths and Legends), 1958.

Collections of Myths and Legends

Belting, Natalia M.: *Calendar Moon,* ill. by Bernarda Bryson, Holt, 1964. Myths related to the months of the year.

Bulfinch, Thomas: *Age of Fable; or, Stories of Gods and Heroes,* introduction by Dudley Fitts, ill. by Joe Mugnaini, Heritage, 1958.

Colum, Padraic: *Children of Odin,* ill. by Willy Pogány, Macmillan, 1920, 1962.

Coolidge, Olivia E.: *Greek Myths,* ill. by Edouard Sandoz, Houghton Mifflin, 1949.

D'Aulaire, Ingri, and Edgar Parin: *Book of Greek Myths,* ill. by authors, Doubleday, 1962.

Hawthorne, Nathaniel: *A Wonder Book; and Tanglewood Tales,* ill. by Maxfield Parrish, Dodd, Mead, 1934.

Kingsley, Charles: *The Heroes* (1856), ill. by Joan Kiddell-Monroe, Dutton, 1963. Perseus, the Argonauts, Theseus, and the twelve labors of Heracles.

Sellew, Catharine: *Adventures with the Gods,* ill. by George and Doris Hauman, Little, Brown, 1945.

————: *Adventures with the Heroes,* ill. by Steele Savage, Little, Brown, 1954.

Sewell, Helen: *A Book of Myths,* sel. from Bulfinch's *Age of Fable,* ill. by author, Macmillan, 1942.

CHAPTER 4

WHO
USES
CHILDREN'S
BOOKS
—AND WHY?

$\mathcal{C}$hildren's literature today is so many different things—it includes such a variety of purpose and means—that most people who have turned their serious attention to it have at one time or another despaired of making any sense of it and have given themselves over to feeling it is impossible to deal with children's books in a logical, methodical way.

But there *are* ways of classifying children's books so that one can look at groups and tendencies rather than try to consider each of the thousands of books by itself. One may, for instance, classify all children's books by subjects—books about locomotives, books about dwarfs, books about mice. This method of classification is not very helpful, though, because the classes include such widely differing things—"rabbits" could include both *Alice in Wonderland* and a simple book on rabbit raising. One may try grouping children's books by sorts of authors—professional children's writers and authors who only occasionally do a child's book ("Sunday writers"), authors of different periods, authors from different countries. One may group books according to authors' purposes or intentions—to amuse, to instruct, to do both, to put children to sleep, to earn money. Or one may place in different categories books in different styles—"simple vocabulary," "colloquial," "rather elaborate." Another mode of getting children's books into some order is according to age levels—preschool, primary, middle grades, adolescence. And there are still others—by cost, by publishers or kinds of publishers, by the amount or kind of illustrations in the books, by book size.

Before we are through with our consideration of children's literature, we shall have used almost all of the ways of classification just now mentioned.

But it would seem particularly useful in the early stages of our study to classify children's books in terms of their audience and use—not their *intended* audience and not how they are intended to be used, but the various groups of people who *actually* use them and their reasons for doing so. The question, "Who uses children's books—and why?" would seem to call for settlement before we get deeper into questions of content and style. It might, incidentally, be pointed out that this is a useful method of thinking about all kinds of media. It is very illuminating to think of popular musicians, from Elvis Presley to Duke Ellington, in terms of the kinds of listeners they have and why these listeners listen. Likewise, it is clarifying to break up movies into groups according to the audiences that view them and their reasons for doing so.

The Three Adult Audiences

The name *children's literature* is misleading insofar as it suggests literature that is meant for, and reaches, only children, because it can obscure the fact that many adults are involved in the selection and use of children's books, too.

In our culture, adults process almost everything that reaches children, and books are no exception. Adult audiences stand between the publication of a book and the child audience for the book; indeed, the reactions of these adult audiences may mean that the book never gets a child audience, or at least that it gets it under inauspicious circumstances.

There are today three main adult audiences for children's books— parents, teachers, and librarians. These groups may overlap and may share some of the same interests and attitudes, but they are different enough in important ways to justify their being described separately.

Parents and Their Purposes

The first gantlet books for children must run is parents of children. Parents generally buy the books that get to their children within the home, and often they read them to their children, or at least explain them and answer (or sometimes refuse to answer) questions about them. This means that the books are looked at—perhaps merely glanced at, more likely skimmed quickly, and even possibly read thoroughly—by parents before children read them. The adults may form an audience for children's books only briefly and sporadically; but it is nevertheless an influential audience because it has the purchase money and some authority.

Now *why* do parents get certain books for their children and then read them to the children or see that the children read them? There are as many reasons as there are kinds of parents and kinds of children, but they can be reduced to several rough categories of general intentions:

1   To Amuse the Children   A parent may wish to make a child laugh happily, giggle hysterically, or smile quietly and contentedly—that is, to entertain him. This desire, of course, may arise from widely differing motives or causes. Parents may hope to distract their children from some particular activity—for instance, teasing the cat or marking the furniture or crying—by getting them interested in some new and less obnoxious sort of amusement. Parents may wish to quiet their children, to bring them down from some sharp and uncomfortable peak of excitement; for instance, after a neighborhood crisis, a storm, or an uncustomary evening out, the children may be overexcited and need to be edged toward sleep. Many parents rely heavily on books for this purpose; there are even books built on the principle of going to sleep. On the other hand, parents (the same ones, conceivably) may use reading to stimulate children, to puncture lethargy, real or imagined—say, in the dog days of summer, when a mood of whimpering weariness may easily settle down on whole neighborhoods of children, or during the long days of a long illness.

Parents may use books to console—to bring new interests to an unhappy child or to bring about a calmer, gentler mental state. When buying or selecting books, they may have in mind the quite honorable purpose of simply filling in time which they can see no other way of filling—in other words, the use of books as a last resort. It is not uncommon for parents to get books for their children simply because the parents have learned somewhere, have somehow come to assume, that children *should* be amused and that parents have at least part of the responsibility of amusing them. Some particularly sophisticated parents may go beyond this general amusement principle and believe that children should become accustomed to laughter and fantasy, that any latent germs of humor or imagination should be cultivated in them and that books should be selected toward that end; this motive, generally unrecognized and unstated, is most likley to be found in parents who themselves enjoy the arts and feel most happy when responding to a well-told story or a clever play. And, finally, parents may wish to make their children happy through books in order to achieve the further and ultimate purpose of *instruction;* they conceive of amusement as a disguise for instruction. These parents are in the borderland between entertaining and teaching, a land sometimes fraught with difficult decisions.

2   To Inform the Children   Parents may hope that through reading, their young will become acquainted with the facts of existence and be better able to understand them. Parents may differ, of course, in their conception of what it is important for their children to know, and hence in their choice of informative books. Some may wish them to learn first and mainly about physical phenomena and objects—land, weather, animals, days and nights, seasons, physical laws, inventions. Others may feel it important that their children learn about human society and its history and beliefs—families, nations, cultures, races—the past of this society and its myths and ideas of right and wrong. Some parents who feel the importance of social knowledge may stress the importance of knowledge about the nearby and immediate, and so the books they choose will have a heavy larding of facts about markets, school, the waterworks, the harbor, and trucks. Other parents, sharing the feeling about the importance of social facts but seeing society as going beyond the child's local society, will tend to choose books of biography and autobiography, of nonfiction and fiction about foreign lands and past times.

Some parents want their children to learn general principles that explain disparate facts. These parents think highly of books which explain in children's terms the nature of the universe, the reason for the tides, the cause of day and night, which give a notion about time, an awareness of distance, a sense of the relation of things to the persons who observe them.

3 To Advise Children in Matters of Behavior and to Develop Certain Behavior Patterns   Through their children's reading, parents may hope to influence their attitudes and actions toward family, neighborhood, school, church, nation, or the world society. They may use books to shape a child's values, to create or change his ideals. Such counsel, embodied in fiction, poetry, or nonfiction, may cover a tremendous range of behavior matters— obedience, independence, physical safety, doing chores, being honest, study habits, hygiene, attitudes toward school, being kind to animals. For many parents the book is still primarily a moral agent, an influence upon belief and behavior.

The Ways Parents Choose

All these parents, whatever their motives and whatever their individual degrees of attention, constitute part of the audience for juvenile literature. They all inspect the books in some degree, and they all react to them— happily, enthusiastically, cautiously, with boredom, angrily, etc. They are all users of children's literature. There are great contrasts, however, in the ways they deal with these juvenile materials. Some do it the hard way, with much worry and much consulting of recommended lists and reading of reviews in parents' magazines, much checking on the progress of their children's reading, often considerable direct participation in the reading. Others take their children's reading more lightly; they may pick up titles on the run at drugstore or department-store counters or on a buying spree at Christmas, and they are inclined to let the child develop his own interpretations and his own reading tastes and not to worry about the results.

Most parents of both the worrying kind and the more complacent sort are consciously unsure about children's books. They feel ignorant and confused about almost all aspects of juvenile literature—what is available, how to judge it, what children want, what children really feel about the books provided them, how children of various ages may differ in their reading tastes. But the more complacent parents and the worriers express this uncertainty in different ways. The more complacent rely upon chance, hoping for everything to work out; they feel children's books and children are so many and so varied that one might as well shut his eyes and blindly choose. The worrying sort lean heavily and with touching hope on authorities—famous educators, the children's teachers, librarians, reviewers, bookstore salespeople, writers of children's books. In both cases, the parents are really depending on chance, taking a big chance. The difference is that the second group *think* they aren't.

Another point of difference among parent users of children's books is that some lean toward the conventional in both ideas and presentation, and others lean toward the unusual, the unconventional. The former, for various reasons, are anxious to find the things that are classified as standard, classic, or popular. (They are beloved by publishers, for they provide a sure market.) The latter parents, a considerably smaller group, are anxious to find the offbeat, the "fresh" book for their chidren—the kind of book over which visitors to their homes are likely to shudder or giggle nervously. Their choices are likely to be books generally classified as adult books, books about controversial subjects, books about new developments, books on unusual specialties such as collecting saddles or watching the weather, or books illustrated in highly original, individualistic styles.

Teachers

Teachers—teachers in public schools, private schools, and Sunday schools —compose a second main group of adults who use children's books and so shape children's reading.

The extent to which teachers use children's books is determined to a large extent by the fullness and variety of the school's reading activities. In a school where free, individualized reading is held desirable, the teachers are likely to become close followers of children's books; and this is even more likely if the school makes ample provision for book purchases. A second factor that may affect teachers' use of children's books, in both amount and kind, is the role played in children's reading by *other* agents of education, such as parents, libraries, churches, and clubs. If other providers of reading experience fall down on their jobs, teachers may, without really realizing what they are doing, try to fill the gap, and this will bring them into closer contact with the flow of children's books. Or if the children are obviously getting elsewhere a large dose of certain kinds of reading—say Freddy the Pig books or horse stories or fairy tales—the teacher may turn in other directions for appropriate reading materials.

Teachers' purposes in finding and using children's books include all those we found parents have—to amuse (and for all the same reasons), to inform (and in all the same areas), and to influence behavior—and this would seem to give some strength to the argument that the teacher's and the parent's roles are not essentially different, or at least not as different as some critics of education believe.

There is, however, one important difference. For teachers the information purpose of reading tends to become the most important one. In most communities the school is popularly viewed as a place of *learning*, and the learning that should be done there is generally thought to be the learning of facts and formulas, with amusement and the assimilation of desirable ideas and habits held to be important but not of *first* importance. In the kindergarten and primary grades, where reading is not yet a mastered craft, the pressure for the fact-learning function of reading is still countered by pressures to use literature for its amusement and indoctrination functions. But through the grades, reading is generally judged increasingly by the amount of information children seem to gather by means of it. More and more it is used to inform the child about his physical environment (biological, physical, chemical facts) and the social world (government, cultures of past and present) and to help him gather facts on any special project of his own or of his group. The logical conclusion of this process could be said to have been reached when a high school senior frantically devotes all his reading time to the nip-and-tuck completion of a term paper in one of his classes.

In one sense, then, teachers are not quite as free agents as parents in their use of children's literature: they are expected to get as much information learning as possible out of children's reading activities. This pressure sometimes takes the form of specific curricular requirements— the expectation that a child will have covered such and such material by the end of the fourth grade, the need for a child to be able to deliver certain facts on entrance examinations and for promotion from grade to grade. These requirements may be built into a school system's curricula, or they may be the personal will of certain administrative superiors or influential parent groups or even of articulate individual parents. Other limitations on the amount and variety of reading done by children in school may be created by limited school budgets; no matter how eager certain teachers in a school may be to have their children read widely, they cannot have this accomplished within their school pattern if their school's library is being starved almost into nonexistence.

Yet in spite of this and other factors limiting school reading, school is still held by the public mind and by most pedagogic minds to be the most appropriate place for reading. Indeed, in some minds school is almost *synonymous* with reading, to the exclusion of many other activities. And so the reading of books, even of books that can only by much stretching of the imagination be considered informative or didactic, is open to less question than other activities, such as music, dancing, or games, might be.

Teachers may use reading material in many ways. Reading may be done as part of regular assignments for class or for outside reading assignments. It may be done as part of an entirely free reading program. Children may read books as part of a literature program, or they may read books in relation to certain subject fields, such as American history or music. Books may be read aloud by the teacher or silently by the students. Or all of these methods may be combined in a full, many-sided reading program.

Librarians

Children's librarians, both school and public, compose a small but influential group of adult users of children's literature. They too, like parents and teachers, can be directly intent on amusing, informing, and counseling the child through his reading and will look at books with these purposes in mind. However, because of their peculiar go-between position, their use of children's books has a special character. Besides satisfying their own tastes in children's literature, they must try to meet the reading needs felt by children, parents, and teachers. And so part of their job is to ascertain and meet the demands of these several groups of users of children's books. Theirs is a specially *auxiliary* function; parents and teachers are presumed to have the eventual child listeners or child reader in mind when scouting through books, but the librarian must consider not only the child but his parents and teachers—all the adults around him—when selecting children's books. Also, the librarian's use of children's books is her main activity—it is the heart of her work, while for parents and teachers it is only one among a number of very important responsibilities—and this tends to make for a more rigorous, intensive consideration of children's reading materials by librarians.

Children

It is logical that this audience should be mentioned last, since it is often the last to get to look at children's books. Generally, by the time the child opens a book that book has already been used in some way by at least one kind of adult reader.

The great difference, of course, between the child audience and the adult audience for children's books is that children use these books primarily to satisfy their own needs rather than to do things to or for other people. In this way, they are like that small minority of parents and teachers who insist on personally getting a kick out of children's books or else refuse to have anything to do with them.

Why do children use books? For what particular reasons or purposes do they read books instead of turning cartwheels, drawing with crayons, building or breaking, swinging, or just sitting on the steps?

Before considering their own personal satisfactions, we might note that children *may* use books to meet not their own needs, but the demands of others, much as most adults do. For instance, a child may read a book to please his parents or teachers or just to meet, mechanically, a school assignment; he may feel the reading is expected of him and try to live up—or read up—to the expectation. Through books he may also try to meet the demands of other children, of what other children expect him to know and even to like; here is the pressure of fashion, and it may become strong in the world of the child, particularly in junior and senior high school. Another boy has a new Walt Disney picture book; why can't he? Another girl has built up a Sue Barton library of twelve titles; shouldn't she, then have thirteen? So the books are acquired and devoured.

Such reading, done because of pressures from adults or other children, is fundamentally a social use of literature, and one not to be forgotten by the adult who has anything to do with children's literature.

The main reason why children read, though, is *to satisfy their own many and varied wants.*

It is easy to be glib about children's needs and to make up impressively short simplifying lists or impressively long exhaustive lists of them, seizing on the terminology of certain educational philosophies or psychological schools. (We seem to need such terminologies in order to think clearly of children's needs and their satisfaction through reading.) But however we classify child readers' needs, it is important to remember (1) that children's reading is primarily an attempt to satisfy these needs, and (2) that these needs are characterized by multiplicity and variability. The child reader is not a passive, unwanting stick, and his wants differ from other children's and shift and change among themselves from year to year, even from month to month.

One may quickly and quietly agree with these two generalizations and feel them to be so obvious they should be taken for granted and not thought on further. Yet many actual practices would seem to be based on the denial of these premises. For example, books are often chosen for children simply because their names are on a required school list. If the criteria for the list itself are not asked for, then the teacher or parent is not seriously considering the individual readers themselves. Or choices may be based on unannotated lists of "Best Books for Children" or "100 Greatest Children's Books." People who choose books for children from such lists without asking that "best" and "greatest" be defined are not thinking of what the reader will do with these books, and they are also assuming that a good book now is a good book later, that the effect of a book never varies significantly from time to time or from place to place. The uncritical, unquestioning choice of classics for children's reading and the insistence upon their being read by *all* children would seem to be in large part founded on this sort of thinking. It is a kind of absolutist thinking—thinking of goodness in books without considering *for whom* and *how* these books will be good. A teacher who feels this way will feel that a book which is amusing to a fast reader will be so to a slow reader, that a good fairy tale will amuse all children, that a book which enthralled him as a boy will inevitably spellbind the boys in his class. Actually, it is quite probable that this sort of thinking about children's reading is much more common than the view which relates children's reading to their specific, changing needs. "Children's needs" has become a slogan, a piece of jargon, and it is said by a lot of people who do not carry it into practice.

Perhaps the avoidance of this approach in practice is due in part to its calling for much more work on the part of the adult in selecting books for children. He can no longer merely get hold of a list and use it. He must now think about children—try to find what their wants are and *keep* doing so, since those wants may change under altered circumstances. And then he must investigate the different kinds of children's books to see how well they meet these various and changing requirements. Yet like many another long way round, this relativistic approach generally proves highly rewarding—it makes for more enthusiastic, effective, and continued reading by children, for less wasted effort in trying to force on readers reading of an irrelevant kind. And it proves in the long run easier, in that the reading children do makes better sense to them and so is likely to lead into fewer reading problems, fewer situations in which the adult feels he is dragging unwilling victims to a dignified but meaningless sacrificial altar. Teachers and parents who have tried to feed "important" or "good to know" books to children without considering the books in relation to the children know how much strain and pointless effort go into such an undertaking. Thinking of the child and his reading *in relation to one another* can obviate the need for much of this customary sweat and overall tiredness. In short, the more complex, difficult road may very well be the surer road to where we would like to go in children's reading.

Why Children Read

I have suggested as a useful basis for the study of children's reading *their reasons for reading.* The nature of these reasons and ways of satisfying them will be considered at length in later chapters of this book, but briefly listing and describing the more important reasons at this point may make clearer this whole basic conception and may give useful hints as to what we may be on the lookout for later in our study of children's literature.

1   A child may read a story, poem, or newspaper article *to meet again what he already knows or half knows.* This is probably at least one of the reasons why he listens intently to—and looks at—the Mr. Small accounts of very ordinary daily living, why he follows closely a book of the "we go to the supermarket" variety, why he may listen to a parent or older sister repeating in detail the story of a trip he himself has taken and so knows about. It is one reason for girls' reading long series of rather uneventful books about families of a quite ordinary sort. It is most likely one reason for a child's rereading a book many times. This is reading for the fun of recognition—the satisfaction of being able to identify oneself with another person and one's own experiences with other situations. The child derives from it the reassurance that comes from encountering the familiar.

2   Children may read *to find out the facts of living,* to learn more about what they already know exists and to find what else exists. In differing

degrees and ways, children are curious about their own existence (their own daily routines, their bodies) and the environment in which they exist (the plants and animals around them, the city and country, the past, present, and future, machines, the universe). This curiosity often is to some extent utilitarian in its origin; a boy may read a book about pigeons so he can raise pigeons successfully or a book about Lincoln so he can give a report on Lincoln in his social studies class. But it is certain that children's wanting to know is not explainable in only utilitarian terms. A child may just have an itch to know what happened and why and how. Like his elders, he may want to know about reality both because he needs to and because he wants to, because he needs to understand reality to handle it and because it is pleasant to comprehend reality.

3   Besides using reading to meet what he already knows and what he does not know, a child may seek through his reading *to turn reality on its head*—in a way, to destroy it. He may turn to reading to be helped in pretending that what does not exist really exists, that the probable is improbable and the improbable altogether probable. The world is simply not nice enough, or it is not unnice enough. He may wish to create or to have created for him a world of nonsense which challenges the daily world of sense, the fabric of facts and probabilities. For this reason he may read or listen to nonsense verse, to such nonsense as *The Dragons of Blueland* or Dr. Seuss's *Beyond Zebra* or *The Wizard of Oz* or *The Hobbit* or *The Enchanted Schoolhouse,* to folktales full of magic. That world replaces the world of fact temporarily; it is not subject to the criteria he uses in examining the world of fact.

4   A desire related to the preceding one but not altogether synonymous with it is the desire *to come up against the strange and the somewhat threatening.* This is the recurring longing for change, for the chill of newness and unfamiliarity. It may cause a child to seek out the fresh slant of a story about life in another land like the d'Aulaires' *Nils* or *Ola* or Elizabeth Foreman Lewis's *To Beat a Tiger* or Taro Yashima's books about Japanese children; it may attract him to the terror of the unknown evoked by an Arthur Conan Doyle or Edgar Allan Poe or Hardy Boys mystery story or an interplanetary-travel tale by H. G. Wells or Robert Heinlein. This desire is like the compulsion of the child to risk putting his foot on slightly hardened mud that may not bear his weight. In his reading he seeks vicarious dangers and excitement.

5   Children, perhaps the very same ones, may seek *reassurance and calmness* through their reading. They may read to lull themselves into complete contentment and the certainty that things are just right and won't suddenly change. This is the primary attraction of the lullaby, the comfortable little Peter Rabbit story, the vast series of tales of affectionate family life, and the happy ending of books that up to that ending may cater to quite different emotional demands. There is a sort of escape from the complex problems of real life, but it is escape into unusual calm and harmony, not into unusual excitement.

6　A child may want *people whom he can admire,* particularly if he can identify himself with them and so participate in their superiority and in their achievements. And so he reads or listens to tales of daring—Jason's or Robin Hood's or Davy Crockett's or Admiral Byrd's or the astronauts'— and tales of achievement—Bach's or Franklin's or Carver's or Fleming's. At the same time, it is not uncommon for child readers to want something to hate as well as to admire; in this they are not essentially different from adult readers. And so there are the giants and bad stepmothers for little children, the Long John Silvers and the bad beasts of the wild-horse herd for the older ones.

7　Children can fall in love with *language,* much as their elders frequently do. They can become enamored of the pattern and music of the language symbols, and so may listen and read for the enjoyment of these patterns, the very exercise of handling language symbols. For some children language can become a reason for not reading, but for other children it may become a real and important reason for reading.

There are certainly other reasons, and other ways of classifying reasons, why children read. But the above are enough to indicate the general nature of children's reasons for reading and to get one working out his own hypothetical pattern of them.

It is more important, though, to realize that children's reasons for reading cannot be reduced to one or two. Children read for a large number of reasons. One child may read for quite a number of different reasons. Too, his reasons may change over a period of time and under changing conditions. And his reasons may be significantly different from the reasons of other children because of differences in intelligence, interests, social and cultural backgrounds, immediate problems, emotional pressures, and language skill.

The child reading public is really the child reading *publics.*

Many Targets

We now have a view of children's books as a mass of various materials used in various ways for various reasons with various results by various kinds of children and adults. This is a complex view, which means that in this book and outside of it we need to take our time in developing and testing it. To do so will be interesting, because our path will be full of concrete—and surprising—experiences. The view presented here makes our job as sponsors of children's reading an open-ended, exploratory one.

SUGGESTED SOURCES

Some Books on Children's Literature for Adults

Arbuthnot, May Hill: *Children and Books,* 3d ed., Scott, Foresman, 1964.
Burger, I. Victor: *Bringing Children and Books Together,* Library Club of America, 1956.

Chase, Mary Ellen: *Recipe for a Magic Childhood,* Macmillan, 1953.

Colby, Jean: *The Children's Book Field,* ill. by Greta Franzen, Pellegrini and Cudahy, 1952.

Crouch, Marcus (compiler): *Chosen for Children,* Library Association, London, 1957.

Duff, Annis: *Bequest of Wings: A Family's Pleasure with Books,* Viking, 1944.

————: *Longer Flight: A Family Grows Up with Books,* Viking, 1956.

Eaton, Anne T.: *Reading with Children,* Viking, 1940.

Fenner, Phyllis: *The Proof of the Pudding: What Children Read,* John Day, 1957.

Ferris, Helen (ed.): *Writing Books for Boys and Girls,* Garden City, 1952. The contributors tell why they wrote children's books.

Fisher, Margery: *Intent upon Reading: A Critical Appraisal of Modern Fiction for Children,* Watts, 1962.

Frank, Josette: *Your Child's Reading Today,* Doubleday, 1954.

Gates, Doris: *Helping Children Discover Books,* ill. by Lois Axeman, Science Research, 1956.

Hazard, Paul: *Books, Children and Men,* trans. by Margaret Mitchell, Horn Book, 1944.

Hewins Lectures 1947–1962, ed. by Siri Andrews, Horn Book, 1963. Lectures on important aspects of children's literature.

Hollowell, Lillian: *A Book of Children's Literature,* Rinehart, 1950.

A Horn Book Sampler: On Children's Books and Reading, ed. by Norma R. Fryatt, Horn Book, 1959. Selected from *The Horn Book,* 1924 to 1948.

Huck, Charlotte S., and Doris A. Young: *Literature in the Elementary School,* Holt, 1961.

Johnson, Edna, et al.: *Anthology of Children's Literature,* 3d ed., Houghton Mifflin, 1959. Introductions to sections contain useful discussions of important critical questions about children's reading.

Larrick, Nancy: *A Parent's Guide to Children's Reading,* rev. ed., Doubleday, 1964.

————: *A Teacher's Guide to Children's Reading,* Merrill, 1960.

Mahony, Bertha E., and Elinor Whitney: *Realms of Gold in Children's Books,* 5th ed., Doubleday, 1929.

Meigs, Cornelia, et al.: *A Critical History of Children's Literature,* Macmillan, 1953.

Miller, Bertha Mahony, and Elinor Whitney Field, (eds.): *Caldecott Medal Books: 1938–1957,* vol. II of *Horn Book Papers,* Horn Book, 1957.

————: *Newbery Medal Books: 1922–1955,* Horn Book, 1955.

Norvell, George W.: *What Boys and Girls Like to Read,* Silver Burdette, 1958.

Sayers, Frances Clarke: *Summoned by Books,* Viking, 1965.

Shedlock, Marie L.: *The Art of the Story-teller,* 3d ed., Dover, 1951.

Smith, Irene: *A History of the Newbery and Caldecott Medals,* Viking, 1957.

Smith, Lillian: *The Unreluctant Years,* American Library Association, 1953.

Strang, Ruth, et al.: *Gateway to Readable Books,* 3d ed., H. W. Wilson, 1958.

Viguers, Ruth H.: *Margin for Surprise: About Books, Children, and Librarians,* Little, Brown, 1964.

White, Dorothy: *Books before Five,* ill. by Joan Smith, Oxford University Press, 1954.

CHAPTER 5

ADULT LITERATURE AS A PART OF CHILDREN'S LITERATURE

*O*ccasionally a literary work appears which, whether or not it is meant for children or for adults or for both, can be read with pleasure by both children and adults without any significant omission, addition, or other alteration. Not everyone likes A. A. Milne's Pooh stories, but the distinction between approvers and nonapprovers certainly does not accord to age differences; Pooh's most ardent devotees may be found both among six-year-old children and among mature adults. Grahame's gentle, witty *The Wind in the Willows*, with its shrewdly observed human little animals Toad, Rat, Mole, etc., likewise can appeal to both the very young and the much older reader. Some of Kipling's *Jungle Books* are for the child of eleven or twelve but can also, if read for the first time, grip the adult reader; and the more sophisticated his reading tastes, the more likely he is not to dismiss the tales as childish. A good many funny cartoon books, such as Ludwig Bemelmans's *Madeline*, Munro Leaf and Robert Lawson's *Ferdinand* and Lawson's *Ben and Me*, Jean de Brunhoff's *Babar* and Roger Duvoisin's *Petunia* and *Veronica*, bring child and adult together in laughter, and similar laughter. A good deal of folk literature has become children's reading, but, at least for the mature adult reader, this body of folktales and balladry has retained its power. The silly jingles of Edward Lear have their nonsense meaning for both children and adults. Some children and some adults find *Alice in Wonderland* heady and delightful just as it is, without change. Thurber's and E. B. White's delicate fantasies can entertain the child and the adult who reads them to the child.

And then there are, as noted previously, adult books whose main elements make them appropriate to both adults and children; nineteenth-century romantic-adventure tales like Scott's and Cooper's straddle easily. There is some excellent writing for adults which proves to be eminently satisfying to younger readers.

But unfortunately we soon run out of such titles, readings that are unquestionably and in similar ways both children's and adults' literature. If there were more of them, our job with children's literature as parents and teachers and librarians would be much simpler, and this chapter would scarcely need to be written, or might at least be short.

As I indicated in Chapter 2, literary values are specific and particular rather than general. Books are good or fair or poor in particular ways, for various reasons. This means, among other things, that the question, "Is it *not* a children's book?" or "Is it just adult reading?" is not a practical question. We need to face the fact that there are books which in particular ways are fine adult reading and also fine children's reading, but which may in particular ways not be good as children's reading. How do we recognize the qualities that make this kind of book? And when we encounter them, how do we answer the awkward and complicated question of what to do with such a book—such as the *Iliad, Beowulf, Gulliver's Travels,* or *Lord Jim?* Postpone the reading of it till adulthood and thus lose its particular virtues as childhood reading? Close our eyes to its shortcomings as children's literature and have the child read it all without omission or other change? Omit or alter those aspects of it which do not contribute to its qualities as children's reading?

Such alternatives seem drastic and difficult, but if we turn to a number of such books and examine them with an awareness of their double existence, we shall, I think, find it possible to develop a flexible, practical approach to this considerable and important portion of children's reading.

The *Iliad* and Its Adaptations for Children: A Case Study

Homer's epic poem the *Iliad* tells how Achilles, a Greek warrior at the siege of Troy, became angry because Agamemnon kept a woman prisoner for himself rather than pass her on to Achilles as part of the spoils of war, how her priest father laid a curse on the Greeks, who were almost driven into the sea, how Achilles sulked (the wrath of Achilles) and would not help his fellow warriors, how his close friend Patroclus took his place and was slain, and how Achilles now changed his mind and went forth and slew Hector, the young prince of Troy, thus putting the Greeks once more on the offensive. Among other things, then, the *Iliad* is an exciting tale of danger and daring, filled with the clashing of powerful forces.

The original poem is very long, over three hundred pages in most editions, too long for most children to attend to. Moreover, it piles on a great many individual episodes of various kinds—the fights of particular warriors, fierce battles, spying on the enemy, the connivings of the gods while the mortals are fighting, the exploits of the warriors, and even of their ancestors, in past wars. And finally, the episodes are narrated not directly, chronologically, but in a twisting manner that stresses the important matters; for instance, Homer begins in the middle and then cuts back to pick up the threads that led into the present crisis.

The complex construction obviously reduces the poem's power and effectiveness for young readers, although it may increase them for adults. So adapters reduce the number of episodes, eliminating many of the interesting, vivid stories about the less central warriors and about the gods, and they may straighten out the order of events. This leads to greater speed, simplicity, and obviousness and makes the *Iliad* into better children's reading, but it sacrifices some fine, exciting narratives and very probably weakens one of the epic's great qualities for mature readers—its cumulative and pervasive effect of tragic unity, the feeling that the fates of all these men are interrelated, that these human beings are responsible for one another and to the gods, and that the gods are responsible to men. It may be argued that ability to take in the feelings of these interrelationships and the sense of tragedy depends partly on a reader's experience of life and his maturity of understanding and that therefore they would be lost on children anyway, so that no harm is done by such omission and reordering. It may also be argued, however, that since this tragic unity is one of the great achievements of the work, the epic should be held back until a reader is ready to appreciate it in such terms.

This complex work develops a number of themes, some of which can be real to children, some perhaps less so. The question of victory or defeat for the Greeks is present, but in a peripheral way. It is not really so important in the *Iliad* whether or not the Greeks win; it is more important what happens to them in winning and to the Trojans in losing. Of course, certain clear, sharp questions arise in the epic, such as whether the boats will be destroyed, whether the Greeks will be shoved into the sea; and these specific crises may be interesting to the child. Likewise, the simple questions of whether Achilles and Patroclus and Hector and the others will live or not are there, and may be important for a young reader.

But in Homer's poem such questions are *not* as significant as the question of death's fatedness. After all, Homer keeps us aware of the inevitability of Achilles' early death. *Why* is he doomed, because of what human actions or nonhuman forces? And *how* will the human being meet his fate? One needs to decide whether the reader of, say, eleven to fourteen years of age can yet feel the significance of *these* questions. One needs to decide whether most child readers will be able to sense the nature and significance of the theme of fate, how real it can become to them. Is it beyond most children? One may go still farther and consider whether, in our culture, the question of fate may lack significance for many, possibly most, adults. (Frequently it pays one, in thinking about children and their books, to push the question being asked toward adults and *their* books.) Then, if one wants to preserve this thematic aspect of fate, he will leave in the poem the commentaries of the poet and his protagonists on these matters and will retain the sections where the gods ponder the fate of mortals and how much autonomy to permit them; this, of course, will slow down the pace and also obscure other more limited themes.

The theme of death—its omnipresence, its nature, its bitterness, man's hatred of it, his acceptance of it as a complement of life—intertwines with the theme of fate throughout the epic. It is often the motivation of the warriors' behavior—the fear of death causes some to flee, acceptance of it makes others fight against great odds, his awareness of approaching early death enters into the intensity of Achilles' feelings and his shifting actions. Again and again in the *Iliad** the nature of death is commented on:

Meges the mighty spearman caught up this man and struck him with his sharp lance on the nape of the neck. The point came through between his jaws and severed his tongue at the root. He fell down in the dust and bit the cold bronze with his teeth.

And Apollo speaks of mortals as

". . . men, those wretched creatures who, like the leaves, flourish for a little while on the bounty of the earth and flaunt their brilliance, but in a moment droop and fade away."

Adapters for children omit or greatly reduce the number of such comments; and of course in so doing they almost banish a central theme of the poem and drastically change the poem's tone. Their rationale, of course, is the assumption that young readers are not yet ready to face the facts of death and its significance or that they should not be asked to. This, of course, is a recurrent and central question the adult must consider in thinking about children's literature; for on the one hand, he finds a great many teachers and parents arrayed against death as a literary subject, and on the other hand, he realizes that most writers have been deeply aware of death and concerned with it and have addressed themselves to it in much of their best work.

Still, there are in the *Iliad* themes certainly not beyond children's comprehension and interest, themes which, without tampering, can come through to children. Physical skill and courage—these two attributes of the heroes are constantly in evidence, and a recurring theme is the degree to which the various heroes live up to ideals of physical courage and skill—Ulysses' skill in strategy, Achilles' and Hector's spear handling and bravery. Another theme, loyalty, runs all through the epic—Achilles' failure in loyalty to his chief (who he feels has let him down), Patroclus's loyalty to his lord Achilles, Achilles' final loyalty to his fellow Greeks and Hector's to the Trojan cause—and it is here in an obvious enough form to be recognized and responded to by the young reader.

How are all these subjects treated in the *Iliad*? The *Iliad* is, of course, epic poetry, and so there are certain conventions of epic style that will be unfamiliar to most child readers, just as they are to many adult readers—

the formal invocation of the muses, the use of an elaborate superhuman machinery, the relating of protagonists and events at some length to prior history and to deities, repetition of certain modes of description and narrative (''wine-dark sea,'' ''armor clanged around him''), and Homeric similes. For example:

. . . the incoming troops, who had issued, tribe on tribe, from their ship and huts by the wide sea-sands to march in battalions to the meeting place, like buzzing swarms of bees that come out in relays from a hollow rock and scatter by companies right and left, to fall in clusters on the flowers of spring.

This elaborate comparison certainly stops the action, but also it may intensify and deepen its significance for the reader. This is *poetry*, poetic speech. If, then, the *Iliad* is approached in a natural way as poetry and the child has not yet built up a prejudice against all poetry, these special poetic conventions should not seem confusing or silly and should actually make the poem more attractive to him. Reading the *Iliad* aloud or hearing it read aloud is a great help in keeping these poetic conventions from becoming stumbling blocks to understanding and enjoyment.

The epic writer may at times seem to pause to take on a load of factual information about genealogies, gods, etc., but for the most part, the Homeric epic tells its story swiftly, not so much through local color as through movement and action—what happens. In the *Iliad* there are backgrounds, but these are mainly in terms of action—sailoring, fighting, athletic games. The reader does come to know in considerable detail the techniques of ancient fighting and sailing the Mediterranean. These become a major source of appeal to young readers of the *Iliad*. Still, there is constant referring to ancient Greek family and tribal relationships, religious ceremonies (thanksgiving, marriage, funeral customs), and the Greek pantheon, and this rich context *may* be confusing to the child reader, partly because it is not part of his normal cultural exposure and partly because of the casual obliqueness of its introduction. Homer could assume his listeners knew more than he actually said about a particular god or godlike hero; he did not need to stop to explain in any detail who Thetis or Artemis or Poseidon was. Simply leaving out much of this context is one fairly common solution of this problem; but doing this seems to reduce the poem's significance, to transform it from a broad drama of a whole culture to a simple adventure tale (does Achilles finally kill off Hector?), and so proves that Homer's epic is a whole work of art, that it is more than its story. Some adaptations try to have the cake and eat it by including explanatory notes; this too is distracting, and it changes the tone to that of an encyclopedia. Another strategy is to retain most of these references but to drop some.

This is in part a language obstacle. The unfamiliarity of the Greek names of people, deities, and places and the uncertainty about pronunciation may make for confusion and a feeling of unsureness and self-consciousness in the reader. But this need not be in any way a major problem if adults try to avoid inculcating in young readers too intense a worry about accurate pronunciation (an *oral* problem, mainly); also, a little early suggesting of the most common pronunciation stumpers may clear up much needless worry—hard *k* in Achilles, *oo* sound in Zeus, etc.

Vocabulary is a greatly exaggerated stumbling block in the way of children's reading of the *Iliad* and other ancient epics. Some of the translations have tried to approximate the poetic form of the original and so have used a special English poetic vocabulary, but in the prose translations—and the most effective ones for children appear to be in prose—there is a tendency to flatten out the vocabulary somewhat, make it less special. So what one gets in, say, the Jane Werner Watson Golden Book adaptation is a rich enough but not particularly complex or rare vocabulary; the strangeness results mainly from unfamiliarity with the objects and actions to which the language refers. Although the language of Homer's *Iliad* at first worries adults who think of it as part of a child's reading, this should not be their primary consideration. The Golden Book adaptation, again, is within the language range of good eleven- and twelve-year-old readers.

The *major* possible block between the young reader and the *Iliad* is its complexity of thought and feeling, the maturity and seriousness of the thematic content. The *Iliad* is the product, not of an unsophisticated, primitive society, but of an already highly developed society with rich history, traditions, and ethical and aesthetic codes of its own, and the advanced state of that society is reflected in this epic poem. Achilles, for example, although at first he may seem a rather spoiled, pouting boy of muscle and little else, acquires more and more dimensions as we follow him through the torturing weeks of his wrath; we discover in him much self-doubt mingled with pride, a poignant awareness of death and a love of life, an intense struggle between impulsive egotism and a sense of responsibility to his fellow men. And the other heroes are not simple, brutish warriors, either, but many-sided human beings—Ulysses brave but also cautious, eager to use cunning whenever possible instead of the frontal attack; old Nestor wise and in some ways a learned man; Hector intense, refined, touched with melancholy, able to cover up his personal feelings under the robe of warrior prince. And warfare is portrayed in all its complexity of political plotting, angry impulse, bold attack, courage and fear, and, as in Hector and Andromache particularly, sense of personal loss. And these people are swept by various feelings of trust and distrust of the divine order. This is adult thinking, and it is an integral part of the whole poem. Try leaving it out and you drastically alter the poem; it is no longer Homer's *Iliad,* and you might then as well invent a wholly new story about an assault on a fort in the pioneer days of the American West. If you leave it in, the reader will not see it through adult eyes, and it may get in the way of the elements he *can* respond to.

So we have in the *Iliad* a *poetic* account of *action* which does not move in a single or straight line, a poem of feats of physical strength, skill and great valor, but at the same time a poem crowded with a thoroughly mature awareness of life's frustrating complexity, a work of art full of questions and ambiguous answers, and an overspreading sense of fate and human tragedy. It is safe to conclude that the original *Iliad* in translation is adult in too many ways to be comprehended and enjoyed by most children. So the full version will need to wait, in most cases, until the reader has grown up; otherwise, he will be defeated by a work he might later really be able to get into.

Nevertheless, the *Iliad* does have much that children want and that we may want them to get—vigorous and significant action, the excitement of daring deeds, ideals of courage and loyalty and effort, a poetry rich and sturdy, even in prose translation. The problem, then, is to decide whether or not we can, in a superior adaptation, get the latter without those elements that create special difficulties for children. And this is part of a larger question: *can* the great epics be adapted and used as children's reading without causing their young readers to lose potentially great artistic experiences later on?

The *Odyssey:* A Different Kind of Case

The *Odyssey* tells of Odysseus' (Ulysses') many adventures in his long effort to get home to his wife Penelope and son Telemachus—his stay in the land of the lotus-eaters, his blinding the giant herdsman Polyphemus, his encounter with the cannibal giants, his being delayed by the enchantress Circe (who turns his companions into swine), his voyage past the Sirens, his seven years' detention by the goddess Calypso after loss of his whole ship and company in a storm, his being cast up on the shore of Scheria and entertained by King Alcinous and his daughter Nausicaa, his eventual return home, and his destruction of all the courtiers who have been trying to replace him during his long absence.

Much that we have said about the *Iliad* applies to the *Odyssey.* It has the same characteristics of style, the same epic conventions, the same historical and mythical contexts. Like the *Iliad,* it deals with adult problems, in this instance exile and sexual fidelity. Also it shows a similar awareness of the complexity of human problems and character; for instance, its central figure Odysseus is a many-sided man in whom are combined physical courage, practical skills, and a shrewdness and caution that set him apart. It, too, is episodic, intricate, long. Yet the general tone is different from that of the *Iliad,* and this difference makes it much more easily adaptable for children's reading.

This is partly a difference between the characters of Achilles and Odysseus—Achilles brooding, tied up in suspicion and self-doubt, weighed down by a knowledge of his own brief destiny, Odysseus the man of action, less dark and uncertain, not generally given to brooding and inner fret. Odysseus is pretty much an optimistic man of action, and he dominates the poem. Also, although there are in the *Odyssey*, as in the *Iliad*, violence and death and an awareness of fate, these are much less central, more incidental, in the *Odyssey*. The question of dying or not is less significant than the question of *getting home* over an obstacle course that calls for skill, daring, and almost superhuman endurance. The *Odyssey* is a tale, not of a bitter, confused impasse, a stubborn clash of angry wills, as the *Iliad* is, but of an adventurous voyage. There is actually little of the wonderful in the *Iliad*, whereas the *Odyssey* is a succession of successful encounters with thrilling unknowns and marvels. Odysseus is never stalemated; instead, he is always on the move, taking care of each monster or whirlpool or one-eyed giant as it appears. There is less occasion for commentaries on the presence of death and the bitterness of man's fate. And in keeping with the brighter tone of the poem is the successful outcome for Odysseus; the epic has an appropriate, untricky happy ending. Unentangled with melancholy or nostalgic regret or hectic desire, it is a magnificent tale of movement, adventure, and wonder.

Obviously, then, the *Odyssey* has a great deal to offer younger readers and, unlike the *Iliad*, little that is incomprehensible or that in any way could be considered too old for them. It is essentially a young story, just as the *Iliad* is fundamentally an adult, old story. When we talk, then, of children's reading Homer, we need to distinguish between the two epics, for the reading situations and problems of the two are quite different from one another.

Adapting the Homeric Epics

If we agree that the *Odyssey* and, perhaps, the *Iliad* have too many elements that can be valuable to children to be left until adulthood, we need to decide between the originals and the adaptations, and then, if the latter, among adaptations. In the light of our survey of the particular elements in these epics, it would seem that except for children of quite unusual cultural and reading background, some adapting of the originals would be preferable. Then which adaptations?

One which, like Padraic Colum's version of the *Odyssey**, preserves something of the work's poetic spirit but at the same time makes clear sense in modern prose would appear most desirable. Here is a brief passage from Colum, in which Odysseus begins to tell King Alcinous the story of his travels after the fall of Troy:

"*The wind bore my ships from the coast of Troy, and with our white sails hoisted we came to the cape that is called Malea. Now if we had been able to double this cape we should soon have come to our own country, all unhurt. But the north wind came and swept us from our course and drove us wandering past Cythera.*

"*Then for nine days we were borne onward by terrible winds and away from all known lands. On the tenth day we came to a strange country. Many of my men landed there. The people of that land were harmless and friendly, but the land itself was most dangerous. For there grew there the honey-sweet fruit of the lotus that makes all men forgetful of their past and neglectful of their future. And those of my men who ate the lotus that the dwellers of that land offered them became forgetful of their country and of the way before them. They wanted to abide forever in the land of the lotus. They wept when they thought of all the toils before them and of all they had endured. I led them back to the ships, and I had to place them beneath the benches and leave them in bonds. And I commanded those who had ate of the lotus to go at once aboard the ships. Then, when I had got all my men upon the ships, we made haste to sail away."*

One need not be at a loss for variety of adaptations. Among them are Alfred Church's *The Odyssey of Homer,* told freshly, chronologically; Catherine Sellew's *Adventures with the Gods,* written in a simple, direct way for younger children; Colum's *The Adventures of Odysseus and the Tale of Troy;* Aubrey De Sélincourt's *Odysseus the Wanderer,* a vigorous retelling; Sally Benson's *Stories of the Gods and Heroes,* a clear account but one which perhaps does not convey much of the Greek spirit and background; Jane Werner Watson's imaginatively done Golden Book *The Iliad and the Odyssey,* appropriately illustrated by Alice and Martin Provensen; and the barer retelling or outlines in the various mythologies of Thomas Bulfinch, Edith Hamilton, and others.

The *Aeneid, Beowulf,* and *The Song of Roland*

These three epics all share in greater or lesser degree the major virtues and limitations of the Homeric poems as children's reading. They are all poetry and use certain poetic conventions; for example, the *Aeneid* begins with an invocation of the muse and uses elaborate Homeric similes. They are all episodic in arrangement and are all filled with a great many occurrences, mainly of warlike adventure and daring in the face of magical wonders. They all describe courage—in the persons of the heroes Aeneas, Beowulf, and Roland and their liege men—in the face of overwhelming odds. Aeneas sails along the Mediterranean and at last encounters and defeats the Latin tribes of central Italy and establishes the beginnings of the Roman Empire. Beowulf waits in the Hall of Heorot for the onslaught of the monster Grendel and eventually fights his last bloody fight with its mother. And Roland, waging a hopeless rearguard action against the Saracens, dies a hero's death. For the most part, the episodes are physical encounters with giants or other terrifying forms and forces, but in each case the poem is much more than a Buck Rogers adventure. Each epic is informed with characteristic values, awarenesses, and questions. Virgil's *Aeneid,* although composed of adventures similar to those treated in the

Odyssey, expresses a different outlook—a romantic melancholy and at the same time a cynical, worldly materialism not found in Homer. *Beowulf* suggests a more terrified sense of the uncontrolled powers of nature than do the Greek and Roman epics, at the same time giving forth a note of Christian hope. And *The Song of Roland* is crowded with the values and symbols of medieval chivalry.

In each case the versions for children have done fundamentally the same things: they have picked out the astonishing and greathearted deeds and the magical wonders and have eliminated a good many episodes, such as additional duels by the same persons, that seemed to the adapters repetitious or extraneous (although they might not seem so to other adult readers); and they have cut out elements that appear inappropriate for children for one reason or another, such as the family hatreds in *Beowulf* or the love of Aeneas and Dido and his betrayal of her or the ugly betrayal in *The Song of Roland.* And much of the original special tone—of grandeur, complication, fear, melancholy, pride—has been lost. What remains is usually a pretty good action yarn, a sort of western. This, of course, may be plenty—especially if it has led such an illustrator as Howard Pyle, N. C. Wyeth, or Peter Hurd to create vivid drawings and paintings for it.

An English Epic, the *Morte d'Arthur*

In their accounts of marvels, action, and human courage, all of the epic works we have so far considered quite obviously have much for children. At the same time they contain important elements that may partially unsuit them as reading for many children—complex episodic narrative, the interests and attitudes of adults, and the special knowledge and values of cultures deeply different from ours. The last may seem an added reason for children's reading them, but it may also be argued that one needs to have a fuller, slower learning of Greek values than an explanatory sentence about how the Greeks believed in the ideal of the balanced, well-rounded human being. And of course the epics lose much of their poetry in translation. This, however, is not peculiar to them as children's books; the adult reader confronts the same possible limitation in reading Dante's *Divine Comedy* or Goethe's *Faust.*

In the Arthurian tales, a body of lore made for adults in one culture and appropriated by the children of another, we have in some respects a quite different situation. These too are hero tales and wonder legends that have collected around a central hero; also, they are full of magic, physical achievement, and warlike valor and express indirectly a set of cultural values, in this case a medieval pagan-Christian view. But the source from which the Arthurian tales in most children's collections are mainly taken, Sir Thomas Malory's *Morte d'Arthur**, is *a prose account,* and this means that a retelling may not do as much violence to the original spirit of the narrative as would a prose retelling of an epic poem. Moreover, Malory's version of the legends is *in English,* a fifteenth-century English not easily read by twentieth-century English-speaking people but still basically English in vocabulary and syntax. This means that an adapter, if he chooses, may make the most of Malory's own pungent way of telling the story. He needs only a somewhat modernized sentence order and spelling and the occasional substitution of a better-known word for an archaism. He may, of course, as did Howard Pyle, seek to suggest the past with archaic words (*thee, prithee*) and an occasional trace of earlier syntax.

Here is the beginning of Malory's own fifteenth-century account of the episode of the sword in the stone by which Arthur proved himself King of Britain:

Then stood the realm in great jeopardy long while, for every lord that was mighty of men made him strong, and many weened to have been kind. Then Merlin went to the Archbishop of Canterbury, and counselled him for to send for all the lords of the realm, and all the gentlemen of arms, that they should to London come by Christmas, upon pain of cursing and for this cause, that Jesus, that was born on that night, that he would of his great mercy show some miracle, as he was come to be king of mankind, for to show some miracle who should be rightwise king of this realm. So the Archbishop, by the advice of Merlin, sent for all the lords and gentlemen of arms that they should come by Christmas even unto London. And many of them made them clean of their life, that their prayer might be the more acceptable unto God. So in the greatest church of London, whether it were Paul's or not the French book maketh no mention, all the estates were long or day in the church for to pray. And when matins and the first mass was done, there was seen in the churchyard, against the high altar, a great stone four square, like unto a marble stone; and in midst thereof was like an anvil of steel a foot on high, and therein stuck a fair sword naked by the point, and letters there were written in gold about the sword that said thus:—Whoso pulleth out this sword of this stone and anvil, is rightwise king born of all England. Then the people marvelled, and told it to the Archbishop. I command, said the Archbishop, that ye keep you within your church and pray unto God still, that no man touch the sword till the high mass be all done. So when all masses were done all the lords went to behold the stone and the sword. And when they saw the scripture some assayed, such as would have been king. But none might stir the sword nor move it.

Now here is the same episode as retold by Mary Macleod in her *Book of King Arthur and His Noble Knights,** an edition intended for children:

When several years had passed, Merlin went to the Archbishop of Canterbury and counselled him to send for all the lords of the realm, and all the gentlemen of arms, that they should come to

London at Christmas, and for this cause—that a miracle would show who should be rightly king of the realm. So all the lords and gentlemen made themselves ready, and came to London, and long before dawn on Christmas Day they were all gathered in the great church of St. Paul's to pray.

When the first service was over, there was seen in the churchyard a large stone, four-square, like marble, and in the midst of it was like an anvil of steel, a foot high. In this was stuck by the point a beautiful sword, with naked blade, and there were letters written in gold about the sword, which said thus: Whoso pulleth this sword out of this stone and anvil is rightly King of all England.

Then the people marvelled, and told it to the Archbishop.

"I command," said the Archbishop, "that you keep within the church, and pray unto God still; and that no man touch the sword till the service is over."

So when the prayers in church were over, all the lords went to behold the stone and the sword; and when they read the writing some of them—such as wished to be king—tried to pull the sword out of the anvil. But not one could make it stir.

The language and the literary form of the modern adapters have probably caused them less worry than some of the subject matter and its ethical implications—the dark theme of intrigue and treason that runs somberly under and through the pattern of noble deeds, the medieval court of love and the dalliances of Lancelot and Guinevere, Tristram and Iseult. In most of the adaptations these parts of the legend are left vague, obscure; but even with such de-emphasis or omission the Arthurian tales, in all their strange and magical happenings and in the efforts of the Knights of the Round Table to live up to the chivalric code, retain much of their underlying spirit and fervor. Furthermore, the Arthurian tales do not have the interwoven, elaborate kind of mythology that the adapter must leave out or explain in the epics of the Mediterranean and Norse worlds. There is instead a fairy element, easy enough for children to comprehend, that gives to the whole series of tales a unifying magical aura—the sword in the stone, Merlin the magician, the magical carrying off of Arthur to Avalon.

John Bunyan's *Pilgrim's Progress*

Now let us consider a classic work in which, in contrast to those we have been discussing, language offers no major problem at all. Although written over two hundred years ago, the language of Bunyan's *Pilgrim's Progress** seems almost meant for children speaking twentieth-century English. Its syntax is very simple and regular; its vocabulary is plain and vigorous. The following passage is typical:

As I walked through the wilderness of this world, I lighted on a certain place where was a Den, and I laid me down in that place to sleep: and as I slept I dreamed a dream. I dreamed, and behold I saw a man clothed with rags, standing in a certain place, with his face from his own house, a book in his hand, and a great burden upon his back. I looked, and saw him open the book and read therein; and as he read, he wept and trembled; and not being able longer to contain, he brake out with a lamentable cry, saying, "What shall I do?"

Here language is no special obstacle to understanding and interested reading. And the incidents and the characters present few barriers to children, for whom *Pilgrim's Progress* can be an exciting story of an expedition taken into a strange and hostile land against great odds. Its events are intensely exciting, enacted by simplified human beings moved by recognizable human feelings of love, jealousy, fear, and anger; and the accounts of these events are filled with physical reality and a sense of swarming crowds—a vivid visualness that still makes the book tempting to illustrators. The Slough of Despond, the Valley of Humiliation, Vanity Fair, and the House Beautiful have both a precision and a solidity that make them very immediate and real to children.

Pilgrim's Progress is a clear, swift account of a wonderful journey, a kind of *Odyssey*, and yet its intention was to change men's minds and thereby their whole lives and afterlives; it is a Puritan document, a sermon, a Protestant allegory. Most child readers do not realize this, except in the very general sense of the work's being about good versus evil, a lesson in the art of being virtuous. Why can it be a doctrinal tract and at the same time a great adventure tale for children, one that scarcely calls for any adaptation whatsoever?

The clearest reason is that what happens in *Pilgrim's Progress* is in terms of *action, not thought;* it is a chain of physical hardships and adventures, the allegorizing of the spiritual hazards that were altogether real to the Baptist Bunyan. Also, the figures are generalized, so that the child reader can create his own figures for Greed, Jealousy, and the others. And yet the individual persons, scenes, and places are very specific and concrete, filled with a sense of *physical* reality. *Pilgrim's Progress* is in this way very close to the folktales of generalized brave, good boys or princes going out to reach a castle, kill a giant, free a maiden, or break a spell. It contains all the elements of a north European folktale.

Gulliver's Travels and Other Unchildlike Works

Jonathan Swift's *Gulliver's Travels* is a classic instance of thoroughly adult literature that is so completely unchildlike in all respects except one that only that single element of the work can be kept: it uses a wonder tale as a skeleton on which to hang the author's *real* story. The result: all the children's adaptations are essentially *new* stories, owing something to the original tale in only the most mechanical way.

The borrowed idea—a human being among creatures very much smaller or larger than himself—is not an unusual one in literature. There are *Hop o' My Thumb*, the *Odyssey* with its giant shepherds, *Jack and the Beanstalk*, *Alice in Wonderland*, *The Borrowers*, *The Amiable Giant*, and many more. In *Gulliver's Travels* the traveler first wanders among little people, then among giants; this is what has been borrowed to make the *children's Gulliver's Travels*.

But Swift's *whole* tale is a quite different entity: it attacks hypocrisy, selfishness, misrule, and unreason as he saw them in the European society of his time, and it does so by having the Lilliputians and Brobdignagians reflect with harsh intensity those qualities in their actions. Not only are the petty, gross, beastly, and irrational actions described with startling frankness; their pettiness, grossness, etc., are underlined. Thus, in the view of most adults, many of the accounts of specific incidents would be something for adults to observe and assimilate but without point for children, since the satirical implications would largely escape them. And both the very adult anger—Swift's impatience with humankind accumulated through long and greatly diverse experience with them—and the humaneness behind his rage would be out of the range of all but precocious children.

The language, however, is quite within children's range. It is like that of the almost contemporary Bunyan in that respect: modern English syntax, vigorous and concrete vocabulary. Swift uses a language children of eleven or twelve can understand, but to tell a tale they probably cannot comprehend, the tale of evil in modern society as Swift felt it.

All that Swift has for children is the adventure yarn, the wonder tale, and out of this germ have developed all the children's *Gullivers*, from the brief résumés in many collections of tales for children and the longer telling illustrated by Arthur Rackham to Walt Disney's ingenious fairy tale. So it is realistic to consider these as *original* children's literature.

This is true of a number of famous modern books that have a surface of physical adventure and a core of mature thinking. They are metaphors, and the new children's books that have come from them consist of one side of the metaphor. An example is Herman Melville's *Moby Dick*. Its events are those of pure adventure story—clipper-ship sailing, whale hunting, the search for a great whale. But in all other respects—the philsophical questions and conceptions, the rich, shifting, many-layered language, the probing, groping characterizations—it is, except for the child with special intellectual and language background, almost entirely nonjuvenile fare. Similar to *Moby Dick* in this respect are the novels of Joseph Conrad—*Lord Jim*, *Almayer's Folly*, *Typhoon*, *Heart of Darkness*, etc. Superficially novels of adventure at sea and in the jungle, they have an intricately knotted metaphysical core, often ambiguous and puzzling human characters, an indirect, sinuous kind of narration, and various levels of symbolic significance.

This means that in adaptations for children the only things retained from the original are the *outlines* of the adventures, a few general ideas, such as the survival of man against whale or jungle, and accounts of such physical crises as armed attacks or tempests. In short, these books become adventure tales, much as *Gulliver* becomes a wonder tale. All the incidents that do not have high action value, all the character searching, all the artful and intricate fitting together of the pieces of the author's cosmic puzzle—these the adapter omits. He may rewrite the retained crisis passages; the originals he feels are too intricate, indirect, allusive. And so what he turns out is a fairly orthodox action tale that could have been written for *The American Boy* or the *Saturday Evening Post*. It is realistic to think of these as simply new action tales for children and not as works by Conrad, Melville, Swift, etc. The names of their authors and the reputation of the works should therefore carry no special weight when these books are published as children's literature.

Adult Tales of Adventure and Mystery

But there is a large class of adult literature whose adventure or wonder elements can be made available to children without any need for changing the book in any important way: the tale of romantic adventure, often with a historical setting, written *for* its external, physical movement and color and to stir feelings by uncomplicated problems and emotions. Sir Walter Scott's *Ivanhoe* and *The Talisman* are of this kind; the books are successions of sieges, battles, duels, and escapes, and the protagonists are pretty much black and white characters—the fair Rowena, noble Ivanhoe, villainous Sir Brian de Bois-Guilbert, Richard the Lion-hearted. Many more of Scott's books would be equally appealing to children without adaptation but for his use of Scottish dialect. The pace may for many readers be slow. In *The Talisman* and *Ivanhoe* it is not markedly so, however; and for good readers of eleven or twelve and over, Scott's sometimes elaborate, flowery vocabulary offers no special trouble, for it is clearly ornamentation and covers up no really puzzling experiences or ideas.

This kind of adult fiction, given its great impetus in the early nineteenth century by Scott and carried on without any ascertainable tapering off into this present time, is responsible for many books that now pass for children's literature—Alexandre Dumas's *The Count of Monte Cristo* and *The Three Musketeers*, James Fenimore Cooper's *Last of the Mohicans*, Richard D. Blackmore's *Lorna Doone*, Rafael Sabatini's *Scaramouche* and *Captain Blood*, Charles Reade's *The Cloister and the Hearth*, George Eliot's *Romola*, Charles Dickens's *A Tale of Two Cities*, Winston Churchill's *The Crisis*, Henryk Sienkiewicz's *Quo Vadis*, John Buchan's *Prester John*, Walter Edmonds's *Chad Hanna*. These historical novels are essentially adventure tales, with historical settings and perhaps historical meaning, but they do not have the underpinning or overlaying of social, philosophical, psychological meanings you find in certain books that bear them a superficial resemblance but are much more complex and mature—books like Thackeray's

Vanity Fair and Tolstoy's *War and Peace*. Books like Dumas's and C. S. Forester's (the Hornblower series) are essentially successions of dangers, pursuits, captures, hairbreadth escapes, physicaı combats, and happy endings, and the authors left the action uncomplicated by complex human characters and motives.

Occasionally, of course, modern writers of this historical-adventure type of novel show the contemporary inclination to refer in frank naturalistic detail to acts of sex and violence that their predecessors might have avoided. This may sometimes make a present-day historical novel seem more adult than it is; also, in the view of some adults, it may make a novel postponable for the children for whom it is otherwise unquestionably appropriate.

In general, this great field of historical adventure is one meeting ground of the child readers and writers for adult readers where there exists no need for intervention by an adapter. The reason is, in the main, that the writers of this type of literature have been largely concerned with the surface color and movement of life, less given to eliciting its significances. Moreover, most teachers, parents, and librarians have generally encouraged children's taking these books as their own because of the more or less historically factual content. This kind of writing has had cultural sanction.

Child readers and writers for adult readers again meet on common ground in that traditional type of popular fiction whose subject is outdoor adventure. The outdoors may be the American West, the African jungle, the South Sea Islands, the baseball diamond or football stadium, or interplanetary space. Whatever the setting, characters and events are essentially similar—simple heroes or heroines encountering dangers and hardships, generally of a physical, outdoor sort, and overcoming them. The characters are one-dimensional, the place and time are conceived in generalized terms (pioneer days, a rough lumber camp, a jungle of snakes and poisoned arrows), and there are no difficult or profound questions and ideas implied in, or growing out of, what happens in the story. The style may be spare and journalistic or romantically overblown, but it is seldom of so special a kind as to give reader, adult or child, any cause for concern.

Typical of the genre are Zane Grey's seemingly endless series of westerns, Edgar Rice Burroughs's Tarzan series, the space fantasies that fill *Amazing Stories* and the other science-fiction journals, Stewart Edward White's stories of the West, Rider Haggard's *She*, and Kipling's *Kim* and *Captains Courageous*. Such stories may appear first in magazines or books intended as light reading for some fictitious figure called "the general reader," presumably adult. But these stories are generally fated to become the reading of the *young* "general reader"—the reader from eleven to sixteen or seventeen years old.

Still another popular type of adult reading that because of its most important ingredient needs little if any change to become children's reading is the romantic, mist-filled mystery, from Charlotte Brontë's *Jane Eyre* to W. H. Hudson's *Green Mansions* and Daphne du Maurier's *Rebecca*. Such mystery is also one of the dominant elements in much of Dickens's writing and Stevenson's shorter tales and John Buchan's stories.

Great Adult Books That Are Also Great Children's Books

These last two kinds of books for adults can without change become children's reading mainly because, whatever, other qualities they may have or lack, they do not generally carry important intellectual freight, any complex view of life or human character, any unconventional perspectives. Still, there occasionally appears a work which has considerable intellectual vigor but which at the same time manages to become a children's book without major alterations or without any at all. There are not many of this sort, but they are significant works of both adult and children's literary art. In general, they are written in an unornamented, direct style, and their idea content is implicit in the characters and actions of the protagonists. Occasionally the presence of clear humor or of unapologetic fantasy explains the appeal to both adults and children.

Daniel Defoe's *Robinson Crusoe** satisfies intelligent adult readers and at the same time, without adaptation, holds a deep and sure appeal for children. For adults it is a beautifully lean, economical narrative of a man's nip-and-tuck struggle against both nature and his fellow man to survive and to go on to create the elements of a civilization. It has a satisfying simplicity and singleness of direction, a moving unity, and yet it achieves this through a multiplicity of varied episodes presented in equally satisfying concrete detail. There is no close scrutiny of Crusoe; Defoe presents him as a man sharing the elemental desires and capabilities of his species. He is a simple man—or, more accurately, *simply man.*

Now what does the child of, say, eleven or twelve, find when he comes to this adult masterpiece? First, he gets one action-filled episode after another in swift succession—a fight with pirates, the wreck, Crusoe's recovery of the stores from the ship, his building a house and domesticating animals, his encountering human signs, his saving Friday, and their rescue from the island. All of these episodes involve much physical activity, much *doing.* Many of them suggest danger and the need for courage; all of them call for accomplishment, the solution of problems. In other words, each part *moves,* in terms of both physical action and the development and resolution of a problem. And Crusoe's are concrete problems and situations that, for the most part, a child can comprehend. Shipwreck, saving objects and animals from the sea, living in a cave, making a garden, raising animals, building a house—these are elemental if not all widely shared human experiences. And they are created intensively in full factual detail; the child thus gets the concreteness of *The Big Book of Trucks* and its like. But, in addition, here in *Robinson Crusoe* things happen to a special person in wonderful circumstances—a seaman afloat alone on a wide sea, then marooned alone on an uninhabited island, then finding a footprint from nowhere. So the episodes that compose the tale have everything a child might want—action, concrete factual information, and even a certain strangeness, a suggestion of other fresh, new worlds, untouched and waiting to be explored. Perhaps this last element is what has made this work most deeply appealing to adult and child alike for nearly three hundred years—the conception of a new, clean world which a man has now the chance of shaping, of civilizing as he wills. Defoe created a firstness, a virgin quality, that can hold a man and bewitch a child.

As for Defoe's language, it is direct talk a young reader can understand. The word order is regular; the vocabulary is concrete and vivid. This description of Robinson's building of a shelter is typical of Defoe's language.

In search of a place proper for this, I found a little plain on the side of a rising hill, whose front towards this little plain was steep as a house-side, so that nothing could come down upon me from the top; on the side of this rock there was a hollow place worn a little way in like the entrance or door of a cave, but there was not really any cave or way into the rock at all.

On the flat of the green, just before this hollow place, I resolved to pitch my tent. This plain was not above an hundred yards broad, and about twice as long, and lay like a green before my door, and at the end of it descended irregularly every way down into the low grounds by the seaside. It was on the north-northwest side of the hill, so that I was sheltered from the heat every day, till it came to a west and by south sun, or thereabout, which in those countries is near the setting.

Before I set up my tent, I drew a half circle before the hollow place, which took in about ten yards in its semi-diameter from the rock, and twenty yards in its diameter, from its beginning and ending.

In this half circle I pitched two rows of strong stakes, driving them into the ground till they stood very firm like piles, the biggest end being out of the ground about five foot and a half, and sharpened on the top. The two rows did not stand above six inches from one another.

Then I took the pieces of cable which I had cut in the ship, and laid them in rows one upon another, within the circle between these two rows of stakes, up to the top, placing other stakes in the inside, leaning against them, about two foot and a half high, like a spur to a post; and this fence was so strong that neither man nor beast could get into it or over it. This cost me a great deal of time and labour, especially to cut the piles in the woods, bring them to the place, and drive them into the earth.

The entrance into this place I made to be, not by a door, but by a short ladder to go over the top, which ladder, when I was in, I lifted over after me, and so I was completely fenced in, and fortified, as I thought, from all the world, and consequently slept secure in the night, which otherwise I could not have done, though, as it appeared afterwards, there was not need of all this caution from the enemies that I apprehended danger from.

This English shares with Swift's writing in *Gulliver's Travels* and much of Bunyan's in *Pilgrim's Progress* a flexible, wiry, utilitarian quality that permits the present-day child access to all the action that occurs and all the many objects that move through this tale, so eminently a children's story in subject and mood.

Richard Dana's *Two Years before the Mast** resembles *Robinson Crusoe* in much more than their both being tales of the sea. It is an adult book whose themes and language make it, like *Robinson Crusoe*, appropriate for children from, say, eleven on. Again like *Robinson Crusoe*, it is a series of vivid, almost independent episodes full of physical activity, the doing of things—a young man's struggle with seasickness on his first voyage, a chase by what seems to be a pirate ship, fighting through the storms off Cape Horn, hauling in the rigging in storms. In each episode Dana holds the young reader's attention with physical, tangible detail. This is a typical episode:

Our chief reliance, the prevailing westerly gales, was thus cut; and here we were, nearly seven hundred miles to the westward of the Cape, with a gale dead from the eastward, and the weather so thick that we could not see the ice with which we were surrounded, until it was directly under our bows.

At four P.M. (it was then quite dark) all hands were called, and sent aloft in a violent squall of hail and rain to take in sail. We had now all got on our "Cape Horn rig"—thick boots, southwesters coming down over our necks and ears, thick trousers and jackets, and some with oilcloth suits over all. Mittens, too, we wore on deck, but it would not do to go aloft with them on, for it was impossible to work with them, and being wet and stiff, they might let a man slip overboard, for all the hold he could get upon a rope; so, we were obliged to work with bare hands, which, as well as our faces, were often cut with the hailstones, which fell thick and large.

Our ship was now all cased with ice—hull, spars, and standard rigging; and the running rigging so stiff that we could hardly bend it so as to belay it, or, still worse, take a knot with it; and the sails nearly as stiff as sheet iron. One at a time (for it was a long piece of work and required many hands), we furled the courses, mizzen topsail, and fore-topmast and staysail, and close-reefed the fore and main topsails, and hove the ship to under the fore, with the main hauled

*up by the clew lines and buntlines and ready to be sheeted home,
if we found it necessary to make sail to get to windward of an
island. A regular lookout was then set, and kept by each watch in
turn, until the morning.*

As in *Robinson Crusoe,* the central character is intelligent but not particularly complex or many-leveled; he is simply very much concerned with
surviving in the situations where he finds himself. Some of these call for
endurance or courage, such as the long fight back around the Horn in
freezing storms, dodging icebergs; others call for ingenuity. As in *Robinson
Crusoe,* these episodes move forward compellingly along the line of a single,
clear theme and essentially the same one—surviving. Furthermore, this
chronicle of epic struggle is told, like Defoe's tale, in commonplace, everyday terms—in terms of eating, shelter, the mechanics of operating ships,
curing and loading hides. And in a way highly attractive to children, *Two
Years before the Mast* also combines this sense of the real, even the
prosaically real, with the sense of unreality—the strangenes of far lands,
remoteness from normal, at-home living, a special intensity of experience.
The following passage illustrates this combination that characterizes Dana's
narrative:

*One night, while we were in these tropics, I went out to the end
of the flying jib boom, upon some duty, and, having finished it,
turned round, and lay over the boom for a long time, admiring the
beauty of the sight before me. Being so far out from the deck, I
could look at the ship, as at a separate vessel;—and there rose up
from the water, supported only by the small black hull a pyramid
of canvas, spreading out far beyond the hull, and towering up almost, as it seemed in the indistinct night air, to the clouds.*

*The sea was as still as an inland lake; the light trade wind was
gently and steadily breathing from astern; the dark blue sky was
studded with the tropical stars; there was no sound but the rippling
of the water under the stem; and the sails were spread out, wide and
high; the two lower studding sails stretching, on each side, far beyond the deck; the topmast studding sails, like wings to the topsails; the topgallant studding sails spreading fearlessly out above
them; still higher, the two royal studding sails, looking like two kites
flying from the same string; and highest of all, the little skysail, the
apex of the pyramid, seeming actually to touch the stars, and to be
out of reach of human hands. So quiet, too, was the sea, and so steady
the breeze, that if these sails had been sculptured marble, they could
not have been more motionless. Not a ripple upon the surface of the
canvas; not even a quivering of the extreme edges of the sail—so
perfectly were they distended by the breeze.*

And through all of Dana's narrative runs a kind of proud confidence in

men's ability to meet whatever comes their way. This open, eager acceptance can be for children a compelling element, particularly as it is offered
in terms of vivid, concrete experiences rather than of abstraction and
generalization.

The direct, concrete language offers no obstacle to the fairly accomplished child reader. It permits him to get at the attractive matter of the
tale:

*One of the finest sights that I have ever seen, was an albatross
asleep upon the water, during a calm, off Cape Horn, when a heavy
sea was running.*

*There being no breeze, the surface of the water was unbroken, but a
long, heavy swell was rolling, and we saw the fellow, all white, directly ahead of us, asleep upon the waves, with his head under his
wing; now rising on the top of a huge billow, and then falling slowly
until he was lost in the hollow between. He was undisturbed for some
time, until the noise of our bows, gradually approaching, roused him,
when, lifting his head, he stared upon us for a moment, and then
spread his wide wings and took his flight.*

Tom Sawyer and *Huckleberry Finn* and Other Adult Books about Children

The popular conceptions of Mark Twain's writings illustrate how unanalytic
our thinking about literature often is. The fact that the ostensible subject
matter of both *Tom Sawyer* and *Huckleberry Finn* is boys and boyhood
does not make them necessarily children's books, but we tend to think that
it does; if this were so, then James's *The Turn of the Screw*, Anderson's
Winesburg, Ohio, Hughes's *A High Wind in Jamaica*, and Golding's *Lord of
the Flies* would make admirable children's reading. Another common assumption is that because they involve the same characters, *Tom Sawyer*
and *Huckleberry Finn* must be alike (people who do not really know the
books often think of them as a single book); actually, they are as different
in one important way as it is possible for two books by the same author
to be.

The two books do have a number of important things in common. They
have some of the same central characters. They share the same picaresque
pattern of rather loosely related exciting adventures that happen to the
two boys; in both books the boys are runaways, and in both books they get
involved with criminals and are instrumental in bringing the criminals to
justice. And in both books Huckleberry Finn's joining or not joining the
respectable community is a continuing question.

And the two novels do share certain characteristics that make them
children's books, whatever the author's original intention in this regard.
A great many of the episodes in each book cluster around matters of special interest to children—secret gang brotherhoods, rivers, rafts, ghosts,

picnics, mammoth caves, mischief, going to school and not going to school. And these subjects are treated in terms of vigorous action—fence painting, going down a river on a raft, exploring bat caves. And in both books all these events, credible or incredible, domestic and ordinary or romantic and extraordinary, are told in language, Twain's and Huck's, that provides the child reader with a constant sense of life, a feeling for the scratchiness and imperfectness of real persons. And finally—probably the most notable characteristic in common and an important reason for their undeniable power to attract and convince young readers—both books reflect Twain's very special gift for the creation of high adventure, the romantic discovery of an exciting far-off world in a context of psychological and physical reality. Like *Treasure Island* and *Westward Ho!* and *Moonfleet*, both narratives embed the wildest of children's (and adults') dreams in a gritty matrix of realistic experience.

But unified though they are in these respects, the two books read differently for mature adult readers; for their perspective is different, and consequently their implications are different. This is not just a matter of different sets of events or of unlike narrative techniques (*Tom Sawyer* is told by Twain, *Huckleberry Finn* by Huck himself); it is a fundamental difference in spirit and in attitude toward people and the things that happen to them. In *Tom Sawyer* the world is seen as a pretty exciting place and as delightful because of its excitement, the constant movement on the surface of things. In *Huckleberry Finn* the world witnessed is much the same, but the perspective has shifted, has become the soberer, more uncertain view of a tired man. Cruelty, deceit, loss of freedom, the imprisonment of the mind as well as the body, the loss of innocence in all human experience—the awareness of these aspects of a boy's life has partially replaced the joyful effervescence and youthful excitement of *Tom Sawyer*. Only partially, but enough to make the two books quite different experiences for mature adult readers.

This difference, however, should probably not be an important one for juvenile readers, simply because the books possess certain attributes of which children are more aware and about which they will be more eager— the fantasy of adventure, the recognizable impulses and questions of childhood, the surface physical realities of the town and the river, Twain's broad humor, his rich, vivid language. These are what pull young readers to the books and make them great children's books, whereas the special place of the books in the consciousness of the adult reader may relate more closely to the clear happiness of *Tom Sawyer* and the brooding wryness in *Huckleberry Finn*, the fresh openness in the one and the unsureness, the huddledness, in the other.

There are other stories about children told from an adult point of view for adults but at the same time, as they stand, comprehensible and enjoyable to children, but their numbers are rather few. Among them are James Barrie's *Sentimental Tommy*, part of Lincoln Steffens's *Autobiography*, Kipling's *Kim* and *Captains Courageous*, and Dickens's *David Copperfield*.

The scarcity is perhaps explained by the fact that a book about children by adults for adults will very likely reflect adult experience as well as childhood experience, or rather will reflect childhood experience *through* adult experience. In Kipling's *Puck of Pook's Hill,* for instance, although many of the adventures are what children could have or could conceive having, the latter-day tiredness and wistfulness of the middle-aged Kipling show through and color the entire book. Or the book becomes coyly sentimental and quaint, as Hugh Walpole's *Jeremy* does at times (though perhaps the Jeremy books have unjustly suffered in the wholesale rejection of Walpole as a writer by the present generation). The boyhood parts of autobiographies are, for similar reasons, often not particularly readable by children. One exception is Lincoln Steffens's *Autobiography,* in which he reports simply but fully and without adult hindsight childhood experiences wonderful to a child—going to a ranch, getting and training a horse, etc. Booth Tarkington's Penrod books have become children books—but they have almost ceased to be adult books because in them Tarkington did not go beyond superficial observation, which is not the same as writing simply.

Dickens's *David Copperfield** is preeminent among books written about children for adults but full of attractive meaning for children. The major part of the book is the account of the childhood and early youth of the central character, David Copperfield, and the book is filled with other children—Little Emily, Tommy Traddles, the young Micawbers, and many others. But more significantly, the kinds of people and things that crowd the pages—the droll aunt Miss Betsey Trotwood and Micawber and Barkis and Peggoty, the exciting wonderland Dickens created out of rook-filled woods and bustling London streets, that magnificent invention for children, the Ark—for various reasons possess a special interest for children and are seen as children might see them. Dickens's bright eccentrics and fantastics, who are his vaudevillians, and Uriah Heep and Steerforth and Murdstone, his melodramatic villains, provide just the right props for the child's drama. All this fascinating world is borne along on waves of action, physical movement—storms, shipwrecks, stagecoach rides. And the characters constantly act—pound tables, carry children on their shoulders, drink toasts—and seldom does Dickens dip behind the dramatic action, vivid colorings, and realistic artifacts of his Copperfield world to suggest complex motives, to find anything more than sweet innocence and simple ingenuousness and dark villainy. When he does, as in the later pages where he tells of the sweet but silly Dora and a weary, confused David Copperfield, the book becomes less clearly a child's. On the other hand, the very qualities which make *David Copperfield* gripping for children may lessen its interest for some readers who come to it for the first time as adults. There would seem to be some truth in the common saying that one ought to read Dickens, Scott, and Dumas before he is eighteen. Not quite true, but partly.

David Copperfield is frequently adapted for children, but such tampering does not seem necessary. Very few, if any, sections of the book are devoid of the melodramatic events and dramatic figures, fantastic scenes, and broad clowning that make the novel particularly attractive to children. The pace of the book makes it easily read; there is seldom a time lacking either the promise of action or action itself. Dickens's vocabulary is large, but it is a colorful, expressive language in which the total effect can be more important than the understanding of a particular word or phrase. The words suggest gloom, joy, terror, and confidence, even if exact meanings do not come through to the reader. And the very concreteness and tangibleness of Dickens's writing—the colors, smells, sounds, movements— make this writing relatively easy reading for children in their early teens.

Here is a typical example of Dickens's rich but not frustrating language. David Copperfield is in the lawyers' quarters in London looking for his old friend Traddles, who, unknown to Copperfield, has just gotten married:

Number two in the Court was soon reached; and an inscription on the door-post informing me that Mr. Traddles occupied a set of chambers on the top story, I ascended the staircase. A crazy old staircase I found it to be, feebly lighted on each landing by a club-headed little oil wick, dying away in a little dungeon of dirty glass.

In the course of my stumbling upstairs, I fancied I heard a pleasant sound of laughter; and not the laughter of an attorney or barrister, or attorney's clerk, but of two or three merry girls. Happening, however, as I stopped to listen, to put my foot in a hole where the Honourable Society of Gray's Inn had left a plank deficient, I fell down with some noise, and when I recovered my footing all was silent.

Groping my way more carefully, for the rest of the journey, my heart beat high when I found the outer door, which had MR. TRADDLES *painted on it, open. I knocked. A considerable scuffling within ensued, but nothing else. I therefore knocked again.*

A small, sharp-looking lad, half-footboy and half-clerk, who was very much out of breath, but who looked at me as if he defied me to prove it legally, presented himself.

"Is Mr. Traddles within?" I said.

"Yes, sir, but he's engaged."

"I want to see him."

After a moment's survey of me, the sharp-looking lad decided to let me in; and opening the door wider for that purpose, admitted me, first, into a little closet of a hall, and next into a little sitting-room; where I came into the persence of my old friend (also out of breath), seated at a table, and bending over papers.

"Good God!" cried Traddles, looking up. "It's Copperfield!" and rushed into my arms, where I held him tight.

"All well, my dear Traddles?"

"All well, my dear, dear Copperfield, and nothing but good news!"

We cried with pleasure, both of us.

But the book's great appeal for children lies in the fact that it is so thoroughly a children's world in which very real children are among the chief protagonists, in which most of the other main people—Peggoty, Micawber, and the others—are in their accentuated characteristics rather young, and in which objects and events, whatever else their significance, all seem to have been created for the entertainment of children.

Another example of an adults' book about children and with much of a child's view is Marjorie Kinnan Rawlings's *The Yearling.* Its protagonist, the boy Jodie, does many things that children do and recognize, but Jodie does them in a forest of difference, of adventure, much as Crusoe meets his familiar problems in a sea of strangeness. But as in *David Copperfield,* there is a child's sense of the significance and wonder of these things, rather than an adult's. Rawlings, for the most part, looks at an animal as a child would do; the boy joyfully lets himself become involved with the animal and only gradually, reluctantly, discovers the realities of life and death. The adult's view, the lesson the adult wants the child to learn, is there, but it grows out of what happens and how Jodie feels about what happens. At least, the major perspectives of the book are those of Jodie, a child whose world has come to pivot on the possession, care, and love of an animal.

Steinbeck's *The Red Pony,* like Rawlings's story, went first to an adult audience and only later found its way to younger readers. In *The Red Pony* there is much the same kind of central situation, a boy's love for an animal and his losing the creature, but the adult's theory about this world is more important, more in the foreground, than it is in Rawlings's *The Yearling.* Maybe another way of putting the difference is that in Steinbeck's story the horse and what happens to him are more inescapably symbolic of Steinbeck's conception of nature than is the yearling. The yearling's relation to the boy and its meaning for the boy, with all his not wholly developed philosophy and acceptance, are more constantly and fully in the light of the writer's and reader's attention; *The Red Pony,* through action and characters, constantly points to a nature red in tooth and claw and expresses an adult pity for mortals caught up in the inexorable impersonal struggle of species for survival. *The Red Pony* is really a kind of morality play, a drama about good and evil as seen by a modern man—Steinbeck—influenced, more or less indirectly, by Darwin, Freud, two world wars, and modern science. The Rawlings novel has a moral,—but the moral does not constitute the whole fabric of the story.

The Place of Adult Books in Children's Reading

In the foregoing examinations of a variety of adult books, what have we noted that might go toward shaping a sensible, sensitive policy in the use of adult writing as a part of children's literature?

Obviously, the common assumption that children's literature and adult literature are two entirely unlike worlds with an unbridgeable chasm between them is a mistaken one. Adult books can become children's books, provided they have some of the particular things child readers may want.

An adult book, of course, is well on its way to being a children's book if its subject matter interests children—children themselves, families, animals, dangerous adventures. It is closer to being a children's book if its subject or subjects are viewed, at least in part, in terms of a child's knowledge and interests, the aspects of the subject comprehensible and significant to him; for this reason, Captains Courageous and Thomas Bailey Aldrich's Story of a Bad Boy are more clearly children's adult books than Moby Dick or a Conrad sea novel. And a double life as adult and children's literature is made more even likely if, besides dealing with matters interesting to children and from a child's viewpoint, the writer has told his story in concrete, specific terms of external action—if people sail, run, fight, leap, duck, hide, swim, row, dig, flee, chase, build, if they do not confine their behavior mainly to thinking and talking about action. These three things—children's subject, children's focus, and externalized behavior—would seem, while not absolutely essential, at least of prime importance in an adult book's chances of becoming a juvenile book.

These other elements may make any radical adaptation unnecessary: (1) a vocabulary and syntax comprehensible to the contemporary child, (2) brevity and speed of telling, (3) a cultural context with which the child has already become acquainted through experience or other reading. Thus Robinson Crusoe needs no change of language, no shortening of chapters or total book, no omission or simplification of parts of the narrative. Many adult books, for instance, the epics, are potentially children's books but require some adaptation of language, perhaps shortening, perhaps some omission or retelling to make the story more comprehensible and interesting to the child reader.

We have noted the common ingredients of adult books that can also be children's books, and we have seen them to be variables—not always all present and certainly not always of equal importance. If this is a sound analysis of such literature, then are there certain general principles we can follow in thinking about and using adult literature as part of children's reading?

1   We should recognize that when the book's elements requiring change for juvenile use are among the central characteristics of the original book, we have in the children's edition essentially another book. Perhaps we may feel such change is altogether legitimate and worth doing. But whether we feel that way or not, we need to recognize that the children's Gulliver's Travels is now an adventure yarn and fairy tale, which it was not in any significant way in Swift's narrative; that the child's Homer is not the Homeric epics. And we may also feel, particularly with older children, that the children, too, ought to be made aware of this distinction. But it is more important that we adults keep the difference in mind; if we do, we may avoid drifting into the mistaken assumption that by thus introducing such "classics" to young readers, we are giving them a head start on great

literature and helping them to see what makes such writing great. If we realize what and how much we are leaving out, we will also be in a better position to understand the peculiar qualities and attraction of what we are leaving in—that is, of the new book we have made.

2   If we realize that maturity of interest, accumulation of experience, and growth of language skill and cultural range will eventually make these books in their original form available to the older readers, then we will probably see there is no point in *forcing* such books, adapted or not, upon child readers. We will see that whether we give the child an adapted, wonder-story form of *Gulliver* or the *Odyssey* or *The Song of Roland* or do not give him the book at all, we are not depriving him of knowledge of a great work; we will know that exposure to the essential great work must come when the reader can respond to the particular elements in which its greatness lies. This awareness will take some of the pressure off—off us and off children—and leave us free to postpone the reading experience or to use the book, in adapted form, for whatever imaginative elements we think it has for the child on his own level of experience and language.

But we should be careful that we do not slip from this position into taking a book's interest for mature adults as evidence that it is *ipso facto* not a book for children. I may personally conclude that the full *Morte d'Arthur* can wait and that, in the meantime, retellings of the Arthurian tales will do, that there is no hurry in getting some classics into the hands of young readers if I am fairly certain they will miss too many good things at this early feasting. But at the same time I would make an effort to get to children any adult books—in their original form, that is—which would have their full and special impact upon children as well as adults. The fact that *David Copperfield, Ivanhoe, Two Years before the Mast,* and *The Count of Monte Cristo* are, along with the *Aeneid* and *Gulliver's Travels,* all classics for adults is no reason to conclude that the first four could not be great books for children. We are saved from the too common all-or-nothing approach to adult literature for children if we think, not of children's books and adult books, but of *elements in books*—juvenile and adult elements *in* adults' books. In this way we consider the subject, theme, narrative focus, length, technique, and language of the book as more or less appropriate to children. If none of these elements appears to be too far out of the child reader's ken, then we think of the original book as children's reading. If some of the elements seem to make it a nonchildren's book while others make it a children's book, then we do not hesitate to use an adapted form, provided the adaptation itself is a vivid imaginative literary experience for the child reader.

The question of adult literature as a part of children's literature is essentially the same as that we face as parents and teachers in exposing the child to any experience, in bringing him to anything we think important: how much, if any, sifting of the materials—history, mathematics, science, literature, or whatever—is needed, and if some is needed, then what kind of mesh will let through the things the child can assimilate?

SUGGESTED SOURCES

Children's Adaptations of Epics

Greek and Roman Epics

Church, Alfred: *The Aeneid for Boys and Girls*, Macmillan, 1918. Simple, direct prose.

————: *The Iliad of Homer*, ill. by John Flaxman, Macmillan (New Children's Classics), 1951.

————: *The Odyssey of Homer*, ill. by John Flaxman, Macmillan, (New Children's Classics), 1951.

Colum, Padraic: *The Adventures of Odysseus and the Tale of Troy*, ill. by Willy Pogány, Macmillan, 1918. Poetic prose; deft combining of the two Homeric epics.

————: *The Golden Fleece and the Heroes Who Lived before Achilles*, ill. by Willy Pogány, Macmillan, 1934.

De Sélincourt, Aubrey: *Odysseus the Wanderer*, ill. by Norman Meredith, Criterion, 1956. Vigorous adaptation.

Graves, Robert: *The Siege and Fall of Troy*, ill. by C. Walter Hodges, Doubleday, 1962.

Green, Roger Lancelyn: *Heroes of Greece and Troy*, ill. by Heather Copley and Christopher Chamberlain, Walck, 1961.

Lang, Andrew: *The Adventures of Odysseus* (1907), ill. by Joan Kiddell-Monroe, Dutton, 1962.

Picard, Barbara Leonie: *The Iliad of Homer*, ill. by Joan Kiddell-Monroe, Walck, 1960.

————: *The Odyssey of Homer*, ill. by Joan Kiddell-Monroe, Walck, 1952.

Sellew, Catherine: *Adventures with the Gods*, Little, Brown, 1945.

Taylor, N. B.: *The Aeneid of Virgil*, ill. by Joan Kiddell-Monroe, Walck, 1961.

Watson, Jane Werner: *The Iliad and the Odyssey*, ill. by Alice and Martin Provensen, Simon and Schuster, 1956. A sensitive, effective adaptation; the Provensens' many striking illustrations suggest the designs of Greek vase painting.

Norse Epic Tales

Baldwin, James: *The Story of Siegfried*, ill. by Peter Hurd, Scribner (Scribner Illustrated Classics), 1931.

Colum, Padraic: *Children of Odin*, ill. by Willy Pogány, Macmillan, 1920, 1962.

Hosford, Dorothy C.: *Sons of the Volsungs*, ill. by Frank Dobias, Holt, 1949.

Sellew, Catherine: *Adventures with the Heroes*, ill. by Steele Savage, Little, Brown, 1954. Stories of the Volsungs and the Nibelungs.

Beowulf

Hosford, Dorothy: *By His Own Might: the Battles of Beowulf,* ill. by Lasslo Matulay, Holt, 1947. Good prose version.

Serraillier, Ian: *Beowulf, the Warrior,* ill. by Severin, Walck, 1961.

Sutcliff, Rosemary: *Beowulf,* ill. by Charles Keeping, Dutton, 1962. Fine prose version by author of many distinguished historical novels for children.

Arthurian Tales

Lanier, Sidney: *The Boys' King Arthur; Being Sir Thomas Malory's History of King Arthur and His Knights of the Round Table,* ill. by N. C. Wyeth, Scribner (Scribner Illustrated Classics), 1917.

Macleod, Mary: *Book of King Arthur and His Noble Knights,* ill. by Henry C. Pitz, Lippincott (Lippincott Classics), 1949.

Pyle, Howard: *The Story of King Arthur and His Knights,* Brandywine ed., ill. by author, Scribner, 1933.

The Song of Roland

Baldwin, James: *The Story of Roland,* ill. by Peter Hurd, Scribner (Scribner Illustrated Classics), 1930.

Sherwood, Merriam: *Song of Roland,* ill. by Edith Emerson, McKay, 1938.

Other Epics

Deutsch, Babette: *Heroes of the Kalevala: Finland's Saga,* ill. by Fritz Eichenberg, Messner, 1940.

Gaer, Joseph: *The Adventures of Rama,* ill. by Randy Monk, Little, Brown, 1954.

Mukerji, Dhan Gopal: *Rama, the Hero of India,* Dutton, 1930. Poetic prose version.

Historical Novels as Children's Adventure Tales

Blackmore, Richard D.: *Lorna Doone*

Buchan, John: *Prester John*

————: *Salute to Adventurers*

Bulwer-Lytton, Edward: *The Last Days of Pompeii*

————: *The Last of the Barons*

————: *Rienzi*

Churchill, Winston: *The Crisis*

————: *Richard Carvel*

Cooper, James Fenimore: *The Deerslayer*

————: *Last of the Mohicans*

————: *The Pathfinder*

Craik, Dinah (Mulock): *John Halifax, Gentleman*

Dickens, Charles: *Barnaby Rudge*

————: *A Tale of Two Cities*

Doyle, Arthur Conan: *The White Company*

Dumas, Alexandre: *The Black Tulip*

————: *The Count of Monte Cristo*

————: *The Man in the Iron Mask*

————: *The Three Musketeers*

Edmonds, Walter: *Chad Hanna*

————: *Rome Haul*

Eliot, George: *Romola*

Ferber, Edna: *Cimarron*

————: *Show Boat*

Forester, C. S.: *Beat to Quarters*

————: *Captain Horatio Hornblower*

Hawthorne, Nathaniel: *The House of Seven Gables*

Hugo, Victor: *Notre-Dame de Paris*

Kingsley, Charles: *Westward Ho!*

Mitchell, Margaret: *Gone with the Wind*

Mitchell, S. Weir: *Hugh Wynne, Free Quaker*

Porter, Jane: *Scottish Chiefs*

Reade, Charles: *The Cloister and the Hearth*

Rolvaag, Ole E.: *Giants in the Earth*

Sabatini, Rafael: *Captain Blood*

————: *Scaramouche*

————: *The Sea Hawk*

Scott, Sir Walter: *The Heart of Midlothian*

————: *Ivanhoe*

————: *Old Mortality*

————: *Quentin Durward*

————: *Rob Roy*

————: *The Talisman*

Sienkiewicz, Henryk: *Quo Vadis*

————: *With Fire and Sword*

Tarkington, Booth: *Monsieur Beaucaire*

Thackeray, William Makepeace: *Henry Esmond*

Verne, Jules: *Michael Strogoff*

Some Romantic Adult Books Readable by Children

Barrie, James Matthew: *The Little Minister*

————: *Sentimental Tommy*

Brontë, Charlotte: *Jane Eyre*

Du Maurier, Daphne: *Rebecca*

Hudson, W. H.: *Green Mansions*

Jackson, Helen Hunt: *Ramona*

Ouida (Louise de la Ramée): *A Dog of Flanders*

Stevenson, Robert Louis: *New Arabian Nights*

Wallace, Lew: *Ben Hur*

Walpole, Hugh: *Fortitude*

Some Adult Adventure Stories Readable by Children

Buchan, John: *John Macnab, The Thirty-nine Steps, The Watcher by the Threshold*

Chesterton, G. K.: *The Innocence of Father Brown, The Secret of Father Brown*

Collins, Wilkie: *The Moonstone*

Davis, Richard Harding: *The Bar Sinister*

————: *Gallagher and Other Stories*

Defoe, Daniel: *Robinson Crusoe*

Doyle, Arthur Conan, *Adventures of Sherlock Holmes*

————: *The Hound of the Baskervilles*

————: *The Lost World*

Grey, Zane: *Nevada*

Haggard, E. Rider: *She*

Haggard, R.: *King Solomon's Mines*

Harte, Bret: *The Luck of Roaring Camp and Other Sketches*

Hilton, James: *Lost Horizon*

Hope, Anthony: *The Prisoner of Zenda*

Hough, E.: *The Covered Wagon*

Kipling, Rudyard: *Captains Courageous*

————: *Kim*

————: *The Light that Failed*

Lever, Charles: *Charles O'Malley, the Irish Dragoon*
London, Jack: *The Call of the Wild*
————: *White Fang·*
Marryat, Frederick: *Mr. Midshipman Easy*
Orczy, Emmuska: *The Scarlet Pimpernel*
Poe, Edgar Allan: *The Gold Bug and other stories*
Stewart, George: *Fire*
————: *Storm*
Verne, Jules: *Around the World in Eighty Days*
————: *Journey to the Center of the Earth*
————: *20,000 Leagues under the Sea*
Wells, H. G.: *The Invisible Man*
————: *The Time Machine*
————: *War of the Worlds*
White, Steward Edward: *Gold*
————: *The Long Rifle*
Wister, Owen: *The Virginian*
Wyss, J. R.: *The Swiss Family Robinson*

Books about Childhood for Adults and Interesting to Children

Aldrich, Thomas Bailey: *The Story of a Bad Boy*
Barrie, James Matthew: *Sentimental Tommy*
Dickens, Charles: *David Copperfield*
————: *Nicholas Nickleby*
————: *Oliver Twist*
Kipling, Rudyard: *Captains Courageous*
————: *Puck of Pook's Hill*
Rawlings, Marjorie Kinnan: *The Yearling*
Steffens, Lincoln: *Autobiography of Lincoln Steffens*
Steinbeck, John: *The Red Pony*
Tarkington, Booth: *Penrod and Sam*
Twain, Mark (pseud. for Samuel Langhorne Clemens): *The Adventures of Huckleberry Finn*
————: *The Adventures of Tom Sawyer*
Walpole, Hugh: *Jeremy*

CHAPTER 6

CHILDREN'S CLASSICS

*P*eople persist in making lists of classics and, perhaps unfortunately, using them. We can, I think, assume that as long as there is literature, there will be lists of bests or "must reads" or classics, if for no other reason than that they are fun to do; and that as long as there are children's books, those who deal with them professionally will continue to make lists of children's classics.

It does little good to point out their general uselessness, their inutility for the person who does not know about them and so takes them on trust or for the person who already knows them and so does not need someone else's score sheet, and it does little good to point out the danger of their becoming a substitute for one's own reading and judgment. Regardless of their limitations, lists of children's classics will continue to come from children's librarians, college teachers of teachers, the new teachers themselves when they find a little time and confidence, earnest committees of parent organizations, professional reviewers of children's books, critics temporarily adrift from their normal moorings in adult literature (perhaps with rather limited knowledge of the deep waters of children's literature), and publishers with series of "Children's Illustrated Classics" or "Junior Classics." We are apparently going to continue to live in a world filled with lists of children's classics.

A better policy, then, than disregarding them or placing them under a blanket condemnation would be to realize what they essentially are, what the particular premises of the various lists are, and to keep on the watch both for tired, indefensible, but constantly recurring items in existing lists and for desirable additions.

Often the consideration of children's classics begins—and ends—with the question, "*Should* children read the classics?" or "*Why* should children read the classics?" This approach is unfortunate, for it leaves the classics themselves unexamined, unanalyzed. A prior and more rewarding question would be, "What kinds of elements do we find in the books generally classified as children's classics, and which of these make a book worth keeping as part of a child's reading?" Such a query would at least lead directly into the alleged classics themselves.

How Books Become Classics

Classics tend to become very set. They get established and come to be regarded as being beyond critical analysis. So-called new lists of classics are usually based on *other* lists, and so the lists lose contact with valid, announced criteria. A book keeps bobbing up on list after list for probably no better reason than that it was on earlier lists or that it has a name easier to remember than some books the bibliographer might otherwise have borrowed from them. Often a title gets onto lists in much the way a man in public life may acquire honorary titles with increasing rapidity because of his already possessing some. Making lists of classics thus becomes a kind of game; something that should be qualitative turns quite quantitative. Getting on a couple of lists improves a book's chances for getting on *more* lists. Our lists of classics or bests become potpourris of titles which are there for all sorts of reasons, good, bad, and indifferent.

Perhaps a title is on the list merely because it was required reading when we were in school; we too quickly assume that anything thrown at us in academic circles must have been given us for good reasons. We may have trouble recalling the book or even remembering whether it was one of the reading assignments we succeeded in dodging altogether, but hazy or not, *Hiawatha, Snowbound, Ivanhoe, The Lady of the Lake, The Mill on the Floss, Quentin Durward, A Tale of Two Cities, Idylls of the King, Two Years before the Mast, The Call of the Wild,* and *Giants in the Earth* were studied in our literature classes and so seem to us automatically deserving of inclusion on any roster of greats. Yet the original reasons for their use in school may not have been altogether defensible. Titles can make school lists through all sorts of pressures—one teacher's now-forgotten enthusiasm, a school board's timidity or haste, a buyer's ignorance, a publisher's hard sell, the lower cost of the book, its easier availability in large numbers when needed, a passing wave of popularity coinciding with the school's decision on a new curriculum.

It is a grim fact of children's literature that many book titles originally attain lists of bests or classics for children without the lister's knowing the least thing about their content or style. It is another grim fact that makers of lists, especially the famous scholars and critics who are asked to suggest classics for children, often have to grope suddenly and desperately for names in a field of reading they have paid little attention to during their own professional careers, and so come up with titles of books read long ago, names that remained in their consciousness for miscellaneous reasons, many of them entirely unrelated to any personal recollection of the books themselves. Even the unusual shortness or other oddness of a name can occasionally explain why one remembered this book instead of that book.

Some books may be on a list because the list maker recalled his own enjoyment of them as a child; he remembered laughing at *Mrs. Wiggs* or being unable to go to sleep until he had finished *Treasure Island* or being kept eager for school by the promised afternoon reading of *Pinocchio*. (I confess that in surveying lists of classics, I discover that most of the books for which I had a strong personal regard as a boy—the enthusiasm to stay up late with, to read and reread on my own—were *not* on the lists of classics. The classics, unlike *The Boy Allies, The Rover Boys,* or the Tom Swift series, were ordinarily read with someone or under someone's sponsorship.) Books may sometimes be listed because they were pleasantly encountered in *late* childhood or early adulthood; in high school or college literature courses a list maker may have read or reread Carroll's *Alice in Wonderland*, Dickens's *Great Expectations*, Thackeray's *Vanity Fair,* Twain's *Huckleberry Finn,* Tennyson's *Idylls of the King,* Cooper's *Deerslayer,* or Hawthorne's *House of Seven Gables* and thus enjoyed it recently enough to recall the book when he tried to make up his list. Or possibly he had never read the book either as child or adult, but friends or teachers whom he respected had done so, or other authorities—lecturers, book reviewers, critics, anthologists—were for the book. So he had taken their word.

Now in view of these chancy, heterogeneous origins of children's classics lists, it would seem necessary to be very much on guard against the tendency of such lists to get set and sacred. Classics listings, instead of being revered, should always remain a little suspect. We need (1) to note with some frequency the common assumptions, possibly sound but not necessarily so, behind the selecting and using of classics, (2) to ascertain the elements present and lacking in the lists of classics, and (3) to constantly revise the lists, giving them a shaking up that will cause rather ordinary works to drop out and make room for new candidates of greater worth.

One Common Assumption: The Intrinsic Merit of All Classics

Implicit in much of the confidence in classics is the assumption that if many members of previous generations have been required to read a book, in school or at home, then it must possess special merit and should be read by most, preferably all, children. According to this view, since for several generations Eliot's *Silas Marner, Toby Tyler, Mrs. Wiggs,* and *Swiss Family Robinson* have been on many lists, school reading lists and others, we can safely assume that these books must be outstanding in some respects and so still deserve our children's attention; since *Lady of the Lake* and *Hiawatha* have persisted in school curricula for a good many years and O. E. Rolvaag's *Giants in the Earth* got into the required reading of many English curricula a generation ago, all these books are somehow particularly meritorious and should remain a part of children's reading. In this way the decisions of the curriculum makers, librarians, and parents of generations prior to our own become of great significance to us, much in the same way as stop and go traffic signals determine our behavior at street intersections. Their decisions largely take the place of our own analysis of books on the classics lists and of works for adding to the lists. And of course, many before us have already followed their lead. And so, having long been generally regarded as a classic, an honored member of publishers' and others' lists of classics, *Black Beauty* or *Little Lord Fauntleroy* continues to be named almost automatically, on trust, to our new selections for reading and, by occupying a niche, to exclude some newer candidate for a place of honor.

Widespread though it is, this assumption of the intrinsic merit of all classics proves to be extremely weak on the most cursory examination, for at its core lies a faith in the validity of past popularity as a criterion of present literary value. Particular generations value particular things and so select books in which they find them; it is not hard to see why *Five Little Peppers* and *Rebecca of Sunnybrook Farm* appealed to a reading public that specially prized tender sentimentality and so were put on many reading lists for children. But this is quite obviously no good reason for retaining these titles on the reading rolls, for tastes change. There is a very real contradiction in the past-popularity basis for selecting classics: One is in the untenable position of holding, on the one hand, that the popularity of certain works among certain groups at certain times in the past is an argument in support of their superiority and, on the other hand, that a classic somehow possesses lasting, universal qualities. That a children's book was very well thought of by the makers of classics lists eighty years ago may signify that the book met contemporary standards of taste then but does not mean that it would necessarily meet *our* standards or satisfy the children reading it today.

If we presume quality merely on the basis of past reputation, we also overlook the fact that a classic's becoming and remaining high in the prestige race may involve factors entirely extrinsic to the book's own qualities. A publishing firm may have a big stake in keeping one of its popular books going by a steady berth on classics; a teacher or librarian may get a special stake in the limiting of reading lists to a safely small number of books he or she already knows. Extrinsic factors *not* involving promotion by anyone directly interested in a book's fate can be important in determining whether a book will become and remain a children's classic. Books like *Pilgrim's Progress* or *Little Women* may so completely represent and satisfy the needs of a certain system of ethical belief that they will secure firm niches in the lists of "must reads" regardless of any imaginative qualities they may or may not possess. *Pilgrim's Progress*, Alcott's novels, *The Secret Garden, Idylls of the King,* and *The Happy Prince* certainly owed a considerable part of their first momentum to the popularity of the religious beliefs and moral codes they seemed to promulgate. And there is the cumulative effect of our simply seeing and saying frequently encountered titles, and the new life injected into old books, or at least into old titles, by movie, radio, and television dramatizations and comic-book versions.

Clearly, then, past and continued success is a flimsy base for unquestioning uncritical acceptance of books as classics to be read by most children; not all the forces that go to make a children's book a household word need be related to the intrinsic and lasting merits of the book.

A Second Common Assumption: The Universality of Classics

A second common assumption, that a book is good for *all* children, underlies the firm faith in children's reading classics; and it, too, cannot bear real scrutiny. Are we willing to agree that a well-told adventure tale will be as moving an imaginative experience for girls as for boys? that the sentimentality of *Heidi* will stir all children? that the rich verbal play of Lear and Carroll is an appropriate intellectual imaginative playground for all children, no matter what their language background? that MacDonald's moral earnestness combined with his fantasy in such books as *At the Back of the North Wind* is for all? Clearly, if we begin to think closely about particular classics, we come to realize that content, styles, tones, and themes are relative to certain groups of children in certain societies, and that the creative writer can reach the creative young reader in a great variety of ways, in many more ways than an unthinking reliance on lists of classics is likely to foster or even to permit.

The Characteristics of Classic Lists

It would seem wiser, then, not to accept children's classics lists as automatically important in children's reading, but rather to look at their items as individual books calling for examination on their own merits, as books to be classified according to subject, purposes, and style and to be judged in these respects in relation to other children's books. Thus the relevant general question about children's classics becomes one that is relevant to *all* children's books: What is worthy of preservation and distribution in these particular pieces of children's reading?

When we look at the books which compose most lists of children's classics, what do we find—what kinds of subject, purpose, and style, what levels of quality? What kinds of books tend to be included? What kinds tend to be omitted?

A striking characteristic of most lists of children's classics is that they pay scarcely any attention to the very young, preschool children, a little more to the seven- to nine-year-olds, and most attention to older readers. See the Breakdown of Classics Lists on page 117. Only one book with strong appeal to very young children, *Pinocchio*, appears on most of the lists analyzed, and no other books for young readers, like *Peter Rabbit* or *Just So Stories* or *A Child's Garden of Verses*, were among those listed on five or more lists out of ten. The great majority of the titles listed are clearly reading for older children—books like Dodge's *Hans Brinker*, *Heidi*, Stevenson's *Treasure Island* and *Kidnapped*, Twain's *Huckleberry Finn* and *Tom Sawyer*, *Alice in Wonderland*, *Swiss Family Robinson*, *Black Beauty*, Kipling's *Jungle Books*, *Tom Brown's School Days*, James Otis's *Toby Tyler*, Verne's *20,000 Leagues under the Sea*, Alcott's stories, *Master Skylark*, Aldrich's *Story of a Bad Boy*, *The Moffats*, Kingsley's *Westward Ho!*, the Lambs' *Tales from Shakespeare*, Scott's *Ivanhoe*, Tarkington's *Penrod*. Also, many of the books commonly listed were not written for a juvenile audience and still hold interest for older readers; such are *Robinson Crusoe*, the Grimm tales, Twain's works, Dana's *Two Years before the Mast*, the *Iliad* and the *Odyssey*, Bunyan's *Pilgrim's Progress*, Irving's writings, Cooper's *Last of the Mohicans*, Scott's novels, perhaps Jules Verne's tales, Selma Lagerlöf's *Adventures of Nils*. A considerable number of classics list regulars, moreover, while clearly meant for and appealing to children, possess qualities that make them adult reading— Grahame's *Wind in the Willows*, Carroll's *Alice in Wonderland*, Milne's *Winnie the Pooh*, Kipling's *Just So Stories*. Also, the lists contain adaptations of adult works, such as *Gulliver's Travels* and the *Iliad*.

So most lists of classics for children definitely lean toward adulthood and are consequently more useful with older than with younger children. The possible reasons for this slant are many—adults' choosing works *they* still like, their memories of later childhood reading being fresher than their memories of early childhood reading, the influence of formal school reading curricula on the selection and publishing of classics, the assumption that literary values in children's and adult literature are identical or that in adult literature they are superior. Whatever the causes—and they are surely quite complex—the tendency to rely on the classics lists as guidelines means a rather indiscriminate "adultizing" of children's reading.

Besides getting older reading fare, children whose reading is somewhat guided by classics selections are also more likely to read according to the dictates of nineteenth-century English and American literary taste than if they read more randomly. The great majority of books on the classics lists came out between 1840 and 1900 in England and America and reflect the values of that particular period and those particular places. The sentimentality, moral earnestness, and religious piety of the Victorian era are prominent ingredients in many of the continuing classics—*Black Beauty*, *Heidi*, the Alcott novels, Frances H. Burnett's *The Secret Garden* and *Little Lord Fauntleroy*, Wiggin's *Rebecca of Sunnybrook Farm*, MacDonald's *At the Back of the North Wind*, Kingsley's *Water-babies*, Carlo Collodi's

Pinocchio, Five Little Peppers, Ruskin's *King of the Golden River*, Craik's *Little Lame Prince*. The confident optimism and bouncy vigor that were one facet of that complex period characterize such standard classics as *Swiss Family Robinson*, Kingsley's books, Verne's adventurous tales, Pyle's telling of the Robin Hood adventures, Dana's *Two Years before the Mast*, Stevenson's yarns, Lucretia P. Hale's happy, silly *Peterkin Papers*, and Aldrich's vigorous *Story of a Bad Boy*.

This Victorian stamp on the classics lists can partly be explained by the undeniable fact that the middle and late nineteenth century was a great flowering time in children's literature, for in those years some of the finest creative talents turned to the writing of fine fiction and poetry for children, particularly older children. Also, children's literature got institutionalized in the late nineteenth century, and one of the inheritances from that organizing time has been the list of children's classics, even to the titles on the list. Since, as we have noted, classics lists tend to reflect established modes of taste and thought, and to go on reflecting the same ones, our listings are still largely those which got under way in the 1890s and the early decades of this century. The lists contain relatively few books from the past forty years, a period marked not only by a vast outpouring of children's books but by many outstanding imaginative works certainly superior to many titles already on the lists, titles like *Toby Tyler, Swiss Family Robinson*, and Burnett's *The Secret Garden*.

The making of book lists, a conservative influence on literary taste, reminds us of some of the good things of the past and so keeps us from being altogether the helpless followers of every new fad and fancy, but one of its inevitable limitations is that it conserves whatever mediocrity chanced to be dominant in the taste of the time when the lists began and that these tired leftovers keep more deserving newcomers out—out of sight and so out of mind.

Obviously, most of the current classics lists are full of treasures. But just as certainly, they reflect the dominant judgment of a certain period and a certain sort of society, as well as diverse forces which have more or less accidentally determined the continuing popularity of book titles, such as memory and publishing campaigns. And so the lists contain much quite ordinary stuff, along with the greatest achievements.

Breakdown of Classics Lists

The following titles appear from two to nine times in ten current and widely distributed lists of "Children's Classics," "Best Books for Children," etc. None appeared ten times.

On nine lists:
Collodi, *Pinocchio*
Dodge, *Hans Brinker; or, the Silver Skates*

On eight:
Defoe, *Robinson Crusoe*
Grimms, *Household Tales*
Spyri, *Heidi*
Stevenson, *Treasure Island*

On seven:
Andersen, *Tales*
Carroll, *Alice in Wonderland*
Swift, *Gulliver's Travels*
Twain, *Huckleberry Finn*

On six:
Alcott, *Little Women*
Wyss, *Swiss Family Robinson*
Sewell, *Black Beauty*
Stevenson, *Kidnapped*
Twain, *Tom Sawyer*

On five:
Arabian Nights
Dana, *Two Years before the Mast*
Kingsley, *Water-babies*
Kipling, *Jungle Books*

On four:
Lambs, *Tales from Shakespeare*
MacDonald, *At the Back of the North Wind*
Odyssey
Otis, *Toby Tyler*
Stevenson, *Child's Garden of Verses*
Verne, *20,000 Leagues under the Sea*

On three:
Aldrich, *Story of a Bad Boy*
Barrie, *Peter Pan and Wendy*
Bunyan, *Pilgrim's Progress*
Burnett, *The Secret Garden*
Grahame, *Wind in the Willows*
Hale, *The Peterkin Papers*
Potter, *Tale of Peter Rabbit*
Pyle, *Merry Tale of Robin Hood*
Ruskin, *King of the Golden River*
Travers, *Mary Poppins*
Wiggin, *Rebecca of Sunnybrook Farm*

On two:
Alcott, *Little Men*
Bennett, *Master Skylark*
Bible (adapted)

Book of Golden Deeds
Cooper, *Last of the Mohicans*
Craik, *Little Lame Prince*
Dickens, *A Christmas Carol*
Estes, *The Moffats*
Gág, *Millions of Cats*
Harris, *Uncle Remus*
Hughes, *Tom Brown's Schooldays*
Irving, *Alhambra*
Irving, *Legend of Sleepy Hollow*
Irving, *Rip van Winkle*
Jacobs, *English Fairy Tales*
Kingsley, *Westward Ho!*
Kipling, *Just So Stories*
Lagerlöf, *Adventures of Nils*
Lang, *The Blue Fairy Book*
London, *The Call of the Wild*
MacDonald, *The Princess and the Goblin*
Marryat, *Children of the New Forest*
Milne, *Winnie the Pooh*
Scott, *Ivanhoe*
Sidney, *The Five Little Peppers*
Song of Roland
Tarkington, *Penrod*
Wilder, *Little House in the Big Woods*

Revising the Lists

It is because of this simple but often unrecognized fact—that children's classics lists are indeed very spotty in quality—that we should, as I recommended earlier in this chapter, constantly revise our lists, shake them up so that the ordinary, the once maybe interesting but now tired, will screen out and leave slots for promising newcomers that seem to contain elements of special worth.

This shaking up will leave in their places of honor a good many books that have long been standard classics. I would, I think, retain the following: the Grimms' tales and *The Arabian Nights* (in Colum's edition for children), two of the greatest collections of traditional tales; Andersen's stories, *The Adventures of Pinocchio*, Kipling's *Jungle Books*, *The Wind in the Willows*, and *Alice in Wonderland*, in all of which fantasies the author has created a very special, complete, self-sufficient world; Beatrix Potter's *Tale of Peter Rabbit*, a quiet work of genius for the very young; *Treasure Island*, *Robinson Crusoe*, *20,000 Leagues under the Sea*, and *The Last of the Mohicans*, because they are brilliantly told tales of high adventure; *Hans Brinker*, *Heidi*, and Alcott's *Little Women*, which tell with literary grace the domestic sort of story that still has meaning to most children; and *Tom Sawyer* and Aldrich's *Story of a Bad Boy*, because they capture so completely a boy's sense of excitement at the possibilities of adventure in boyhood. I would not, however, try to keep on my list such old standbys as Tennyson's *Idylls of the King*, Hawthorne's *Wonder-book* and *Tanglewood Tales*, Lamb's *Tales from Shakespeare*, *Lorna Doone*, and *Swiss Family Robinson*. Although all these books have thrilling subject matter for children, they are just a bit spindly and forlorn from a literary point of view; in each case the writing has certain defects that somewhat reduce its vigor and intensity. As for *Five Little Peppers*, *Mrs. Wiggs of the Cabbage Patch*, *Rebecca of Sunnybrook Farm*, and *Toby Tyler*—old reliables of the classics lists— they are good enough second-rate, run-of-the-mill writing for children and will not hurt anybody, but their continued presence on so many literary honor rolls must be attributed to some mixture of cultural accident and personal sentiment. MacDonald's *At the Back of the North Wind?* Here I beg off. I simply cannot decide to keep or exclude this lively but woolly and ponderously didactic tale.

But I would really not be eager to *eliminate* titles from the classics. It would be unfortunate if someone left a book—any book—unread just because of a list. If a good case can be made for the retention of titles, fine; let us keep them, without worrying too much about the list's size. What we really need is that the lists be opened up to new blood, with or without the dropping of present place holders. The conception of what is best needs to be kept both tough and flexible and, above all, fresh.

Suggested Criteria

We need to have definite reasons for putting a book on a classics list. We need constantly to *reexamine* books and ask *why* they should be on or off the classics list. These two steps are often not taken in the manufacturing of such lists, and they are vital if we are going to indulge in the luxury of listing classics.

If I were making a list, my basic criterion for a classic would be that, for one reason or another, I should hate to see a person miss reading it before he got out of childhood. The reasons for hoping child and book will collide can be of several kinds. They include the following:

1   The book is a specially effective grappling, at the children's level of experience and understanding, with significant facts of human existence— birth and death, friendship and enmity, loyalty and disloyalty, justice and injustice, being puzzled and discovering an answer or not discovering one. This is one of the reasons why, if I were making a list of classics, I would put on it the Grimms' tales, most of Andersen's, Dickens's *David Copperfield* and *Christmas Carol*, L. M. Boston's *The Children of Green Knowe*, Rosemary Sutcliff's *Knight's Fee*, E. B. White's *Charlotte's Web*, and Sheila Burnford's *Incredible Journey*.

2   The book invents a great adventure, a situation full of dangers, that a child will participate in fervently and wholly. *Treasure Island* does this. So

do J. Meade Falkner's *Moonfleet*, Arthur Conan Doyle's *Adventures of Sherlock Holmes*, Elizabeth Gray's *Adam of the Road*, Charles Kingsley's *Westward Ho!*, Armstrong Sperry's *Call It Courage*, and Fritz Muhlenweg's *Big Tiger and Christian*.

3   The book creates essentially real people (a rare feat in art), and they are people a child can comprehend, encountered in situations that for him reinforce their significance. Some books which seem eminently capable of doing this: E. Nesbit's *The Railway Children*, Carol Ryrie Brink's *Caddie Woodlawn*, Marcel Aymé's *The Wonderful Farm*, Elizabeth Coatsworth's *Away Goes Sally*, Elizabeth Enright's *The Saturdays*, Joseph Krumgold's *And Now Miguel*, and Laura Ingalls Wilder's *Little House in the Big Woods*.

4   The book successfully creates a fantastic world the child can live in temporarily. This might well be the most desirable book of all for inclusion in a children's list, for by the time the individual is in high school he is generally less capable of responding with his total imaginative equipment to the lures of magic and so might never read a great fantasy if it is left to his adult years. Here are some books of this kind: J. R. Tolkien's *The Hobbit*, C. S. Lewis's *The Lion, the Witch and the Wardrobe*, Walter de la Mare's *The Three Royal Monkeys*, and Mary Norton's *The Borrowers*.

5   The book captures and illuminates with unusual vividness and sensitivity the reality of the physical world around the child. Some books that do this: Margaret Wise Brown's *The Little Island*, Will James's *Smoky, the Cow Horse*, and Harriet Huntington's *Let's Go Outdoors*.

6   The book creates, in a specially effective way, humor of situation, of character, or of language, humor which the child can share. Some books one might list mainly because they meet this criterion: Edward Lear's *Complete Nonsense Book* (with Lear's illustrations), Lucretia P. Hale's *The Peterkin Papers*, Jean de Brunhoff's *Story of Babar, the Little Elephant*, Ludwig Bemelmans's Madeline books, Eleanor Estes's *The Moffats*, Richard Chase's collection of *Jack Tales*, Pamela Travers's *Mary Poppins*, and Astrid Lindgren's *Pippi Longstocking*.

Different from one another though they seem, all these reasons for including a book on a children's classics list come down to this: *the book provides some special imaginative experience which the child is not likely to get from other sources—or at least in the same degree of intensity— and which it would be a shame for him to miss.*

I would not give much heed to a number of more common criteria. One of these is the conception of a classic as a favorite, a book that is very popular with large numbers of children and/or their elders. Many of the books I would place on a list *are* widely and appreciatively read by children, but their popularity would not be the reason for listing them. Nor would I use a related criterion, the length of time the book has been around. Most of the titles would probably not be *very* recent, but survival would not in itself be a basis for judgment.

When a classic is not defended simply on grounds of its popularity or its proved ability to survive, the justification usually offered for its selection is that it *ought* to be read by *all* children. This sense of urgency may have many different kinds of roots—the book's possession of certain aesthetic qualities in the highest degree, the soundness of its ethical teachings, the importance and accuracy of its factual information, its introduction of the child to values and experiences he will need in order to appreciate adult literature, the social importance of his having read certain books. In making my title suggestions, I would not feel that for these or other reasons everybody had to, or should, read *these* particular books. Reading is many roads; the opening up and development of a child's imaginative and cognitive life does not depend on his exposure to a certain small number of works. If he does not read *Treasure Island,* he may still lose himself in the fierce world of danger he discovers in such reasonably well-written books as Charles Hawes's *The Dark Frigate,* Jack O'Brien's *Silver Chief, Dog of the North,* and Louise Kent's *He Went with Marco Polo,* or in the host of altogether undistinguished books concocted specifically to satisfy this need. But the potentiality of a *more intense, more complete* literary experience of this sort lies in *Treasure Island* and *Moonfleet*—and *that* is why they would find places on my list. *Classics,* if we are going to continue to use the word and concept, should be conditional *desirables* rather than imperative *musts.*

SUGGESTED SOURCES

Points of View on the Children's Classics—and Some Lists

Adams, Bess Porter: "Books for Children," *Vogue,* vol. 125, Mar. 15, 1955.

Bell, A. E.: "Best Books We Never Read," *Peabody Journal of Education,* vol. 37, May, 1960.

Blount, C.: "Must Children Read the Classics?" *Parents' Magazine,* vol. 36, November, 1961.

Cerf, Bennet: "Trade Winds," column on Baxter list of children's classics. *Saturday Review,* vol. 38, June 18, 1955.

Commager, Henry S.: "When Majors Wrote for Minors," *Saturday Review,* vol. 35, May 10, 1952.

Emans, R.: "Treasure Island: The Classic and the Classic Comic," *Elementary Schools Journal,* February, 1960.

Fadiman, Clifton: "Party of One," *Holiday,* vol. 12, August, 1952. With reply by A. B. McGuire, *Wilson Library Bulletin,* vol. 27, October, 1952.

"Favorite Books of Childhood," *Good Housekeeping,* vol. 125, September, 1947.

Hurley, R. J.: "Old Favorites and the New Look: Classics Edited, Abridged, Adapted, Modernized, Simplified," *Senior Scholastic,* vol. 71, Nov. 1, 1957.

Jackson, Shirley: "Lost Kingdom of Oz," *Reporter,* vol. 21, Dec. 10, 1959.

Jacobsen, S. V.: "100 Books Every Child Should Know," *Parents' Magazine,* vol. 26, November, 1951.

Janeway, Elizabeth: "Young Readers' Companions," *New York Times Book Review,* Nov. 12, 1963.

Lelande, Dorothy A. E. (compiler): "Fifty Books for a Young Child's Library," *Parents' Magazine,* vol. 29, December, 1954.

McCreary, A. P.: "Reconsideration of Classics for Children," *Elementary English,* vol. 39, April, 1962.

"100 Best Books for Children," sel. by Virginia Haviland, Ruth Gagliardo, and Elizabeth Nesbitt, *McCall's Magazine,* vol. 84, November, 1956.

Pritchett, V. S.: "Improvers and Infidels," New Statesman, vol. 58, Aug. 8, 1959.

Rose, Ada Campbell: "Speaking Out: Are Children's Books Trash?" *Saturday Evening Post,* vol. 234, Nov. 25, 1961.

Sayers, Frances Clarke: "Books That Enchant: What Makes a Classic?" *National Education Association Journal,* vol. 46, January, 1957.

Thompson, Dorothy: "Why and What Should Johnny Read?" *Ladies Home Journal,* October, 1956.

Trilling, Lionel: "Rearing and Reading," *Vogue,* vol. 131, May, 1958.

Wallace, Robert: "Kids' Books: A Happy Few amid the Junk," *Life,* vol. 57, Dec. 11, 1964.

Welty, Eudora: "Sweet Devouring," *Mademoiselle,* vol. 46, December, 1957.

Wilson, Ellen J.: "Books We Got for Christmas," *American Heritage,* vol. 8, December, 1956.

CHAPTER 7

SENSE
AND
SENSIBILITY
IN
CHILDREN'S
LITERATURE:
Part 1.
Sense

*A*n adult unfamiliar with children's books might well be startled by the apparent taste of children for diverse sorts of book fare. He might, for instance, find the same child reading everyday-life tales and fantasies—involved in the family problems of the Hugginses and the doings of men from Mars, the familiar details of dog raising and the unfamiliar problems of fairyland, Mr. Small's small world of real mechanisms and the wide, fantastic world of the Pet of the Met or of the goose Petunia flying above New York City. And if he carefully examined the contents of the shelves in a children's library or bookstore, he would find the same polarity, the same division between books whose primary appeal would seem to be to an interest in the narrowly real and books whose attraction lies chiefly in their flight from such reality.

One helpful way of analyzing the vast body of children's literature is to divide it into those materials which seem to represent mainly the world of familiar things and those which create a new world of fantasy.

The Familiar and the Strange in Children's Literature

A boy of four may scrutinize cows, barns, and trains in a picture book with an eye to accuracy of representation and also have in his personal mental zoo a cow that jumps over the moon and a gander that throws its master downstairs. This same child a little later—say, at the age of seven or eight—may be very much interested in the operation of tugs, planes, and trucks and at the same time be completely entranced by such Dr. Seuss fantastics as Thidwick the bighearted moose, on whose antlers all the creatures of the forest made their home, Bartholomew Cubbins, on whose head one magical cap appeared after another, and the dream fish McElligot fishes for in his pool. Suppose this boy has a twin sister. At seven or eight she is quite likely to couple a liking for Snow White or Cinderella with devotion to the Bobbsey Twins. At ten or eleven, these children may get even more complex in their literary proclivities. (It is no great feat for a ten- or eleven-year-old girl to live simultaneously in the world of Rapunzel and that of a very ordinary American girl from some fictional Brown's Corners.) They may become devotees of family-fiction pieces like Alcott's *Little Women* or *Blue Willow* or *Thee, Hannah!* and of Dick Tracy, the men from Mars, *The Borrowers, Alice in Wonderland,* and their own ghost stories. And a few years later they may be scaring themselves into chattering fright with nightmarish interplanetary horror tales at the same time that they are becoming very insistent on accuracy in animal fiction and curious about the way girls train to become nurses or how real machines operate with real electricity and real oil.

And this divided state need not be assumed to stop with the end of childhood. After all, the children's father quite possibly reads the stock-market reports and scientific fiction or adventure yarns with equal appetite, and their mother may combine a taste for cookbooks with a failing for romantic fiction involving semitropical evenings. Parents, like their children, may be realist-romantics, captives of both sense and sensibility—only the parents may be more quickly and easily confused and insulted by any hint that this is the case.

It would be interesting to probe into the reasons for this split as it exists in children, but it would not notably advance our inquiry into children's literature. It is enough to recognize that numerous explanations may be advanced—that from an early age human beings are both idealists and realists, that the child needs the comforting security of knowing and the exciting insecurity of not knowing, that human nature in its restlessness must be constantly on the move to new things, that reality itself may involve a certain ambivalence as to what are real things and what are fancies, that the child wants both to know and to create. Possibly these explanations are all essentially the same. Or maybe they are different but not opposed to one another; maybe they can all be true of some children all the time or of all children some of the time. It would seem presumptuous, and altogether unnecessary here, to come out for any of these suggestions as *the* explanation.

However, whatever the explanation or explanations, we may observe one very remarkable characteristic shared by the two kinds of preferences: each sphere—the realistic and the fantastic—is wonderful, that is, *full of wonder,* for those who choose to live in it.

Wonder, the Common Denominator

It is true, as noted earlier, that children tend to be drawn more strongly to realistic literature in some parts of their childhood and more strongly to fantasy in other parts. Perceptive parents and teachers notice that from two or three to about six or perhaps seven, children are frequently luke-warm about fairyland and may be quite intrigued, sometimes to the ex-asperation of their bored elders, with the routine of buying the family groceries at the market or of taking the car into the service station to get it gassed up. Some parents and teachers worry about this, feeling it indi-cates a lack of imagination in the child. In doing so, they forget that for the very young child these experiences are still pretty new and, for that reason, exciting and fresh, full of wonder. Even going upstairs and down-stairs is a sufficiently new—and difficult—feat to enchant the four-year-old with its intricacies. In the triter minds of many adults mountains are likely to be associated with imaginative, aspirational, or inspirational thinking and the stairs are not—but is there really anything a 15,000-foot mountain has for an adult that a 15-step staircase does not have for a two- or three-year-old, or for a five- or six-year-old if he is permitted to build a camp on the middle landing? For the tired adult the supermarket has probably lost its glamor, but for the small child it is a wonderland of whirling gates, mountains of multicolored vegetables, walls and columns of cans, pyramids of cardboard boxes, caverns of steaming ice, bright caravans of metal carts in which one may ride regally, and plunkity-plunk magical machines from which a girl in white pulls out a long strip of paper. And the intricacies of a trip through one's own neighborhood may have all the marvelousness that Wonderland had for the older Alice—mysterious fences, deep piles of crackly leaves, huge bicycles that eight-year-olds ride on, deep-baying dogs, piping-voiced fox terriers, houses with many windows, and, strangely enough, houses with no windows.

Why are these things wonderful? For the same reason that a vision, nightmare, or fairy tale is wonderful: as the experience is new, it has nothing to be compared with, to be measured against, and so it must be wondered about. Fairyland would not be wonderful in a land of wonders; indeed, that may be one reason why fairyland is not very intriguing to some five- to seven-year-olds; for them everything is new enough and so amazing enough to take the edge off goblins, fairies in the dell, magical spells, or frogs who become princes.

Everyday experience is eventually mastered by the child and so grows gray, commonplace, *normal*—and at that point wonder must change its base of operations from domestic and mercantile scenes to magic barrows, fairy castles, witches, and hobgoblins. These cannot be made everyday, and so they serve the growing child as a stronghold against the tiresomeness of repeated, familiar experience. The boy who at four found a visit to bears in the zoo altogether astonishing may now, at eight or nine, turn for his diet of amazement to marshland dragons, e.g., *The Dragons of Blueland*. And when these fragile fancies get pierced too often to remain whole, the real biographies of extraordinary people give him the extraordinariness which, as a human being, he demands.

I have here suggested that the wonderful is not a particular *subject*, but rather is what is new, surprising, unbelievable by the criteria of everyday experience. And so a poem or story about any experience will be wonderful to a person, whether child or adult, if he has not had that experience and if he is still eager and curious about unknown things. Most young children are still very curious, and since most things in our ordinary physical and social environment are new to them and unexplored, they find these ordinary things extraordinary.

Now to most adults with all their wits these commonplace experiences are no longer new and so no longer wonderful. This means that when an adult writes or reads to children a children's book about commonplace things, such as a trip to a supermarket, he has three alternatives: to make no effort at all to be excited himself and thus to rely on the objective account to stimulate the child much as the experience itself would do; to try to recall his own childhood excitement over these no longer stirring matters, an exceedingly difficult thing to do; or to try to become excited about the market or whatever else the subject is.

The final alternative almost always has unfortunate results; it leads to ponderous cuteness, a patronizing tone, and gushiness. Nor are the other two alternatives without their drawbacks. To get back through memory to one's childhood view of things without letting it be colored by all the years between is an impossible task. In addition, there is the simple fact that the everyday environment of one's own childhood was greatly different from that of today's child—the grocery of twenty or thirty years ago is only a distant cousin of today's "super-supermarket," and the living room used to have no television set as its focal point. Probably the most satisfactory of the three possible choices would be simply to report—to relate the process of filling a gas tank at the service station, to describe the various kinds of vegetables carried on the supermarket shelves, to describe the species of animals the child will meet if he goes to the country this summer. For adults this kind of telling will almost certainly lack any spice, unless they keep their attention more on the children than on the limited world of real things they are revealing to the children. Lois Lenski's *Little Auto* may be slightly amusing to the adult on first reading, mainly because of its unpretentious, simplified little drawings of the Small family and their activities. But if (as he is most likely to do) the child persists in having it read to him, with much pointing, for a dozen times in a row, the adult's relish for the small book may change to boredom and at last to fuming dislike. Perhaps there is no avoiding this eventual satiety on the part of adults—but one way of postponing it is to forget that the book is limited and note the intensity of the child's curiosity, his unlimited concentration and pleasure.

Reality as the Subject Matter of Wonder

Inquiring into the children's literature centered on the wonderfulness of reality, one discovers two interesting facts: (1) that the real world supplies a great variety of subjects to be used as raw material, and (2) that these kinds of subjects provide the bases for many of the most common and important kinds of children's books.

The children's writer who wants to appeal through reality to the child's desire for wonder may draw on these kinds of realities: things (material objects), processes (routines and how they are carried out), animals, places, and people.

Household Surroundings as a Source of Wonder

When you stop to think of it, the child's world is crowded with objects, and these objects are marvelously varied in kind. There are many differently shaped dishes—bowls, cups and saucers, dinner plates and salad plates, gravy dishes—and innumerable kinds of food and drink to go into the dishes. Then there is furniture; even a rather plain room will have an interesting diversity of furniture shapes and functions—straight-backed chairs with knobs on the legs, morris chairs, rocking chairs, round and square tables, little end tables, bookshelves, carpets, lamps of different sizes and shapes. And these shapes are found in many different kinds of houses, too—from one-story homes to many-storied apartments, from cottages to mansions. These houses have in them marvelous features like steps, closets, basements and attics, garages, oilstoves and wood stoves and fireplaces and furnaces. And in the house, too, are strange and intricate machines—clocks, washing machines and dishwashers, electric eggbeaters, television and radio sets, electric switches, even sometimes elevators.

Some houses have more objects and more kinds of objects that other houses have, but they all have them in sufficient number and variety to make them a highly suggestive world of wonder for the small child and a rich source of story *and of verse* for the writers for small children. The traditional verse called nursery rhymes or Mother Goose occasionally centers around these household furnishings—Old Mother Hubbard's cupboard, the old men of Gotham's tub, the candlestick Jack must jump over, "upstairs and downstairs and in my lady's chamber"—but modern verse for children has made itself thoroughly at home in the home. Many children's poets have made poetry out of the house and common domestic pieces of equipment, such as Stevenson in "My Bed Is a Boat," Hilda Conkling in "The Cellar," Milne in "Stairs," Walter de la Mare in "The Cupboard," Dorothy Aldis in "Radiator Lions," James Tippett in "Fourth Floor," Rachel Field in "Doorbells," Aileen Fisher in "A Coffeepot Face."

But children's writers who use household objects as subject matter are not all alike in what they make out of them. They may do what children often do with their immediate environment: they may use it as a starting point for a fanciful invention, an imaginary voyage, a problem. Rugs become magical flying machines; chairs turn into towers or bears or cars. The commonplace piece of domestic equipment becomes more than it was; it is arbitrarily transformed into an altogether different object, as in the innumerable poems and semistories about children playing house—for example, Ruth Krauss's book *A Very Special House*. Or it becomes an object in a private amusement, a mental game of one's own, as in Stevenson's "My Bed Is a Boat." In Dorothy Baruch's "Lawn-mower" * a lawn becomes something else that bemuses children, a barbershop:

I'm the gardener today.
I push the lawn-mower
Across the grass.
    Zwuzz, wisssh, zwizz, wisssh.

I'm the lawn's barber.
I'm cutting
Its green hair
        Short.
I push the lawn-mower
Across the grass.
    Zwuzz, wisssh.

The accoutrements of domestic existence provide the props for a personal flight into fancy in Mary Norton's book *The Borrowers*. She has an English family just a few inches high inhabit the very real house of a natural-sized English family, and she has given her little people furtive but otherwise full use of the thrown-away or lost small articles of the big-sized human family—thimbles, scissors, pins, postage stamps, etc.

In this literature, whether poetry or fiction, the domestic scene is borrowed for purposes of inventing, of "let's pretend." The commonplace becomes the uncommonplace; the prosaic becomes the strange. This can be a rather modest little imagining, like Stevenson's bed-boat or his armies in the fire, or it can be a full-scale, elaborate invention like C. S. Lewis's world of Narnia, which his children discover in the dark recesses of a big, empty wardrobe, in *The Lion, the Witch, and the Wardrobe*. Many of us have felt, most probably as children, a sense of endlessness as we groped into the darkness of a clothes closet or wardrobe. In Lewis's tale this fairly common object and a relatively common feeling about it become springboards for a leap into a new and mysterious existence.

Using a different and perhaps more appropriate metaphor, one might say that such writers use the commonplace pieces of our commonplace lives as building blocks, much as a child uses building blocks to help him imagine armies, cities, garages, and ships. Like children, such writers exploit the house and its belongings to meet, in some degree, the child's need for transformation of the near into the far, the small into the great, the ordinary into the extraordinary.

Still, these commonplace furnishings and structures can be to small children strange and wonderful just as they are, without becoming anything else, and writers for children may content themselves—and the children—with this *wonder of the thing itself;* in poems and stories the object itself is explored and described thoroughly enough to bring it close to the listening and looking child. Walter de la Mare describes a grandmother's fascinating cupboard *:

I know a little cupboard
With a teeny, tiny key,
And there's a jar of lollypops
For me, me, me.

Typical of this reliance on the object's inherent wonderfulness is Elizabeth Manson Scott's "My Bed" *:

I have a little bed
Just for me.
Brother's too big for it.
Mummy's too big for it.
Daddy's too big for it.
Do you see?—

I have a little bed,
Do you see?
But—pussy's too small for it.
Puppy's too small for it.
Baby's too small for it.
It's just for me.

In the short poems of Tippett the important discovery may be that the floors and apartments in an apartment building have numbers *:

"Fourth floor!"
Is what I say
When I come in
From play.

My home
Is on that floor.
It has a seven
On the door.

Six other doors
Are on our hall
With a different family
Behind them all.

And in many picture books, or picture-story books, for little children the authors have apparently felt that the making or handling or living with household things provides sufficient subject for a book. For example,

Blossom Budney's *Huff Puff Hickory Hill*, illustrated by Kurt Werth, is simply the straightforward account of a family's first day in a new house. Berta and Elmer Hader, in *The Little Stone House*, tell in some detail how two little children help their parents build a house—how they put in foundations, install plumbing, etc. Some of Lois Lenski's Mr. Small books deal largely with the possessions of a small family—its house, furniture, car, etc. There are many frankly nonfiction picture books devoted to listing and giving elementary descriptions of the parts of a house and the various kinds of household gadgetry.

Perhaps for adults stories and poems about everyday surroundings and objects become unbearably mundane, and they may find it very hard to imagine what children find so interesting in them. But a house is to a child a much larger place than it later becomes, and a more complex one, too, full of dark corners and hidden backs of chairs and window blinds and dark chests. That is perhaps enough mystery for a five- or six-year-old's story.

Personal Possessions

The most familiar of all things in the child's physical world, his personal possessions, similarly provide likely subject matter for a child's reading and looking, and they can be treated both realistically and fantastically. On the one hand, a child can be intrigued by a description of his own clothing and the process of putting it on, as in Edna W. Chandler's *The New Red Jacket* and Leone Adelson's *All Ready for Winter*, or by a "do it yourself" toy-book that requires him to tie laces, look in a mirror, brush his teeth. And on the other hand, he can, in the spirit of Beatrice de Regniers's *What Can You Do with a Shoe?* fool around imaginatively with almost any common object—his shoe, pencil, watch, chair, doll. He can go on all sorts of adventures with such as these. The wooden puppet Pinocchio becomes a funny fugitive who at last is transformed into a real boy. In Milne's Pooh books Christopher Robin's stuffed toys—Pooh, Eeyore, Piglet, and the others—have birthday parties, seek Heffalumps, and visit one another in their little wood. The adventures of Hitty, an English doll, provide the plot of Rachel Field's *Hitty, Her First Hundred Years;* dolls do the same for Rumer Godden's *The Doll's House* and *Impunity Jane;* a toy rabbit is the central figure of Margery Williams Bianco's famous *The Velveteen Rabbit;* and in Andersen's *The Steadfast Tin Soldier* a lead soldier and a tinsel dancer share brief but exciting lives.

These stories of animated possessions are easily convincing to children. Children quite generally give speech and character to their own possessions; so there is for them nothing unusual in the living and talking of fictional toys and other possessions. The excitement lies both in the appearance of the possessions and in any adventures the writer can dream up for them—journeys through sewers, visits to tinsel palaces, flights through the air.

One very convenient characteristic of a personal possession like a toy, pen, or watch is that it is an easy device for carrying the ideas, scenes, or characters of a story. The doll or toy soldier, for instance, can journey to many places—the maker's factory, the store, the homes of its owners. A chest or an old coat can go into and out of the possession of many people and so serve as a string on which to hang many plots and places and people. Such an object can journey through *time*, too; Rachel Field's doll Hitty goes through the events of a hundred years. And in traveling through space and time the personal possession can serve to tell a great deal about its owners; in *Impunity Jane* we learn not only about the doll but about the boy, Gideon, who carried off the doll from her protected doll's house into the more adventurous world of his toy boats, wigwams, and planes.

The pathetic fallacy—the assumption that inanimate objects feel and think like people—may become a bothersome and artificial thing in adult literature, but it creates little awkwardness for most child readers and does not ring false to them, for to children the participation of our things in our lives still seems natural and not to be questioned. Hence, stories and poems involving such participation need not be touched with the coyness or artificiality that could very easily creep into such a tale intended for adult readers.

The Neighborhood

Away from the child's own person and home but within his immediate neighborhood lies a great variety of things to be experienced and appropriated to the uses of the imagination—houses and streets, yards and swings, trees and flowers, stores and their windows, cars and buses, streets and bridges, streetlights and stoplights, playgrounds, nursery schools and kindergarten classrooms.

These neighborhood subjects appear to hold such special interest for the child of five to seven or eight, most likely because he is making the big break, alone, out into the world beyond the limits of his own yard. Teachers, moreover, are specially interested in furthering this interest in his neighborhood; they want him to get to know his community and, in an elementary way, to begin to be aware of primary social realities—buying and selling, safety, community health, related social problems. In some school systems these have been built into study units. These facts may partially account for the tremendous mass of realistic neighborhood books. The world of the supermarket, neighborhood apartment, and school has been done full justice in the children's books of the past thirty years.

Many of these books make no attempt to go much beyond reporting the surface facts of the corner drugstore, the market, the gas station, the post office, the library, the classroom. They offer a simplified account, largely by pictures, of a market—the various food sections, the cash register, the turnstile, the packaging, maybe even the parking lot outside the store—or a city's transportation system (Mary Ann and Norman Hoberman's *How Do I Go?* and Ethel Kessler's *Big Red Bus*), traffic (Margaret Wise Brown and Leonard Weisgard's *Red Light, Green Light*) or the main parts and functions of a whole city (Lorraine Beim's *Benjamin Busybody*, Margaret Wise Brown and Crockett Johnson's *Willie's Adventures*).

Some books of this sort simply offer a generalized report, largely by pictures—my (or your) city, its bus system, the steps in getting a letter from sender to destination; whatever excitement there is, apart from that inherent in the child's wonder about what he does not yet know well, comes from the visual excitement of colorful abstract designs. Other books of this general type hang a lot of miscellaneous facts on a simple idea—the blinking of red and green lights throughout day and night in the city streets, the succession of morning, afternoon, and night. Many others suspend the same sort of material on a very slight story—the visit of a child and his mother to the store, the family's getting the car gassed and lubed at the neighborhood gas station, a visit to the library, a holiday outing in the park. The children have names but are any children; the adventure is either a routine event, like the weekly marketing, or a transparent device, like a child's needing to visit the main parts of a department store in deciding what to buy for his mother's birthday. Such books have a snug, close-to-home feeling that perhaps compensates for the lack of warmth that fancy might bring; the book makes the child's own environment seem important and his own. Polly Curren and Robert J. Lee's *This Is a Town*, one such book, starts and ends with the sentence, "This is a town—a fine friendly town—much like the town where you live." From such books the child may get a sense of the strange in the familiar, the new in the old, the exciting in the secure. Most such books, except when saved by a specially talented artist, are thoroughly run-of-the-mill, but for small children they can be very interesting for a while.

The Larger World

The threat of flatness and monotony that is implicit in the familiar subject matter of home and neighborhood lessens as the child's reading about real things reaches beyond his immediate environment to the outer world—to the whole city beyond his neighborhood, in such books as the Haders' *Big City*, Virginia Lee Burton's *Mike Mulligan and His Steam Shovel*, Marjorie Flack's *The Boats on the River*, and *The Big Book of Real Trucks*; beyond the city, as in Jean George's *The Hole in the Tree*, Margaret Wise Brown's *The Little Farmer* and *The Little Island*, Alice C. and Fleming H. Gall's *Here and There and Everywhere*, Valenti Angelo's *Look Out Yonder*, Leo Politi's *The Butterflies Come*, and Robert McCloskey's *Time of Wonder*; to the diverse regions of the country, as in Will James's books about cowboy life, McCloskey's *One Morning in Main*, Politi's picture stories of the environments of Mexican, Italian, or Chinese children in the United States, Wilfred S. Bronson's story of pueblo life in *Pinto's Journey*, Ann Nolan Clark's *In My Mother's House*, Ellis Credle's *Down, down the Mountain*

(Southern hill country), and Lois Lenski's stories about Midwestern farm life; and to foreign lands, as in Françoise's *Jeanne-Marie in Gay Paris,* Bemelmans's Madeline stories and his *Hansi,* Elizabeth Coatsworth's *Lonely Maria* (about a little girl in the West Indies), the d'Aulaires' books about Scandinavia, Eleanor Lattimore's *Little Pear,* and Taro Yashima's stories of child life in Japanese villages.

People as Subject

This world of physical objects, processes, animals, and places is a tremendously rich source of subject matter for children's realistic reading, partly because children are still uninformed and curious about *things* and partly because children, at least when little, have no difficulty in breaking down any barriers between such categories as inanimate and animate, nontalking and talking, nonhuman and human.

But as children grow older, they become increasingly aware of, and interested in, another element of the real environment around them: the human beings who inhabit it. The appearance and behavior of individual human beings would seem to be of *relatively* small interest to the four- or five-year-old compared to his concern with the physical world he has to understand and handle, but by the age of ten or eleven the child may very well have become fascinated by human beings' puzzling complexity and variety; and as he grows into adulthood, he may come to focus his reading largely, although not exclusively, on human character. This shift, though not inevitable, is general enough to be a probability for the teacher and librarian to keep in mind and to use.

This rise of children's interest in book people is likely to follow the general pattern of their developing interest in their physical environment—to move from the immediate to the more remote, from the relatively simple to the very complex.

Thus the two- to four-year-old may be intrigued by meeting "Mama" and "Papa" and his brothers and sisters in his books; these people are simply generalized figures, and the plots of their stories tend to be abstractions of the very ordinary routines of most middle-class families in the child's culture, as in Lenski's Small books, Myra Brown's *Company's Coming for Dinner,* or Marguerite de Angeli's *Ted and Nina Have a Happy Rainy Day.* Then gradually he develops a liking for encounters with *neighborhood types*—policeman, fireman, postman, grocer, librarian, bus driver, other children. And what he seeks in other children gradually becomes more complex. To meet this enlarging interest in the kinds of people and activities in the larger environment beyond his home is clearly the intention of little books like Margaret Wise Brown's *The Little Farmer* and her *Willie's Adventures* and the innumerable books about playgrounds and neighborhood children (Bernice Bryant's *Follow the Leader,* Ezra Keats and Pat Cherr's *My Dog Is Lost!,* about the little boy seeking his dog among children speaking other languages than his own).

Domestic Fiction

Still later, about the age of eight or nine, most children become increasingly interested in the more complex, beneath-the-surface aspects of domestic life and family relationships. It is now that Louisa Alcott's stories of the March family and all the vast outpouring of domestic fiction since her time become a staple of children's reading.

Louisa Alcott placed her fictional boys and girls in a middle-class family that is peculiarly Victorian but not dissimilar from many middle-class families today in its main concerns—family budgets, clashes and reconciliations among brothers and sisters, making friends outside the family and bringing them in, getting educated, celebrating conventional holidays in conventional ways, choosing careers and trying to get started in them, courtship. One could make tales of Victorian life quite special and exotic (many authors have done this) simply by focusing on the very special Victorian practices and attitudes, but Alcott did not do so. A present-day child will find much of the life of the novels oddly familiar and comprehensible. The central and supporting events of Alcott's books are of a surprisingly commonplace sort—preparing Christmas gifts, having parties, saving money, buying clothes, doing lessons—and they may interest children because they know and like them. But the really special characteristic of Alcott's writings is that they deal in a head-on manner with emotional problems and states of mind that adolescents are beginning to know and by which they are puzzled and therefore fascinated. In Jo March, for instance, Alcott portrayed a girl beset by conflicting impulses to continue a tomboy and to conduct herself in a more responsible womanly manner, and in all the girls of Little Women Alcott recreated the tug-of-war between the individual and the family group.

Alcott's girls and boys are not very complex people; although they have more than one dimension, each dimension is clearly and unmistakably projected, and each trait is darkened or brightened by deep Victorian coloring—Beth's sweet, almost saintly invalidism, Jo's self-sacrifice, Meg's striving for propriety, Amy's vanity. Yet to ten- to twelve-year-olds this fictional world does suggest a psychological complexity which has been hitherto uncommon in their reading and which they are only now beginning to realize exists in themselves and in the people around them. In stories set beyond the domestic scene they may still be contented with highly simplified fictional people—brave heroes, romantic heroines, very bad badmen—but in stories of family life they are more likely to appreciate more complexity, as they are now becoming more aware of it in the puzzling inconsistencies and obscure motivations of their own relatives and friends and the difficulties encountered in getting along with their own families. So, if the writer, teacher, or librarian is concerned about helping to develop the child's sense of psychological realities, he or she will find no better way of beginning than through the domestic novel.

A tremendous number of works of domestic fiction have been written, having a surprising range of styles, language levels, experience levels, and moods.

The simplest sort of domestic fiction for children, and to most adults probably one of the less interesting, is typified by Carolyn Haywood's Betsy books (*"B" Is for Betsy, Betsy and the Boys, Back to School with Betsy, Betsy's Busy Summer*) and the Eddie stories (*Little Eddie, Eddie and His Big Deal*, and others). Focused on the daily routines of children in the elementary grades, they generally lack any major climax, offering, instead, a series of minor crises—birthdays, the choice of a summer vacation, the first day of the new school year, a new neighbor. And through these familiar events the child reader encounters boys and girls and a few adults who are set off by rather broad traits—the worrying mother, the friendly little fellow, the harum-scarum tomboy, the friendly storekeeper.

For slightly older children and marked by more shaping of both plot and characters—in short, more significant storytelling—are those stories, again often developing into series, which are about commonplace family life but go beyond the elementary appeal of familiar incidents to the development of somewhat rounded, complex human beings with human problems and motivations. These are most clearly in the Alcott tradition. The genre thrived in the early years of this century with the appearance of Susan Coolidge's *What Katy Did*, Alice Hegan Rice's *Mrs. Wiggs of the Cabbage Patch*, Margaret Sidney's *The Five Little Peppers*, and Kate Douglas Wiggin's *Rebecca of Sunnybrook Farm*. The continuing appeal of these slow-paced, sentimental stories would seem to testify to the fundamentalness of the appeal of this type of fiction. The genre has been represented in more recent years by such books—many of them superior storytelling—as Eleanor Estes's Moffat books (*The Moffats, The Middle Moffat, Rufus M.*) and *Ginger Pye*, and *Pinky Pye*; Elizabeth Enright's *The Saturdays, The Four Story Mistake*, and *Then There Were Five*; Mayde Lee Chastain's stories of the Fripsey family (*Bright Days, Fripsey Summer, Fripsey Fun*); Hilda Van Stockum's *The Mitchells, Canadian Summer*, and *The Cottage at Bantry Bay*; Beverly Cleary's Henry Huggins stories (*Henry Huggins, Henry and Beezus*, etc.); Hazel Wilson's Herbert stories (*Herbert, Herbert Again, More Fun with Herbert*, etc.) and *The Owen Boys*; Maud Hart Lovelace's Betsy-Tacy series (*Betsy-Tacy, Betsy-Tacy and Tib, Betsy and Tacy Go over the Big Hill*, etc.); Carol Ryrie Brink's *Family Grandstand* and *Family Sabbatical*; and Sydney Taylor's stories of Jewish family life, *All-of-a-kind Family* and *More All-of-a-kind Family*.

All these stories are loosely knit chains of fairly common domestic situations and events in which there is sufficient originality and depth of character interpretation to create interest and unity beyond simply that of familiar domestic scenes. In *The Saturdays*, for instance, a rather superficial sort of unity is contributed by having each child in the family choose how he will use their pooled resources on a given Saturday in New York

City; but because the inclinations of each of the children begin to be discernible early and continue to unfold and exhibit themselves, the book has the additional unity of these developing attitudes.

The Moffat books, outstanding representatives of juvenile domestic fiction, ramble through various experiences of the Moffat children, a rather loose series of incidents, without major unifying crises; in these several books each of the children reveals, but not all at once, a set of distinctive personal characteristics. Rufus is a sturdily independent character who invents his own rituals (for instance, his always circling the library lamppost each time he visits the library) and sets his own goals (for instance, his wish, before he has learned to read, to have a library card so he can "read" a book just as his older brothers and sisters do). These are not stock characters. They are individuals but not so eccentric the child reader cannot associate them with children he knows. And they are given an extra boost out of the "Jones family" rut by the author's humorous perceptiveness, her noting innumerable details of human consistency and inconsistency, congruity and incongruity. In short, the Moffat stories are about characters and so come to have their own special character; they explore personalities and reflect, in the noting of the selected details, the individual personality of the author. In their appeal they are certainly cousins to the "Daddy, Momsy, and me" kind of series, but they are accurate and imaginative in ways it is not.

Domestic Fiction for Adolescents

The appeal of domestic subject matter in reading continues on into later adolescence for girls, with a shift of emphasis from essentially children's problems to those of semiadults—membership in more or less formally organized groups (the Y, school clubs, church groups), romance, physical appearance, high school and college studies, money, vocational preparation and choice, beginning to deal as adults with older adults, starting to raise families (baby care from the point of view of mothers). The stories are still family-centered, but matters related to sex and vocation get more attention. Typical of such books are Rebecca Caudill's *The House of the Fifers* (about a spoiled girl); Beverly Cleary's *Fifteen;* Maureen Daly's *Seventeenth Summer;* Vivian Breck's *Maggie;* Mary Stolz's *The Organdy Cupcakes* (about student nurses), *The Sea Gulls Woke Me,* and *To Tell Your Love;* Betty Cavanna's *A Girl Can Dream, Going on Sixteen,* and *Six on Easy Street;* and the Sue Barton series by Helen Boylston. The formulas here are rather rigid. The standard ingredients are essentially those of soap opera; indeed, it would seem that many girls in their reading stay almost completely in the little fictionalized world of dating, clique making and breaking, marriage, and child care.

It is interesting to note that whereas domestic fiction for younger children has produced many sturdy, original tales of real literary quality, the teen-age domestic fiction is depressingly uniform in its drab lack of distinction. It is hard to say why. Perhaps one explanation is that bright children from about thirteen to sixteen appropriate adult fiction to their own use and so find there the imaginative re-creation of all the domestic problems they may crave—in such diverse novels as *David Copperfield*, *Pride and Prejudice* and *Sense and Sensibility*, Mazo de la Roche's Jalna books, Margaret Mitchell's *Gone with the Wind*, Thackeray's *Vanity Fair*, Sinclair Lewis's *Main Street*, Mann's *Buddenbrooks*, Galsworthy's *Forsyte Saga*, Edith Wharton's novels, Wolfe's *Look Homeward, Angel*, D. H. Lawrence's *Sons and Lovers*, Tolstoy's *Anna Karenina*, Willa Cather's novels, Ellen Glasgow's fiction, and Arnold Bennett's *The Old Wives' Tale*—while less critical or skillful adolescent readers feel happier with the earlier simplified emotional diet (and, indeed, may continue to feel so all their lives). Still another reason may be the very nature of the domestic events intriguing to younger children—parties, jokes, tricks, hikes, holidays, pets, physical games, camping. All these easily involve humor, whereas the job choosing and mate choosing and baby rearing of adolescent domestic fiction may not so readily or frequently lead to laughter. So laughter in the domestic fiction for younger readers may keep their writers' inventiveness awake in a way that is unlikely, maybe impossible, in the lugubrious atmosphere of the teen-age "dramatic home situation." At any rate, it is a sad fact that domestic fiction for adolescents is and always has been in a sad state. This is one of the few areas of nonadult literature that has failed to produce much literature of value beyond the immediate satisfaction of the needs of its age group.

Regional and Historical Fiction for Younger Children

Along with children's growing engrossment with real people within the domestic circle come an increasing interest in the real people of other times and places and its expression in a turning to regional and historical fiction. And here again, as with neighborhood and home realism, we first find concern with the outer physical aspects of people and events and then a gradual shift to fascination with personal thinking and problems and social reality.

The small child, intrigued by the family life of McCloskey's little loose-toothed Sal or the small Smalls or the Marjorie Flack dog-centered homes (the Angus stories), may begin to find the real children of far places just about as fascinating as his brothers, sisters, and friends. But in books about them he looks for children like himself, with basically similar activities and problems. And so he may look and listen to elementary little accounts of how a Swiss boy takes care of sheep in mountain meadows, how Pelle raised the wool for his new suit, how Eleanor Lattimore's Little Pear grows up in a Chinese village, or how Ping, another Chinese boy, got into and out of mild scrapes.

Soon—at about seven to nine—he may become absorbed in more detailed accounts of foreign lands—accounts that tell him about children (again really himself) bearing the names of other cultures, wearing the clothes of other cultures, living in their houses, doing the chores of their children, celebrating their holidays, playing their games. Relying much upon illustrations suggestive of Scandinavian peasant design, the d'Aulaires' books *Ola, Ola and Blakken, Nils,* and *Children of the Northlights* tell him how it would be to be a child in Norway; he gets a fairly detailed picture, attached to a loose narrative, of the outer, routine physical facts of life in the north. Similarly, through Kathleen Morrow Elliot's writing and Roger Duvoisin's illustrations, children can put themselves in the place of Jo-Yo (*Jo-Yo's Idea*), Riema (*Riema, Little Brown Girl of Java*), and Soomoon (*Soomoon, Boy of Bali*). Such books generally do not have a particularly tight and gripping story line or close, original characterization; they tend to depend for their interest on the lure of information, the sense of realness they can convey. The sense of the *immediacy* of these realities, their close-to-us quality, is assured by keeping in the center of the scene and action little children generalized enough in their feelings and interests to be easily linked to himself by the child reader. This is a simple way of connecting the remote real with the immediate real; the faraway is made to seem more real through its association with the child's familiar world.

As for his reading of historical fiction, the child in these early years is somewhat handicapped by his lack of a strong sense of history, the conception of a succession of related events in time. The distant in time is harder for him to comprehend and to get excited about than the spatially distant, the faraway land. The fairy tales which he already knows gave him no trouble in this respect because they happened simply once upon a time. They happened really any old time, and so are essentially timeless; their time could even be now, or at least yesterday. If the child reading a historical tale can be made to feel the *anytime* of the events, rather than their *then* time, he may be excited by their timeless realness rather than, as will later become the case, by their special time-bound realness, their realness in a particular past time. But this is not easy to do without making the story altogether fiberless, meaningless. Historical fiction is one field of children's book publishing in which there seems to be a paucity of material for the younger child. The reasons seem pretty clear. It is difficult to appeal to a child's feeling for reality when he may not even really believe the past to be real.

This sense of the past is slow and erratic in arriving, but once it *has* come for the individual child, it is absorbing and intense; indeed, it may become a consuming passion from ten or eleven years on. At this age level, the child will find a tremendous number of books, many of them excellent, to satisfy his wish for past realness. Besides, this is an interest generally catered to and underwritten by teachers and librarians. The great popularity of *adult* historical fiction has perhaps contributed to children's historical fiction by interesting writers and editors in making and publishing historical novels and by accustoming parents, teachers, and librarians to thinking of history as reading content.

Patterns in Children's Historical Fiction

Children's stories based on history, well written or not, have come to follow a general pattern. The principal figures are usually children, and the books generally split into boys' books and girls' books according to the sex of the children who fill these central roles. The simplest bridge from the child reader to the past, so different from the child's world, would be childhood itself—the sharing of childhood by the reader and by the characters in his book. One will encounter this bridge almost everywhere in modern historical fiction for children—J. Meade Falkner's *Moonfleet* (a boy gets involved with smugglers along the English seacoast), Stevenson's *Kidnapped* (a boy in turbulent Scotland of the eighteenth century), Esther Forbes's *Johnny Tremain* (a boy apprentice fights through the American Revolution), Rachel Field's *Calico Bush* (a "bound girl" endures privation with a pioneer family in colonial Maine), Walter D. Edmonds's *Two Logs Crossing* (a boy on the middle frontier), Louise A. Kent's *He Went with Magellan* and succeeding books on boys who accompanied other explorers, Marian Magoon's *Little Dusty Foot* (a young boy wandering across the medieval world with Charlemagne's merchants), Stephen W. Meader's *River of the Wolves* (boys held captive by Indians on the early frontier), Bruce Catton's *Banners at Shenandoah* (a boy's experiences on that Civil War battleground), Howard Pyle's *Otto of the Silver Hand* (a little boy caught in the clash of medieval barons). In these and in thousands of other historical novels for children the past is seen through the eyes of youth and is sometimes shaped by its will and hand.

Faithfulness to the spirit of a past age *may* make the use of childhood characters as bridges more difficult, for, being characteristic children of their own very special time in history, the book's child characters will *not* be twentieth-century children. Thus Marchette Chute's stories of medieval and Elizabethan England, *The Innocent Wayfaring* and *The Wonderful Winter,* may lose some child readers because the children of these stories mirror the world they lived in—its high and particular enthusiasms, its lyricism, its roughness and vulgarity and delicacy. This might easily happen, too, in the case of Caroline Dale Snedeker's richly detailed stories of ancient Rome— *The Forgotten Daughter, The White Isle,* and *A Triumph for Flavius*—in which the children are very definitely ancient Roman children, not simply modern American boys and girls transported to old Rome for an exciting on-the-spot observation. For the mature reader, of course, this part of their realistic appeal can make such books all the more compelling, all the more convincing; and even less mature readers may be imaginative enough to take their cue from *the characters' being children* and let themselves slide into the characters of those far-off children without being frustrated by differences in habits and values.

When children are replaced in the central roles of juvenile historical fiction, the substitutes are seldom adult human beings. They are likely to be either animals "who were there," such as the mouse in Lawson's *Ben* and Me or the horse in his *Paul Revere and I,* or inanimate objects, such as the doll in *Hitty* or a dress or trunk or house. As noted earlier, the use of the inanimate object makes it easy for the author to bring in whatever exciting or colorful events he wishes, simply by his transferring ownership of the object to people who where present at those events. He can appropriate an object that has a logical relationship to the event; Holling C. Holling, for instance, in his *Tree in the Trail,* has focused his many-sided, many-purposed narrative on the tree which, in an arid, almost treeless land, attracted to itself preconquest Indians, conquistadores, and immigrants seeking water and coolness and eventually the tree's own wood for an oxen yoke.

In this use of inanimate objects the historical novelist for children does something quite in keeping with the inclinations of children. In their younger years children are accustomed to dramatic play with toys or any other objects—sticks, stones, buttons, anything—and so there is no strain, for most children up to the age of nine or ten, in the writer's bringing a doll or toy soldier to life and parading the little figure through great events and vivid pageantry.

In the weaving of fictional patterns around their child characters or inanimate-object characters the writers of juvenile historical fiction have shown considerable variety and ingenuity.

The novel may take its children, toy soldiers, dolls, or whatnots through series of loosely related, historically significant episodes lacking any unity beyond that of general atmosphere or the continued activity of certain characters, or it may put them into a more closely knit unified situation or problem leading to a climax and resolution of the difficulties. Typical of the first alternative are Laura Ingalls Wilder's stories of pioneer families in the Western woods and on the plains (*Little House in the Big Woods, On the Banks of Plum Creek*), Carol Ryrie Brink's *Caddie Woodlawn,* and Marguerite de Angeli's *Thee, Hannah!* The children have various experiences typical of a particular place and time; there is no major theme or problem to be worked out through the particular incidents. Typical of the second, more unified kind of historical novel is Stevenson's *Kidnapped,* in which all the action relates to David Balfour's legacy. The unifying thread of Enid Meadowcroft's *By Secret Railway* is a white boy's attempt to rescue a freed Negro from the South; William O. Steele's *Winter Danger* tells of a boy's experiences on a frontier farm during an Indian uprising; in *Wilderness Journey,* Steele tells of another boy's hazardous journey. These novels create strong unifying questions around the characters: Will they survive? Will they achieve what they are trying to do?

There is, of course, for the writer of historical fiction, adult or juvenile, a great temptation to introduce all sorts of colorful scenes and events and so to trot his people in and out of happenings. This can loosen up the whole piece of fiction to the point where it almost stops telling a story and becomes a pageant. This feeling of pageantry, of witnessing a constantly changing panorama, is strong in such sweeping, inclusive novels as Elizabeth Janet Gray's *Adam of the Road*, Cynthia Harnett's *Caxton's Challenge*, and Rachel Varble's *Pepys' Boy*; this pageantry, indeed, is one of their most appealing aspects. Pageants have their place in the imaginative life of a society, and certainly a pageant—for instance, a parade—is to a child a major experience. By its nature it is surface, lacking depth of meaning and human characterization, but it has its own values. There are imaginative, vivid, moving pageants, and there are dull, ponderous ones. Some are very lively and exciting; others are just gaudy and repetitious. And so it is with the pageant-like novel based on history.

Another way in which children's historical tales may differ from one another is in the placing of the central child characters in relation to major events or themes. The child character may be a direct participant in historically significant happenings—sail on the *Santa Maria* as a cabin boy, fight off Indians in a settlement raid, be a drummer boy with Washington's army, or be a page at the court of Queen Elizabeth. Thus in Chute's *The Wonderful Winter* the young runaway, Sir Robert Wakefield, comes into close contact with many of the great figures of the Elizabethan theater, including Shakespeare and John Heminge. In Lynn Bronson's *The Runaway* the runaway boy meets Captain Ulysses Grant in Oregon Territory; in *Niko, Sculptor's Apprentice* Isabelle Lawrence has her apprentice very much in the midst of the glorious building days of Pericles and Phidias in fifth-century Athens; in Lucile Morrison's *The Lost Queen of Egypt* the young central characters are themselves King Tutankhamon and his Queen Ankhsenamon of ancient Egypt; in Alice Dalgliesh's *Thanksgiving Story* the children are on the *Mayflower*. In such books the child hero or heroine is a leading actor in the historical drama, and so the child reader is given the feeling of being one too, or at least of occupying a front-row seat. This arrangement, of course, takes a good deal of ingenious manipulation by the author to get his characters to the right place at the right time and to see to it that they have always an active role in the goings-on. It may place something of a strain on the reader's credulity that Johnny Tremain should be in on the Boston Tea Party, the Boston Massacre, Paul Revere's ride, Washington's crossing the Delaware, and the Battle of Trenton. Still, a skillful author may make likely the unlikely by careful spacing, timing, and telescoping.

Many children's historical tales skirt this difficulty by having their boy and girl principals moving just on the periphery of important events. In this sort of story the major plot of the book is contributed not by the historical event but by some personal problem of the characters or their families, with larger historical events and trends supplying a backdrop. The events may affect the lives of the children—for instance, cause Puritans to flee Europe for America or cause middle-borderers to move farther west in search of free land—but in all these tales the major historical events are simply a sort of accompaniment to the personal lives of the protagonists. Thus in Brink's *Caddie Woodlawn* the great pressures and conflicts of the western movement in America are certainly implied in the novel's middle-border settings, the news of Indian troubles elsewhere, and the struggles of Caddie Woodlawn's family; but Caddie's own limited childhood adventures on the farm are the novel's central concern. So in Coatsworth's *Five Bushel Farm*, her *Away Goes Sally*, and her *The Fair American*, in Clyde Robert Bulla's *Down the Mississippi* (the great western movement suggested in the boy's adventures in storms, during an Indian raid, on a log raft), in Janet Gray's *Adam of the Road* (a minstrel boy's wandering across medieval England), and in Isabel McMeekin's *Journey Cake*. And of course many historical novels fall somewhere between these extremes, freely interweaving factuality with romantic coloring; something of this freedom characterizes Coatsworth's books, de Angeli's *Door in the Wall*, Eric Kelly's *Trumpeter of Krakow*, Joseph A. Altsheler's Civil War tales, and Pyle's fighting-filled, fact-crowded *Men of Iron* and *Otto of the Silver Hand.*

Obviously, then, children's historical fiction varies greatly both in the amount of history it offers and in historical accuracy. In some tales there is merely a suggestion of general setting, perhaps by a few references to special costumes or architectural details or a few common words and phrases of the period, just enough to identify the setting. It may simply be mentioned that the boy was in the army of General Grant at Vicksburg or in a fort on the Oregon frontier, and the author may then concern himself with invented events and characters that lack any special historically factual basis. A children's historical novel may, on the other hand, be so full of historical data that the child may come to think of the novel as history. In short, the historical texture of the book may be quite rough or very close and fine.

In this matter of historical accuracy, it is important to recognize that there is more than one kind of accuracy. There is literal accuracy and there is overall accuracy, or faithfulness to the spirit of the event, and they need not go together. For example, in a fictional account of a prairie-wagon journey through Indian country, an author may spill a liberal bag of facts about the routines of wagon travel and all the details of days wheeling westward (much as many diaries did) and create a very dull chronicle that neither captures the actual feeling of people traveling under threat of attack nor creates a vicariously thrilling experience; on the other hand, by a judicious selection of facts and by imaginative invention of what he thinks might happen under such circumstances, an author can create a scene both thrilling and close to the way such things really were.

Perhaps the majority of historical novels for children that take place in the seventeenth-century colonial settlements or in the days of the push into Kentucky or the later crossing of the Great Plains are essentially frontier-adventure tales, with the particular frontier and its special characteristics, events, and personalities so sketchily suggested that whether the book is pinned down to 1680 or 1790 or 1850 is of little matter; in these books the historical atmosphere is general, the fabric of historical fact quite thin. (This, of course, does not make them good or poor, impressive or innocuous, as fiction.) A relatively small number of chronicles drawing on the western movement in America, such as Elizabeth Gray's novels of North Carolina settlement or John Buchan's *Salute to Adventurers* or Walter Edmonds's *Rome Haul* or Hazel Wilson's *His Indian Brother* (Maine in the 1800s), are tapestry-rich in the circumstances and feeling of a particular place and time in the western migrations.

Subject-matter Focuses in Children's Historical Fiction

When we turn to consider the history on which writers of historical fiction for children have mainly drawn, we find they have tended to crowd into certain areas, principally because of general public interest. The history most fully represented on American library shelves is American history, with the westward movement bulking largest by far; the early colonial period and the Revolution have also attracted many writers for children, and in recent years the Civil War has provided themes and backgrounds for much juvenile fiction. These concentrations are easily explained by national pride and school curricula, but also the action and danger and conflict inherent in these historical subjects have lured writers into writing great numbers of juvenile historical novels about them. Other historical areas on which writers have drawn in a major way are (1) the exploration of North and South America, (2) Renaissance Europe of the sixteenth and seventeenth centuries, (3) medieval Europe, (4) the ancient world of Greece, Rome, and Egypt, and (5) the prehistoric world of the cavemen.

Certain historical areas have been de-emphasized or almost omitted, for fairly obvious reasons. For children the *recent* past—the last eighty years or so—lacks the impact of present reality, but it is yet too like the present to possess the romantic wonder, the glamor, of the more *past* past. For authors too the recent past may be deader than the years back of it. Moreover, some recent events may, at least at close view, not seem to lend themselves to dramatic fictions about individuals; the world wars and the recent mass movements, political and economic and physical, do not easily or obviously provide the seeker of individualistic adventure with the material he wants. And certainly they seldom suggest virtue clearly triumphant or even virtue nobly slain. There is much tragedy, but tragedy with an ironic twist that makes these recent events extremely hard for the children's writer to handle unless he rejects the widely accepted notion that most children are not ready to cope with adult tragedies and ironies.

And for similar reasons, the scientific and industrial revolution of the eighteenth and nineteenth centuries have not produced much children's historical fiction. The scientific revolution of the past two centuries has been too intellectual to lend itself readily to vivid action fiction; there is little of the pageant about science, seldom a dramatic showdown between good and evil. And the world of business—even the freewheeling business ventures of the nineteenth century—has apparently not seemed to writers of historical fiction to provide themes and protagonists that would hold child readers. Tariffs, the stock market, the railroad financiers, Wall Street and Threadneedle Street, Black Friday—these have not often stimulated writers for young readers to write fiction.

In American juvenile fiction the national crises and undertakings of other countries—Britain's colonial expansion, the Napoleonic wars, the Suez Canal—have taken a back seat to our own national crises and ventures of a similar kind. Likewise, English writers for children, e.g., G. A. Henty, have concentrated on British history, and so use our Civil War and other important national events only occasionally.

The history of the *early* Middle Ages in Europe has not been a common source of material for children's historical-fiction writers; this is not surprising, for those times are relatively unfamiliar to modern writers and readers in comparison with the age of chivalry. For this same reason—unfamiliarity—the history of Asia and Africa, except for ancient Egypt, has been somewhat neglected. A writer naturally draws on cultures and periods he has some knowledge of and interest in, and even then he may feel his audience needs already to have some orientation to the culture, so that he will not have to build his theater from the very ground. That a child is likely to know more about the lives of prehistoric cavemen than about medieval Arabia gives the former topic a strong advantage.

Style in Children's Historical Fiction

A final sort of difference one finds in historical novels for children is a less tangible, less easily defined difference: it is one of style, the mode of telling, the things which make a difference that are not in the plot or overall plan or in the facts used.

Style in children's historical fiction ranges from a fairly crisp, spare narrative style, somewhat like a news report of events (Elizabeth Gray's *Beppy Marlowe of Charles Town*) through a somewhat poetic, warm, expressive manner (Elizabeth Coatsworth, Esther Forbes, Rachel Field, Cornelia Meigs) or an intentionally archaic, elegant mode (Howard Pyle) to a highly excited, emotionally colored manner (James Daugherty).

A striking aspect of juvenile historical fiction is the surprisingly high level of originality and literary effectiveness in the styles of its practitioners. Capable writers with evocative personal styles are many—Robert Louis Stevenson, Pyle, Coatsworth, Laura Ingalls Wilder, Walter Edmonds, Field, Forbes, Gray, Bruce Catton, Marguerite de Angeli, Marchette Chute, Joseph Altsheler, John Bennett, Irving Bacheller, John Buchan, Arthur Conan Doyle. There is, in short, a wealth of fresh, thoroughly good writing in this genre for children—a condition not always matched in other sorts of children's books.

Several reasons suggest themselves as likely ones. Because it combines elements of fact and fancy, familiarity and the unknown and strange, children's historical fiction has attracted a large variety of writers. Also, historical fiction primarily intended for an adult audience got off to a good start in the nineteenth century with some practitioners of special literary merit. Cooper, Dickens, Thackeray, Eliot, Scott, Reade, and Stevenson established a strong tradition of historical fiction in English and American literature; so did Dumas, Hugo, Stendhal, Chateaubriand, Sienkiewicz, in Continental writing. Very soon it became clear that meritorious adult historical fiction might, with little or no adaptation, be read eagerly by children from about eleven or twelve years of age. And so it has never seemed strange to writers, editors, librarians, or teachers that adult historical fiction should also be good children's fiction.

In this field there never has been the assumption, so characteristic of most other kinds of children's writing, that writing for children is somehow of an intrinsically inferior kind and that therefore it is not worth the serious attention of talented writers. Many writers of children's historical fiction—Coatsworth, Brink, Wilder, and many others—are people of information, narrative skill, and imagination. Many good writers of fiction and nonfiction for adults have turned to writing historical tales for children—Stevenson, Arthur Conan Doyle, Rachel Field, Chute, and Edmonds, to name a few. Perhaps the level has been kept high partly because of the competition of those works of adult historical fiction which prove appealing to children; in other words, there is no chance for the growth of a feeling that children's writers are isolated and have a little field all to themselves. When you are working in the same vineyards with men of the imaginative stature of Scott, Dickens, Thackeray, Hugo, and Stendhal, you are a little more likely to keep on your toes, to stretch and strain.

A further reason for the high level of style in children's historical fiction may lie in the nature of the material historical novelists work with. They use fact, but fact touched with the mist and color of pastness, and so they may be encouraged to keep in touch with reality at the same time they are moved to imagine, to fancy. Also, they are comparatively free from the temptation toward excessive, soap-opera sentimentality that lies in the domestic family story (although, of course, a good many historical stories are combined with the family-story genre). And because of the distance of historical figures and events from present-day realities, there is perhaps not the tug of prosaic dullness that weakens much realistic fiction about present-day children, the school, neighborhood, park, and summer camp.

Finally, historical-novel writers for children have the advantage of knowing they possess the support and encouragement of many adults. Many teachers, parents, and librarians feel that factual information is an especially good reason for reading. And since history concerns fact (it is, of course, not simply fact), they are likely to be happier about history-linked reading by children than about family stories, dog stories, and other popular types of juvenile fiction. Historical fiction relates to children's formal schooling and so becomes a staple of both the required and outside reading programs of the schools. Consequently it gets constant attention from the adult world on which children's literature is so dependent.

SUGGESTED SOURCES

Poetry of the Commonplace: Poems Having the Ordinary Experiences of Childhood as Their Starting Point

Aldis, Dorothy: *All Together: A Child's Treasury of Verse,* ill. by Helen D. Jameson, Marjorie Flack, and Margaret Freeman, Putnam, 1952.

————: *Hello Day,* ill. by Susan Elson, Putnam, 1959.

Brooks, Gwendolyn: *Bronzeville Boys and Girls,* ill. by Ronni Solbert, Harper & Row, 1956.

Brown, Margaret Wise: *Nibble Nibble: Poems for Children,* ill. by Leonard Weisgard, Young Scott Books.

Conkling, Hilda: *Poems by a Little Girl,* Lippincott, 1920.

————: *Shoes of the Wind,* Lippincott, 1922.

Field, Rachel: *Poems,* ill. by author, Macmillan, 1951.

————: *The Pointed People,* ill. by author, Macmillan, 1933.

————: *Taxis and Toadstools,* ill. by author, Doubleday, 1926.

Fisher, Aileen: *Going Barefoot,* ill. by Adrienne Adams, Crowell, 1960.

————: *Where Does Everyone Go?* ill. by Adrienne Adams, Crowell, 1961.

Flanders, Michael: *Creatures Great and Small,* ill. by Marcello Minale, Holt, 1965.

Frost, Frances: *The Little Naturalist,* ill. by Kurt Werth, Whittlesey, 1952.

Greenaway, Kate: *Marigold Garden: Pictures and Rhymes,* Warne.

Hoberman, Mary Ann and Norman: *All My Shoes Come in Twos,* Little, Brown, 1957. Poetry about kinds of children's shoes.

Krauss, Ruth: *A Very Special House,* ill. by Maurice Sendak, Harper & Row, 1953.

Stevenson, Robert Louis: *A Child's Garden of Verses,* ill. by Tasha Tudor, Walck, 1947. Many other editions.

Tippett, James: *I Go a-Traveling,* ill. by Elizabeth T. Wolcott, Beacon Press, 1957.

————: *I Live in a City,* Harper, 1927.

————: *I Spend the Summer,* ill. by Elizabeth T. Wolcott, Harper, 1930.

Wynne, Annette: *All through the Year: Three Hundred and Sixty-five New Poems for Holidays and Every Day,* Stokes, 1932.

Realistic Fiction about Children's More or Less Commonplace Environment

Adelson, Leone: *All Ready for Winter,* ill. by Kathleen Elgin, McKay, 1952.

Association for Childhood Education Literature Committee: *Told under the Blue Umbrella,* ill. by Marguerite Davis, Macmillan, 1933, 1962. Realistic stories.

Ayars, James Sterling: *Caboose on the Roof,* ill. by Bob Hodgell, Abelard-Schuman, 1956. Train watching.

Bechdolt, Jack: *Oliver Becomes a Weatherman,* ill. by Ralph Ramstad, Messner, 1953.

Beim, Jerrold: *Andy and the School Bus,* ill. by Leonard Shortall, Morrow, 1947.

————: *Smallest Boy in the Class,* ill. by Meg Wohlberg, Morrow, 1949.

Beim, Lorraine: *Benjamin Busybody,* ill. by Violet LaMont, Harcourt, Brace & World, 1947.

Beim, Lorraine and Jerrold: *Two is a Team,* ill. by Ernest Crichlow, Harcourt, Brace & World, 1945.

Bendick, Jeanne: *All around You: A First Look at the World,* ill. by author, Whittlesey, 1951.

————: *What Could You See? Adventures in Looking,* ill. by author, Whittlesey, 1957.

Beskow, Elsa: *Pelle's New Suit,* ill. by author, Harper, 1929. The making of a new suit for a little boy, from shearing the sheep to stitching.

Bianco, Marguery: *Forward Commandos!* ill. by Rafaello Busoni, Viking, 1944. Boys' play.

Borten, Helen: *Do You Hear What I Hear?* ill. by author, Abelard-Schuman, 1960.

————: *Do You See What I See?* ill. by author, Abelard-Schuman, 1959.

Brown, Margaret Wise: *The Dead Bird,* ill. by Remy Charlip, Young Scott Books, 1958.

————: *The Little Farmer,* ill. by Esphyr Slobodkin, Scott, 1948.

————: *The Little Island,* ill. by Leonard Weisgard, Doubleday, 1946.

————: *The Little Lost Lamb,* ill. by Leonard Weisgard, Doubleday, 1944.

————: *The Noon Balloon,* ill. by Leonard Weisgard, Harper & Row, 1952.

————: *Red Light, Green Light,* ill. by Leonard Weisgard, Doubleday, 1946.

————: *Willie's Adventures,* ill. by Crockett Johnson, Scott, 1954.

Brown, Myra Berry: *Company's Coming for Dinner,* ill. by Dorothy Marino, F. Watts, 1959.

Bryant, Bernice: *Follow the Leader,* ill. by Beryl Bailey-Jones, Houghton Mifflin, 1950.

Budney, Blossom: *Huff Puff Hickory Hill,* ill. by Kurt Werth, Lothrop, 1955. A family's moving into a new house.

Burton, Virginia Lee: *Katy and the Big Snow,* ill. by author, Houghton Mifflin, 1943.

————: *The Little House,* ill. by author, Houghton Mifflin, 1947.

————: *Mike Mulligan and His Steam Shovel,* ill. by author, Houghton Mifflin, 1939.

Chandler, Edna W.: *The New Red Jacket,* ill. by Robert Miller, Whitman, 1962.

Collier, Ethel: *The Birthday Tree,* ill. by Honoré Guilbeau, Scott, 1961. A little girl replanting a tree after visit to the country.

Curren, Polly, and Robert J. Lee: *This Is a Town,* ill. by Robert J. Lee, Follett, 1957.

Dawson, Rosemary and Richard: *A Walk in the City,* ill. by authors, Viking, 1950.

De Angeli, Marguerite: *Ted and Nina Go to the Grocery Store,* ill. by author, Doubleday, 1935.

————: *Ted and Nina Have a Happy Rainy Day,* ill. by author, Doubleday, 1936.

De Regniers, Beatrice Schenk: *A Little House of Your Own,* ill. by Irene Haas, Harcourt, Brace & World, 1955.

————: *The Snow Party,* ill. by Reiner Zimnik, Pantheon, 1959.

————: *What Can You Do with a Shoe?* ill. by Maurice Sendak, Harper & Row, 1955.

Enright, Elizabeth: *Gone-away Lake,* ill. by Beth and Joe Krush, Harcourt, Brace & World, 1957. Children's play in woods.

Fisher, Aileen: *Summer of Little Rain,* ill. by Gloria Stevens, Nelson, 1961.

Flack, Marjorie: *The Boats on the River,* ill. by Jay Hyde Barnum, Viking, 1946. Kinds of boats on the river.

————: *Wait for Williams,* ill. by author and R. A. Holberg, Houghton Mifflin, 1935.

Hader, Berta and Elmer: *Big City,* ill. by authors, Macmillan, 1956.

————: *The Big Snow,* ill. by authors, Macmillan, 1948.

————: *The Little Stone House,* ill. by authors, Macmillan, 1944.

Hughes, Thomas: *Tom Brown's Schooldays,* Collins (Nelson's Classics).

Hurd, Edith Thacher and Clement: *Mr. Charlie's Gas Station,* ill. by authors, Lippincott, 1956.

Kay, Helen: *City Springtime,* ill. by Barbara Cooney, Hastings House, 1957.

Keats, Ezra Jack, and Pat Cherr: *My Dog Is Lost!* Crowell, 1960. A boy from Puerto Rico tries to describe his lost dog to Chinese, Italian, and other children in Spanish and with gestures; an elementary lesson in Spanish and internationalism.

Kessler, Ethel and Leonard: *The Big Red Bus,* Doubleday, 1957.

————: *Plink Plink!* Doubleday, 1954. About water. Followed by *Crunch Crunch,* 1955, about food.

Koch, Dorothy: *I Play at the Beach,* ill. by Feodor Rojankovsky, Holiday, 1955.

Lenski, Lois: *I Like Winter*, ill. by author, Oxford University Press, 1950.

————: *Let's Play House*, ill. by author, Walck, 1944.

————: *The Little Auto*, ill. by author, Walck, 1940. Also *The Little Farm*, *The Little Sailboat*, etc.

————: *Papa Small*, ill. by author, Oxford, Oxford University Press, 1951.

McCloskey, Robert: *Make Way for Ducklings*, ill. by author, Viking, 1941. A duck family in downtown Boston.

————: *One Morning in Maine*, ill. by author, Viking, 1952. A little girl's morning at the seashore.

————: *Time of Wonder*, ill. by author, Viking, 1957. A Maine vacation treated lovingly in poetic prose and vivid watercolor.

Merrill, Jean: *Tell about the Cowbarn, Daddy*, ill. by Lili Cassel Wronker, Young Scott Books, 1963. An account of milk making with big colorful pictures.

Neurath, Marie: *I'll Show You How It Happens*, ill. by author, Chanticleer Press, 1950. Boat locks, dragonfly birth, engines, etc.

Rand, Ann and Paul: *I Know a Lot of Things*, ill. by authors, Harcourt, Brace & World, 1956.

Sauer, Julia: *Mike's House*, ill. by Don Freeman, Viking, 1954. "Mike's house" is the library which contains a small boy's favorite book, *Mike Mulligan and His Steam Shovel*.

Schick, Eleanor: *The Little School at Cottonwood Corners*, Harper & Row, 1965. Picture book about a small child's first visit to school.

Schlein, Miriam: *City Boy, Country Boy*, ill. by Katherine Evans, Children's Press, 1955.

————: *Henry's Ride*, ill. by Vana Earle Abingdon, 1956. Elderly gentleman's pleasant ride through country.

————: *How Do You Travel?* ill. by Paul Galdone, Abingdon, 1954.

————: *Who?* ill. by Harvey Weiss, Walck, 1963.

Seignobosc, Françoise (Françoise): *What Do You Want to Be?* ill. by author, Scribner, 1957.

Shortall, Leonard: *Ben on the Ski Trail*, ill. by author, Morrow, 1965. A small boy's learning to ski.

Smith, Robert Paul: *When I Am Big*, ill. by Lillian Hoban, Harper & Row, 1965. A child's dreams of such adult activities as changing tires and shoveling snow.

Stolz, Mary: *A Dog on Barkham Street*, ill. by Leonard Shortall, Harper & Row, 1960.

Tresselt, Alvin: *Hi, Mister Robin!* ill. by Roger Duvoisin, Lothrop, 1950.

————: *Johnny Mapleleaf*, ill. by Roger Duvoisin, Lothrop, 1949.

————: *Rain Drop Splash*, ill. by Leonard Weisgard, Lothrop, 1946.

————: *White Snow, Bright Snow*, ill. by Roger Duvoisin, Lothrop, 1947. Caldecott Medal.

Tudor, Tasha: *Around the Year*, ill. by author, Walck, 1957.

Uchida, Yoshiko: *The Promised Year*, ill. by William M. Hutchinson, Harcourt, Brace & World, 1959.

Weisgard, Leonard: *Who Dreams of Cheese?* ill. by author, Scribner, 1950. Describes ways of life of various animals.

Yashima, Taro (pseud. for Jun Iwamatsu): *Momo's Kitten*, ill. by author, Viking, 1962.

————: *Youngest One*, ill. by author, Viking, 1962. Neighborhood girl and baby boy become friends.

Zolotow, Charlotte: *Over and Over*, ill. by Garth Williams, Harper & Row, 1957. Little girl gets acquainted with each holiday, then her birthday, and wishes to have it all ''over and over.''

————: *The Storm Book*, ill. by Margaret B. Graham, Harper & Row, 1952. Little boy sees a summer storm.

Books about Familiar Kinds of People in Familiar Environments: Family Stories

Alcott, Louisa May: *Little Men*, ill. by Hilda Van Stockum, World (Rainbow Classics), 1959.

————: *Little Women*, ill. by Barbara Cooney, Crowell, 1955.

————: *Old-fashioned Girl*, ill. by Elenore Abbot, Little, Brown, 1924.

Armer, Alberta: *Screwball*, ill. by W. T. Mars, World, 1963. The development of a crippled boy's mechanical aptitudes, expressed in his building cars for soapbox derby. Similar in its factual tone: *Steve and the Guide Dogs*, ill. by J. C. Kocsis, World, 1965.

Bader, Laura Nelson: *The Dahlbe Family Horse*, ill. by Paul E. Kennedy, Dial Press, 1964. Life on a Norwegian farm.

Bonham, Frank: *Durango Street*, Dutton, 1965. Teen-age gangs.

Bontemps, Arna W.: *Sad-faced Boy*, ill. by Virginia Lee Burton, Houghton Mifflin, 1937. Negro boyhood.

Boylston, Helen: *Sue Barton, Senior Nurse*, Little, Brown, 1937. Long series.

Breck, Vivian (pseud. for Vivian G. Breckenfeld): *Maggie*, Doubleday, 1954.

Brink, Carol Ryrie: *Family Grandstand*, ill. by Jean Macdonald Porter, Viking, 1952.

————: *Family Sabbatical*, ill. by Susan Foster, Viking, 1956.

Carlson, Natalie: *The Empty Schoolhouse*, ill. by John Kaufmann, Harper & Row, 1965. An integrated school in Louisiana.

Caudill, Rebecca: *The House of the Fifers,* ill. by Genia, McKay, 1954.

Cavanna, Betty (pseud. for Elizabeth Headley): *Going on Sixteen,* Westminster, 1946. Many others about adolescent girlhood, such as *A Girl Can Dream,* Westminster, 1948, and *Six on Easy Street,* Westminster, 1954.

Chastain, Madye Lee: *Bright Days,* ill. by author, Harcourt, Brace & World, 1952.

————: *Fripsey Summer,* ill. by author, Harcourt, Brace & World, 1953. Also *Fripsey Fun,* 1955.

Cleary, Beverly: *Emily's Runaway Imagination,* ill. by Beth and Joe Krush, Morrow, 1961. Girl starts town library; small-town life.

————: *Fifteen,* ill. by Joe and Beth Krush, Morrow, 1956.

————: *Henry Huggins,* ill. by Louis Darling, Morrow, 1950. A series of very funny incidents concerning a small boy, Henry Huggins. Followed by *Henry and Beezus, Beezus and Ramona, Henry and the Clubhouse,* etc.

Coolidge, Susan (pseud. for Sarah Chauncey Woolsey): *What Katy Did,* ill. by Ralph Coleman, Collins, 1924.

Daly, Maureen: *Seventeenth Summer,* Dodd, Mead, 1942.

De Angeli, Marguerite: *Turkey for Christmas,* ill. by author, Westminster, 1965. About a family of five children and their attitudes towards Christmas.

Emery, Anne: *The Losing Game,* Westminster Press, 1965. Cheating in high school.

Enright, Elizabeth: *The Four-story Mistake,* ill. by author, Holt, 1941.

————: *The Saturdays,* ill. by author, Holt, 1941. One of the best of Enright's well-written family stories.

————: *Spiderweb for Two: A Melendy Maze,* ill. by author, Holt, 1951.

————: *Then There Were Five,* ill. by author, Holt, 1944.

————: *Thimble Summer,* ill. by author, Holt, 1938. Newbery Medal.

Estes, Eleanor: *Ginger Pye,* ill. by author, Harcourt, Brace & World, 1951. Newbery Medal.

————: *The Moffats,* ill. by Louis Slobodkin, Harcourt, Brace & World, 1941. Followed by other very funny stories—*The Middle Moffat* and *Rufus M.*—about the Moffat children.

————: *Pinky Pye,* ill. by Edward Ardizzone, Harcourt, Brace, 1958.

Friis, Babbis: *Kristy's Courage,* trans. from Norwegian by Lise Sømme McKinnon, ill. by Charles Geer, Harcourt, Brace & World, 1965. The school experiences of a disfigured girl.

Haywood, Carolyn: *"B" Is for Betsy,* ill. by author, Harcourt, Brace, 1939. One in series of stories about ordinary home and school experiences of children.

————: *Little Eddie,* ill. by author, Morrow, 1947. One of a series about a little boy's everyday problems. *Eddie and His Big Deals*, 1955, is one of the best.

L'Engle, Madeline: *Camilla*, Crowell, 1965. A girl caught between angry parents.

Lovelace, Maud Hart: *Betsy-Tacy*, ill. by Lois Lenski, Crowell, 1940. Followed by long series about girl and friends.

Nesbit, E.: *The Railway Children*, 1906, ill. by C. E. Brock, Penguin (Puffin), 1960.

Rice, Alice Hegan (Alice Caldwell Hegan): *Mrs. Wiggs of the Cabbage Patch*, Century, 1901.

Sachs, Marilyn: *Laura's Luck*, ill. by Ib Ohlsson, Doubleday, 1965. Two sisters at summer camp.

Sidney, Margaret (pseud. for Harriet Mulford Lothrop): *The Five Little Peppers*, ill. by William Sharp, Grosset & Dunlap, 1948.

Sorensen, Virginia: *Miracles on Maple Hill*, ill. by Beth and Joe Krush, Harcourt, Brace & World, 1956. A family moves from city to country.

Spykman, E. C.: *A Lemon and a Star*, Harcourt, Brace & World, 1955. About the motherless Care children; sequel, *The Wild Angel*, 1957.

Stolz, Mary: *The Organdy Cupcakes*, Harper & Row, 1951. And other fiction about adolescence, like *The Sea Gulls Woke Me*, Harper & Row, 1951, and *To Tell Your Love*, Harper & Row, 1950.

Taylor, Sidney: *All-of-a-kind Family*, ill. by Helen John, Follett, 1951. Jewish family life in New York City. Followed by *More All-of-a-kind Family*, ill. by Mary Stevens, 1954, and *All-of-a-kind Family Uptown*, ill. by Mary Stevens, 1958.

Van Stockum, Hilda: *Canadian Summer*, ill. by author, Viking, 1948. A family holiday.

————: *The Cottage at Bantry Bay*, ill. by author, Viking, 1938.

————: *The Mitchells*, ill. by author, Viking, 1945.

Viereck, Phillip: *The Summer I Was Lost*, ill. by Ellen Viereck, John Day, 1965. Lost at a summer camp.

Wiggin, Kate Douglas: *Rebecca of Sunnybrook Farm*, ill. by H. H. Grose, Houghton Mifflin, 1903.

Wilson, Hazel: *Herbert*, ill. by John N. Barron, Knopf, 1950. Followed by other amusing Herbert stories.

————: *The Owen Boys*, Abingdon Press, 1947. Family story, unusual in that it is mainly about boys.

Realistic Fiction about Nature

Adrian, Mary: *Gray Squirrel*, ill. by Walter Ferguson, Holiday, 1955.

————: *Honeybee*, ill. by Barbara Latham, Holiday, 1952.

Anderson, Clarence W.: *Billy and Blaze,* ill. by author, Macmillan, 1936. About a boy and his pony; first of a series.

Atkinson, Eleanor: *Greyfriars Bobby,* ill. by Marguerite Kirmse, Harper, 1929. About a faithful dog in Edinburgh.

Beebe, B. F.: *Run, Light Buck, Run,* ill. by Larry Toschik, McKay, 1962. A pronghorn in Arizona.

Bronson, Lynn (pseud. for Evelyn S. Lampman): *The Runaway,* Lippincott, 1953.

Bronson, Wilfrid S.: *Polwiggle's Progress,* ill. by author, Macmillan, 1930. A frog's life.

Brown, Margaret Wise: *The Sleepy Little Lion,* with photography by Ylla, Harper & Row, 1948.

Burgess, Thornton: *The Burgess Animal Book for Children,* ill. by L. A. Fuertes, Little, Brown, 1920.

Carroll, Ruth and Latrobe: *Beanie,* ill. by authors, Walck, 1953. Also *Tough Enough,* 1954, and *Tough Enough's Trip,* 1956.

————: *Sniffles,* Oxford University Press, 1943.

Davis, Lavinia R.: *The Wild Birthday Cake,* ill. by Hildegard Woodward, Doubleday, 1949. Johnny's hike; his finding a duck for professor's birthday.

Denison, Carol: *What Every Young Rabbit Should Know,* ill. by Kurt Wiese, Dodd, Mead, 1948.

Dennis, Wesley: *Flip and the Cows,* ill. by author, Viking, 1942.

Ets, Marie Hall: *Play with Me,* ill. by author, Viking, 1955.

Farley, Walter: *Black Stallion,* ill. by Keith Ward, Random House, 1941. Also *Black Stallion Returns.*

Flack, Marjorie: *Angus and the Ducks,* ill. by author, Doubleday, 1930. Followed by *Angus and the Cat,* 1931, and *Angus Lost,* 1932—all stories about a Scotch terrier.

————: *The Story about Ping,* ill. by Kurt Wiese, Viking, 1933.

————: *Wag-tail Bess,* ill. by author, Doubleday, 1956.

Gall, Alice, and Fleming H. Crew: *Here and There and Everywhere,* ill. by Nils Hogner, Oxford University Press, 1950.

————: *Wagtail,* ill. by Kurt Wiese, Oxford University Press, 1932.

Gay, Zhenya: *Who Is It?* ill. by author, Viking, 1957. Identifying animals.

George, Jean: *The Hole in the Tree,* ill. by author, Dutton, 1957. Two children follow development of a hole in tree from a bark beetle's small hole to raccoon's shelter.

————: *My Side of the Mountain,* ill. by author, Dutton, 1959. A boy's living alone in Catskills in winter and observing nature.

Gipson, Fred: *Old Yeller,* ill. by Carl Burger, Harper & Row, 1956. Dog story set in Texas hill country of the 1860s.

Goudey, Alice E.: *Here Come the Beavers!* ill. by Garry MacKenzie, Scribner, 1957.

Henry, Marguerite: *Misty of Chincoteague,* ill. by Wesley Dennis, Rand McNally, 1947. Other horse stories by Henry and Dennis: *King of the Wind,* 1948 (Newbery Medal); *Sea Star: Orphan of Chincoteague,* 1949; *Born to Trot,* 1950; *Brighty of the Grand Canyon,* 1953, *Justin Morgan Had a Horse,* 1954; and *Black Gold,* 1957.

Hogan, Inez: *Twin Otters and the Indians,* ill. by author, Dutton, 1962.

James, Will: *Will James' Book of Cowboy Stories,* ill. by author, Scribner, 1954.

Johnson, Margaret S.: *Kelpie, a Shetland Pony,* ill. by author, Morrow, 1962.

Kingman, Lee: *Peter's Long Walk,* ill. by Barbara Cooney, Doubleday, 1953. About Peter's walk to closed school, and all the animals he met on the way.

Kipling, Rudyard: *The Jungle Books* (1895), ill. by Aldren Watson, Doubleday, 1948.

Knight, Eric: *Lassie Come Home,* ill. by Cyrus LeRoy Baldridge, Holt, 1940.

London, Jack: *The Call of the Wild,* ill. by Robert Todd, Macmillan, 1963.

McCloskey, Robert: *Make Way for Ducklings,* ill. by author, Viking, 1941.

McClung, Robert M.: *Otus: the Story of a Screech Owl,* ill. by Lloyd Sandford, Morrow, 1959.

Murphy, Robert: *The Golden Eagle,* ill. by John Schoenherr, Dutton, 1965.

Newberry, Clare Turlay: *Frosty,* ill. by author, Harper & Row, 1961. Also *April's Kittens,* 1940.

O'Hara, Mary: *My Friend Flicka,* Lippincott, 1941.

Pace, Mildred Mastin, Henry V. Larom, and Peggie Cannam: *Three Great Horse Stories,* ill. by Wesley Dennis and Ross Santee, Whittlesey, 1957.

Palazzo, Tony: *Bianco and the New World,* Viking, 1957.

Rawlings, Marjorie Kinnan: *The Yearling,* ill. by N. C. Wyeth, Scribner, 1939.

Sanger, Marjory Bartlett: *Greenwood Summer,* ill. by Christine Price, Dutton, 1958.

Seton, Ernest Thompson: *The Biography of a Grizzly,* ill. by author, Century, 1900. Full of information about grizzly bears, with sentimental, allegorical ending.

White, Anne H.: *The Uninvited Donkey,* ill. by Don Freeman, Viking, 1957. Summer vacation complicated by donkey.

Realistic Stories about Children and Families
in Particular Regions and other Countries

Anckarsvard, Karin: *Aunt Vinnie's Invasion,* trans. by Annabelle MacMillan, ill. by William M. Hutchinson, Harcourt, Brace & World, 1962. Swedish children live a year with their aunt.

Angelo, Valenti: *Look Out Yonder,* ill. by author, Viking, 1943. About a farm family in California.

————: *The Marble Fountain,* ill. by author, Viking, 1951. Postwar Italian village.

————: *Nino,* ill. by author, Viking, 1938. Boy's life in Italy.

Armer, Laura Adams: *Dark Circle of Branches,* ill. by Sidney Armer, Longmans, 1933.

————: *Waterless Mountain,* ill. by Sidney Armer and author, Longmans, 1931. Newbery Award.

Arora, Shirley L.: *What Then, Raman?* ill. by Hans Guggenheim, Follett, 1960. A boy's life in a poor family in India.

Ayer, Jacqueline: *Nu Dang and His Kite,* ill. by author, Harcourt, Brace & World, 1959. Siamese boy's search for his lost kite; much about Siamese life.

————: *The Paper Flower Tree,* ill. by author, Harcourt, Brace & World, 1962.

————: *A Wish for Little Sister,* ill. by author, Harcourt, Brace & World, 1960. Siamese life.

Bannon, Laura: *Gregorio and the White Llama,* ill. by author, Whitman, 1944. Peruvian boy with llama train.

————: *Manuela's Birthday in Old Mexico,* ill. by author, Whitman, 1939.

Beim, Lorraine and Jerrold: *The Burro That Had a Name,* ill. by Howard Simon, Harcourt, Brace, 1939.

Bemelmans, Ludwig: *Hansi,* ill. by author, Viking, 1934. Hansi's Christmas in the Tirol; fine illustrations.

————: *Madeline in London,* ill. by author, Viking, 1961.

Benary-Isbert, Margot: *The Ark,* trans. by Clara and Richard Winston, Harcourt, Brace & World, 1953. Sequel, *Rowan Farm,* 1954.

Bettina (Bettina Ehrlich): *Cocolo,* ill. by author, Harper & Row, 1945. About Italian donkey; distinctive drawings. Also *Cocolo Comes to America,* Harper & Row, 1949.

————: *Pantaloni,* ill. by author, Harper & Row, 1957. Italian village life; boy looking for his dog.

Bothwell, Jean: *River Boy of Kashmir,* ill. by Margaret Ayer, Morrow, 1946.

Bronson, Wilfrid S.: *Pinto's Journey*, ill. by author, Messner, 1948. About a Pueblo Indian boy in New Mexico.

Brown, Marcia: *Henry—Fisherman*, ill. by author, Scribner, 1949. A boy's life in Virgin Islands.

Buck, Pearl: *The Big Wave*, ill. with woodcuts of Hiroshige and Hokusai, John Day, 1948.

Buff, Mary and Conrad: *Kobi: A Boy of Switzerland*, ill. by Conrad Buff, Viking, 1939. Life of a Swiss herdboy.

————: *Magic Maize*, ill. by authors, Houghton Mifflin, 1953.

Bulla, Clyde Robert: *Eagle Feather*, ill. by Tom Two Arrows, Crowell, 1953.

Carlson, Natalie Savage: *A Brother for the Orphelines*, ill. by Garth Williams, Harper & Row, 1959. Life near Paris.

Clark, Ann Nolan: *In My Mother's House*, ill. by Veline Herrera, Viking, 1941. The daily life of an Indian child in the Southwest.

————: *Little Navaho Bluebird*, ill. by Paul Lantz, Viking, 1943.

————: *Looking-for-something: The Story of a Stray Burro of Ecuador*, ill. by Leo Politi, Viking, 1952.

————: *Magic Money*, ill. by Leo Politi, Viking, 1950. Children in Costa Rica.

Coatsworth, Elizabeth: *Lonely Maria*, ill. by Evaline Ness, Pantheon, 1960. Little girl on a West Indies island.

————: *The Noble Doll*, ill. by Leo Politi, Viking, 1961. Mexican village.

Credle, Ellis: *Down, down the Mountain*, ill. by author, Nelson, 1934. Vigorously told pictures-and-words story of the efforts of two Southern hill children to get "squeaky-creaky shoes."

Darbois, Dominique: *Achouna: Boy of the Arctic*, ill. with photographs by author, Follett, 1962.

————: *Agossou: Boy of Africa*, ill. with photographs by author, Follett, 1962.

D'Aulaire, Ingri and Edgar Parin: *Children of the Northlights*, ill. by authors, Viking, 1935. Lapp children.

————: *The Magic Meadow*, ill. by authors, Doubleday, 1958.

————: *Nils*, ill. by authors, Doubleday, 1948.

————: *Ola*, ill. by authors, Doubleday, 1932. About a Norwegian boy's life.

————: *Ola and Blakken*, Doubleday, 1933.

————: *Wings for Per*, ill. by authors, Doubleday, 1944.

Davis, Norman: *Picken's Exciting Summer*, ill. by Winslade, Oxford University Press, 1951. Africa.

————: *Picken's Great Adventure*, ill. by Winslade, Oxford University Press, 1951. Africa.

DeJong, Meindert: *Dirk's Dog, Bello,* ill. by Kurt Wiese, Harper, 1939. About a Dutch boy and his dog.

————: *The Wheel on the School,* ill. by Maurice Sendak, Harper & Row, 1954. Vivid story of children in Dutch fishing village.

Dodge, Mary Mapes: *Hans Brinker, or the Silver Skates,* ill. by Peter Spier, Scribner, 1958. Deservedly still popular story of two Dutch children.

Elliot, Kathleen Morrow: *Riema, Little Brown Girl of Java,* ill. by Roger Duvoisin, Knopf, 1937. And other stories of children in Asia—*Jo-Yo's Idea,* Knopf, 1939, and *Soomoon, Boy of Bali,* Knopf, 1938.

Ets, Marie Hall, and Aurora Labastida: *Nine Days to Christmas,* ill. by Marie Hall Ets, Viking, 1959. Mexican Christmas.

Fletcher, David: *Confetti for Cortorelli,* ill. by George W. Thompson, Pantheon, 1957. An orphan in Sicily; vivid picture of carnival time.

Françoise: *Jeanne-Marie in Gay Paris,* ill. by author, Scribner, 1956.

Gray, Elizabeth Janet: *The Cheerful Heart,* ill. by Kazue Mizumura, Viking, 1959. A Japanese girl's adjustment to new homeplace after war.

Gallant, Kathryn: *The Flute Player of Beppu,* ill. by Kurt Wiese, Coward-McCann, 1960.

Garnett, Richard: *The White Dragon,* ill. by Garham Oakley, Vanguard, 1964. Boys and iceboat in British fen country.

Gates, Doris: *Blue Willow,* ill. by Paul Lantz, Viking, 1940. About a child of migrant workers in California.

Hader, Berta and Elmer: *Little Appaloosa,* ill. by authors, Macmillan, 1949.

Handforth, Thomas: *Mei Li,* ill. by author, Doubleday, 1938. About Chinese family life; Caldecott Medal.

Jones, Elizabeth Orton: *Maminka's Children,* ill. by author, Macmillan, 1946. A Bohemian family in America.

Justus, May: *Luck for Little Lihu,* Aladdin, 1950. Tennessee mountain life.

Kelsey, Vera: *Maria Rose,* ill. by Candido Portinari, Doubleday, 1942. Carnival time in Brazil; imaginative illustrations by famous Brazilian artist.

Kingman, Lee: *The Best Christmas,* ill. by Barbara Cooney, Doubleday, 1949. A Finnish family in America.

————: *Pierre Pidgeon,* ill. by Arnold E. Bare, Houghton Mifflin, 1943. A little French boy on the Gaspé Peninsula in French Canada.

Krumgold, Joseph: *And Now Miguel,* ill. by Jean Charlot, Crowell, 1953. A sheepherding boy in New Mexico; Newbery Award.

Lattimore, Eleanor Frances: *Junior: A Colored Boy of Charleston,* ill. by author, Harcourt, Brace, 1938.

————: *Little Pear,* ill. by author, Harcourt, Brace, 1931. Other stories about the little Chinese boy: *Little Pear and His Friends,* Harcourt, Brace, 1934, and *Little Pear and the Rabbits,* Morrow, 1956.

Lattimore, Eleanor Frances: *The Little Tumbler,* ill. by author, Morrow, 1963. Life in China.

Lauritzen, Jonreed: *The Ordeal of the Young Hunter,* ill. by Hoke Denetsosie, Little, Brown, 1954. Story of a Southwest Indian boy.

Lenski, Lois: *Blue Ridge Billy,* ill. by author, Lippincott, 1946.

————: *Boom Town Boy,* ill. by the author, Lippincott, 1948. A boy in the Oklahoma oil boom.

————: *Corn Farm Boy,* ill. by author, Lippincott, 1954.

————: *Cotton in My Sack,* ill. by author, Lippincott, 1948.

————: *Prairie School,* ill. by author, Lippincott, 1951.

————: *Strawberry Girl,* ill. by author, Lippincott, 1945. Realistic story about girl in poor Florida family; Newbery Award.

Lewis, Elizabeth Foreman: *To Beat a Tiger, One Needs a Brother's Help,* ill. by John Huehnergarth, Holt, 1953. A gang of Chinese boys all struggling to survive.

————: *Young Fu of the Upper Yangtze,* ill. by Kurt Wiese, Holt, 1932. Newbery Medal.

Lindquist, Willis: *Burma Boy,* ill. by Nicolas Mordvinov, Whittlesey, 1953.

Louden, Claire and George: *Far into the Night: A Story of Bali,* Scribner, 1955. Balinese child's home and community life, slightly fictionalized.

MacDonald, Golden (pseud. for Margaret Wise Brown): *Little Lost Lamb,* ill. by Leonard Weisgard, Doubleday, 1945.

Matsuno, Masako: *A Pair of Red Clogs,* ill. by Kazue Mizumura, World, 1960. Japanese girl's fancy clogs prove impractical.

Milhous, Katherine: *Appolonia's Valentine,* ill. by author, Scribner, 1954. Children in Pennsylvania Dutch country.

————: *The Egg Tree,* ill. by author, Scribner, 1950. Easter on a Pennsylvania Dutch farm.

Mirsky, Reba: *Seven Grandmothers,* ill. by W. T. Mars, Follett, 1955. Zulu family life.

————: *Thirty-one Brothers and Sisters,* ill. by W. T. Mars, Follett, 1952.

Morrow, Elizabeth: *The Painted Pig,* ill. by René d'Harnoncourt, Knopf, 1949. Simple little story of Mexican life, with bright illustrations.

O'Dell, Scott: *Island of the Blue Dolphins,* Houghton Mifflin, 1960. Somber honest story about California Indians on offshore islands.

Perkins, Lucy Fitch: *The Eskimo Twins,* Houghton Mifflin, 1914. Others in the series: *The Dutch Twins, The Chinese Twins, The Japanese Twins, The Norwegian Twins, The Filipino Twins, The Irish Twins.*

Politi, Leo: *The Butterflies Come,* ill. by author, Scribner, 1957. About children in California near Monterey.

————: *Juanita,* ill. by author, Scribner, 1948.

————: *Little Leo,* ill. by author, Scribner, 1951. About a little California Italian boy's trip to Italy.

————: *Moy Moy,* ill. by author, Scribner, 1960. Chinese children in America.

————: *Pedro, the Angel of Olvera Street,* ill. by author, Scribner, 1946. Mexican children in Los Angeles.

————: *Song of the Swallows,* ill. by author, Scribner, 1949. A child at San Juan Capistrano Mission.

Rankin, Louise: *Daughter of the Mountains,* ill. by Kurt Wiese, Viking, 1948. A child follows her dog from Tibet to Calcutta.

Reyher, Becky: *My Mother Is the Most Beautiful Woman in the World,* ill. by Ruth Gannett, Lothrop, 1945. Russian peasant life.

Rugh, Belle Dorman: *Crystal Mountain,* ill. by Ernest H. Shepard, Houghton Mifflin, 1955. About American family in Lebanon.

Sandburg, Carl: *Prairie-town Boy* (taken from *Always the Young Strangers*), ill. by Joe Krush, Harcourt, Brace & World, 1955.

Sandoz, Mari: *The Story Catcher,* ill. by Elsie J. McCorkell, Westminster Press, 1958.

Sauer, Julia L.: *The Light at Tern Rock,* ill. by Georges Schreiber, Viking, 1951. Boy and aunt act as substitute lighthouse keepers on rocky coast.

Sawyer, Ruth: *The Least One,* ill. by Leo Politi, Viking, 1941. About a Mexican boy and his donkey.

Sayers, Frances Clarke: *Blue Bonnets for Lucinda,* ill. by Helen Sewell, Viking, 1934. About a child in Texas.

————: *Tag-along Tooloo,* ill. by Helen Sewell, Viking, 1941.

Schaefer, Jack: *Old Ramon,* ill. by Harold West, Houghton Mifflin, 1960. Old shepherd and boy on plains.

Shannon, Monica: *Dobry,* ill. by Atanas Katchamakoff, Viking, 1934. About Hungarian peasant boy who wants to become a sculptor; Newbery Medal.

Shannon, Terry: *Little Wolf the Rain Dancer,* ill. by Charles Payzant, Whitman, 1954.

Simpson, Dorothy: *The Honest Dollar,* Lippincott, 1957. Fisherman's children on a Maine island.

Singh, Reginald Las, and Eloise Lownsbery: *Gift of the Forest,* ill. by Anne Vaughan, McKay, 1958. Village life in India; a boy adopts a tiger cub.

Sorensen, Virginia: *Plain Girl,* ill. by Charles Gier, Harcourt, Brace & World, 1955. Story of the Amish people.

Spyri, Johanna: *Heidi,* new ed., ill. by Agnes Tait, Lippincott, 1948.

Stuart, Jesse: *The Beatinest Boy,* ill. by Robert Henneberger, Whittlesey, 1953. Anecdotal piece about a Southern mountain boy.

Tarshis, Elizabeth K.: *The Village That Learned to Read,* ill. by Harold Haydon, Houghton Mifflin, 1941. Mexican village life.

Undset, Sigrid: *Happy Times in Norway,* trans. by Joran Birkeland, Knopf, 1961.

Van Stockum, Hilda: *Cottage at Bantry Bay,* ill. by author, Viking, 1938. Story of a family in Ireland, with sequel, *Pegeen.*

Waltrip, Lela and Rufus: *Quiet Boy,* ill. by Theresa Kalab Smith, Longmans, 1961. Arizona Indians today.

Weilerstein, Sadie Rose: *Ten and a Kid,* ill. by Janina Domanska, Double-day, 1961. About a Jewish family in Lithuania.

Wood, Esther: *Silk and Satin Lane,* ill. by Kurt Wiese, McKay, 1939. About Ching-ling, an orphan Chinese girl.

Wuorio, Eva Lis: *The Island of Fish in the Trees,* ill. by Edward Ardizzone, World, 1962. A day in Balearic Islands with two little sisters.

————: *The Land of Up and Down,* ill. by Edward Ardizzone, World, 1964. A girl collecting butterflies in Andorra.

Yashima, Taro (pseud. for Jun Iwamatsu): *Crow Boy,* ill. by author, Viking, 1955. Vividly illustrated story about a lonely little Japanese boy and his special understanding of birds.

————: *The Village Tree,* ill. by author, Viking, 1953. Boy's games in Japanese village.

Yashima, Taro and Mitsu: *Plenty to Watch,* Viking, 1954. Village life in Japan.

The Your Fair Land series, ed. by Erick Berry. Novels set in America's national parks. Examples: Vanya Oakes, *Island of Flame* (Hawaii National Park); Jack Steffan, *The Gift of Wilderness* (Grand Canyon National Park); Dale White, *Hold Back the Hunter* (Yellowstone).

Zolotow, Charlotte: *The Night When Mother Was Away,* ill. by Reisie Lonette, Lothrop, 1958.

Historical Fiction for Children

Aldis, Dorothy: *Lucky Year,* Rand McNally, 1951. An Indiana town's preparations for Jenny Lind's visit a century ago.

Altsheler, Joseph A.: *The Guns of Bull Run,* Appleton-Century-Crofts, 1914. Also *The Sword of Antietam, The Rock of Chickamauga,* etc.

Bacmeister, Rhoda W.: *Voices in the Night,* ill. by Ann Grifalconi, Bobbs-Merrill, 1965. The Underground Railroad in New England during the Civil War.

Ball, Zachary (pseud.): *North to Abilene,* Holiday, 1960. Orphan boy on cattle drive to Kansas from Texas.

Bennett, John: *Master Skylark,* ill. by Reginald Birch, Grosset & Dunlap, 1924. Story of a boy of Shakespeare's time.

Bothwell, Jean: *Dancing Princess,* Harcourt, Brace & World, 1965. Romantic story of sixteenth-century India.

Bowers, Gwendolyn: *The Lost Dragon of Wessex,* ill. by Charles Geer, Walck, 1957. A boy at the court of Alfred the Great.

Brink, Carol Ryrie: *Caddie Woodlawn,* ill. by Kate Seredy, Macmillan, 1935.

————: *Magical Melons: More Stories about Caddie Woodlawn,* ill. by Marguerite Davis, Macmillan, 1944.

Brown, Frances Williams: *Looking for Orlando,* Criterion, 1961. Antislavery sympathy in the North.

Buchan, John: *Salute to Adventurers,* Houghton Mifflin, 1930.

Buff, Mary: *The Apple and the Arrow,* ill. by Conrad Buff, Houghton Mifflin, 1951. Story about William Tell; richly illustrated.

Buff, Mary and Conrad: *Hah-Nee of the Cliff Dwellers,* ill. by Conrad Buff, Houghton Mifflin, 1956. A vividly illustrated story of life among the cliff dwellers of the thirteenth century.

Bulla, Clyde Robert: *Down the Mississippi,* ill. by Peter Burchard, Crowell, 1954. About a cook's helper on a log raft down the Mississippi.

————: *Riding the Pony Express,* ill. by Grace Paull, Crowell, 1949.

————: *The Secret Valley,* ill. by Grace Paull, Crowell, 1949. Gold-rush days.

————: *The Sword in the Tree,* ill. by Paul Galdone, Crowell, 1956. Days of King Arthur.

Bunce, William H.: *Dragon Prows Westward,* Harcourt, Brace & World, 1946. Erik the Viking's adventures in America.

Burchard, Peter: *Jed: The Story of a Yankee Soldier and a Southern Boy,* ill. by author, Coward-McCann, 1960.

Catton, Bruce: *Banners at Shenandoah,* Doubleday, 1955. Civil War.

Caudill, Rebecca: *Tree of Freedom,* ill. by Dorothy Bayley Morse, Viking, 1949. American Revolution.

Chute, Marchette: *The Innocent Wayfaring,* ill. by author, Dutton, 1955. A girl's and a poet's adventures in Chaucer's England.

————: *The Wonderful Winter,* ill. by Grace Golden, Dutton, 1954. Elizabethan times.

Coatsworth, Elizabeth: *Away Goes Sally,* ill. by Helen Sewell, Macmillan, 1934. Pioneers in Maine. Sequels: *Five Bushel Farm,* 1939, and *The Fair American,* 1940.

————: *Dancing Tom,* ill. by Grace Paull, Macmillan, 1944. A dancing pig with pioneer family on Mississippi flatboat.

————: *First Adventure,* ill. by Ralph Kay, Macmillan, 1950. A child of a *Mayflower* family gets lost and is cared for by Indians.

Coolidge, Olivia: *Men of Athens,* ill. by Milton Johnson, Houghton Mifflin, 1962. Short stories about Athens's Golden Age.

Dalgliesh Alice: *Adam and the Golden Cock*, ill. by Leonard Weisgard, Scribner, 1959. Story of the American Revolution.

————: *The Bears on Hemlock Mountain*, ill. by Hildegard Woodward, Macmillan, 1952. Well-told story of a pioneer boy's fears of the forest.

————: *The Courage of Sarah Noble*, ill. by Leonard Weisgard, Scribner, 1952. Pioneers in Connecticut of pre-Revolutionary days.

————: *The Thanksgiving Story*, ill. by Helen Sewell, Scribner, 1954.

De Angeli, Marguerite: *The Black Fox of Lorne*, ill. by author, Doubleday, 1956. Days of the Vikings in Scotland.

————: *The Door in the Wall*, ill. by author, Doubleday, 1949. Well-written tale about the crippled son of a thirteenth-century nobleman; Newbery Medal.

————: *Thee, Hannah!* ill. by author, Doubleday, 1949. About a Quaker girl of the mid-nineteenth century.

Doyle, Arthur Conan: *The White Company*, ill. by N. C. Wyeth, McKay, 1955.

Edmonds, Walter D.: *Cadmus Henry*, Dodd, Mead, 1949. About a Confederate observer in balloon in Union territory.

————: *The Matchlock Gun*, ill. by Paul Lantz, Dodd, Mead, 1941. Thrilling story of Indian frontier raids; for young readers; Newbery Medal.

————: *Rome Haul*, Modern Library, 1938.

————: *Tom Whipple*, ill. by Paul Lantz, Dodd, Mead, 1942. Story for older children about a boy's sailing before the mast to northern Europe in the early nineteenth century.

————: *Two Logs Crossing*, ill. by Tibor Gergely, Dodd, Mead, 1943.

————: *Wilderness Clearing*, ill. by John de Martelly, Dodd, Mead, 1945. Indian raids in backwoods of New York State during the American Revolution.

Falk, Elsa: *Winter Journey*, Follett, 1955. A boy's journey of many hardships into Minnesota Territory.

Falkner, J. Meade: *Moonfleet*, ill. by Fritz Kredel, Little, Brown, 1951. A boy with smugglers on English coast in the eighteenth century; a well-told tale.

Field, Rachel: *Calico Bush*, ill. by Allen Lewis, Macmillan, 1931. Story of a French girl's adventures with a pioneer family in Maine.

————: *Hitty: Her First Hundred Years*, ill. by Dorothy Lathrop, Macmillan, 1929. The nineteenth century through the travels of a doll.

Finger, Charles J.: *Courageous Companions*, ill. by James H. Daugherty, McKay, 1929.

Fisher, Aileen: *A Lantern in the Window*, Nelson, 1957. Story of the Underground Railroad.

Fleischman, Sid: *Mr. Mysterious & Company*, ill. by Eric von Schmidt,

Little, Brown, 1962. A family makes its way to a California ranch by giving magic shows on frontier.

Forbes, Esther: *Johnny Tremain,* ill. by Lynd Ward, Houghton Mifflin, 1943. Well-told tale of a silversmith's apprentice's adventures in the American Revolution; Newbery Medal.

Garland, Hamlin: *Boy Life on the Prairie,* ill. by Edward W. Deming, Ungar, 1959.

Gordon, Patricia: *Boy Jones,* Viking, 1943. Young chimney sweep's adventure in Buckingham Palace in Victoria's reign.

————: *Romany Luck,* ill. by Rafaello Busoni, Viking, 1946. Gypsies during Elizabeth I's reign.

Gray, Elizabeth Janet: *Adam of the Road,* ill. by Robert Lawson, Viking, 1942. Fine tale of a minstrel boy in the Middle Ages; Newbery Medal.

————: *Beppy Marlowe of Charles Town,* ill. by Loren Barton, Viking, 1936.

————: *I Will Adventure,* ill. by Corydon Bell, Viking, 1962.

Hall, Anna Gertrude: *Cyrus Holt and the Civil War,* ill. by Dorothy Bayley Morse, Viking, 1964.

Harnett, Cynthia: *Caxton's Challenge,* ill. by author, World, 1960. About an apprentice to printer Caxton in the fifteenth century.

————: *Nicholas and the Wool-pack,* ill. by author, Putnam, 1953. A mystery with medieval setting.

————: *Stars of Fortune,* ill. by author, Putnam, 1956. An adventure tale of Elizabethan England.

Harris, Christie: *West with the White Chiefs,* ill. by Walter Ferro, Atheneum, 1965. Frontier adventure.

Havighurst, Walter and Marion: *High Prairie,* Holt, 1944. A Norwegian family's journey to Minnesota and then to the Dakota Territory.

————: *Song of the Pines,* Holt, 1949. A Norwegian boy in Wisconsin lumbering.

Hawes, Charles B.: *Dark Frigate,* Little, Brown, 1924. Sea adventure during time of the Stuarts; Newbery Medal.

————: *The Mutineers; A Tale of Old Days at Sea,* ill. by Anton Otto Fischer, Little, Brown, 1919. Violent adventures, melodrama.

Hawthorne, Hildegarde: *Lone Rider,* ill. by R. H. Rogers, Longmans, 1935. Pony-express adventure.

Henty, G. A.: *With Clive in India,* Latimer House, 1953. Slightly abridged edition of one story from Henty's long series of boys' historical-adventure tales.

Hodges, Cyril Walter: *Columbus Sails,* ill. by author, Coward-McCann, 1950.

————: *The Namesake*, ill. by author, Coward-McCann, 1964. Concerning King Alfred and the Danish invasions.

Hoff, Carol: *Johnny Texas*, Wilcox, 1950. A German boy in early Texas.

Holling, Holling C.: *Tree in the Trail*, ill. by author, Houghton Mifflin, 1942. The events that occurred around a cottonwood tree on the Santa Fe trail; much factual information.

Jones, Ruth Fosdick: *Boy of the Pyramids: A Mystery of Ancient Egypt*, ill. by Dorothy Bayley Morse, Random House, 1952. Capture of a tomb thief.

Jones, Weyman: *The Talking Leaf*, ill. by Harper Johnson, Dial Press, 1965. Life among the Cherokees.

Judson, Clara Ingram: *They Came from France*, Houghton Mifflin, 1943. Early New Orleans.

Kelly, Eric P.: *The Blacksmith of Vilno*, ill. by Angela Pruszynska, Macmillan 1930. Adventures in Poland in the early nineteenth century.

————: *The Trumpeter of Krakow*, ill. by Angela Pruszynska, Macmillan, 1928. Well-told tale of medieval Poland; Newbery Medal.

Kent, Louise Andrews: *He Went with Magellan*, ill. by Paul Quinn, Houghton Mifflin, 1943. Also in series: books about boys sailing with Vasco da Gama and Marco Polo.

Latham, Jean: *This Dear-bought Land*, ill. by Jacob Landau, Harper & Row, 1957. Settlement of Jamestown.

Lawrence, Isabelle: *Niko, Sculptor's Apprentice*, ill. by Arthur Marokvia, Viking, 1956. About an Athenian boy of the fifth century B.C.

Lawson, Robert: *Ben and Me*, ill. by author, Little, Brown, 1939. Merry picture tale of Ben Franklin and his helpful mouse companion.

————: *Mr. Revere and I*, ill. by author, Little, Brown, 1953. As told by Paul Revere's horse.

————: *They Were Strong and Good*, ill. by author, Viking, 1940. Earnest account of American pioneers; Newbery Award.

Lenski, Lois: *Indian Captive: The Story of Mary Jamison*, ill. by author, Lippincott, 1941. About a girl captured by Indians in the eighteenth century.

Lownsbery, Eloise: *A Camel for a Throne*, ill. by Elizabeth Tyler Wolcott, Houghton Mifflin, 1941. A tale of ancient Egypt.

————: *The Boy Knight of Reims*, ill. by Elizabeth Tyler Wolcott, Houghton Miffin, 1927: Building the Cathedral of Reims.

Magoon, Marian Austin: *Little Dusty Foot*, ill. by Christine Price, Longmans, 1948. Story of a boy who traveled with merchants in the time of Charlemagne.

Malkus, Alida Simms: *Eastward Sweeps the Current*, ill. by Dan Sweeney, Winston, 1937. Oriental navigators coming to shores of the Americas in the time of the Incas.

Mason, Miriam: *Caroline and Her Kettle Named Maud,* ill. by Kathleen Voute, Macmillan, 1951. A story of pioneer life in the midwest.

————: *Susannah, the Pioneer Cow,* ill. by Maud and Miska Petersham, Macmillan, 1941. Another story of pioneer life.

McGraw, Eloise Jarvis: *The Golden Goblet,* Coward-McCann, 1961. An apprentice in ancient Egypt captures tomb robbers.

————: *Mara: Daughter of the Nile,* Coward-McCann, 1953.

McMeekin, Isabel McLennan: *Journey Cake,* ill. by Nicholas Panesis, Messner, 1942. Pioneers in Kentucky. Sequel, *Juba's New Moon.*

Meader, Stephen W.: *Boy with a Pack,* ill. by Edward Shenton, Harcourt, Brace, 1939. A young Yankee peddler in the early nineteenth century.

————: *The Fish Hawk's Nest,* ill. by Edward Shenton, Harcourt, Brace & World, 1952. Smugglers on the New Jersey coast in the early nineteenth century.

————: *River of the Wolves,* ill. by Edward Shenton, Harcourt, Brace & World, 1948. A boy in the French-Indian wars.

————: *Who Rides in the Dark?* ill. by James MacDonald, Harcourt, Brace, 1937. Mystery at a stagecoach inn in New Hampshire.

Meadowcroft, Enid: *By Secret Railway,* ill. by Henry C. Pitz, Crowell, 1948.

Meigs, Cornelia: *The Covered Bridge,* ill. by Marguerite de Angeli, Macmillan, 1936. A tale, like the following four, about pioneer life.

————: *Master Simon's Garden,* new ed., ill. by John Rae, Macmillan, 1929. Three generations, from early colonial village to end of American Revolution.

————: *Swift Rivers,* Little, Brown, 1932.

————: *The Willow Whistle,* ill. by E. Boyd Smith, Macmillan, 1931.

————: *Wind in the Chimney,* ill. by Louise Mansfield, Macmillan, 1934.

Morrison, Lucile: *The Lost Queen of Egypt,* ill. by Franz Geritz and Winifred Brunton, Lippincott, 1937.

Oliver, Jane (pseud.): *Faraway Princess,* ill. by Jane Paton, St. Martin's, 1962. A princess's flight to Scotland after the Norman Conquest.

Payne, Joan Balfour: *General Billycock's Pigs,* Hastings House, 1961. Story of post-American Revolutionary days in Tennessee.

Pyle, Howard: *Men of Iron,* ill. by author, Harper, 1891. Tale of medieval knighthood.

————: *Otto of the Silver Hand,* ill. by author, Scribner, 1888.

Ray, Mary: *The Voice of Apollo,* ill. by Enrico Arno, Ariel Books, 1965. Two boys at Delphi in ancient Greece.

Robertson, Keith: *The Pilgrim Goose,* ill. by Erick B. Berry, Viking, 1956. Pioneer life in Connecticut told through the account of geese brought over on the Mayflower.

Seredy, Kate: *The White Stag*, ill. by author, Viking, 1937. Based on Hungarian legendry; Newbery Medal.

Skinner, Constance Lindsay: *Silent Scot, Frontier Scout*, Macmillan, 1925. Scouts in Tennessee mountains during the American Revolution.

Snedeker, Caroline Dale: *Beckoning Road*, ill. by M. De V. Lee, Doubleday, 1929. A Quaker girl, Dencey, at Robert Owen's utopian colony, New Harmony, in Indiana.

————: *Downright Dencey*, ill. by M. V. Barney, Doubleday, 1927. About a Quaker girl of Nantucket.

————: *The Forgotten Daughter*, ill. by Dorothy Lathrop, Doubleday, 1933. Ancient Rome.

————: *Theras and His Town*, ill. by Dimitris Davis, Doubleday, 1961. Life of a boy in Sparta, contrasting with Athenian life.

————: *A Triumph for Flavius*, ill. by Cedric Rogers, Lothrop, 1955. Early Roman Christian times.

————: *The White Isle*, ill. by Fritz Kredel, Doubleday, 1940. A story of Roman Britain.

Speare, Elizabeth George: *Calico Captive*, ill. by W. T. Mars, Houghton Mifflin, 1957. Well-written story of a family carried off into slavery in the French-Indian wars.

————: *The Witch of Blackbird Pond*, Houghton Mifflin, 1958. A girl comes to Puritan Connecticut in the late seventeenth century and almost becomes a victim of witchcraft hysteria.

Steele, William O.: *The Buffalo Knife*, ill. by Paul Galdone, Harcourt, Brace & World, 1952.

————: *Far Frontier*, ill. by Paul Galdone, Harcourt, Brace & World, 1959.

————: *The Lone Hunt*, ill. by Paul Galdone, Harcourt, Brace & World, 1956.

————: *Wilderness Journey*, ill. by Paul Galdone, Harcourt, Brace & World, 1953.

————: *Winter Danger*, ill. by Paul Galdone, Harcourt, Brace & World, 1954.

Stevens, Mary Ellen, and E. B. Sayles: *Little Cloud and the Great Plains Hunters 15,000 Years Ago*, ill. by Barton Wright, Reilly & Lee, 1962.

Stevenson, Robert Louis: *The Black Arrow: A Tale of the Two Roses*, ill. by N. C. Wyeth, Scribner, 1955.

————: *Kidnapped*, ill. by N. C. Wyeth, Scribner, 1941.

Sutcliff, Rosemary: *Dawn Wind*, ill. by Charles Keeping, Walck, 1962. England in the sixth century; remarkable writing.

————: *The Eagle of the Ninth*, ill. by C. Walter Hodges, Walck, 1954. A lost Roman legion in Britain in the second century.

————: *The Mark of the Horse Lord*, Walck, 1965. Scotland in the second century.

————: *The Outcast*, ill. by Richard Kennedy, Walck, 1955. About an outcast from both Britons and Romans.

————: *The Shield Ring*, ill. by C. Walter Hodges, Walck, 1957. Eleventh-century England during the Norman invasion; one of Sutcliff's best.

————: *The Silver Branch*, Walck, 1958. Struggle among Romans for control of Roman Britain.

————: *Warrior Scarlet*, ill. by Charles Keeping, Walck, 1958. England during the Bronze Age.

Trease, Geoffrey: *Message to Hadrian*, Vanguard, 1955. Rich historical fiction of ancient Rome and Britain.

Treece, Henry: *Viking's Dawn*, ill. by Christine Price, Criterion, 1956. Sea voyages of a Viking in the eighth century. Followed by *The Road to Miklagard*, 1957, and *Viking's Sunset*, 1961.

Trevino, Elizabeth de: *I, Juan de Pareja*, Farrar, Straus & Cudahy, 1965. Vivid picture of Spain in time of Velasquez; centered on his slave.

Varble, Rachel M.: *Pepys' Boy*, ill. by Kurt Werth, Doubleday, 1955.

Weisgard, Leonard: *Mr. Peaceable Paints*, ill. by author, Scribner, 1956. About a sign painter in a village in colonial New England; vivid pictures of colonial life.

Wibberley, Leonard: *John Treegate's Musket*, Farrar, Straus & Cudahy, 1959. One of four novels about the Treegates in Revolutionary days.

————: *Kevin O'Connor and the Light Brigade*, Ariel Books, 1957. An Irish boy's adventures at home in rebellious Ireland and then in the Crimea.

————: *The King's Beard*, ill. by Christine Price, Ariel Books, 1952. English boy's experiences in the English-Spanish struggle in the sixteenth century.

Wilder, Laura Ingalls: *Little House in the Big Woods*, ill. by Helen Sewell, Harper, 1932. First of a series on pioneer life in the Middle West; others include *Little House on the Prairie*, 1935; *On the Banks of Plum Creek*, 1937; *By the Shores of Silver Lake*, 1939; *Little Town on the Prairie*, 1941; *The Long Winter*, 1940; and *Happy Golden Years*, 1943.

Wilson, Hazel: *His Indian Brother*, ill. by Robert Henneberger, Abingdon, 1955.

Winterfeld, Henry: *Detectives in Togas*, trans. by Richard and Clara Winston, ill. by Charlotte Kleinert, Harcourt, Brace & World, 1956.

CHAPTER 8

**SENSE
AND
SENSIBILITY
IN
CHILDREN'S
LITERATURE:**
Part 2.
Sensibility

A large body of children's literature—that which I might here nickname, without any intention of disparagement, "literature of the supermarket"— is related to outer, real physical and social experiences and owes to that linkage a certain measure of its attractiveness. But as the analogy to the supermarket rather than to just any market may suggest, in literature the experience carries with it some specialness that makes it super, wonderful, worthy of wonder. The original experience itself, the facts, may occasionally be enough to make the wonder, but generally not; more often the subject must be selected, revised, arranged, and set forth in a way that creates, preserves, and heightens its wonderfulness. From *Mr. Small, The Little Engine That Could,* and the *Noisy Books* to *Treasure Island, The Moffats,* Fred Gipson's *Old Yeller,* and Rosemary Sutcliff's *The Shield Ring,* the realistic literature rises out of, and owes a considerable part of its importance to, reality; but it is *literature,* not reality. It is the real thing with the specialness added.

But this has never been super enough to entirely satisfy children. They want from their reading and listening something more—something very, very special and unusual. They want that which is so incredible as to be wonderful, that which is worthy of remark because of its unexpectedness, its distance from the norms. These norms, of course, vary according to the actual experience and education of the children, but always children have insisted, with good sense, that some of their reading and listening depart from the norms of expectable experience. Hence, fantasy—and its importance as a part of children's literature.

Children's literary fantasy, as I am using the term here, is the literature of *outright invention.* In this literature wonder is owing not to the exciting knowledge that the thing told about could exist but to the equally exciting awareness that it could *not* exist, that it is an invention, something new. The incredibility of this literature may lie in its unbelievable protagonists and in the unbelievable things they do and say or in the unbelievable world in which they act so incredibly or in all of these together. This is the literary world of "superman."

Fantasy literature, though the creation of something hitherto not a part of human experience, does have significance to human beings—in the case of the literature with which we are dealing, young human beings. In this respect, then, it is not altogether cut off from actual human experience, things seen, done, heard, and touched. It is strange, but also it in some way says something to one. To label fantasy "escape literature" is to misunderstand it, to miss altogether the sources of its continuing, many-formed appeal, if by "escape" one means just *going away from;* if one means going from one kind of mental environment into another, then no damage is done, perhaps. Authors and readers, adults and children, escape into fantastic inventions. But there would be no impulsion toward escaping into these inventions, these "thought-ups," if they did not have *meaning* for human beings. A common connotation of "escape" in literaure is that of a free, open landscape with very little in it or going on in it. This is not true of fantasy in literature; the landscape is full of things—created, invented things. They have a very real existence.

What is Fantasy and What Is Not?

What kinds of invention populate the fantasy world of children's literature?

Right off, let us distinguish between fundamental, thoroughgoing fantasy in children's literature—inventions that appeal because of their fantasy— and that literature in which certain odd things happen not so much for their own interest as for the purposes of getting a story told, often a story with highly realistic appeal. Inanimate objects and animals may be gifted with human speech—the animals may even wear human garments—in a story or poem which in other respects is highly unfantastic and whose first appeal lies in the sense of its physical or psychological realities; in a story or poem of this kind the talking does not itself excite wonder but is mainly a device for developing a situation, creating a character. That Puss in *Puss in Boots* should talk is accepted without question or wonder by the child as one of the conditions of his getting to know the events of the story, a story that has in it little of the extraordinary; its tone is matter-of-fact, familiar, social. Black Beauty talks, and at considerable length, but certainly the spirit of fantastic invention is remote from Anna Sewell's tale of Black Beauty's many ordeals in nineteenth-century England. The animals in Lawson's *Rabbit Hill* and *The Tough Winter* converse like people, but by and large theirs is a real animal world, and the speech and other human habits come to be taken by the reader as incidental. So with Beatrix Potter's stories; speaking, dressing, and acting like people, her little creatures forego any aura of strangeness and become quite convincing people with human problems and inclinations. And so with Hitty, Miss Flora Mc-Flimsey, and other dolls who are maneuvered through situations which suggest the real world rather than any unreal existence. And so with *The Little House,* in which the personification is really a device to get the reader into a real situation—little house in urban squeeze. In these and many other children's books the characters' possession of untypical attributes is primarily a storytelling means, not an end or an important appeal, and does not in any way detract from the story's suggestion of the possible.

The tall tale, however, in which objects like chairs, hoes, rocks, and fish suddenly and disconcertingly begin talking back to human beings, makes the gift of speech a thing of wonder, an esoteric skill, that is, does not simply use it as a means for conveying information. In the context of Potter's story, Peter Rabbit's wearing a little boy's clothing is not strange at all, but seems the most normal thing in that world, which is really a world not of rabbits, but of little boys; but in *Alice's Adventures in Wonderland* the white rabbit's possessing a watch and other articles normally worn by human beings *is* offered as upsettingly strange, at least to Alice, and is consistent with all the topsy-turvy, magical things Alice afterward encounters. In the nursery rhyme the fork and spoon cavorting on a moonlit landscape are fantastic, whereas in Virginia Burton's *The Little House* the house's seeming to smile as it is moved from the city slum to the countryside does not amaze, for it is simply a way of underlining the author's point; it is primarily a device. In many contemporary stories machines, bridges, and cars are animated, sometimes given names and even dialogue, merely in order to make clear the information the author wants to convey about them.

The real spirit of fantasy in children's literature, then, is something other than an expedient transfer of speech, clothing, etc. It comes into being through *invention,* the creating of people, animals, objects, and conditions that *are not so* and much of whose interest for the reader rests in the wonderful fact that they are not so. The world of fantasy is a world we create, imagine, make up—a world that never was until we summoned it into being, but then continues to exist as a mental reality. It may suggest the normal world of experience, by analogy reminding us of ourselves, what we do, and what we know, but its essence is its newness, its being an invention, and its deepest, most lasting power is its capacity for astonishing, amazing, exciting.

Different individuals experience this world of fantasy at different levels of awareness and acceptance. For some a fantastic account may be an exciting game, a made-up situation in which one says to himself, "Wouldn't it be fun if . . . ?" Other individuals, or the same ones at other times, may come close to accepting the tale as a description of the actual, at least temporarily. By some children, though not many and not often, the story may be taken wholly and completely as a literal report of actualities. For others, the tale itself may not seem to be real but may analogically suggest something that could be. They would think of it in "like this" terms; the troll story might not convince them that there are real trolls, but it might leave them with a stronger sense that all is not sweetness and light, that evilness may lurk close by. And many children may have mixed feelings about the realness of the story and may move from one feeling to another. Also, the teller of the tale may see it on one level of realness, his readers on another; James Barrie conceived Peter Pan out of a belief, not in his literal existence, but in the reality of the human longing for eternal childhood, whereas his child readers may range from outright rejection of Peter Pan to an acceptance of him as fact. And the storyteller, too, may be uncertain at just what level he is telling the story; the traditional Irish spinner of stories about the fairies tells them, like Ella Young, in a "well, yes and no" way.

But these differences and shiftings in the acceptance of fantasy as reality do not detract from the most important effect of literary fantasy: that it surprises and bemuses by its farness from the ranges of normal. human experience, the expected and expectable. Adults today often waste time and thought by getting themselves into a blind argument about the relation of fantasy to children's knowledge and sense of reality; this main effect of fantasy can come about whether or not the child accepts it as a game, as literal truth, as concrete illustration of a general truth, or as all. The river of diamonds, the bear-man, the magical phrase, the one-eyed giant, the fairies' ring, Maurice Sendak's big-toothed, grinning "wild things," the flying elephant—these inventions engender a commotion of the imagination, a heightened sensibility, a stirred state of mind, which has no necessary connection with the kind of acceptance we might call believing. This commotion is not altogether unlike the excitement stirred by the child's discovery that an elevator carries him to the tenth floor or that the zoo monkeys swing by their tails and eat peanuts, for this commotion is essentially *a sense of wonder*, and as we have seen, reality can be a source of wonder too. But the wonder we are discussing now has a different source: it is created not by observation of the real and its transformation into something special, but by the creating, the inventing, of a new kind of experience.

A Variety of Inventions

In this invented world—whether it be created in ancient myths, folktales, tall tales, medieval romances, modern wonder tales, fairy poems, or ghost stories—the ordinary laws and procedures of life as we know them are suspended. Thus, in children's fantasy the earth has in it holes—great or small, winding or slantwise or straight down—by means of which men can go into the earth's core. In the Greek myths Orpheus sought Eurydice in the underworld, and Persephone returned to her mother Demeter there.

The little men of Celtic folklore emerge from holes in the earth and reenter them, sometimes followed down by curious human beings; in somewhat the same spirit the contemporary author Tolkien has Bilbo, his brave little Hobbit, seek hidden treasure in tunnels and lake-filled caves deep in the earth, and the miner and his son Curdie, central characters of George MacDonald's *The Princess and the Goblin* and *The Princess and Curdie*, are tunnelers. The road to Alice's Wonderland is a hole in the ground. The deep probe beneath the earth's surface is the physical and psychological crux of Jules Verne's *A Journey to the Center of the Earth* and his *The Mysterious Island.*

Sometimes the descent is into the depths of the ocean, as in the legends and folktales about the sea-gods (Neptune, the king of the sea Sadko, whose dancing made the ocean storms) and in the innumerable stories and poems about mermaids (Andersen's *The Mermaid*, Kingsley's *Water-babies*, Matthew Arnold's "The Forsaken Merman"). Scientific fiction has gone to sea bottom with such tales as Verne's *20,000 Leagues under the Sea.* And the upper reaches of the air have always fostered fantasies, such as the Greek myths of Icarus and Daedalus (Daedalus and his son Icarus's flight on wings of feathers and wax, Icarus's prideful flight too near the sun, and his fall into the sea when the wings melted) and of the fatal attempt of the mortal Phaeton to drive the chariot of his father the sun; the innumerable folktales about flying people and objects (Sindbad and the giant bird, the flying carpet, the princess's search for her bewitched husband on the back of the north wind); modern fantasies like George MacDonald's *At the Back of the North Wind*, William Pène du Bois's *Twenty-one Balloons*, Betty Babcock's *The Expandable Pig* (flight on a balloon-like pig), and Selma Lagerlöf's *The Wonderful Adventures of Nils* (flight on a gander over Sweden); the tremendous amount of scientific fiction set in space, from Jules Verne's *From the Earth to the Moon* and H. G. Wells's *The First Men in the Moon* to the comic books like *Superman;* and the comic Miss Pickerell's Martian adventures and such flights of scientific fancy as Robert Heinlein's *Have Space Suit—Will Travel* and *Rocket Ship Galileo*, Eleanor Cameron's *Stowaway to the Mushroom Planet* and *The Wonderful Flight to the Mushroom Planet*, and Jay Williams and Raymond Abrashkin's *Danny Dunn and the Anti-gravity Paint*. Of course, with each further conquest of earth, sea, or space, a little of the potentiality of these regions as a source of fantasy has been impaired; these domains, with their atomic submarines, space missiles, and scientific earth probes, are becoming increasingly sources of that different wonder generated by the knowable. Yet even though children today see planes in the air above them, in movies, and on television, and hear and see accounts of flights into outer space, they still find Daedalus's flight on waxen wings or Verne's heroes' flight in a balloon strange, too.

In regions of fantasy, be they in air, earth, or sea or on the earth's surface, things have taken on new characteristics. There are hills of glass. Houses are made of gingerbread or emeralds or, like the snow queen's, of ice; or, like the Russian witch Baba Yaga's, they walk on chicken legs. Cities like Oz and everything in them may be all of one color. Geese lay golden eggs; the flying ram that carried Phryxus to safety had a fleece of gold, which became the object of Jason's great adventure. The zoo in Dr. Seuss's *If I Ran the Zoo* and the ocean in his *McElligot's Pool* are filled with animals of fantastic shape, color, and general demeanor. Lewis Carroll's flamingos can be used as croquet mallets; his caterpillar smokes a hookah; and a Cheshire cat smiles in a tree. Bucking broncos bounce to the moon and back. Cows are purple. Creatures half human and half fish inhabit the sea. Mike Mulligan's steam shovel digs itself into a hole in the earth and becomes a boiler for the new city hall.

Transformations

This fantasy world and the things in it are capable of all sorts of sudden transformation, and thus they give the reader an excitement he does not obtain from his daily living, where, although everything constantly changes, it often seems not to and, when it does change, does so only slowly for the most part. Animals change into men, men into animals. Myth and folklore are crowded with creatures capable of such transformation—the frog prince of the Grimm tale, Cinderella's horses, the polar bear of *East of the Sun, West of the Moon* who by night is a handsome prince, the sailors changed by Bacchus into dolphins, the girl Arachne whose pride in her weaving causes Athena to change her into a spider, the beast transformed in *Beauty and the Beast*, the ogre who in *Puss in Boots* takes the form of a mouse and is consequently gobbled up, Jupiter (a very human god) who turns into bull, swan, etc., and Odysseus's sailors transformed by Circe into swine. In modern fantasy Andersen tells in *The Marsh King's Daughter* of the marsh princess who changed back and forth between mean girl and kind, gentle frog; in Carroll's *Alice's Adventures in Wonderland* the duchess's baby turns into a pig; in William Lipkind and Nicolas Mordvinoff's *Chaga* the proud elephant Chaga eats grass that makes him very small; Alf Proysen's main character in *Little Old Mrs. Pepperpot* can quickly shrink in size; in Oliver Butterworth's *The Enormous Egg* an ordinary hen lays a dinosaur egg.

In this fantasy world physical objects can become other things, and persons can become things: the physical world is constantly shifting, changing. Thus palaces become hovels, and hovels suddenly change into palaces; Cinderella's pumpkin becomes her coach and as suddenly is transformed back into pumpkin. In Ruskin's *The King of the Golden River* a jug melts into the king of the golden river. Tamlane in the fairy tale is changed by fairy spells successively into ice, fire, adder, snake, dove, swan, red-hot iron, and man. Myth and folktale are full of such interchanges—Niobe becoming a stone fountain in her grief for her lost children, Clytie in her adoration of the sun turning into a sunflower, the loving old couple Baucis and Philemon being changed into neighboring oak and linden, the dragon's teeth being sown by Jason and springing up behind him as armies, the turning of men to stone by a glance at the Medusa head, the beautiful Pygmalion emerging from the sculptor's carved stone, the phoenix arising from its own ashes, Midas's possessions all changing into gold.

And in a world of such easy change things can suddenly come out of nothing at all or vanish into nothingness. Rumpelstiltskin and many another evil "thing" disappear suddenly and totally at the saying of the right word or the arrival of an enemy of evil; in Julia Sauer's *Fog Magic* the little girl and the reader come to know that the old town on the Nova Scotia coast is insubstantial, coming and going with fog and human dreams; and in Philippa Pearce's *Tom's Midnight Garden* Tom, at the stroke of thirteen on the grandfather's clock discovers a new playmate, Hatty, while the *real* Hatty, now an old lady, dreams of the past.

To this element of transformation, to this changing and constant immanence of change, fantasy literature owes much of its excitement. The fact that change is a basic fact of our daily existence and yet is often almost unnoticeable and seldom dramatic there means that when it happens swiftly and violently it seems a strange and wonderful thing. There is little fantastic literature—from the ancient myths to de La Mare and P. L. Travers—which is not permeated by the expectation of sudden and complete metamorphosis (Ovid's collection of myths he aptly called *Metamorphoses*).

Magic in Fantasy

In this changeful world of fantasy a major power—not the only causal agent, but certainly one operative enough to be taken for granted as an integral part of it—is magic. This is a power that persons, animals, objects, places, and even words or numbers can possess, by means of which they can change things, suspend the normal trend of events, without waiting for nature to take its course—that is, without operating within the normal rules and patterns. Through the power of magic certain potions can kill or cure, put to sleep or awaken; magical waters can restore youth, in some cases life; evil apples will kill or transform one into a hideous creature. Through this magical power animals, chairs, and tables will speak, and by its means people can speak the language of animals; magical tablecloths, like the one in the folktale *Little One-eye, Two-eyes, and Three-eyes,* produce food; possessing this power, carpets can make you airborne, mirrors will reveal the past and the future, and wands will put you to sleep or awaken you or change your appearance. Magical shirts thrown over the eleven swans in Andersen's *The Wild Swans* turn them back into handsome princes. Fiddles, whistles, and other instruments can charm animals into compliance or drive them mad; the faery flag of Dunvegan Castle three times protected the MacLeod clan when waved in crises but brought their downfall when a MacLeod waved it sceptically to disprove its magic. Magic was the power in Thor's hammer, belt, and iron gloves, in the Norse Idun's apples of youth, in the wonderstone of the little monkey Nod in de la Mare's *Three Royal Monkeys,* in Arthur's sword Excalibur and Odin's sword Branstock, in Aladdin's lamp; half magic was the power in a coin that made it possible for the children in Edward Eager's *Half Magic* to get half of any wish they made.

Magic can be a power held over other beings by certain creatures— fairies, witches, devils. Sometimes this power is inherent in a place, such as a mountain, wood, stream, palace, or country, so that when one is there he is not his own master but is in the power of the spirit of the place; within the fairy ring, one is in the fairies' power; caught up in the enchantment of the undersea palace, Urashima Taro in the Japanese folktale thought that his three hundred years' stay there had been only three years. Sometimes one has the magical power through contact with certain elements; Antaeus was unconquerable so long as he could touch the earth, a secret discovered to Antaeus's sorrow by Hercules. Particular words or phrases—charms—make brooms sweep, as in the folktale *The Sorcerer's Apprentice,* have the power to open doors, bridge rivers, paralyze enemies, or even kill or restore to life; singing such as that of the Rhine maidens or particular songs such as the magic song Medea sang to the dragon guarding the golden fleece can cast a spell over men or beasts and make them powerless.

Children's literature contains thousands of persons, objects, places, words, and songs endowed with these magical powers of control, and innumerable instances of their use. They are more common and important in the old inherited part of children's literature—the ancient myths, legends, and folktales—than in today's fantasy, but fantasy characters like Alice continue to drink potions that change their height; or, like the children in Eager's *Half Magic,* they wish themselves back in time; or, like the witch in Patricia Gordon's *The Witch of Scrapfaggot Green,* they play tricks on modern men; or, like the queen of Narnia in C. S. Lewis's fantasies, they hold other creatures under magic spells. By wearing the magical March wind's hat, the boy in Inez Rice's *The March Wind* became a soldier, cowboy, judge, and entertainer; the rabbit in Lawson's *Robbut* got from a goblin apothecary a tail-growing potion that succeeded all too well.

Man and Superman

The inventors of these fantastic regions of abnormal topography, sudden change, and magical powers have often introduced real people and animals—that is, probable creatures—into these fantastic regions; in the folktales cloddish peasants and sharp-eyed merchants move among fairies and elves and through enchanted forests, and Carroll's Alice and, in *Oz,* Baum's Dorothy are recognizable enough little late-nineteenth-century girls in the midst of wild inventions. Indeed, it would be very difficult to find any fantasy in which all of the protagonists were fantastic inventions; no matter where we look, be it in European, Oriental, or African folktale, in Greek, Nordic, or American Indian myth and legend, or in Andersen's or Baum's or other modern fantasy, the human and other species wander in their ordinariness through the extraordinary. One might even get the feeling that the good storyteller, the really imaginative inventor, is aware, subconsciously if not consciously, that the presence of the more ordinary wonders of actual experience can heighten the wonderfulness of utter invention, of fantasy. The familiar town on the shore underlines the foreignness of the forsaken merman and his little family; the humanness of the two sisters in Christina Rossetti's *Goblin Market* makes their goblin market in the glen even more of a threat to common sense, even to life; all the rich barnyard detail that precedes our introduction to the wonderful spider of *Charlotte's Web* may make even more startling her ability to write messages. Be this as it may, the great mass of fantastic literature has shown a decided disinclination to expel the human species and its works from its fantastic countries.

But at the same time the makers of fantastic tales and poems have created a diverse population of beings endowed with characteristics—including the possession of magical powers—not encountered among ordinary men and animals.

Some of these characters are essentially human but possess one or more superhuman qualities, or normal abilities to a superhuman degree. They are ordinary human beings in all but one or two respects. Their special gift may be some variety of magic; this may reside in a personal possession, like a stone or memorized phrase or cloak or shoes or loaf of bread, or it may be a generalized magical power, like that of the fairies' Queen Mab, a witch, or Merlin. The superhuman power may be great physical strength, like that of Hercules, of supermen like Mike Fink and John Henry, of the English folk heroine Mollie Whuppie (a killer of giants), or in our own time, of Astrid Lindgren's powerful little girl Pippi Longstocking. It may be almost incredible courage, a quality found in the heroes of myth and legend—Jason, Perseus, Achilles, Beowulf, Siegfried, Roland, King Arthur and his Knights of the Round Table, the Cid. These heroes fight against fantastic odds, and even where they fail to overcome their enemies (as they infrequently do), their daring lends a superhuman splendor to the tale. The fantasy figure, in other respects not far beyond other men, may be endowed with a special degree and kind of wisdom, like the shrewd Ulysses, the wise men in many a folktale, Merlin, and Sherlock Holmes of the sharp eye and unfailing logic. Heroes may have a special ability to communicate with other species, like Doctor Dolittle, Marie Ets's Mr. T. W. Anthony Woo, Azor of Maude Crowley's *Azor and the Haddock* and *Azor and the Blue-eyed Cow,* and the farm children in Marcel Aymé's *The Wonderful Farm.* Often the beauty of a hero or heroine contributes to the tale's air of wonder; in folktales the usual hero, at least after he reveals himself, is an extremely handsome prince, and the heroine "the most beautiful princess in the world''; sometimes, as with Rapunzel, the heroine's hair is incredibly long, or, as with Cinderella, her feet are very delicate and tiny, or, as with Snow White, her complexion is astonishingly fair.

Children's literature is thickly populated with these beings essentially human but *superhumanly* endowed with one or two human qualities—physical strength, wisdom, intellect, courage, beauty, knowledge—and these creatures are responsible for much of the feeling of superhuman perfection that pervades the literature of fantasy, and at the same time for something of the sense of human significance that holds its own, too, in that literature. The Robin Hoods and William Tells never miss a shot with their arrows; the Galahads take on all comers, never flinch at the most fearsome peril; the beauty of the princesses admits of not the slightest flaw; the wise men are masters of all lore, can answer all questions. Their endowments are all human endowments, but possessed beyond all human expectation; these creatures are fantasies of perfection. Thus they bring together human experience and human dream, fact and fancy.

New Creatures

But the literature of fantasy would be much less wonderful than it is if it restricted itself to exaggeration and the glorifying and idealizing of experience, if the human imagination did not invent altogether *new* creatures—nonhuman, not a part of our human experience. Fortunately these, in tremendous variety, crowd the fantasies of children's literature and are responsible for much of their appeal.

There are the inventions of fantastically small or large creatures: tiny perfect human beings like Tom Thumb, and Andersen's Thumbelina, and Isun Bashi the One-inch Lad of the Japanese folktale, and giants, sometimes fiendish and full of hatred for mankind like the giant Jack killed and Thurber's Hunder in *The Great Quillow,* sometimes genial and benevolent, like Louis Slobodkin's giant in *The Amiable Giant* and the friendly giant seven stories tall in William Pène du Bois's *The Giant.* There are many sorts of malevolent figures, embodiments of evil who threaten men's bodies and souls—witches, from Circe through the conventional Halloween witch on broomstick to C. S. Lewis' white witch, devils and demons, many of them capable of assuming disarmingly pleasant forms, and trolls. There are mermaids and mermen. There are the wandering spirits of dead men—bogles, Flying Dutchmen, headless horsemen. And of special importance in children's literature are the legions of the great twilight kingdom of fairyland, whose main characteristic is that whatever they be—fairies, dwarfs, elves, brownies, leprechauns, gnomes, goblins, water nixies, kelpies, satyrs, fauns, nymphs, naiads—they somehow cannot survive human invasion and domination. They find it difficult to live in the light of day, and their normal habitats are groves, dark glens, caverns, and thick grass, into which they may bring their own uncanny lights. Some of them, many elves, for instance, are unfriendly to the human race; others, like most fairies, are well inclined toward human beings and may even help them achieve their human ends; but none of them would seem given to easy human fraternization, and all, even the Jinns of Eastern folklore and the house spirits Lob Lie-by-the-Fire and Aiken Drum, live existences different from, and quite apart from, men's normal daily lives. Some may resemble human beings closely, even in size, although they tend to tininess, and in the cities they build and the occupations they follow, but no matter: they always seem to be divided from humanity, even when the division's nature is unclear. The fairy ring, men's losing their senses at a glimpse of fairyland, their difficulties in trying to get back from fairyland, the remoteness of the fairy regions from villages and towns—all these things underline the nonhumanness of these creatures. They do not belong to the world of men, nor do men belong to theirs, and in this separation lie many plots of fairy tales and much of their enchantment.

Sometimes they have kings and queens, but generally their social organizations are loose and seldom figure in the stories and poems about them. But they do have meetings and festivals, and sometimes, like those witnessed by Rip van Winkle and those seen by the two sisters in Rossetti's *Goblin Market*, they are brawling and riotous. Although they usually keep to themselves, the creatures of fairyland occasionally are portrayed raiding human communities and doing impish mischief, or luring a lone human being into the forest or marsh.

All these nonhuman inventions, fantastic as they are, reveal in one way or another their human origins, their cousinship with man. They generally walk upright, talk like men, and share human feelings—love, hatred, jealousy, confidence and fear, greed, pride. This level of imagining is like an added dimension of humanity; there are fair human princesses and even lovelier, more ethereal fairy princesses; some men are ugly and brutal, but the trolls are uglier and more brutal and fierce than any angry men; human impishness and drollery are concentrated in the imps, elves, and gnomes; and the deep human experience of being outcasts is reflected in all the varied tribes of fairy, leprechaun, gnome, witch, mermaid, giant, and ogre.

But the human imagination has also imagined into existence a great congeries of creatures remote from human form and spirit, and these, whatever their extremely varied sources, are responsible for much grotesquerie behind humor, much weirdness behind mystery, and much terror in the fantasies of children's literature.

At a level possessing just a touch of familiarity there are the wonderful animals—huge, often savage dogs like Cerberus, gargantuan horses like the Norse Dappelgrim and the Russian horse of power, winged horses like Pegasus, Bellerophon's steed, great and savage wild boars like the Calydonian boar sent by the goddess Artemis to ravage the land of Calydon and the boar Jack disposed of through trickery in one of the American

Jack Tales, magical birds like the firebird of Russian legend and the phoenix, giant birds like the roc that snatched up Sindbad. And there are the hybrids, the mixed-up animals, sometimes grotesquely funny and other times uncanny and terrifying—the centaurs (half horse, half man) of Greek mythology, the birdlike harpies, the serpent-haired woman, the chimera, the sphinx, the minotaur, the unicorn, the stalk-eyed, furry Psammead in E. Nesbit's *Five Children and It*, William Pène du Bois's Great Geppy, Dr. Seuss's hybrids (birds like animals, animals like birds, fishes like both). This category should probably also include those otherwise recognizable species who, like Louis Fatio's happy lion, C. S. Lewis's wise and friendly lion Aslan the Great in *The Lion, the Witch, and the Wardrobe*, and Seuss's egg-sitting Horton, possess characteristics and perform deeds quite uncharacteristic of their species. And always there are the monsters—dragons, usually heavy-sheathed, long-tailed, and spitting fire, serpents of every description except naturalistic, many-headed or many-eyed or many-legged monsters, and some, like Doctor Dolittle's pushmi-pullyu and the elusive Woozle of the Pooh stories and Tolkien's Gollum encountered by the Hobbit in the underground lake ("dark as darkness except for his two big round pale eyes"), that are altogether ambiguous in nature. And now there are the mechanical monsters from outer space—great, soulless, usually malevolent things that, in their pitiless antipathy toward civilized human beings, remind one of the dragons of medieval legend.

The Characteristics of Fantastic Creatures

Man's inventiveness and imaginativeness are clearly evident in any lining up of the monsters and grotesques of fantasy, but one may also be impressed by the recurrence of characteristics. Certain conventions have dominated the imagining of nonhuman creatures; especially is this true in folktale and myth, which are responsible for so much of the fantasy now embedded in children's reading. In most European folktales dragons are fiery and hateful; the unicorn, besides having the essential single horn, is usually white and shy. In general, these legendary beings were not highly particularized; rather, they were given one or two characteristic attributes—for instance, anger and great size—and the listener or reader was left to provide them with more specific natures if he wished. As was true of most figures in folklore and myth, the outlandish creature's nature was pretty much established by his activities in the plot; the role of most such animals was harassment of the human communities or the guarding of some treasure or region, and so they lurked, attacked, and protected.

But modern fantasy, in borrowing the standard grotesques and terrifiers, often fills out the general conception with a great many particulars—details of size, color, smell, movement, diet, hideout, feelings—and sometimes altogether departs from the convention. Seuss, with the aid of his own particularizing illustrations, has created a whole aviary of quite distinct plumed monstrosities, varying in color, size, shape, nesting habits, eggs, and personality. And many of the new creatures of modern fantasy have not followed in the footsteps of their ancestors; Kenneth Grahame's reluctant dragon wants nothing to do with his kind's customary "rampaging, and skirmishing, and scouring the desert sands, and pacing the margin of the sea, and chasing knights all over the place, and devouring damsels, and going on generally." This eccentricity of the dragon creates the story's plot by taking away from St. George his required foe and jeopardizing his job of dragon fighter. Ruth Stiles Gannett's candy-striped dragons of Blueland are unlike the traditional dragons in their stripes and their general sweetness of disposition. Dexter the dragon in Jan Thayer's *The Popcorn Dragon* proves quite useful because he can pop corn with his hot breath; in Glen Dines's *The Useful Dragon of Sam Ling Toy* the dragon which Toy had raised from babyhood to frightened dragon adulthood became a useful substitute for the paper dragon in San Francisco's Chinese festival. This, of course, is what has happened to much of the modern writer's inheritance from traditional literature: he has filled it in with his own imagined particulars, sometimes has even forsaken the traditional conception, and has turned whatever he has kept to the making of his own special statement.

The Essence of Fantasy

These, then, are the fantastic inventions—the imagined places, conditions, events, beings—that compose the fantasy of children's literature and give to it the wonderfulness of accepted unreality. Whatever the style and whatever the particular mind and purposes of the teller, these fantastic inventions are the fundamental thing that makes fantasy fantasy; it is their being made up, their being fancied and invented, that gives fantasy its own place and character, distinguishing it from all those imagined literary worlds where there is a constant reflection of that existence to which we are accustomed or which we know by hearsay. The literature of the supermarket is made up too, is not real life; but it clearly relates to real life and owes something of its control over the reader's attention to this relationship. The literature of superman, on the other hand, relates primarily, though not exclusively, to unreality, the invented, and owes its own special control over the reader's attention to that relationship.

Fantasy and the Reader's Age

The fantastic, of course, is not solely the prerogative of children. As we have seen, much traditional fantasy—the Mother Goose rhymed imaginings, the folk and fairy tales, the heroic legends and myths—in large part began as adult literature, and for sophisticated, well-educated adults in contemporary society traditional fantasy retains much of its importance and appeal; witness the borrowings from folktale and myth by such writers as O'Neill, Joyce, Jeffers, Dunsany, Synge, Robinson, D. H. Lawrence, and Yeats. And in recent years writers writing with adults in mind have been particularly inclined to fantastic invention—for instance, Dinesen, Collier, Cocteau, Capek, Thurber, White, Kafka, C. S. Lewis, and E. M. Forster. Still, at least quantitatively, fantasy would seem to bulk larger in modern children's literature than it does in the adult literature of the past two hundred years, where the various kinds of realistic literature have sometimes seemed to thrive at the expense of fantasy. And that adult literature has perhaps become less fully, richly fantastic than it once was, while children's literature has kept and added to its store of fantastic wonders, may in part account for the growing strength in our culture of the erroneous notion that fairies, monsters, goblins, and the like are fine for children, are kids' stuff, but that mature adults put them aside for something called real life.

This notion obscures an important fact about the real place of fantasy in childhood reading: that its place is not equally firm and important throughout childhood. Rather obviously, fantasy appeals in different degrees and in different ways to different children, but the strength and nature of that appeal also changes for the majority of children as they grow older. "Fairyland equals childhood" is not a realistic or helpful equation. As we have noted, for the very young child the near world of real, daily experience is often new enough to satisfy with wonders. Not that the child will find *Little Red Riding Hood* dull or be bored by trolls trying to frighten billy goats at the bridge or by other uncomplex plots and simple characters of a fantastic sort. Not at all, but he is likely not to find them any more fascinating than stories about himself and people around him. Most little children are not yet especially lured by fairyland, by the armies of strange creatures floating in air and working underground, the elaborate magic of *Sleeping Beauty, Beauty and the Beast,* or *Snow White and Rose Red.* After all, the child's eventual recognition of the *absence* of such fascinating beings as fairies and witches in his immediate environment needs to take place before he can recognize their special wonder and their desirability as a part of his life.

For most children fantasy comes to have more interest about eight or nine, and generally this interest declines in early adolescence; it may reassert itself as the person approaches full maturity. The important point is not that we need to find definite periods of liking for fantasy, which there aren't, but that children go through shiftings of allegiance between the world of possible real experience and the world of the impossible, the fantastic, and that the basis for their allegiance may also alter over the years. Five- or six-year-olds may follow with interest the contest of wits and courage Hansel and Gretel have with the witch, but they may not yet quite follow and become concerned about Pandora's temptation to open the mysterious box and what happens when she does. Nor will they probably comprehend what is happening in the search for the water of life in the old German tale, or attend long or closely enough to the lassie's seeking her white bear prince east of the sun and west of the moon, for the search to become really important to them or be able to recognize the significance of the spells and curses in many a folktale and become caught up in the working out of these spells and curses. Given a year or two, these same children may well find these tales exciting and easy to follow to their end; at the same time they may understand and follow the story on a quite literal level: Does the younger son really get the treasure? Does the prince find the spellbound princess and break the spell? Does the princess have to marry the monster? Will the magic amulet work? Perhaps when they come back to the tale as adolescents or adults, they will see still other dimensions to it—the psychological crises and tensions intimated by the stories, the moral crises and their resolutions. For some individuals this may have happened earlier. For many it will never happen.

Fantasy—and the wonder it stirs in human minds—is not a steadfast, consistent thing in one child's reading even at a given time, for some imaginings may impress him or intrigue him, whereas others may seem not fantastic enough or too bewildering; the twilight fancies of Celtic imagination may not break through his sense of reality to touch wonder, while the boisterous inventions of the Finnish *Kalevala* or of a Western tall tale may do so. Fantasy takes many forms, and it creates many different states of mind in its readers and listeners.

Fantasy and Literary Value

Two other, opposite misconceptions of fantasy often have unfortunate effects on our approach to it as a part of children's literature. One of these is that fantasy is somehow a *superior* kind of literature; its opposite is that it is somehow an *inferior* sort. There is a widely held and quite unsupportable view of all fantasy as being, by its very nature, a more imaginative, somehow finer literature than any writing which seeks significance within the frames of ordinary human experience. Thus it is assumed that fantasies will be better, and better *for* children, than a family, dog, or airplane story, and that somehow fairy poetry will reach heights poetry about cats and cars cannot. And on the other hand, there is the generalized feeling that fantasy is not a part of real life and therefore makes less vital, less significant literature than realism.

In describing fantasy as the inventing of occasions for wonder, in contrast to observing, developing, and arranging experience for wonder, I have suggested nothing that *ipso facto* leads to the idea of a more imaginative or in any other way superior kind of literature. We have seen the literature of fantasy to be the creating of beings, situations, places, and events that stir the reader's imagination through their remoteness from the experienceable rather than through the discovery of interesting sides of the known or knowable. The fanstasist seeks to devise a fantastic set of experiences to amaze, tease, amuse, excite, trouble his reader. His efforts, like those of creators of other imaginative literature, may partly or wholly fail. A great deal of children's fantasy is only a pallid shade of the reality which its maker could not really escape; some of it is strained or cute, revealing how hard the maker worked at his job; some of it nervously shuttles back and forth between fancy and experience, trying to explain the former by the latter; some of it is so generalized and vague it fails to take on the concreteness all literary experience, fantastic or realistic, has to have; and some of its gets so bogged down in concrete details it cannot stir. In some of it the symbolism, particularly analogy, is made so inescapable that it crushes the story. Much fantasy has been written by people who have no knack for it, any real ability to *invent,* and so come forth with counterfeit fancies, something perhaps more unfortunate, particularly in developing sure taste in children, than merely dull, unimaginative writing about some set of facts which itself may be enough to stir an imaginative child to do his own inventing. And the misapprehension that fantasy is somehow always successful imagining is to some degree responsible for the tendency to accept quite uncritically the bogus in place of the really original dream.

The Mixture of Fantasy and Realism

There is another fallacy to be dealt with here: the misconception of fantasy as a completely independent type of children's literature. This arbitrary cutting off, or pigeonholing, of fantasy strengthens the mistaken inclination to find either fantasy or realism superior and to neglect the other category, for it is easier to do this when one does not consider fantasy and realism as *elements* in a single story or poem influencing one another. Also, this misconception can easily lead to adults' neglect of writing where fantasy and nonfantasy are inextricably combined, where there is no clear predominance of supermarket or superman—and this includes a great deal of the best writing for children. And it can make selection of literature for children too polar, too confined to the most easily classifiable—not necessarily the best, most interesting—representatives of each category. Drifting, as many people do, into extreme positions is simply not justified by the nature of supermarket and superman literature as we have analyzed each of them—that is, as different kinds of imaginings, both in their own ways meant to stir the reader to excited participation in the imagining. The two different *elements* of imagining can work together to create a special hybrid. Mary Poppins's fantastic adventures, for instance, occur to an English lady who, aside from her few very remarkable peculiarities, is a convincing representative of English womanhood, and they happen in a proper middle-class environment contrasting strongly with the mad events. Much of the early action of *Mr. Popper's Penguins* centers on a bathtub and a refrigerator, almost symbols of our clean and cool daily routine. In the folktales most of the peasants who wander into fairyland or onto the hostile ground of witches and demons are themselves quite convincing representatives of humanity and its common concerns.

In many mixtures of the fantastic with the nonfantastic the reader starts out with the latter and gradually moves toward the former. In Carroll's tale we first meet a little English girl, with the very common name of Alice, on an English afternoon in an English countryside, above an English rabbit hole. In Grahame's *Wind in the Willows* it is only near the end of this book full of marsh animals, cars, and recognizable human eccentricities that we meet the most complete fantasy in the piper at the gates of dawn. In the Azor books we come to know the little boy Azor before we discover his special involvement with the fishes. Peter Pan begins in a London bedroom where little children are sleeping, then moves into remote regions where all the rules of normal living seem to be suspended. Dorothy's adventures among the wonders of Oz begin back on a Kansas ranch. A great many—perhaps the majority—of folktales begin with a woodcutter going to the forest, a farmer leaving for his fields or for market, a hunter pursuing a deer through the forest, a farmer making his will, a merchant settling a dowry on his daughter, or a king arranging his affairs before he dies.

This pattern has the advantage of getting us into the story by way of the believable before asking us momentarily to suspend reason upon encountering the fantastic; this makes a bridge into the created existence of the story, and at the same time can make the strange seem stranger by contrast with commonplace things. Often there is a special satisfaction when the circle is completed by the return of the wanderers from fairyland or Oz or whatever strange regions they have visited to the circle and activities whence they came. This circularity—this tight formal pattern— is the source of some of the satisfaction in Wanda Gág's *Millions of Cats*, Seuss's *And to Think That I Saw It on Mulberry Street* and his *Cat in the Hat*, Maurice Sendak's *Where the Wild Things Are*, and Washington Irving's *Rip van Winkle*. The dream story, in which someone drifts from ordinary life into a fantastic dream and then back out of the dream, may seem not quite legitimate, a trick on the reader, but it does make for a certain aesthetic satisfaction in that it puts all its people and events into a neat circle and returns to the point on the circle where it started.

Whatever the particular chronological arrangement of the realistic elements of a story or poem in relation to the fantastic ones—before them, before and after, or mixed with them—there can be and often is a special thematic relationship, a suggested parallelism, of sense and nonsense, reality and fantasy, supermarket and superman. As they appear, the fantastic events, places, and creatures may implicitly or explicitly bring reality with them, like a kind of shadow or reflection. The chronic ill temper of gnomes, the evil cacklings and shrillings of witches, the roarings of giants and dragons, the white beauty of fairies in green forests—all these may seem to echo, to suggest, human emotions. The constant transformations of the magical world, the changing of form into form, may waken in the reader a sense of the reality of change, the uncertainties and ambiguities of experience itself. The breaking of spells by princely lovers and the freeing of maidens from dragon-guarded caverns or monster-

haunted rocks and other riskings of a daring man's life at seemingly impossible tasks need not all be narrowly interpreted as symbols of love,
courage, and faith, yet they can easily shadow forth the fact that human
beings do sacrifice themselves for causes. The beauty and terror of nature
may be caught in the beautiful and terrible inventions of the fantasist,
by the concrete myths of life and death. The silliness of Alice's Wonderland and the many little worlds of Lear's limericks and longer nonsense
poems constantly tease with uncanny familiarity; when everything is upside down, it can seem to mirror us and our friends. And of course in such
modern moralities as Godden's *The Mousewife*, Dinah Mulock's *The Little
Lame Prince*, MacDonald's *At the Back of the North Wind*, Wilde's *The
Happy Prince* and *The Selfish Giant*, and Norton Juster's *The Phantom
Tollbooth*, the symbolic meanings, the intended parallels to human experience, are almost thrust upon the reader by the writer's conceptions.

The Symbolic Meanings of Fantasy

Except where thorough spelling out of meaning makes the symbolism, or
at least the fact that it is there, hard to miss, the symbolic reflection of
reality may escape most children, who still may find and understand the
wonder in the fantasy. *The Frog Prince*'s splendid suggestion of the themes
of evil and human duty is probably lost on children who at the same time
find it a gripping wonder tale, and on many adults, too. Children may find
memorable the myths of Demeter and Persephone and of Orpheus and
Eurydice without perceiving in any clear way their themes of life and
death. They may not discover Andersen's bitterness and sentimentality
simply because they may not observe the bitter and sentimental themes in
The Snow Queen, but at the level of fantastic wonders they may well find
his tale satisfying. Maurice Druon's *Tistou of the Green Thumbs* may be
for most child readers a compelling description of a little boy's magical
powers to make flowers grow everywhere, even in the cannon of his
munitions-maker father, and *not* at the same time a serious allegory of
creativeness and destructiveness in modern life. Many children may not
detect the ancient symbolism—and the new—to be found in *The Goose
Girl* or *Faithful John* or *Rapunzel* or *Cupid and Psyche* or *The Firebird* or
the tale of Connla the fiery-haired one and his following the fairy maiden
into the western sea; yet for these same children the tales may be vivid
evocations of the unexperienced, the wonderful, all colored by human hope
and search, wish and conflict.

This, if so, means that two common reasons for having children read
fantasy can be set aside as only rarely significant. These are the idea that
children will be effectively exposed to the conceptions presumed to be
implicit in the tales and the idea that they will, by such exposure, learn
to read literature for deeper meanings, to sense the presence of symbolic
significance in art. But significant symbolic meaning is not something laid
away in a story, like a nut in a squirrel hole, waiting to be taken out of the

events, persons, and words used by any reader. Occasionally a child, while not fully realizing the symbolic suggestions of a myth of the life-death cycle or of Andersen's *Snow Queen* may sense the presence there of *some* feeling, *some* notion, about the nature of things; the child may become cognizant of a note of seriousness running through the narrative and under the surface themes. But this possibility is a thin reason for trusting that the symbolism of fantasies in children's literature will reach them, sink in, and so establish an openness for symbolic meaning later. If this happens, fine—but it cannot be counted on. Then it may be urged that even though the symbolic overtones do not reach the child, his early reading will leave the imprint of vivid characters and incidents and that this will "put him that much farther ahead" when he reads the tale later, in fuller maturity. This, though, places a great deal of faith in the retentive powers of readers' nervous systems. Also, if the book is to become a rich, imaginative commentary on human life when it is read later, then it must become that *in reading,* in the concrete experience of reading the story, not by the memory of what earlier readings had been.

Fantasy and Message

An unfortunate by-product of the concern over the symbolic content of fantasy in children's literature is that it can lead to emphasis on the message and on the less artistic, least aesthetically satisfying fantasies. The effort to connect fantastic inventions with life, to make them correspond with human characteristics, problems, and events, generally dulls down the fantasies. When the literary creation has to be explained, the artistry may lose its burnish, even its reason for being. Clear instances of this are Wilde's *The Happy Prince,* Mulock's *The Little Lame Prince,* Kingsley's *Water-babies,* and the many strenuous efforts to point out to child readers possible interpretations of Greek and Norse myths and to tag explanations to folktales like *Beauty and the Beast* and *The Firebird.* The wish to have children become aware of philosophical meaning in fantasy can result in poorer fantasy literature. It can lead to literature where the meanings are more obvious, and at least in the art of fantasy, obviousness is usually not a close friend of vivid creation; so this desire can ironically result in a confusing and lowering of literary values.

Fantasy and Humor

The marriage of fantasy with social and philosophical meanings may often, at least in children's literature, seem forced, but another marriage, that of fantasy and humor, does not. Many of the fantastic characters of traditional folk literature (elves, dwarfs, gnomes, etc.) are comic; and some of them are themselves imbued with a sense of fun, a relish for practical joking—turning milk sour, upsetting pans, getting identities scrambled, or impishly setting up situations in which human beings will behave foolishly. The fantasy of folktale, legend, and myth is not particularly humorous, but fun, especially broad fun, is certainly not foreign to it. And when we turn to modern children's literature, we find that much fantasy can as justifiably be called humorous literature; indeed, modern fantasies and modern children's humor call for a great deal of cross filing. Hans Christian Andersen often became fantastic and humorous at the same moment. Lear, Carroll, Carlo Lorenzini, Helen Bannerman, Joel Chandler Harris, Gág, Hugh Lofting, Mary Norton, Carl Sandburg, Seuss, Ets, Astrid Lindgren, Tolkien, E. B. White, Thurber, Ogden Nash, Bemelmans, Lawson, McCloskey—these are all in their individual ways humorous fantasists, or fantastic humorists. We do not need to dismiss coincidence altogether, but it would seem quite natural for a writer who sees things humorously to conceive them in fantastic terms and for a writer who invents new things to discover the humorous possibilities in them. For both fantasy and humor involve an appreciation of incongruity, a delighted awareness of the failure of things to match. Invented names like Seuss's, Lofting's, or Lear's are funny because, although they are still recognizably names, they are not the names to which we are accustomed; Duvoisin's Petunia is funny in her affectation of un-gooseness; Seuss's ridiculous birds with their hairy head-tufts are funny in their eccentric non-birdness; a cat that, like Carroll's Cheshire cat, comes and goes is funny and fantastic in its uncertainness; most dwarfs, at least in literature, are funny, and some of their humorousness lies in their combination of human attributes with uncommon smallness.

Summary and Conclusion: Supermarket and Superman as Complementary

The division of our study of realism and fantasy in children's literature into two chapters and their sharing of the title "Sources of Wonder" represent the basic structure of the present analysis. In this analysis children's realistic and fantastic literature are seen to possess a common denominator: each creates a new experience which, because of its novelty for the reader, causes him to feel a sense of wonder. But in this analysis children's realistic literature and children's fantastic literature are at the same time considered to be different kinds of created experiences that serve as sources of wonder: on the one hand, we have literary experiences that suggest the familiar, or at least the possible, and that owe some of their excitement to that relationship; on the other, we have literary experiences that are inventions and owe their impact to their remoteness from the familiar or the possible.

This is not, although it may at first have seemed so, a division of children's books by *subject matter*. In both the literature of the supermarket, realism, and the literature of superman, fantasy, the actual subject for the reader is the *newness*, or *freshness*, of the material the teller has selected—that is, its potentialities for exciting attention and wonder. In literature the airplane is no more real and potentially impressive than Daedalus's wings or the magic carpet or a spaceman's rocket; the neighborhood family in a book is no more real than a band of little men trooping down the glen or a family of unicorns. The distinction is between the familiar and the unfamiliar, the likely and the unlikely, the expected and the unexpected. Both provide—or are—the subject matter from which the imaginative writer seeks to create a story or poem that in turn excites the child's imagination. And in the effective story or poem, that is, in the story or poem effective as literature, he succeeds in doing so; the work is less effective insofar as he fails to capture the possibilities for wonder in the realistic or fantastic materials.

In looking at children's literature in this way we sidestep the pitfall of thinking of it as more or less imaginative simply by virtue of the kinds of experience it starts with. We avoid splitting literature so that its aspects cannot be thought of together. In this way we can bring together the realistic and the fey or fairy folktales, the Alcott stories and the Lear bits of madness, and at the same time we can see more clearly some of the actual differences between them as literary experiences of the child.

By viewing realism and fantasy as actually two elements in the same kind of experience, a procedure I have followed in these two last chapters, I have found it possible to describe the two kinds of literature without lining them up in opposing camps and without becoming involved in battles over their rival claims. At this point, with this kind of general description to work from, we can see and grant the merits of many of the claims regularly made in partisan support of supermarket and superman literature.

We can grant the relevance of certain claims made for each—literary realism and fantasy—on ethical grounds. Granted that children ought to acquire in their growing up a knowledge of things as they are, so they may have a firm basis for their behavior as mature human beings in that world; and granted that stories and poetry related to real life—society, nature, science, the historical and prehistoric past—can help contribute to this foundation or knowledge and understanding. But it can also be granted that the literature of fantasy, in inventing and so making life larger and fuller than it is, stretches existence, idealizes it, and thus gives children a sense of possibilities, the wisdom of myth, of ifs; this is the argument based on the ideal as a moral force, an exciter to action, and it does not necessarily negate the first.

Too, we can grant, without uneasiness, certain claims made for both elements in children's literature on psychological grounds. Granted that literature about familiar and recognizable life may provide the mental comfort that comes with knowing something or with knowing that things can be known; granted, too, that it may act as a sort of brake on, if not an obstacle to, escape into make-believe from a life one must understand. And at the same time one can recognize the therapeutic effect of fantasy in creating fresh, new wonders, in giving our capacity for wonder even more room to work in than it has with the natural and social world of experience.

Finally, we can see bases for the aesthetic claims made for realism and fantasy in literature, without getting caught up in the ancient argument over literature as truth and as fancy, as experience and as inspiration. Granted that literature related to experience can capture and transfer to the reader some of the beauty inherent in actual experience; also, granted that reality gives art a context, a point of comparison and contrast, something with which the writer's imagination can play; granted also that the literature more or less closely meshed with actual experience gives the child something on which he can work—room in which to use his own imagination, invent his own additions. But granted also that the art of fantasy gives the writer more freedom in which to invent and, more importantly, a sense of that freedom, knowing what he makes does not need to stand comparison with a previous experience; granted also that fantasy thus can provide readers with involvements and excitements in addition to those lying ready to hand.

We can allow the justness and importance of turning to these qualities in support of realism and in support of fantasy in children's books; indeed, our finding a common denominator would seem to strengthen all of the arguments on both sides and so show that both realism and fantasy are needed. But clinching proof that both the realistic and the fantastic have their rightful places in children's reading is simply (1) that the great works of children's literature include primarily realistic works and primarily fantastic ones—*Big Claus and Little Claus* and *Beauty and the Beast*, Stevenson's *Treasure Island* and *Peter Pan*, *David Copperfield* and *Alice's Adventures in Wonderland*, *Smoky* and *The Hobbit*—and (2) that there are also great numbers of dull, poorly conceived, weakly imagined realistic stories and great numbers of dull, poorly conceived, weakly imagined fantasies.

SUGGESTED SOURCES

Magic

Andersen, Hans Christian: *The Wild Swans,* in *The Complete Andersen,* trans. by Jean Hersholt, ill. by Fritz Kredel, Heritage, 1952.

Baum, L. Frank: *The Wizard of Oz,* Grosset & Dunlap, (Junior Library), 1958. And many other Oz books.

Benary-Isbert, Margot: *The Wicked Enchantment,* ill. by Enrico Arno, Harcourt, Brace & World, 1955. Amusing tale of the wicked enchantment of an entire town.

Dalgliesh, Alice (ed.): *The Enchanted Book,* ill. by Concetta Cacciola, Scribner, 1947. Stories about people or animals under a spell.

De la Mare, Walter: *The Three Royal Monkeys,* ill. by Mildred Eldridge, Knopf, 1948. Originally published as *The Three Mulla-Mulgars.* Imaginative, evocative tale of the magical journey of the three royal monkeys.

Dickens, Charles: *The Magic Fishbone,* ill. by F. D. Bedford, Warne.

Dolbier, Maurice: *The Magic Shop,* ill. by Fritz Eichenberg, Random House, 1946.

————: *Torten's Christmas Secret,* ill. by R. G. Henneberger, Little, Brown, 1951.

Eager, Edward M.: *Half Magic,* ill. by N. M. Bodecker, Harcourt, Brace & World, 1954. Also sequel, *Magic by the Lake.* Humorous fantasy in contemporary setting.

Farjeon, Eleanor: *The Glass Slipper,* ill. by Ernest H. Shepard, Viking, 1955.

Gordon, Patricia: *The Witch of Scrapfaggot Green,* ill. by William Pène du Bois, Viking, 1948.

Henry, Jan: *Tiger's Chance,* ill. by Hilary Knight, Harcourt, Brace & World, 1957. Children's trip to India on a magical tiger rug; considerable wit.

Lathrop, Dorothy P.: *The Colt from Moon Mountain,* Macmillan, 1956.

Lawson, Robert: *Robbut, A Tale of Tails,* ill. by author, Viking, 1948.

Mayne, William: *The Blue Boat,* ill. by Geraldine Spence, Dutton, 1960.

O'Faolain, Eileen: *King of the Cats,* ill. by Vera Brock, Morrow, 1941. Irish magic.

————: *The Little Black Hen,* ill. by Aldren Watson, Random House, 1940. The rescue of a kitchen maid from the fairy queen.

————: *Miss Pennyfeather and the Pooka,* ill. by Aldren Watson, Random House, 1946. Tale of a half-fairy horse.

Pyle, Howard: *Pepper and Salt; or Seasoning for Young Folk,* ill. by author, Harper, 1913. Tales full of fantasy.

————: *The Wonder Clock,* ill. by author, Harper, 1887.

Rice, Inez: *The March Wind,* ill. by Vladimir Bobri, Lothrop, 1957.

Sawyer, Ruth: *The Enchanted Schoolhouse,* ill. by Hugh Troy, Viking, 1956. An Irish boy and a leprechaun bring enchantment to an American schoolhouse.

Sleigh, Barbara: *Carbonel: The King of the Cats,* ill. by V. H. Drummond, Bobbs-Merrill, 1957. Two children rescue the king of the cats from a witch's spell.

————: *The Kingdom of Carbonel,* ill. by D. M. Leonard, Bobbs-Merrill, 1960.

Weales, Gerald: *Miss Grimsbee Is a Witch,* ill. by Lita Scheel, Little, Brown, 1957. A present-day witch changes a teacher into an alligator purse and in other ways upsets a town.

Created Creatures

Andersen, Hans Christian: *Thumbelina*, in *The Complete Andersen*, trans. by Jean Hersholt, ill. by Fritz Kredel, Heritage, 1952.

Bailey, Carolyn Sherwin: *Miss Hickory*, ill. by Ruth Gannett, Knopf, 1946. A hickory-nut doll.

Behn, Harry: *The Faraway Lurs*, World, 1963.

Bright, Robert: *Georgie to the Rescue*, ill. by author, Doubleday, 1956. And other *Georgie* stories. Georgie is a nice little ghost.

Butterworth, Oliver: *The Enormous Egg*, ill. by Louis Darling, Little, Brown, 1956. Concerning the dinosaur Triceratops.

Cox, Palmer: *The Brownies: Their Book*, ill. by author, Century, 1887.

De Regniers, Beatrice Schenk: *The Giant Story*, ill. by Maurice Sendak, Harper & Row, 1953. A child's dream of being a giant.

Dines, Glen: *The Useful Dragon of Sam Ling Toy*, ill. by author, Macmillan, 1956. A well-meaning dragon in San Francisco's Chinatown.

Du Bois, William Pène: *The Giant*, ill. by author, Viking, 1954.

————: *The Great Keppy*, ill. by author, Viking, 1940. About a striped horse who is also a detective.

Embry, Margaret: *The Blue-nosed Witch*, ill. by Carl Rose, Holiday, 1956. A young witch joins a Halloween party. Typical example of efforts to give traditional fantasy a contemporary context.

Enright, Elizabeth: *Tatsinda*, ill. by Irene Haas, Harcourt, Brace & World, 1963. Fairy tale.

————: *Zeee*, ill. by Irene Haas, Harcourt, Brace & World, 1965. About a fairy who cannot find a home until given one in a dollhouse.

Estes, Eleanor: *The Witch Family*, ill. by Edward Ardizzone, Harcourt, Brace & World, 1960.

Ewing, Juliana Horatia: *The Brownies*. Adapted and ill. by Katherine Milhous, Scribner, 1946.

————: *Lob Lie-by-the-Fire and Other Tales*, ill. by Gordon Browne, Macmillan.

Fatio, Louise: *The Happy Lion*, ill. by Roger Duvoisin, Whittlesey, 1954.

Fenner, Phyllis R. (ed.): *Giants and Witches and a Dragon or Two*, ill. by Henry C. Pitz, Knopf, 1943.

Ford, Nancy K.: *Baba Yaga's Secret*, ill by Kurt Werth, Lippincott, 1959. Followed by other Baba Yaga tales.

Gág, Wanda: *The Funny Thing*, ill. by author, Coward-McCann, 1929.

Gannett, Ruth Stiles: *My Father's Dragon*, ill. by Ruth Chrisman Gannett, Random House, 1948. Elmer Elevator's adventures involving gentle, candy-striped dragons. Followed by other stories—*The Dragons of Blueland*, 1951, and *Elmer and the Dragon*, 1950.

Grahame, Kenneth: *The Reluctant Dragon*, ill. by E. H. Shepard, Holiday, 1938. A whimsical, shrewd tale about a boy's acting as go-between for a peace-loving dragon and St. George.

Hoff, Syd: *Danny and the Dinosaur*, ill. by author, Harper, 1958.

Jones, Elizabeth Orton: *Twig*, ill. by author, Macmillan, 1942. A fairy in a tomato can in a city yard.

Kendall, Carol: *The Gammage Cup*, ill. by Erik Blegvad, Harcourt, Brace & World, 1959. Revolt of the Minnipins—little people. Sequel, *The Whisper of Glocken*, ill. by Imero Gobbato, Harcourt, Brace & World, 1965.

Kumin, Maxine W.: *Sebastian and the Dragon*, ill. by William D. Hayes, Putnam, 1960. Rhyming story about how a small boy caught a dragon for the zoo.

Lindgren, Astrid: *The Tomten*, adapted from poem by Viktor Rydberg, ill. by Harald Wiberg, Coward-McCann, 1961. A kind troll helps animals and people in difficulty; book given special distinction by Rydberg's full-page illustrations.

Lofting, Hugh: *The Story of Doctor Dolittle*, ill. by author, Lippincott, 1920. And other Doctor Dolittle stories.

Mulock, Dinah Maria (Mrs. Craik): *The Adventures of a Brownie*, ill. by Edwin J. Prittie, Winston, 1929.

Nesbit, E.: *Five Children and It*, Penguin (Puffin), 1959.

Sendak, Maurice: *Where the Wild Things Are*, ill. by author, Harper & Rowe, 1963.

Seuss, Dr. (pseud. for Theodor Seuss Geisel): *Horton Hatches the Egg*, ill. by author, Vanguard, 1940. Followed by many others, including *McElligot's Pool*, 1947; *Bartholomew and the Oobleck*, 1949; *Scrambled Eggs Super!* 1953; and *The Cat in the Hat*, 1957.

————: *If I Ran the Circus*, Random House, 1956.

————: *If I Ran the Zoo*, Random House, 1950.

Slobodkin, Louis: *The Amiable Giant*, ill. by author, Macmillan, 1955.

Stockton, Frank R.: *The Griffin and the Minor Canon*, ill. by Maurice Sendak, Holt, 1963. Well-told tale of the consequences of a griffin's visit to a church to see a carving of himself there.

Thayer, Jan: *The Popcorn Dragon*, ill. by Jay Hyde Barnum, Morrow, 1953.

Thurber, James: *The Great Quillow*, ill. by Doris Lee, Harcourt, Brace & World, 1944.

Tolkien, John R. R.: *Farmer Giles of Ham*, ill. by Pauline Diana Baynes, Nelson, 1962. Farmer saves village from dragons.

————: *The Hobbit*, ill. by author, Houghton Mifflin, 1938. A humorous, richly imaginative account of Hobbits, gnomes, trolls, etc.

Tales of Transformation

Andersen, Hans Christian: *The Marsh King's Daughter* and *The Wild Swans*, in *The Complete Andersen*, trans. by Jean Hersholt, ill. by Fritz Kredel, Heritage, 1952.

Asbjörnsen, Peter C., and Jörgen Moe: *East o' the Sun, West o' the Moon*, ill. by Hedvig Collin, Macmillan, 1953.

Beaumont, Leprince de: *Beauty and the Beast*, in *All the French Fairy Tales*, retold, with a foreword by Louis Untermeyer, ill. by Gustave Doré, Didier, 1946.

Boston, L. M.: *The Castle of Yew*, ill. by Margery Gill, Harcourt, Brace & World, 1965. Children's minds transform a garden: yews become chessmen.

————: *The Children of Green Knowe*, ill. by Peter Boston, Harcourt, Brace & World, 1955. Sensitively written tale of a little English boy's making friends with three spirits from the seventeenth century. Followed by *Treasure of Green Knowe*, 1958, and *The River at Green Knowe*, 1959.

Butterworth, Oliver: *The Enormous Egg*, ill. by Louis Darling, Little, Brown, 1956.

Carroll, Lewis (pseud. for Charles Lutwidge Dodgson): *Alice's Adventures in Wonderland* and *Through the Looking Glass*, ill. by John Tenniel, Macmillan, 1963.

The Frog King, in *Grimm's Tales*, complete ed., ed. by Josef Schnarl, Pantheon, 1944.

Gág, Wanda: *Nothing at All*, ill. by author, Coward-McCann, 1941. Invisible puppy becomes visible through use of magical phrase.

Krauss, Ruth: *The Backward Day*, ill. by Marc Simont, Harper & Row, 1950.

————: *How to Make an Earthquake*, ill. by Crockett Johnson, Harper & Row, 1954.

————: *I Want to Paint My Bathroom Blue*, ill. by Maurice Sendak, Harper & Row, 1956. A child's dream fantasy about things he'd like to do.

————: *A Very Special House*, ill. by Maurice Sendak, Harper & Row, 1953. A boy's imaginings, ending with a "Bung" as the dreaming boy comes back to earth.

Lipkind, William: *Chaga*, ill. by Nicolas Mordvinoff, Harcourt, Brace & World, 1955. An elephant becomes small as a rabbit.

Myths in any good collection, such as Sally Benson's *Stories of the Gods and Heroes*, Helen Sewell's *A Book of Myths*, and the d'Aulaires' *Book of Greek Myths*. Many, many tales based on transformation of one thing into another—gods and goddesses into human beings, animals into men and men into animals, living things into rocks, etc., and inanimate objects into human beings.

Nesbit, E. (pseud. for Edith Bland): *The Story of the Treasure Seekers* (1899), ill. by C. Walter Hodges, Coward-McCann, 1948.

————: *The Wouldbegoods*, ill. by Arthur H. Buckland and John Hassall, Coward-McCann, 1950.

Pearce, A. Philippa: *Tom's Midnight Garden*, ill. by Susan Einzig, Lippincott, 1959.

Prøysen, Alf: *Little Old Mrs. Pepperpot and Other Stories*, trans. by Marianne Helweg, ill. by Bjorn Berg, McDowell, Obolensky, 1960.

Rice, Inez: *The March Wind*, ill. by Vladimir Bobri, Lothrop, 1957. A little boy finds an old hat and uses it to become a soldier, a cowboy, etc.

Ruskin, John: *The King of the Golden River*, ill. by Fritz Kredel, World Publishing, 1946.

Sauer, Julia: *Fog Magic*, ill. by Lynd Ward, Viking, 1943. A little girl discovers a "come and go" village.

Seuss, Dr. (pseud. for Theodor Seuss Geisel): *And to Think That I Saw It on Mulberry Street*, ill. by author, Vanguard, 1937. Story of a boy's imaginings.

————: *The 500 Hats of Bartholomew Cubbins*, ill. by author, Vanguard, 1938.

Fantasy: Into the Earth, the Sea, and the Air

Babcock, Betty: *The Expandable Pig*, ill. by author, Scribner, 1949.

Beatty, Jerome, Jr.: *Matthew Looney's Voyage to the Earth*, ill. by Gahan Wilson, Scott, 1961.

Cameron, Eleanor: *Stowaway to the Mushroom Planet*, ill. by Robert Henneberger, Little, Brown, 1956.

————: *The Wonderful Flight to the Mushroom Planet*, ill. by Robert Henneberger, Little Brown, 1954.

Carroll, Lewis (pseud. for Charles Lutwidge Dodgson): *Alice's Adventures in Wonderland* and *Through the Looking Glass*, ill. by John Tenniel, World, 1946.

Du Bois, William Pène: *Peter Graves*, ill. by author, Viking, 1950. About results of discovery of an antigravity compound.

————: *The Twenty-one Balloons*, ill. by author, Viking, 1947. This account of an aerial trip is an intriguing mixture of science and fancy; Newbery Medal.

Heinlein, Robert A.: *Have Space Suit—Will Travel*, Scribner, 1958.

————: *Red Planet: A Colonial Boy on Mars,* ill. by Clifford Geary, Scribner, 1949.

————: *Rocket Ship Galileo,* ill. by Thomas Voter, Scribner, 1947.

————: *Space Cadet,* ill. by Clifford N. Geary, Scribner, 1948.

Johnson, Crockett (pseud. for David J. Leisk): *Harold's Trip to the Sky,* ill by author, Harper & Row, 1957. Harold draws his own sky adventures.

Kingsley, Charles: *The Water-babies: A Fairy Tale for a Land-baby,* ill. by W. Heath Robinson, Houghton Mifflin, 1923.

Lagerlöf, Selma: *The Wonderful Adventures of Nils,* trans. from the Swedish by Velma Swanston Howard, ill. by H. Baumhauer, Pantheon, 1947. A boy's adventures in flight over Sweden with wild geese.

MacDonald, George: *At the Back of the North Wind,* ill. by George and Doris Hauman, Macmillan, 1950.

————: *The Princess and Curdie,* ill. by Dorothy Lathrop, Macmillan, 1926.

————: *The Princess and the Goblin,* ill. by Nora S. Unwin, Macmillan, 1951.

MacGregor, Ellen: *Miss Pickerell Goes to Mars,* ill. by Paul Galdone, Whittlesey, 1951.

Parrish, Anne: *Floating Island,* ill. by author, Harper, 1930.

Seuss, Dr. (pseud. for Theodor Seuss Geisel): *McElligot's Pool,* ill. by author, Random House, 1947. Through an underground channel to the sea, whose fantastic creatures Seuss describes.

Slobodkin, Louis: *Space Ship under the Apple Tree,* ill. by author, Macmillan, 1952. A little spaceman from Mars visits boy during latter's vacation.

Tolkien, John R.: *The Hobbit,* ill. by author, Houghton Mifflin, 1938. Underground adventure, much of it droll, all of it exciting, involving Hobbits, dwarfs, elves, etc.

Verne, Jules: *From the Earth to the Moon,* Associated Booksellers, 1959.

————: *A Journey to the Centre of the Earth,* Collier, 1959.

————: *The Mysterious Island,* ill. by N. C. Wyeth, Scribner, 1946.

————: *Twenty Thousand Leagues under the Sea,* ill. by W. J. Aylward, Scribner (Scribner Illustrated Classics), 1952.

Wells, H. G.: *The First Men in the Moon,* Collins, 1960.

Williams, Jay, and Raymond Abrashkin: *Danny Dunn and the Anti-gravity Paint,* ill. by Ezra Jack Keats, Whittlesey, 1956.

————: *Danny Dunn on the Ocean Floor,* ill. by Brinton Turkle, Whittlesey, 1960.

Mixture of the Ordinary and the Extraordinary

Atwater, Richard and Florence: *Mr. Popper's Penguins,* ill. by Robert Lawson, Little, Brown, 1938. A lively piece of nonsense about a man whose life became filled with penguins.

Aymé, Marcel: *The Wonderful Farm,* trans. by Norman Denny, ill. by Maurice Sendak, Harper & Row, 1951.

Bettina: *Cocolo Comes to America,* ill. by author, Harper & Row, 1949. Mixture of fantasy and realism.

Bianco, Margery Williams: *The Velveteen Rabbit, or, How Toys Became Real,* ill. by William Nicholson, Doubleday, 1926.

Bontemps, Arna, and Jack Conroy: *The Fast Sooner Hound,* ill. by Virginia Lee Burton, Houghton Mifflin, 1942.

Brunhoff, Jean de: *The Story of Babar, the Little Elephant,* ill. by author, Random House, 1937. The first of a long series—including *Babar the King, Babar's Picnic, Babar and Father Christmas*—about the daily routines and topsy-turvy adventures of very human elephants.

Crowley, Maude: *Azor,* ill. by Helen Sewell, Walck, 1948. Followed by other Azor books about a boy who knows what animals say to him.

De Regniers, Beatrice Schenk: *A Child's Book of Dreams,* ill. by Bill Sokol, Harcourt, Brace & World, 1957.

Ets, Marie Hall: *Mr. T. W. Anthony Woo,* ill. by author, Viking, 1951.

Farjeon, Eleanor: *The Little Bookroom,* ill. by Edward Ardizzone, Oxford, 1956. A collection of Farjeon's fantasies.

Godden, Rumer: *The Doll's House,* ill. by Dana Saintsbury, Viking, 1948.

————: *Home Is the Sailor,* ill. by Jean Primrose, Viking, 1964. More doll play.

————: *Impunity Jane,* ill. by Adrienne Adams, Viking, 1954.

————: *Miss Happiness and Miss Flower,* ill. by Jean Primrose, Viking, 1960. About two Japanese dolls who live in a Japanese dollhouse and influence the children around them.

Grahame, Kenneth: *The Wind in the Willows,* ill. by Ernest H. Shepard, Scribner, 1933. The adventures—ranging from picnics, car rides, and boating expeditions to meeting the piper at the Gates of Dawn—of a mole, water rat, badger, and toad. Ingratiating humor.

Gramatky, Hardie: *Little Toot,* ill. by author, Putnam, 1939. Personified tugboat's adventures. Followed by *Loopy, Sparky,* etc.

Kraus, Robert: *I Mouse,* ill. by author, Harper & Row, 1958. Mouse finally wins family's attention by biting burglar.

Lawson, Robert: *Rabbit Hill,* ill. by author, Viking, 1944. Newbery Medal. Followed by sequel, *The Tough Winter,* 1954. Small animals, endowed with human feelings and speech, encounter real animal problems, such as whizzing cars and hunger.

————: *Robbut, a Tale of Tails,* ill. by author, Viking, 1948. Merry fantasy with humanized little animals.

Lindgren, Astrid: *Pippi Goes on Board,* trans. by Florence Lamborn, ill. by Louis S. Glanzman, Viking, 1957.

Lofting, Hugh: *The Story of Doctor Dolittle,* ill. by author, Lippincott, 1920. Followed by many other Dolittle books.

McCloskey, Robert: *Homer Price,* ill. by author, Viking, 1943. Followed by *Centerburg Tales,* 1951. Both books are collections of tall tales rising out of small-town boys' activities.

McGinley, Phyllis: *The Horse Who Had His Picture in the Paper,* ill. by Helen Stone, Lippincott, 1951.

Milne, A. A.: *The World of Pooh,* including *Winnie-the-Pooh* and *The House at Pooh Corner,* ill. by E. H. Shepard, Dutton, 1955. A very special mixture of wit, sentiment, and droll fantasy built around Christopher Robin and his nursery toys—Pooh, Eeyore, Piglet, and others

Norton, Mary: *Bed-knob and Broomstick,* ill. by Erik Blegvad, Harcourt, Brace & World, 1957. Wilson children learn some magic from Miss Price.

————: *The Borrowers,* ill. by Beth and Joe Krush, Harcourt, Brace & World, 1953. Followed by *The Borrowers Afield,* 1955; *The Borrowers Afloat,* 1959; and *The Borrowers Aloft,* 1961. All concerned with the adventures of tiny but very real working-class English people.

Sandburg, Carl: *Rootabaga Stories,* ill. by Maud and Miska Petersham, Harcourt, Brace, 1922.

Selden, George: *The Cricket in Times Square,* ill. by Garth Williams, Farrar, Straus & Cudahy (Ariel Books), 1960. Fantasy in a New York subway station.

Titus, Eve: *Anatole and the Cat,* Whittlesey, 1957. A lively version of the belling-the-cat tale; mixture of realism and the fantastic.

Travers, Pamela L.: *Mary Poppins,* ill. by Mary Shepard, Harcourt, Brace, 1934.

————: *Mary Poppins Comes Back,* ill. by Mary Shepard, Harcourt, Brace, 1935.

————: *Mary Poppins Opens the Door,* ill. by Mary Shepard and Agnes Sims, Harcourt, Brace, 1943.

Ungerer, Toni: *The Mellops Go Flying,* ill. by author, Harper & Row, 1957. About little pig people who build planes, are caught by Indians, and undergo miscellaneous other mad adventures.

White, E. B.: *Charlotte's Web,* ill. by Garth Williams, Harper & Row, 1952.

Like *Stuart Little,* a wise and humorous fantasy filled with a sense of daily life.

————: *Stuart Little,* ill. by Garth Williams, Harper & Row, 1945.

Symbolism

Alexander, Lloyd: *The Book of Three,* Holt, 1964. About an imaginary kingdom and a hero who goes against the evil horned king. Sequel, *The Black Cauldron,* Holt, 1965.

Andersen, Hans Christian: *Fairy Tales,* new ed., trans. by Jean Hersholt, ill. by Fritz Kredel, Heritage, 1944. The majority of Andersen's stories are richly symbolic. Typical of Andersen's symbolic approach is *The Snow Queen.*

Barrie, James M.: *Peter Pan,* ill. by Nora S. Unwin, Scribner, 1950.

Carroll, Lewis: *Alice's Adventures in Wonderland* and *Through the Looking Glass,* ill. by John Tenniel, Heritage, 1944.

Coatsworth, Elizabeth: *The Cat Who Went to Heaven,* ill. by Lynd Ward, Macmillan, 1959. A miracle results from the kindness of a Japanese artist to his cat; Newbery Medal.

Collodi, Carlo (pseud. for Carlo Lorenzini): *Pinocchio, the Tale of a Puppet,* ill. by Anne Heyneman, Lippincott (Lippincott Classics), 1948.

De la Mare, Walter: *The Three Royal Monkeys,* ill. by Dorothy Lathrop, Knopf, 1948.

Druon, Maurice: *Tistou of the Green Thumbs,* ill. by Jacqueline Duhème, Scribner, 1958.

Godden, Rumer: *The Mousewife,* ill. by William Pène du Bois, Viking, 1951. Delicate little fable of the friendship of a mouse and a dove.

————: *The Fairy Doll,* ill. by Adrienne Adams, Viking, 1956. A little girl's discovery of herself through the fairy doll on the Christmas tree.

Heyward, DuBose: *The Country Bunny and the Little Gold Shoes,* ill. by Marjorie Flack, Houghton Mifflin, 1939.

Juster, Norton: *The Phantom Tollbooth,* ill. by Jules Feiffer, Random House, 1961.

Kingsley, Charles: *The Water-babies: A Fairy Tale for a Land-baby,* ill. by W. Heath Robinson, Houghton Mifflin, 1923. A fairy tale filled with ethical ideas and facts about nature.

Lewis, Clive Staples: *The Lion, The Witch, and the Wardrobe,* ill. by Pauline Baynes, Macmillan, 1950. Others: *Prince Caspian,* 1951; *The Voyage of the Dawn Treader,* 1952; *The Silver Chair,* 1953; *The Magician's Nephew,* 1955; and *The Last Battle,* 1956. In these books Lewis creates the world of Narnia, in which the good lion Aslan and the bad witch compete for supremacy.

MacDonald, George: *At the Back of the North Wind,* ill. by F. D. Bedford, Macmillan, 1924.

Mulock, Dinah Craik: *The Little Lame Prince* and *The Adventures of a Brownie,* ill. by Colleen Browning, Garden City, 1956. The former full of moral symbolism.

Ruskin, John: *The King of the Golden River,* ill. by Arthur Rackham, Lippincott, 1932.

Saint-Exupéry, Antoine de: *The Little Prince,* trans. by Katharine Woods, ill. by author, Harcourt, Brace & World, 1943.

Sendak, Maurice: *Kenny's Window,* ill. by author, Harper & Row, 1955. A rooster gives a boy seven riddles to solve, which he does because of his loving heart.

Thurber, James: *Many Moons,* ill. by Louis Slobodkin, Harcourt, Brace & World, 1943. Caldecott Medal. A gently funny fantasy that contains an idea about which Thurber was serious.

Tolkien, John R. R.: *The Lord of the Rings* (3 vols.), Houghton Mifflin, 1963. Trilogy, crowded with rich fantasy, consists of *The Fellowship of the Ring, The Two Towers,* and *The Return of the King.*

Wilde, Oscar: *The Happy Prince and Other Fairy Tales,* ill. by Everett Shinn, Garden City, 1940.

Yamaguchi, Tohr: *Two Crabs and the Moonlight,* ill. by Marianne Yamaguchi, Holt, 1965. Theme of self-sacrifice: crab willing to give up shell if moon will rescue his mother from fishnet.

CHAPTER 9

THE
HOOT
OF
LITTLE
VOICES:
Humor in
Children's
Books

*T*o many of us, the whole matter of humor and humorous literature often seems so obvious as not to call for much analysis. Humor? Why, that's something that is funny. When is something funny, or humorous? When it makes us laugh. Why does it make us laugh? The humor in it. But why does this humor make us laugh? Well, it tickles our funny bone. What's that? Our sense of humor. Yet obviously, there is an atmosphere of vagueness and circular reasoning here, and our sense of a sense of humor could do with a little refurbishing.

This atmosphere exists in children's literature as it does elsewhere. Indeed, no aspect of children's literature is more carelessly thought about than its humor; unexamined assumptions about children's humor and children's humorous literature thrive. Here are some of them:

1   Children and laughter are just about synonymous. Children love fun, and they laugh much—much more than adults do. So children's literature becomes almost identified with funny literature. If children don't laugh at a children's story, it is assumed that the story failed to find its target, the funny bone of the juvenile reader. If an adult book shows a knack for making adults laugh, it is very likely (unless certain aspects of subject and language seem improper for the young) to come in for consideration as a conscript to the ranks of children's books.

2   Humor is some absolute quality which a children's book either has or doesn't have. Thus the humor of a book is incapable of analysis; there is merely the question, "Is the book humorous or not?" There is no question, "Humorous in what way or ways?" or "What kind of child will find

it humorous?'' We assume there are no significant differences among the things that different children laugh at.

It is embarrassingly simple to explode both sorts of assumptions. Thus, the assumption that laughter is the predominant and almost exclusive possession of childhood disregards the quite undeniable fact that some adults laugh a great deal. It ignores the great many children who are little sobersides, not given to the easy jest and slow to respond to other persons' attempts at fun. It overlooks the great popularity of many juvenile books of past and present that are not notable for their humor—*Black Beauty, Treasure Island, Hans Brinker, King of the Golden River.* For every Edward Lear or Lewis Carroll, there are many solemn, no-nonsense Frances Hodgson Burnetts, Horatio Algers, and Anna Sewells. And the run-of-the-mill series for children, from Tom Swift and the Rover Boys to Nancy Drew, are certainly not books of high merriment.

As for assumptions of the second sort: Clearly, humor is not just one simple thing, for different humorous stories make different people laugh, and sometimes the same story makes different people laugh for quite different reasons, and a humorous story may cause different laughers to laugh in different degrees of abandon. Children who may not crack a smile over *Alice in Wonderland* or even evince enough interest to ask a question may be thrown into fits of laughter by Dr. Seuss; the child who just barely listens through the passages of language fun in *Pooh* (misspellings, nonsense rhymes, etc.) may come alive when Owl's house is turned upside down or when Eeyore is pushed into the brook. The fact that most humorists try quite consciously, as artists, to make their writing *more* amusing indicates that humor is not just something you've got or not got.

Why, then, do such assumptions about children's humor continue dominant? And indeed, why is there a tendency for thoughts about humor in general to be vague? Why does humor tend to remain a highly approved but unexamined, uncomprehended phenomenon?

One clue may be the commonplaceness of humor. So many people laugh that laughter comes to be accepted as a sort of divine order of things—universal, not to be comprehended by the little individual. The thing that is everywhere may fail to draw attention. Another possible clue may be that as soon as you look into it, humor becomes a multiplicity of kinds of humor; it becomes so complex that it seems to defy comprehension, reduction to common denominators. And our task looks the more difficult because for a full understanding of humor we must draw on so many disciplines—psychology, physiology, aesthetics, sociology, literature, art, anthropology, history. A special combination of ordinariness and complexity usually makes for the easy acceptance of unexamined, unproved generalizations—witness those about politics, crime, and taxes.

Yet humor is not so complex as to be unanalyzable. And certainly some understanding of it, no matter how arrived at, can be quite helpful, can save one from making embarrassingly unsuccessful jests, from taking funniness in dead earnest or from boring schoolchildren with a tale or poem that a number of well-educated adults think is really very funny. The teacher who has done a little elementary analysis of humor for himself, and particularly in relation to children, has not assured that his classes will laugh at the humorous stories he chooses for them to read, but he has certainly reduced the chances that he will completely miss this target.

The Theory of Incongruity

There are a number of theories of humor—ideas about the causes of laughter. For the psychologist, humor may be conceived as an escape from personal blind alleys, from uncontrollable conditions and unsolvable problems. The physiologist may define it in terms of glandular secretion and blood pressure. The television comedian may conceive it as a collection of sure gags that will provide a certain number of laughs per minute. For the philosopher, humor may be a particular point of view toward existence, say, an attitude of objectivity or of acceptance. And there are other theories, and all have their particular uses and degrees of usefulness. But for the adult working with children and their reading, the broader and more fundamental the theory the better, for the simple reason that children laugh at such different things, at such different kinds of reading.

One such concept is that the common denominator of the various kinds of humor is the awareness of incongruity—that people find funny those experiences which involve some element of oddness, the lack of a close fit. According to this theory, things tend to strike us as funny—as a cause for quiet, inner amusement, smiles, chuckles, or unrestrained laughter—when we observe in them an element of inappropriateness. According to this theory, we laugh when we encounter the unexpected, the thing that does not happen according to plan, the breaking of the regular and expected pattern, the departure from the normal. *Unexpectedness, surprise, breaking, irregularity, contrast*—these words all suggest something of the element this theory considers the common denominator of humor. The claim for this theory as a useful tool is that it helps to explain why different people laugh at apparently entirely different situations. Let us consider some examples:

A solemn-faced gentleman in a shiny bowler hat (itself an oddity today in America) marches very erectly up the street, slips on a banana peel, and is suddenly horizontal and minus his hat. Some of us laugh; probably most of us do at first. A baseball player confidently gets up to bat; he takes a tremendous swing at the ball and spins all the way around, a result not at all commensurate with his intention and effort. If he is on the other team, many of us will find this airy swing cause for laughter, possibly edged with a bit of malice. A very tall comedian and a very short comedian called The Long and the Short of It carry on an argument from their different elevations. The sight of this pair, plus their seeming unawareness of the picture they present, will strike some of us as uproarious. A high school boy brings a classmate home to meet his "attractive younger sister," and she turns out to be three years old. The brother laughs at the surprise he has brought off; the friend may laugh at the surprise he has experienced. A small child with an adult vocabulary usually makes his elders laugh; a septuagenarian who addresses his juniors with the salutation "Hi ya, kids" may stir general laughter. Mistaken identities cause a man to propose to the wrong girl, a staple of comedy in the theater. Mrs. Malaprop uses big words in the wrong places in Sheridan's *The Rivals;* this strikes as funny an audience that knows the right meanings for the words. When an actor in a girl scout play gets tangled in her costume and falls as she makes her entrance, some waggish parent labels her "a crashing success"—and laughs loudly at his own jest. A friend of mine has a very broad Scottish accent and yet is constantly puzzled when people recognize him for a Scot; his astonishment makes his friends laugh. One hundred thousand people, two of the most powerful football teams in the country, and a half-dozen exasperated officials await the removal of one small dog from a football stadium; this is a regular Saturday afternoon joke in the fall. At Halloween we laugh at bulbous noses, padded stomachs, and oversize pants in which small children threaten to get lost. Sometimes we find reason for laughter in an adolescent trying to behave like an adult or in an older person trying to act young, as when a very stern and dignified old bachelor suddenly becomes quite kittenish and silly in the pursuit of a pretty young thing who caught his fancy. We may find very funny a large man methodically emerging from a small foreign car. A novelist like Thackeray or Thomas Hardy may find cause for sober ironic laughter in the confusions of human existence, the contrasts between what people plan and what really happens.

These instances of humor vary widely in the people who will laugh, the reasons for the laughter, and the degree or abandon of the laughter—yet they are all essentially similar in that they contain this element of unexpectedness, surprise. It may be physical incongruity (The Long and the Short of It), language incongruity (Mrs. Malaprop), or incongruity in situation (the small dog as king of the football field), or incongruity of character (the very proper elderly man starting to act silly over the young girl). But in all these instances something doesn't quite altogether fit the regular or expected pattern. Something goes kerflooie or gets out of whack. The phrase *merry mix-up* catches something of this particular aspect of humor.

If, however, any incongruous situation involves us personally, either physically or emotionally, the element of humor may be significantly reduced or may altogether disappear. The person who slips on a banana peel is unlikely to find the event laughable; and some of the laughers will soon come to feel vicarious pain or worry over the fallen walker, stop laughing, and possibly inquire seriously about his condition. Amusement over an elderly man pursuing a young girl may turn into a feeling of pity or compassion for him. We do not laugh at the wide-swinging batter so readily if he is on the team we want to win. If a boy has built up a hopeful dream image of someone's younger sister only to discover that the younger sister is three years old, the situation may seem humorous to other people but not so very humorous to him. The butt of a practical joke usually gets less enjoyment out of it than anyone else. Most funny characters are unable to find anything funny in themselves. We generally do not laugh at ourselves; it is a very rare human being who does.

It would seem, then, that in addition to the incongruous element in the situation, there must be some degree of objectivity in the person who sees the incongruity. He should be at some distance, physical or psychological or both, from the cause for laughter; he needs to be far enough off from it to be able to see it. If he is close to the cause for laughter, he runs a greater chance of becoming entangled in it and not being able to see it as something apart from himself. (May this be one reason why we sometimes become able after a lapse of time to laugh at something over which we were formerly deeply concerned?) Many incongruous situations are uncomfortable or even painful to the participants; but even when the circumstances are not unhappy ones for the people directly affected, they usually cannot perceive the incongruous elements clearly enough to see what's so funny. The malapropian manhandler of language can see nothing funny about his speech because it's *his* natural way of speaking. The merry drunk lurching along the street is often completely unconscious of the curious figure he is making and tolerantly bemused when people laugh at him. The person who unwittingly contradicts himself may strike us as funny for his self-contradictions, but his unconsciousness of what he is doing keeps him happily unaware of the cause of others' laughter.

Perhaps in the element of incongruity as seen from a distance we have a useful means of analyzing the humor that children respond to. Perhaps it will help us see *why* there is humor for them in each of the different kinds of children's humorous literature.

Physical Humor in Children's Literature

Probably the most common of all sources of children's humor is the physical situation with its obvious elements of contrast and surprise.

To begin with, sudden physical disasters (skiddings, stumblings, and tumblings, dousings, head bumpings, whackings) and grotesque physical appearance and costumes have been part of the equipment of the traditional comic-strip artist. From the Yellow Kid down through can-topped Happy Hooligan, Mutt and Jeff, the Katzenjammer Kids (with the walrus-moustached captain), Krazy Kat, Moon Mullins, Popeye, and Li'l Abner, the cartoonist has placed ridiculous-looking, weirdly dressed characters in puddles, on collision courses, on breaking branches, and on the receiving end of flying bricks.

Traditional verse for little children is filled with, and depends for much of its fun on, physical mix-up and smashup, confusion and mishap: Jack and Jill fall down the hill, the old lady is tossed up in a basket seventeen times as high as the moon, Goosey Gander is flung downstairs, Humpty Dumpty falls off his wall, a blackbird snips off the maid's nose, Tom the piper's son runs howling down the street. And

As I was going to sell my eggs,
I met a man with bandy legs;
Bandy legs and crooked toes,
I tripped up his heels and he fell on his nose.

Then there was Doctor Foster, who

. . . stepped in a puddle
Right up to his middle
And never went there again.

And on miniature stage and in verse Punch and July have banged and flopped:

Punch and Judy
  Fought for a pie;
Punch gave Judy
  A knock in the eye.
Says Punch to Judy,
  Will you have any more?
Says Judy to Punch,
  My eye is too sore.

The world created by nursery rhymes is a world of physical confusion and mishap.

Incongruity of appearance likewise is liberally spread through traditional children's rhymes—Humpty Dumpty teetering on his wall, the old man clothed all in leather, the fine lady upon a white horse with rings on her fingers and bells on her toes, the crooked man who walked a crooked mile. And situations in which persons, animals, objects, and circumstances are combined in surprising and ludicrous ways are a regular staple of these short, gusty rhymes. An old lady living in a shoe or, like Mother Shuttle, living in a coal scuttle, a cow jumping over the moon and a dog laughing at it, Mother Goose riding on a goose through the air, blackbirds singing out of an opened pie, the old men of Gotham at sea in a bowl, Simple Simon fishing to catch a whale in his mother's pail—all these situations are fantastic and ludicrous combinations of common, familiar things. It is a scrambled world that the children's traditional verses give the child, in which things are out of joint—but without particularly serious consequences, or at least without results we are asked to fret over.

Folktale literature is not markedly humorous as a whole, but a boisterous, physical sort of humor runs through a good many folktales, particularly those which have been appropriated by children. A witch or giant can be a terrifying object, but the witch's weird appearance and her utter divorce from sensible, down-to-earth behavior may make her a funny character, and the giant's clumsiness can make him a laughingstock. Trolls, dwarfs, and goblins can lead to laughter by their droll appearance and eccentric behavior. Sometimes, also, the folktale explodes into a frenzy of slapstick. In *The Three Billy Goats Gruff*, after the two smaller billy goats gruff get the troll to wait for the *big* billy goat gruff, the latter "flew at the troll and poked his eyes out with his horns, and crushed him to bits, body and bones, and tossed him out into the burn." The Irish tale of *Hudden and Dudden and Donald O'Neary*, in which meek O'Neary outwits the two greedy farmers Hudden and Dudden, is a succession of blows, kicks, tossings in sacks, and leaps into lakes. Much of the hilarity of *The Sorcerer's Apprentice* comes from the apprentice's frantic efforts to stop the spellbound brooms from sloshing more buckets of water into his master's house.

This sort of rough-and-tumble goings-on is an integral part of most tall tales—the Jack Tales, Mark Twain's Western yarns, the stories about Paul Bunyan, those about Pecos Bill, etc. Typical of tall-tale humor is the predicament of Pecos Bill's girl friend when she tries to ride the horse Widowmaker and bounces up to the moon and back and forth, without anyone being able to catch her between bounces. And the tall tales derive much of their humor from the half-recognized contrast between normal physical existence and a world in which Pecos Bill tames Widowmaker, in which Jack outsmarts giants and monstrous hogs, and in which a big tree that a woodsman has felled continues to slide from one side of a valley to the other until it has worn itself down to a toothpick, which the woodsman narrator is happy to draw from his vest pocket as undeniable evidence. Most such tales start in a matter-of-fact way, offering recognizable commonplace physical realities (backcountry cabins, logging camps, farm animals, ranch routines), and then gradually stretch our credulity farther and farther. The contrast is the funniest part. Of course, when *everything* gets tremendous and superhumanly powerful, the element of contrast becomes less important, and the tale may become a bit monotonous and so less humorous. In a world of clowns, a clown is not funny; it is his difference that makes him funny.

A great deal of the humor in modern literature written directly for children is rooted in physical incongruity—Lear's grotesque figures with their long noses and towering wigs and stilt-like legs, Laura Richards's Misses Wobblechin and Snipkin, Alice's constantly changing size, the tigers wearing Little Black Sambo's bright-colored clothes, Pinocchio's long nose. Indeed, when we turn to contemporary humor fashioned for children, we find that some of the most popular funny books depend for their funniness primarily on physical incongruity. Dr. Seuss's books, for example. In most of them the central pattern is a vigorous, persistent outraging of the familiar world. In *On beyond Zebra* he exhausts the alphabet and so has to go "beyond zebra" and invent a new one, with appropriately fantastic creatures to illustrate it. In *And to Think That I Saw It on Mulberry Street* he populates Mulberry Street with reindeer, elephants, charioteers. In *Thidwick: The Big-hearted Moose* all the birds and beasts and insects of the woods come to rest on the antlers of one poor moose. For *If I Ran the Zoo* Seuss invented a whole zooful of monstrosities. In *The Cat in the Hat* the cat creates one chaos after another in the quiet home of two ordinary little children, and each chaos is more chaotic than the last. In story after story, Seuss thinks up a world of physical topsy-turviness in which normalcy is more and more subverted. His animals have exceedingly knobby knees and ferociously hairy heads; his birds erupt in fountains of feathers, his fish in surgings of spines. Also, his books have a constant action and reaction that is in the vaudeville tradition of collision and collapse. A sizable part of Seuss's humor depends on the bang on head, the flop on nose or chin, the custard-pie type of event carried along in rhythmic doggerel involving *whoosh* and *smash* and *garrumph*. Seuss's splashy colors and swirling drawings reinforce this impression of hilarious jumping, bounding, and sudden stopping. The total effect of his subjects, distortions, explosive events, and rhythmic doggerel and cartooning is one of broad, unsubtle, almost surefire comicness.

The modern children's literature of physical humor has many other well-known practitioners. Robert McCloskey, in *Homer Price and Centerburg Tales,* tells with great zest stories like that of the unstoppable doughnut machine that spills thousands of doughnuts into the doughnut shop. Virginia Kahl, in *The Duchess Bakes a Cake,* creates a similarly mad situation out of the duchess's inability to prevent the dough, on which she is sitting, from rising higher and higher into the sky and taking her ever farther from her bewildered family. P. L. Travers's Mary Poppins slides up banisters and sails off into the sky, feats altogether at odds with her excessively plain dress and frame. Hardie Gramatky's Little Toot, Loopy, and other machine heroes get involved in all sorts of madcap adventures on waves, clouds, etc. Roger Duvoisin's white goose Petunia has funny adventures of a very similar kind when she dares the open sky and country on her flight south. Many comic stories derive much of their humor from the physical misadventures of pets—Kahl's Wolfgang in *Away Went Wolfgang!,* Hans Rey's Curious George, Flack's Angus. Hugh Lofting's Doctor Dolittle and his animal friends get into all sorts of confused situations and physically grotesque complications; the Freddy the Pig series is a somewhat broader form of the same loud humor—animals on boats, cars, etc., going through all sorts of strident adventures. Much of the fun of *Pippi Longstocking* derives from the little girl's ability to do altogether astonishing physical feats. And of course, many of today's movie cartoons depend for almost all their humor on physical smashup—the chase in which a big tough bulldog encounters a series of immovable objects, which take an impression from his massive form; the falling traps, axes, thrown bricks, collapsed trees, yanked rugs, and explosives that are the standard equipment of Bugs Bunny and his like. In all this highly popular modern children's humor the incongruous physical event is a prime component. And in some more offbeat humor of today, such as that of Ruth Krauss or that of Beatrice de Regniers, the pleasure of turning existence upside down and rearranging it in mad ways is the principal source of the fun. In de Regniers and Maurice Sendak's *What Can You Do with a Shoe?* the little child suddenly puts a shoe to all sorts of uncustomary uses—as a hat, a cup, a boat, etc.

In much modern children's humor, then, from Seuss's hairy birds and winged animals through Bugs Bunny's wall smashing to the imaginings of a little boy with a shoe, the funniness lies mainly in the cracking of the ordinary physical world. Things look or happen differently from how they are expected to look or happen, or the ordinary *is* there but is suddenly placed in dramatic and funny contrast to a new and unfamiliar way of existence.

Physical humor seems to have more appeal to very young children than do other kinds of humor, but this does not signify that it ceases to move older children and adults to laughter. Obviously, physical humor causes people of all ages to laugh—instinctively, unreasoningly, with unintellectual belly laughter. And the thread of physical funniness runs through most comic art—Chaplin's comedies, Shakespeare's Falstaff and Malvolio and Sir Andrew Aguecheek, Cervantes' Don Quixote and Sancho Panza, Humphrey Clinker. Thus the good reader of thirteen or fourteen who laughs appreciatively at the grotesqueness of some of Dickens's characters in *David Copperfield* may be responding for much the same reason that the three-year-old burbles over the girl who lost her nose to the blackbird in the clothesyard. There is a significant difference, however: in Dickens, the available causes for laughter are much more diverse and complex.

Physical humor blends imperceptibly into *situation* humor, in which the odd scrambling of people and events creates a funny situation not entirely physical but only in a minor way dependent on *language* or *character* for its fun. Some of the examples of physical humor already discussed show this blending, and children find humor of this kind in Bemelmans's Madeline and the appendix scar of which she was so proud, the big farmer and little farmer of Margaret Wise Brown, Munro Leaf's Wee Gillis blowing on tremendous bagpipes, Ferdinand the flower lover's being expected to put on a bullish performance, little old Miss Pickerell's adventures on Mars, Stuart Little the all-American mouse and his adventures in the midst of middle-class city living.

Language as a Source of Children's Humor

Language humor in children's literature seems to be better understood and appreciated by literate adults than is the purely physical sort of fun or even situation humor. This may be because they are more accustomed to language as an ingredient of adult humorous literature, and this in turn may be because as adults they have had more experience with language, know more of it and about it, and so are readier for humor based on it. But whatever the reason, it is common for parents and teachers to find language humor an especially worthy ingredient of children's books and so to push for the inclusion of books that contain it in their children's reading.

Among other things, language is a set of sounds we form into words and use to represent the particulars of experience and our generalizations about them, and when the sounds come into odd relation to other sounds or get shifted from their ordinary meanings, then we may find the language funny.

Sounds that have been borrowed or made up may not agree with the kind of sounds we are accustomed to hearing, and the disagreement may cause us to laugh. Thus Chinese, in itself not funny, may sound funny when we don't hear it often. This also may be a reason why nonsense lines in verse can make children laugh. Sounds like *winkle wankle wunk—jinkle jankle junk* or *hickory dickory dock* may suggest nothing at all except their remoteness from what one is accustomed to hear; it would seem, then, that if they are funny, it is the difference from normal language that is humorous. It should be noted, however, that the appeal of nonsense language need not be entirely or even primarily in its humor. Have you ever watched children making up nonsense rhymes or shouting them as they played games? Often in so doing they are quite solemn. It would seem that nonsense language can appeal simply as exploration and experimentation, which are often serious business. In other instances, like

Here we go dancing jingo-ring,
Jingo-ring, jingo-ring,

the nonsense words may simply create an easy kind of music.

The language of some nonsense verse seems funny because it is just a bit off normal, not too far off but just a bit, and so sets up a kind of teasing similarity and difference at the same time, something like dissonance in music. This may be part of the amusingness of Carroll's

'Twas brillig and the slithy toves
Did gyre and gimble in the wabe;
All mimsy were the borogroves
And the mome wraths outgrabe

or Lear's

On the top of the Crumpetty Tree
The Quangle Wangle sat

or his

And in twenty years they all came back,
In twenty years or more;
And everyone said. "How tall they've grown
For they've been to the Lakes, and the Terrible Zone
And the Hills of the Chankly Bore"

or Laura E. Richards's ending every third line of her "Legend of Okeefinokee" with a word ending startlingly in -ee or -y (*spokee, jokee, oaky, smokee, brokee*).

Similarly, baby talk and stories and poems that use it seem funny, not because of what is said, but because of the fumbling of our normal way of speaking. The double-talk dear to many children is funny because it skirts the edge of sense. Foreign accents and dialects can seem funny; again the reason is probably the not very great discrepancy between them and what we commonly hear. This kind of discrepancy seems to be dwindling as a source of children's humor today, perhaps because of adult sensitivity to the dangers of setting national, racial, and ethnic minority groups apart; but it was a central element in some of the funny poetry for children written in the late nineteenth century by James Whitcomb Riley ("Little Orphant Annie") and Eugene Field, in old-time poems and stories about Negroes (*Epaminondas*), in Daly's poems of New York immigrant dialects. And of course the cruel folk verse of the playgrounds which imitates stutterers and lispers depends for its "humorous" effect on this kind of disparity.

A variation of this sort of language play that is capable of much complex development is to take words from a particular social, cultural, or vocational context and to use them in some other context or at some other level. For instance, highfalutin language may be used to describe ordinary things on which such language is not customarily lavished ("Will you honor our mansion with your presence?" for "Come into our house," "pedal extremities" for feet, or Micawber's fancy talk of mundane things). It is a favorite adolescent jest to use the jargon of some specialized field of activity for quite ordinary activities, such as scientific terminology for eating, sleeping, and walking. And to take language in the reverse direction is another common source of youthful humor—to call the important person such as the school principal or the President of the United States "that guy," resolutely to use such plain language as "bang" for explosion, "chow" for dinner, "gut" for stomach. When a gray-headed grandfather uses jive talk or an elegant matron indulges in pithy lower-class speech or a small boy comes out with jawbreaking terms and elaborate syntax— in each case the speaker is relying for any desired laughter on the listener's surprise at the gap between the language he expected and the language he gets.

The foregoing language humor basically depends on our encountering sounds we do not expect. Some language jesting originates in another sort of language variation: a shift of *meanings* for sounds, or, more directly, words. The meaning of a word or group of words is changed from that it ordinarily has, or it keeps its old meaning at the same time that it acquires a new one. This is that ancient form of humor, the pun. During the past century some have occasionally considered the pun gauche and therefore rather disgraceful. But the pun is persistent; in disgrace or not, it plays a part in adults' and in children's humor, though it plays a less important part in the latter because it depends so heavily on language knowledge. Many of the riddles of which fifth and sixth graders are fond are based on double or triple meanings, and children of ten or eleven may catch on to the punning in Lear or Carroll or in Thomas Hood's nonsense poems* like

Ben Battle was a soldier bold,
And used to war's alarms,
But a cannon-ball took off his legs,
So he laid down his arms!

or in popular doggerel bits like

Flo was fond of Ebenezer—
"Eb," for short, she called her beau.
Talk of "tide of love"—great Caesar!
You should see 'em, Eb and Flo.

In all these language jests, from the broadest of nonsense chatter to the relatively intellectual pun, it is getting the *unexpected*—unexpected sounds and unexpected shifts in the meanings of words—that calls forth the laughter.

It is evident, from this brief breakdown of language humor, that language play is a staple in children's fun but also that children vary in their responses to it. The broad fun of nonsensical language seems to have its strongest appeal to the very young; jests based on changes in word meaning become more important as the child grows older. The amount of fun a child finds in language depends to a considerable extent on the language interest and awareness in his family and, later, in his town and school environment. Where adults concern themselves with words—pronounce them, compare them, discuss them—and where they do much conversing and/or reading, there is greater likelihood that language will be for them a source of fun, and that the child among them will accordingly be more responsive to language jokes—nonsense sounds, dialect variants, puns. This may be an important reason for the special joy some children appear to find in reading that involves language gymnastics—*Alice in Wonderland*, the Pooh books, and Krauss's word fun (*A Hole Is to Dig*, etc.)—and for other children's finding it somewhat puzzling and on the whole not very funny.

Language humor forms one of the few bridges of common appreciation between adults and children in children's books. Lear's fanciful names, his use of words in startlingly unexpected frames, Carroll's sound non-sense, the gentle ridiculousness of Pooh's songs, Ogden Nash's gram-mar stretching—the literate adult generally has little difficulty warming up to these sources of the children's fun. Of course, there is a tendency for such adults to imagine a mutuality of appreciation even when it does not really exist.

Character as a Source of Humor

Another bridge between child and adult, though a less important one, is the humor of character—the fun of discovering incongruities *within* a character or strange contrasts *between* characters. Here again there is something the child already finds funny and mature people find increas-ingly humorous. But unlike language humor, the humor of character holds relatively little attraction for the child until the middle and adolescent years. For this reason most of the clear examples of it we find are in books for children from ten or eleven on.

Children's traditional verse contains little humor of this kind. Characters complex enough to have inner contrasts are almost nonexistent in *Mother Goose*, and contrasting characters, such as Jack Sprat and his wife, are uncommon there. In folktales there is little inner complexity to make for comedy; characters are likely to be entirely crafty (Puss in *Puss in Boots*) or gullible (Gudbrand, who continued to trade his possessions for those of less value until he had only a stick), good or bad, wise or foolish, greedy or kind. However, folktales do have considerable comedy arising out of the encounters of unlike characters with one another; dwarfs and giants create a ludicrous strain in many folktales, as do long-nosed witches and fairy princesses, and all of these make a strong contrast with ordinary folk.

As children grow older, complex characters and amusing contrasts be-tween characters come to be of more concern to them. A *confused* witch may now become funnier than a simply weird-looking old crone. Kenneth Grahame's reluctant dragon is supposed to be ferocious and aggressive, instead of which we find him quite gentle and unaggressive, with a taste for people's company rather than their flesh and for poetry rather than battle; and Grahame's St. George, who is supposed to be entirely the uncompromising fighter, turns out to be a peace-loving soul who fights mainly because he must stay in character and do what people expect of him. In James Thurber's *Many Moons* much of the humor lies in the fact that the so-called wise men really do not comprehend the problem set them by the king, whereas the so-called fool, the king's jester, emerges with all the right, wise answers. And Thurber's people are funny mixtures inside themselves—the pompous statesmen with their very unimposing ignorance of practically everything, concerned with high matters of state and also having to do their wives' shopping. The lord high chamberlain reads a list of rare objects obtained for the king—peacocks, black orchids, unicorns' horns—and finds himself reading "two dozen eggs, and a sack of flour," his wife's instructions to him.

E. B. White's *Charlotte's Web* is funny to children for many reasons, but probably the principal one is its character mix-ups. Wilbur the Pig's given name contrasts with his barnyard environment, and his piggish form is delightfully out of keeping with his gentle, lonely personality; Charlotte's loyal, cooperative, domestic personality makes a funny contrast with our normal picture of a spider. And they are set off by selfish, scheming Templeton the rat.

Much of the humor of *The Wind in the Willows* comes from this sort of character contrast: the faddish, modish character of Mr. Toad in contrast with the simple, unpretentious Ratty and Mole and Badger, and also Toad's illusions set over against reality. In the world of Alice in *Alice in Wonderland* the rabbit, who is always late, frets over his watch, Alice keeps changing and losing her identity, the duchess is torn by fits of anger, the lugubrious Mock-turtle breaks down under the trials of existence, the stiffish, huffish caterpillar dignifiedly smokes his hookah on a toadstool and keeps Alice guessing. It is a world filled with the aberrations and confusions of human character; but even the utterly fantastic characters have habitual responses that are very human indeed.

Once the child, at nine or ten or older, begins to like meeting people from daily life in his stories, his reading will come to have more and more of its humor rooted in its characters. Although some of the fun in the Mary Poppins books is the broad comedy of ludicrous physical happenings, the books owe much of their ability to provoke laughter to the ludicrously out-of-place figure of Mary Poppins—the old-fashioned—looking maiden lady who is given to sudden flights at the end of her umbrella. Much of the humor in the family stories that eleven- and twelve-year-old children read so avidly—Alcott's *Little Women,* Eleanor Estes's Moffat series, Elizabeth Enright's *The Saturdays* and *Thimble Summer,* Hilda Van Stockum's *The Mitchells* and *Canadian Summer,* Beverly Cleary's stories of Henry Huggins and Beezus—has its source in the books' characters. In *Rufus M.,* for instance, Rufus is an amusingly independent-minded little boy whose growing up is marked by many funny encounters with older brothers and sisters, librarians, and other authorities. Jo in *Little Women* has a constant conflict between her tomboyishness and her ladylike propensities.

Humorous books for adolescents generally center their laughter in contrasts between characters and in complications within fictional people such as Tom Sawyer and Huckleberry Finn, or Mary Norton's "borrowers," those 6-inch-high people who are cantankerous and illogical just like their "biggers." It should be noted, though, that one will not find as *many* humorous books for adolescents as for younger children, for children beyond the ages of twelve or thirteen seem to prefer (or perhaps are just *expected* to prefer) deadly serious romantic love or adventure or, on the other hand, "real-life books"—travel, mechanics, science, biography, etc.

Children's Humor and Adults' Humor

As this brief glance at the various sorts of children's humor clearly indicates, children's fun has much the same kinds of sources as those we find in adult humor. Both children and adults laugh at striking physical adventures and ludicrous situations. Both child and adult may find language play funny. And both child and adult may find laughter in striking contrasts between characters and in contrasts between the different sides of a single character. In short, we do not discover such a thing as exclusively children's humor or adult humor. But—and this is extremely important— juvenile and adult humor *are* different in significant ways: the *same sort* of physical situation or language play or character incongruity is not likely to satisfy both child and adult, at least in equal degrees. We need not expect that the thing which rocks father will send his nine-year-old boy or girl into hysterics; it is not to be assumed that children's humor will always, or even most of the time, keep the teacher or librarian amused while it is providing amusement for the children. There are a number of major differences between things that make children laugh and what adults are likely to find amusing, and if children's humorous literature is to be dealt with sensibly and sensitively, these differences need to be recognized.

Except for language *nonsense,* language as a source of humor for children is limited. This is because the child only gradually and slowly comes to acquire knowledge and control of his language. Most young children do not yet have a sufficient grasp of vocabulary and syntax to appreciate play with word sounds, spellings, and meanings. Before one can appreciate incongruities and departures, one must know the norm being abandoned, the rule being broken.

The development of a sense for language humor will vary tremendously according to the child's own language background—the importance of language to the adults around him, the richness and variety of his exposures to language—so one cannot set up any realistic lower age limits for language humor. Rather, one must simply recognize that for *most* three- to five-year-olds nonsense sounds or sounds that sound like funny things are the only important language play; that broad distortions in pronunciation and spelling may become funnier as the child goes on through elementary grades and comes to pronounce and spell more accurately himself; that in junior and high school years the contrast between language used and the situation in which it is used becomes funnier, since children are now growing more aware, through their own experience, of usage levels and vocabulary levels; and that except in fairly set forms like riddles, the pun is not generally appreciated until a child's mastery of language becomes quite sophisticated and flexible. One might guess that humor heavily larded with puns would be dull to most nine- or ten-year-olds. Yet one could not arbitrarily say that an elaborate pun jest such as Lear's poem "The Sage" would be *only* for older children or adults. In that poem the whole joke is a play on the two meanings of the word *sage*—

"wise man" and "a plant and the spice that is derived from it." *Some* young children might know these two meanings and be interested enough in language to put them together and laugh (and a good many adults in the general population might *not* have the necessary information and alertness to do this). Likewise, the punning part of Ogden Nash's humor may be appreciated by the occasional nine-year old. But again, Nash's facile punning will become effective with most children only when they get older, for it is based on considerable language knowledge and ease and demands a fair degree of that in the listener or reader.

For somewhat similar reasons the humor of character—humorous contrasts between characters and funny combinations of traits within characters—is likely to form only a minor component of young children's humor and to become more important as they grow older. Growing up is, among other things, the accumulation of knowledge of people. The child gradually comes to know more kinds of people and so to be more aware of possibilities of difference between them, and he also gradually learns something of the complexities within individuals. He has to get some knowledge of human contrasts before he can recognize them. And his social perception requires training and practice, so that he can come to recognize specific cues to character traits in people's outward behavior. It is only slowly, for instance, that a person comes to realize that although a banging fist on a table may indicate certainty and be funny because it is so startlingly loud, a fist banging on a table may really be the result of uncertainty and frustration in the banger and may thus be in funny contrast to what he really feels.

A deep appreciation of the foolish and irrational in human behavior—of how seemingly wise people may be very unwise, of how people who seem to have reasons for doing things may have no reasons, at least conscious ones—this enters last of all into one's developing sense of humor. For this is essentially a philosophical attitude that comes about as the result of not only experience with human folly but also a mature intelligence, a mature sense of balance. This appreciation is not something we develop easily or quickly, and many adults never develop it; certainly it can come only with years. And especially if there is a possibility we share a kind of foolishness or a bit of craziness, it is not easy to appreciate it deeply and go on to laugh at it.

This humor of human folly is one of the kinds of humor we find in *Alice in Wonderland,* as well as in some of Thurber. Perhaps it is the source of some adults' enthusiasm for *Alice* and the puzzlement of many young children who are given the book early. One of Carroll's great gifts was his feeling for the nonsensical in seemingly sensible, quite self-satisfied people, and this aspect of his writing is lost on many of his younger readers. They may laugh at the grotesque situations and even at the language japery and yet miss the irony underlying Alice's constant inability to be the appropriate size, the great joke underlying the hatter's tea party, the solemn meaningless questions of the caterpillar, the fantastic goings-on at the court of the king and queen of hearts. Thurber's clowns are wise, and his proper, respectable, "sensible" people turn out to be pretty ignorant and shallow. And something of the same awareness of the human predicament that Carroll had—the awareness of human intelligence trying to cope with problems often too big for it—characterizes all Thurber's work, including his books for children.

If we realize that differences in appreciation of certain kinds of humor exist between younger and older human beings, we can select certain stories and poems as more suitable for children than others without being patronizing, without fear that we are coddling or retarding them. At the same time, we must realize that there is nothing *essentially* higher or lower about broad physical comedy or word play or character humor, that these are just different *expressions* of our awareness of the imperfect fits which make up the comic part of our existence. In many of the great comic works of adult humor all of these varieties of humor are present. The comedies of Aristophanes are comically thoughtful, and at the same time are shot through with the broadest slapstick farce and the sharpest word fencing. Shakespeare's comedies, such as *The Taming of the Shrew* or *Twelfth Night* or *A Midsummer Night's Dream*, contain genuinely funny characters, lots of language frolicking (puns, blunders, etc), and a good deal of broad physical roistering and tumbling; and Molière found fun in human folly, in mad confusion, and in clever verbal wit.

If we maintain this balance—if we are aware of differences of appreciation but also of the deep roots of all kinds of humor—our working policy will be to introduce *as much* humor and humor of as *many different kinds* as the child seems capable of understanding, to keep expanding the bases of the child's fun as fast as possible but with a realization that the child's experience and particular skills in part determine what he will find funny.

Other Views of Humor in Children's Literature

This relativistic view of children's humor which I have just presented is only one among a number of possible views. It is not, perhaps, the most generally accepted and practiced. The others are usually not stated in so many words; nevertheless, they underlie policies that often determine the buying and using of children's books of humor.

1 The Undesirability of Humor   Thus far we have been assuming that humor is and should be a part of children's literature. But not everyone feels this way. There is the opposed dogma that humor is bad for children and to be excluded from their literary intake.

This dogma can stem from any one of a number of notions about life in general, but most often involves a combination of them. One is the notion that life is a vale of tears and that it is therefore futile, or at least highly inappropriate, to try to bring laughter into it; merriness is discord in such a serious universe. Then there is the conviction that man is sinful and so must be chastened, must pay for his sinfulness, in a sense work it off. From cradle to grave, he must not enjoy himself; even the child must be punished by the sacrifice of laughter. Related to this outlook is the notion that life is a serious business, that if one is to become a responsible, useful, respected member of society, he has little time for laughter; he had better develop sober habits early and not get into frivolous ways with such nonsense as games, music, and Dr. Seuss. This latter is the position of expediency: that though humor may not be evil, it simply does not pay, that we have no time to waste in dancing, movies, or reading books other than books of useful information.

These various notions were widely adhered to in the seventeenth and eighteenth centuries, and this meant that the reading of *most* children, particularly from the Puritan middle class, was mostly humorless. Some parents and teachers felt that reading humorous books was sinful because it was especially pleasant in itself and therefore a carnal indulgence. Others felt it might *lead* to sin through the reader's vicarious participation in worldly pleasures. Still others—and this remained true of many nineteenth-century adults who had relinquished something of the stern Puritan creed—discouraged the reading of humorous books because they feared the books themselves would lead to lazy, self-indulgent habits and because they felt that to read them was to waste time that could be spent in preparation for the business of earning a living. Reading for information and for ethical improvement could be justified, but not reading for the enjoyment of humor—or for enjoyment at all, for that matter.

This basic antagonism to humor in children's literature is no longer dominant, as it once was, and not nearly so much in evidence. But it has by no means disappeared. Although it may be unconscious or concealed, uneasiness about humor as a part of the child's world is still something to be reckoned with. Some adults confine their children's humorous reading to the preschool and primary years, in the belief that the very young child is not yet able to take in much useful information and so can be permitted to mark time for a few years, after which any hilarity is suspect as a dangerous extravagance. A good many parents and teachers do not openly object to humor but simply concentrate on sober fare and so make humor scarce. To a funny tale they will prefer a lesson-teaching story about little boys and girls, or a facts-of-life account (*The Postoffice, My Trip to the Harbor,* the Pogo series about the dog Pogo and his master's learning about planes, etc.). Large areas of children's reading—school readers, the many series of historical novels for children, the family series, and the children's magazines—seem startlingly lacking in humor of any sort, and this absence may indicate, if not hostility, certainly indifference to laughter as a major ingredient of children's literature.

The inclination to steer away from funny writing seems to be most marked in teachers. Whether or not commendable, this is understandable, for they are the adults most immediately involved with the imparting of information and the cultivating of certain skills. And some teachers keep humor at a distance, not because of their own dislike for it or any reasoned conception of children's reading, but because of fear of public criticism; they are on edge lest there will be unfavorable public reaction against levity as frivolous and time-wasting. The recent worry about "frills" in education and increased emphasis on subject mastery and accelerated learning have made some teachers hesitate to bring as much humorous literature into the classroom as they otherwise would.

So although the massive disapproval of humor for children has gone, there are still enough felt reasons for de-emphasizing humor to keep its presence limited in children's reading.

2 The Inappropriateness of Subtle Humor   People who do not positively feel that humor is bad for children may still believe that it will not be appreciated by children, that it is beyond them and so need not be a significant part of their literary fare.

It would be extremely hard to swallow the idea that children do not react to broad, physical humor—weird appearances, physical tumbles, and mixed-up situations—and so the inclusion of this sort of humor in children's reading is pretty generally unopposed on the grounds that it won't be appreciated. The real rub comes with humor based largely on language or character. Language and character may not be as funny to young children as they will become for them later, but also, children are highly variable in this matter, and it is important only in selecting reading for quite young children. The qualifications, though, sometimes get lost, and a good many teachers and parents conclude that the broadest sort of humor is "the only kind the kids will go for" and leave almost all language wit and character humor for "the maturity of adulthood." Thus when they select humor for children, they are likely to draw heavily on Seuss, energetic Disney cartooning, *Little Toot* and Rey's *Curious George*, and the Miss Pickerell series, and to ignore or use only sparingly the gently funny Pooh books, *Babar, The Wind in the Willows, The Hobbit*, the Borrowers, and the sensitive, cerebral humor of E. B White.

This view assumes that a great gap exists between the child and the grown-up. It ignores the possibility of any basic similarity throughout all humor and the likelihood that the development of a feeling for complex fun may be a gradual, uneven process. The fact that it is founded in a partial truth makes this oversimplified view that subtlety is not for children difficult to counter.

3 The Single Standard for Humor   An oversimplified view that stands in strong contrast to this one is held by a highly literate minority of adult selectors of children's reading. This is the concept that good humor is good humor *for all*, for children and adults together. Far from putting children's and adults' fun into separate pigeonholes, these people are given to assuming a single standard for jesting and so conclude that the book that both adult and child can laugh at is the better one and look for books of this kind. This means that they will ignore a great many books of children's humor as infantile and dull and will concentrate mainly on books like *Alice in Wonderland, The Hobbit, Ferdinand,* and Grahame's *Wind in the Willows* and *The Reluctant Dragon,* which satisfy them as adults. Thus their general theory that good humor is good humor anywhere, anytime, for any age, usually works out in favor of the adult; good humor is what appeals to both child and adult, poor humor is what appeals to neither *or* what fails to appeal to the adult. Under these selective principles, children are likely to get a fairly adult diet of language fun from Lear, Carroll, and Milne, mellow Thurber, and E. B. White. Perhaps Seuss creeps in, and some Krauss, mainly for the language play in each. And the laughter of Dickens is hustled to the children as fast as they can take it, chosen by adult standards of literacy and appreciation. The reading resulting from this policy is a somewhat exclusive sort; it leaves out more than it includes.

4 *An Unanalytic Approach*   In contrast to all these views of humor in children's literature is that of adults who are convinced that children crave and must have a literary diet consisting almost entirely of humor, and that it does not matter what kinds of humor they get. The generalizations of these people are as big as those of antihumor moralists. They believe that all children, or almost all children, love humor, but they feel no special need for analyzing humor into kinds of humor; for them, "Humor is humor," and enough said. And so they do not feel any special need for discrimination in the selection of humorous literature for children; they do not worry about the special tone of a tale or its suitability to particular groups of children. When these unanalytic adults think of children's books, they think of funny children's books—Bemelmans, *Johnny Crow's Garden, Fun, Fun, Fun,* Seuss's many books, *Pooh, Tom Sawyer*—and the books they get for the young are mainly funny stories. This view, essentially an uncritical one, is widespread, and partly accounts for the prominence of funny books in the juvenile sections of bookstores.

Conclusion

The central implication of this whole chapter is that our adult thinking about humor in children's literature is generally very sloppy and vague. All too frequently it starts with sweeping but very rickety assumptions about both humor and children, and much of the time we do not recognize the nature of the assumptions we are using.

It is ironic, but perhaps not surprising, that we should be so confident and cavalier in regard to one of the elements of children's literature about which we have probably done the least amount of truly critical thinking.

Some people might say this is not altogether unfortunate; they might hold that thinking about fun would make it less funny, would defuse it. This position, I think, is altogether mistaken: humor can take analysis.

SUGGESTED SOURCES

Suggestions for Further Study of Sources of Humor in Children's Literature

Physical Humor

In the following selection from children's literature physical humor is a major, although not necessarily the sole, humorous element:

Bontemps, Arna, and Jack Conroy: *The Fast Sooner Hound* and *Sam Patch, the High, Wide and Handsome Jumper*

Brooke, Leslie: *Johnny Crow's Garden*, etc.

Brooks, Walter: *Freddy and the Men from Mars, Freddy and the Ignoramus*, and other Freddy stories

De Regniers, Beatrice: *What Can You Do with a Shoe?*

Duvoisin, Roger: Petunia and Veronica series

Folktales like *The Three Billy Goats Gruff* and *The Pancake*

Gramatky, Hardie: *Little Toot, Loopy*, etc.

Kahl, Virginia: *Away Went Wolfgang!, The Duchess Bakes a Cake*, etc.

Lindgren, Astrid: The Pippi Longstocking books

Lofting, Hugh: The Doctor Dolittle series

McCloskey, Robert: *Centerburg Tales* and *Homer Price*

Mother Goose verses

Rey, Hans: The Curious George books

Seuss, Dr.: *Bartholomew and the Oobleck, The Cat in the Hat, If I Ran the Zoo, McElligot's Pool, Scrambled Eggs Super!, On beyond Zebra*, etc.

Sendak, Maurice: *Where the Wild Things Are*

Tall tales like Jack Tales and Pecos Bill, Mike Fink, and Paul Bunyan tales

Situation Humor

In the following selections situation humor is a major ingredient:

Atwater, Richard and Florence: *Mr. Popper's Penguins*

Bemelmans, Ludwig: The Madeline books

Bond, Michael: The Paddington books, about a very amusing bear

Bright, Robert: *Georgie to the Rescue*, etc.

Brown, Margaret Wise: *The Little Farmer* and *The Runaway Bunny*

Butterworth, Oliver: *The Enormous Egg* and *The Trouble with Jenny's Ear*

Collodi, Carlo: *Pinocchio*

Corbett, Scott: *The Lemonade Trick*

Du Bois, William Pène: *Bear Party*, *The Great Geppy*, *The Giant*, and *The Alligator Case*

Fleischman, Sid: *McBroom Tells the Truth*

Folktales of simpletons, like *Gudbrand of the Hillside*, *Clever Elsie*, *Silly Jean*, and *The Three Sneezes*, or of trickery, like the Uncle Remus stories

Freeman, Lydia and Don: *Pet of the Met*, etc.

Gág, Wanda: *Nothing at All* and *Millions of Cats*

Hale, Lucretia: *The Peterkin Papers*

Fatio, Louis: *The Happy Lion* series

Krasilovsky, Phyllis: *The Man Who Didn't Wash His Dishes*

Lawson, Robert: *Ben and Me*, *Mr. Revere and I*, *McWhinney's Jaunt*, and *Mr. Twigg's Mistake*

Leaf, Munro, and Robert Lawson: *Ferdinand* and *Wee Gillis*

McCloskey, Robert: *Blueberries for Sal* and *Lentil*

MacDonald, Betty: The *Mrs. Piggle Wiggle* stories

MacGregor, Ellen: The *Miss Pickerell* series

Mian, Mary: *The Nip and Tuck War*

Selden, George: *Sparrow Socks*, about socks for cold sparrows

Seuss, Dr.: *The Five Hundred Hats of Bartholomew Cubbins*, *Horton Hatches the Egg*, *Horton Hears a Who*, *Thidwick: The Big-hearted Moose*, and *I Had Trouble in Getting to Solla Sollew*

Stong, Phil: *Honk: The Moose*

Titus, Eve: The *Anatole* books, with the French mouse Anatole as their hero

White, E. B.: *Stuart Little*

Language Humor

In the following books language is a main source of humor:

Carroll, Lewis: *Alice in Wonderland* and *Through the Looking-glass*

Ciardi, John: *The Reason for the Pelican*, etc.

Hood, Thomas: *The Works of Thomas Hood, Comic and Serious, in Prose and Verse*

Krauss, Ruth: *A Hole Is to Dig: A First Book ot First Definitions* and *A Banquet of Littles*

Kuskin, Karla: *Roar and More*

Lear, Edward: *The Complete Book of Nonsense*

Milne, A. A.: The Pooh stories; also Milne's poetry

Morrison, Lillian (compiler): *A Dillar, a Dollar; Yours Till Niagara Falls* and *Remember Me When This You See*, autograph-verse collections

Nash, Ogden: *Parents Keep Out: Elderly Poems for Youngerly Readers*

Richards, Laura E.: *Tirra Lirra*

Riley, James Whitcomb: *Rhymes of Childhood*

Seuss, Dr.: *Fox in Socks*, tongue twisters

Withers, Carl (ed.): *Rocket in My Pocket*

Humor of Character

Character is a primary source of humor in the following selections:

Alcott, Louisa: *Little Women, Jo's Boys*, etc.

Cleary, Beverly: The Henry Huggins and Beezus stories

Enright, Elizabeth: *The Saturdays* and *Thimble Summer*

Estes, Eleanor: The Moffat stories

Grahame, Kenneth: *The Wind in the Willows*

Norton, Mary: The Borrowers series

Thurber, James: *Many Moons*

Travers, P. L.: *Mary Poppins* and other Mary Poppins stories

Twain, Mark (Samuel Clemens): *The Adventures of Tom Sawyer* and *The Adventures of Huckleberry Finn*

White, E. B.: *Charlotte's Web*

CHAPTER 10

A
READY-MADE
AUDIENCE
FOR
POETRY

*I*f you wander past front yards or playgrounds where little children are playing, you will hear poetry. It may not be good poetry—although some of it may be surprisingly good—but there will be plenty of it. You may hear chants like

One's a twozy, two's a twozy,
Three's a twozy, four. . . .

or

One, two,
Buckle my shoe. . . .

or

Here is the church, and here is the steeple;
Open the door and here are the people.
Here is the parson going upstairs,
And here he is a-saying his prayers.

or

Charlie Chaplin went to France
To show the ladies how to dance.

227

First your heel, then your toe,
Lift up your skirt and round you go.

or

I'm the king, I'm the king,
I'm the king, the king, the king;
See me, see me, I'm the king. . . .

or

Hickory dickory dock,
The mouse ran up the clock. . . .

or

I scream, you scream,
We all scream
For ice cream.

or

Fuzzywuzzy was a bear,
Fuzzywuzzy had no hair.
Fuzzywuzzy wasn't fuzzy,
Wuz he?

or

How much wood could a woodchuck chuck
If a woodchuck could chuck wood?

or

Smarty
had a party
and nobody came.

or

Marguerite, go wash your feet;
The board of health's across the street.

or, borrowed from television watching and radio listening,

Like a [clap] cigarette should.

or

Double your flavor, double your fun,
With double-good, double-good Doublemint Gum.

There is no denying the fact that little children use great amounts of poetry and that they do it of their own volition, for their own purposes. They use borrowed poetry or poetry of their own making in their games and dances. They adapt poems to the music they hum and sing or make up words for it. In solitary play they mumble over learned snatches of verse and also create vast amounts of rhythmic verbal pattern. Poetry comes easily to little children. They do not call it poetry or anything else; they simply use it more than they ever will at any later period in their lives.

And mothers, fathers, and other adults read poetry to little children with less self-consciousness or uneasiness than they ever experience in using poetry for their own purposes. They often read them Mother Goose verses with much relish and verve, and will sometimes participate in their making up of verses, and do not feel apologetic for all this poetic activity. And, in kindergarten and the primary grades poetry is a very important part of the children's day—out on the playground and in the classroom too. Teachers introduce poetry into classroom activities. They search for poems in anthologies and juvenile magazines; they find folk songs a source of poetry that most children can be brought to like. Some of them may even encourage children to say or write down their own poetic notions.

Some parents and teachers view this poetic activity as just fun, a welcome recreational activity; others consider it a means of preserving and encouraging creativity in the young child; still others use it as a device for teaching moral principles (kindness to animals, obedience to parents, traffic safety) or for dropping information pleasantly into the child's mind (how the beaver builds his dam, the animals on a farm). But whatever their motives, parents and teachers apparently sense no inappropriateness in poetry for children up to, say, eight or nine years of age, or through the third or fourth grade. The use of poetry by and for little children is not problematic.

The Shift Away from Poetry in Later Childhood

But when children are somewhere in the middle grades—say, by the age of ten—the attitudes of both children and adults to poetry undergo a significant change. Children come to use poetry somewhat less in games and as free verbal play, although they may still sing the lyrics of popular songs and the advertising jingles they hear on television and radio. They come to *make* poetry much less; a tendency develops for them to rely more on poetry borrowed from the contemporary adult world, such as the popular songs and jingles, than on their own inventions or their own versions of traditional verses. Adults—parents and teachers—become less ready to go along with children's own poetic tastes. They are likely to leave out nonsense poetry—in fact, most humorous poetry—and to supplant it with "more refined" verse (usually inferior) about nature and admirable moral traits such as courage and kindness. They are likely to draw on the poetry of the Victorians—Tennyson, Kipling, Longfellow, Whittier, Lowell. Gradually, poetry ceases to be considered a basic and normal sort of human expression and comes to be thought of as a very special—"higher," "more imaginative"—form of expression. It becomes less something in which children can take part and more an aesthetic expression to be made for them and brought to them. It is more and more thought of as being rhymed verse with very regular meter; the possible forms of poetry become few. In classes, poetry is drained off into assigned lessons. It gets collected into card indexes and associated with weighty anthologies.

By the time they reach high school, many children have a store of thoroughly stultifying and wrongheaded misconceptions of poetry. They consider poetry to be a trivial sideline that has no connection with the important purposes and problems of living; and at the same time they think of it as something inspired, "divine"—and so beyond the spheres of ordinary men. When they do permit it to enter their environment unchallenged, it is under the guise of performance—as something to be memorized and recited in class, a show to be presented. The only poetry to escape the charge of triviality is moralizing verse, poetry that teaches ethical lessons. And large sections of human expression—nonsense verse, children's Mother Goose rhymes, songs, hymns, the Bible—get shoved out of the poetry category altogether.

In summary, between early childhood and adolescence poetry moves from a central to a peripheral position in children's lives. It slips from unquestioned acceptance to neglected respectability.

What underlies the young child's freedom with poetry and the shift away from it that takes place as he grows up?

Explanations

There are within the natures of young children several reasons why they usually find nothing too strange or too boring, nothing unreachably divine or unspeakably trivial, about poetry.

First, young children's failure to find a sharp distinction between the real world and their own mental world makes poetry, with its disregard of any such distinction, seem more normal, more regular, than it can ever be for most adults. Young children are not ordinarily bothered by the question, "Do giants, dragons, fairies, trolls, and ghosts really exist?" and so they are not puzzled or stopped by that poetry in which such creatures play a prominent part. Nor are they worried by the attributing of human qualities to winds, leaves, cockroaches, flowers, rocks, and brooks. The commonsense question, "Can trees really feel?" is not so likely to bother the young child, and the poem in which the poet has put himself inside the tree will probably not give the young child pause. Coleridge's "willing suspension of disbelief" seems to require much less will in younger than in older children and adults.

The young child, moreover, feels freer to indulge his play impulses than he will be later, to play around with experiences, to pretend that dogs can fly, that maybe *he* can, that the moon is a man, and that animals can talk. As he grows older, this becomes harder for him to do; and if he is still doing it in his teens, he is likely to be considered very odd, maybe even in need of psychiatric attention.

The small child's urge to play around extends beyond the tangible, physical world to language. He feels no shame in just jabbering, playing with pleasant or sometimes unpleasant sounds, making up nonsensical words. In middle childhood he may restrain himself from such sound play, but he may indulge in such forms of language fooling as pig Latin, double-talk, and jive talk. In the adult world, however, he comes under pressure not to experiment with language; playing word games persists but is held to be disrespectful to language, which we have naively come to give the status of reality itself. The whimsy of "All mimsy were the borogoves" becomes unrespectable, just as pretending jabberwocks really exist does.

It may be reasonably argued that playfulness does not necessarily diminish with age, that it is not intrinsically the property of youth—but *in our culture* most of us lose some of our verve for play and our ability to play as we grow older. Both our experience and our words about it are put into straitjackets, as it were. And so it is hard for poetry, which is in considerable part an experimenting with experience and language, to remain central in the consciousness of older children and adults.

Two other important elements of poetry, concrete imagery and rhythm, are quite acceptable to the young child but become very much less so with the accumulation of years.

The young child's language is characteristically concrete. It consists mainly of words for things he senses—sees, smells, tastes, hears, feels— and words for actions—walking, running, bumping, falling, shouting, etc. He is more likely to say, "Mary's crying" than the more abstract "Mary is unhappy" or "Mary is in trouble." He will say, "This is a stone," not "This is a hard, round thing." But, for many reasons, as we grow older we bring into our language use great numbers of abstract terms and substitute them for many of the concrete terms we first learned. Now the language of much poetry (not all, of course) is very concrete. The poet says, "My love is like a red, red rose," not "My love is beautiful"; he says "Go and catch a falling star," and "Tiger, tiger, shining bright/ In the forest of the night." "Red rose," "falling star," "tiger . . . forest . . . night"—all concrete, particular images. Poetic imagery is full of—indeed, rests upon—particular sensory experiences. For this reason, much poetry is closer to the language of the young child than is the more highly abstract speech of adults in our culture.

And the young child customarily uses regular, accentuated rhythms in his daily physical activities—in running, skipping, jumping, "calling names," even in sitting and moving around in a chair. The rhythms of poetry are not particularly strange to a child who jiggles and jumps and chants many minutes a day.

All these common denominators—ways in which childhood experience and language are akin to poetic experience and language—are positive factors working *for* poetry in our early years. Now let us concentrate on the negative factors working *against* it as we get older.

In some segments of present-day American culture poetry has become associated with effeminacy, has come to be thought of as something sweet and pretty and delicate that girls and girlish boys like; and so there is a widespread feeling that as a boy approaches manhood, he ought to put aside poetry, along with childish clothes and the girlish tendency to weep. This association completely ignores the historical fact that poetry has been an integral part of cultures not noted for their lack of virile masculinity—Greek, Celtic, European Renaissance, for example—but there is no denying the fact that this present linking in people's minds retards enthusiasm for poetry on the part of the boy and also of the parents and teachers who might encourage him with books and advice.

Likewise, our society, tolerant of uselessness in the activities of little children but not in those of older children and adults, views poetry as useless and harmless to the little child but definitely harmful in its uselessness as he grows to adulthood. The attitude toward poetry is, in this respect, like that toward playing marbles or mumblety-peg—quite all right for little children but to be dropped at an early age. One finds among the parents of kindergartners and primary graders no worry at all over their children's using poetry in their class activities, but a good many parents would disapprove of their children's taking courses in poetry in high school and college. This utilitarian pressure often works in a less overt way: the children themselves come to feel that school subjects should help them get jobs or college recommendations and then degrees and so jobs, and become convinced that though poetry may somehow be great stuff, it is not useful in these ways and so is something they had better not fool around with. It achieves the reputation of being an educational frill.

The positive and negative factors that I have set forth go far toward explaining the high status of poetry among young children and its shift to a peripheral position in the imaginative experience of older children and adults, but the way poetry is presented by its advocates in our schools suggests a whole cluster of additional reasons for the shift.

In the course of twelve years' or more exposure to poetry the student comes to associate it with certain special activities—memorization, reciting, getting grades, taking tests—which teachers impose on him but which do not go outside of school; it comes to be accepted as an academic activity, ending at the classroom door. That teachers put poems under the general category of classics further links them with school, and to many young people their own feelings of embarrassment about anything "classical" are enough to make poetry seem remote, not for them. The extravagant claims made for poetry along the academic way perhaps serve to deepen this sense of its remoteness for many growing people; poetry is often taught as a sort of mystery, and to the student it remains a mystery, a mystery that seems to belong to shy men and elderly ladies. And the setting up of rigid linguistic differences between poetry and prose (partly due to the linguistic unsophistication of many teachers) seems to give some sort of justification for putting poetry off in a corner by itself. And generally the main emphasis, especially in the later grades, is placed on lyric poetry, which by and large seems to students the farthest removed from everyday feelings, concerns, and speech; indeed, this is often taught as "the truly real poetry," "the most poetic poetry."

What Can Be Done?

In all these ways teachers have unwittingly accelerated the process of removing poetry from the active consciousness of the growing boy and girl. It would seem, then, that the exiling of poetry from the growing child's experience could be slowed down, perhaps stopped, by modifying or abolishing these academic practices. The unusualness of poetry might thus be left relatively unstressed, so that children would be less likely to drift into the conclusion that poetry, being something very special, is not for them.

Teachers need not link poetry constantly with individual performance, written or oral, under glaring test conditions. They need not refer to poetry constantly in terms of classics, and they might refrain generally from a stance of awe in its presence. They can, without being mechanical or too insistent about it, mingle poetry with history, social studies, school plays, and club activities, at the same time not making it bulk so large in English that it somehow gets irrevocably associated with the English class. (Of course, in linking poetry with student's other activities, teachers need to be careful that they don't handle poetry simply as a vehicle or channel for factual information and ethical teachings and that they do not, accordingly, introduce weak poetry in the name of factual accuracy and ideational soundness.) Classes might work as much with philosophical, narrative, and other kinds of poetry as with lyric poetry. Teachers might introduce poetic prose, in which one can rather easily be led to see the special but not rare qualities that make language poetic. They might well expose children to some contemporary poetry—Frost, Rukeyser, Eliot, Cummings, Spender, Shapiro, Roethke, and others—to help them sense the immediacy of poetry, its close relation to human experience. In so doing, however, a teacher might well choose not to stress today's more highly intellectualized symbolic poetry, which can prove frustrating to the young reader.

Such restraints and activities can do much to reduce the tremendous flight from poetry during the years of later childhood and youth, but in the very nature of poetry and in society (at least, our society) there are, as we have seen, forces that make poetry increasingly less acceptable and natural in the older years. The hardening distinction between things in here and out there, or between mental and real, the growing emphasis on abstract thought and language, the various social pressures that move poetry into a special, more limited enclosure on the edge of our living— these things perhaps we may as well recognize as facts of life, at least in our time. Perhaps too much time is wasted in lamenting the narrowness of poetry's dominion—the fact that few adults read poetry with any understanding and relish—and in condemning the mass of people for being so unappreciative of poetry, so apparently immune to the muse's influence. In our world poetry is not everyone's meat, and not *all* poetry is for everyone who uses poetry in his life, and it would seem to be more sensible to face such facts. Then we could see what, within existing limits, can be done to keep the atrophy of children's feelings for poetry from going farther than it need go.

The best way to start resisting this atrophy, I submit, would be for teachers and parents themselves to achieve a more realistic conception of the nature of poetry. Importantly, they should learn the *range* of poetry, the very different things that poetry is and can do, and they should learn what to select from this variety of poetic kinds for particular individuals and groups of children. Thus they would think not in terms of poetry as a whole, but rather of certain poetic elements and of certain kinds of poetry in which these particular elements are relatively important. Nor would they think primarily in terms of great poetry; instead, they would consider the different kinds of things poetry can do and then consider what poems will do these things. The dreamy wishing for some perfect absolute in art, for some *one thing* that art is—this constitutes one of the most pernicious enemies of the *use* of poetic or any other art.

Classifying Children's Poetry

One method of classifying children's poetry is by the author's intention. But this kind of classification is not very useful, partly because it is often very difficult to determine what an author's intention was and partly because knowing an author's intention has little to do with determining what he has finally made and its effect on his readers. Another method is to classify by subject matter—nature, fairies, animals, famous men, holidays, courageous deeds. But this kind of classification does nothing to help us distinguish poetic writing from any other kind of writing or different poetic approaches to experience from one another; thus a nonsense verse about cats gets lumped in with an altogether different sort of poem urging kindness to cats or with a realistic little poem describing a particular cat.

A classification of children's poetry more useful than either of these two is according to *what the poet mainly did*. Why he did it or whether he wrote a poem about a cat or a mouse or an ancient battle is not the basic question; rather the basic question is what he did with his subject—what sort of poetry he created out of his subject.

Five main things that poets do in children's poetry, that is, in poems which children read or listen to, are (1) make sense, (2) make nonsense, (3) tell a story, (4) make ethical recommendations, and (5) fancy or imagine a mode of existence. And in doing each of these things, we shall find, poets use in various ways the diverse elements of experience and language.

Making Sense

The poetry that chiefly makes sense is probably the kind closest to non-poetry, its language the closest to prose. It is based in sensory experience, and its primary appeal lies in the vividness of its recreation of the things seen, smelled, felt, heard. It may use very little imagery, as in Dorothy Baruch's or James Tippett's verse or much as in Walter de la Mare's poems about the fields and woods. It may use conventional and definite patterns of rhythm and rhyme as in the poetry of Dorothy Aldis and Tippett, or unconventional, experimental free-verse patterns, as in much of Baruch's. But whatever the particular use of imagery, rhythm, rhyme, and other poetic devices, such poetry of sense is above all a vivid, intense capturing of a moment experienced, an experience observed—a circus clown bounding, a curled, purring cat, a white daisy, a black bear, washing the family car, a beach picnic, visiting the neighborhood market.

Sometimes the writer tries to get at the special moment very directly and quickly by selecting certain facts from it and reporting them, with just a little reinforcing from rhythms, rhymes, etc. For example, Lois Lenski in "Supermarket"*:

Open the door,
Go get a cart,
Pick up some soup
Just for a start.
Here is the fruit,
Fill up your sack;
Bread's up front,
Soap's in the back.
Cookies are here,
Crackers are there,
Where is the salt?
Tea anywhere?
See all the shelves,
Cans in a row;
Fill up your cart,
Pay as you go!

The unknown author of "The Milkman's Horse"* tried to do a similar thing:

On summer mornings, when it's hot,

The milkman's horse can't even trot,
But pokes along like this—
Klip-klop, klip-klop, klip-klop.

But in the winter brisk,
He perks right up and wants to frisk,
And then he goes like this—
Klippty-klip, klippty-klip, klippty-klip.

The following poem, Eleanor Chaffee's "The Cobbler," * is an economical little report on certain aspects of shoemaking and shoe shops:

Crooked heels
  And scuffy toes
Are all the kinds
  Of shoes he knows.

He patches up
  The broken places,
Sews the seams
  And shines their faces.

Many of James Tippett's poems, such as "Ferryboats," * are almost aggressively blunt reports of events interesting to children:

Over the river,
Over the bay,
Ferryboats travel
Every day.

Most of the people
Crowd to the side
Just to enjoy
Their ferryboat ride.

Watching the sea gulls,
Laughing with friends,
I'm always sorry
When the ride ends.

There is no imagery at all here, no metaphor, no symbolism; there are simply four generalizations about ferry travel—that ferries travel every day, that people crowd to the side, that they watch gulls and laugh, and that the poet is sorry at the end of the ride. Still, the rhythm and rhyme lend a feeling of specialness to the occasion, and there is somewhat more selection and therefore speed here than would be true of an ordinary prose account; the ferry ride is separated from the rest of experience and is looked at quickly.

Still staying close to the observed object and reporting it in some detail, Rose Fyleman in "Mice"* does more shaping and so creates a poem whose reporting is somewhat camouflaged by the formal patterns she creates— the neat contrast of her view of mice with everyone else's, her surrounding their ordinary view by hers in the opening and closing statements:

I think mice
  Are rather nice.

    Their tails are long,
    Their faces small,
    They haven't any
    Chins at all.
    Their ears are pink,
    Their teeth are white,
    They run about
    The house at night,
    They nibble things
    They shouldn't touch
    And no one seems
    To like them much.

But I think mice
Are nice.

Here the poet has used little imagery and no figures of speech, but with other patterns has created a plaintive little poetic observation.

In the following poem, "Whisky Frisky,"* the anonymous poet uses more elaborate poetic means to get us to see the particular thing he has seen:

Whisky Frisky,
Hippity hop,
Up he goes
To the tree top!

Whirly, twirly,
Round and round,
Down he scampers
To the ground.

Furly, curly,
What a tail!
Tall as a feather,
Broad as a sail!

Where's his supper?
In the shell.
Snappy, cracky,
Out it fell.

Like "Mice," "Whisky Frisky" arbitrarily establishes a little cycle of action as the boundaries of the poem——up to the top of the tree for a meal and down with it to the bottom, where it is cracked open. In addition, the poet has suggested the action by sounds (*Whisky frisky, Hippity hop, Whirly, twirly, Snappy, cracky*) and has used evocative images (*"furly, curly"*) and similes ("Tall as a feather" and "Broad as a sail"). All of these poetic effects contribute to the vividness of the picture of the object——the busy squirrel.

Still seeking to give a vivid image of a particular thing but going farther than any of the foregoing poems in transforming it into other things is Hilda Conkling's "Little Snail"*:

I saw a snail
Come down the garden walk,
He wagged his head this way . . . that way . . .
Like a clown in a circus.
He looked from side to side
As though he were from a different country.
I have always said he carries his house on his back . . .
Today in the rain
I saw that it was his umbrella.

Here, as with the milkman's horse, the cobbler, the mice, and the nut-gathering squirrel, we are given a clear report of a particular object at a particular moment; but here we get it in more personal terms, as experienced by one person who sees the snail not only as wagging its head but also as carrying a house and toting an umbrella. The author's fancy is given a little more play; still, her imaginings help to make more vivid a single, observable thing and event——a snail out in the rain.

The poets of sense may be diverse in their poetic means, but they all convey as well as they can the sense of a particular experience, a feeling that it really is or was, that it is not altogether a dream, a created thing. Perhaps the most widely read children's poet to do this in his poetry is Robert Louis Stevenson. The great majority of the poems in his *Child's Garden of Verses* are about common experiences most children know something about——being sick in bed and having to amuse oneself by inventing games on the bed, going up in the air in a swing, riding in a railway carriage, watching the fire in a grate, leaving a farm, digging holes in the sand at the beach, playing with blocks, watching the rain.

Many of Stevenson's poems are primarily clear, direct reports of things sharply noted. Typical of this kind of Stevenson poetic recording is "The Cow"*:

The friendly cow all red and white,
*   I love with all my heart:*
She gives me cream, with all her might,
*   To eat with apple-tart.*

She wanders lowing here and there,
And yet she cannot stray,
All in the pleasant open air,
The pleasant light of day;

And blown by all the winds that pass
And wet with all the showers,
She walks among the meadow grass
And eats the meadow flowers.

In "Farewell to the Farm"* the things a child would realize he was leaving are described in the summarizing stanza:

To house and garden, field and lawn,
The meadow-gates we swung upon,
To pump and stable, tree and swing,
Good-bye, good-bye, to everything.

And in "At the Sea-side"* Stevenson precisely points to what is most memorable to a child in his sand digging:

When I was down beside the sea
A wooden spade they gave to me
To dig the sandy shore.

My holes were empty like a cup.
In every hole the sea came up,
Till it could come no more.

In all these poems Stevenson has gone to what may be for a child the important facts of an experience and has stated them just about as simply and directly as he can, with, of course, the heightened intensity that may come from the regular rhythms, the recurring rhyme sounds, and the neat aural-visual patterns of the stanzas.

In many other poems Stevenson just as straightforwardly describes children's imagining, their playing "pretend"—in "Block City," "Shadow," "A Good Play," "Pirate Story," "Land of Story Books," "Foreign Lands," "My Bed Is a Boat," "Armies in the Fire," and "The Land of Counterpane," for example. In such poems the poet first makes clear the actual situation (sick child in bed, child with building blocks, child watching fire), then describes what the child pretends, and, usually, ends with a reminder that the child returns to reality. "Block City," * for instance, starts this way:

What are you able to build with your blocks?
Castles and palaces, temples and docks.
Rain may keep raining, and others go roam,
But I can be happy and building at home.

Let the sofa be mountains, the carpet be sea,
There I'll establish a city for me:
A kirk and a mill and a palace beside,
And a harbor as well where my vessels may ride.

Then for two stanzas he describes his pretending—ships mooring, sailors singing, kings "coming and going with presents and things." Then he tells how he knocks the blocks down and ends with the thought that he will forever remember what he has imagined:

And as long as I live and where'er I may be,
I'll always remember my town by the sea.

Many of Stevenson's verses, then, contain fancies, but they are characteristically the fancies of the children he is writing about and not his own; he merely records them with precision and sensitivity. Thus even in these poems Stevenson is not basically different from Aldis, Tippett, and the others who have described as accurately as they could the experiences of childhood; here too he is, like them, a poet of sense, one who sets out to make a particular experience intensely vivid and real.

Except when the conventionally hallowed or respected name of Stevenson is attached, a good many adults are inclined to exclude the poetry of sense from their category of poetry; somehow they feel that this poetry brings us too close to experience to be considered poetry, that all poetry should help us to escape from experience rather than confront us with it, as this poetry does. In the foregoing discussion I have not made this assumption. Some poetry can assist in such an escape, but not *all* poetry need do so. The quality that I am asking for in poetry is *the intensity of the realized occasion,* whether it be an actual experience recognized by poet and reader or a poet's journey to fairyland or any other occasion. And the best of these children's poems about real experience are characterized by this intensity. Indeed, they have more of it than do some poems where the effort to soar and plunge and somehow have a special sort of experience is altogether obvious; and adults who fail to recognize this fact are failing one test of their poetic appreciation.

Making Nonsense

The poetry of sense and the poetry of nonsense both have considerable difficulty being accepted as poetry by many editors, teachers, and other arbiters of children's poetry. A reason why this is true in the case of the poetry of sense has been suggested above; it is simply the prevalence of the view that poetry should help us *escape* from experience. An oddly contrasting reason why the poetry of nonsense has difficulty winning acceptance will be suggested in the course of the following brief consideration.

There can be nonsense when a normal life situation is turned topsy-turvy, and there can be nonsense when language contradicts the expected; and nonsense poetry, or verse (people who find it hard to think of nonsense as ever being poetic prefer the term *verse*), can be based on either kind of nonsense, situation or language, or on both occurring together.

A nonsensical situation—specifically, a running away from one's own body—is the whole content of Mary E. Wilkins Freeman's "The Ostrich Is a Silly Bird" *:

The ostrich is a silly bird,
With scarcely any mind.
He often runs so very fast
He leaves himself behind.

And when he gets there, has to stand
And hang about till night,
Without a blessed thing to do
Until he comes in sight.

Another nonsensical situation is the whole focus of Goldsmith's "Elegy on the Death of a Mad Dog," which concludes with these lines:

The man recovered of the bite,
The dog it was that died.

In his "A Tragic Story" William Makepeace Thackeray devotes six stanzas to telling how a "sage" tried vainly to make his pigtail hang in front of him. In his "Purple Cow" Gelett Burgess contemplates the nonsense of seeing a purple cow and the silliness of being one too. A great many of Lear's limericks are little experiments in the denial of ordinary living—playing a harp with one's chin; welcoming all the birds in the air to sit on one's bonnet; twirling around in making a curtsey, like the old lady of Chertsey, till one sinks underground. And most of Lear's longer poems, pieces like "The Jumblies," "The Duck and the Kangaroo," and "The Owl and the Pussy-Cat," are more fully imagined contradictions of normalcy—the Jumblies' going to sea in a sieve and, what's more, coming home in it, how the owl and the pussy-cat went to sea in a beautiful pea-green boat and

. . . took some honey, and plenty of money
Wrapped up in a five-pound note

and the duck's wearing worsted socks so he would not chill the kangaroo as he rode on his tail. And a skimming of any large Mother Goose collection will turn up dozens of little poems whose reason for being is their non-sensical scrambling of reality—an egg sitting on a wall, Mother Hubbard's dog alive and dead and alive again, a dish running with a spoon, etc.

In the poetry of *language* nonsense the lack of sense, the silly turned-arounds, lies primarily in the words. An anonymous limerick-maker conceived this out of two broad puns and a protracted repetition of sounds:

A flea and a fly in a flue
Were imprisoned; so what could they do?
  Said the fly, "Let us flee,"
  Said the flea, "Let us fly,"
So they flew through a flaw in the flue.

More often than not in nonsense poetry, the nonsense is actually both of situation and of language. For instance, in

Hi diddle diddle, the cat and the fiddle,
The cow jumped over the moon

we have the unorthodox combination of the cat with fiddle and cow kicking her heels at normalcy and the "hi diddle diddle" running away from sense too. Another example of this sort of combination, one in which there is an equal balance of far-out language and far-out situation, exists in the following verse:

There was a young lady from Woosester
Who ussessed to crow like a roosester.
  She ussessed to climb
  Seven trees at a time—
But her sissester ussessed to boosester.

And in Laura Richards's "Eletelephony" * we find a ridiculous situation tangle all tangled up with a ridiculous language tangle:

Once there was an elephant,
Who tried to use the telephant—
No! no! I mean an elephone
Who tried to use the telephone—
(Dear me! I am not certain quite
That even now I've got it right.)

Howe'er it was, he got his trunk
Entangled in the telephunk;
The more he tried to get it free,
The louder buzzed the telephee—
(I fear I'd better drop the song
Of elephop and telephong!)

Now one may say—and there are a good many people who do—that although such verse is obviously more or less effective nonsense, it is not poetry. But this exclusion of the great mass of children's nonsense verse from poetry seems altogether unjustified and unfortunate. In the verses quoted above one finds many of the language devices often used to achieve poetic effects—rhyme, rhythm, assonance, stanzaic patterns. These devices are not necessarily identical with poetry, but they do help to create a departure from ordinary patterns of thought; and this shift is one, if only one, of the elements of poetry. But also, nonsense verse in the very nature of its content, opposed to normalcy as this is, achieves specialness and stretches the imagination, as does *all* poetry in one way or another. Thus one will find a great deal of nonsense verse essentially poetic—that is, if one does not assume that all poetry must be sober high seriousness, that humor is inimical to poetry. Nonsense poetry is full of fantastic invention, from Lear's peculiar limerick people to Lewis Carroll's and Ogden Nash's language foolery, and this invention can be a source of the poetic experience.

Another source of the poetic experience, intensity, can be achieved in nonsense poetry if the nonsense world be telephunks or borogoves is fully and consistently imagined, so that one gets the full sense of the author's created nonsense world, and if the poet has made use of various appropriate devices of poetic intensification, such as clattering or syncopated rhythms, rhymes and assonance, and vivid imagery.

Not all nonsense verse is poetic, but a great deal of it contains poetic elements. Therefore nonsense verse, with its lure of humor, provides a bridge over the gulf that forms between children and poetry. This bridge is far too often left unused, mainly because of the unjustifiable assumption that nonsense and poetry are in antithesis.

Narrating in Poetry

Narrative poetry is not made poetic by its being narrative. A story is in itself not poetic, although certain kinds of events may have quite a lot of the rough material for poetry. And the stories about the Pied Piper of Hamelin and Hiawatha and Paul Revere and Gunga Din could be told, though differently, in prose. But tellers of stories have often chosen the poetic forms and modes for telling them, perhaps most often when some such quality as terror or daring or mystery in a situation seemed exciting enough to justify poetic reinforcement. And by so doing, they have contributed something to their particular tales, have somehow enlarged them, and so have been able to heighten the intensity of their readers' (or listeners') feelings, their sense of the significance of incidents.

The poet-storyteller characteristically seeks to build a sense of urgency about the events he is presenting, and this he may do in various ways and combinations of ways. For instance, he may suggest physical speed and onrushing by strong, insistent rhythms, short vowels and explosive consonants, and repetitions of sound and words, as does Alfred Noyes in "The Highwayman" *:

The wind was a torrent of darkness among the gusty trees,
The moon was a ghostly galleon tossed upon cloudy seas,
The road was a ribbon of moonlight over the purple moor,
And the highwayman came riding—
  Riding—riding—
The highwayman came riding, up to the old inn-door.

or as does Browning in "How They Brought the Good News from Ghent to Aix":

I sprang to the stirrup, and Joris, and he;
I galloped, Dirck galloped, we galloped all three;

Usually he chooses a definite rhythm and adheres to it throughout the telling of his story; thus the reader is made to feel he is on a journey to a certain destination, without freedom to dawdle at games or in contemplation along the way. The regularly recurring beat seems to force him onward. And the regular recurrence of the same stanza form establishes, as the events pass, another sort of beat that propels one forward. Furthermore, the verse narrator may get down to the actions themselves, omitting all but the most essential information, and giving as much of that as he can in terms of action, what was done. And this action account he may put into the mouths of the participants in the events, so that one feels he is moving along with, or even inside, the events. The narrator may even plunge us into the middle of events and let us catch up with the first stages by clues dropped in the latter stages of the development.

All of these devices are ways of making a verse narrative move swiftly and thereby building sense of urgency; and this swift movement, created by these devices, characterizes much of the narrative verse that has been appropriated by children and also much of that written mainly with children in mind. The traditional ballads—tales in verse like "Edward," "Lord Randall," "Bonnie George Campbell," "Barbara Allen," "Patrick Spens," "Raggle, Taggle Gypsies," "The Wife of Usher's Well"—use it to create the sense of urgency. And the modern ballads which have sought to capture the spirit of the traditional story songs have used it to the same end.

Charles Kingsley's "Ballad of Earl Haldan's Daughter" * is one of these. The first stanza firmly establishes a quick, easy rhythm, within a stanza pattern which is adhered to till the end, and describes the basic situation, partly through the words of one of the two chief characters:

It was Earl Haldan's daughter,
  She looked across the sea;
She looked across the water,

> *And long and loud laughed she:*
> *"The locks of six princesses*
> *Must be my marriage fee:*
> *So, hey, bonny boat, and ho, bonny boat,*
> *Who comes a-wooing me!"*

We are already well on into the narrative, and a clear beat and a refrain have already been established. In the second stanza we are introduced to the second main actor in the drama:

> *It was Earl Haldan's daughter,*
> *She walked along the sand,*
> *When she was aware of a knight so fair,*
> *Come sailing to the land.*
> *His sails were all of velvet,*
> *His mast of beaten gold,*
> *And "Hey, bonny boat, and ho, bonny boat,*
> *Who saileth here so bold?"*

Here the few descriptive details serve to establish the visitor as a person of great wealth and importance, not to be scorned by Earl Haldan's daughter. The third stanza quickly confronts the daughter, and us, with the fact that this visitor is very close to being the man she had waited for:

> *"The locks of five princesses*
> *I won beyond the sea;*
> *I shore their golden tresses*
> *To fringe a cloak for thee.*
> *One handful yet is wanting,*
> *But one of all the tale;*
> *So, hey, bonny boat, and ho, bonny boat,*
> *Furl up thy velvet sail!"*

And the brief poem explodes into a finale of action:

> *He leapt into the water,*
> *That rover young and bold;*
> *He gript Earl Haldan's daughter,*
> *He shore her locks of gold:*
> *"Go weep, go weep, proud maiden,*
> *The tale is full today.*
> *Now, hey, bonny boat, and ho, bonny boat,*
> *Sail Westward ho, and away!"*

And so it is with the work in this genre by many of its most skillful practitioners—Scott, Browning, Coleridge ("Rime of the Ancient Mariner") Thomas Campbell ("Lord Ullin's Daughter"), Wordsworth, Southey ("Inchcape Rock"), Longfellow, Stephen Vincent Benét ("The Ballad of William Sycamore"), William Rose Benét, Alfred Noyes. They all use the same devices to create swift movement and so the sense of urgency, of hurry, of crowding toward a conclusion.

In most of the narrative poems less clearly related to the traditional ballad, such ballad devices as narration through dialogue and the conventional ballad rhythms may not be used. But in these poem-stories one does move quickly with the poet into the heart of the action and, with the aid of other vigorous rhythms and singing sounds, on through the action steps to the final action. Such poems are Whittier's "Maud Muller," Tennyson's "Charge of the Light Brigade" and "Sir Galahad," Burns's "Tam O'Shanter," Arnold's "Forsaken Merman," de la Mare's "The Listeners," Noyes's "Song of Sherwood" and "The Admiral's Ghost," William Rose Benét and Rosemary Benét's "Johnny Appleseed," "Drake's Drum" by Henry Newbolt, Kipling's "Gunga Din."

A story may also be intensified, made more poetic, by deepening the colors of the telling, enriching by imagery of sight, sound, touch, and smell. Much narrative poetry, and particularly that written for children or found appealing to them, acquires what poetic specialness it has through narrative tempo, but still there is a considerable body of poetic story-telling in which the imagery reinforces the intensifying effect of speed; occasionally, however, as in some of Noyes's verse-stories, or Vachel Lindsay's, the imagery becomes so rich it almost displaces the action or sense of action.

The power of Coleridge's "Rime of the Ancient Mariner" * can be attributed to both the speed of his telling and the vividness of the imagery he chooses to use. Tremendous impetus is gained in such stanzas as his first:

It is an ancient Mariner,
And he stoppeth one of three.
"By thy long grey beard and glittering eye,
Now wherefore stopp'st thou me?"

and as this:

The ship was cheered, the harbor cleared,
Merrily did we drop
Below the kirk, below the hill,
Below the lighthouse top.

and as this:

The Sun now rose upon the right:
Out of the sea came he,
Still hid in mist, and on the left
Went down into the sea.

But throughout the narrative one encounters the gleam and fire of imagery. For example:

And now there came both mist and snow,
And it grew wondrous cold:
And ice, mast-high, came floating by,
As green as emerald

and

All in a hot and copper sky,
The bloody Sun, at noon,
Right up above the mast did stand,
No bigger than the moon

and

As idle as a painted ship
Upon a painted ocean

and

The water, like a witch's oils,
Burnt green, and blue, and white.

In Coleridge's poem this vivid imagining is nearly always enmeshed with action. Thus the imagery seldom stops the story; indeed, it often advances the story at the same time that it deepens it, makes it more memorable.

In Stephen Vincent Benét's "The Ballad of William Sycamore" * the imagery frequently enough supports the action for it not to weaken the narrative line, but the imagery seems to come away from the narrative fabric more often than in Coleridge's poem, to be less thoroughly of a piece with the action. In the first stanza a variety of qualities of Sycamore's father are noted, and the description is furthered by two vivid figures of speech:

My father, he was a mountaineer,
His fist was a knotty hammer;
He was quick on his feet as a running deer,
And he spoke with a Yankee stammer.

In the next four stanzas Benét gets Sycamore born and uses colorful figures of speech and immediate images to give us a sense of the wilderness in which he was born:

My mother, she was merry and brave,
And so she came to her labor,

With a tall green fir for her doctor grave
And a stream for her comforting neighbor.

And some are wrapped in linen fine,
And some like a godling's scion;
But I was cradled on twigs of pine
In the skin of a mountain lion.

And some remember a white, starched lap
And a ewer with silver handles;
But I remember a coonskin cap
And the smell of bayberry candles.

The cabin logs, with the bark still rough,
And my mother who laughted at trifles,
And the tall, lank visitors, brown as snuff,
With their long, straight squirrel rifles.

In later stanzas we follow the westward wanderings of a Sycamore now tall "as the Indian corn," and are told that he found

A woman straight as a hunting-knife,
With eyes as bright as the Dipper!

that he sowed sons

. . . like appleseed
On the trail of the Western wagons

and that now he lies

. . . in the heart of the fat, black soil,
Like the seed of a prairie thistle.

The tale gets told, but in cluster upon cluster of sensory images and comparisons, even to the point where the reader becomes aware of their constant clustering. Indeed, the obviousness of this sensory coloring may well be considered a weakness of this poem; the poet's machinery becomes too much in evidence.

Telling in "The Forsaken Merman" * of the desertion of a merman by a woman of the land, his wife and the mother of his children, Matthew Arnold, speaking as the merman, first tells what is happening now, after the event:

Come, dear children, let us away;
Down and away below!

Now my brothers call from the bay,
Now the salt tides seaward flow;
Now the wild white horses play,
Champ and chafe and toss in the spray.
Children dear, let us away!
This way, this way!

Call her once before you go—
Call once yet!
In a voice that she will know:
"Margaret! Margaret!"
Children's voices should be dear
(Call once more) to a mother's ear;
Children's voices, wild with pain—
Surely she will come again!

This is spare dramatic narrative; there are not many sensory images—"salt tides," "wild white horses," "voices, wild with pain"—and those there are precisely outline the action. But soon the merman turns from the present to the origin of the present pain—to the day when the wife and mother heard from the bottom of the sea the sound of church bells on the land; and here there is a sudden welling up of eloquent physical details:

Children dear, was it yesterday
We heard the sweet bells over the bay?
In the caverns where we lay,
Through the surf and through the swell,
The far-off sound of a silver bell?
Sand-strewn caverns, cool and deep,
Where the winds are all asleep;
Where the spent lights quiver and gleam,
Where the salt weed sways in the stream
Where the sea beasts, ranged all round,
Feed in the ooze of their pasture ground;
Where the sea snakes coil and twine,
Dry their mail and bask in the brine;
Where great whales come sailing by,
Sail and sail, with unshut eye,
Round the world forever and aye?
When did music come this way?
Children dear, was it yesterday?

Here physical details are not simply extras, atmospheric embellishments, but rather a way of deepening one's sense of what the woman has left behind in the sea—how shimmering and bright and wonderful it was.

After a further account of her leaving, the merman tells how he and the children went seeking her

. . . up the beach, by the sandy down
Where the sea-stocks bloom, to the white-walled town;
Through the narrow paved streets, where all was still,
To the little gray church on the windy hill

and how they sought her at the church, climbing on the gravestones to see her and call to her, and how they see her spinning in her room and sometimes looking out at the sea, and how they must now leave. All this is once more rather spare narration, not thick with imagery. But then, in the final lines of the poem, Arnold stresses once more the abandonment and the merman's loneliness with which the poem began, and to do this he makes the barrier, the shore, vivid with images that are made all the more vivid by their contrast to the earlier images of the bottom of the sea.

But, children, at midnight,
When soft the winds blow,
When clear falls the moonlight,
When spring tides are low;
When sweet airs come seaward
From heaths starred with broom,
And high rocks throw mildly
On the blanched sands a gloom;
Up the still, glistening beaches,
Up the creeks we will hie,
Over banks of bright seaweed
The ebb tide leaves dry.
We will gaze, from the sand-hills,
At the white sleeping town;
At the church on the hillside—
And then come back down,
Singing, "There dwells a loved one,
But cruel is she!
She left lonely forever
The kings of the sea."

In this poem the emotional tone of the tale—the heartbroken longing, the sense of separation—is created partly by the clear outline of the poignant situation and partly by the sensory imagery, which makes the separation and heartbreak both more understandable and harder to accept. This brings us to a final important point about the use of imagery in narrative poetry. Objects and events and the sensory images they call forth come to have symbolic meaning. The blackness of night, the grayness of stone walls, the redness of roses and blood, the greenness of grass and water, the whiteness of skin and ivory, the windiness of headlands, the lonely flatness of white beaches—such sensory images come to stand, in the consciousness of many of us, for certain experiences and states of mind. And when they are well used in narrative poetry, as they are here in "The Forsaken Merman," they draw on the emotional force of our experience and so bring poetic life to the tale.

The Special Place of Narrative Poetry in Children's Poetry

I have tried to suggest how in narrative poetry the rapid succession of events, the musical qualities of words, the rhythms of metrical schemes and of repeated sounds and words, an absence or minimum of explanatory or expository details, the presence of vivid sensory images, and the symbolic significance of such images all may contribute to the intensification of experience that is one of the main functions of poetry. Through these qualities story poetry can be poetic in its essential spirit and effect, not merely in its surface forms.

For this reason there is much to be said for the fairly common emphasis on narrative poetry in children's poetry anthologies and in course work in the middle grades. Many poets have found it possible to tell an exciting story, which most children like, in the form and spirit of poetry, which not all children (at least after the customary conditioning in our culture) greatly care for. Narrative poetry is therefore one of the easiest ways of bringing poetry to the child who may have already begun to build walls between himself and poetic experience. And the general poetic level of the narrative poetry in children's anthologies is very high; no apology on account of poetic imagination and intensity need be made for a genre of poetry which includes the great body of anonymous balladry and some of the best poems of Scott, Tennyson, Browning, Lindsay, Kipling, Masefield, Noyes, Longfellow, Whittier, Frost, and Stephen Vincent Benét. This is one instance where literature seems to lend itself to the creation of superior art at the children's level; another instance is historical fiction. The same cannot be said for that poetry whose central content and purpose are ethical, as we shall now see.

Being Ethical in Poetry

Didactic poetry—poetry that seeks to lead to ethical improvement—is frequently published, in comparison with most other poetry, in children's books, magazines, and anthologies; clearly, it is highly favored for children's use by a considerable number of adults. The ethical qualities recommended in this mass of didactic poetry have wide acceptance in our society—honesty, courage, kindness to animals, love of parents and family, unselfishness, cooperativeness, cheerfulness, friendliness, politeness, hard work, belief in deity, respect for authority, individualism, ambition, physical safety, cleanliness, neatness, noncheating, self-reliance, obeying the law.

The moral lessons didactic poetry teaches are usually made obvious enough; there is little attempt to disguise its ethical purpose. How *effective* it is as a moral instrument, how well it actually teaches, is a moot question. There can be little question however, about the poetic qualities of this poetry: they are generally of a quite inferior order; indeed, this is probably the *least poetic* of all the poetry either written or collected for children. A simple way to put this statement to the proof is to compare the children's anthology sections which have names like "Life Lessons" and "Wisdom" with the other sections. If one keeps in mind *poetic* criteria, not standards of belief and behavior, he will be startled by the comparatively low poetic level—or, let us say, the unpoetic nature—of the poetry in the former sections.

Some of this verse is quite directly utilitarian, sharply focused on very particular lessons that adults want children to learn—to do their homework, to be careful at the corner, etc. For instance:

Hearts, like doors, will ope with ease
To very, very little keys,
And don't forget that two of these
Are "I thank you" and "If you please."

Even more unpretentious (and the unpretentiousness of this utilitarian verse is probably its most praiseworthy literary quality) is this little safety lesson:

When you're at the corner,
  Waiting to go,
Be sure to remember:
  Green's Yes,
  And red's No!

Many such poems urge kindness to animals, as this anonymous poem does:

Little children, never give
Pain to things that feel and live;
Let the gentle robin come
For the crumbs you save at home,—
As his meat you throw along
He'll repay you with a song;
Never hurt the timid hare
Peeping from her green grass lair,
Let her come and sport and play
On the lawn at close of day;
The little lark goes soaring high
To the bright windows of the sky,
Singing as if 'twere always spring,

And fluttering on an untired wing,—
Oh! let him sing his happy song,
Nor do these gentle creatures wrong.

This last poem uses a little imagery and so gives us some sense of place and the creatures in it, but it still moves inexorably along one moral line of thought.

More abstract than the foregoing in thought and more sweeping in moral purpose are those poems which are sometimes lumped under such titles as "Inspirational Verse" and "Golden Thoughts." These poems are often selected for children and also used by many adults for their own reading. Much of the popular verse of Edgar A. Guest was of this sort. Here is part of his "See It Through" *:

You may fail, but fall still fighting;
    Don't give up, whate'er you do;
Eyes front, head high to the finish.
    See it through.

Much of this kind of verse is very familiar to most of us, which would suggest how widely acceptable and accepted it has been and still is. There is, for instance, Henry Van Dyke's "Four Things" *:

Four things a man must learn to do
If he would make his record true:
To think without confusion clearly;
To love his fellow-men sincerely;
To act from honest motives purely;
To trust in God and Heaven securely.

or Sam Walter Foss's "House by the Side of the Road," * the last stanza of which goes:

Let me live in my house by the side of the road,
    Where the race of men go by—
They are good, they are bad, they are weak, they are strong,
    Wise, foolish—so am I.
Then why should I sit in the scorner's seat,
    Or hurl the cynic's ban?
Let me live in my house by the side of the road
    And be a friend to man.

or Kipling's "If," * so familiar a part of childhood learning that the final stanza should recall almost the whole to many of us:

If you can talk with crowds and keep your virtue,
    Or walk with Kings—nor lose the common touch,

If neither foes nor loving friends can hurt you,
If all men count with you, but none too much;
If you can fill the unforgiving minute
With sixty seconds' worth of distance run,
Yours is the Earth and everything that's in it,
And—which is more—you'll be a Man, my son!

or Longfellow's "A Psalm of Life" *:

Tell me not, in mournful numbers,
Life is but an empty dream!—
For the soul is dead that slumbers,
And things are not what they seem.

with its much-quoted last stanza:

Let us, then, be up and doing,
With a heart for any fate;
Still achieving, still pursuing,
Learn to labor and to wait.

As is evident just from examples quoted so far, this didactic verse that holds such a prominent place in children's poetry covers a considerable range of poetic techniques and vocabularies and skills in their use; but all of it is characterized by certain qualities that work against both the poetic intensity of feeling and the transcending of ordinary experience that poetry in some degree achieves. For the most part, this poetry is filled with, indeed, built with, abstractions—"hearts," "wrong," "true," "a friend to man," "still achieving." The poems consist mainly of generalizations applicable to large classes of situations and persons. They use very few images and so generally do not achieve concreteness and vividness. They seldom evoke the feelings of a particular place and time—the smells, textures, lights and darks and particular hues, sounds, and movements that help to achieve the poetic heightening of experience—and the absence of these particulars means there are few ladders of symbolic meaning which the reader can climb up. And with the absence of particulars there is an absence of complexity, a dulling simplification of reds, oranges, and blues into "color," of yesterday and the sixteenth of last month and tomorrow into "time," of each of us into "man." This may be intellectually satisfying and may even be in certain ways an aesthetic experience, but it tends away from *poetic* experience.

Relatively infrequently a didactic poem achieves some poetic as well as moralistic vigor. Such a poem will be found to derive its poetic quality, I think, from the concreteness and sensuousness that have found their way into it. Such poems illustrate the struggle in poetry between the abstract and the concrete. For instance, Isaac Watts's "How Doth the

Little Busy Bee'' * is a thorough little sermon, with no effort made to disguise that fact, but it attains a modest degree of the poetic intensity lacking in the examples from Guest, Van Dyke, Foss, Kipling, and Longfellow:

How doth the little busy bee
  Improve each shining hour,
And gather honey all the day
  From every opening flow'r!

How skillfully she builds her cell!
  How neat she spreads the wax!
And labors hard to store it well
  With the sweet food she makes.

In these two opening stanzas Watts has anchored any idea that is to come firmly in a visualized particular, the little busy bee, and one he clearly feels excited about. In the third stanza he introduces his moral lesson but still in fairly unabstract terms of himself and Satan, neither of them made concrete or complex here but both certainly less abstract than ''man'' and ''sin'':

In works of labor or of skill,
  I would be busy too;
For Satan finds some mischief still
  For idle hands to do.

In books, or work, or healthful play,
  Let my first years be past,
That I may give for ev'ry day
  Some good account at last.

The poetry is almost all gone by the last line, but enough impetus was given by the little of it at the beginning to maintain a slight suggestion of it into the final stanza.

Another modest poem, Jane Taylor's well-known ''I Like Little Pussy,'' * quite straightforwardly presents a preachment but, again because it is rooted in a particular that the poet has feelings about, achieves a quiet little satisfaction of a poetic kind:

I like little Pussy,
  Her coat is so warm;
And if I don't hurt her
  She'll do me no harm.
So I'll not pull her tail,
  Nor drive her away,

But Pussy and I
  Very gently will play;
She shall sit by my side,
  And I'll give her some food;
And she'll love me because
  I am gentle and good.

I'll pat little Pussy,
  And then she will purr,
And thus show her thanks
  For my kindness to her;
I'll not pinch her ears,
  Nor tread on her paw,
Lest I should provoke her
  To use her sharp claw;
I never will vex her,
  Nor make her displeased,
For Pussy can't bear
  To be worried or teased.

Warm coat, pulling tail, gentle playing, cat's food, purring, pinched ears and untrod-on paw, sharp claws, "little Pussy"—these sensory notings and the author's feeling about them all make this poem a more poetic work (although a quite minor one) than any of the more pretentious "inspirational verse" quoted above. Perhaps this kind of didactic poem is not common because people with messages have already passed beyond the personal and particular experience into the generalization, where the original perceptions and emotions have become diluted, thinned out.

Some of the technical means of conveying and heightening poetic feeling—manipulation of rhythms to underline shift in idea, selecting language sounds appropriate to the idea, bodying forth a concept in appropriate imagery—are permitted to lie unused in the poetry of moral lessons written for, or given to, children. Thus all the examples I have given above, even the superior ones, have a mechanical regularity of rhyme and rhythm and therefore lack the special excitement that can be generated through appropriate variations in rhyme and rhythms; and in this they are all typical of this poetry.

A number of probable reasons why it is not easy to find effective poetry of clear ethical purpose for children suggest themselves.

1   Many adults want to improve children's minds and behavior, and to them poetry appears to be a handy vehicle for their ethical messages. Alas! there are never very many good poets, and the fact that a teacher or parent has a desirable suggestion to make does not automatically place him among the ranks of the poetically elect, the skillful and imaginative singers; yet, perhaps liking poetry as well as knowing that people may be

reached by it, he tries to put his unpoetic thoughts into poetic form, with unimpressive results. But these results may not seem unimpressive to the many other parents and teachers who often confuse good behavior with good poetry; so they may welcome the bad poetry that has been turned out and perhaps reject some better ethical poetry in the process. It may be that many do this because they cannot find the moral, or "point," plainly enough stated for them in the more "poetic" poetry. "The birds sang" or "My heart is like a watered shoot" is not as obvious and superficially graspable a statement of happiness as "The birds were happy" or "I am happy."

2   Furthermore, it may be that the ethical generalizations sometimes seem at odds with, or at least not to make a neat fit with, the concrete facts of experience in all their baffling particularity and irregularity, and this makes the good poet wary of ethical generalizations. It is hard for a person who likes neat moral maxims to find one, at least one that will stick, in, say, Frost's "Stopping by Woods on a Snowy Evening" or his "Mending Wall."

3   Many readers, then, may be inclined either to force one out of Frost's tantalizing, ambiguous, concrete imagery or to turn away from Frost, for instance, and look for some approvable moral in a less poetic versifier.

4   This conflict between generalization and particulars in thinking about human behavior may adversely affect the poet's work, often without his realizing it is going on, and this may be the basis for the lack of critical appreciation of his poetic thinking on the part of the adult readers of children's didactic verse.

Making Fantasy in Poetry

The popularity of ethics-teaching poetry with adults is equaled by their enthusiasm, no more discriminating, for the poetry of outright fantasy, the poetry of fairyland. Indeed, many adults—and then children, following their lead and identifying poetry with what they are exposed to under that name—equate poetry with fairy poetry. They make an automatic connection between poetry and any sort of elfin goings-on, no matter how stodgy and inept the poetry may be. The result is unfortunate; an undue proportion of poetry for children comes to have just this one subject and mood.

The basic error is in linking poetry with a particular subject and thus losing sight of the most helpful notion that poetry is a method, or approach, not a subject. One cannot really understand painting so long as he persists in identifying it with pretty women and flowers and spring landscapes and dissociating it from butcher shops, garbage cans, and empty bottles and apples on a white table. And one will encounter needless difficulties in placing poetry in his own mental existence if he has come to believe that poetry is always fairy stuff and not ever writing about everyday sensory experience or about noneveryday nonsensical experience.

However, this is no argument for reducing or blocking the supply of fantasy in children's poetry, but simply a complication that needs to be seen and understood. For children's fantasy poetry contains, along with some of the limpest, weakest, least poetic children's poetry, some of the finest children's poetry—William Allingham's fairy songs, Shakespeare's, Christina Rosetti's *Goblin Market,* Rose Fyleman's poems, Elizabeth Coatsworth's, Sara Teasdale's, James Hogg's, Walter de la Mare's, and Hilda Conkling's.

In discussing other poetry genres, I have been suggesting that poetry mainly tends to do two things, sometimes at the same time but not necessarily so: (1) to intensify our feelings about the various aspects of our individual existences, and (2) to free us momentarily from the ordinariness of life and take us into special experience. In the more effective fairy poetry for children the second of these gets done.

Whether one takes magic and fairies and wee men for reality or for invention, for deeper reality or for unreality, they are not the surface reality of life, that is, the usual, expected arrangements and conjunctions of our experience; and so the poetry that deals with them is a turning away, in art, toward the strange and unexpected. Thus the introduction of fairy characters and magical events can start the reader of a poem in the direction of a special poetic experience. But this is only a beginning; simply introducing fairy lore and characters, without giving them a very special kind of substance, will not take the reader very far in this direction. Much children's fairy verse does no more, however. For example, Abbie Farwell Brown's "The Fairy Book" * begins:

When Mother takes the Fairy Book
  And we curl up to hear,
'Tis "All aboard for Fairyland!"
  Which seems to be so near.

The remainder of the poem is pretty much a listing of fairy things:

. . . .
Where birdies sing the hour of day,
  And flowers talk in rhyme;

Where Bobby is a velvet Prince,
  And where I am a Queen;
Where one can talk with animals,
  And walk about unseen;

Where Little People live in nuts,
  And ride on butterflies,
And wonders kindly come to pass
  Before your very eyes;

Where candy grows on every bush,
  And playthings on the trees,

And visitors pick basketfuls
As often as they please

It is the nicest time of day—
Though Bedtime is so near,—
When Mother takes the Fairy Book
And we curl up to hear.

In this poem the strangeness is just the rather slight strangeness of the subjects. There is little in this pleasant little story in verse that works to-ward poetry. Similarly Rose Fyleman, by placing a fairy on a bus on a busy fashionable London shopping street in "Yesterday in Oxford Street," * has given her reader a *slight* shove out of the everyday:

Yesterday in Oxford Street, oh, what d'you think, my dears?
I had the most exciting time I've had for years and years;
The buildings looked so straight and tall, the sky was blue between,
And, riding on a motor-bus, I saw the fairy queen!

Sitting there upon the rail and bobbing up and down,
The sun was shining on her wings and on her golden crown;
And looking at the shops she was, the pretty silks and lace—
She seemed to think that Oxford street was quite a lovely place.

The overall tone of the poem is actually rather cozy, chatty, suggesting the elegant but not the marvelous; Rose Fyleman has relied mainly on the introduction of the subject, a fairy riding a London bus, to give her a foot up on the tree of the strange and special. Imagery is used only a little, and then in fairly conventional ways, and the rhythm and rhymes are quite elementary.

But the poet, having let his fairy subject matter initiate the special poetic experience, can (as Fyleman does in many other poems) seek to deepen and intensify the acceptance of otherworldliness, of the fairy reality, by drawing on the special means at the poet's hand.

Vivid and varied imagery can do much to create a magical world, a realm of faerie, delicate and yet substantial enough to escape into. The finest children's poetry of fairyland—de la Mare's, Shakespeare's, Hilda Conkling's, and some of Fyleman's and Allingham's—is made fine, that is, imaginatively real, by physical images which create a sense of more than stage machinery and hocus-pocus, an awareness of real nonbeings who live on wonderful planes. And this sense can be strengthened and sharp-ened by evocative sounds and groupings of sounds, appropriate rhythms, and melodic invention.

Without describing the fairy folk, Walter de la Mare, in the first two stanzas of "Sleepyhead," * suggests their delicate, ambiguous presence by a subtly shifting rhythm, a melody of long vowel and *n* sounds, and the suggestion of whiteness and faintness:

As I lay awake in the white moonlight,
I heard a faint singing in the wood,
  "Out of bed,
  Sleepyhead,
  Put your white foot now,
  Here are we,
  Neath the tree
  Singing round the root now!"

I looked out of the window, in the white moonlight,
The trees were like snow in the wood—
  "Come away,
  Child, and play
  Light with the gnomies;
  In a mound,
  Green and round,
  That's where their home is."

In the third stanza the unseen singer shifts into a listing of only slightly described but evocative particulars:

"Honey sweet,
Curds to eat,
Cream and fruménty,
Shells and beads,
Poppy seeds,
You shall have plenty."

Then in the fourth and final stanza de la Mare turns again to the carefully selected images of light and sound and the melody of long vowels and *n* sounds:

But soon as I stooped in the dim moonlight
To put on my stocking and my shoe,
The sweet, sweet singing died sadly away,
And the light of the morning peeped through:
Then instead of the gnomies there came a red robin
To sing of the buttercups and dew.

The last statement ends the faint whiteness of fairy-filled night with a touch of vivid red and the firmness of a little robin. Without ever introducing fairies de la Mare has brought them to life and at the last moment taken them away, by means of color-and-sound words and a complex melody and sound harmony.

A different use of the same poetic resources in making a different kind of fantasy is exemplified by Rachel Field's "The Visitor." * Here the magical otherworld boldly asserts itself as a definite but very special set of figures and actions. The rhymed lines, although full of accent shifts, set up a certain brisk regularity that contributes to the vigor of the poem's fancy. The poem starts in a flurry:

Feather-footed and swift as a mouse
An elfin gentleman came to our house;

Field quickly creates the unearthly creature with vivid images:

Knocked his wee brown knuckles upon our door;
Bowed till his peaked cap swept the floor.
His shiny eyes blinked bright at me
As he asked for bread and a sup of tea,
"And plenty of honey, please," he said,
For I'm fond of honey on my bread!"

Now the crisis created by the visitor is told by a cluster of words for color and sound:

Cross-legged he sat, with never a word,
But the old black kettle sang like a bird;
The red geranium burst in bloom
With the blaze of firelight in the room,
The china rattled on every shelf,
And the broom danced merrily all by itself.

With sparing touches of sensory detail Field recounts the solution:

Quick to the pantry than I ran
For to serve that elfin gentleman.
I brewed him tea, I brought him bread
With clover honey thickly spread.
One sip he took, one Elfin bite,
But his ears they twitched with sheer delight.
He smacked his lips and he smiled at me.
"May good luck follow you, child!" said he.

The end of the elfin episode is told almost entirely through vivid sensory images of color, temperature, and light:

He circled me round like a gay green flame
Before he was off the way he came,
Leaving me there in the kitchen dim,
Sighing and staring after him,
With the fire low and the tea grown cold,

And the moon through the window sharp and old,
Only before me—instead of honey,
That bread was golden with thick-spread money!

"The Visitor" compels attention not so much by the extraordinariness of the invented situation, though this does have its effect, as by the poetic fabric created by Rachel Field out of imagery and sound.

Christina Rossetti's *Goblin Market,** one of the finest of all fairy poems, is probably the best example one could find of children's poetry that creates an intensely felt imagined existence by means of invented magic— a whole world of nonmundane people and happenings—and by language magic—appropriate, evocative imagery, exciting rhythms and sound patterns. This amazing poem creates the various kinds of poetry that one may find separately in the works of de la Mare and Allingham and Thomas Hood and other makers of fairy poems, but somehow here they form a unified, magical whole. The poem is, unfortunately, far too long to be used in its entirety here for illustration and analysis; representative parts of it, however, may suggest the variety of means the poet employed and their effectiveness.

The poem tells how the goblins tempted two sisters, Laura and Lizzie, with their magical, ensnaring fruits, how Laura bought and ate some of these and then began to waste away in her longing for more, how Lizzie went to the wood and gave the goblins her coin but instead of eating the fatal fruit forced the goblins to squeeze the fruit against her face, how tasting the juice on her sister drove Laura into final, almost fatal ecstasy, and how she recovered and afterward found herself freed by her sister's love from the magic spell of the goblin men.

Rossetti plunges into the heart of the matter with

Morning and evening
Maids heard the goblins cry:
"Come buy our orchard fruits,
Come buy, come buy"

and at each important step in the narrative she announces the development directly and swiftly. In this way, and by the clattering, quick, short lines, Rossetti achieves a kind of impetuousness and velocity in the telling that underlines the relentless pressure of the goblin merchants on the human beings they seek to control.

The goblins sing out their wares in long listings that sound like magical charms, creating a sense of both earthly and unearthly riches:

"Apples and quinces,
Lemons and oranges,
Plump unpecked cherries,
Melons and raspberries,

Bloom-down-cheeked peaches,
Swart-headed mulberries,
Wild free-born cranberries,
Crab-apples, dewberries,
Pine-apples, blackberries,
Apricots, strawberries;—
All ripe together
In summer weather,—
Morns that pass by,
Fair eves that fly;
Come buy, come buy:
Our grapes fresh from the vine,
Pomegranates full and fine,
Dates and sharp bullaces,
Rare pears and greengages,
Damsons and bilberries,
Taste them and try:
Currants and gooseberries,
Bright-fire-like barberries,
Figs to fill your mouth,
Citrons from the South,
Sweet to tongue and sound to eye,
Come buy, come buy.''

These chants, picked up periodically in the poem, are made spell-like partly by the repeated sounds—*berries* and other words with initial *b*, *f*'s ("Fair eves that fly," "fresh from the vine," "full and fine," "Bright-fire-like barberries,/Figs to fill your mouth")—and partly by the sheer piling on of names in series of similarly structured lines, the names being all the more enchanting when we are not sure we understand what they are. The same spell casting is achieved in much the same ways later when we are introduced to the goblins:

One had a cat's face,
One whisked a tail,
One tramped at a rat's pace,
One crawled like a snail,
One like a wombat prowled obtuse and furry,
One like a ratel tumbled hurry skurry.
She heard a voice like voice of doves
Cooing all together:
They sounded kind and full of loves
In the pleasant weather.

Here again are the repeated sounds—*One*, the *at* sound in *cat's*, *rat's*, *wombat*, *ratel*, and the words ending in *urry*—and repetition of the same line structure. Here again is evocativeness through physical imagery—"like a wombat prowled obtuse and furry," "a rat's pace," "like a snail," "a voice like voice of doves/ Cooing all together." And the spell is maintained by the delicate imagery of the similes with which Laura is described at this moment:

Laura stretched her gleaming neck
Like a rush-imbedded swan,
Like a lily from the beck,
Like a moonlit poplar branch,
Like a vessel at the launch
When its last restraint is gone.

Later, Laura's image-laden telling of how the fruit tasted establishes the indescribable specialness of fairyland:

"You cannot think what figs
My teeth have met in,
What melons icy-cold
Piled on a dish of gold
Too huge for me to hold,
What peaches with a velvet nap,
Pellucid grapes without one seed"

And Rossetti concludes this first magical encounter with phrases which, while describing the girls going to sleep, really seem to take us away into an unworldly place of spells:

Golden head by golden head,
Like two pigeons in one nest,
Folded in each other's wings,
They lay down in their curtained bed:
Like two blossoms on one stem,
Like two flakes of new-fall'n snow,
Like two wands of ivory
Tipped with gold for awful kings.

(Anyone still puzzled as to why the poetry in a poem is not just the point or idea or subject or rhyme or rhythm might do well to look hard at this last line, particularly in its context here.)

In the remainder of the poem, which tells of Laura's sick longing and Lizzie's self-sacrificing visit to the goblins, the poet succeeds, by a highly ingenious but easy use of poetic devices, in preserving the sense of spell and this magical world she has created. Here is how Lizzie sees the goblins when she dares to go in the dusk to meet them:

> *Laughed every goblin*
> *When they spied her peeping:*
> *Came toward her hobbling,*
> *Flying, running, leaping,*
> *Puffing and blowing,*
> *Chuckling, clapping, crowing,*
> *Clucking and gobbling,*
> *Mopping and mowing,*
> *Full of airs and graces,*
> *Pulling wry faces,*
> *Demure grimaces,*
> *Cat-like and rat-like,*
> *Ratel- and wombat-like,*
> *Snail-paced in a hurry,*
> *Parrot-voiced and whistler,*
> *Helter-skelter, hurry skurry,*
> *Chattering like magpies,*
> *Fluttering like pigeons,*
> *Gliding like fishes,—*

To the end of the poem Rossetti sustains the sense these lines have of frenzy and of almost nightmarish reality of the otherworld of goblinry, at the same time that she winds through the poem a sweet, lyric pattern of delicate imagery like that in the following passage:

> *White and golden Lizzie stood,*
> *Like a lily in a flood,—*
> *Like a rock of blue-veined stone*
> *Lashed by tides obstreperously,—*
> *Like a beacon left alone*
> *In a hoary roaring sea,*
> *Sending up a golden fire,—*
> *Like a fruit-crowned orange-tree,*
> *White with blossoms honey-sweet . . .*

Rossetti's rich, vigorous, complex account of

> *. . . the haunted glen,*
> *The wicked quaint fruit-merchant men*

achieves the excitement of poetry by creating a separate, remote state of being with its own laws, its own language, its own special air. Still, the elements of superior fairy poetry (like the elements of superior poetry of any kind) remain similar, if not identical. In Rossetti's *Goblin Market* and the de la Mare and Rachel Field poems, different from one another as they are, we find a similar lack of straining for effect, a similar appropriate use of imagery to make a certain feeling more intense, a similar appropriate use of other poetic instruments, such as rhythms and harmonies of sound. In run-of-the-mill children's verse of fairyland we find either a trite, flat, not particularly poetic reporting or a pretentious overblownness, an over-doing, the use of all the poet's armory in a self-conscious attempt to create fairy effects, the latter complex being very common and therefore especially damaging to the development of children's taste in poetry. Un-fortunately, the world of children's verse has been so inundated with the latter sort of poetic fantasy that fairy poetry has, in many quarters, come to be almost synonymous with this most strained and saccharine kind of fairy poetry.

Somewhat typical of the kind is Eugene Field's well-known "The Rock-a-By Lady" and the less well-known "Fairy and Child." "Fairy and Child" begins in a cloud of conventional suggestions of fairyland's remoteness and sweetness:

Oh, listen, little Dear-My-Soul,
*   To the fairy voices calling,*
For the moon is high in the misty sky
*   And the honey dew is falling;*
To the midnight feast in the clover bloom
*   The Bluebells are a-ringing,*
And it's "Come away to the land of fay"
*   That the katydid is singing.*

Here the images tend toward the vague and overused—a moon "high," a "misty sky," "honey dew."; and "land of fay" is straining for specialness.

Oh, slumber, little Dear-My-Soul,
*   And hand in hand we'll wander—*
Hand in hand to the beautiful land
*   Of Balow, away off yonder;*
Or we'll sail along in a lily leaf
*   Into the white moon's halo—*
Over a stream of mist and dream
*   Into the land of Balow.*

"Slumber," "hand in hand," "wander," "the beautiful land," "away off yonder," and "a stream of mist and dream" are all general, unvivid, a bit tarnished by usage—and are being used in an obvious effort to call forth a standardized "Fairyland!" reaction much like the standardized reaction to the misty-mountain-and-blue-lake illustrations Maxfield Parrish did for the popular 1904 edition.

Or, you shall have two beautiful wings—
*   Two gossamer wings and airy,*

And all the while shall the old moon smile
  And think you a little fairy;
And you shall dance in the velvet sky,
  And the silvery stars shall twinkle
And dream sweet dreams as over their beams
  Your footfalls softly tinkle.

Throughout the last stanza the poet, seeking more concreteness, uses the conventional trappings of fairyland—"gossamer wings," "a little fairy," "velvet sky," "silvery stars," "sweet dreams."—and does not stamp his imaginings with any original impression, any particular way of seeing. But the lack of vivid, private conception is most manifest in the last line, where the author is pushed into the strained and meaningless metaphor of footfalls that tinkle.

Now this and *Goblin Market* and de la Mare's poetry are all fairy poetry—but how different Rossetti and de la Mare are in what they do as poets, in the tellingness, the intensity, of the poetry they make!

Conclusion

The ability to see the differences in how the poets sing—or, put differently, in what they make of whatever subject they start with—is what this chapter has, by implication, called for in the adult who is trying to judge, select, and use poetry with children. A much more common approach to poetry is in terms of subject matter—the child's daily environment, nature, witches, holidays, seasons. Here this was not our focus. Instead, our starting point was what the author *did*. Did he make nonsense of whatever situation or person or events interested him? Did he make sense of a real experience—observe it and extract from it a special meaning and feeling? Did he narrate a series of events grippingly, excitingly? Did he inculcate certain ideas or attitudes? Did he create an illusionary world of magic and wonder?

We found that the poet, in trying to do these various things, tended to intensify one's experience of reality, to make the sensing of it keener and clearer, or to move one beyond and out of reality into the more rarified atmosphere of the imagined—or, sometimes, to do both together. And also we noted how in doing things poetically on various levels, the poet used various poetic techniques of rhythm, sound, language imagery, and overall poetic structure to achieve his desired effect, or poem.

Poetry is not simply *about something*. Certainly, in trying to create certain imaginings or to make particular feelings vivid, poets may be inclined to draw more on some subjects than on others, but the subject does not make the poetry. It is *what the poet does* that makes the great difference, and it is this that the person who wishes to understand, enjoy, and select and use poetry wisely needs to concern himself with.

Such a focus—on what is created and how it is created—should help to preserve the breadth and flexibility that I earlier suggested should characterize the adult in his approach to children's poetry, for the range of possible poetic creations is much, much greater than the range of possible subjects. It should also assist us toward more *controllable* and *precise* poetic criteria, for it places the question of value squarely in the work in front of us, rather than in the world of subjects back of the poem.

SUGGESTED SOURCES

Mother Goose Material

Alexander, Frances: *Mother Goose on the Rio Grande,* ill. by Charlotte Baker, Banks Upshaw, 1960.

Benét, William Rose (compiler): *Mother Goose: A Comprehensive Collection of the Rhymes,* ill. by Roger Duvoisin, Heritage, 1936.

Brian Wildsmith's Mother Goose, ill. by Brian Wildsmith, F. Watts, 1964.

Caldecott, Randolph: *Hey Diddle Diddle Picture Book,* ill. by author, Warne.

Crane, Walter: *Baby's Bouquet: A Fresh Bunch of Old Rhymes and Tunes,* ill. by author, Warne, 1900.

Evans, Patricia: *Rimbles: A Book of Children's Classic Games, Rhymes, Songs, and Sayings,* ill. by Gioia Fiammenghi, Doubleday, 1961.

Fish, Helen Dean (compiler): *Four & Twenty Blackbirds: Nursery Rhymes of Yesterday Recalled for Children of Today,* ill. by Robert Lawson, Stokes, 1937.

In a Pumpkin Shell, ill. by Joan Walsh Anglund, Harcourt, Brace & World, 1958.

Justus, May: *Peddler's Pack,* ill. by Jean Tamburine, Holt, 1957. A book of play-party games, songs, and rhymes of the Great Smoky Mountains.

Lang, Andrew (ed.): *Nursery Rhyme Book,* ill. by L. Leslie Brooke, Warne, 1897.

Lines, Kathleen (ed.): *Lavender's Blue,* ill. by Harold Jones, F. Watts, 1954.

Little Mother Goose, ill. by Jessie Willcox Smith, Dodd, Mead, 1918.

Low, Joseph and Ruth: *Mother Goose Riddle Rhymes,* ill. by Joseph Low, Harcourt, Brace & World, 1953.

Marguerite de Angeli's Book of Nursery and Mother Goose Rhymes, ill. by Marguerite de Angeli, Doubleday, 1954.

Montgomerie, Norah (ed.): *A Book of Scottish Nursery Rhymes,* ill. by T. Ritchie and N. Montgomerie, Oxford University Press, 1965.

Morrison, Lillian (compiler): *Black Within and Red Without,* ill. by Jo Spier, Crowell, 1953.

————: *A Dillar, a Dollar,* ill. by Marjorie Bauernschmidt, Crowell, 1955.

————: *Touch Blue,* ill. by Doris Lee, Crowell, 1958.

————: *Yours Till Niagara Falls,* ill. by Marjorie Bauernschmidt, Crowell, 1950.

Mother Goose; or, the Old Nursery Rhymes, ill. by Kate Greenaway, Warne.

Mother Goose: Seventy-seven Verses, ill. by Tasha Tudor, Oxford University Press, 1944.

Mother Goose: The Old Nursery Rhymes, ill. by Arthur Rackham, William Heinemann, 1913, 1958.

Opie, Iona and Peter (compilers): *The Oxford Nursery Rhyme Book,* ill. from old chapbooks, with additional pictures by Joan Hassall, Walck, 1955.

Petersham, Maud and Miska (eds.): *The Rooster Crows: A Book of American Rhymes and Jingles,* ill. by eds., Macmillan, 1945.

Potter, Charles Francis (compiler): *Tongue Tanglers,* ill. by William Wiesner, World, 1962.

The Real Mother Mother Goose, ill. by Blanche Fisher Wright, Rand McNally, 1916.

Ring o' Roses: A Nursery Rhyme Picture Book, ill. by L. Leslie Brooke, Warne.

The Tall Book of Mother Goose, ill. by Feodor Rojankovsky, Harper & Row, 1942.

The Tenggren Mother Goose, ill. by Gustav Tenggren, Little, Brown, 1940.

Untermeyer, Louis: *The Golden Treasury of Poetry,* ill. by Joan Walsh Anglund, Golden Press, 1959.

Walter, L. E. (ed.): *Mother Goose's Nursery Rhymes,* ill. by Charles Folkard, Macmillan, 1922.

Wheeler, Opal: *Sing Mother Goose,* ill. by Marjorie Torrey, Dutton, 1946.

Withers, Carl (ed.): *A Rocket in My Pocket,* ill. by Susanne Suba, Holt, 1948.

————: *I Saw a Rocket Walk a Mile: Nonsense Tales, Chants and Songs from Many Lands,* ill. by John E. Johnson, Holt, 1965.

Wood, Ray (ed.): *The American Mother Goose,* ill. by Ed Hargis, Lippincott, 1938.

————: *Fun in American Folk Rhymes,* ill. by Ed Hargis, Lippincott, 1952.

Poetry Anthologies

Adshead, Gladys L., and Annis Duff (eds.): *An Inheritance of Poetry,* ill. by Nora S. Unwin, Houghton Mifflin, 1948.

Arbuthnot, May Hill (ed.): *Time for Poetry,* ill. by Arthur Paul, Scott, Foresman, 1952.

Association for Childhood Education, Literature Committee: *Sung under the Silver Umbrella,* ill. by Dorothy Lathrop, Macmillan, 1936.

Beyond the High Hills: A Book of Eskimo Poems, with photographs by Guy Mary-Rousselière, World, 1961.

Blishen, Edward (compiler): *Oxford Book of Poetry for Children,* ill. by Brian Wildsmith, Watts, 1963.

Brewton, John E. (ed.): *Gaily We Parade,* ill. by Robert Lawson, Macmillan, 1952.

————: *Under the Tent of the Sky: A Collection of Poems about Animals Large and Small,* ill. by Robert Lawson, Macmillan, 1937.

Brewton, Sara and John (eds.): *Birthday Candles Burning Bright: A Treasury of Birthday Poetry,* ill. by Vera Bock, Macmillan, 1960.

————: *Sing a Song of Seasons,* ill. by Vera Bock, Macmillan, 1955.

Brown, Helen A., and Harry J. Helt (eds.): *Let's-read-together Poems,* Harper & Row, 1954.

Coatsworth, Elizabeth: *Poems,* ill. by Vee Guthrie, Macmillan, 1957. Much of Coatsworth's poetry is scattered through her novels.

Cole, William (ed.): *The Birds and the Beasts Were There,* ill. by Helen Siegl, World, 1963.

————: *Humorous Poetry for Children,* ill. by Ervine Metzl, World, 1955.

————: *I Went to the Animal Fair,* ill. Colette Rosselli, World, 1958.

————: *Poems of Magic and Spells,* ill. by Peggy Bacon, World, 1960.

————: *Story Poems New and Old,* ill. by Walter Buehr, World, 1957.

De la Mare, Walter (ed.): *Come Hither,* ill. by Warren Chappell, Knopf, 1957.

————: *Tom Tiddler's Ground,* ill. by Margery Gill, Knopf, 1961.

Ferris, Helen (ed.): *Favorite Poems Old and New,* ill. by Leonard Weisgard, Doubleday, 1957.

First Book of Short Verse, sel. by Coralie Howard, ill. by Mamoru Funai, F. Watts, 1964.

Geismer, Barbara Peck, and Antoinette Brown Suter: *Very Young Verses,* ill. by Mildred Bronson, Houghton Mifflin, 1945.

Gregory, Horace, and Marya Zaturenska (eds.): *The Crystal Cabinet,* ill. by Diana Bloomfield, Holt, 1962. Selection by two important contemporary poets.

Huffard, Grace Thompson, and Laura Mae Carlisle: *My Poetry Book: An Anthology of Modern Verse for Boys and Girls,* rev. ed., ill. by Willy Pogány, Holt, 1956.

Larrick, Nancy (compiler): *Piper, Pipe That Song Again: Poems for Boys and Girls,* ill. by Kelly Oechsli, Random House, 1965.

Lewis, C. Day (ed.): *The Echoing Green: An Anthology of Verse* (3 vols.), Blackwell, 1960–1963.

Love, Katherine (ed.): *A Little Laughter*, ill. by Walter Lorraine, Crowell, 1957.

————: *A Pocketful of Rhymes*, ill. by Henrietta Jones, Crowell, 1946.

McDonald, Gerald D. (ed.): *A Way of Knowing: A Collection of Poems for Boys*, ill. by Clare and John Ross, Crowell, 1959.

McEwen, Catherine Schaefer (ed.): *Away We Go!* ill. by Barbara Cooney, Crowell, 1956.

McFarland, Wilma (ed.): *For a Child*, ill. by Ninon, Westminster Press, 1957.

Morrison, Lillian (ed.): *A Dillar, a Dollar and Sayings for the Ten o'Clock Scholar*, ill. by Marjorie Bauernschmidt, Crowell, 1955.

————: *Touch Blue*, ill. by Doris Lee, Crowell, 1958.

————: *Yours Till Niagara Falls*, ill. by Marjorie Bauernschmidt, Crowell, 1950.

Nash, Ogden (ed.): *Everybody Ought to Know*, Lippincott, 1961.

————: *The Moon Is Shining Bright as Day*, Lippincott, 1953.

Parker, Elinor (ed.): *100 Story Poems*, ill. by Peter Spier, Crowell, 1951. *Also 100 More Story Poems*, ill. by Peter Spier, Crowell, 1960.

————: *The Singing and the Gold*, ill. by Clare Leighton, Crowell, 1962. Large collection of translated poems.

Peterson, Isabel J. (ed.): *The First Book of Poetry*, ill. by Kathleen Elgin, F. Watts, 1954.

Plotz, Helen (ed.): *Imagination's Other Place*, ill. by Clare Leighton, Crowell, 1955.

————: *Untune the Sky: Poems of Music and the Dance*, ill. by Clare Leighton, Crowell, 1957.

Read, Herbert (compiler): *This Way, Delight: A Book of Poetry for the Young*, ill. by Juliet Kepes, Pantheon, 1956.

Sechrist, Elizabeth Hough: *One Thousand Poems for Children*, ill. by Henry C. Pitz, Macrae Smith, 1946.

Sheldon, William D., et al.: *The Reading of Poetry*, Allyn and Bacon, 1963. Large, lively collection.

Smith, Janet Adam (ed.): *The Faber Book of Children's Verse*, Faber, 1953.

Stevenson, Burton Egbert: *The Home Book of Verse for Young Folks*, rev. ed., ill. by Willy Pogány, Holt, 1929.

Thompson, Blanche (ed.): *More Silver Pennies*, ill. by Pelagie Doane, Macmillan, 1938.

————: *Silver Pennies*, ill. by Winifred Bromhall, Macmillan, 1925.

Thompson, Jean McKee (ed.): *Poems to Grow On*, ill. by Gobin Stair, Beacon Press, 1957.

Tudor, Tasha (ed.): *Wings from the Wind*, ill. by ed., Lippincott, 1964.

Untermeyer, Louis (ed.): *The Golden Treasury of Poetry*, ill. by Joan Walsh Anglund, Golden Press, 1959.

————: *Rainbow in the Sky*, ill. by Reginald Birch, Harcourt, Brace, 1935.

————: *Stars to Steer by*, ill. by Dorothy Bailey, Harcourt, Brace & World, 1941.

————: *This Singing World*, ill. by Florence Wyman Ivins, Harcourt, Brace, 1923.

Wiggin, Kate Douglas, and Nora Archibald Smith (eds.): *Golden Numbers: A Book of Verse for Youth*, Doubleday, 1926.

————: *The Posy Ring: A Book of Verse for Children*, Doubleday, 1955.

A Selective Bibliography of Poetry Volumes by Individual Poets

Aiken, Conrad: *Cats and Bats and Things with Wings*, ill. by Milton Glaser, Atheneum, 1965.

Aldis, Dorothy: *All Together*, ill. by Marjorie Flack, Margaret Frieman, and Helen D. Jameson, Putnam, 1925.

————: *Is Anybody Hungry?* ill. by Artur Marokvia, Putnam, 1964.

Baruch, Dorothy: *I Like Machinery*, Harper, 1933.

————: *I Would Like to Be a Pony and Other Wishes*, ill. by Mary Chambers, Harper & Row, 1959.

Becker, John: *New Feathers for the Old Goose*, ill. by Virginia Campbell, Pantheon, 1956.

Behn, Harry (author-illustrator): *The House beyond the Meadow*, Pantheon, 1955.

————: *The Little Hill*, Harcourt, Brace & World, 1949.

————: *Windy Morning*, Harcourt, Brace & World, 1953.

————: *The Wizard In the Well*, Harcourt, Brace & World, 1956.

Benét, Rosemary and Stephen Vincent: *A Book of Americans*, ill. by Charles Child, Holt, 1933.

Chute, Marchette: *Around and About*, ill. by author, Dutton, 1957.

Ciardi, John: *I Met a Man*, ill. by Robert Osborn, Houghton Mifflin, 1961.

————: *John J. Plenty and Fiddler Dan: A New Fable of the Grasshopper and the Ant*, ill. by Madeleine Gekiere, Lippincott, 1963.

————: *The Reason for the Pelican*, ill. by Madeleine Gekiere, Lippincott, 1959.

————: *You Know Who*, ill. by Edward Gorey, Lippincott, 1964.

————: *You Read to Me, I'll Read to You*, ill. by Edward Gorey, Lippincott, 1962.

Coatsworth, Elizabeth: *Poems*, ill. by Vee Guthrie, Macmillan, 1958.

————: *Summer Green*, ill. by Nora Unwin, Macmillan, 1948.

Conkling, Hilda: *Poems by a Little Girl*, Lippincott, 1920

————: *Shoes of the Wind*, Lippincott, 1922.

De la Mare, Walter: *Peacock Pie*, ill. by Barbara Cooney, Knopf, 1961.

Farjeon, Eleanor: *The Children's Bells*, ill. by Peggy Fortnum, Walck, 1960.

————: *Eleanor Farjeon's Poems for Children*, Lippincott, 1951.

Field, Eugene: *Poems of Childhood*, ill. by Maxfield Parrish, Scribner, 1920.

Field, Rachel: *Poems*, ill. by author, Macmillan, 1951.

————: *The Pointed People*, ill. by author, Macmillan, 1933.

————: *Taxis and Toadstools*, ill. by author, Doubleday, 1926.

Fisher, Aileen: *Runny Days, Sunny Days*, ill. by author, Abelard-Shuman, 1933.

————: *That's Why*, ill. by author, Nelson, 1946.

Frost, Frances: *The Little Naturalist*, ill. by Kurt Werth, Whittlesey, 1959.

————: *The Little Whistler*, ill. by Roger Duvoisin, Whittlesey, 1949.

Frost, Robert: *You Come Too: Favorite Poems for Young Readers*, ill. by Thomas W. Nason, Holt, 1959.

Fyleman, Rose: *Fairies and Chimneys*, Doubleday, 1920.

Greenaway, Kate: *Marigold Garden: Pictures and Rhymes*, ill. by author, Warne.

Kuskin, Karla: *In the Middle of the Trees*, ill. by author, Harper & Row, 1958.

————: *Alexander Soames: His Poems*, Harper & Row, 1962.

Lear, Edward: *The Complete Nonsense Book*, Dodd, Mead, 1946.

Lindsay, Vachel: *Johnny Appleseed, and Other Poems*, ill. by George Richards, Macmillan, 1928.

McCord, David: *Far and Few*, ill. by Henry B. Kane, Little, Brown, 1952.

Merriam, Eve: *It Dosen't Always Have to Rhyme*, ill. by Malcolm Spooner, Atheneum, 1964.

Milne, A. A.: *The Pooh Song Book*, music by H. Fraser-Simson, ill. by E. H. Shepard, Dutton, 1961.

————: *The World of Christopher Robin: The Complete When We Were Young and Now We Are Six*, ill. by E. H. Shepard, Dutton, 1958.

Nash, Ogden: *The New Nutcracker Suite and Other Innocent Verses*, ill. by Ivan Chermayeff, Little, Brown, 1962.

Potter, Beatrix: *Appley Dapply's Nursery Rhymes*, Warne.

Richards, Laura E.: *Tirra Lirra*, ill. by Marguerite, Little, Brown, 1955.

Rien, E. V.: *The Flattered Flying Fish,* ill. by E. H. Shepard, Dutton, 1962.

Riley, James Whitcomb: *Rhymes of Childhood,* Bobbs-Merrill, 1900.

Roberts, Elizabeth Madox: *Under the Tree,* ill. by F. D. Bedford, Viking, 1930.

Rossetti, Christina: *Goblin Market,* ill. by Arthur Rackham, Lippincott.

————: *Sing-song,* ill. by Marguerite Davis, Macmillan (Little Library), 1924.

Sandburg, Carl: *Early Moon,* ill. by James Daugherty, Harcourt, Brace, 1930.

Seeds of Time: Selections from Shakespeare, ed. by Bernice Grohskopf, ill. by Kelly Oechsli, Atheneum, 1963.

Stevenson, Robert Louis: *A Child's Garden of Verses,* ill. by Tasha Tudor, Oxford University Press, 1947.

Teasdale, Sara: *Stars Tonight,* ill. by Dorothy Lathrop, Macmillan, 1954.

Tippett, James: *I Go a-Traveling,* ill. by Elizabeth T. Wolcott, Harper, 1929.

————: *I Live in a City,* Harper, 1927.

————: *I Spend the Summer,* Harper, 1930.

Books about poetry

Arnstein, Flora: *Adventure into Poetry,* Stanford, 1951. Record of a creative-writing experiment with elementary school children.

Brooks, Cleanth, and Robert Penn Warren: *Understanding Poetry,* 3d ed., Holt, 1960.

Barrows, Herbert, et al.: *How Does a Poem Mean?* Houghton Mifflin, 1959.

Drew, Elizabeth, and George Connor: *Discovering Modern Poetry,* Holt, 1961.

Frankenberg, Lloyd: *Pleasure Dome: On Reading Modern Poetry,* Houghton Mifflin, 1949.

Isaacs, J.: *The Background of Modern Poetry,* Dutton, 1952.

MacLeish, Archibald: *Poetry and Experience,* Houghton Mifflin, 1960.

Perrine, Laurence: *Sound and Sense: An Introduction to Poetry,* 2d ed., Harcourt, Brace & World, 1963.

Reid, James M., et al.: *Poetry: A Closer Look,* Harcourt, Brace & World, 1963.

CHAPTER 11

THE
CHILD
AND
THE
FACTS:
Nonfiction
for Children

*T*wo basic facts about facts, as far as children's reading is concerned, are that most children most of the time want them and that most adults want them to have them.

The Childs Own Reasons for Knowing

Why do children generally want to know more about the physical and social world around them?

Usually the small child does not *need* to know facts in order to survive and be comfortable—his elders will see that he is fed, clothed, kept out of wintry weather, provided with most of the playthings he may wish, and taken to places he would like to go to. Yet the small child is apt to be full of questions. He wants to know who that is, what this is, what it is for, why it is made like that, what will happen to it if you do such and such. Will you do such and such? If not, why not? He seems to be impelled by a curiosity about the world around him, a desire to control that world mentally. The great mass of things small children want to know they do not have a need to know for their own physical preservation and well-being; they have *mental* need to know them.

Perhaps we are working here with something noted earlier in our consideration of fiction: that the real may be a source of wonder, a stimulant of the imagination, a base for its operation. A small child's openmouthed wonder at a big color picture of a horse in a book of animals may be very close to his excitement over sudden transformation; facts are strange, the first time around. Perhaps we are working here with an aesthetic factor in knowledge getting—the pleasure one obtains through acquiring knowledge, quite apart from the later consequences of one's having it. We need not theorize, although it would be interesting to do so, about the components of this curiosity. All we need for our purposes is to recognize that the discovery of realities is something that children very early begin to want and insist on, something that apparently satisfies them apart from any utilitarian considerations.

Also, of course, there *is* the motivation of wanting to know things that have some conceivable direct use—whether a certain sharp object will cut, what the name of that candy is that one might want to buy, where the nail goes into the wooden side of the crate-wagon, whether puppies like oatmeal or not. Children share with adults the desire to know so that they can understand their environment and in some degree actively control it. In the early years this motive appears to be rather unimportant, at least to be less important than intellectual curiosity; but it becomes increasingly important as the child grows older. Indeed, by the time the individual has become a man, he may have lost most of his curiosity and seek almost exclusively those facts he thinks he can use. But in childhood the two motivations work together to make children fact seekers—which means that if given the chance, children will look for information in books and magazines.

Adult Pressure

The second important fact about facts is that adults generally want children to have them. Parents and teachers want the child to learn facts and to know them, to "acquire knowledge," to "become better informed." They want him to learn facts that will help him meet present problems—to learn that the contents of the drug cabinets are dangerous so he won't swallow them, to learn about numbers and clocks so that he will be able to count and tell time, to learn what the red and green signal lights at the corner mean. And they also want him to learn facts that will prepare him for *future* learning—something about the physical nature of the world, the history of at least some parts of the world, etc. Often a set of facts will be wanted for both present and future purposes. Adults may disagree among themselves and with their children over what facts will help them and what facts should be given priority, but most adults are in agreement that children should obtain facts *for utilitarian reasons.*

And there is another motive in many adults' wanting their children to have facts: the wish that their children, their own children or their pupils, should know more than other children. This motive, often unconscious and when conscious generally not admitted, is the adults' desire for prestige; they want their children to learn facts for the sake of winning the game of "Who's best?" And of course prestige can become a direct factor in children's fact-finding. For them getting information can become a kind of competition—to know more than somebody else, to get a better grade. Sometimes competition becomes the primary motivation for acquiring knowledge.

Problems in Presenting Facts to Children

These two forces, children's variously motivated wish for facts and adults' variously motivated desire that they have facts, create a tremendous audience for the writer of books of information for children. Children's information books do not have to face the sceptical parental questions sometimes damaging to a child's chances of getting a novel or poem to read: "Will it really be useful? What good is it?" and in the schools, where teachers and administrators feel compelled to justify their courses of study in terms of usefulness (even though they may feel these terms are narrow, unrealistic, and impractical), the book of information does not have to go over the hurdles of doubt a fantasy or humorous story may have to jump. Obviously, then, there is an overwhelming demand for juvenile books of facts.

Still, all is not clear sailing for the writers of these books. The nature of children and the nature of facts create certain problems in the presentation of factual information to children:

1 Small children, though very curious, are likely to be inquisitive about facts within a relatively narrow sphere, facts limited by their own house or block and by their own day. The dining room, the kitchen, the car, the backyard, the nearby market, the kinds of weather—such are the matters about which they are likely to want to know more. So the writer who wants to reach small children with facts is going to have to restrict himself pretty much to this kind of very commonplace material.

2 Living is a cumulative matter; an experience gains meaning from other experiences we have had. Thus a child reader's understanding of what he experiences through his reading depends to some degree on what he has *previously* experienced, through his reading or in other ways. A play by Shakespeare may make more sense in the reading if he has been taken to see the play produced. A book on space travel is one thing to the child who has read little about the universe and a different thing to the child who has read much. The word *storm* means more to a child if he has come across electric storms, cyclones, blizzards, ocean storms, and dust storms in his reading. *Wild animals* mean more to a child after he has had an eye-opening visit to a large zoo.

Now in the normal course of events, a bright child of six has had fewer kinds of experiences—and fewer samplings of each kind—than a bright child of nine, and it is going to be harder to explain many things to the six-year-old simply because he has less experience to go on. Explanation may have to be given to the younger child in more elementary terms and at a slower pace. This is one reason, although not the only one, why there are relatively few books for six- to eight-year-olds on ancient history, microscopic organisms, orchestral music, and chemical and physical processes. But this problem is a major one for the writer of informational books for children of all ages. He cannot count on the possession of helpful knowledge that he may expect the intelligent, well-educated adult to have, and so he may need either just to skip the presentation of certain facts requiring this preknowledge or to offer the preliminaries along with the facts he wants the child reader to have. And teacher and parents, if they are aware of this problem, will ask themselves whether a particular book of facts requires of a child knowledge he does not yet have. And when they are getting a child to use reference sources, such as encyclopedias, almanacs, and yearbooks, they will consider what kinds of facts he will need to have in order to use each of the available sources.

3   Some experiences may enter into an individual's accumulation of knowledge at almost any age—for instance, breathing at a high altitude or seeing a magnet attract steel filings. But some experiences are, by their very nature, *later* experiences, so essentially adult, or at least adolescent, that children are not in a position to comprehend them at all fully. Vocational experiences—getting jobs, working in factories and stores and offices, belonging to unions, getting paid, having social security numbers— are primarily adult and so are difficult for children to comprehend. A father's work is most likely to be "what Daddy does" and to have little more meaning than just that. Children do not have husbands or wives and families, do not take part in politics as voters or officeholders, do not own property, do not enter the armed forces, do not belong to adult fraternal organizations; all these experiences are rather remote from children's own living and so pretty impossible for them to figure out. Education of various kinds occurs at different age levels; high school and college experiences are remote from the elementary school child. It can usually be assumed, therefore, that he will have no way of knowing, and will not know, what a major subject is, or an elective.

Faced with this situation, the writer for children is likely to avoid as subjects these various facts of adult life, which partly explains the comparative infrequency, in children's books, of plot situations based on industrial and business routines, of factual descriptions of university life, politics, marriage. Or he may try, like some of the writers on subjects not so essentially far from children, to provide much explanation an older person would not require, to give that additional fill-in. This is a difficult path to take, and many who take it end by being condescending in the abundance and worriedness of their explanations, their leaving nothing to the imagination.

4   In every field of knowledge and action the mastery of *abstract principles* is essential to understanding and effective control. A person who is acquainted with matches, gasoline, wood, and water hoses but does not know the principle of combustion is not likely to have good luck in avoiding fire dangers or fighting a bad fire. The boy to whom history is a series of unrelated events is not nearly so likely to understand, and become in-

terested in, human events beyond his own small sphere as is the boy who has somehow got hold of a concept of continuity in human events. The child's relations with animals are likely to improve greatly when he "gets the idea" that mauling pets angers them and may make them bite. Grasping abstractions is a way of learning—one of the best.

But it is also one of man's most difficult tasks. Time, history (as distinguished from the passing of time), space, birth, life, death, movement, speed and slowness, coldness and hotness, science, art, religion, government, freedom and captivity, singleness and manyness—these are all abstractions. We never experience abstractions directly; rather we experience a series of particular concrete events and then *think out* any abstract quality they all share. And we need to have a sizable succession of such particular experiences first before we are in a good position to see the principle involved in them. And it also takes time for our skills in abstract thinking to develop; indeed, great numbers of us adults never come to really understand most principles, even those with which we are daily concerned, such as time and heat and space and intelligence. So it is to be expected that explaining general principles to children will be a very demanding task. Yet if we do not try, then we are justifiably bothered by the uneasy feeling that all the pieces of information about fires, trucks, eggs, etc., that we give them in pretty books may not really be very useful to them without the sensemaking overall concept.

When we make a moderate effort to present such a concept but still make the particular objects or individuals we are writing about very vivid or dramatic, we risk distracting the child from the general idea we hope he will take away. And when, like Miriam Schlein in *It's about Time* or like Howard Baer in *Now This, Now That: Playing with Points of View,* we try hard to get the general notion across, we run a strong chance of losing the child's attention altogether and so never reaching his ability to understand. There is the unpleasant but inescapable fact that order can be, often is, boring. Ordered thinking, which is really abstract thinking, is likely to lack the suddenness and dramatic contrasts that would amuse. Until the individual has discovered the value of *ordered* facts, as opposed to just fascinating facts, he will find it hard to attend long enough to grasp the principle that is doing the ordering. To most children the recognition of the value of order comes slowly, through long experience.

5   And even if experience were less complex and if children knew more than they do and if abstractions were not so difficult, *vocabulary* would remain an obstacle to the reading child. If the terms for things are unknown to us, then communication about those things is meaningless to us, even when we already know the *things*. Children of six or seven generally have a fuller, more flexible and accurate vocabulary than children of four or five, but the acquisition of an adequate vocabulary to represent our experiences is a slow process, and for all children the words they do not have and the words whose meanings they only partially know form a wall against understanding.

A child, let us say, recognizes the word *bird* and knows it refers to many things that fly. Then he begins to differentiate these flying things from one another, but in order to do so and to understand information about them, he needs to learn a set of new terms—*robin, blue jay,* etc. But if he becomes very interested in knowing about certain kinds of birds, these terms prove quite unhelpful; now he needs to distinguish among Santa Cruz song sparrows, English sparrows, etc. *Water* may be enough for the three-year-old child in dealing with puddles, creeks, rivers, lakes, even oceans, but as he gets older the one general term becomes inadequate for his learning about kinds of bodies of water and he needs a term for each kind; and eventually he finds he must make further distinctions—for instance, between *Atlantic Ocean* and *Pacific Ocean.*

Experiences and the words for them need to go together. Learning is retarded if the words lag behind unduly.

This vocabulary problem has great significance for the writing and use of children's books of information. It is largely responsible for the great reliance on illustration as a means of conveying information and for the fact that even where words are used, the visual image is often used too, just in case. And the continued heavy reliance on illustration may mean a continued limiting of the child's exposure to words and develop in him the habit of relying on the visual image for information.

As already suggested, the limitedness of the child's vocabulary also dictates in some degree the subjects to be dealt with, and the detail and complexity of the coverage. Thus many scientific areas will be dodged or just glancingly touched because of the subjects' special vocabularies; likewise, life in other cultures may be so closely associated with an unfamiliar vocabulary that a writer will have a difficult time describing it to a child and so may dodge it. The children's writer will often restrict himself to the more *general* or *familiar* aspects of his subject because of the restrictedness of the vocabulary he believes his readers have.

6   Finally, a mastery of *methods of investigation* is only slowly developed. For example, formulating clear questions about what one wants to find out is a step that does not occur to most inexperienced investigators—and children are inexperienced investigators. The principle of grouping facts so that one can discover them easily and refer to them does not occur to one automatically; the child may therefore ignore the ordering apparatus provided for him in dictionaries, encyclopedias, and various special kinds of reference works and in the arrangement of a library by the Dewey decimal or Library of Congress system. And even if the child does not ignore such aids, their proper use must be learned, sometimes quite gradually. It takes time and experience to learn the nature and value of a book index, and a great many other aids to investigation that merely puzzle, confuse, and paralyze the person who has not been gradually introduced to their use— bibliographies, newspaper and magazine indexes, encyclopedias and dictionaries for special fields, thesauruses, concordances. Even many college students are clumsy in using these really simple fact-finding tools; and for most young children some of this investigative machinery is out of reach.

As we shall consider in detail later, the unavailability or limited availability of adult methods of investigation is very important in the making of children's reference books; it means that in their presentation and arranging of information special adaptations for children need to be made. Some of the standard equipment, such as indexes and bibliographies, needs to be dropped altogether or employed in rather simplified forms. And this limitation means that the factual material needs to be simplified. There cannot be so much factual data that the inexperienced young investigator would get confused and tired, and there must be such concessions to youth as the placing of dramatic or startling facts early in the account whether or not it is their logical spot, the omission of terms and concepts many children might be unlikely to know yet, and the inclusion of elementary kinds of information that might be omitted from standard reference works.

Further Worries

So far we have considered problems in the presentation of printed information to children that rise out of the very nature of childhood and knowledge—the limitations of the small child's interests, the cumulativeness of experience, the unavailability to the child of some kinds of experience, the slow development of his ability to think abstractly, the complexity of vocabulary and the child's lack of vocabulary in many fields, and his limited ability to make use of systems of investigation.

In addition to these problems, there are problems that rise out of the natures of adults themselves, and the way they run the world. What are these?

1   For various reasons adults may wish to change the pattern of facts that children will see from the pattern of facts that they themselves, as adults, know; they may wish to postpone or slow down children's learning about certain aspects of existence. For instance, many parents and teachers believe children should not encounter the sexual facts of existence. These adults may themselves believe that sex is somehow wrong, or they may just feel embarrassed by it, or they may hold that the child does not yet need to know these particular facts of life or that he does not have the experience and understanding necessary for really comprehending them or simply that "there's no rush." But whatever their reasons, these adults influence writers and publishers (and, of course, include some writers and publishers). And so, for instance, children's biographies of famous men and women either omit or gloss over the facts of courtship and childbearing and generally do not refer to any sort of irregular or socially disapproved sexual behavior. And sex is one phase of biological science that is still handled rather gingerly in science books and children's encyclopedias.

Many adults consider tragic events as matters to be omitted from children's reading matter or euphemistically described. And so great disasters of human history, accidents with mass fatalities, the loss of life in plagues—are often dodged or referred to cautiously in history written for children. And writers sidestep violence and cruelty in nature and in human affairs. They hesitate to describe crimes or even refer to them; the ugly facts of genocide in the modern world are likely to be given a much quicker, lighter treatment in a children's reference work than would be the case in an adult reference work. The preying of one species of animal on other species only gradually comes to have a place in the natural histories for children, as the age level rises.

Just as troublesome for many adults are life's confusions, frustrations, uncertainties. That a cure for a disease has not yet been found, that some-thing has been lost, that certain facts are not known for sure—such truths are hard for many adults to permit youthful readers to swallow. So a children's science writer will mention the positive effects of an invention but not refer to still unsolved problems in its use. Or a children's novelist may even avoid bringing in a tie score in a ball game.

It does not do any real good, however, to condemn *all* such practices as timidity, mollycoddling, or hypocrisy. They can become very silly, but there is no denying that children are *not* adults, that therefore their encounter with the facts of existence is not going to be like that of adults, and that therefore the very same criteria of desirability cannot be used for the presentation of facts to children and adults. Also, one must agree that in practice it is impossible to communicate to children everything we may wish to; they can be given only *some* of the facts. It is, then, the responsi-bility of adults to select facts for children; and this means adults are charged with the complementary task of *omitting facts.* We can theorize about how desirable it might be to open all the doors to children and let them choose, but this does not alter the fact that such free choice is simply impossible.

2   A basic fact that helps to determine what information will be given to children and when and in what form is *school*—the adult-operated aca-demic system which soon takes over much of the child's exposure to knowl-edge. Only a very few years are left free from the academic institution's influence on the present-day child, who is likely to start kindergarten at five or six and to have had one to three years of nursery school prior to that. Thus from the end of infancy to adulthood the child is a member of an organization whose main purpose is to give him information.

One of the main ways in which this institution seeks to achieve this goal is through reading. Moreover, activities connected with school fill a large part of the child's day through most of his educational career. Together, these two facts mean that much of the information he will get will be through the reading he does at school or as assigned homework or recom-mended reading. So the shape of children's reading, and particularly as a source of factual information and opinion, is determined to a large extent by the shape of their formal education. This applies to parents' choice of informative home reading, too, for they will tend to take their cue from what is being done in school and from the books made and chosen by writers, teachers, and librarians, who are influenced by the dominant school needs of the time.

If school systems place special emphasis on formal learning, the fact books their children use are likely to be cast in somewhat adult patterns, within largely traditional and academically acceptable fields of learning—literature, history, biology, etc. If there is less emphasis on formal learning, the fact books for the children will be more experimental, more inclined to give facts in game form, to combine facts from various fields of knowledge, to explore less traditionally academic fields—community life, exploring, industry, commerce, the visual arts, etc. When school systems go in for certain kinds of learning activities—say, alphabet learning or scientific observation or rote memory—these activities are going to be reflected in fact books for children. To take another instance, the spread of the unit system in some large school systems—studying "The Harbor" or "Aircraft" or "The Frontier"—has undoubtedly been one of the main reasons for the proliferation of the series of big-pictured, fact-packed, orderly books on such subjects—the All About series, the Real Books, the True Books, the First Books, the Let's Go To series, and the Big Book series. And the placing of emphasis on certain subjects in certain grades can mean the aiming of books—their vocabulary, interest, tone—at specific age levels.

3   Among some parents, teachers, writers, scholars, and librarians, presenting facts to children in books and articles has taken on a certain stigma; it has come to seem a lower activity than imaginative literature—telling stories, writing poems. As a consequence of this misapprehension (for that it is), this field has been avoided by many excellent scholarly writers who could contribute much to it and been left too often to writers or gadget-minded technicians who may not know either the facts or the children. This unfortunate attitude seems to be disappearing, however, partly because of the economic rewards that lure brilliant as well as dull people and partly because of the increasing prestige of scientific education in the schools. Many leaders in biology, art, music, physics, and other fields are now to be found engaged as both consultants and writers in the presentation of information in attractive books for children.

Some Historical Facts about Facts for Children

The present abundance and richness of factual reading for children are relatively recent developments. The seventeenth- and eighteenth-century books of instruction were largely books of moral instruction, counsel on good and bad conduct. In the eighteenth century the amount of very simple primer information concerning the animal kingdom, geography, and history gradually increased, but ethical generalization and illustrative instance remained the dominant pattern of juvenile instruction through reading.

There gradually came into being, however, with the rise of the middle class a more general desire for the practical instruction of children in arithmetic and reading, with, at times, pretensions to the broader culture that had been central to the education of an aristocratic minority. And the appearance of the knowledge-seeking middle class was paralleled by the great rise of scientific discovery, both theoretical and technological, in Western Europe and America, with its subsequent reflection in adults' desire to have their children know the new scientific facts.

The rise of mass education meant that more children learned to read, that these people as adults thought of reading and books as important, and that more and more reading came to be done in all classes of society at all age levels.

These trends making for the expansion of reading for information coincided with great steps in fact gathering: swifter transportation and communication, the opening of new parts of the world to exploration and settlement, the rise of newspapers and their staffs, the growth of scientific associations and universities and their staffs, the discovery of the microscope and telescope, the development of photography, new laboratory techniques, and the creation of such reference sources as encyclopedias and dictionaries. All these developments meant the creation of a great store of facts which demanded adaptation for children and on which children's writers could draw. All this happened, moreover, at a time when new methods of effective mass reproduction of drawings, maps, photographs, etc., were being discovered.

All of these events and trends of the past two centuries have inevitably created a tremendous wave of books of knowledge for children. Today it is such a complex mass of books that one finds great difficulty in making sense out of it, and at the same time the amount and variety make it absolutely necessary that we do some simplifying, a little cataloging.

The major patterns that have developed in the presentation of facts to children include these: (1) picture books of facts, particularly for the very young, (2) semipictorial "stories" for small children that are a transparent device for giving information on particular subjects, (3) straight information books, which are simply compilations of facts from a limited area of knowledge, (4) idea books, which attach such facts to a unifying concept, (5) "how to" books, and (6) basic reference tools, especially encyclopedias and dictionaries, adapted for children.

The Picture Book of Facts

The ancestor of the modern picture book of facts is the small seventeenth-century woodcut of Jonah's whale, the walls of Jericho, a martyr at the stake, or a strange African beast, the woodcut illustrating a verbal message. In many modern picture books of facts, however, the pictures are the book; whatever words may be there are there merely to clarify the picture.

The purpose of the picture book is to give information about object, event, place, person, or idea by means of the visual image; the pictures teach. But they vary in how much they try to accomplish. A picture can simply be a credible likeness of the object—say, a bear or porcupine or fire truck—in its normal environment, the kind of impression one gets in one or two quick glances. Photography can do this; much so-called realistic painting and drawing is of this sort. The great majority of animal books for little children use this general, impressionistic realism. Or a picture can try to tell the child more than he might actually see in a general look at the object; it will show the thing in more detail—all four feet of the bear, with all the claws showing, the individual spikes of the porcupine, or the individual hoses on the fire truck. This approach can be carried to the extreme point of *diagramming*, where essential parts are picked out and examined analytically—the inside of an ocean liner, for instance. Many of the picture books in such series as the Big Books (trucks, trains, etc.) are essentially of this kind; the aim of these books is to tell their looker-readers as much as possible about the parts and functions of the objects under consideration.

Facts in Story Disguise

Many information books for the very young child present information under the guise of a story—a very simple and really plotless story about one or more people going through a routine, doing a task, using something that the author wants to inform the child about. Instead of merely describing a library and the processes of getting out a book, this author would take Johnny and Mary on a tour of the library, have the librarian show them the different kinds of books, and perhaps have them choose and check out books. Lois Lenski conveys a great deal of information about housekeeping, farms, airplanes, and autos by having her Mr. Small and his family keep house, tend farms, and operate planes and autos. Much realistic fiction, such as Norman Bate's *Who Fishes for Oil?* or Jo and Ernest Norling's *Pogo's Sea Trip: A Story of Boats* or Carl Denison's *What Every Young Rabbit Should Know*, actually performs this sort of function for slightly older children, too. In such books the facts are the most interesting things; the slight story line and characterizations are simply added attractions. (See in Chapter 7 the related discussion of books about household surroundings, personal possessions, and neighborhood.) These books rely heavily on visual description too.

Straight Information Books and Their Methods of Presenting Information

These are books on limited areas of information in which no attempt is made to disguise information as something else; the book is straightforwardly offered as a source of facts. As the child moves out of the primary grades, these books come to be major sources of information for him.

There are a great many ways of offering facts as facts. Let us consider briefly the main ones used in these books on limited areas of information. Later we shall turn to the problem of presenting knowledge in encyclopedic, reference form.

The simplest, most arbitrary, least intellectual way of arranging data within a subject area is by alphabetic order. Handbooks (botany, ornithology, biography, geography) are generally arranged in this way. The great and obvious advantage of this method is quickness of reference; one of its main uses is identification. Its limitation is one of logic and unity; alphabetic arrangement does not facilitate the making of connections among facts. And this sort of book does not lend itself to continuous reading. Such books as Doubleday's Pocket Nature Library (*Wild Flowers East of the Rockies*, etc.) are primarily "look it up" books and, as such, are small cousins of the large encyclopedia and dictionary. Of course, this alphabetic ordering may be used in combination with other ways of classifying information.

The most common kinds of order in children's straight information books are these: (1) interest, (2) historical chronology, (3) place and spatial relations, (4) cause and effect, (5) uses, (6) similarity and contrast, (7) discovery or invention, and (8) degree of familiarity. All grow out of the subject itself or the author's special purposes, or both.

1 Order of Interest to the Author or Reader   One may or may not consider this a bona fide method of arranging facts. The author merely groups his information according to its interest to himself or his readers. Rather than group according to logical connections, he decides to place what he considers his most interesting facts first or, seeking some climax, last; or he tries to scatter them among the less interesting facts. And pictures are placed not so much where they will clarify as where they will capture attention and then recapture it whenever it may flag; the most ferocious-looking dinosaur may be in the front of the book. The book that uses this method, most common among the "primary" books, is really intended as an attention getter; its information value is relatively low.

2 Historical Chronology   A subject may be treated in terms of what came first, what came second, etc. Any subject may be dealt with by this method, but it is more appropriate for certain kinds of subjects than for others. The history of a country or culture or region can easily be treated in this manner; so might the history of a family or the history of a person, biography; the life cycles of animals may be most easily described thus. A modification of this order is to begin with the most recent happening and to go on back.

One argument for the chronological type of arrangement is that it may contribute to the child's developing sense of time, his feeling for historical order. But chronological order frequently goes counter to purposes of amusement and attention getting and keeping. With quite young children the feeling for time may be so slight that a chronological ordering merely confuses and baffles. Also, though event 1 may be interesting and significant to a child, events 2 and 3 and 4 may be less so, and the child's interest may be lost before he gets to that interesting fifth point; one may omit the duller events, but this may sacrifice the sense of sequence. And many times the historical order is less informative than some other kind.

3   *Place and Spatial Relations*   Facts may be grouped according to place and, often, the relations between places. Instead of describing world events chronologically, one may present them according to the places where the events occurred—America, Europe, Asia, Africa. In describing how foods come to market, one may start with the point farthest away, the farm, and work in to the closest, the market, or go in the opposite direction. This method is most commonly used in presenting geographic information, including travel facts—facts about Chicago, then facts about Detroit, then Cleveland, then, moving still farther east, New York. Again, as with the chronological arrangement (with which it obviously is sometimes combined), this order may run counter to the actual significance or interest of the facts, but it is easy to use, conveys a sense of movement, and may assist the child in getting a clear sense of his physical world, from his home to the entire universe.

4   *Arrangement by Cause and Effect*   The facts about a subject may be presented in terms of cause and effect, including, of course, effect first and then cause. Thus the parts of a manufacturing process may be described along with the specific effects meant to come from each of those steps, or each event in a man's later life may be described along with its particular causes in his earlier life. A most obvious example of this type of organization is the question-answer book: "Why does it rain?" "Why do some liquids change their color?" This method means that the author each time takes on himself the responsibility for pointing out *this* as the cause or effect of *that*. In many matters, of course, this is impossible, or at least rash; and even when this method could easily be used, an author may wish to leave the drawing of cause-effect connections up to the child.

5   *Uses*   This grouping is related to cause and effect, but here the organizing principle is the *use* to which the facts can be put. For example, facts about fruit, sugar, and bacteria that might be relevant in canning would be placed under the heading "Fruit Canning"; facts about animal anatomy and physiology, forests, tracks, weather, and weapons that might be related to trapping would be placed under "Trapping"; facts about England, Scotland, Russia, and Argentina related to games would be

grouped under "Games." Typical of this way of presenting information is the First Book series—*First Book of Cotton*, etc. The strength of this method lies in its general practicality; its weak point is its tendency to dump masses of quite different kinds of fact together simply because of one more or less accidental connection.

6 *Similarity and Contrast*   One of the simplest and most orderly methods of arranging facts is by similarity and contrast. An obvious example of such an arrangement is the dictionary's grouping of the synonyms and antonyms of a word. This method is quite frequently used in children's informational books—partly, perhaps, because it is so orderly. Some common examples of this method: comparing domestic animals and the wild forebears of each; contrasting types of houses, or various forms of the skyscraper; contrasting facts about life in ancient times and today, the "then and now" approach. The advantage and the limitation of this way of grouping facts are that it imposes a *definite* arrangement on them; this makes for orderliness and clarity but at the same time risks oversimplification and moving the child to conceive things in unrealistic black-and-white terms.

7 *Discovery or Invention*   Still another way in which facts may be grouped for exposition is to present them in relation to their discovery or in relation to an invention. This approach, then, is a biographical one. Thus facts about atomic physics may be set forth in a book on the Curies. A history of flight and an account of the engineering principles involved may be given through presenting the lives of the Wrights. A book about astronauts may convey much information about space flight. This basing on biography has two opposite major dangers: the biographical facts may tend to shove the scientific problems and facts around, or the scientific facts may create a one-sided picture of the man.

8 *Degree of Familiarity*   The probable degree of readers' familiarity with facts can determine how these facts will be given to them; a writer may decide to give the familiar facts on each matter first, to cluster the unfamiliar around the familiar. For example, a book on printing might start with information on the printing of today's paper and then move into the history of printing, rather than begin with the more unfamiliar medieval printing. Or a boat book might start with the most familiar craft—perhaps a canoe or rowboat—and then move into a coverage of boats increasingly complex and unfamiliar. Or a book on American Revolutionary times might start with the more famous figures of the period, such as Washington and Franklin, and move on to the less widely known, such as Madison and the Adamses.

The Idea Book

In these eight methods of arranging facts for children the emphasis is *on the facts themselves* and pretty much on the facts as *separate* facts, any one of which one might wish to consider by and for itself. Some relationship, such as time or place or cause and effect, is used, but it is not basic; that is, the facts are not presented as elements of an *idea*. But there *is* a type of book which presents facts to children as elements of an idea, an abstract concept; and, indeed, in this type of book the idea is the primary target, reached by way of the facts.

In the past two decades a relatively small number of authors—among them Schlein, Alvin Tresselt, Krauss, G. Warren Schloat, Dahlov Ipcar, Glenn O. Blough, Irma E. Webber, Jeanne Bendick—have done a large number of these facts-to-idea, or idea-through-facts, books. Some typical books of this genre are Schlein's *It's about Time, Heavy Is a Hippopotamus,* and *Fast Is Not a Ladybug;* Margaret Wise Brown's Noisy Books; Blough's *After the Sun Goes Down* (the ways different things behave at night); May Garelick's *What's Inside;* Olive Earle's *Paws, Hoofs and Flippers;* Dorothy Koch's *I Play at the Beach;* Tresselt's *Sun Up* (what happens first thing in the morning), his *Follow the Wind,* and his *I Saw the Sea Come In* (experiencing a tide); Schloat's *The Wonderful Egg;* Irma E. Webber's *Bits That Grow Big: Where Plants Come from;* Jeanne Bendick's *How Much and How Many;* John E. Bechdolt's *Going Up: The Story of Vertical Transportation;* Herman and Nina Schneider's *Follow the Sunset* and *How Big Is Big?* and Irma Simonton Black's *Big Puppy and Little Puppy.*

In Schlein's *It's about Time* a great many miscellaneous facts are given—about clocks, ancient timekeeping methods, calendars, holidays—but they are organized to help the child grasp some concept of time as a flow which we arbitrarily divide up for the sake of convenience. This, by the way, is an extremely difficult, complex concept, one which some cultures have scarcely sensed and with which many adults in our own culture have barely a nodding acquaintance. In *Fast Is Not a Ladybug* the child is first introduced to something faster than himself and then to things all progressively faster, then to various degrees of slowness, even to that of a ladybug. In this manner the child is supposed to pick up the concept of speed as relative; along the way he has become acquainted with many faster and slower animals and machines. The Schneiders' *How Big Is Big?* is organized in a similar way and with a similar purpose. The reader starts with his own size, then explores smaller and smaller organisms, down to microscopic animals, then goes up the ladder of size all the way to the sun. By then he has been exposed to many animals, some of them probably new to him, and to outer space and rocket travel and perhaps has also recognized a very difficult and tricky abstract idea, relativity of size.

There are many such abstract concepts that human beings need to come to understand if they are to master their environment, such as relativivy of speed, time relativity, size relativity, heat and light, birth and growth and decay, germ theory, electricity. And in social relationships there are other complex principles, such as peace and war, commerce, individuality and society, law, government, toleration, reward and punishment, taxation history, and education. Social concepts generally wait longer than physical ones to be presented in book form to children. Still, even at primary level this may be attempted, as in Margaret Wise Brown's *Red Light, Green Light,* which suggests the whole notion of regulating traffic, or Nina Schneider's *While Susie Sleeps,* which, by noting the many kinds of work going on at night, suggests that people are working for our well-being all the time, even at night while most of us sleep. Joan Anglund, in her *Look out the Window,* notes the many things you can see from a window and, in so doing, points out that everything, everyone, is individual, single, that every child is different from the onlooker, "because you're the only one in this whole wide world that is you." For children a little older, Munro Leaf suggests, in his *History Can Be Fun,* what the historical past is and how we can think about and use it and, in his *Reading Can Be Fun,* the purposes and rewards of books. For still older children, general ideas can be embedded in books of biography and history. For instance, the idea of free speech gives structure to, and may be conveyed through, Tom Galt's biography of Peter Zenger, who went to court rather than submit to censorship rules he considered unjust. Similarly, Robert Lawson's concepts of the American pioneering spirit are embodied in the biographical sketches of his *They Were Strong and Good.*

There is, however, no sharp line between straight information books and idea books. Both present facts from a limited area of information; and also, the idea book shades off into the straight information book. A book of facts may contain *no* overall idea, or it may have one more or less incidentally suggested by the facts, or it may present an overriding central idea by means of any facts which seem relevant to that purpose. Sometimes, as in William Bridges's *Zoo Babies* or Krauss's *A Very Special House* or Lee Kingman's *Peter's Long Walk* or Phyllis McGinley's *All around the Town,* a general concept seems really an excuse for bringing together a lot of facts of interest to children. And even where the idea is clearly central, a child may take the facts without getting the abstract notion running through those facts.

The "How to do it" Book

Finally, information may be presented to children in such a way that it can be used to carry out certain tasks, solve certain problems. This is done in "how to do it" books. Again, they shade off into straight information books, because the facts are sometimes offered in a rather "take them or leave them" or "do anything you want with them" manner. Their central intention, however, is different from that of straight information books: they set out to focus the facts on the accomplishment of a certain task. Only the facts about the engine or boat that will be of some practical use will be included. This is the book of *applied* knowledge. If it has an index, that is probably organized so the user can easily find what he wants at each step of his project.

The great mass of "how to do it" books for children are not fundamentally different from their counterparts for adults. They do use a more limited vocabulary, place more reliance on visual than verbal explanation, and may have a touch more amusement or teasing wonder. But these children's books on how to make a table, catch fish, repair a radio, perform elementary physics experiments, or whatever are very close to their adult prototypes.

The "how to do it" element may be incorporated into books of the other types. For example, plans for a weekend camping trip may be included in a general handbook on nature study; how to build a bird station can be told in a handbook; to tell how to perform a simple experiment is one way of explaining a chemical or physical conception.

Books of General Reference

The information books which we have been considering are all concerned with limited areas of knowledge. They focus on certain kinds of facts or facts linked to certain situations, problems, localities, persons. Another type of information book, the basic general reference book, is closely related to the preceding types but different in one fundamental respect: it presumes to give information on *all*, or at least most, areas of human knowledge. Its contents can be referred to in seeking information in any of its main aspects. There are three broad types of reference work: the encyclopedia; the dictionary; and the index, bibliography, or summary of other sources of information. The two especially important for children's use are the encyclopedia and the dictionary.

Differences between Adult and Child Users of Reference Materials

Children inquiring are not adults inquiring. There are a number of fundamental ways in which they differ:

1 Interests The kinds of information which the child will want to run down will tend to be different from the kinds which adults will most frequently look up. The child's inquiries will be mainly about the physical world—first the immediate world of insects, animals, trees, and rivers and then the wider physical universe. The adult, besides wanting information on these subjects, will have questions on history (the past), psychology (the mind), art, philosophy, science, religion, education. The world of adult interests differs from that of children, and so the information adults and children will seek out differs.

2 Background   The amounts of knowledge children and older readers already have and bring with them to a reference book will differ. The child has not had as much experience as the adult, and he has not had as much opportunity to read and investigate. So to understand certain things, he will need to be given information the adult probably already knows; for instance, in a discussion of batteries, the child may well need a definition of the term *batteries*. A well-educated adult is likely to know more than a child about American Puritanism, its Reformation background, for instance. So, on the one hand, information given the child on American Puritanism may need to be simple, so as not to swamp him with too many new facts; the writer will need to assume that more of the facts will be new to the child. On the other hand, the writer will need to give *more* information than an adult might need, so that the child can come to understand the subject as a unified whole.

3 Language Vocabulary   The child's vocabulary is likely to be more limited than an adult's. Hence, the presentation of facts for children will need to differ from the presentation of facts in an encyclopedia for adults. The adults' presentation may assume a wider language base—*more words* and a *wider range of meanings*. And the child will not be helped much by a dictionary explanation of an unknown word meaning if the explanation itself is couched in words he has not encountered.

4 Children's Reading Skills   The fact that children only gradually acquire the various reading skills means dependence on various sorts of assistance in using reference books. At first the child needs the assistance of someone else in reading; later he still needs fairly normal syntax, recurring words, largish print, and considerable white space, and more use of picture explanation than an adult would need.

5 Attention   The child's relatively short atttention span is a critical element in his use of reference materials. Where amusement is a primary objective, the writer can get and retain attention by a great many devices—suspense, colorful language, exaggeration—pretty much as he needs to. But where the main intention is to inform accurately and clearly, the writer may be more limited in what he can do to keep a wandering or fatigued mind on a given track. In any case, the children's writer on geography, government, and history cannot count on as long forbearance by the reader as can the writer for adults on those subjects. His articles need to be briefer, less detailed, and more buttressed with visual illustration.

6   *Techniques of Fact-finding*   As already noted, efficient investigation involves the ability to use certain tools—indexes by author or title or subject, cross-indexes, bibliographies, pronunciation keys, library cataloging systems, etc.—and it may take some years for the child to become easy in their use, even after he knows the theory of their use. And when the child looks for reference books in a school or public library, there is the need for mastering the location of the stacks and the local system for tracing wanted books.

There are two ways of reacting to these differences between adult and child fact seekers. One is to hold that they do not matter, which in effect means to wait until the child can use adult reference materials and then have him use them—adult encyclopedias such as the *Encyclopaedia Britannica* or *Encyclopedia Americana* or *Collier's*, adult dictionaries such as *Webster's* or *Funk and Wagnall's* or the *American Collegiate Dictionary*. The second alternative is have the child use, and help him to use, reference sources designed primarily for children, books that these differences have brought into existence.

Characteristics of Children's Reference Books

Special children's references differ from adult references in several major ways; they follow major patterns of their own.

1   Most of the children's encyclopedias group their facts in *general articles or sections*. Thus their information on armadillos is more likely to be treated in an article called "Armored Animals" or "Strange Animals" or "South American Animals" than in an article called "Armadillos"; or the material on famous American statesmen may be brought together in an article called "Great Leaders of our Country." And in some children's encyclopedias the facts are strung together in *narrative form*, as elements of a story. Children's encyclopedias vary tremendously, however, in the degree to which they weave particular subjects into general groupings with such narrative and thematic continuity. Thus some, such as *Childcraft*, present all their facts in very general subject or problem groupings or chapters. Such a work is really a series of separate books on various large subjects—animals, industry, art, literature. Others, such as *Junior Britannica, Compton's Pictured Encyclopedia, The World Book,* and *Our Wonderful World*, have alphabetic arrangement of factual articles on specific subjects, but these also group their material in rather large, thematic packages—e.g., a big article on lumbering, including wood, forests, sawmill processing, and conservation, rather than separate articles on these particular facets of lumbering.

This difference between children's and adults' encyclopedias reveals itself in the lesser usefulness of the alphabetic arrangement of the children's work (where it *is* alphabetized) and the greater convenience of the children's work for the reader who is browsing, reading on and on. The children's encyclopedia is more designed for continuous, consecutive reading, the adult encyclopedia for looking things up.

2   The children's encyclopedia generally covers *fewer subjects* than the adult encyclopedia, the selection being based on various kinds of criteria—what the child may be able to understand, what will interest him, what in the adult's opinion the child should know, what he should not know, what he needs or will be expected to know. Children's encyclopedias vary all the way from a high degree of exclusion to relatively little exclusion of matters that would be dealt with in an adult's reference. Likewise, dictionaries for children have fewer items than most regular abridged dictionaries, and they too range from much to little selectivity.

3   The children's encyclopedia generally has *fewer facts* on a given subject. There tends to be less factual *packing,* more selecting of facts, and this normally means smaller articles. In dictionaries for children some of the kinds of information included under a word in adult dictionaries are often omitted, e.g., derivations and special uses and forms.

4   Most juvenile reference books employ a *vocabulary* the editors believe will create no special hurdles for intelligent children. They try to use words which, normally, children will have encountered in their reading and relatively simple, direct constructions. Again, they range from making concessions to children with small vocabularies to making only small allowances on this score.

5   Children's encyclopedias tend to rely more heavily on *visual* forms of information—drawings, photographs, charts, maps—than adult encyclopedias do, and the illustrations are usually an integral part of the exposition rather than an extra help. Some children's encyclopedias are almost picture books. Children's dictionaries, too, show a tendency to use a relatively large amount of illustration.

6   Children's encyclopedias try in various ways to have simple *index systems.* For instance, some do without a back-of-book index and try to rely on a table of contents as a sufficient key. This is at one pole. Others have an index with a little summary of information under each index item.

7   Most children's encyclopedias use larger print and more white paper.

Though, as we have just seen, present-day reference works for children differ from one another as well as from adult references, the differences tend to group themselves so that one has a range of identifiable types of references to choose from. Thus the children's encyclopedia whose editors have decided to make it thoroughly a child's book of facts will very likely be organized into chapters, be about a relatively small number of categories, have relatively few facts in those categories, contain facts chosen for their special interest to small children, lack an index, draw on simple vocabulary, rely on illustrations for much of the explanation, be light and small enough for easy handling, and have spacious pages and large print. Children's encyclopedias which try to incorporate the advantages of the adult encylcopedia may have smaller sections but still the thematic approach, more subjects covered (and those of an increasingly adult interest), more data on given subjects, an index but a fairly general one, a richer, more varied and technical vocabulary, fewer and less prominent illustrations, and smaller print and a more crowded page. And then there are children's encyclopedias which are quite close to their adult counterparts, but just a bit smaller and less inclusive. There is a comparable range of types of children's dictionaries. In both categories, the great differences lie in the degree to which the reference work allows for presumed limitations in the child user.

Conclusion

The central implication of this chapter has been that in the making and selecting and use of children's books of information of all types one needs to consider special problems that do not exist, at least in nearly the same degree, in children's fictional literature.

1   Arousing and Keeping Children's Interest   To what extent can the facts be relied on to catch and keep the child reader's interests, and at what point may interest catching interfere with the conveying of information? This kind of question applies, of course, to adult factual books as well, but there the question takes a somewhat less critical form, with the attention, background-information, experience, and reading-facility factors much less acute.

Most makers of children's information books seem to be agreed that to interest most children, they cannot just give the facts. And most adults would, I think, agree that a Freeman many-volumed biography of Lee or Washington is not likely to attract an intelligent young reader, that the entire life of Jefferson, including his wide reading in eighteenth-century philosophy, would not intrigue him, that the details of Lincoln's state business will not interest him as much as Lincoln's frontier boyhood or his later dramatic public appearances. But here the agreement ends. Adults disagree on how far the makers of books should go and just what should be done in adapting factual presentation to the task of keeping children amused and happy.

For example, in the life of a biologist the years of quiet laboratory work and reading and thinking out of new concepts, although centrally significant in the man's life, will almost certainly not intrigue most children— but his capturing live specimens will, and so the biographer for children will be tempted to give a chapter to this matter and to briefly mention the less dramatic periods of the man's life or try to add drama to them, touch them up. Similarly one may try to make a journey stormier than it was, to have the Indians be more warlike than they were at a particular time and place. Or, if a subject is difficult to make exciting without too much distortion, one may just overlook it and write about some other more exciting subject in the same general category. Darwin may get pushed aside by the snake specialist Ditmars, the microscope by the telescope, the building of Rome's viaducts and great buildings by the gory Colosseum spectacles, the variety of small fish by the whale. Or if a subject seems hard to make interesting to children because of its complexity and unfamiliarity it may be given little or no attention. Of course, all subjects may to a considerable degree be presented visually to catch and keep children's wandering attentions, but this may blur fine points, oversimplify, capture just the external aspects of things; for instance, to present modern science pictorially, it would be most easy to concentrate on *machinery;* objects, rather than ideas, will be portrayed visually. And the space given to pictures reduces the space given to full verbal explanation of factual details.

Certainly, the factually sound account need not be uninteresting to children, nor need the enthralling collection of pictures and anecdotes be inaccurate; but in children's information books the problem of obtaining and keeping interest is more acute than in factual books for adults, and the temptation to sacrifice accuracy to interest is greater.

2   Being Simple, Comprehensible, and Accurate at the Same Time   A certain number of facts about a situation need to be known for accuracy and understanding, but if the reader is swamped by more facts than he can handle or by facts too far out of his range, then the facts themselves work against his understanding. This is a problem in all exposition, but an especially pressing one for children's books of information, in view of the physical and emotional growth yet to take place and the amount of information to be acquired before a firmly useful background is established. Thus the writer needs to simplify but not too much, to eliminate but not leave out too much, to get the essentials but avoid seeming to offer a bunch of bare bones.

3   Making Information Available to the Child   Attention factors and children's lack of training in data gathering make it especially necessary that their fact books be of such a size and arrangement that the facts will be easily available. Here again many times a compromise needs to be struck between an efficient, logical classification system for adults and an easier-to-use, less complex system for children. And there is the need for introducing the child to more complex, advanced methods of fact collecting and presenting *at the same time* that he is getting through a simpler, more elementary system the facts he wants and needs right now. He needs, furthermore, continued practice in the development of habits of vigorous, detailed investigation, critical-mindedness, and accuracy.

SUGGESTED SOURCES

Examples of Various Kinds of Direct Presentation of Information

Allee, Veva Elwell: *The Frozen Foods Plant,* with photographs by Robert Fogata, Melmont, 1955. Straight exposition, with large photo for each step in process.

Baumann, Hans: *The Caves of the Great Hunters,* rev. ed., Pantheon, 1962. Full account of cave paintings and their discovery.

Blough, Glenn O.: *Not Only for Ducks: The Story of Rain,* ill. by Jeanne Bendick, Whittlesey, 1954.

Britten, Benjamin, and Imogen Holst: *The Wonderful World of Music,* ill. by Ceri Richards, Doubleday, 1958.

Bucheimer, Naomi: *Let's Go to the Library,* ill. by Vee Guthrie, Putnam, 1957.

Buehr, Walter: *Railroads Today and Yesterday,* ill. by author, Putnam, 1958.

Chase, Alice Elizabeth: *Famous Paintings: An Introduction to Art,* Platt, 1962. Many reproductions, organized mainly around subjects, e.g., "Trains and Stations," "Heir to the Throne," "Bridges," "Horses, Horses, Horses."

Chilton, Charles: *The Book of the West: An Epic of America's Wild Frontier and the Men Who Created Its Legends,* ill. by Eric Tansley, Bobbs-Merrill, 1962.

Craven, Thomas: *The Rainbow Book of Art,* World, 1956.

Dillon, Ina K.: *Policemen,* ill. by Robert Bartram, Melmont, 1957.

Foster, Genevieve: *Abraham Lincoln's World 1809–1865,* ill. by author, Scribner, 1944.

————: *Augustus Caesar's World: A Story of Ideas and Events from* B.C. *44 to 14* A.D., ill. by author, Scribner, 1947.

————: *George Washington's World,* ill. by author, Scribner, 1941.

Glubok, Shirley: *The Art of Ancient Egypt,* ill. by Gerard Nook, Atheneum, 1962.

————: *The Art of Lands in the Bible,* ill. by Gerard Nook, Atheneum, 1963.

Huntington, Harriet E.: *Let's Go Outdoors,* with photographs by Preston Duncan, Doubleday, 1939. Followed by others in series—*Let's Go to the Brook,* etc.

Johnson, Gerald W.: *America Is Born: A History for Peter,* ill. by Leonard Everett Fisher, Morrow, 1959. With exciting drawings.

Leaf, Munro: *History Can Be Fun,* ill. by author, Lippincott, 1950. Also *Geography Can Be Fun,* etc.

Lent, Henry B.: *Here Come the Trucks,* ill. by Renée George, Macmillan, 1954.

Lingstrom, Freda: *The Seeing Eye: How to Look at Natural and Man-made Things with Pleasure and Understanding,* Studio Books, London, 1960.

Lucas, Mary Seymour: *Vast Horizons,* ill. by C. B. Falls, Viking, 1943.

McNeer, May: *The Canadian Story,* ill. by Lynd Ward, Ariel Books, 1958. Also *The Mexican Story,* 1953.

Mead, Margaret: *People and Places,* ill. by W. T. Mars and Jan Fairservis, and with photographs, World, 1959. Basic anthropology.

Nugent, Frances Roberts: *Jan Van Eyck: Master Painter,* ill. by author, also reproductions of Van Eyck paintings, Rand McNally, 1962.

Peterson, Roger Tory: *How to Know the Birds,* Houghton Mifflin, 1949.

Pistorius, Anna: *What Bird Is It?* ill. by author, Follett, 1945. Also in series, books on butterflies, dinosaurs, etc.

Pocket Nature Library, Doubleday. *Wild Flowers East of the Rockies,* etc.

Price, Christine: *Made in the Middle Ages,* ill. by author, Dutton, 1961.

Price, Willard DeMille: *Rivers I Have Known,* John Day, 1965.

Reed, W. Maxsell, and Wilfred S. Bronson: *The Sea for Sam,* rev. ed. by Paul F. Brandwein, ill. with photographs, Harcourt, Brace & World, 1960. Also *The Earth for Sam,* etc.

Rey, H. A.: *Find the Constellations,* ill. by author, Houghton Mifflin, 1954. Many diagrams, with several little red figures making comments on them.

Sasek, Miroslav: *This Is Hong Kong,* Macmillan, 1965. One of a lively series on great cities.

Scheele, William E.: *Prehistoric Animals,* ill. by author, World, 1954. Many pictures, diagrams, and charts.

Snedigar, Robert (ed.): *Life in the Forest,* ill. by Edwin Huff, Encyclopaedia Britannica (Britannica Books), 1962.

Swain, Su Zan Noguchi: *Insects in Their World,* Doubleday, 1955.

Tunis, Edwin: *Colonial Living,* ill. by author, World, 1957. Big book full of factual accounts and drawings. Also in series: *Indians; Wheels; Weapons; Oars, Sail and Steam.*

Van Loon, Hendrik Willem: *The Story of Mankind,* rev. ed., ill. by author, Liveright, 1951.

White, Anne Terry: *Lost Worlds: The Romance of Archaeology,* Random House, 1941.

Concept Books: Presentation of Facts
as Related to an Idea or Point of View

Adelson, Leone: *All Ready for Winter,* ill. by Kathleen Elgin, McKay, 1952. How horses, mice, etc., prepare for winter.

————: *All Ready for Summer,* ill. by Kathleen Elgin, McKay, 1956.

Anglund, Joan Walsh: *Look Out the Window,* ill. by author, Harcourt, Brace & World, 1959.

Baer, Howard: *Now This, Now That: Playing with Points of View,* Holiday, 1957.

Barker, Melvern: *The Different Twins,* Lippincott, 1957.

Bechdolt, John E.: *Going Up: The Story of Vertical Transportation,* ill. by Jeanne Bendick, Abingdon, 1948.

Bendick, Jeanne: *All around You: A First Look at the World,* ill. by author, Whittlesey, 1951.

————: *How Much and How Many,* Whittlesey, 1947.

Berkley, Ethel S. (Ethel S. Berkowitz): *The Size of It,* Scott, 1951.

————: *Ups and Downs: A First Book about Space,* ill. by Kathleen Elgin, Scott, 1951.

Black, Irma Simonton: *Big Puppy and Little Puppy,* ill. by Theresa Sherman, Holiday, 1960.

————: *Busy Water,* ill. by Jane Castle, Holiday, 1958. Rain falling on hair, squirrel's nose, etc., then to brook, lake, dam, city and ocean; numerous facts on houses, industry, and weather.

Blough, Glenn O.: *Who Lives in This Meadow?* ill. by Jeanne Bendick, Whittlesey, 1961.

Borten, Helen: *Do You Hear What I Hear?* Abelard-Schuman, 1960. How sounds made by kettles, glasses, rattlesnakes, sea, pigeons, clocks, etc., make one feel.

Bridges William: *Zoo Babies,* ill. with photographs, Morrow, 1953.

Brown, Margaret Wise, *The City Noisy Book,* ill. by Leonard Weisgard, Harper, 1939. And other Noisy Books.

————: *The Important Book,* ill. by Leonard Weisgard, Harper & Row, 1950.

————: *Red Light, Green Light,* ill. by Leonard Weisgard, Doubleday, 1946.

Browner, Richard: *Look Again!* ill. by Emma Landau, Atheneum, 1962.

Craig, M. Jean: *Spring Is like the Morning,* ill. by Don Almquist, Putnam, 1965.

Earle, Olive: *Paws, Hoofs and Flippers,* ill. by author, Morrow, 1954.

Elting, Mary: *Machines at Work,* ill. by Lazlo Roth, Garden City, 1953.

———— **and Margaret Gossett:** *Lollypop Factory—and Lots of Others,* Doubleday, 1946. Mass production of ice cream, dolls, sweaters, etc.

Garelick, May: *What's Inside,* with photos by Rena Jakobsen, Scott, 1955.

————: *Where Does the Butterfly Go When It Rains?* ill. by Leonard Weisgard, Scott, 1961.

Goudey, Alice E.: *Houses from the Sea,* ill. by Adrienne Adams, Scribner, 1959.

Gruenberg, Sidonie M.: *The Wonderful Story of How You Were Born,* rev. ed., ill. by Hildegard Woodward, Garden City, 1959.

Johnson, Crockett: *Who's Upside Down?* ill. by author, Scott, 1952.

Kessler, Leonard P.: *What's in a Line?* Scott, 1951.

Koch, Dorothy: *I Play at the Beach,* ill. by Feodor Rojankovsky, Holiday, 1955.

Lathrop, Dorothy: *Let Them Live,* ill. by author, Macmillan, 1951. Conservation.

MacAgy, Douglas and Elizabeth: *Going for a Walk with a Line,* Doubleday, 1959.

O'Neill, Mary: *Hailstones and Halibut Bones: Adventures in Color,* ill. by Leonard Weisgard, Doubleday, 1961.

Schlein, Miriam: *Fast Is Not a Ladybug,* ill. by Leonard Kessler, Scott, 1953.

————: *Heavy Is a Hippopotamus,* ill. by Leonard Kessler, Scott, 1954.

————: *It's about Time,* ill. by Leonard Kessler, Scott, 1955.

Schloat, G. Warren: *The Wonderful Egg,* Scribner, 1952.

Schneider, Herman and Nina: *Follow the Sunset,* ill. by Lucille Corcos, Doubleday, 1952.

————: *How Big Is Big?* ill. by Symeon Shimin, Scott, 1950.

————: *Let's Look inside Your House,* ill. by Barbara Ivins, Scott, 1948.

————: *Let's Look under the City,* ill. by Bill Ballantine, Scott, 1954.

————: *You, among the Stars,* ill. by Symeon Shimin, Scott, 1951.

Schneider, Nina: *While Susie Sleeps,* Scott, 1948. Night activities.

Schwartz, Julius: *I Know a Magic House,* ill. by Marc Simont, Whittlesey, 1956.

Selsam, Millicent: *All Kinds of Babies and How They Grow,* ill. by Helen Ludwig, Scott, 1953.

Skaar, Grace: *What Do They Say?* Scott, 1950. Language.

Slobodkin, Louis: *The Friendly Animals,* ill. by author, Vanguard.

Tresselt, Alvin: *Follow the Wind,* ill. by Roger Duvoisin, Lothrop, 1950. Picture-book impression of wind.

————: *I Saw the Sea Come In,* ill. by Roger Duvoisin, Lothrop, 1954.

————: *Sun Up,* ill. by Roger Duvoisin, Lothrop, 1949.

Webber, Irma E.: *Travelers All: The Story of How Planets Go Places,* ill. by author, Scott, 1944.

————: *Bits That Grow Big: Where Plants Come from,* ill. by author, Scott, 1949.

Weyl, Peter K.: *Men, Ants & Elephants: Size in the Animal World,* ill. by Anthony Ravielli, Viking, 1959.

Wyler, Rose, and Gerald Ames: *What Makes It Go?* ill. by Bernice Myers, Whittlesey, 1958.

Zion, Gene: *All Falling Down,* ill. by Margaret Bloy Graham, Harper, 1951.

Stories for the Facts' Sake: Stories as Pretexts

Anglund, Joan Walsh: *The Brave Cowboy,* ill. by author, Harcourt, Brace & World, 1959.

Barnum, Jay Hyde: *The Little Old Truck,* ill. by author, Morrow, 1953. Trucking berries to market in floods.

Barr, Jene: *Dan the Weatherman,* ill. by P. J. Hoff, Whitman, 1958.

————: *Good Morning, Teacher,* ill. by Lucy and John Hawkinson, Whitman, 1957. Other books of the same kind by Jene Barr: *Busy Service Station, Mr. Mailman, Policeman Paul,* and *Fireman Fred.*

Bate, Norman: *Vulcan,* Scribners, 1960. Old locomotive is melted down and made into a warning buoy.

————: *Who Built the Highway?* ill. by author, Scribner, 1953.

————: *Who Fishes for Oil?* ill. by author, Scribner, 1955. Shrimp boat observes oil drilling, assists in storm.

Bauer, Helen: *Good Times at Home,* with photos by Hubert A. Lowman, Melmont, 1954. Also *Good Times at the Fair, Good Times at the Park,* etc.

Blough, Glenn: *Who Lives in This House?* ill. by Jeanne Bendick, Whittlesey, 1957. About the animal families that live in a deserted house.

Brock, Emma L.: *Mr. Wren's House,* ill. by author, Knopf, 1944. Rhythmic account of nest building, with imitations of bird sounds.

Brown, Margaret Wise: *The Little Brass Band,* ill. by Clement Hurd, Harper & Row, 1955. Introduction to the instruments in medieval band.

————: *Little Chicken,* ill. by Leonard Weisgard, Harper & Row, 1943. A little chick meets various creatures—butterflies, caterpillars, beaver, man, bears, etc.

———— **and Edith Thacker Hurd:** *Two Little Gardeners,* ill. by Gertrude Elliott, Simon and Schuster, 1951. Rhythmic account of how children raised a garden.

Buckheimer, Naomi: *Night Outdoors,* ill. by Dorothy Teichman, Putnam, 1960.

Buff, Mary and Conrad: *Big Three,* ill. by authors, Viking, 1946.

————: *Elf Owl,* ill. by authors, Viking, 1958.

Burton, Virginia: *Life Story: The Story of Life on Our Earth from Its Beginning up to Now,* ill. by author, Houghton Mifflin, 1962. Projected on a stage in Burton's typical spherical patterns.

Carrighar, Sally: *One Day on Beetle Rock,* ill. by Henry B. Kane, Knopf, 1946. About all the animals at Beetle Rock.

Denison, Karl: *What Every Young Rabbit Should Know,* ill. by Kurt Wiese, Dodd, Mead, 1948.

George, Jean: *Gull Number 737,* Crowell, 1964. A boy and father doing research on gulls.

Harris, Isobel: *Little Boy Brown,* ill. by André François, Lippincott, 1949. A boy's life in the city—skyscrapers, subways, etc.

Holling, Holling C.: *Minn of the Mississippi,* ill. by author, Houghton Mifflin, 1951. Conveys all sorts of information about the Mississippi Basin as it follows a turtle from the river's headwaters to the Gulf.

————: *Paddle-to-the-sea,* ill. by author, Houghton Mifflin, 1941.

————: *Pagoo,* ill. by author and Lucille Webster Holling, Houghton Mifflin, 1957.

————: *Seabird,* ill. by author, Houghton Miffin, 1948.

————: *Tree in the Trail,* ill. by author, Houghton Mifflin, 1942.

Lenski, Lois: *Davy's Day,* ill. by author, Walck, 1943.

————: *We Live in the Country,* ill. by author, Lippincott, 1960. Others in series.

McClung, Robert: *Whitefoot: The Story of a Wood Mouse,* ill. by author, Morrow, 1961.

Norling, Jo and Ernest: *Pogo's Sea Trip; A Story of Boats,* Holt, 1949. And other Pogo books about houses, airplanes, mining, paper, wool, etc.

Schloat, G. Warren: *Andy's Wonderful Telescope,* ill. by author, Scribner, 1958.

Scott, William R.: *This Is the Milk That Jack Drank,* Scott, 1944. Jingle.

Children's Encyclopedias and Encyclopedia-like Works

The Book of Knowledge (20 vols.), The Grolier Society. Organized under departments, not alphabetically—"The Earth," "Golden Deeds," etc.

The Bookshelf for Boys and Girls (10 vols.), The University Society.

Britannica Junior Encyclopaedia for Boys and Girls (15 vols.), Encyclopaedia Britannica.

Childcraft: The How and Why Library (15 vols.), Field Enterprises.

Compton's Pictured Encyclopedia and Fact Index (15 vols.), Compton.

The Golden Book Encyclopedia of Natural Science (15 vols.), Herbert Zim, editor-in-chief, Golden Press. Most valuable for free exploratory reading.

The New Wonder World (10 vols.), *Parents' Magazine's* Education Press. Most suitable for exploratory reading.

Our Wonderful World: An Encyclopedic Anthology for the Entire Family (18 vols.), Spencer Press, 1962. Somewhat story-like presentation.

The World Book Encyclopedia (20 vols.), Field Enterprises Educational Corp. Close to adult type of encyclopedia.

Book Series: Factual Information

All about . . . [*Dinosaurs, Electricity, the Flowering World,* etc.], Random House.

Editors of American Heritage: American Heritage Junior Library, American Heritage Publishing Co., *Thomas Jefferson and His World, Great Days of the Circus, Indians of the Plains, The California Gold Rush, Pirates of the Spanish Main, Trappers and Mountain Men, Discoverers of the New World, Steamboats of the Mississippi,* etc.

The Big Book of . . . [*Real Building and Wrecking Machines, Real Fire Engines, Real Trains, Real Boats and Ships,* etc.], ill. by George Zaffo, Grosset & Dunlap.

Buck, Margaret Waring: *In . . .* [*Ponds and Streams, Yards and Gardens,* etc.], ill. by author, Abingdon.

Exploring . . . [*the Moon, Mars, the Universe, the Weather, Chemistry,* etc.], ill. by Roy A. Gallant and Lee J. Ames, Garden City Books.

The First Book of . . . [*Plants, Rhythms, Public Libraries,* etc.], F. Watts.

The Golden series, Golden Press. *Golden Geography, Golden History of the World, Golden Treasury of National History, Golden Book of Science, Golden Book of the American Revolution,* etc.

The Illustrated Book of . . . [*the Sea,* etc.], Grosset & Dunlap.

I Want to Be a . . . [*Bus Driver,* etc.], ill. by Katherine Evans, Children's Press.

Junior Scientist series, Rand McNally. Includes *Around the Corner, In Your Neighborhood, Here and Away, Far and Wide,* and *Your Science World.*

Let's Go to . . . [*an Airport, the Library, a Garage, a Zoo,* etc.], Putnam.

My Easy to Read True Book of . . . [*Dinosaurs,* etc.], Grosset & Dunlap.

Pocket Nature Library, Doubleday. *Wild Flowers East of the Rockies,* etc.

The Real Book about . . . [*Space, Trains, Canada,* etc.], Garden City.

The True Book of . . . [*Your Body and You,* etc.], Children's Press.

The Wonderful World of . . . [*Medicine,* by Ritchie Calder; *The Sea,* by James Fisher; *Energy,* by Lancelot Hogben; *Mathematics,* by Hogben; *Archaeology,* by Ronald Jessup, etc.], Garden City.

The World Library series, sponsored by *Life.* Includes *Australia and New Zealand,* by Colin MacInnes and Editors of *Life,* 1964.

A Sampling of Biographies for Children

Brown, John Mason: *Daniel Boone: The Opening of the Wilderness,* ill. by Lee J. Ames, Random House, 1952. A Landmark Book.

Busoni, Rafaello: *Stanley's Africa*, Viking, 1944.

Dalgliesh, Alice: *Ride on the Wind* (told from Charles A. Lindbergh's *The Spirit of St. Louis*), ill. by Georges Schreiber, Scribner, 1956.

Daugherty, James: *Of Courage Undaunted: Across the Continent with Lewis and Clark*, ill. by author, Viking, 1951.

D'Aulaire, Ingri and Edgar: *Buffalo Bill*, ill. by authors, Doubleday, 1952.

Forbes, Esther: *America's Paul Revere*, ill. by Lynd Ward, Houghton Mifflin, 1946.

Franchere, Ruth: *Willa*, ill. by Leonard Weisgard, Crowell, 1958. Fictionized childhood of Willa Cather.

Holbrook, Stewart: *America's Ethan Allen*, ill. by Lynd Ward, Houghton Mifflin, 1949.

Judson, Clara Ingram: *Thomas Jefferson, Champion of the People*, Follett, 1952.

Lauber, Patricia: *The Quest of Louis Pasteur*, ill. by Lee J. Ames, Garden City, 1960. Big, vividly illustrated book.

Lawson, Robert: *The Great Wheel*, ill. by author, Viking, 1957. On the development of the ferris wheel.

Petry, Ann: *Harriet Tubman: Conductor on the Underground Railroad*, Crowell, 1955.

Sandburg, Carl: *Abe Lincoln Grows up* (reprinted from *Abraham Lincoln: The Prairie Years*, the first 27 chapters), ill. by James Daugherty, Harcourt, Brace, 1931.

Steffens, Lincoln: *Boy on Horseback* (reprinted from *The Autobiography of Lincoln Steffens*), ill. by Sanford Tousey, Harcourt, Brace, 1931.

Stevenson, Augusta: *Squanto, Young Indian Hunter*, ill. by Nathan Goldstein, Bobbs-Merrill, 1962. One of many by Stevenson and others in Childhood of Famous Americans series.

Swift, Hildegarde Hoyt: *The Edge of April*, ill. by Lynd Ward, Morrow, 1957. Biography of John Burroughs.

————: *From the Eagle's Wing: A Biography of John Muir*, ill. by Lynd Ward, Morrow, 1962.

Wheeler, Opal: *Handel at the Court of Kings*, ill. by Mary Greenwalt, Dutton, 1943.

———— **and Sybil Deucher:** *Joseph Haydn*, ill. by Mary Greenwalt, Dutton, 1936. With music.

Whipple, H. B. C.: *Hero of Trafalgar*, ill. by William Hofmann, Random House, 1963. A biography of Lord Nelson; concentrates on his naval career, skims over his private life. A Landmark Book.

CHAPTER 12

TO READ, TO LOOK:
The
Illustrating
of Children's
Books

*C*hildren's reading is part *looking*. Their books are visual art as well as verbal art. This is a basic fact of children's literature and one of the primary distinctions between children's books and adults' books. One cannot ignore—although some adults may try to—the visual ingredient in most children's literature.

The Reasons for the Importance of Illustration in Children's Books

Publishing for children has not always been as visual as it is today, but the centralness of the picture to writing for children is nothing new. The seventeen-century catechisms, alphabets, blunt ethical verses, and horrible and good examples relied as much on the force of the crude woodcuts as on the equally crude verses and fables for their chastizing or inspirational effects. And on through the eighteenth century and the early nineteenth century engravers, with increasing skill and sensitivity, created black-and-white woodcuts and engravings for books for children. Then in the mid-nineteenth century there was a gaudy bursting of high artistry in drawing for children, and in our twentieth century there has been the seeming dominance of the colorist.

Some critics may cry "Fad!" or "Plot!" but it is the result of no fad, fluke, trick, or plot that children's books should be thoroughly grounded in the *pictured*, as well as in the *told*, story and poem. There are good reasons for this.

For the prereading child the verbal world is only heard; he lacks the visual language symbol. Thus the visual representation of the situation or object is invaluable as a reinforcer, a giver of meaning to the heard word. And even heard language is just becoming a principal means of having experience for this child; he still relies to a great degree on the objects themselves or their visual representations. To him, even the latter are less abstract than even the simplest words like cow and hat. Moreover, this child is still avidly exploring his physical environment—new shapes, colors, textures, etc.—and the drawn world of his books complements that activity.

This learning through visual representation of experience remains through the elementary grades a significant and inescapable part of the child's learning, gradually diminishing as his ability to handle language abstractions improves. There is *always* the aesthetic appeal and stimulus of line and color and shape and texture; this never lessens at all, or at least need not and should not.

Such reasons for illustrated children's books are implicit in the nature of the child, language, and sensory experience. There are also other reasons for the present importance of art in juvenile publishing. Publishers have come to believe that bright, unusual, bold illustrations attract adult buyers and so help sell a book; and they and other adults—parents, librarians, teachers—may feel that vivid, aesthetically satisfying pictures give a book an added appeal for children and so will make them more likely to read it. Moreover, the visual image has in our day become an accepted part of formal schooling. And all these factors have a cumulative effect: when many children's books use many illustrations, publishers and buyers and teachers come to believe in their inevitability, to assume that children's books mean illustrations.

Whatever the causes may be, almost everyone concerned with the making and selection of children's books today is a critic of illustration as well as of text. The writer-illustrator has become a major figure in juvenile publishing. Reviewers give as serious consideration to the illustrations as to the text of most children's books, and especially those for the small child; the Caldecott Medal for the best book illustration holds equal prominence with the Newbery Medal. For better or worse, anybody involved with children's literature has to attend closely to its visual side.

The Illustration of Children's Literature in the Past

Until the nineteenth century the visual image in children's books was black-and-white. The seventeenth- and eighteenth-century illustrations of alphabets and moral tales and aphorisms were woodcuts, generally simplified, bold, dramatic. In the main, they were not remarkable for their aesthetic qualities but did their journalistic job well enough, told their story unambiguously, and, importantly, had a sense of action. And the general practice of the time was to provide one drawing for each poem or anecdote. This is a practice that has much to be said for it, and some critics have urged it be followed more widely in new editions of Mother Goose and comparable books. If a drawing can reinforce one rhyme, why not a drawing for every rhyme? Moreover, the omission of drawings for certain pieces creates disappointment, and there is a possibility of confusion over which poem to relate the picture to.

In the eighteenth and nineteenth centuries great technical achievements were made in illustrating books—new developments in metal engraving, the invention of lithography, the first steps in color printing, and the reduction of mass-printing costs—and this technical progress corresponded with the appearance of some of the greatest of illustrators for children. The nursery-rhyme wood engravings of Thomas Bewick (1753–1828) are magnificently deft in their intricacy of pattern, their combination of realistic detail with decorative line and shape. (Their inclusion in the 1960 Opie *Oxford Nursery Rhyme Book*, along with Joan Hassall's engravings, contributes much to the liveliness of that remarkable work.)

The dominant trend in nineteenth-century book illustration, including juvenile book illustration, was a sort of romantic naturalism—recognizable representation of things and events combined with a love of elegant elaboration, rhythmic gracefulness and delicacy, and melodramatic contrast. Illustration was both realistic and romantic, and it was frequently sentimental. This was the age of the Academicians, the genre painters, the Hudson River school (which painted nature in its dashing aspects), and the Pre-Raphaelites (Rossetti, Millais, Burne-Jones). An acquaintance with the popular gallery art of the mid-nineteenth century can help one recognize what he is getting in Kate Greenaway, Arthur Rackham, and Randolph Caldecott. These illustrations reflect the same values and attitudes.

A most interesting fact in the children's book illustrating of the nineteenth century—a century, by the way, marked by an outburst of children's writers with their own individual styles—is that the fine children's book illustrators succeeded in doing their representational reporting job and at the same time developed their own highly personal and recognizable styles—Kate Greenaway's quiet, low-toned, delicately linear drawings for *Mother Goose* and her own books, George Cruikshank's vigorous, dramatic drawings, verging on grotesquerie, John Tenniel's witty and grotesque *Alice in Wonderland*, Walter Crane's imaginative and decorative *Baby's Bouquet*, Arthur Rackham's *fin-de-siècle* elegance, Caldecott's combination of academy elegance with the cartoonist's drollery, and Howard Pyle's complex, rich draftsmanship for his books of medieval tales. All these artists were fine *narrative* artists; they could either create a sense of a particular event or complement and support the verbal account closely and accurately. Yet none of them was *simply* an accurate illustrator of the told tale or poem. Each created his own highly individual world of color, line, and form. Rackham's drawings for *Wind in the Willows* have stamped that work as almost as much Rackham's as Grahame's, and Pyle's medieval world is instantly recognizable as Pyle's and nobody else's.

The styles that all these artists developed became established modes of illustration, models for numerous other artists or artist-storytellers to follow; indeed, these artists were so widely and slavishly imitated that there came to be whole schools of Pyle-like illustrators, Rackhamish evokers of twilight woodlands and English meadows, and so forth. And in addition, these mid- and late-nineteenth century artists succeeded in establishing both the importance of illustration as an inherent part of children's books and the close relationship between text and art in children's books. In short, they did much to determine the course of juvenile book illustration since their time.

The Importance of Illustration in the Twentieth Century

The complete acceptance today of illustration as an essential part of children's books—indeed, its almost overwhelming importance in the juvenile book field—is evidenced in a great many ways. One may find in all corners the signs of what some worried critics have called illustrationitis or pictureitis but unworried critics feel is simply the long due recognition of the natural place of the visual image alongside the verbal image in children's books.

When publishers consider a children's book for publication, they almost always begin thinking immediately of illustratability, a possible illustrator, the use of color, etc., and writers share such concerns. Correspondence between writer and publisher very early introduces questions of illustration. Publisher to writer: "Can you illustrate this, or do you have an illustrator in mind"? Writer to publisher: "I think bright background blocks of color with rather free, scratchy ink drawings might be appropriate for this book: Do you agree?" Writer to publisher, hopefully: "Don't you think there should be one cut for each poem?" One of the major concerns of any publisher putting out new editions of previously printed works is the illustrator: "Whose drawing or painting is most appropriate?" "Whose work will constitute an additional attraction to readers?" Publishers are very happy when they find a talented writer-artist, one who can provide them with one source for two ingredients they have come to consider of just about equal importance. And they frequently try to sell a book as much by the illustrator's name as by the author's. Garth Williams, Louis Slobodkin, James Daugherty, Marcia Brown, Roger Duvoisin, Dorothy Lathrop, Helen Sewell, Lynd Ward, Leonard Weisgard—such illustrators' names are prominently displayed in the advertisements, and on the jackets and title pages. The name of the illustrator may even be in the same type as the author's.

And there are many indications that modern selectors of children's books concur in this emphasis on the visual. The illustrations are nearly always a major factor in a librarian's acceptance of a book for purchase. Librarians' lists of recommended books show much concern over the illustrators, and their shoptalk, as reflected in such professional journals as *The Horn Book* and *Elementary English*, tends to deal almost as much with illustration as with text. It is also manifest that the schools—school librarians, teachers, textbook-selection committees, supervisors—stress the pictorial aspect in book selection. Preschool and kindergarten tables and shelves are naturally going to hold many picture books; but also, all text-book series, from the beginning grades right up through senior high school, are plentifully illustrated, offering a startling contrast to textbooks of seventy or eighty years ago. Blown-up reproductions of the illustrations from *Pooh, Babar,* and *Alice in Wonderland* have gone to the walls and bulletin boards of the classroom. Outside the classroom and library the children's book is automatically taken to be an illustrated book. An inter-view with salesmen in any children's department of a bookstore or a half hour spent eavesdropping there will convince you that in buying books for children, most adults to a great extent buy the illustrations; often they will look only at the pictures. Occasionally the prestige of an author's name or a title—Grimm, Andersen, Stevenson, *Heidi*—will determine a purchase, but a colorfully illustrated edition of the prestigious work is most likely to be favored over a plain one, and an unknown but especially colorfully illus-trated story is very likely to win out over both.

As for children's own feeling about the importance of pictures, one need only recall how children hunt for the comics section of the daily newspaper or watch a child attending to a book: whether he is reading a book or hav-ing it read to him, he will keep moving back and forth between word and picture; and if he is being read to he will often keep up a running comment in detail surprising to an adult on the correspondence of picture to text. Another sign of the importance of the picture to the child is that when we grow up, we recall a great many of our childhood reading experiences first and mainly in terms of illustrations—the flamingo-mallet croquet game in *Alice* by Tenniel, N. C. Wyeth's ships and golden sails and towering clouds for *Treasure Island,* Jessie Willcox Smith's *Heidi,* Lawson's Ben the mouse. We recall particular *Mother Goose* editions by their illustrations—Feodor Rojankovsky's saucily realistic, warm-colored drawings, Duvoisin's bright, splashy designs, Greenaway's quiet, precise watercolors, Tasha Tudor's softly romantic evocations, the brightly colored realism of Blanche Fisher Wright's *Real Mother Goose.*

Clearly, then, all of us who may have anything to do with children's reading—publishers, librarians, school people, parents, children, and, of course, illustrators themselves—take for granted that a children's book will be a book of pictures as well as a book of words. And indeed, children's book illustration is no longer, at least for books for children up to eleven or twelve, a matter of pictures *accompanying* story or poem; it is often an equal partnership, a collaboration, a unity of picture and word. And, some-times the roles have become reversed, so that the story really accompanies, or "illustrates," the picture.

A final strong indication of the significance of the visual image in modern juvenile book publishing is the large amount of artistic talent of a high caliber that children's bookmaking has attracted to itself during the past half century. The world of juvenile book illustration has developed its own highly skilled specialized practitioners—excellent artists for children, such as Roger Duvoisin, Gustav Tenggren, Garth Williams, Maud and Miska

Petersham, Ernest Shepard, Leonard Weisgard, and Maurice Sendak, and author-artists, such as Ingri and Edgar d'Aulaire, James Daugherty, Wanda Gág, Kurt Wiese, Robert McCloskey, Kate Seredy, Wilfred Bronson, Dr. Seuss, Berta and Elmer Hader, Marguerite de Angeli, William Pène du Bois, Marjorie Flack, Robert Lawson, Jack Keats, and Taro Yashima. But the world of juvenile book illustration has also drawn to it the talents of artists primarily identified with art outside the field of book illustration—well-known artists like Jean Charlot, Alexander Calder, Carlos Merida, Georges Schreiber, Lynd Ward, Reginald Marsh, William Gropper, Peter Hurd, Dong Kingman, Doris Lee, Antonio Frasconi, Peggy Bacon, Thomas Hart Benton, and Candido Portinari. At the end of this chapter you will find a representative list of children's artists, author-artists, and other artists who have done children's book illustrations, with a selection of books illustrated by each. The participation of all these artists from outside the book field suggests that in the eyes of many artists, there is room in the children's book for the original *visual* artist as well as for the original *verbal* artist, and that the painter's or woodcut artist's participation in such enterprises in no way places him in a subordinate or captive role.

The quality and main directions of children's book art (a more accurate term than *illustration*), however, are established mainly by those artists and author-artists who concentrate on children's books. And, like *writers* for children, they are related to the world of creating for adults but do work under certain special conditions and hence cannot be understood and judged solely in terms appropriate to work for adults.

Diversity in Contemporary Children's Book Illustration

One cannot reduce all modern art to one or two characteristics. Perhaps one may say that the aims of abstract expressionism—the use of new shape-line-color-texture patterns to create or express a feeling—have tended to dominate the art of the twentieth century, but these aims have manifested themselves in forms so diverse that frequently it is very difficult, if not a waste of effort, to try to find a common denominator. Moreover, former aims and methods have not been supplanted by new ones; the old and the new have gone on side by side, and very often they have combined forces. Much the same things may be said of the art that we find in the children's books of the past fifty years or so. In this juvenile book art we find many manifestations of the abstract and expressionistic tendencies characteristic of the age of Cézanne, Gauguin, van Gogh, Picasso, Vlaminck, Marin, Klee, Beckmann, Moore, Orozco, Graves, Rouault, Chagall, Matisse, Pollock, Hofmann, and Sutherland, and we find these tendencies flowing into much the same diversity of forms. And here too the newer modes are accompanied by and often joined with former, more traditional modes; the illustrators of children's books, while often simplifying or abstracting or using impressionistic suggestion and symbolism, have continued to represent reality, so that modern children's book art is a mixture of conservative and radical in art, of conventional and experimental, of past styles and present. This mixture is complex and at first seemingly chaotic. Still, it is possible, and helpful, to distinguish among all this diversity and interbreeding a number of especially strong and common approaches to the task of the artist in children's books—some main currents—without superimposing an unreal pattern of schools or influences.

Representational Art in Modern Children's Books

Despite the first impression of decorative abstraction and freewheeling impressionistic and expressionistic art which one may get from skimming a collection of children's books in a library or bookstore, by far the greater number of artists in this field have worked within the representational tradition developed by the nineteenth-century illustrators. They have stuck to the storytelling, place-describing, person-portraying purposes of George Cruikshank, Richard Doyle, Kate Greenaway, Randolph Caldecott, and Howard Pyle, and have "gone to school" to some of these forerunners; still, like these great nineteenth-century representationalists, they have developed their own highly distinctive styles, their own personal ways of seeing and telling.

In the late 1800s and the first decade of the present century Howard Pyle created book after book of pen-and-ink drawings of costume, weaponry, architecture, and natural landscape, all scrupulously detailed yet distinguished by his highly personal, wiry, linear style. Pyle's visual world was a late Victorian combination of realism and elegant, pageant-like romanticism, but it was certainly his own. Indebted to it but with the added romantic effulgence of glowing color and blue and purple shadow was the art of his pupil N. C. Wyeth (1882–1945). The latter artist partly determined how thousands of child readers since the 1920s have seen the castles of *Ivanhoe*, Robinson Crusoe's island, Jim Hawkins's Treasure Island. He created a world of highly credible, recognizable objects—real rope, real velvet, real rock and dust and sand, real jaws grayed with grizzled beard—but he filled it with a bigger-than-life, melodramatic sense of the villainous and the virtuous, the craven and the heroic. Another of Pyle's pupils, Jessie Willcox Smith (1863–1935), carried into her illustrations for *The Water-babies*, *Little Women*, *A Child's Garden of Verses*, and many other children's books a similar sense of romantic splendor; her work, though, was somewhat quieter, more static, than Pyle's or Wyeth's. Pyle, Wyeth, and Smith still remain a vital part of present-day children's books through the reprinting of the various series of classics which they illustrated decades ago.

Realistic storytelling that is evocative of place and situation but lacks the romantic, heroic suggestion of Pyle and Wyeth has been practiced by such artists as Elsa Beskow (*Pelle's New Suit*), Pelagie Doane (*A Child's Garden of Verses*), Berta and Elmer Hader, Lois Lenski (that is, in her books for older children, not the abstract drawings for the Mr. Small series), and Holling C. Holling. This reportorial sort of realism has been turned especially to the representation of animals, particularly animals in action, by Kurt Wiese, Clare Turlay Newberry, Marjorie Flack, Glen Rounds, Wilfred Bronson, Conrad Buff, Wesley Dennis, and Will James. All these artists portray animal life accurately and faithfully, but not slavishly so; their impressions range from the soft, blurry contours of Newberry's cats and the gentle tonal gradations of Buff's animal forms to Wiese's clear, bold drawing and James's shorthand sketchiness.

Accurate in representational detail but gently expressive, even at times sweetly sentimental, is the work of such artists as Marguerite de Angeli, Elizabeth Orton Jones, and Tasha Tudor. These artists, with their pastel colors and careful detail and their sweet-faced children and animals, stay within the tradition developed in the nineteenth century by Kate Greenaway and Beatrix Potter. All have reflected the world of physical reality, but in a way that has eliminated the hard edges, the pain, the disconcerting contrasts of existence; they have left out the coarse grit of daily reality and made all things quaint and picturesque.

The diversity possible within realism and the way this diversity comes about are both made clear if we compare artists like Tudor and de Angeli, who select the forms, colors, and lines that will gentle down reality, with artists like McCloskey and Robert Lawson, who select those real details that will suggest the ridiculous and silly, the comic. The techniques of the latter group verge on caricature; they are a blend of careful, almost photographic representation with the satirist's distortion. The leggy gawkiness of McCloskey's little girls, the cracker-barrel quality of his elderly Centerburg citizenry, the virile stringiness of Lawson's Robbut, the squatness of Lawson's Ben Franklin and the clutter of his quarters, the ricketiness of the toreadors who face Lawson's Ferdinand—such qualities as these are the result, and they are far indeed from the qualities created by Tudor and de Angeli. But in the work of all these artists there is still a detailed representation of physical reality.

The Disney School

A step or so from this comic realism—not really so far as it might at first seem—are the comic art of Walt Disney and all the mass of Disneyish drawing that now comes to children through movies, television advertising, and magazine illustration, as well as innumerable books. Disney's early drawing is full of amusing inventions—Mickey Mouse, Pluto, Donald Duck, the Three Pigs—and he has continued to create funny new toy figures, such as Sleepy, Dopey, and Dumbo; but over the decades the Disney picture world has become both more realistic in its careful detail and more slickly decorative. Snow White, Bambi, Pinocchio, and Cinderella, the books and the movies, are actually very canny compromises; they offer children many unusual, invented creatures like Cinderella's mouse horses, the fearsome witch, and the Disney squirrels, but in a world of quite conventional representation of conventional objects and experiences, all against a background of decorative abstractions—simplified mountains, stage-set trees, etc. A freer use of abstract line and color in Disney's illustration has increased in recent years, possibly partly as a result of the pioneering work UPA artists did in motion-picture cartooning in the forties and early fifties.

The style of Disney's children's books and the other children's books that have resulted from his work is an amalgam of the prettiness of postcards, the mad distortion of the comic strip, and the surface realism of the magazine advertisement. This does not mean that the Disney and Disney-like books, which loom large in juvenile publishing today, are necessarily inferior, for Disney's mixing of these elements is undeniably a very special mix, and in such books as *Cinderella* a rather appealing one. But these are important difficulties: the combination has become a set formula for Disney and his many imitators and has been used too often, and often crudely and mechanically. It is a special deficiency of such books—though this is no inherent fault of the books themselves—that a child encounters forms and fancies there that he is constantly meeting elsewhere. He meets them on television, in movies, in newspaper and magazine advertising, on milk bottles—indeed, everywhere. The books, then, give him the same old diet to which he is accustomed. Disney's images have simply become part of the American popular culture, the American cultural landscape, and so do not often provide the child with a new, fresh element when he encounters them in books. Of course, he may not mind this; indeed, he may like Disney-style books for their giving him something he knows.

The Comic Style of Dr. Seuss

Another distinctive comic style, and one which, like Disney's, at times has threatened to crowd out other comic art for the young, is that of Dr. Seuss (Theodor Seuss Geisel). Over the years Dr. Seuss's style has settled into a formula, as has Disney's, but Seuss's world is essentially a more fantastic and irrational visual world than Disney's; in Seuss's there is a greater proportion of distortions and outright inventions. Disney's funny dream world is usually a little like American suburbia; Seuss's is closer to a witches' Sabbath or a jokester's version of Hieronymous Bosch's conception of hell.

Violent primary colors predominate; the drawings swirl in frenzied movement and burst into explosions of ragged splatterings and dangerous-looking bubbles; the bone joints and feathers and hairs of animals all erupt grotesquely. Whereas Disney much of the time exaggerates in the direction of sweetness and decorative prettiness, Seuss exaggerates into weirdness and hilarious madness. And in each of Seuss's books the degree of madness increases; we proceed from a misleadingly quiet beginning to a wildly insane climax. A distinction needs to be made here, though, between the visual and verbal ingredients of Seuss's spicy dish. The things that happen—the fantastic parade a small boy pretends he has witnessed on Mulberry Street, Bartholomew Cubbins's growing hats on his head, a cat taking over and disrupting a household, the elephant Horton sitting on the egg of a bird too lazy to do her own hatching, Thidwick the bighearted moose carrying a whole forestful of animals and birds on his antlers—all quite fantastic, and so is Seuss's drawing of these goings-on. But his language, even when he indulges in making up silly names, is not nearly so unusual and inventive. In itself, the doggerel Seuss relies on eventually becomes monotonous, and to some extent it leans on fairly common jokes and slang. Without the drawings, Seuss's humor is much quieter and much more ordinary than it is with the drawings. The very special fantasy of Dr. Seuss lies primarily in his visual creation.

Other Styles of Humorous Illustration

There are other major artists of children's books who have developed their own special cartoon styles—Hardie Gramatky (*Loopy*), Tony Palazzo (Lear's *Nonsense Book*), Don Freeman (*Pet of the Met*), Crockett Johnson (*Harold and the Purple Crayon*), Edward Ardizzone (*Little Tim and the Brave Sea Captain*, etc.), N. D. Bodecker (*Edward Eager's Half Magic*), H. A. Rey (*Curious George, Katy-No-Pocket*). Their styles lie somewhere between the slickly pat, rather realistic fantasy of Disney and the bumptious, explosive fantasy of Seuss.

Contributing to humorous illustration in modern children's books but in various ways far from both the McCloskey-Lawson realistic funniness and the cartooning of Disney, Seuss, Gramatky, et al., are a number of artists whose visual humor derives from a highly individualized kind of sophisticated impressionism—Louis Slobodkin, Ernest Shepard, Maurice Sendak, Susanne Suba, and Beth and Joe Krush. The two things they all have in common are a quiet drollery and an economy of means, a seemingly casual sketchiness; although their techniques vary widely, these artists all depend heavily on the eloquence of the drawn line. Occasionally these artists use color, but color seems to add little to their art. In Shepard's *Pooh* the ink sketches seem much more eloquent than the colored drawings. Perhaps black-and-white is more in keeping with the directness and seeming offhandedness in the art of these illustrators.

Abstraction

It is not far—but it *is* a turn—from the deft, highly personal impressionism of Slobodkin and Shepard to the kind of book illustration in which a single bold line or one plane of solid color suggests a figure and in which one is as conscious of the new design as of the original objects which suggested it—that is, nonnaturalistic, nonrepresentational art, or abstract art. All art, of course, involves abstraction—the omission of certain aspects of an object and the reconstruction from what is left. Kate Greenaway omitted bright colors and retained the soft tones, left out sudden angles and emphasized the remaining gentle contours; in painting a clipper ship, Wyeth dropped much detail and stressed the white bulgings of sails and the sunlight hitting the great prow; and Shepard, in creating Pooh Bear, left out a great deal of the toy bear to create his own suggestions of a roly-poly, rather clumsy, small, and pleasant Pooh. Indeed, every individualistic style is so because of the kinds of things the artist omits and what he tends to abstract and reassemble. But, the degree of abstractness is clearly much greater in the simplified blocks of color for apples, etc., in Antonio Frasconi's *See and Say* or in Leonard Weisgard's illustrations for the Noisy Books or in Esphyr Slobodkin's pattern for Margaret Wise Brown's *The Little Farmer* than it is in Shepard's still somewhat naturalistic impressions of toy animals or in Pyle's patterned but still meticulously detailed drawings of medieval knights and ladies. Louis Darling's drawings of boys and girls and dogs running, in *Henry and Beezus*, and Tasha Tudor's delicate portraits of little Pennsylvania Dutch children suggest their subjects quite directly, so that we may be scarcely aware of the drawings themselves, whereas the flat, bright designs by the Provensens in Margaret Boni's Fireside books of folk songs and their stark designs, suggestive of Greek vase painting, in the Golden Book edition of *The Iliad and the Odyssey* make us immediately aware of *themselves* as visual experiences, while at the same time but much more indirectly suggesting the forms of boats, horses, human beings, and waves.

Many of the most original and lively contributors to children's books of the past half century have designed abstractly in the service of stories and poems; they have found it possible to get at the spirit of a poem or at the point or plot of a story by simplifying and recomposing nature into a new and attractive pattern that both does the utilitarian task of imitating and creates a new aesthetic experience of its own, with its own values. Helen Sewell's severe black-and-white patterns suggestive of the Olympian remoteness of the Greek myths; Virginia Lee Burton's rhythmic line and echoing color patterns in *The Little House, Mike Mulligan and His Steam Shovel,* and *Katy and the Big Snow;* the stiff, quaint d'Aulaire illustrations in *Abraham Lincoln, Benjamin Franklin,* and *Leif the Lucky,* suggestive of both Norwegian peasant art, itself quite abstract, and modern abstractionism; Lynd Ward's dramatic woodcuts for *The Cat Who Went to Heaven* and *Johnny Tremain;* Leonard Weisgard's bright blocks of color suggesting the noise world of a blindfolded pup in the Noisy Books series and his softer impressionism in *The Little Island;* Katherine Milhous's elegant, decorative *Egg Tree,* suggestive of Pennsylvania Dutch design, itself highly abstract; Marcia Brown's subtly flattened, thin-lined, bright-hued patterns for *Cinderella* and *Puss in Boots* and her more brilliant-lined, swirling-lined *Felice* (all about a stray cat in Venice); Gustav Tenggren's elaborately decorative *Mother Goose*—these are all examples of restrained, middle-of-the-road adaptation of abstraction to the tasks of narration and scene

Y was a Yew tree
which grew in the Park
Where all the year round
it was shady and dark.

Y—
gloomy old yew

Y was once a little yew,
Yewdy,
Fewdy,
Crudy,
Yewdy,
Growdy, grewdy,
Little yew!

From *Lear Alphabet ABC*. Penned and Illustrated by Edward Lear. Copyright © 1965 by Theodore Besterman. Used with permission of McGraw-Hill Book Company. (Book 5 by 7¼)

ROBIN HOOD MEETETH THE TALL STRANGER ON THE BRIDGE

From *The Merry Adventures of Robin Hood*. Written and illustrated by Howard Pyle. Copyright 1946 by Charles Scribner's Sons. Reproduced by permission of Charles Scribner's Sons. (Book 6½ by 9)

From *Song of Robin Hood*. Selected and edited by Anne Malcolmson. Designed and illustrated by Virginia Lee Burton. Copyright 1947 by Anne Burnett Malcolmson and Virginia Lee Demetrios. Reproduced by permission of Houghton Mifflin Co. (Book 9 by 11)

Reproduced with the permission of Charles Scribner's Sons from *Puss In Boots*, a free translation from the French of Charles Perrault, illustrated by Marcia Brown. Copyright 1952 by Marcia Brown. (Book 8¼ by 10½)

Illustrated by Hans Fischer. Reproduced from his volume, *Puss In Boots*, by permission of Harcourt, Brace & World, Inc. and Ernest Benn Limited. (Book 8¼ by 10¾)

From *Alice's Adventures in Wonderland* by Lewis Carroll. Illustrated by Sir John Tenniel. Rare Book Room. New York Public Library. (Book 6 by 8)

From *Alice's Adventures Under Ground* by Lewis Carroll. Hardcover edition published by McGraw-Hill Book Company, 1966. (Book 6 by 9)

suggestion and mood evoking. In the work of all these artists the narrative and the representation of place and object are all quite clear, and the drawing carries in addition a very definite sense of decorative or symbolic form. Leonard Weisgard's mountains for *The Little Lost Lamb* are themselves excitingly fearsome in their cubistic jaggedness; one remembers Tenggren's bright, gay elegant abstract patterns after he has forgotten the particular poems being illustrated. Virginia Lee Burton's bright spirals in *The Little House* are both pleasing in themselves, as patterns, and effectively suggestive of the natural contours of rolling farming country.

But this post-Cézanne sort of abstracting, which seemed experimental and daring in the 1930s and 1940s, has now become altogether common and almost a cliché, a formula, except in the hands of fresh artists like Weisgard, Pène du Bois, Duvoisin, and the Provensens. Occasional steps farther away from naturalistic representation toward abstract expressionism may be noted here and there in the art of children's books during the past several decades, but these are still rare enough to be remarked as experiments. Partly because illustration itself involves description and narration and partly because illustrating stories and poetry *for children* seems to involve special limitations on the freedom of narrator and illustrator, the prevalent feeling being that children need a representation of reality, children's book illustration has followed abstraction in modern art only to where it is still easy to see the relation between the new forms and the ones which suggested them; it has stopped at about where abstract art was working in the late thirties and early forties, with the simplification to be found in Orozco, Rivera, Dufy, Matisse, Marsden Hartley, and John Nash. The expressionistic forms to be found in Frasconi's *See and Say* or in Paul Rand's *I Know a Lot of Things* suggest only mildly the free expressionism with which many painters have been working during the past two decades. This, of course, does not *mean* that the influence of artists like Pollock, de Kooning, and Klein will not eventually break strongly into children's book illustration. After all, the work of Cézanne and van Gogh was four or five decades past before the abstract designing of children's books by Weisgard, the Petershams, and Ward became a fact.

It is interesting to note that books on scientific ideas—relativity, speed, weight, birth and aging, change—have opened their pages more often than have other children's books to highly abstract design. Colored cubes, stark lines, bright dots, contrasts of solid and mottled colors, directional lines— these abstract creations are often just what is needed to explain a highly abstract idea without benefit of much language. Indeed, the introduction of representation—dogs, people, cars, airplanes—can lead the child away from the author's target, the general concept, to the particular experience. And experimenters with the use of abstract illustration in books on scientific ideas, such as Miriam Schlein, Herman and Nina Schneider, and Margaret Bloy Graham, have shown that whatever the understanding effected, the result is often an attractive book that is exciting to the child sensorily, in the way bright building blocks or balloons are.

Trends in Layout, Printing, and Relating Illustration to Text

A quick ramble through a representative group of modern children's books might impress one with just the quality and diversity of drawing and painting he finds therein; such are the aspects we have so far been considering. A second ramble, though, should make one aware of another kind of revolution in the visual form of children's books: all sorts of experimentation in total design. Indeed, the increased diversity in page format, use of color, size and shape of books, type design, and use of special devices, such as foldouts, might give one the impression that more emphasis is laid on the visual appearance of juvenile books than on their verbal content.

In the eighteenth century and on through the nineteenth century the illustrations—woodcuts, engravings, etchings—were generally fairly small in relation to the page and amount of text. Still, there were often *many* of these small illustrations in a particular book. In books of poems there was generally one cut per poem, with the relation of picture to print quite clear. In fiction or nonfiction prose, the illustrations were at the book's beginning—a frontispiece—and on following separate pages; the reference of a picture to a particular passage was made clear mainly by captions. These illustration-and-text arrangements were normally rather formal and mechanical. During the past forty to fifty years the relationship of illustration and text has become much more flexible, itself a way of creating emphasis and pace. The illustrator is now much more a participant in the creating of the poem or story than he formerly was, and his illustrations are an integral part of the poem or story. The book now tends to be *one unit* of words and drawings, rather than the two units, with the illustration unit clearly auxiliary to the language unit, that it normally used to be. Whether or not author and artist happen to be the same person, text and pictures are a close partnership today.

This integration can be arrived at in a number of ways. Most obviously, one can have the illustrations *run through* the text. Thus the pictures are placed as close as possible to what they are about; they often flow into, coil through and around the printed matter, even into the printing itself. When the narrating calls for special clarification or emphasis, then there may be much illustration at that spot; and when there seems less need for this, or a greater need for verbal emphasis, then there will be less pictorial work. Often the old formal institution of the frontispiece is abandoned. Instead, the artist may start with the cover itself and then leave a visual symbol or impressionistic design inside the covers and on the title page, in this way getting the story or poems started before the verbal telling.

The drawing itself can tell part of the story, not merely retell it. For instance, blocks of different colors may suggest the different seasons of the story (as in Weisgard's illustrations for *The Little Island* and for Tresselt's *Rain Drop Splash*) or the succession of night and day (as in Golden MacDonald's *Red Light, Green Light* and Tresselt's *Wake Up, City*, both illustrated by Weisgard, and as in Brown's *Good Night Moon,* illustrated by Clement Hurd). Both devices are splendidly used in McCloskey's *Time of Wonder.* Dominant colors may relate to the physical setting or atmosphere of an event—the vivid, gaudy colors of circuses, parades, and holidays, the blues and greens of the sea and sky, the yellows and tans of beaches and deserts. The artist may wish to suggest by his choice of dominant colors or by their arrangement within the book a rather more general or intangible spirit—quietness (as in Zolotow's *Sleepy Book,* illustrated by Vladimir Bobri), excitement (James Flora's illustrations for his *The Fabulous Firework Family*), gaiety (Zolotow's *One Step, Two . . .,* illustrated by Duvoisin). The artist's lines and shapes, too, may assist in telling the story, as do Shepard's gentle little sketches for *Pooh,* Dr. Seuss's dashing, swirling lines, the blocky forms in Charlot's drawings of Mexican peasant life, the Provensens' formal, sharply outlined patterns in their *Iliad and Odyssey* Golden Book, Daugherty's nervous twisting line throughout his black-and-white drawings for *Daniel Boone* and many another melodramatic work, Norman Bate's bold, explosive lines suggestive of great busyness in his *Vulcan* (about steel mills) and *Who Fishes for Oil?* (oil drilling), de Brunhoff's neat, tidy drawings for his neat, tidy accounts of the neat tidy middle-class lives of his little elephants, Babar and his family and friends.

This closer relationship of illustration to verbal text is probably the principal manifestation but is not the only manifestation of the tendency to think about a children's book as a unified whole in which every element is intended to help tell the story or evoke the poetic idea or get certain information to the child. The page format itself is another important consideration: how much white space, and where should it be distributed? What areas can focus attention, indicate breaks between parts of a story, suggest groupings of poems and facts, and give the reader a rest and help him get set for the next important group of words? They can contribute to the tone of the telling by creating a sense of spaciousness or crowdedness, of openness or of confinement, clutter or comfortable coziness; the large amounts of white space around Maurice Sendak's drawings for Beatrice Schenk de Regniers's *What Can You Do with a Shoe?* and around Irene Haas's drawings for *A Little House of Your Own,* also by de Regniers, reinforce one's feeling of experimental play, the freedom to move anywhere and try anything.

Also, what kind of typography should be used? One primary consideration here is the child's ability to read the type without discomfort. Furthermore, the size, darkness, and shape of the type can help to establish the book's mood (calmness or excitement, orderliness or confusion, formality or informality), to place it in a certain culture (present-day large American city, backcountry, Africa, the Orient, medieval Europe, ancient Greece), to determine how important the told story will be in relation to the pictured story, to emphasize certain parts of the story. In the Babar books the very neat, precise, rather small script gives to Babar's exciting adventures just the amount of calm casualness, social propriety, and order appropriate to a nice French middle-class elephant. The roughhewn, zigzag look of Dr. Seuss's titles foretells and leads into the slashing, zigzagging pictures and mad narrative, and the black, very prosaic type used in the body of the narrative seems altogether appropriate to the jiggety-jogging doggerel.

The size and shape of the book have also come to be considered integral parts of the book and contributors to its total effect. And so we have the very small Mr. Small books of Lois Lenski, the large flat volumes that almost announce they are picture books to be laid out flat, the small volumes of James Tippett's brief, unpretentious poems, *I Live in a City, I Spend the Summer,* and *I Go a-Traveling,* and the startlingly tall Mother Goose book that hints at the liveliness and sassiness of Rojankovsky's drawings inside.

In summary, today's children's books are astonishing in the experimentation and diversity evident in the visual aspects—illustrations, page format, typography, size and shape, and binding and jackets too—and in the degree to which the visual characteristics are used to achieve the books' effects. Book illustrators and designers have shown a great flare for collaboration in experiment.

The main limitation on all this is economic: it tends to be expensive. For example, in thinking about possible visual effects in his planned book, the artist may have to limit himself to certain colors, or even to just black-and-white, since color processes are still more expensive than black-and-white. Or he may not be able to try out several alternative ways of telling a story in pictures, for that would take time, and time in publishing is expensive. Or, although he may feel that each of the rhymes in a Mother Goose collection needs illustration, he may find that that would cost too much money and so may settle for one picture for every third or fourth rhyme.

Another limiting economic fact is that except for the small number of limited editions, children's books need to sell large numbers of copies if they are going to break even; thus they must appeal to the tastes of large numbers of the adults who mainly buy children's books. And since these adults are inevitably going to be very much influenced by a book's physical appearance, publishers are going to be most enthusiastic about the illustrations and layouts that are more or less bound to be popular with them, and these are often not the new and experimental, nor are they always appropriate to the particular book.

This pressure of the already proved, the style that has become popular and safe, partly explains the domination of a period by certain successful modes—some years ago the Greenaway mode, a bit later the Pyle and Wyeth modes, more recently the Disney and Seuss and Weisgard. Where a product depends for its existence on large-scale consumption, the pressure of majority taste—or what is *guessed* to be majority taste—tends to restrict and control, even though a large public may have recently risen to greet its fresh appearance in the first place. And this is true, I think, of children's book design and illustration in our culture. Here is a great, relatively new field for the artist, but the need for meeting consumer demand may limit what he can do in it. Yet this is by no means an automatic control, for the degree to which it will be allowed to operate depends on the publishers, editors, illustrators, designers, and authors who create the books—how inventive they are, how adventurous and willing to take a chance, how sensitive to as yet unrevealed desires in the buyers and readers. The tremendous diversity of book design and illustration available in modern children's books cannot be explained simply in terms of meeting popular demand.

Dangers and Ways of Coping with Them

The designing and illustrating of children's books has become in itself an exhilarating field of creative activity; indeed, it can well be argued, as David Bland does in his *History of Book Illustration,** that "it is here that the best contemporary work [in the whole area of book design and book illustration] is often to be seen." But the obvious attractiveness of the visual book to both makers and consumers of children's books can obscure the existence of, and even promote, dangers that lie in this very importance of graphic arts in children's books; and there are several .of them. They need to be recognized.

Superior *visual* storytelling can obscure inferior *verbal* storytelling, and it may be that the concern with obtaining a fine *illustrated* book can lead to lack of concern with the words in the book. But whether or not the latter is common enough for us to worry about, it is an important fact that impressive, imaginative, colorful pictures make it harder to become aware of literary flaws. Not all the books illustrated by Louis Slobodkin are equal, in their verbal part, to the *Many Moons* of Thurber that he did, nor are all Weisgard's many children's books, visually attractive as they may be, all equally well told verbally, but the differences tend to be obscured by Slobodkin's and Weisgard's art. Visual freshness can cover over, or seem to compensate for, tired, flabby plot (or the lack of any at all), unperceptive characterization, stale, hackneyed language, and lack of wit and fancy. A book's lack of the latter qualities does not weaken it as a work of visual art; the danger lies in the fact that its visual attractiveness may make us less alert to its verbal telling.

Visual art not only may obscure literary weaknesses in a book; it may also hide literary merits. Occasionally an excellent text is so buried under the weight of masterful painting or drawing or lithography or wood engraving that it takes considerable effort to attend to the text at all; and the impression may be so overpoweringly visual that one takes away only the pictures and cannot recall the word-told story. The child reader is likely to take such a book as solely a picture book; the adult reader may be so distracted by the art that he may fail to note a fresh new story or a bright style. The text is lost in the illustrator's onslaught. This point can be illustrated, I think, by comparing an edition of Edward Lear illustrated by himself with the large-sized, elaborate edition by Tony Palazzo, or an edition of

Alice in Wonderland illustrated in small black-and-whites by Tenniel with the big-sized edition of Alice vividly illustrated in color by Leonard Weisgard. In each case the visual impact of the second volume is so great, at least at first, that a kind of unity breaks up into two kinds of art, verbal storytelling and visual storytelling, and the latter outglitters, or outshouts, the other. And one might go on to imagine how much more important is this in the child's experience with the book, for he comes to the book already accustomed to books that tell by pictures and perhaps still more unsure of himself in language than in visual communication; the pictures can completely knock out even a well-told story or fine poem. Another test might be to see how difficult it is to read the well-written text of a vividly illustrated Holling C. Holling book, such as *Minn of the Mississippi* or *The Tree in the Trail;* one's eyes keep moving back to the pictures. Or one might try to stick with the text of one of the Golden Books (*Golden Book of Science, Golden Book of Geography*) or with one of the Wonderful World series (*The Wonderful World of Mathematics, The Wonderful World of Archaeology*); the pictures always take over.

One need not argue, as too many people do, that simply because in the past a children's book has been primarily a literary experience, it should not also be a visual one. The visual possibilities of the children's book are great and should be used, but it is important to keep in mind in this day of the children's book illustrator that a unity of word and picture is most desirable, that a fine artist may waste his art on a poor story, and that a fine artist may cast into the shade a fine teller of tales.

A more important danger *may be* that too great reliance on pictures by makers of children's books and by the parents and teachers who bring them to children may tend to shut up the child's imagination in a visual world, the closet of the artist's visual conception. It is sometimes feared that for a child to have a succession of experiences in which he is so overwhelmed by the visual telling of a story that he does not hear or read the story with real attention will lead him to imagine things mainly in visual terms and cause his verbal imagination, his conceiving of things and events in words, to lie fallow. A special form of this worry is the fear that such experiences will limit the child's linguistic skills and interests—his word recognition, feeling for word meanings, appreciation of verbal distinctions, sense of style in language. The validity of both of these worries, the more general and the more limited, is highly debatable; they have at present to rest on too little evidence. But whether or not today's child's diet of heavily illustrated books ties him to the picture and limits his appreciation and use of language, it can be granted, I think, that the *word* story and poem still have the special values of verbal imagining. The experience of savoring the word story should not be sacrificed, and so adults should try to have children exposed to that kind of experience in a book as well as the first and more direct visual experience of its pictures. Furthermore, it can be sensibly urged that since books *are* a source of language experience and the learning of language, they should be read for practice with language, and that looking at the pictures should not be permitted to reduce the possibilities of the child's so learning. These are not arguments for books with few or poor illustrations. They *are* arguments for teachers' simultaneously telling the story and showing the pictures, for much talking about the story, told and pictured, in the class, and for choosing books in which the words as well as the pictures are worthy of a child's attention. And similarly for parents, at home.

It must be conceded that emphasis on picture telling tends to remove children's reading farther than ever from the *oral tradition* of storytelling. This is a loss. The printed book was the great step in this direction, of course, and long before the rise of the modern illustrated book, the printed page had come to replace listening as the main source of our stories and poems and reports. Still, we should recognize that looking is not listening and that if we want to have children get the additional feel of the *spoken* tale, we must get it told in some way—read aloud by ourselves or by children or told on records or tape. The accompanying of the telling with pictures may make more effective the oral telling; to urge and carry out this combination would seem to be the best and most pertinent answer to people who see in the attractively illustrated children's book a final death-blow to the fine old tradition of the told story, recited poem, sung song, or acted play.

Clear Gains

Conceding some need for caution in the handling of our newly acquired visual riches in children's books, we cannot deny the positive benefits of the use of illustration in them.

Good illustration makes possible a simultaneous two-way attack upon the reader's attention. He gets E. B. White's pawky, down-to-earth word account of Charlotte the Spider and Wilbur the Pig—and White is a consummate artist with words. At the same time he receives Garth Williams's delicate, ironic picture account—and Williams is an imaginative artist. In Katherine Milhous's *The Egg Tree* the young reader reads about Pennsylvania Dutch life and art, and in the Milhous drawings he is exposed to that art. Wanda Gág's stories dip and curl and repeat, in a folktale way, and so does her black-and-white design, like German peasant art. Stevenson's *Treasure Island* tells of moving ships and hulking pirates, and so do Wyeth's illustrations for Stevenson's story. For most of us the reading we recall most vividly from childhood, at least from *early* childhood, is a coupling of story and pictures—*Mother Goose* with Rajankovsky's or Tudor's or Wright's illustrations, Pyle's Arthurian tales with his ink drawings, *Peter Rabbit* with Beatrix Potter's pastel drawings, Caldecott's drawings with *John Gilpin's Ride*, Richard Doyle's drawings with Ruskin's *King of the Golden River*, A. B. Frost's little drawings with *Uncle Remus*, Shepard's Pooh and Eeyore and Piglet with Milne's Pooh stories. A well-illustrated book is, for a child, a natural combination. The child wants to see *and* hear the story; he is not yet conditioned, as we adults are, to simply reading it, getting it only one way at a time.

Besides complementing the word story, the visual patterns provide a stimulus to the child's own verbal storytelling, his own imagination in language. They lead him to make up his own word stories. Prereading children find little difficulty in creating word stories from the pictures they are looking at, and they continue to add to their later reading by thus imagining out the pictures. There is a strong defense of illustration in children's books in the contention that pictures stimulate, rather than deaden, the child's language interests and abilities.

Pictures, in books as well as elsewhere, constitute a source of information and experience when for various reasons—physical, mental, social—children cannot obtain it through language. For the child who does not yet read, pictures are a main source of knowledge, along with oral counsels, and they continue of necessity to be important sources for children whose reading abilities do not match their capacity to absorb and comprehend experience. This is not so much a matter of using illustrations to improve a child's reading as one of helping the child keep up in all his various kinds of learning; when his reading does not help him enough, then he needs the assistance of illustration. Needless prolonging of reliance on visual learning is wasteful and perhaps dangerous, but visual experience can generally be to some degree helpful, and for many children a necessity if they are to learn up to their capacities. In this respect it is important to remind ourselves that language, while in our culture it is one central way of learning and usually the most important, is still *one* way of learning among a number of ways, and that learning, by whatever means, is still our main concern.

Language is also an aesthetic experience, with its own satisfactions, and so the linguistic abilities of the child need to be fostered, through reading and other means; but this should not blind us to the aesthetic values of visual experience. The word provides aesthetic experience, but so do the visual aspects of a book—its pictures, decorations, format, typography, paper, covers, jacket. For the child the book can be a visual as well as a verbal aesthetic experience, and it can be a step in the development of his aesthetic perception. If we believe that aesthetic awareness can to some degree be developed and if we feel that visual experience is an important part of the child's aesthetic experience, then we will take as much care to select imaginatively illustrated, well-designed, well-printed books for children as we will take to choose excellent stories and poems. We will want a diversity of styles and approaches—realistic and more abstract, flippant and sober, etc.—and we will want a strong representation of the most original and imaginative art available in children's books. We will consider the book as an art experience as well as a literary experience, and as a source of visual understanding and taste as well as literary values.

Summary: Criteria for Juvenile Book Illustration

What qualities should we look for in children's book illustration? In the present discussion I have not recommended too specific and narrow bases for judgment—that children's pictures should be "realistic" or "imaginative" or "decorative," or many or few, or in one style or another, or in one medium or another. Such narrow, rigid criteria are not helpful because they do not conform to the tremendous differences of purposes in children's books and the great diversity of ways of seeing among the artists who turn their talents to illustrating them. Instead of recommending particular criteria, I have in this chapter implied several rather broad criteria:

That, generally speaking, the illustration and other visual aspects of the book should complement the text, should be in a close partnership with it, achieving mutual effects rather than vying with it for the child's attention or operating irrelevantly.

That illustration should foster, rather than stop, the child's conceptions, verbal and visual.

That the illustrations of a book should themselves provide an enjoyable aesthetic experience.

SUGGESTED SOURCES

Reference Works on Illustration of Children's Books

The Art of Beatrix Potter, with commentary by Anne Carroll Moore, Warne, 1956.

Bland, David: *History of Book Illustration,* World, 1958.

Colby, Jean Poindexter: *The Children's Book Field,* Farrar, Straus & Cudahy, 1952, chap. 2.

Crouch, Marcus: *Beatrix Potter,* Walck Monograph series, H. Z. Walck, 1961.

————: *Treasure Seekers and Borrowers: Children's Books in Britain, 1900–1960,* Library Association, London, 1962.

Davis, Mary Gould: *Randolph Caldecott 1846–1886: An Appreciation,* Lippincott, 1946.

Hudson, Derek: *Arthur Rackham: His Life and Work,* Scribner, 1960.

Lane, Margaret: *The Tale of Beatrix Potter: A Biography, Illustrated by Beatrix Potter,* Warne, 1946.

Mahony, Bertha E., et al. (compilers): *Illustrators of Children's Books, 1744–1945,* Horn Book, 1947.

Miller, Bertha Mahony, and Elinor Whitney Field (eds.): *Caldecott Medal Books, 1938–1957,* Horn Book, 1957.

Muir, Percy: *English Children's Books, 1600–1900,* Frederick A. Praeger, 1954.

Pitz, Henry C.: *The Practice of Illustration*, Watson-Guptill, 1947. A general study of book illustration.

———— **(ed.):** *A Treasury of American Book Illustration*, Watson-Guptill, 1947. Includes a chapter entitled "Pictures for Childhood."

Scott, Alma: *Wanda Gág: The Story of an Artist*, The University of Minnesota Press, 1949.

Smith, Irene: *A History of the Newbery and Caldecott Medals*, Viking, 1957.

Viguers, Ruth Hill, et al. (compilers): *Illustrators of Children's Books, 1946–1956*, Horn Book, 1958. Supplement to *Illustrators of Children's Books, 1744–1945*.

A Sampling of Illustrators of Children's Books, with Typical Examples of Their Work

The following list is intended to include not all significant artists who have helped to create children's books, but a wide enough range of artists to give one a full view of the variety of children's book illustrations. The illustrator's name is listed first and is followed by a selection of titles of books illustrated, with the name of the author when the author and illustrator were different persons.

Adams, Adrienne: Aileen Fisher, *Going Barefoot*, Crowell, 1960; Alice Goudey, *The Day We Saw the Sun Come Up*, Scribner, 1961.

Angelo, Valenti: Clyde Bulla, *Benito*, Crowell, 1961.

Anglund, Joan Walsh: *Nibble Nibble Mousekin*, Harcourt, Brace & World, 1962.

Ardizzone, Edward: *Little Tim and the Brave Sea Captain*, Walck, 1955; *Tim All Alone*, Walck, 1957; *Nicholas and the Fast Moving Diesel*, Walck, 1959; Walter de la Mare, *Stories from the Bible*, Knopf, 1961; Eleanor Estes, *The Witch Family*, Harcourt, Brace & World, 1960; Eleanor Farjeon, *Mrs. Malone*, Walck, 1962; Eva Lis Wuorio, *The Island of Fish in the Trees*, World, 1962, and *The Land of Up and Down*, World, 1964.

Artzybasheff, Boris: *Seven Simeons: A Russian Tale*, Viking, 1937, reissued from new plates, 1961; Dhan Gopal Mukerji, *Gay Neck*, Dutton, 1927.

Bacon, Peggy: William Cole, *Poems of Magic and Spells*, World, 1960; Tom Robinson, *Buttons*, Viking, 1938.

Bannerman, Helen: *The Story of Little Black Sambo*, Lippincott, 1923.

Barry, Robert E.: *Faint George (Who Wanted to Be a Knight)*, Houghton Mifflin, 1957; *Just Pepper*, Houghton Mifflin, 1958.

Bass, Saul: Leonore Klein, *Henri's Walk to Paris*, Scott, 1962.

Bate, Norman: *Vulcan*, Scribner, 1960; *Who Fishes for Oil?* Scribner, 1955.

Bendick, Jeanne: *What Could You See?* Whittlesey, 1957; Glenn O. Blough, *Who Lives in This Meadow?* Whittlesey, 1961.

Beskow, Elsa: *Pelle's New Suit,* Harper, 1929.

Bettina (Bettina Ehrlich): *Pantaloni,* Harper & Row, 1957.

Birch, Reginald: John Bennett, *Master Skylark,* Grosset & Dunlap, 1924.

Blegvad, Erik: Hans Christian Andersen, *The Swineherd,* Harcourt, Brace & World, 1958; Carol Kendall, *The Gammage Cup,* Harcourt, Brace & World, 1959.

Bobri, Vladimir: Inez Rice, *The March Wind,* Lothrop, 1957; Charlotte Zolotow, *Sleepy Book,* Lothrop, 1958.

Bodecker, W. D.: Edward M. Eager, *Half Magic,* Harcourt, Brace & World, 1954.

Bright, Robert: *I Like Red,* Doubleday, 1955; *Me and the Bears,* Doubleday, 1951.

Brock, Emma L.: *Little Fat Gretchen* (1934), Knopf, 1954; *To Market! to Market!* Knopf, 1930.

Bronson, Wilfred: *Pinto's Journey,* Messner, 1948; *Goats,* Harcourt, Brace & World, 1959.

Brooke, L. Leslie: *The Golden Goose Book,* Warne, 1905; *Ring o' Roses: A Nursery Rhyme Picture Book,* Warne.

Brown, Marcia: P. C. Asbjörnsen and J. E. Möe, *The Three Billy Goats Gruff,* Harcourt, Brace & World, 1957; *Cinderella, or the Little Glass Slipper,* from the French of Charles Perrault, Scribner, 1954; *Dick Whittington and His Cat,* Scribner, 1950; *Felice,* Scribner, 1958; *The Flying Carpet,* Scribner, 1956; *Henry-fisherman: A Story of the Virgin Islands,* Scribner, 1949; *Peter Piper's Alphabet,* Scribner, 1959; *Puss in Boots,* from the French of Charles Perrault, Scribner, 1952.

Brunhoff, Jean de: *The Story of Babar, the Little Elephant,* Random, 1939, and other Babar stories.

Buff, Conrad: Mary Buff, *Dancing Cloud,* rev. ed., Viking, 1957; *Dash and Dart,* Viking, 1942; *Elf Owl,* Viking, 1962; *Hah-Nee,* Houghton Mifflin, 1956; *Hurry, Skurry, and Flurry,* Viking, 1954.

Burton, Virginia: *Choo Choo,* Houghton Mifflin, 1937; *Katy and the Big Snow,* Houghton Mifflin, 1943; *The Little House,* Houghton Mifflin, 1942, Caldecott Medal; *Mike Mulligan and His Steam Shovel,* Houghton Mifflin, 1939; Anne Malcolmson (ed.) *Song of Robin Hood,* Houghton Mifflin, 1947.

Caldecott, Randolph: *The Diverting History of John Gilpin,* George Routledge & Sons, 1878. *The Hey Diddle Diddle Picture Book,* Warne; *R. Caldecott's Picture Book* (containing *The House That Jack Built, Sing a Song of Sixpence, The Queen of Hearts*), Warne.

Carigiet, Alois: Selina Chong, *A Bell for Ursli,* Walck, 1953.

Chappell, Warren: Walter de la Mare (ed.), *Come Hither,* 3d ed., Knopf, 1957; *The Sleeping Beauty* (from *Tales of Charles Perrault*), Knopf, 1961.

Charlot, Jean: Anita Brenner, *A Hero by Mistake*, Scott, 1953; Margaret Wise Brown, *A Child's Good Night Book*, Scott, 1943; Joseph Krumgold, *And Now Miguel*, Crowell, 1954, Newbery Award; Miriam Schlein, *When Will the World Be Mine?* Scott, 1953.

Cooney, Barbara: Louisa Alcott, *Little Women*, Crowell, 1955; *Chanticleer and the Fox*, Crowell, 1958; *The Little Juggler*, Hastings House, 1961; Ruth Crawford Seeger, *American Folk Songs for Children: In Home, School and Nursery School*, Doubleday, 1948.

Cox, Palmer: *The Brownies: Their Book*, Century, 1887.

Crane, Walter: *Baby's Opera*, Warne; *Baby's Bouquet*, Warne, 1900.

Cruikshank, George: *George Cruikshank's Fairy Library: Hop-o-my-thumb, Jack and the Bean-stalk, Cinderella, Puss in Boots*, Bell and Daldy, 1870.

Darling, Louis: Oliver Butterworth, *The Enormous Egg*, Little, Brown, 1956; Beverly Cleary, *Henry and Beezus*, Morrow, 1952; Beverly Cleary, *Henry Huggins*, Morrow, 1950.

Daugherty, James: *Abraham Lincoln*, Viking, 1943; *Andy and the Lion*, Viking, 1938; *Daniel Boone*, Viking, 1939; *Marcus and Narcissa Whitman: Pioneers of Oregon*, Viking, 1953; *Of Courage Undaunted: Across the Continent with Lewis and Clark*, Viking, 1951; *Poor Richard*, Viking, 1941; Benjamin Elkin, *Gillespie and the Guards*, Viking, 1956.

D'Aulaire, Ingri and Edgar: *Abraham Lincoln*, Doubleday, 1955; *Benjamin Franklin*, Doubleday, 1950; *Book of Greek Myths*, Doubleday, 1962; *Buffalo Bill*, Doubleday, 1952; *Columbus*, Doubleday, 1955; *Don't Count Your Chickens*, Doubleday, 1943; *George Washington*, Doubleday, 1936; *Leif the Lucky*, Doubleday, 1951.

De Angeli, Marguerite: *Door in the Wall*, Doubleday, 1949; *Mother Goose*, Doubleday, 1954; *Thee, Hannah!* Doubleday, 1940; *Yonie Wondernose*, Doubleday, 1944.

Dennis, Wesley: Marguerite Henry, *Black Gold*, Rand McNally, 1957; Marguerite Henry, *Justin Morgan Had a Horse*, Rand McNally, 1954.

DeWitt, Cornelius: Jane W. Watson, *The Golden History of the World*, Golden Press, 1955.

Doane, Pelagie: Robert Louis Stevenson, *A Child's Garden of Verses*, Garden City Books, 1942.

Doré, Gustave: Charles Perrault, *French Fairy Tales*, retold by Louis Untermeyer, Didier, 1945.

Doyle, Richard: John Ruskin, *King of the Golden River*, 2d ed., Smith, Elder, 1851.

Du Bois, William Pène: *The Alligator Case*, Harper, 1965; *Bear Party*, Viking, 1951, 1963; *The Giant*, Viking, 1954; *Great Geppy*, Viking, 1940; *Lion*, Viking, 1956; *Three Policemen*, Viking, 1938, 1960; *Twenty-one Balloons*, Viking, 1947; Edward Lear, *The Owl and the Pussy-Cat*, Doubleday, 1962.

Duvoisin, Roger: *A for the Ark,* Lothrop, 1952; *Petunia,* Knopf, 1950; *Veronica,* Knopf, 1961; *Veronica's Smile,* Knopf, 1964; William Rose Benét (compiler), *Mother Goose: A Comprehensive Collection of the Rhymes,* Heritage, 1936; Mary Calhoun, *The Nine Lives of Homer C. Cat,* Morrow, 1961; Herbert Coggins, *Busby & Co.,* Whittlesey, 1952; Louise Fatio, *The Happy Lion,* Whittlesey, 1954, and other books in the Happy Lion series; Louise Fatio, *Red Bantam,* Whittlesey, 1963; Alvin Tresselt, *The Frog in the Well,* Lothrop, 1958; Alvin Tresselt, *Hide and Seek Fog,* Lothrop, 1965; Alvin Tresselt, *Hi, Mister Robin!* Lothrop, 1950; Alvin Tresselt, *I Saw the Sea Come In,* Lothrop, 1954; Alvin Tresselt, *White Snow, Bright Snow,* Lothrop, 1947, Caldecott Medal; Jack Tworkov, *The Camel Who Took a Walk,* Aladdin, 1951; Charlotte Zolotow, *One Step, Two . . . ,* Lothrop, 1955.

Eichenberg, Fritz: *Ape in a Cape,* Harcourt, Brace & World, 1952; Rudyard Kipling, *The Jungle Book,* Grosset & Dunlap, 1950.

Ets, Marie Hall: *In the Forest,* Viking, 1944; *Mister Penny,* Viking, 1935; Marie Hall Ets and Aurora Labastida, *Nine Days to Christmas,* Viking, 1959, Caldecott Medal.

Evans, Katherine: Benjamin Elkin, *Six Foolish Fishermen* (based on a folk-tale in *Ashton's Chap-books of the Eighteenth Century,* 1882), Children's Press, 1957, sparkling illustrations.

Fischer, Hans: *The Good-for-nothings* (retold from the Grimms), Harcourt, Brace & World, 1945; *The Traveling Musicians* (retold from the Grimms), Harcourt, Brace & World, 1944; Charles Perrault, *Puss in Boots,* Harcourt, Brace & World, 1959.

Flack, Marjorie: *Angus and the Ducks,* Macmillan, 1930, and other Angus books; *Ask Mr. Bear,* Macmillan, 1932.

Françoise (Françoise Seignobosc): *Jeanne-Marie in Gay Paris,* Scribner, 1956; *Small-trot,* Scribner, 1952.

Frasconi, Antonio: *The House That Jack Built,* Harcourt, Brace & World, 1958; *See and Say: A Picture Book in Four Languages,* Harcourt, Brace & World, 1955.

Freeman, Don: Julia Sauer, *Mike's House,* Viking, 1954.

Frost, A. B.: Joel Chandler Harris, *Uncle Remus: His Songs and Sayings,* rev. ed., Appleton-Century-Crofts, 1947.

Gág, Wanda: *Gone Is Gone; or the Story of a Man Who Wanted to Do Housework,* Coward-McCann, 1935; *Millions of Cats,* Coward-McCann, 1941; *Nothing at All,* Coward-McCann, 1941; *Snippy and Snappy,* Coward-McCann, 1931; *Snow White and the Seven Dwarfs,* Coward-McCann, 1938.

Galdone, Paul: Irma Simonton Black, *Night Cat,* Holiday, 1957; William O. Steele, *The Buffalo Knife,* Harcourt, Brace & World, 1952; Eve Titus,

Anatole, Whittlesey, 1956; Eve Titus, *Anatole and the Poodle*, McGraw-Hill, 1965.

Gekiere, Madeleine: Ray Bradbury, *Switch on the Night*, Pantheon, 1958, very imaginative illustrations closely integrated with story; John Ciardi, *John J. Plenty and Fiddler Dan*, Lippincott, 1963; *The Fisherman and His Wife* (from Grimm), Pantheon, 1957.

Graham, Margaret B.: Gene Zion, *All Falling Down*, Harper & Row, 1951; Charlotte Zolotow, *The Storm Book*, Harper & Row, 1952.

Gramatky, Hardie: *Little Toot*, Putnam, 1939.

Greenaway, Kate: *Under the Window*, Warne; Robert Browning, *The Pied Piper of Hamelin*, Warne; *Mother Goose*, Warne.

Haas, Irene: Beatrice Schenk de Regniers, *A Little House of Your Own*, Harcourt, Brace & World, 1954; *Something Special*, Harcourt, Brace & World, 1958; Elizabeth Enright, *Tatsinda*, Harcourt, Brace & World, 1963; Paul Kapp (ed. and music arranger), *A Cat Came Fiddling and Other Rhymes of Childhood*, Harcourt, Brace & World, 1956.

Hader, Berta and Elmer: *The Big Snow*, Macmillan, 1948, Caldecott Medal.

Henneberger, Robert: Jesse Stuart, *The Beatinest Boy*, Whittlesey, 1953; Hazel Wilson, *His Indian Brother*, Abingdon, 1955.

Hoffman, Felix: *The Sleeping Beauty*, Harcourt, Brace & World, 1960; *The Wolf and the Seven Little Kids* (from Grimm), 1st American ed., Harcourt, Brace & World, 1959.

Hogrogian, Nonny: Sorche Nic Leodhas (pseud. for Leclaire Alger), *Always Room for One More*, Holt, 1965, Caldecott Award.

Holling, Holling C.: *Minn of the Mississippi*, Houghton Mifflin, 1951; *Tree in the Trail*, Houghton Mifflin, 1942.

Hurd, Clement: Margaret Wise Brown, *Good Night Moon*, Harper & Row, 1947; Margaret Wise Brown, *The Runaway Bunny*, Harper & Row, 1942; Evans G. Valens, Jr., *Wingfin and Topple*, World, 1962.

Hurd, Peter: James Baldwin, *The Story of Siegfried*, Scribner, 1931.

James, Will: *Smoky, the Cowhorse*, Scribner, 1926, Newbery Medal.

Johnson, Crockett (pseud. for David J. Leisk): *Harold and the Purple Crayon*, Harper & Row, 1955.

Jones, Elizabeth Orton: Rachel Field, *Prayer for a Child*, Macmillan, 1944, Caldecott Medal; Jessie Orton Jones, *This Is the Way*, Viking, 1951.

Jones, Harold: William Blake, *Songs of Innocence*, Barnes, 1961; Kathleen Lines (ed.), *Lavender's Blue*, F. Watts, 1954.

Keats, Ezra Jack: *John Henry: An American Legend*, Pantheon, 1965; *The Snowy Day*, Viking, 1962, Caldecott Medal; Ann Nolan Clark, *Tia Maria's Garden*. Viking, 1963; Verne T. Davis, *Time of the Wolves*, Morrow, 1962.

Kent, Rockwell: Esther Shepard, *Paul Bunyan*, Harcourt, Brace & World, 1941.

Kessler, Leonard: Miriam Schlein, *It's about Time*, Scott, 1955.

Kiddell-Monroe, Joan: Kathleen Arnott, *African Myths and Legends*, Walck, 1963.

Krush, Beth and Joe: Florence Hightower, *Mrs. Wappinger's Secret*, Houghton Mifflin, 1956; John Langstaff, *Ol' Dan Tucker*, Harcourt, Brace & World, 1963.

Kuskin, Karla: *The Animals and the Ark*, Harper & Row, 1958; *The Bear Who Saw the Spring*, Harper & Row, 1961; *Roar and More*, Harper & Row, 1956.

Lantz, Paul: Walter D. Edmonds, *The Matchlock Gun*, Dodd, Mead, 1941; *Tom Whipple*, Dodd, Mead, 1942; Evelyn Lampman, *Navaho Sister*, Doubleday, 1956.

Lathrop, Dorothy: *Hide and Go Seek*, Macmillan, 1938; *Who Goes There?* Macmillan, 1935; Helen Dean Fish (ed.), *Animals of the Bible, a Picture Book*, Stokes, 1937, Caldecott Medal; Sara Teasdale, *Stars Tonight*, Macmillan, 1930.

Lawson, Robert: *Ben and Me*, Little, Brown, 1939; *Mr. Revere and I*, Little, Brown, 1953; *Rabbit Hill*, Viking, 1944; *The Tough Winter*, Viking, 1954; Richard and Florence Atwater, *Mr. Popper's Penguins*, Little, Brown, 1938; John Brewton (ed.), *Gaily We Parade*, Macmillan, 1940; John Bunyan, *Pilgrim's Progress*, Stokes, 1939; Elizabeth Janet Gray, *Adam of the Road*, Viking, 1942; Munro Leaf, *The Story of Ferdinand*, Viking, 1936; Munro Leaf, *Wee Gillis*, Viking, 1938.

Leaf, Munro: *Geography Can Be Fun*, rev. ed., Lippincott, 1962, and others in series.

Lee, Doris: Lillian Morrison (compiler), *Touch Blue*, Crowell, 1958.

Leighton, Clare: Helen Plotz (compiler), *Imagination's Other Place: Poems of Science and Mathematics*, Crowell, 1955.

Lenski, Lois: *Papa Small*, Walck, 1951, and other Small books; *Strawberry Girl*, Lippincott, 1945.

Lionni, Leo: *Inch by Inch*, Ivan Abolensky, 1960, exciting illustration.

Low, Joseph: Walter de la Mare, *Jack and the Beanstalk*, Knopf, 1959, abstract linear designs.

McCloskey, Robert: *Burt Dow, Deep-water Man*, Viking, 1963; *One Morning in Maine*, Viking, 1952; *Time of Wonder*, Viking, 1957; Keith Robertson, *Henry Reed, Inc.*, Viking, 1958; Tom Robinson, *Trigger John's Son*, Viking, 1949; Ruth Sawyer, *Journey Cake, Ho!* Viking, 1953.

McClung, Robert: *Whitefoot: The Story of a Wood Mouse*, Morrow, 1961.

Mariana: Janice (Janice Brustlein), *Little Bear's Sunday Breakfast*, Lothrop, 1958.

Milhous, Katherine: *Appolonia's Valentine,* Scribner, 1954; *The Egg Tree,* Scribner, 1950; *With Bells On: A Christmas Story,* Scribner, 1955.

Mordvinoff, Nicolas: Will and Nicolas (William Lipkind and Nicolas Mordvinoff), *Finders Keepers,* Harcourt, Brace & World, 1951, Caldecott Medal; *The Two Reds,* Harcourt, Brace & World, 1950.

Munari, Bruno: *Bruno Munari's A B C,* World, 1960, Big, bright illustrations. Other books include *Animals for Sale, The Birthday Present,* and *Zoo.*

Ness, Evaline: *Tom Tit Tot,* Scribner, 1965.

Newberry, Clare Turlay: *April's Kittens,* Harper, 1940. Also *Babette,* 1937; *Marshmallow,* 1942; *Mittens,* 1936; *Percy, Polly, and Pete,* 1952; *Smudge,* 1948.

Palazzo, Tony: *Bianco and the New World,* Viking, 1957; *The Story of Snowman the Cinderella Horse,* Duell, Sloan & Pearce, 1962; Jacob and Wilhelm Grimm, *The Four Musicians,* Doubleday, 1962; Edward Lear, *Nonsense Book,* Doubleday, 1956.

Parrish, Maxfield: Eugene Field, *Poems of Childhood,* Scribner, 1904.

Petersham, Maud and Miska: *An American A B C,* Macmillan, 1941; *The Rooster Crows: A Book of American Rhymes and Jingles,* Macmillan, 1945.

Pogány, Willy: Grace T. Huffard et al. (eds.), *My Poetry Book,* rev. ed., Holt, 1956.

Politi, Leo: *Juanita,* Scribner, 1948; *Little Leo,* Scribner, 1951; *Moy Moy,* Scribner, 1960; *Saint Francis and the Animals,* Scribner, 1959; *Song of the Swallows,* Scribner, 1949; Alice Dalgliesh, *The Columbus Story,* Scribner, 1955.

Potter, Beatrix: *The Tale of Peter Rabbit,* Warne, 1901, and many other similar little books; Margaret Lane, *The Tale of Beatrix Potter: A Biography,* Warne, 1946.

Provensen, Alice and Martin: *Aesop's Fables,* ed. by Louis Untermeyer, Golden Press, 1965; Margaret B. Boni, *Fireside Book of Folk Songs,* Simon and Schuster, 1947; Robert Louis Stevenson, *A Child's Garden of Verses,* Golden Press, 1951; Jane Werner Watson (adapter), *The Iliad and the Odyssey,* Golden Press, 1956; Anne Terry White (adapter), *The Golden Treasury of Myths and Legends,* Golden Press, 1959.

Pyle, Howard: *Men of Iron,* Harper, 1891; *The Merry Adventures of Robin Hood,* Scribner, 1946; *Wonder Clock,* (1887), Harper & Row, 1943.

Rackham, Arthur: *Aesop's Fables,* trans. by V. S. Vernon Jones, Doubleday, 1912; *The Arthur Rackham Fairy Book,* Lippincott; *English Fairy Tales,* Macmillan, 1918; John Ruskin, *The King of the Golden River,* Harrap, 1932.

Rand, Paul: Ann and Paul Rand, *Sparkle and Spin,* Harcourt, Brace & World, 1957. Bright abstract patterns.

Rand, Paul and Ann: *I Know a Lot of Things*, Harcourt, Brace & World, 1956.

Rey, H. A.: *Curious George*, Houghton Mifflin, 1941, and other books about Curious George; Emmy Payne, *Katy No-pocket*, Houghton Mifflin, 1944.

Rockwell, Norman: Mark Twain (Samuel Clemens), *The Adventures of Tom Sawyer and the Adventures of Huckleberry Finn*, Heritage, 1952.

Rojankovsky, Feodor: John Langstaff, *Frog Went a' Courtin'*, Harcourt, Brace & World, 1955, Caldecott Award; John Langstaff (ed.), *Over in the Meadow*, Harcourt, Brace & World, 1957; *The Tall Book of Mother Goose*, Harper & Row, 1942; *The Tall Book of Nursery Tales*, Harper & Row, 1944.

Rounds, Glen: *The Blind Colt*, Holiday, 1941; *Ol' Paul, the Mighty Logger*, Holiday, 1949; *Stolen Pony*, Holiday, 1948; *Whitey's First Roundup*, Holiday, 1960.

Sasek, Miroslav: *This Is New York*, Macmillan, 1960, and others in series of books about cities.

Schreiber, Georges: Claire Huchet Bishop, *Pancakes-Paris*, Viking, 1947; Alice Dalgliesh, *Ride on the Wind*, Scribner, 1956.

Sendak, Maurice: *All Around: An Alphabet*, Harper & Row, 1962; *Chicken Soup with Rice*, Harper & Row, 1962; *One Was Johnny: A Counting Book*, Harper & Row, 1962; *Where the Wild Things Are*, Harper & Row, 1963; Marcel Aymé, *The Wonderful Farm*, trans. by Norman Denny, Harper & Row, 1951; Beatrice de Regniers, *What Can You Do with a Shoe?* Harper & Row, 1955; Wilhelm Hauff, *Dwarf Long-nose*, trans. by Doris Orgel, Random House, 1960; Ruth Krauss, *Open House for Butterflies*, Harper & Row, 1960; Else Holmelund Minarik, *Little Bear*, Harper & Row, 1957; Janice May Udry, *The Moon Jumpers*, Harper & Row, 1959; Alec Wilder, *Lullabies and Night Songs*, ed. by William Engvick, Harper & Row, 1965.

Seredy, Kate: *The Good Master*, Viking, 1935; *The White Stag*, Viking, 1937.

Seuss, Dr. (pseud. for Theodor Seuss Geisel): *And to Think That I Saw It on Mulberry Street*, Vanguard, 1937. Other books include *Fox in Socks*, 1965; *Horton Hatches the Egg*, 1940; *McElligot's Pool*, 1947; and *Scrambled Eggs Super!* 1953.

Sewell, Helen: *A Book of Myths*, Macmillan, 1942; Elizabeth Coatsworth, *Away Goes Sally*, Macmillan, 1940; Elizabeth Coatsworth, *Five Bushel Farm*, Macmillan, 1939; Alice Dalgliesh, *The Bears on Hemlock Mountain*, Scribner, 1952.

Shepard, Ernest H.: Kenneth Grahame, *The Reluctant Dragon*, Holiday, 1938; Kenneth Grahame, *The Wind in the Willows*, Scribner, 1933; A. A. Milne, *Now We Are Six*, Dutton, 1927; A. A. Milne, *When We Were Very Young*, Dutton, 1924; A. A. Milne, *The World of Pooh*, Dutton, 1957.

Shimin, Symeon: Herman and Nina Schneider, *How Big Is Big*, Scott, 1950; Herman and Nina Schneider, *You, among the Stars*, Scott, 1951.

Sidjakov, Nicolas: Laura Baker, *The Friendly Beasts*, Parnassus Press, 1957; Ruth Robbins, *Baboushka and the Three Kings*, Parnassus Press, 1960, Caldecott Medal.

Simont, Marc: Ruth Krauss, *Happy Day*, Harper & Row, 1949; Janice May Udry, *A Tree Is Nice*, Harper & Row, 1956.

Slobodkin, Esphyr: Margaret Wise Brown, *The Little Farmer*, Scott, 1948.

Slobodkin, Louis: *The Late Cuckoo*, Vanguard, 1962; *Magic Michael*, Macmillan, 1944; Helen E. Bill, *The Shoes Fit for a King*, F. Watts, 1956; Eleanor Estes, *The Moffats*, Harcourt, Brace & World, 1941, and other Moffat stories; James Thurber, *Many Moons*, Harcourt, Brace & World, 1943.

Smith, E. Boyd: *The Boyd Smith Mother Goose*, collected by Lawrence Elmendorf, Putnam, 1919; *Chicken World*, Putnam, 1910.

Smith, Jessie Willcox: Louisa May Alcott, *Little Women*, Little, Brown, 1934; Charles Kingsley, *The Water-babies*, Dodd, Mead, 1916; Johanna Spyri, *Heidi*, Scribner, 1958; Robert Louis Stevenson, *A Child's Garden of Verses*, Scribner, 1905.

Sperry, Armstrong: *All about the Arctic and Antarctic*, Random House, 1957; *Call It Courage*, Macmillan, 1940, Newbery Medal.

Stamm, Claus: *Three Strong Women: A Tall Tale from Japan*, Viking, 1962.

Suba, Susanna: Virginia Haviland (collector), *Favorite Fairy Tales Told in Germany*, Little, Brown, 1959; Carl Withers (ed.), *A Rocket in My Pocket: The Rhymes and Chants of Young Americans*, Holt, 1948.

Tenggren, Gustav: *The Tenggren Mother Goose*, Little, Brown, 1940.

Tudor, Tasha: *Dorcas Porkus*, Walck, 1942; *Pumpkin Moonshine*, Walck, 1938, 1962; *The Tasha Tudor Book of Fairy Tales*, Platt, 1961; Frances Hodgson Burnett, *The Secret Garden*, Lippincott, 1962.

Ungerer, Toni: *Rufus*, Harper & Row, 1961.

Unwin, Nora: James Barrie, *Peter Pan*, Scribner, 1950; Elizabeth Yates, *Amos Fortune, Free Man*, Aladdin, 1950, Newbery Medal; *Mountain Born*, Coward-McCann, 1943.

Van Loon, Hendrick Willem: *The Story of Mankind*, rev. ed., Liveright, 1951.

Walt Disney Studios: *Little Pig's Picnic and Other Stories*, told by Margaret Wise Brown, Heath, 1939; *Walt Disney's Sleeping Beauty*, told by Jane Werner Watson, Simon and Schuster, 1957.

Ward, Lynd: *The Biggest Bear*, Houghton Mifflin, 1952, Caldecott Medal; Elizabeth Coatsworth, *The Cat Who Went to Heaven*, Macmillan, 1930, 1959; Padraic Colum (ed.), *The Arabian Nights: Tales of Wonder and Magnificence*, Macmillan, 1953; Esther Forbes, *America's Paul Revere*, Houghton Mifflin, 1946; Esther Forbes, *Johnny Tremain*, Houghton Mifflin,

1943; May McNeer, *America's Mark Twain*, Houghton Mifflin, 1962; May McNeer and Lynd Ward, *Armed with Courage*, Abingdon, 1957.

Weisgard, Leonard: Gerald Ames and Rose Wyler, *First Days of the World*, Harper & Row, 1958; Margaret Wise Brown, *The Golden Egg Book*, Simon and Schuster, 1947; Margaret Wise Brown, *The Little Island*, Doubleday, 1946, Caldecott Medal; Margaret Wise Brown, *The Noisy Book*, Scott, 1939; Lewis Carroll, *Alice in Wonderland*, Harper, 1949; Hila Colman, *Watch That Watch*, Morrow, 1962; Virginia Haviland (ed.), *Favorite Fairy Tales Told in Norway*, Little, Brown, 1961; Johanna Johnston, *Penguin's Way*, Doubleday, 1962; Golden MacDonald (pseud. for Margaret Wise Brown) *Little Lost Lamb*, Doubleday, 1945; Golden MacDonald (pseud. for Margaret Wise Brown), *Red Light, Green Light*, Doubleday, 1944; Mary O'Neill, *Hailstones and Halibut Bones*, Doubleday, 1961; Alvin Tresselt, *Rain Drops Splash*, Lothrop, 1946.

Wiberg, Harald: *The Tomten*, adapted by Astrid Lindgren from a poem by Viktor Rydberg, Coward-McCann, 1963.

Wiese, Kurt: *Fish in the Air*, Viking, 1948; *You Can Write Chinese*, Viking, 1945; Claire Huchet Bishop, *The Five Chinese Brothers*, Coward-McCann, 1938; Kathryn Gallant, *The Flute Player of Beppu*, Coward-McCann, 1960; Joseph Jacobs (ed.), *The Fables of Aesop*, Macmillan, 1950; Elizabeth Foreman Lewis, *Young Fu of the Upper Yangtze* (1932), Holt, 1960; Phil Stong, *Honk: The Moose*, Dodd, Mead, 1935; Theodore J. Waldeck, *The White Panther*, Viking, 1941.

Wildsmith, Brian: *Brian Wildsmith's Mother Goose: A Collection of Nursery Rhymes*, F. Watts, 1964; Edward Blishen (compiler), *Oxford Book of Poetry for Children*, Oxford University Press, 1963.

Williams, Garth: Natalie Carlson, *A Brother for the Orphelines*, Harper & Row, 1959; George Selden, *The Cricket in Times Square*, Farrar, 1960; Margery Sharp, *The Rescuers*, Little, Brown, 1959; E. B. White, *Charlotte's Web*, Harper & Row, 1952.

Wright, Blanche Fisher: *The Real Mother Goose*, Rand McNally, 1916.

Wyeth, N. C.: Daniel Defoe, *Robinson Crusoe*, Scribner (Scribner Illustrated Classics), 1957; Sidney Lanier, *The Boy's King Arthur*, Scribner, 1912; Marjorie Kinnan Rawlings, *The Yearling*, Scribner, 1939; Robert Louis Stevenson, *Treasure Island*, Scribner, 1911.

Yamaguchi, Marianne: Tohr Yamaguchi, *The Golden Crane: A Japanese Folktale*, Holt, 1963.

Yashima, Taro (pseud. for Jun Iwamatsu): *Crow Boy*, Viking, 1955; *Umbrella*, Viking, 1958; *The Village Tree*, Viking, 1953; Taro and Mitsu Yashima (pseuds. for Jun and Tomoe Iwamatsu), *Momo's Kitten*, Viking, 1961; Taro and Mitsu Yashima, *Plenty to Watch*, Viking, 1954.

Zaffo, George J.: *The Big Book of Real Fire Engines*, Grosset & Dunlap, 1951, and other Big Books.

CHAPTER 13

*H*ow should literature be introduced into children's lives? How should children do their reading, as a separate activity with its own values and benefits or as an auxiliary to some other activity? Is their reading something good in itself or something good only insofar as it aids in the achievement of some other, extraliterary aim? Should a child's reading be considered as having intrinsic values mainly, or are its important values extrinsic, relating to ends beyond the reading and the pleasure obtained from it?

This matter of intrinsic versus extrinsic values arises in adult reading too. When adults say they are reading certain books just for pleasure or for the fun of it, they are thinking of reading as a good in itself; they do not really mean that *for* to imply any result beyond the minutes or hours they spend reading. They are voicing the feeling that the activity of reading, just so long as it is pleasurable, need not be measured by any other criteria whatsoever. Contrarily, when they say they are reading (or would like to read) certain books to become better informed or to learn more about such and such or to find how to do such and such, they are referring to extrinsic criteria. They are expecting literature to be good *for something*, not just good in the aesthetic sense of pleasurable, beautiful, etc. They want and expect literature to help them in something else, to perform an auxiliary function—to help them be better voters or conversationalists or mothers, to help them get a job, to help them find out something that will help them find out something else. And adults feel one way or the other about specific books or batches of books—that they are good in themselves or that they are good for some purpose outside themselves.

But the question of literature in general for itself or for extrinsic ends arises in relation to children's reading more abruptly and demandingly than in relation to adults' reading. Why?

The Educational Role of Children's Reading

Adult reading is less generally and closely linked with purposive education than children's reading is. More often than not, the adult reader is through school and is reading books unrelated to any particular course or course assignment, and so the question of instruction or pleasure is not a pressing one, and the issue is not likely to force itself upon our attention. But so much of children's learning is done through reading that juvenile reading comes to be considered primarily a teaching tool; hence its utilitarian value is placed over, and often against, its aesthetic effects. Children read assignments and problems, explanations of how to proceed in doing them, and they read about defined subjects. And so their reading gets related to the idea of learning what to do and how to do it and also becomes linked with the notion of learning particular kinds of things—history, science, art, political science. Furthermore, given the very high degree of formality and routine existing in schools, activities become thoroughly channeled, and subjects become well separated—and so the question of what goes with what becomes a pressing one more quickly and readily than it does outside the classroom and very easily becomes associated with the reading that is an integral and central aspect of much teaching.

Such separation and channeling are really very special and unusual apart from children's schooling. In ordinary conversation, for example, someone may refer to a money question, say, the rising cost of living, without calling it economics, and what he says about the cost of living today may remind someone else of the days when costs were lower; so he describes the dinner he could get ten years ago for a dollar, without its occurring to anyone that the conversation has shifted from economics to home economics (or storytelling). Someone in the group may remember and describe a period of high inflation and how it affected people's way of living; this, without being so called, is history. Another may wonder how people would react if there were a quick slump, and we find ourselves trying to think about mass psychology; maybe someone wonders about the effect of ads in the newspaper urging labor unions and businesses to "hold the line in wages and prices." The wage-price spiral may remind someone of a funny story illustrating the futility of man's attempts to control events. And so the several people in the discussion will, in the course of it, create stories, maybe repeat pieces from articles or poems, recite history, argue logic, suggest and illustrate political and economic theories, consider human psychology—and all this without feeling they are crossing the boundaries between "fields." This sort of free mental movement is common enough outside of formal education. But inside it, even in the most so-called progressive education, there is considerable classifying in terms of subjects and educational purposes, and reading inevitably gets involved in this; so reading becomes reading history, reading biography, reading fiction, and all children's literature becomes tied in with "school," "learning," "education."

In our culture, this "educationizing" of children's reading has had many factors working in its favor. People are naturally more inclined to worry about the formation of character and mind of young people than that of older persons, and so they pay more attention to the *effects* of children's activities, including their reading; they may be more inclined to ask "what for" of a child's reading than of an adult's. Also, in Protestant northern Europe and America reading was for a long time associated primarily with the reading of the Bible and other religious literature (tracts, martyrs' lives, etc.); other reading was generally regarded as frivolous, if not downright dangerous. And the rise of the middle class over the past several centuries has made the utilitarian emphasis more and more important in education; thus reading has come to be viewed as a tool to make men better clerks, engineers, doctors, teachers, and scientists.

Children's reading, then, has definitely become linked in our thinking with extraliterary, utilitarian purposes. But at the same time, reading for itself has retained a certain prestige in our society, and the two emphases frequently pose a choice in children's reading. A great question which anyone who has anything to do with children's reading answers in one way or another is that of the extent to which he sees a children's book as instruction and the extent to which he sees it as aesthetic experience. How far does he consider the child's reading a secondary, complementary activity tied to the kite of a learning program? There are two general positions, from each of which stem certain sets of values, inferences, and courses of action. There is, first, the position that children's reading is significant primarily as a way of teaching facts, principles, and values. The second position is that children's reading is significant primarily as an aesthetic experience.

Children's Literature as a Vehicle for Facts, Principles, and Values

The premise behind this general position would seem to be incontrovertible—that children's literature contains the subject matter of the various fields of human knowledge—history, science, the arts, etc.—and contains material referable to society's ethical standards. Characters in books take part in certain activities and perform certain processes with certain objects in certain places and times, and they tell the truth or lie, value this or that, stand up for what they believe in or deny it. Children's literature, therefore, can be used to inculcate information, ideas, attitudes, and habits. This awareness underlies the general view of children's literature as instruction.

This position can lead a teacher to any one of three levels of using literature for extraliterary purposes: (1) that of using it *primarily* to give children aesthetic experience but not discounting the incidental effect on the child's store of information and attitudes; (2) that of using it *primarily* for content of information and ethical teaching; and (3) that of using it *only* for what information and attitudes it can teach.

1   Using Books Primarily for Aesthetic Experience   An elementary teacher who operates on the first of these three levels may pick *Ben and Me*, Lawson's biography of the mouse who helped Ben Franklin do most of the things for which he became famous, to read to her seven- and eight-year-olds in story time because she thinks they will find it funny. She may go further and think that Lawson's exaggeration and contrasts are intelligent fun and will give these children good practice in appreciating humor. The historical information she notes but does not consider important, and she will not underline it in her reading aloud. And if she had come across a Dr. Seuss at the time of picking a book and had thought it was funnier, she would have taken it instead. In choosing books for her fourth-grade reading shelves, a teacher selects McCloskey's *Homer Price* because she thinks the mixture of the familiar boy and setting with Bunyanesque fantasy makes interesting reading; that the book presents realistically certain aspects of American boyhood is for her incidental. A teacher of older children may assign J. Meade Falkner's *Moonfleet* for a student's individual reading because she thinks it is an artistically told, thrilling tale of adventure and she wants this student to get to like really well-told, imaginative adventure tales; she is, at the same time, aware that the book has captured something of eighteenth-century smuggling in England, but that does not account for her assigning the story. She may suggest various historical-fiction titles—Charles Boardman Hawes's *The Dark Frigate* (English seamen in the seventeenth century) and his *The Mutineers* (American seamen in the early nineteenth), Charles Finger's *Courageous Companions* (about an English boy who shipped with Magellan), Eric Kelly's *Trumpeter of Krakow* (Poland in the fifteenth century). As a book for students to read on Asia, a high school teacher chooses Muhlenweg's *Big Tiger and Christian*, not so much for the accuracy of its portrayal of Asian history and life (which the teacher may be in no position to judge) as for the effectiveness of its telling.

In considering a book for classroom shelves or a reading list, all these teachers will first ask, "Is it a good story? What are its qualities as a story? Is it imaginative? original? vigorously or delicately funny? effectively exciting?" and like questions. Then they may note quite secondarily and incidentally that the book could leave in the child's mind a residue of information about people, times, places, and processes, or that the heroes show admirable qualities, or that the book involves an important ethical choice. Such a teacher might be glad to use a fine imaginative work which happened to provide informational stimulus and background for a subject being studied in regular classwork. For instance, a sixth- or seventh-grade teacher whose class was studying Indians might like to have some pupils read Laura Armer's *Waterless Mountain* for the imaginative power of its legend and also for its picture of Indian life; or the teacher of a ninth-grade class studying frontier America might be happy to use Walter Edmonds's *Rome Haul,* William O. Steele's *Wilderness Journey,* or Rachel Feld's *Calico Bush* as a vigorous, intelligent piece of storytelling and also as a work that might whet and support interest in frontier America. But such a teacher's enthusiasm would be first and foremost for the literary merit of the story at hand.

2 Using Books Primarily for Information and Ethical Teaching   The choices of teachers who operate at this second level will be quite differently based, even when the books chosen are the same ones. Here again an elementary teacher may use *Ben and Me,* but she will do so mainly because of its painlessly absorbable background of American history. She may use Dr. Seuss, but she will most likely choose a Seuss book that she feels clearly has a moral lesson in it and then set out to emphasize that lesson in her use of the book, though she may also be pleased if the children find the book funny. One such book would be *Thidwick: the Big-hearted Moose.* Thidwick's misplaced hospitality to all the birds and animals of the forest shows you need to discriminate among friends. In later grades, stories with little information that is new to students or relevant to subjects they are studying are likely to get relatively little attention from teachers who operate at this level. Thus stories like *Homer Price, The Borrowers,* and *Tom Sawyer* may easily be supplanted by heavily backgrounded historical stories, such as Coatsworth's *The Fair American,* Elizabeth Janet Gray's *Adam of the Road,* Isabel McMeekin's *Journey Cake* (Kentucky), Cornelia Meigs's *Master Simon's Garden,* and Hildegarde Swift's *Railroad to Freedom* (a fictionalized life of Harriet Tubman, Negro leader), or by true stories of science, such as the lives of Pasteur, Curie, and Fleming. And if a teacher has to choose between acquiring *Treasure Island* and acquiring Daugherty's *Daniel Boone* at a time when the American frontier is the big subject of class study, *Daniel Boone* it will probably be. In making such choices, however, such a teacher may have qualms if a book that doesn't fit in has exceptional merit as a work of imagination.

In general, nonfiction and fictionalized history and biography will tend to get prime attention in all grades from teachers working on this level. Fictionalized history and some kinds of science fiction will have the edge over stories with no background specially connected with regular school studies. A teacher who is much concerned with certain behavior patterns will probably stress fiction with pretty obvious moral teachings, such as Tunis's *All-American* and his *Keystone Kids* (the problem of anti-Semitism), Lorraine and Jerrold Beim's *Two Is a Team,* and Eleanor Estes's *The Hundred Dresses.* Folktales and modern fantasies will be somewhat de-emphasized except where a tale clearly reflects a culture or a social problem, and they will be used ordinarily when a class is studying the country or society that brought forth the story. Poetry will tend to receive less attention than it might from teachers of the first type. And in reading stories and poems out loud, the teacher who operates at the second level will be more inclined to point out and ask questions about matters of fact (the background information, the ideas offered) than internal questions (the plot structure of a story, the expression of the feeling in a poem), although these may not be excluded.

3 *Using Books Only for Information and Ethical Teaching*   At this *third* level, books are selected and used *only* for their connection with certain educational objectives, for what they can achieve in line with these. Very likely a teacher with this outlook would never choose Seuss, Duvoisin, McCloskey, *Moonfleet*, Twain, Edmonds, or *Pooh* unless she felt the vocabulary and reading level of a particular book would be useful at a particular point in the schooling process. A primary teacher who works this way will choose and assign reading that gives just the right vocabulary training for this age group and provides information on whatever subjects are considered important for the young pupil to learn—personal hygiene, safety, school routines, the community. Throughout the grades books will be chosen for their fitting into units—"Industry," "The Harbor"—or into the geography or history study for a particular class. If a book lacks a moving, exciting story line or is confusingly and dully written or lacks vivid characters, it will still be used if the teacher feels it is squarely on the subject being taught. Also, if the teacher is interested in teaching attitudes, books that make a clear ethical point will be sought; for instance, if kindness to animals were a teacher's goal, then *Black Beauty* might very well be that teacher's choice. And probably only those parts of a book that are on the subject will be attended to.

The Results of the Three Degrees of Content Emphasis

Now here is a range of views of children's literature which all assume that books contain information and ideas which can be used in a child's education, that they can provide something beyond the present enjoyment of the work itself. But this is quite a spread, all the way from the teacher who looks first for certain qualities in a story *as a story* and then incidentally for its factual information or ethical teachings to the teacher who looks only for these and cares not at all whether the story shows any artistic qualities.

The first two attitudes quite clearly have much to be said for them. The first type of teacher wants the tale to be original in conception, vivid in the telling, moving the reader in some way, whether or not the informational and ethical content is considerable or relates to other educational goals and activities. But this teacher is not blind to the very real effects upon our knowledge and attitudes a work of imaginative literature can have; she knows, for instance, that many an adult's not too accurate but still lively understanding of Victorian England came from his reading of Dickens, his feeling about colonial America from *The House of Seven Gables* or Washington Irving's *Legend of Sleepy Hollow* or *Rip van Winkle.*

The second type of teacher, the one who looks first for stories and poems *about certain subjects,* is more impressed than the first by the value of information and ideas presented in the guise of art but is also aware of the existence and power of art and does not feel it sensible to ignore aesthetic considerations. When she finds books containing certain facts or raising certain ethical questions, she does not use them indiscriminately. She will, for instance, leave out those pieces in a collection by various writers which, by her standards, are dully written, lack any particular originality of insight, or are empty of interesting characters unless she feels the material they have is quite important. Or if she can choose between using Will James's *Smoky* and using an undistinguished imitation of it, she will use *Smoky*, not because of its reputation, but because it is a better-told tale. She will not overlook various undistinguished series of books about foreign lands and cultures, such as the Twin series, but when she discovers a bright, exciting, well-knit story like Armstrong Sperry's *Call It Courage,* Joseph Krumgold's *And Now Miguel,* Elizabeth K. Tarshis's *The Village That Learned to Read,* Pearl Buck's *The Big Wave* (Japan), or Jean Bothwell's *The Little Flute Player* (India), she will seize on it gladly in place of more pedestrian efforts. She has her eyes open for the extra dividend of superior writing.

But the third type of teacher, who uses literature *only* for its information and ethical contents, is not at all concerned with the package that carries the facts or lessons she wants to get over; indeed, she has separated writing from content and considers the writing as merely the external wrappings. Whether or not the writer has ability to create fresh scenes, incidents, and people and to relate them to one another skillfully in an interesting, original pattern is of no particular importance to this teacher. If a story is simply a dull recital of two bland little children's "wonderful visit to the big, big city," this teacher does not mind, so long as the book has some information on the city and her class has "The City" as its study unit. And she finds it painless to destroy the continuity of books by using just those parts that deal with what the class is doing at the moment— she may pick out for emphasis the part of a story that is illustrative of the dangers of jaywalking or, in high school, assign "the Western part" of a fine novel that should be read from start to finish if at all, just because her class is studying the American West. Or she may use in class any available poem about Columbus because Columbus Day is about to be observed.

The dangers that lie in this third approach to literature should be pretty obvious. Yet many teachers and many parents apparently assume there is no other sensible approach, and many school reading lists transparently reveal this approach to be the working principle behind them. It may be well, then, at least to note the dangers briefly.

Picking pieces of literature, and pieces of those pieces, as illustrations can create an atmosphere of stuffiness, primness, and artificiality—like the atmosphere children feel when an athletic director inserts lectures on sportsmanship into a play period, or adults may feel at an overlabeled art exhibition or on an overlectured tour of a city. When imposed on a child's reading, this practice goes counter to natural tendencies to ramble on and get involved in the thing being read itself, creates a stop-and-go and detour-filled routine. Relatedly, this kind of treatment of literature can weaken and destroy the reader's sense of the form and spirit of the stories and poems he is reading. Concentration on "the important facts here" or on "the lesson to be learned from this" interrupts the reading process and breaks it up into time segments. And it distorts the story in the direction of the data the teacher wants to transmit; scenes, characters, actions, lines, and even words may be shoved out of context. The teacher's extra purpose imposes itself on the author's original purpose. Even a Thurber story can become utterly de-Thurberized by this method.

This extreme but very common conception of reading as a purely service activity can come to dominate entire curricula and whole school systems, so that subjects are organized and books chosen and classroom methods devised all with the purpose of using practically all reading as an auxiliary, a feeder, of some discipline or body of knowledge. Certain kinds of books that are hard to fit into an obvious subject-teaching pigeonhole, such as much fantasy or nonsense poetry, are dropped from the curriculum or relegated to a dark corner of neglect. Highly original books tend to get left out of reading programs simply because the author did not try to cover a standard division of experience—trucks, family, airplanes, American history, national holidays—but, instead, created a new world and for it used whatever pieces from other worlds would help out in this particular bit of imagining. And a demand develops for writing to order—books and book series in which the desired facts and ideas are served up in a thin broth of standard plot and superficial boy and girl characters.

And this kind of thinking about reading leads to an overaccenting of teaching-aid kinds of children's literature not only in individual schools and school systems, but also by publishers, reviewers, and librarians—and so writers. Thus before they know it, all the people connected with children's reading can come perilously close to the sort of excess that marked children's literature in the seventeenth and eighteenth centuries. Many teachers today laugh patronizingly at Puritan literature for children with all its excessive zeal to instruct, without realizing they may be doing essentially the same thing it did in their forcing their pupils' reading to do certain jobs in certain units.

This "put it to use" conception of reading grows to excess easily, particularly today when the schools are increasingly under fire for so-called frills and wasting of time. For this sort of pressure underwrites the widespread notion many teachers and parents have that literature must serve some clear practical purpose.

"Pure Literature": Children's Literature Only for Itself

Ironically, this same devitalizing of children's reading, this same identifying literature with formal school routines, can be, and often is, effected by setting off literary study as a separate experience, as "pure literature."

The second general position on children's reading is that its significance lies in the pleasurable—the aesthetic experience itself. There are many views of the nature of this pleasurable experience of reading—and in the course of this book we have considered the main ones in some detail—but people holding these different views of it are all in agreement that literary experience is not the same as other kinds of experience, including the gathering of scientific, historical, or other knowledge. All agree that literary experience is its own particular kind of human experience and possesses its own special values and therefore does not need to be justified as a road to some other values. Yet, as noted in the discussion of the first general position on children's reading, people who feel this specialness in children's literature may still consider this specialness as just one among many aspects of the reading experience; they would be able to see a historical novel as history as well as an imagined tale, but would not feel the story *had* to be good history to justify itself in a reading program.

But there is an extreme position that originates in the same assumption that literary experiences and values have their own identity: the view that the *only* significance of children's literature lies in the reader's special aesthetic experience, that literature is quite separate from, and exclusive of, other kinds of children's experience and learning. Most people who hold this view do not spell it out, but it is implicit enough in how they think about and use books in children's reading. They think of literary values as confined to fiction, drama, and poetry—and of historical, social, and other information and ideas as obtained *outside of* such literary reading. They set up and emphasize separate story hours or poetry periods; they think of literature in terms of "Literature I and II" and almost in no other way. In dealing with stories and poems they are likely to play down, maybe avoid, discussions of social or ethical implications, science, history, geography, music, art; these connections are seldom considered. Either there is much involvement in matters of diction (and so, reciting), knowing what happened in the story, or metrical questions, or there is the "Did you *enjoy* it?" approach to reading, enthusiasm over the reading experience for its own sake. And there is the accompanying exclusion of literary considerations and values from history and other courses.

The results of this extreme approach to children's reading are unfortunate—and in some respects very much like the effects of the extreme utilitarian approach. This second approach too can make for a stuffy, prim, artificial setting off of literature from other activities and interests of children and also from some of its own content. In this case, literature is set higher than other reading, and in the other it is set lower, or far off to one side out of the range of attention, but in each case the effect is essentially the same.

Most literature *does* have connections with other human activities and concerns, and to pretend it lacks them does violence to both the nature of the literature and to the developing interests of young readers. Literature can in this way be defused—Sandburg's "Chicago" loses its social and historical reality and becomes a peculiar free-verse poem in an English class; the crowd psychology of *Julius Caesar* is ignored; the very central Parisian tone of the Madeline books is left unrecognized; and the satirical core of *Alice in Wonderland* is imagined away. And the quite natural and illuminating connections with social problems, scientific knowledge, historical events, ethical questions, and music and the visual arts are ignored and wasted; for instance, the power of *Johnny Tremain* and Coatsworth's books to feed and shape an interest in American history is left untapped.

Not only does this approach lead to a distortion of literature as literature and of its connections with other human work, but also it contributes to the rise and spread of the mistaken and crippling assumption that literature is "just fun" (which it quite clearly *is not!*) or the assumption that it is a strange set of verbal tricks, a kind of private hobby. It is almost inevitable for children to develop the conception of reading as something just for an idle moment, a completely insignificant pursuit, if their reading of stories and poems is cut off from their other work and play and treated altogether differently.

This approach was characteristic of American schools until twenty or thirty years ago. In some school systems the pendulum has now swung to the other dangerous extreme, at which the single criterion for literature is reference to other educational objectives. In the great majority of schools, however, the view of literature as separate and special is still accepted as the normal state of affairs.

But the result is pretty much the same under either approach: children come to identify reading with formal schooling and courses, literature with certain very limited, assigned educational activities. This is unfortunate, and it is unnecessary.

A Suggested Balance and Some Examples

To obtain some realistic balance between integrating and setting off children's literature is not difficult, provided adults have the imagination—or sense?—to perceive the easy, natural relationships of specific writings to the diverse activities and problems of children, and provided they know when not to push linkings, see when the book world itself, the aesthetic experience, can become the principal or entire experience.

For example, *Mike's House* tells in a sprightly enough way about a little boy who has identified the public library with *Mike Mulligan*, his favorite book, and who gets lost in a snowstorm on his way to the library and tells a puzzled policeman he is looking for Mike's house. The story is a mildly amusing little joke, vigorously illustrated but told in very ordinary prose.

A primary teacher, though, may *also* think of *Mike's House* as a means of fostering in the children in her class a more personal feelings for their neighborhood branch library. And she may decide to follow it up with other little books, such as *A First Book of the Library,* which, through photographs and an almost nonexistent story line attached to a group of children on a library tour, presents somewhat fuller information about the public library.

Later, in the fifth or sixth grade, a teacher might read from Estes's *Rufus M.* the episode in which small Rufus, who cannot yet read or write, tries to get a library card so he can check out his own books from the library, or she might have children read the book for themselves and discover this episode. Either way, she need not stop to point up the library procedures; most children will already know them and will have the fun of recognition in a funny special situation, and the Estes account will be clear enough to the others. But the story can make an easy, natural springboard into a consideration of library use at the children's now more advanced level; and at the same time, without any special devising or tugging, the children will be encountering a sparkling, intelligent kind of humor based on sensitivity to human idiosyncrasies and leading into the creation of credible, three-dimensional characters in fiction. Rufus M.'s ritualistic circling of the lamppost every time he enters the library, his assumption that bigger writing must be better writing, his zealous puncturing of the library card—these will make children laugh. Also, such moments may be hesitated over without undue pointing, for the light they throw on his character. And it would be easy enough to get a discussion going about such in-the-book literary matters as the repetitions of words and actions, the funny words, the characters as people in their own right. And all this could be done along with, or before, the linking up with library-use considerations. Or it might be done without ever tying library use in. The important thing is that here is a book which, unlike *Mike's House,* has both kinds of potentialities. At a later date, more detailed information on the organization of libraries and on their use might be gathered from a text like Carolyn Mott and Leo Baisden's *The Children's Book on How to Use Books and Libraries.*

Again: a teacher may be very much impressed by the visual beauty of Taro Yashima's *Crow Boy*—the highly controlled yet expressive brushwork, the visual unity of the whole little book—or by the vigor and tenderness of the narrative, or by the colorful and yet quite factual impression given of Japan, or by the honest illustration of how real worth may be hidden by superficial cultured differences, or by the book's suggestion that people can see much more than they ordinarily see in their environment. The teacher may respond to several or all of these qualities of *Crow Boy,* and she may use the book with any or all of these things in mind. She might read the book aloud (or have the students read it individually), for the drama and color of the story itself and let it go at that. Or she might bring in the story when a question of differences in intelligence or clothes or habits came up in class or when the class was considering lands in the Pacific, or even crows. Or she might start with the story and then move in any of these directions. In such moving into, or away from, the story there would be no need to separate it from its content; the material is authentic, the story and illustrations are valuable aesthetic experiences, and they harmonize. Indeed, Yashima's art is so casual and unpretentious that it is very easy to move between his story and the things it is about. Incidentally, the teacher could shift easily to the reading of fact-filled fiction or histories and geographies about Japan, in which Yashima's artistry was not present. Or she might read a few of the beautifully told Japanese folktales in *Tales of a Grandmother;* a child may sense in these, without being able to describe it or analyze it, something of the same restrained sensitivity, a kind of understatement, that marks Yashima's art.

Or, again: Suppose a teacher has read Kenneth Grahame's *Wind in the Willows* and knows it to be a wonderful work filled with tantalizing language, shrewd understanding of human nature and a love of its eccentricities and contradictions, and a great deal of fond, sensitive observation of the life of woods and meadowland. She knows it can be for many children a very happy experience, full of incentives for further reading. She is also aware that it is far from a guide to nature, that it is not in the same category as *Justin Morgan Had a Horse* or Dorothy Hogner's *Rufus* or the hundreds of faithful semifictionalized "real life" accounts of animal life; so she will not try to excerpt parts of Grahame's story for "nature passages." She realizes that an essential part of the power and beauty of Grahame's book is its unity, the very special way in which the very human characters in animals' bodies fit into the river-edge world of reeds and willows. For children who need and want information on muskrats, wood rats, and beavers, she will recommend both straight nature guidebooks and the well-told animal fiction of the *Rufus Redtail* variety; and she will assign or recommend reading of these sorts without feeling she is shortchanging literature or science. This teacher will introduce *The Wind in the Willows* whenever and however she can, but not necessarily as part of a literature program; it *could* be part of such a program, but it might be brought in as part of a play activity or free reading or as a sort of footnote to a discussion of rivers and marsh wildlife or as a sequel to some other tale of animals with human characteristics, such as Lawson's *Robbut* or George Selden's *The Cricket in Times Square.* The wise teacher does not think of *The Wind in the Willows* in rigid, exclusive categories; rather, she is aware of it as a book of many facets that might come into the educational program in many roles.

In Scott O'Dell's *Island of the Blue Dolphins* the fifth-grade, sixth-grade, or seventh-grade teacher may recognize a particularly well-told piece of fiction—honest, unsensationalized narrating of a story of human tragedy and endurance, the making of convincing characters, the imaginative, vivid recreating of a vanished Indian island culture—and may welcome it as an addition to her pupils' reading without feeling she needs to relate it to any particular subject concentration. She may simply see in it one more way of deepening the imaginative experience of her pupils. And at the same time she may take mental note of its possible usefulness in relation to the study of the history of whaling, California Indians, the Santa Barbara Islands, and anthropology. She will take *Island of the Blue Dolphins* into her teaching as both an "itself" and an "in with" book.

The thrust of the foregoing comments is simply that teachers attuned to literary values will be able to conceive a story or poem as independent and connected, as a literary experience and as a potential source of non-literary experience. They will sense both the book's autonomy and its connections. They will know when a book is mainly connections—that is, when the book is not significant except insofar as it leads to other matters a child can come to know through it—and they will know when a book, connection or not, is itself an experience worth the having.

SUGGESTED SOURCES

A Comparison of Critical and Bibliographic Works Approaching the Book as Literature with Those Emphasizing Subject Matter

Eakin, Mary K. (ed.): *Good Books for Children*, rev. ed., The University of Chicago Press, 1962.

Hazard, Paul: *Books, Children and Men*, 4th ed., trans. by Marguerite Mitchell, Horn Book, 1960.

Johnson, Edna, et al.: *Anthology of Children's Literature*, 3d ed., Houghton Mifflin, 1959.

National Council of Teachers of English: *Adventuring with Books.* Frequent revisions.

Smith, Lillian: *The Unreluctant Years*, American Library Association, 1953.

American Library Association: *Subject Index to Books for Intermediate Grades*, 3d ed., 1963.

————: *Subject Index to Books for Primary Grades*, 2d ed., 1961.

————: *Subject Index to Poetry for Children and Young People*, 1957.

Books about Negro Life for Children, edited by Augusta Baker, New York Public Library, 1961.

Huck, Charlotte, and Doris Young: *Children's Literature in the Elementary School*, Holt, 1961.

Huus, Helen: *Children's Books to Enrich the Social Studies for the Elementary Grades*, National Council for the Social Studies, 1961.

Kenworthy, Leonard: *Introducing Children to the World in Elementary and Junior High Schools*, Harper & Row, 1956.

Roos, Jean Carolyn: *Patterns in Reading*, 2d ed., American Library Association, 1961.

Tooze, Ruth, and Beatrice Krone: *Literature and Music as Resources for Social Studies*, Prentice-Hall, 1955.

Modern Examples of the Use of Fiction and
Poetry for Moral and Other Instruction

Anglund, Joan Walsh: *A Friend Is Someone Who Likes You,* ill. by author, Harcourt, Brace & World, 1958.

————: *Look out the Window,* ill. by author, Harcourt, Brace & World, 1959. Quaint, bigheaded drawings, low-key colors. Child looks out the window and observes many things—houses, cats, dogs, etc.—and realizes that everything has its own individuality, that "you're the only one in this whole, wide world that is you."

————: *Love Is a Special Way of Feeling,* ill. by author, Harcourt, Brace & World, 1960. Moralizing: "Love is a special way of feeling. . . . It is the safe way we feel when we sit on our mother's lap with her arms around us tight and close."

Barr, Jene: *Big Wheels! Little Wheels!* Whitman, 1955. About trains, buses, scooters, etc.

Beim, Jerrold: *The Smallest Boy in the Class,* ill. by Meg Wohlberg, Morrow, 1959. Very moralizing: how to be big of heart.

Beim, Lorraine and Jerrold: *Two Is a Team,* ill. by Ernest Crichlow, Harcourt, Brace & World, 1945. A white boy and a colored boy discover cooperation is rewarding.

Black, Irma Simonton: *Big Puppy and Little Puppy,* ill. by Teresa Sherman, Holiday, 1960. A big puppy and a little puppy learn about relative size by encountering animals bigger and smaller than they are.

Brenner, Anita: *A Hero by Mistake,* ill. by Jean Charlot, Scott, 1953. Funny story, with moral at end: "How can you be brave when you are afraid? Well, if you do what you are afraid to do, that is brave. That is the bravest thing there is, as a matter of fact. And so Dionisio, the frightened Indian, really became what people believed him to be: a very, very brave man."

Brown, Margaret Wise: *The Diggers,* ill. by Clement Hurd, Harper & Row, 1960. Information strung on theme of diggers—mole, dog, worm, mouse, man, steam shovel.

Brown, Myra Berry: *Benjy's Blanket,* F. Watts, 1962. About Benjy's growing up, symbolized by his giving up a baby blanket.

Bryant, Bernice: *Follow the Leader,* ill. by Beryl Bailey-Jones, Houghton Mifflin, 1950. A little boy's learning from his own sandpile experiences and from a playground supervisor how to play with other children; contrast made between his behavior and that of a bad example, Push Pete.

Buck, Pearl S.: *Welcome Child,* with photographs by Alan D. Haas, John Day, 1963.

Buckley, Helen E.: *The Little Boy and the Birthdays,* ill. by Paul Galdone, Lothrop, 1965. A little boy's giving presents on others' birthdays circled on calendar and thus learning the joy of giving.

Ciardi, John: *John J. Plenty and Fiddler Dan,* ill. by Madeline Gekiere, Lippincott, 1963. This verse telling of the fable of the grasshopper and the ant leads to the conclusions that "the world won't turn without a song" and that music "never stays stopped."

D'Aulaire, Ingri and Edgar Parin: *The Two Cars,* ill. by authors, Doubleday, 1955. A driving-safety lesson in guise of an argument between an old car and a new one.

De Angeli, Marguerite: *Bright April,* ill. by author, Doubleday, 1946. Race problems presented through the experience of a little Negro girl, April, and her cultured family.

Elkin, Benjamin: *The Loudest Noise in the World,* ill. by James Daugherty, Viking, 1956. All the world is to give Prince Hub-bub of Hulla-baloo the biggest noise in world, but all wait to hear others. So, silence—and the prince hears sounds of nature for the first time. The beauty of nature's own sounds is thus made plain.

Estes, Eleanor: *The Hundred Dresses,* ill. by Louis Slobodkin, Harcourt, Brace & World, 1944. A story about a Polish girl whose wearing the same dress every day to school makes her an object of ridicule; moral teaching not oversimplified.

Farjeon, Eleanor: *Mrs. Malone,* ill. by Edward Ardizzone, Walck, 1962. Sentimental poem about old Mrs. Malone's kindness to animals and their carrying her to heaven.

Faulkner, Georgene, and John Becker: *Melindy's Medal,* ill. by Elton C. Fax, Messner, 1945. An eight-year-old Northern Negro girl's ethical problems in the South.

Lindgren, Astrid: *Lotta on Troublemaker Street,* ill. by Ilon Wikland, Macmillan, 1963. Slightly sentimental story about a sloppy little girl's bad-tempered day, her refusal to dress neatly, and her reconciliation with mother.

Sauer, Julia: *Mike's House,* ill. by Don Freeman, Viking, 1954.

Scully, Fred: *Blessed Mother Goose,* Chilton, 1951. The traditional Mother Goose verses adapted to Catholic religious teachings.

Sendak, Maurice: *Pierre: A Cautionary Tale in Five Chapters and a Prologue,* Harper & Row, 1962. A little boy who says, "I don't care!" is eaten by a lion.

Wibberly, Leonard: *The Time of the Lamb,* ill. by Fritz Kredel, Washburn, 1960. A religious moral tale with realistic background of sheepherding.

Wilson, Bettye: *We Are All Americans,* ill. by Carl K. Weiss, Friendly House Publishers, 1959.

CHAPTER 14

CHILDREN'S READING
IN THE
MIDST OF
MUCH ELSE:
The
Cultural Context of
Children's Reading
Today

$\mathcal{A}$ll the time that we have been thinking seriously, closely, critically about children's books many of us have perhaps felt, under all our study and attention, a muted worry that maybe reading books has become a relatively unimportant aspect of children's existence, that therefore the effort on our part to know and understand this activity is largely a waste of time and effort, and that we might well devote what energy and time we have to studying the other, increasingly ubiquitous ways to children's minds. One has perhaps realized that many a child's imaginary world of Alice, Mr. Toad, and Lassie has had its origin in Hollywood studios and not in the books of Carroll, Grahame, and Knight. Or one may have noted children clustered around a television set and have thought to himself, "In watching this televised program, these children are not reading. When, if ever, do they read?" Or one may have remarked how many of the phrases and references heard in children's casual classroom and playground conversation have the mark of television or radio formulas on them, how many children's heroes are television heroes, how many of children's jibes and japes are, at least in part, traceable to television. Constantly exposed to the mass media and seeing children so exposed, it is natural for us in our consideration of children's reading to speculate on the pointlessness, or at least the minor importance, of a study focus on children's literature.

Now without conceding that conclusions of this sort are justified, we would do well to identify the complex *context* within which the present-day child's reading occurs and acknowledge its significance. Thousands of children's books are still published annually; children's libraries increase and grow; great numbers of children still read for information, vicarious experience, emotional satisfaction. But in the world of today's child the *printed* stories, poems, travel books, science books, biographies, etc., are only one kind of source in a great complex of descriptions, expressions, explanations, and amusements *in other forms.* Many sources compete for the attention of today's children, and the printed word is only one of these competitors, often a minor one. Of course, literature has always been only one among others—gossip, the acted drama, the popular cartoon, the storytelling church window, music, dramatic dance, symbolic costume, flags. Children have always had access to a multiplicity of channels of fact and fancy. But during the past half century the spectacular development of other modes of communication has made the struggle for their attention more intense than ever; and indeed, the other modes have often appeared to be winning the competition, pushing printed literature pretty much out of the running. It would be altogether unrealistic to ignore the fact that for all children today the stories they read or have read to them are only one element in a great intake of fact and fiction.

Television

Today television is one of the most constant storytellers to both adults and children. Some of the story is true, that is, ostensibly has happened or exists; news broadcasts, travelogues, sports broadcasts, and science and nature hours provide stories, or the bases for them. Much of the story is fictional, imagined.

Classifying the mass of television material by intended audience, children or adults, has little point. A small number of hours of intentionally juvenile entertainment and instruction are available weekly; this consists largely of cartoons ("Huckleberry Hound," "Woody Woodpecker"), nature trips, occasional dramatizations of such juvenile classics as *Treasure Island, Heidi,* and *Little Women,* a little direct storytelling and teaching. But a great mass of adult television programming is quite immature, not in intention but in outcome. Whether the dramatic content is rerun movies, serials, or the relatively infrequent single dramas produced for television, its situation and subject ingredients are pretty standard and surprisingly few: crime ("77 Sunset Strip"), suspense and horror ("Suspense," "Alfred Hitchcock Presents"), family life, in crisis or not ("Ozzie and Harriet," "My Three Sons," "I Married Joan"), adventure, including westerns and pioneer life ("Gunsmoke," "Wagon Train," "The Lone Ranger," "Rawhide") and war ("Combat," "Hail Navy"), space science ("Outer Limits"). The historical drama, as in the "American Heritage" series, continues to be presented regularly, but not frequently.

Scarcity of Fantasy in Television

Much of this presumably adult dramatic storytelling to which children attend uses the reality of actual things, places, and events as a point of departure, a stepping-off point. Cattle ranches, crowded city streets, tree-shaded suburbs and children on tricycles, four-lane highways, restaurants and nightclubs, football stadiums, hospital wards—these physical realities provide the settings, and directors go to great pains to make them seem very real. In space movies and some horror pieces the settings are strange, far removed from recognizable reality, but the number of these is small in comparison with the "real thing" settings; and even in the fantastic story-telling there is often an effort to suggest laboratories and a test-tube environment that children may already have some acquaintance with through scientific and pseudoscientific information in television advertising, news reports, and movies. Children are not likely to get television tales in which magic is a taken-for-granted part of reality; magical forests, gingerbread houses, witchcraft, flying horses and carpets, and kings of the sea very rarely become a part of the dramatic world of television entertainment. Recognizable, or at least believable, physical reality is the base of the imagined world television gives the child, and in this respect this world differs considerably from the imagined world of children's literature, in which the acceptance of magic as quite real is a central principle. This television world contains little that would correspond to the rich and varied body of children's "superman" literature discussed in Chapter 8; seeing the general dramatic fare offered on television, children will not come into frequent contact with the common ingredients of children's fantasy literature.

Scarcity of Realism in Television

But neither will they be much exposed to the sober spirit, perhaps sometimes commonplace and mundane but honest and truth-seeking, of the children's literature we nicknamed "supermarket" literature; for most television storytelling, while relying for its appeal on a superficial gloss or illusion of real everyday living, treats experience unrealistically, simplifying human character and events, exaggerating, sensationalizing, sentimentalizing. Life is treated in a highly selective way, and the normal criterion for selection is the power to summon quick emotional responses; this is what Schramm et al., in *Television in the Lives of Our Children*, call "the high and still heightening level of excitement in television."

For example, the normal city of the television story has been simplified into a world of jumping neon signs, skyscrapers, harried executives, gun-toting gangsters, honky-tonks—a dream world of extreme luxury and desperateness, of movement and violence. For television, small-town life has become a sweetened Main Street, quaint Victorian city hall and library, idyllic tree-shaded residential streets with comfortable white homes, crackle-voiced merchants and farmers. Domestic life takes two main, generalized forms. One is the cozy middle-sized, middle-income family endowed with mutual understanding, affection, and goodwill and some typical stances— mother's sweet solicitousness, father's good-natured grumpiness, sister's flightiness, big brother's bounciness, little brother's peskiness and inventiveness. The second is the neurotic, divorce-threatened, crisis-swept family beloved by the writers of daytime serials. Civic life and society's problems have been reduced pretty much to cops and robbers, crooks and private eyes, dope peddlers and government agents, cattle thieves and the good cleanup sheriff, Communist agents and counterspies. In all this storytelling the crooked ways of life have been made fantastically crooked, and the more simple have been made fantastically straight. And except where the desired effect is one of complete horror, the story steers toward a happy ending, no matter how farfetched such may be under the imagined circumstances.

In borrowing adult television, then, children get something that, except in its surface treatment, is *not* realism; they take in a story fare that is either a mild, sentimental pap or an undiluted brew of the sensational and the irrational. Both are fantasy in that they have little direct connection with real experience, but unlike the best of fantasy, they lie about reality. They do what folktales and the fairy tales of Andersen seldom, if ever, do; they seek to present their story's events as *not* magical or abnormal, as real (e.g., the constant attempt to remind one that this event took place in San Francisco or Berlin or Columbus), and at the very same time they falsify reality, departing far from the actualities of human experience in their creation of characters and in their working out of dramatic plot. Fantastic as they are, folktales like *Snow White and Rose Red* and *The Frog Prince* and Carol Kendall's *The Gammage Cup* (all about life among the Minnipins) hold close to the central perplexities of human existence, whereas the hard-boiled, private-eye television thrillers, superficially full of real things, seldom actually approach them. Alice, with her pool of tears, her changing size, and the unsettling questions of her reluctant hosts, is much more a real person than is one of Dr. Ben Casey's nurses, with her real-looking tears and very real syringes and white caps.

Unfortunately, the difference between essential truth and slick untruth is often not easy for a child (or an adult, for that matter) to determine. And visual presentation can convey a surface physical realism that is much harder to come by in the nonvisual media. And so, at least if they have a heavy dosage of television and are satisfied with its slick untruths, children may scarcely ever experience essential truth in art or, if they do, recognize the difference.

Genuine fantasy does sometimes slip into television's adult programs—in a modern fantasy like *Amahl and the Night Visitors*, in a production of *Hamlet* or *The Tempest* or *A Midsummer Night's Dream*, in a dramatizations of a Poe tale. When it does, the considerations raised earlier in comparing adult with juvenile fantasy apply. But that is scarcely an important matter here, for this invasion is rare on television and is almost eclipsed by the great mass of the normal superficial realism of adult television.

Vaudeville and Games on Television

The television which children see carries other kinds of entertainment besides drama, and these too can include stories of a sort. There is a constant offering of very popular, rather simpleminded and harmless vaudeville—gags, skits, music and patter, the innocuous, conventionalized kind of jesting represented by Bob Hope, Jack Benny, Danny Kaye, Jackie Gleason, and Dick Van Dyke. These shows to some extent invent and develop characters in terms of one or two traits (for instance, Benny's stinginess, Kaye's helplessness), create little story situations, play with language. On the whole, these variety shows would seem to give children a somewhat richer imaginative diet than television's dramatic efforts.

Then, too, there are the mildly dramatic situations television creates by means of its charades and other guessing games; each of these hours becomes a little drama of mind against mind, against chance, or against time. Rather similar in plot and general spirit are programs built around a real actor or singer making good on the show or revealing in a chatty interview that this is a step on his way to stardom and riches. The Cinderella and Horatio Alger elements in such programs are obvious.

Televised Advertising as Literature

But having noted the regular dramatic programs, the vaudeville, and the games, I have not yet included one of the most widely affective of all the sources of imaginative literature available to children through television: the ads. Young children are inclined to make little distinction between characters on programs and the characters in the advertisements accompanying these programs. In their talk and play you may hear as many references to Mr. Clean, Josephine the Plumber, and the Culligan Man as to the program characters. Elementary teachers and playground supervisors are well aware how thoroughly acquainted with the daily television programs most children are, and they know how many children repeat and improvise on advertising slogans, poems, and songs and allude easily to ideas and information presented in the ads of the preceding evening. They hear children repeating and altering such advertising fragments as the following: "You wonder where the yellow went/ When you brush your teeth with Pepsodent," "21% fewer cavities," "Every woman alive/ Loves Chanel Number Five," "This is Marlboro country," "Does she or doesn't she? Only her hairdresser knows for sure," "Move up to quality, move up to Schlitz," "It's the water," "Pain—tension—pain," "Geritol for tired blood," "Brylcreem—a little dab'll do yuh/ Brylcreem—so friendly to your hair/ So watch out—the gals'll all pursue yuh/ They love to get their fingers in your hair," "That little old winemaker—Me," "Tums for the tummy," and "No more Ouch!" For many children the most important part of their story intake comes from such poetry, song, and drama in the ads.

The advertising literature is of two main sorts. First, there are the "real life" fantasies of lovers smoking as they make friends with pup or horse, housewives turning ecstatic over a detergent and in the process thumbnail sketching a family's daily life, and benighted individuals, social outcasts, dumbfoundedly discovering the miraculous qualities of particular deodorants or toothpastes and subsequently finding social acceptance, business success, and marriage. Their surface realism—the recognizable kitchens and cluttered living rooms, the neighborhood streets, the twangy voices of irritated mothers—helps to make these little ad stories interesting and memorable to small children. Also, the familiarity of their plots—family colds, wanting to go out to play in rainy weather, getting a new pet, placating mother over torn or dirty clothes—gives the ads much the same appeal for children that the supermarket storytelling of Chapter 7 possesses; this is, incidentally, an appeal that characterizes little of the regular television drama. Furthermore, these little ad stories probably reach children easily because, despite adults' impatience with them, they really are, as stories, quite short and so come within the child's attention span.

The second kind of story which television advertising provides children is the skit that uses cartoons, puppets, and other such devices. These skits are often daft and madly comical, sometimes frenzied and grotesque. If one ignores the desperately earnest and ponderous commercial message (and children seem inclined to do so), this kind of story provides a rich enough fare of wild events—explosions, slidings, scootings, chases, upsets, entrances and exits—and funny little characters with big noses, straight-up hair, wide mouths, projecting teeth, outsize shoes, scratchy voices, and silly giggles. Minus the commercials, these little skits have a light, fantastic invention that attracts and holds children's attention; this is probably the most imaginative and stimulating literature television has offered children. Here too, as in the adult dramas and children's hours, the ideas, situations, characters, and jests become limited to recognizable stereotypes that repeat themselves not only in the same ads day after day, but in other ads modeled after them on the principle that if something worked for soap, it should work for life insurance or dog biscuits. Still, this fault is not peculiar to television literature; we have noted this tendency and its limiting effect in the production of children's books by today's publishing industry.

Several Tentative Generalizations about Television and Its Child Audience

When we look at the total television diet available to most children in America today, what generalizations about its tone and quality can we make? The programming of information and entertainment dominating the listening time available to children is not directly aimed at children, but it is not particularly complex or mature adult fare; rather, it is somewhere between being adult or juvenile, somewhat adolescent in its level of understanding and interest. So, like much historical fiction, it offers no major obstacles to a juvenile audience. At the same time, though, some of its regular subject-matter ingredients, such as violent crime and domestic strife, may have a disproportionately heavy place in children's intake of dramatic stories. Also, the television programs children see are not marked, on the whole, by great variety of conception, rich imagining of situation, or inventiveness of language; they are not particularly stimulating of fresh experience. Still, like run-of-the-mill books and magazines for children, they can offer the child starters, the raw material for him to fool with, to manipulate, to adapt and change. And children do take over and alter the often repetitious and unoriginal literature of television much as generations of children appropriated and transformed sometimes dreary medieval romances, the chapbook shockers, and the alehouse songs and political doggerel that have now become an honored part of children's literature; such collections as *Rocket in My Pocket* and the Opie works would seem to give ample evidence that this is happening to the often banal, sometimes tasteless popular literature, including television, of our time.

There is with television the danger that the large amount of time and attention given by children to this one source of dramatic storytelling, with its comparatively few kinds and levels, can simply crowd out other sources—not necessarily superior, but different—and thus limit the imaginative work and play of children. By taking up so much time that might be devoted to reading, games, other listening, etc., and by filling that time with homogeneous stuff that repeats itself and also repeats what the children get from a good deal of their reading, records, and movies, the television set can exercise a restrictive cultural influence. This effect is seriously considered in such major studies as that of Schramm et al. and the British *Television and the Child,* by Himmelweit et al.

But more important in the long run is the possibility that through prolonged and unremitting exposure to particular kinds of television content, children, like their elders, will come to accept and expect from other sources what they have been offered as information and entertainment on their daily television programs. It is yet too early to determine how deep and permanent such carry-over can be, but there is little doubt that individuals do have this happen to them. Millions of readers still reject out of hand poetry, stories, and drama in which they do not recognize the formulas they have come to identify with these art forms; their habits make it difficult for them to see in the new forms what is really there. Likewise, television viewers could demand from their reading the meticulous physical realism television programs give them, the keyed-up melodrama of the television thriller, the easy oral gag, or the constant eye filling of television. A common complaint of classroom teachers today is that some of their pupils find dull and slow the stories read to them and the dramatic play of the classroom, and they often believe the culprit to be television. It would seem rash to ignore all other potential contributing causes and to settle for this one explanation. Like any experience, the television program can come to be a yardstick for other experiences, but we just do not know enough yet to say how common its use as a yardstick is and what other yardsticks may also be in operation. But experience with the development of values in other matters does suggest that people concerned with children's reading need to be alert to the likelihood of children's expecting from books what they find in television and need to consider ways of correcting the misconception, if they think it is one.

Three Special Aspects of Television Watching

We should also keep in mind certain further special characteristics of television watching and be alert to their possible effects, as yet not clearly determined, on the mental activities and tastes of children.

1   Unlike reading, television is more often a group experience than a private one for children. Only infrequently, and then mainly at school, does the child listen to a story with other persons and exchange responses; most of his television viewing is done in a family living room or den and, if television education has arrived there, in a classroom at his school. In these places other people participate in the responding. Gestures, sighs, snores, scuffling of inattention, gasps of excitement, hoots, comments, questions, judgments—all these become a part of the child's television story and make it quite a different experience from the individual's silent reading, where he reads not only to but by himself, without benefit of others' readings. In looking at television he is nearly always in a kind of theater. As a part of a home or school audience, he is a different person from the person he would be if he were sitting alone; he cannot help but respond not only to what he sees but also to the people who are seeing it with him. Hence when we inquire into children's television, we should not overlook the circumstances under which the viewing is done—alone, with other children, with parents or other older persons, at dinner, after dinner, etc. Also, since much television viewing is a group activity, the choice of program may be that of others. In home television viewing the program is often determined by the majority, or by the strongest-minded or loudest-spoken members of the group or by the older people; therefore it might be useful to know something about the people who help to determine what the child sees.

2   It is difficult to read, play cards, sew, draw, make model cars, or do anything else that calls for use of the eyes while looking at television. Television watching reduces the time given to other activities. So, in simple quantitative terms, more television, less reading. Of course, qualitative questions must not be ignored; for instance, though children can read while listening to the radio (and some seem to find radio music almost necessary for any other activity) the kind of reading done and the intensity of the response need to be considered too.

3   Although a verbal-visual medium of communication, television's primary nature and impact are visual. We usually say "look at" television rather than "listen to"; indeed viewers often turn off the sound and watch till something they want to see and listen to comes along. Certainly television further accustoms children to thinking of storytelling literature in visual terms, an expectation strengthened in recent years by the growing importance of illustrations in children's books and by the use of visual methods in the schools. Television viewers both see and hear their dwarfs and their more common cowboys and undercover agents; it is not too much

to assume that, thus conditioned, they should expect as normal the copious illustrating of the books they read or listen to.

Motion Pictures

Face to screen with television as we constantly are, it is easy to forget another significant visual source of story for the young—the movie seen in a theater. This forgetting is made especially easy by the blurring of the distinction between movies and TV—the use of old movies on television, the appropriation of movie directors, actors, and techniques by television, and recently the reverse tendency. But it would be a mistake to assume that seeing motion pictures in a theater, particularly those made for such viewing, is the same experience as seeing a televised show, live or not.

Some important facts are true of both. The motion picture, on theater or television screen, has the same advantage of physical realism, the same powerful impact of the visual image, and the same temptation to rely upon that kind of physical reality as a substitute for other, less tangible kinds of reality—that is, to present slick real-*looking* fantasies masquerading as fact and to dodge fantasy that suggests psychological and social truths. Motion pictures outside television also tend to give the child much the same things he encounters on television, the same actors, the same sorts of plots, characters, language, emotional tone, and pace. But some significant differences remain.

1   *Heidi, The Island of the Blue Dolphins, Mr. Toad,* or *Robinson Crusoe* seen in a theater is not the same as that movie seen at home. At both places it is viewed with other people present, but the crowd at the theater is usually a more impersonal group, unlinked to the individual child by more than proximity; and even when he goes with parents or other children, the size of the theater, the one-way facing, and the size of the screen partially isolate the individual onlooker. There is usually thus more concentration on the verbal-visual telling of the story and a little less distraction by the audience. The experience is a bit more like reading.

2   The theater movie program makes likely, though not inevitable, more selectivity in kind of entertainment and amount. Even in this age of the double bill at the movies, the back-to-back succession of plays, skits, news reports, interviews, concerts, and more plays that crowds three or four hours of television looking is a much more disorganized, many-leveled, unfocused kind of presentation than a double bill in a movie theater. One need not take what he chances to get on television, but children watching for several hours are likely to do so, whereas in an afternoon at the movies their fare is less chancy, uncertain. In practice, this makes it possible, if adults so wish, to exercise somewhat more control over the selecting of offerings than they have over television, even though they may try to read about the television programs ahead of time.

Whatever the children's immediate source of motion-picture entertainment, theater or television program, it is a major cultural fact, and one perhaps frequently overlooked by adults alarmed about the present cultural development of their children, that over the past several decades an impressive list of significant films has become available to children. These films, some based on literary works and others original on the screen, are a rich source of imaginative experience for children and at the same time complement the different experience the child obtains through his reading.

Radio and Phonograph

It has seemed proper to begin this analysis of the cultural context of children's reading by examining media which are primarily visual, because the great new medium of our time, television, is visual and because much of the child's exposure to the creative arts is today visual. Yet an important part in the daily lives of many children is still played by nonvisual, aural media, the radio and the phonograph, and these can be of great importance in complementing children's reading. The phonograph, with the development of better recordings, portable machines, and long-playing, more easily handled records, has retained its place in American homes, and often is the special possession and concern of the children. And it has long been a many-use, integral prerequisite of the classroom. Radios too, now small and easily transportable, have hung on in the many chinks of our communication life not filled by television; radio has become the story-and-entertainment channel to the child's own room, the camp, the beach, wherever it may be impracticable for television to go. And the radio and the phonograph have held their own in our culture, and particularly among the young, not only because technical improvements have made them more practical but also because their own characteristics create advantages peculiar to them. It is a mistake, a common one, to lump television together with the radio and the phonograph and assume we are talking about one mass medium. As with television, the very nature of the radio and the phonograph leads to special kinds of receiving and reaction; the exact significance and depth of these effects may be difficult to determine, but not their existence.

1   The radio and the phonograph, lacking the visual image, leave to the listener the visual filling in of the action. Hersholt's recorded reading of the Grimm version of *Rapunzel* leaves to the listening child the visualizing of the tower, the witch, the lovers, and the violent incidents at the tower; the child may draw from his own experience (towers, long braids of hair, girls he has seen or from pictures in books, movies, and television. Whatever the original source, he does the putting together and so participates in the storytelling in this vision-making way. In this respect the radio-phonograph channel for imaginative experience is like the read-aloud story, or the silently read book with few or no illustrations. For people fearful that the visual image will completely oust the verbal, the use of radio and recordings at home and school promises at least the opportunity for the child

to work with story elements without the visual cue, the coaching of the picture he receives from book illustration, television, and motion pictures. And where one wishes the visual image to assist the verbal, one can easily accompany the aural "picture" with a visual picture—book illustrations, filmstrips, etc.

2   The radio and the phonograph further differ from, and hence complement, television and motion pictures in that they permit other activities, including other communications, to go on simultaneously. Thus radio programs, particularly musical ones, do not block off large chunks of time from reading, one aspect of television watching that has worried many educators and critics of contemporary culture. And other forms of creative activity—drawing, making and arranging objects, dancing, working with numbers—can proceed while children hear a song or instrumental piece or even a story.

3   In various complex ways radio-phonograph communication would seem to facilitate greater selectivity on the part of the individual user, more control over what he will receive. Phonograph users (or their parents or teachers) can make their own choices of particular pieces—the Nutcracker Suite, a folk-song album, a dramatization of Many Moons, music-backgrounded Sleeping Beauty or Bambi, an elaborate Hollywood-produced telling of an Andersen tale or a straightforward reading of it by Paul Wing, Frances Clarke Sayers, Jack Lester, Ruth Sawyer, or Harold Courlander. With the phonograph one does not need to wait on a network's prior selection, and one can determine when he will listen, what parts of a selection he will listen to, and whether he will repeat the listening. Also, advertising is eliminated. In short, there is a much greater chance for personal manipulation, and so control.

Both radio listening and phonograph listening can be a more private thing than television generally is, and privacy can add to the individual's control over what he receives, the things he can imagine. Small, portable radios and phonographs can be more easily moved to where listening can be done alone or under special conditions; earphones make the experience altogether personal. All these factors reduce the likelihood of dictation by the group. Thus again the radio and the phonograph can create conditions roughly equatable with those of silent reading.

4   At present, certain kinds of imaginative experience are more available on radio and recordings than on television and in motion pictures. The amount of music of all types and qualities on radio and recordings is still much greater than that on television. And at least for the present, the reading of imaginative literature, especially poetry, by its creators and other interpreters is still most accessible through recordings.

In noting these four peculiarities of radio and phonograph listening, it becomes obvious that because of them the radio and the phonograph can contribute to our children's diet of literature outside of books a flexibility and fullness it would lack if altogether dominated by television. Overlooking this fact is partly responsible, perhaps, for the anguished note of alarm and helplessness voiced by cultural critics, teachers, and parents when they see the amount and influence of television watching among the young. True, radio programs are formula-ridden, and recordings, whether for the general audience or for children, likewise take their patterns from assumed popular demand; but for the reasons we have noted, listening to the radio and the phonograph seems to be less a contributor to conformity and tawdriness and more a means of increasing the child's cultural resources.

The Rest of the Context

This sort of thinking, not complacent but not hysterical or numbed into depression, may be extended beyond the new electronic means of communication to include a multiplicity of other, less obvious channels constantly bearing to our children various kinds of imagining—fiction, poetry, drama—and the raw stuff of imagining—reports of events, descriptions of places, miscellaneous information. This influx should be observed and kept in mind in our efforts to understand our children's reading in relation to their total imaginative life, the mental context of their reading. This context leaves holes that reading books may fill; it may fill blanks the reading has not filled; it may complement and strengthen or it may counter impressions from reading stories and poems. It is a part of our children's culture, just as their reading is, and should be observed in relation to that culture.

The Comics

Occasional allusions have been made in this book to comic strips and comic books, with no effort to divorce them from children's literature. Customarily, though, they occupy a different pigeonhole in people's thinking and are usually discussed separately, as something beyond, or aside from literature. But whether we call them literature or not, we must recognize that they pour their contents into the same stream, thereby affecting children's imaginative literature.

No art form—and the comics are an art—has become more firmly set into a few grooves, more conventionalized, than the comics, and so it is not difficult or misleading to describe them in the following generalizations:

1 Whether or not a particular comic strip is aimed primarily at an adult or child audience, most comic strips and comic books easily become a part of children's reading because of the visual presentation, which itself can bear much of the narrative, and because of their vocabulary, ordinarily a colloquial, unbookish one that takes the form of short flights rather than long, complicated expositions. Even where the content is in some respects more maturely adult than the usual comics content, as in "Peanuts," "Pogo," "Li'l Abner," and "B.C.," the vocabulary and syntax are not so far beyond child readers as to send them away—and there are the pictures.

2   The majority of the comics—"Dick Tracy," "James Bond," "Apartment 3-G," "On Stage," "Brenda Starr," "Mary Worth," "Orphan Annie," "Rex Morgan, M.D."—are not comic by any reasonable stretching of the term. Most of them are merely the drawings-and-dialogue equivalents of the adventure yarn, the suspense novel or television thriller, the mystery novel or play, space fiction, the melodramatic romantic novel or television drama, the horror tale or movie. This was not true in the early, developing years of the comics, but in the past several decades they have assumed many noncomic assignments. Still, a minority remain comic in some sense, including silly, often slapstick situations ("Li'l Abner," "Mr. Mum," "Pedro," "Henry," "Ferd'nand"), grotesque characters ("Gordo," "Moon Mullins," "Li'l Abner"), the confusions and incongruities of ordinary everyday life ("Bringing Up Father," "Dennis the Menace," "Blondie," "Henry"), funny language ("Pogo," "Peanuts"), and, occasionally, intellectual jottings on the peculiarities of contemporary society ("Peanuts," "Pogo," "B.C.").

3   The comics are closer to being little plays—illustrated dramas, accompanied by printed dialogue—than they are to being stories. Most have become serial dramas; some have come to be much like the television variety shows, centering around a few characters who, week after week, crack much the same sorts of jokes and get into the same kinds of situation; typical of this type are "Nancy," "The Flintstones," "Brother Juniper," "Marty Links," "Emmy Lou," "Andy Capp," and "Beetle Bailey."

4   The comics usually have rather little continuity of plot but considerable continuity in their characters' development. Over a period of time the people of a comic strip generally come to behave in some broadly consistent manner. And most strips possess continuity of style, both visual and verbal; one becomes familiar with the special smudge, blur, jagged line, verbal twist, or slang or jibe characteristic of a particular comic artist.

5   The comics are often serious, vital art, sometimes great art. Some of them have created memorable characters—Barney Google, Charlie Brown, Moon Mullins, Krazy Kat, Pogo, Li'l Abner. Some, such as "Skippy," "Peanuts," "Barnaby," and O. Soglow's "Little King," have imagined human existence from a fresh point of view, probing it experimentally and imaginatively. Some have created charming, sure whimsey, despite all the pitfalls of whimsey; these would surely include "Barnaby," "Mr. Mum," "Pedro," "The Little King," and "Henry." Some, such as "Prince Valiant" and "Buck Rogers," have imagined a romantic, exciting world. Indeed, perhaps the young child comes more frequently into contact with works of creative imagination in the comics than elsewhere in his environment.

The Child's Exposure to Printed Advertising

A second major tributary of print pouring stories and poetry and parts and pieces of stories and poetry into our children's imaginative life today is the mass of advertising and instructions daily printed, lithographed, silk-screened. From getting up in the morning to going to bed at night, the child is exposed to a tremendous bombardment of printed pleadings, urgings, and warnings, a kind of continuing education outside the channels of his conventional education. Splashy labels along his toothpaste tube, on his cereal box factual information about sports heroes or animals or space machines, pictures and essays and even little fictional tales in the morning paper's advertising space and in the family's *Post* or *Life,* similar but bigger pictures and captions on highway billboards, the safety warnings, sometimes with illustrative picture and story, in subways and buses, the innumerable card biographies of athletes, actresses, and historical characters that children accumulate—this outpouring is so constant, so difficult to classify in any orderly way, and seemingly so trivial in its individual items that most adults underestimate its importance in the child's daily imaginative life. But for a child a spaceman is a very important figure, someone to know more about and probably to conceive further adventures about, whether he appears in a story, on a television program, or in a cereal box. A story may be dropped into a child's manipulating consciousness by an earnest safety poster as well as by a book; a rather spare, special kind of wit may reach the child through the car ad, "A Volkswagen can go forward. A Volkswagen can go backward. Isn't that wonderful?" as well as through Lear's or Carroll's punning and general drollery.

Such imaginings do not have to appear in finished form in advertising to become part of the child's personal lore. All the child needs is a starter—one character of a kind or one remark by a character or a drawing and a couple of sentences to suggest a situation—and he will take it from there. Indeed, probably the most significant characteristic of this material, as far as it concerns children, is this fragmentary quality. It is an ever-changing collection of capsules of notions, plots and ideas, little beginnings and endings—raw, undeveloped material that can tease the child into playing with it, filling it out, linking it with his own experience and with stories, characters, and language he has found in his more conventional reading. The value of this unorganized but ever-present miscellaneous stuff may be quite considerable. It can be a kind of enriching mold.

Oral Literature in the Home, in the Neighborhood, and at School

In our concern with the organized, labeled sources of children's stories and story material—books, magazines, television, radio, films, filmstrips, records—we easily overlook other sources so much a part of daily living that we normally fail to consider them sources of communcation, much less think of them as in any way related to literature. These are the oral statements, ranging from long conversations to desultory remarks, of the people children meet in their daily lives.

There is the child's home. Here in his family he overhears his parents, brothers and sisters, family friends, visiting salesmen and tradesmen, and others telling stories, some true and others fictional, some fragments, just glancing references, and others rather full accounts.

The number, length, subjects, language, and tone of these accounts depend on the kind of people in the child's family, their schedules, their relationships with one another and the world outside the family, their articulateness, their educational levels, their experiences. From his father, for instance, the child may hear gossip, brief allusions or long stories, about characters and incidents at his job—if the father is at home when the children are at home and awake, if the mother can and will give him an audience, if he is not too tired to talk about what tired him, if he is not a bottled-up, uncommunicative person, if in his view the things that happened are repeatable before children, if his voice carries across the room to a child's ears, if a television set does not exclude family conversation from the evening's activities, if the child is not so taken up by other activities of his own that he does not listen to what parents may be saying. Or the child may pick up fascinating fishing lore from an older brother who fishes—if the brother is around when the child is, if the brother has had good luck of which he wants to boast, if he tells stories vividly enough to hold a child's attention. Innumerable contingencies determine this kind of source of accidental oral literature. In some families the members seldom or never exchange experiences; in others such exchange is common, and may even become almost a formalized daily ritual. Even the size and shape of the rooms in a house may help to determine what a child hears from the rest of his family. An ill sister, a brother who has to study for examinations, music practice, a new television program that shuts up discussion—these and other incidental factors can affect this source of story. But variable as the source and its conditions may be, what the child hears in his family life must always be a significant element in determining the lore in his head and the appetite he has for stories from other sources, such as books. What a child has read is one helpful kind of clue to the interest and knowledge he will bring to his reading in school; another and sometimes more useful one is what he listens to at home.

The child's neighbors also contribute to his fund of fact, guess, and tale. Simply knowing that a neighbor boy with whom he plays is from a far place called Quebec may be a teasing little datum in the child's imaginative store; and if he hears from the boy about Quebec and the life there, the store is added to. Nearly always a neighborhood provides a child with one or two odd families—a quite bohemian family, a very miserly or stingy one, an extremely religious one, an explosively busy one—and the child gradually hears a good deal of intriguing lore about such families that he could never collect from his own familial world. The children next door, his neighborhood friends' parents, the mailman, the man who cuts the lawn, the workmen eating their lunch at a new building in his block—all or any of them may convey to his ears, intentionally or unintentionally, fascinating story bits and whole narratives that stick in his mind and become part of it.

And there is beyond family and neighborhood still another rich source of oral literature—the child's school. Here again he will be able to do the sort of casual listening in he can do at home and in his neighborhood. The playground lore may range from pets and parties and childhood diseases to fire and murder; at recess a child may be regaled by a big-eyed class-mate with a lurid account of a family argument, a guinea pig that got away, or a television program (identified as such or narrated as an event personally witnessed). But in addition to this quite unstructured, informal storytelling the child will encounter in the classroom a more designed kind of story—his classmates' accounts in story hour or news time, their re-ports of books they looked up or information they were assigned to bring in, the teacher's own descriptions of people and events. And there is, of course, the subject matter—in mathematics, art, music, science, the social sciences, etc.—which may, in spite of whatever efforts may be made to separate the disciplines and facts from imagination and play, break through into the child's private world of imagining, his world of story.

Tendencies in the Present Cultural Context

When we look at the whole range of raw and processed material to which children's imaginations are exposed today, and not just at the television and comic-strip media which receive most attention from social and cul-tural critics, we cannot but be impressed with its variety and complexity, and perhaps we will be bewildered by the variety of elements at work in it and the multiplicity of combinations of influence and the individual child. Thus impressed and bewildered, we may throw up our hands and conclude there are no trends, no emphases, in this cultural context of today's child, or at least nothing that can help us understand it. Such is not the case. Certain important tendencies can be discerned, and they are related to children's reading. In some cases the *significance* of the tendency is rea-sonably clear, in others not.

1   Shift in Importance of Sources   With the rise of radio, television, and motion pictures as major forces in our culture, certain older sources of literature seem to have become less important as contributors to the individual child's imaginative life. Talk within the family, the family inter-play of conversing and recounting and guessing and tale building—this continues as a part of the lives of most children, but often has less time allowed it and, in the crush of other lore from outside, comes to seem less interesting, less worth keeping. So with the neighborhood gossip and yarns, to some extent supplanted by entertainment from the larger world beyond the neighborhood. The new technology has been abetted in this by changes in neighborhood living, such as the increase in apartment living, the car, the closer linking of the family to extrafamily activities in school, church, industry, and elsewhere. And silent reading, like listening to one's father or the neighborhood gossip, has also for many a child been crowded into fewer hours, perhaps back into just school hours, by the image on the white screen in living room or movie theater, the radio disc jockey's patter, the lyrics from the spinning turntable. Quite apart from their very lively stirring of interests that lead back to reading, certainly the development of these sources of communication has *crowded* the child's world of incoming images to an unprecedented degree.

The old sources—books, family, neighborhood and community, schoolroom and playground—remain, and in fact books and the schoolroom, at least, have become richer and more accessible sources than ever before for many children. The difference lies in the strength of the new competitors for time and attention.

2   *The Centralization of Sources*   Under present economic, social, and technological conditions both the more newly important media (television, radio, motion pictures, recordings) and the older ones (printed books, magazines, etc.) tend to have fewer points of origin and a lesser variety of kinds of origins. In our modern culture there is a very strong tendency toward centralization of imaginative talent and activity. This comes partly from the new ease of duplication and simultaneity; it results in part from the tremendously expensive investment of time, money, and personnel; the limited number of communication channels possible in a given area is sometimes a contributing factor. It can be argued that some of the conditions and practices contributing to this centripetal tendency can and will be changed, but certainly the tendency is strong and clear in the mass media as they presently exist.

For instance, a child, in late afternoon or early evening, watches a western that in setting, plot, characterization, photography, pace, and dialogue is almost identical with the westerns he has seen on previous evenings and will see on succeeding programs. It may well be a reshowing, and so he may have seen it before. Other children in his neighborhood and in his class at school will be looking at the same western or a similar one in their homes, and children all over the nation see the same show. Even if other children or their parents had other preferences, they would still likely look at this show, for in most communities the number of channels is quite limited. Also, for various reasons the same shows or same kinds of shows crowd into the same time spots, seeking the same audiences.

Later in the evening the child may see other kinds of programs, but they fall into a surprisingly small number of categories; a typical evening's fare might be a space adventure, a crime story, and a hospital drama. And the child will be given much the same writing formulas on program after program—similar simplifications of character (the space hero is essentially the same person as the undercover agent or the police sergeant or the young doctor), the same sorts of plot (merely shifted to various scenes), the same pace, much the same language in the dialogue. It would be surprising if this were not so, for such programs are written by a comparatively small number of television writers who have received similar training in writing for movies and television and who, rightly or wrongly, feel they are competing for an audience. On these various but not varied programs children see and hear advertisements which emanate from a small number of advertising agencies and show a therefore not unremarkable resemblance in dramatization, acting, photography, cartooning styles, and banter—and are repeated night after night. If they listen to televised music or variety shows, they will hear certain songs over and over again on all of them, and all of these songs fit into a few safe and popular formulas of words and music. Often these songs will be picked up by the commercials, and the children will continue to hear adaptations of them in advertising for months after the original songs have run their brief course. And in all these "different" parts of an evening's television watching the children will repeatedly encounter certain styles in clothes, cars, and manner and speech.

And as a child uses other kinds of communication in his world, he will continue to run into a great sameness, even outright identity. At the movie house he may see pictures he has already seen on television or will see eventually. He will see pictures written, produced, drawn, acted, sung, and danced by people responsible for his television programs, and what they give him here will have the same limited kinds of plot and production technique he got on television; after all they are operating on the principle that they are producing for the same mass audience.

On the radio the child will get, minus visual image, the advertising playlets and jestings he sees on television, and he will hear the same comedians and musicians doing what he has seen them do. His radio listening may give him more music and more kinds of music than come over his television channels, but since much of his radio programming has gone through the kinds of minds that originated his television and cinematic fare, and again often the same minds, most of the music available will not be significantly different. And all this similar music will be surrounded by the same kind of patter from similar kinds of announcers and masters of ceremonies. His record dealers, too, stock up on the same songs and the same entertainers, and his friends and older brothers and sisters play the same records.

In the comic books the child buys or borrows he is confronted by much he is already familiar with on television and radio and in the movies—the same characters, the same plots and gags, the same artists and writers. Many of his comic books will retell or continue stories he has seen or will soon see. On billboards and in magazine advertisements he will again meet the cartoon figures of comics and television, and certainly he will be in the familiar world of luxury cars, adolescent dating, and gadget-filled kitchens. At Disneyland, a world's fair, or one of the Disneyland imitations he will remain in the kind of world he has long known through movies, television, and the comics. And even in the books he reads he will have reunions with the artists and writers who have created an imagined world for him over radio and television. Illustrations, even when drawn by artists he does not already know, will likely be in one of the several styles currently dominant in movie cartooning and television advertising. Often his books will be editions published because of the popularity of a movie or television program.

At school the child will see, as part of the curriculum, movies and taped television programs (taping makes possible and highly likely the further centralizing and homogenizing of storytelling, drama, and music through educational television) and hear recordings like those he has heard everywhere else. And at school, in his neighborhood, and at home the people he lives and communicates with will have supped the same soup too.

This limiting effect of our wealth of communication sources is further intensified by the fact that so many of them are experienced by the individual as part of a *group*. The child at home watches television with others, and often he watches something selected by others. In listening to the radio and records, too, the child, while somewhat more of a free agent, is still very likely to be in company with others; he shares their listening, and they share his, and so there is a sharing of influence and also of reactions to mutual influence.

We cannot, moreover, dismiss as unimportant the fact that the nature of much of this new abundance of cultural material depends upon decisions based on the data of mass consumption—the pollsters' reports on audience size, success at the box office, the ability of the cultural offerings to sell something else, be it toothpaste or cars. Such matters are irrelevant to the quality of a story and to the story's potential popularity with children, but they are important determinants of the literature and the auxiliary literary influences our children are exposed to through the mass media.

Undeniably, and ironically, in this contemporary world of so many possible sources of cultural exposure the actual sources and the circumstances of exposure possess a high degree of homogeneity. A cultural inbreeding characterizes the culture in which our children do their living, learning, and imagining.

On the Other Hand . . .

These sobering facts about mass culture today and its relation to children's literature should not cause us to overlook certain other facts that may make the prospect appear less desperate.

1 Wider Choice   Although the forces that tend to circumscribe and homogenize cultural experience are doubtless strong in our mass-communication culture, all the media are greatly increasing the range of choice. Our children have far more to select from than the children of any preceding time—more authors and kinds of authors, more books and kinds of books, more subjects and styles and levels of understanding, more means and forms of imaginative communication and stimulation. Generally in the past the great problem in the way of children's reading was the technological and economic one of *scarcity;* there were just the printed word and the spoken word of people around us, and the first was often difficult to come by. Now the printed literature is more varied and accessible than ever for more children, and in addition to it there are the spoken words of television and radio and the words-plus-picture of television and motion picture. The primary problem is no longer availability; it is the psychological one of awareness and selectivity. The pressures for uniformity and blandness in our children's imaginative lives are fierce; but the opportunities for making those lives rich and diverse are very great too.

2   The Possibility of Greater Variety of Interpretation   The many and varied sources of literature now easily available within our culture *can* be used, if we so desire, in such a way as to reinforce and supplement one another. The movie or televised story *can* lead a child to the book or give the child the story in another dimension, from another angle. The recorded, read, televised, cinematized, and comic-stripped forms of a story can all be vitally different and so can give the child a richly assorted store from the same cave. Now besides being silently read by the child or read to him by parent or teacher, the Grimm tale can be recorded by a famous actor, with orchestra and special sound effects, or by a quiet-voiced librarian, with no sound effects; or it can be the illustrated tale by Wanda Gág, Marcia Brown, Walt Disney, or Boris Artzybasheff, the filmed cartoon or filmed drama or filmed puppet version, the live televised performance, or the comic-strip Grimm. *Can be* is the important phrase here.

3   The Usualness of Mediocrity   Certainly one is justified in sometimes being struck and depressed by the uniform mediocrity of so much of the literature available, through books and all the other media, to children today; but at the same time we need to remind ourselves that it was ever thus, that the great output of literature, in whatever forms available, has always been mediocre. The great majority of children's books have always been trite, shallow, and temporary in their appeal. The eighteenth-century child's sermonizing books were, for the most part, poorly written; the Victorian child, while he perhaps got hold of *Hans Brinker* or *Tom Sawyer* or *Westward Ho!*, read hundreds of stories lacking any of the qualities of those special works. Most written or oral accounts of an event lack perception, thoughtfulness, imagination, eloquence; and so it should not shock us into hysteria or passiveness to realize how imperceptive, unthoughtful, unimaginative, and ineloquent much of what our children today read, look at, and listen to really is.

4   Children's Ability to Transform   A final—and overriding—consideration and a central theme of this book about children's literature: Children have, in varying degrees, of course, the ability to transform into something else whatever they get. We must not stop short with the movie or comic strip a child saw yesterday; we should also seek to know what he did with it.

SUGGESTED SOURCES

Selected Bibliography on the Cultural Context of Children's Reading

Barnouw, Erik: *Mass Communication: Television, Radio, Film and Press,* Holt, 1956.

Becker, Stephen: *Comic Art in America: A Social History of the Funnies, the Political Cartoons, Magazine Humor, Sporting Cartoons and Animated Cartoons,* Simon and Schuster, 1959.

Boutwell, William D. (ed.): *Using Mass Media in the Schools,* National Council of Teachers of English, 1962. Thoughtful discussions of the place of mass media in our culture and of how schools can assist students in using them.

Bryson, Lyman (ed.): *The Communication of Ideas: A Series of Addresses,* Harper & Row, 1948.

Elliot, William Y. (ed.): *Television's Impact on American Culture,* The Michigan State University Press, 1956.

Emery, Edwin, et al: *Introduction to Mass Communications,* Dodd, Mead, 1960.

Hart, James: *The Popular Book: A History of America's Literary Taste,* University of California Press, 1961.

Himmelweit, Hilde T., et al.: *Television and the Child: An Empirical Study of the Effect of Television on the Young,* Oxford University Press, 1958. Nuffield Foundation study.

Kouenhoven, John: *The Beer Can by the Highway: Essays on What's American about America,* Doubleday, 1961.

Kwiat, Joseph J., and Mary C. Turpie (eds.): *Studies in American Culture: Dominant Ideas and Images,* University of Minnesota Press, 1960

Lynes, Russell: *The Tastemakers,* Harper & Row, 1954. A discussion of the development of the various levels of taste in American society.

Macdonald, Dwight: *Against the American Grain,* Random House, 1962. A number of articles highly critical of the effects of mass media on American culture.

Mass Media and Education, The Fifty-third Yearbook of the National Society for the Study of Education, 1954, part II.

"Mass Media: Their Impact on Children and Family Life in Our Culture," *Child Study,* Summer, 1960. Discussions of effects of mass media on children.

Mead, Margaret: *"Cultural Bases for Understanding Literature,"* Publications of the Modern Language Association, vol. 68, April, 1953.

Mumford, Lewis: *Art and Technics,* Columbia, 1952.

Postman, Neil: *Television and the Teaching of English,* Appleton-Century-Crofts, 1961. For Committee of Television of the National Council of Teachers of English.

Riesman, David: *Individalism Reconsidered and Other Essays,* Doubleday, 1954.

————— **with Nathan Glazer and Reuel Denney:** *The Lonely Crowd: A Study of the Changing American Character,* Yale, 1950; Doubleday (Anchor Books), 1955.

Rosenberg, Bernard, and David Manning White (eds.): *Mass Culture: The Popular Arts in America,* Free Press, 1957. Large collection of essays on popular literature, radio, television, etc., in America today; a worried outlook dominant.

Schramm, Wilbur, et al.: *The People Look at Educational Television,* Stanford, 1963.

—————:*Television in the Lives of Our Children,* Stanford, 1961. Results of study of over six thousand children and questioning of parents and schoolteachers and officials.

Seldes, Gilbert: *The Great Audience,* Simon and Schuster, 1950. Shrewd and stimulating discussion of the American consumer of the arts.

—————: *The Public Arts,* Simon and Schuster, 1956.

Thomas, R. Murray, and Sherwin G. Swartout: *Integrated Teaching Materials,* rev. ed., McKay, 1963. Selection and use of audio-visual materials in the school

CHAPTER 15

HOW
TO
KEEP
AFLOAT:
Practical
Suggestions

*I*n this book my primary purpose has been to point out and clarify basic problems and positions in the selection and use of children's literature. In so doing, I have led us into an informal examination of main types of children's books in which we have looked into representative specimens of these kinds. The recognition of important questions and a beginning acquaintance with the literature itself—these have been our aims.

Now—if one has not done so earlier—one may well ask oneself such questions as these: Even though I understand the basic questions about children's literature and have a fair beginning acquaintance with existing children's literature, how can I remain knowing and proficient in the use of children's books? How can the busy teacher or parent or librarian stay informed about new children's books, series, processes, authors, trends, etc.? How can I become—and stay—informed so that I need not relinquish to others my role as a guide of children's reading? In short, how can I keep afloat?

It is not easy to keep afloat in children's literature, and many adults fail to do so and become dependent on either their memories of a book like this one or whatever books drift their way. At the same time, one can remain reasonably conversant with children's writing, provided he knows some of the simple, available means of doing so and actually uses them.

This final chapter is meant to suggest these practical ways in which one can keep up with the field of children's reading.

Using Bibliographies

A professional in any field—engineering, medicine, teaching, chemistry, labor, entertainment, conservation—needs to keep up with the publications in this field. He cannot possibly read more than a fraction of what is being published in it. So he must rely on bibliographic guides. A teacher with a professional attitude toward his work with children's reading will realize the necessity for knowing what is happening in children's publishing and the impossibility of doing this without bibliographers' help—and there are plenty to help him. He will, therefore, find what bibliographers' tools are available and use those he finds most reliable and adaptable to his own special situation.

Bibliographies of children's literature may be roughly divided into two large kinds—those meant specifically for professionals (librarians, teachers, publishers, writers) in the field and those more popular and informal lists intended for the general public. The teacher can find both useful but will soon discover, if he puts forth the necessary effort to master the slightly more complicated apparatus, that the more professional bibliographies will be more useful.

He should realize that bibliographies have a variety of purposes and so are of many different kinds.

1 More and Less Inclusive   Some lists try to include *all* the publications within announced limits; thus the *Education Index* lists all articles appearing in a large number of education journals; other lists (and these are the more common) *select* titles from within certain limits, by whatever criteria they have decided on, and do not attempt to list everything (e.g., the lists at the end of the chapters in this book, the lists in *The Horn Book* and *Elementary English*). The *Children's Catalog* lists several thousand children's books, but it does not seek to list all children's books; instead, it lists only those its editors believe meet certain standards, and it gives ratings to its selections. A teacher may find the inclusive listing useful if he wants information about a given author or book—what book or books an author has published, who wrote a certain book, publisher and place of publication, date of publication, price. In general, the fuller lists are most useful when one has already decided to use a book and is trying to find it or order it. If one wants to select books, the more selective list is normally the kind he will turn to.

2 Discontinuous and Continuing   A list may be made up to cover books to that date, with or without thought of any continuance of the list. The bibliographer may never revise his list, or he may sometime do a supplement to bring his materials up to date. Such a list can be very valuable in all ways except one—its value stops with the materials published up to the date of the list's own publication. The *continuing* bibliography seeks to remedy this shortcoming by adding titles periodically.

3 Bibliographies Separately Published and Bibliographies Published as Part of a Larger Publication   Some bibliographies are published as separate works. Others are to be found combined in various ways with other materials—as bibliographies in books on certain type of writing, as lists in yearbooks covering various phases of work in the field, as lists attached to periodical articles about children's literature, and as continuing bibliographies in periodicals, such as those in *Elementary English, School Library Journal, The Horn Book,* and *Childhood Education.* The inexperienced worker in this field is likely to overlook these bibliographies in other books or magazines, but they can be very useful, particularly insofar as they are likely to have a special focus on books meeting certain criteria or needs.

4 General and Special Bibliographies   A list may seek to deal with children's literature in general, or it may be confined to just one aspect of the field, say, to biographies or to fantasies or to poetry or to books for good nine- to twelve-year-old readers, or it may be limited by more than one criterion, including, besides literary types and age levels of reading ability and interest, subjects (cars, trains, colonial days, fairies, caterpillars), special functions (books to read in certain units, for special occasions, for remedial reading), quality (classics, best books of . . .), and writers (books by American writers, books by Southern writers). Also, the general bibliography may be organized into sublists according to such special criteria. Such specialization is time-saving for the teacher who already knows the particular type of book he wants to find.

5 Unannotated and Annotated Lists   Unannotated bibliographies are simply lists of names of books and their authors, usually with such discovery information as publisher's name, city of publication and date, and sometimes price. Annotated bibliographies give some idea of what the book is about—its subject, something of the thread of plot or organization, sometimes an indication of its style, tone, and emphasis, and sometimes the lister's judgments of its values and limitations and his recommendations as to its use.

The unannotated list is useful enough if one is using it merely to find names of books one already knows something about, if one knows enough about the author to infer what a new book by him will probably be like, or if one knows enough about the bibliographer to guess what sort of a book is likely to be on his list. For instance, if one comes to know through experience that Mrs. X likes books that point out moral lessons, he may guess that the books on Mrs. X's new list do this, mainly. In short, the unannotated list's usefulness depends on the user's previous knowledge. There is a tendency on the part of many students to overlook this limitation and to take lists on faith, assuming that one person's list is pretty much like any other person's list—and this is just not so. A book list's usefulness depends on one's knowing *why* it contains these titles. This knowledge you can get from what you already know about book or author or lister or from what the lister tells you when he lists a particular book. And what he tells you is useful only insofar as it is definite and specific. "Well told," "original," "very humorous," "of high literary merit," "interesting to young children," "confused," "first rate," "excellent," "mediocre," "delightful,"—these words vaguely express opinions that are meaningless until the list maker has indicated *why* he considers something first rate or whatever, and *what* aspects of the book he is applying his adjective to. An unexplained opinion is useless. It is really worse than useless, for it promises more than it delivers.

Using Reviews of Children's Books

It is but a very short step from the fully annotated bibliography to the book review; indeed, some of the reports in bibliographies like the University of Chicago Graduate Library School's *Bulletin of the Center for Children's Books* may be realistically regarded as serious reviews.

The ostensible purpose of the review is to give the prospective chooser some conception of the general form of a book, its strengths and weaknesses, its possible values. Within this general purpose, a good many different things get done. Reading a review should save the reader time in doing away with his need for looking into obviously irrelevant books. Also, it should give him the benefit of the observation and judgment of *other* readers; their noticing should help him notice more clearly and understandingly.

Reviewers and reviews vary greatly in method and quality. Reviews of children's books range from reviews almost as brief as bibliographic annotations to article-length reviews. They vary from quite objective reports scarcely venturing opinions to reports presenting very strong opinions. Reviewers range from very sweet to very sour—from the school of "Everything is too, too delightful" to that of "More pap for dull children" or "Oh, well, this is a juvenile, so you can't expect a lot"—and they differ widely in the criteria they apply to the books they review. Some concentrate on what a book teaches, others on how well it entertains, others on how well it does both of these at once. Some think much in terms of reading levels and the use of books with children of certain ages; others pay little attention to such criteria. Some focus on what happens, others on the wit, the language, the characterization, the style. Reviewers range from the generally poorly informed to the well-informed, from the general book reviewer drafted into children's book reviewing to the specialist. They include elementary and secondary school teachers, college professors of education, college literature teachers, librarians, journalists, and writers of children's books.

In short, there is such a variety of kind and quality in children's book reviews that anyone using them—and teachers will find this a very rewarding activity—must do some preliminary surveying of the general territory and then settle for the regular consulting of those particular review sources he finds most useful to him.

Reviews of juvenile literature are found principally in three kinds of publication: (1) professional journals in the fields of education and librarianship, (2) parents' magazines and literary magazines, and (3) the general press—newspapers, mass-circulation magazines.

In the long run, the habit of looking regularly into the reviews in one or two professional journals will be especially rewarding. Journals like the *Bulletin of the Center for Children's Books, Childhood Education, Elementary English,* and *The Horn Book* (see list at the end of this chapter) should prove specially useful for their reviews and their fully annotated book lists.

Parents' magazines, such as the *PTA Magazine* and *Parents' Magazine,* frequently have as reviewers librarians and educators of the kind who contribute to the journals, but their reviews are likely to be fewer in number and more irregular in their appearance. Also, they may be more impressionistic, less detailed in their information.

The literary magazine, like the parents' magazine, is only in part concerned with children's books, and so its attention is likely to be only occasional and tied in with some matter of adult reading. But one journal of this kind, the *Saturday Review,* gives a good many columns with some regularity to the reviewing of juvenile literature. So do the book-review sections of the New York *Times* and the London *Times.*

General magazines, such as *McCall's* or *Ladies' Home Journal* or *Redbook* or *Life,* and ordinary newspapers address themselves to the general public, not just that part particularly concerned with children and their books; the reviews of juvenile books in these places, therefore, tend to occur sporadically, to be delegated to nonprofessionals, and to stress topical, newsy aspects of the new books.

Using Articles Presenting Critical Analysis and Describing Research

How important is color in children's book illustration today? How important should it be? Do fast readers absorb as much as slow readers? How should the teacher present a story to nonreaders? Are books for adolescent girls hopelessly sentimental? What correlation, if any, is there between the amount of television viewing and reading among children in the middle grades? How does E. B. White mix the fantastic and the commonplace to create his own special sort of humor? What children's authors are today unjustly neglected? What reading program might be suggested to interest children in music and the fine arts? What new school library programs are being developed in various cities in America?

Anyone seriously concerned from day to day with children's books and reading will often want to have other people's facts and theories on questions of this sort. Or he may want to have such questions drawn to his attention. And there is no dearth of sources of such facts and theories. Each year thousands of professional articles that deal with them appear in dozens of journals—educational, librarian, parent, and general. And yet the great majority of teachers make relatively infrequent use of these sources of professional opinion. Why? One answer is that many teachers do not think about their children's reading, and so questions do not occur to them; they feel no need for critical commentary or research. Another answer is that teachers do not have the time. In many cases this is a just answer; in more, perhaps, it is a rationalization of lassitude or of inability to handle the available materials in such a way as to get the most out of them; the teacher does not know how to pick his way through the jungle. In some cases passivity is simply the result of not knowing where to go for the answers.

Whatever the cause, teachers miss one convenient source of stimulation and suggestion if they do not keep in some sort of regular contact with professional writing on children's literature. The industrial engineer reads *Iron Age;* the medical doctor seeks to keep abreast of current knowledge through such journals as the *AMA Journal;* the librarian keeps up through the *Library Journal.* Likewise, the alert teacher will use his own periodical sources of professional opinion and information. And, as with bibliogarphies and reviews, the key to effective use is knowing in advance what one really wants and knowing where to look for it.

Here again the distinction between the articles meant for a more general audience and those intended for more specialized, professional readers is relevant. The former articles are in broad, general terms and tend to be more prescriptive than descriptive, more inspirational than analytic; the latter tend to be more compressed, businesslike, less entertaining, more filled with data. The more specialized writing assumes previous knowledge of children's literature, as well as of educational psychology and theory. An article in the *Saturday Review* on children's libraries is likely to deal with all kinds of children's libraries, whereas an article in the *School Library Journal* is likely to take up a particular kind of children's library— the school library or the children's section of the public library or the traveling library for children. One should know whether he can get more from considering the more general or more particular aspects of a problem, and then what source will most probably give him what he wants.

Another useful distinction to keep in mind is the distinction between the presentation of the results of research and writing of a critical nature. Neither is often found pure, but articles on children's literature do bend in one or the other direction. In the research article the main purpose is to present new and possibly useful information—a teacher's experimental free reading program, a librarian's report on the borrowing of various types of children's books, an investigator's summary of his study of reading preference among children from different home backgrounds, a biographer's condensed account of the life of a writer. The critical article, while perhaps drawing on such studies, will concern itself mainly with questions of interpretation and evaluation—an analysis of a change perceived in an author's writing over a twenty-year period, a comparison of the humor of two children's writers, a determination of the values and limitations of a certain author, a philosophical consideration of the importance of fantasy in children's lives. A third category might be made for articles on matters of *application*—applying either discovered facts or critical insights to children's reading—but this emphasis is so closely involved with critical analysis that little seems gained by doing so. The more useful distinction seems to be between findings and thinking about the findings.

Now, whichever types of writing about children's literature one wants, how does one find them?

If one has in mind a particular subject, author, or title, he may start by looking it up in an *index*. The most likely source for articles on children's books would be the *Education Index*; more general sources are the *Reader's Guide* and the *International Guide to Periodical Literature*. These are unannotated and do not indicate whether the article is research or criticism; one might infer this, however, from what he already knows about the periodical sources listed.

Besides knowing how to find a particular article, one needs to have a general idea of the usual contents and tone of a half-dozen periodicals in this area, and should keep in touch with a couple of them regularly. Here are some periodicals that one might do well to get acquainted with before settling for one or two regular sources of information and opinion: *Child Study, Childhood Education, Elementary English, The Horn Book, School Library Journal.*

Inspecting New Books and New Editions of Old Ones

Such guides as bibliographies, reviews, and research and critical articles are not substitutes, however, for firsthand acquaintance with the books themselves—they cannot do for us certain things the actual inspection of a book can do. Even when one knows a reviewer's tastes pretty well, he still cannot be sure he would agree with his opinions if he could read the book for himself. And the reviewer or bibliographer is not writing for you alone, and so cannot be alerted to note just those matters that will be most significant to you—points about the use of the book with children the age you are teaching, etc. Also, it is difficult to convey an accurate impression of some aspects of books, particularly the visual. But more importantly, actual contact can do much to stir and preserve interest in children's books, and this personal feeling for the books is essential for adults regularly dealing with children's reading.

There is, then, no denying the value of firsthand inspection of books as a basis for one's knowledge of them and use of them with children. But how does one get this firsthand contact? *Can* one really get anywhere by oneself? Indeed, a good many teachers come to an early negative conclusion and simply do not try to explore for themselves or to seek out the books mentioned in lectures they hear or articles they read. They believe that with all their normal duties, they do not have the time or the energy for doing their own firsthand investigation of children's books. And they are right—if their conception of looking into a book is the common one of going through a book from cover to cover. But this method is only one way of exploring books, and perhaps the least effective. Much more can be found out about far more books if one has developed a *thumbing-through technique.*

This consists essentially of skimming quickly with the eyes open for certain things and then slowing down for a closer look at anything that seems worthy of a second look or that puzzled one on the first look. It is not reading in the sense of reading every word, or even every sentence or paragraph. But it *is* reading if by reading one means taking in as much as one needs to know for his particular purpose in going to a book. This technique is simply the alert once-over, the keying of one's speed and method to one's purpose and the nature of the materials.

Let us assume we are a second-grade teacher browsing through the children's section of the public library in search of twenty books to take out under the teacher-loan sort of arrangement in effect in many cities. Are we this time looking mainly for fiction? If so, let us concentrate on the fiction shelves. We know our children can read on their own but that some of the reading will still be done by the teacher and that, in either case, the children will still do much taking in by picture; also, they do not yet attend to reading for long at a time. Knowing these things narrows our field, makes the job easier. We thus need not worry about unillustrated longish books.

We glance at the title on the cover. Does it suggest the contents? Sometimes yes, sometimes no. *The Hobbit* doesn't help us, but *John's Day in the Country* or *The Elf on the Shelf* or *Come Kitty* probably does. If the title makes clear the book is of a type we have no wish for at present, we need go no further into it. We might, however, note those external physical features of the book which might be relevant to our purposes—such points as size (not too big or awkward if to be handled by the children), binding (important if length of service is important and if children will handle it themselves), and external design characteristics that might themselves suggest the character of the book (wispy and delicate? everydayish? harum-scarum? fantastic?).

Now let's start thumbing.

Any table of contents? If so, what sort of chapter headings do we find? They may tell us a lot, even all we need to know, about the setting and the general plot of a story ("Bob's First Day at School," "Bob's Birthday," etc., or "Lost," "Buried Treasure," "The Pirates' Return," "The Fight," "Search for the Treasure," "Found," "Home Again") and may also suggest the general style and tone of the entire book.

If we still feel we do not have a clear picture of the book, we might skim a few paragraphs here and there—perhaps the first couple, then a scattering of paragraphs later in the first chapter. This may be enough to suggest to us the general plot line or situation, the sort of characters to be met, how fully they are treated, the general tone of the telling (simple and direct? broadly funny? quietly whimsical? fast or leisurely? mysterious or everydayish and familiar? emphasizing action or background and atmosphere?), the vocabulary (easy or difficult for our age level? special in any way?) and whether the book is importantly related to particular interests or information (animals, trains, family life, a foreign country, school, and so forth). And what we look for and how closely and for how long will depend partly on how much we already know about the author's work (his usual subject matter, style, appeal) and how much we may have learned in advance about this particular book. Such information, of course, simply provides clues, not answers.

How long should such an examination take? For a book like one of Seuss's (if one already knows something about him), anywhere from a few seconds, just enough for a glance at the cover to five or six minutes. For a book like one of the Betsy series or Blaze horse stories, about the same range of time. For a Thurber or E. B. White or Pooh type of story of some length, from five minutes to ten or fifteen. It is quite possible for an interested and efficient adult to "get on to" twenty to twenty-five new books in an hour's browsing. And this does not mean that he becomes a reading machine, either; indeed, a person reading the way suggested here will more likely remain interested in his quest because he will not be going through slow, pointless routines.

Types of reading material other than fiction will call for variations in the manner of skimming. In a book of information on the physical world, for instance, the kinds of information and the accuracy of the information would be especially important to notice; this could be done by dipping and sampling here and there, noting authors and consultants, comparing with what one knows. One might also notice the order of presentation (chronological? in order of closeness to children's interests?) and mode of presentation (by topics? in terms of problems?) For biography it might be useful (and easy) to note what kinds of facts the author selects, whether he limits the biography to just one time in the subject's life, and to what extent he embellishes the biographic facts with imagined situations and dialogues.

If we are looking into reference books for older children, we will quickly thumb through and note such things as indexes (any? if so, detailed?), organization into general articles or into articles on specific points of information, the straightness of the presentation of facts (much dramatization and coloring? much entertainment padding placed in the articles?), and the degree to which pictorial aids are depended on.

This skimming, or thumbing-through, technique is a great help, probably a necessity, for anyone who must become familiar and stay familiar with any book field, but it is especially useful for a person working with children's books, for they are many and varied and they are only one among many demands on a teacher's time. And it *is* quite possible. This possibility is what many teachers do not understand. This procedure is simply a matter of reading technique, and there is nothing wonderful or unusual about it. A little extra self-discipline may be necessary at first, for one is inclined to slow down on a book one likes and to go up by-alleys, but after one has established a rough sort of schedule and skimming rhythm, he will find he has still plenty of time for dawdling over favorites, maybe rereading them.

Book Sources

And now that we have a workable method of running through numbers of children's books, where do we find the books to run through? What are the main sources of children's books for the busy teacher or parent?

They are three: (1) bookstores, (2) public libraries, and (3) school libraries. Their relative usefulness depends on many factors, such as locality, economic support, and the individual's transportation and daily schedule.

1 Bookstores   Both children's bookstores and bookstores with useful juvenile collections are confined pretty much to large cities. But they are so useful and enjoyable for the person interested in children's books that one or more of them should be visited at least once or twice a year if at all possible. Also, once one has established contact with the children's departments in bookstores in metropolitan areas, he can usually get on their mailing lists, obtain special information service, and make mailing arrangements. And considerable personal satisfaction, as well as practicality and convenience, is involved in knowing a bookstore and being able to talk shop with its personnel. One gets a feeling of close involvement in the field from chatting over questions about how certain books are doing, what people are asking for, how they are reacting to a new turning in an author's work, what is in the works for a publisher of children's books or on its new list. And there is a perhaps irrational but restorative, therapeutic feeling in handling fresh new paper-packeted books before they have gone into a regular reading-use channel. Too, there is a very real advantage in being able to look at a miscellaneous collection of new books before they have undergone a sifting by librarians, reviewers, and other teachers; one can thus get the feel of current writing for children.

2 Public Libraries   Whether it be a large, semiautonomous institution in a large city's public library system or a little side room off the main reading room of the one public library in town, the children's library is generally the teacher's most useful means of inspecting and keeping up with children's books. Here the teacher has access to a large juvenile collection, and this collection is less likely than the bookstore collection to represent just the tastes and buying pressures of the moment; also, it will very likely be somewhat more representative of all the various kinds of children's reading. Another special advantage: this same collection will probably be one of the primary borrowing sources for one's own pupils, and so being familiar with it will keep one a little closer to what can actually be done in their reading.

The children's section of the public library can be a useful source of book information in other ways, too, besides providing books for inspection. It is generally the best source of bibliographic and review materials; often it supplements the standard book listing with its own special listings. These, perhaps keyed to the available books, may be related to seasonal interests, special events, the interests of particular groups—bird watchers, boy scouts, stamp collectors, model-plane makers. Often a library has a large file of such material but not much of it on display at any one time; one should therefore inquire about the possible existence of such a file. The teacher will find useful the library's listing of its new accessions; the habit of consulting the monthly list is a helpful one. And he will find the library's current book displays helpful in two ways—as a guide to books he himself might want to read and as something he might refer his pupils to. If there is an annual or semiannual book fair in his library, the teacher may find it especially valuable in these ways.

Finally, the children's library can help the teacher find his way among books by making available to him the advice of persons whose job it is to work with children and books. Librarians vary greatly in their knowledge, sharpness of observation, understanding of books and children, articulateness, and eagerness to help; but most librarians can and will help one find out where to find books without wasting time, what new books have come in, which among them are interesting in special ways, what the children are looking for and letting alone, what the young readers tell them about their reading and their wants, what the librarians' publications and meetings have suggested about current developments in children's books. All this is most valuable for the teacher trying to keep afloat in juvenile reading. Librarians work with books in a way different from the ways booksellers and teachers work with books. They are close to both the child and the book at the same moment in a manner neither bookmen nor teachers are; also, the distribution of books is their *chief* concern, not one among many as it is with teachers. Still, the librarian's business overlaps that of bookman and teacher; like booksellers (and publishers), librarians want to have books distributed widely and to have them lead to the reading of other books, and, like teachers, they want to get books into the right hands and to have them understood and to see that they lead to the further intelligent use of books. In a very real sense the public library is the keystone in the present structure of children's books, and the librarian, working at that critical point, is in a position to become very wise in matters relating to children's reading. A teacher should know well at least one children's librarian.

The teacher should be alert to all the ways in which the library's services can be used by him and by the children. He should know and use all special services the library may have for teachers; some libraries, for instance, permit teachers to take out a larger number of children's books than normally allowed and to use them for a longer than normal time, say, a month. Some libraries publish special bibliographies and mimeographed discussion sheets for teachers. Some lend teachers picture collections and book jackets related to books they may wish to use in school. They frequently arrange and conduct library tours for classes. And then there are their services to children that the teacher needs to know about and to rely on—the regular book-loan services, special loan services (book jackets, clippings and reviews of books, pictures of authors and places, art reproductions, maps), book hours and readings by librarians and sometimes by invited guests, special rooms and collections where children can find materials not available in the general collection, and such special arrangements as selections of books for borrowers who are between childhood and adulthood or for readers with foreign-language backgrounds.

It is essential that teachers really study the children's public libraries at their disposal and so come to know both their potentialities and their limitations as sources of children's reading and related activities. This study of library facilities need not be formal or stuffy, but it should be orderly; otherwise one's findings will be vague or tilted in one direction. Some sort of checklist, merely mental or written down, is necessary. Here is a suggested checklist of criteria a teacher might well have in mind during the weeks he comes to know the library on which he and his classes are going to depend most heavily.

Number of books   Are there enough for the children and teachers using this library? Absolute numbers mean nothing; a library of one thousand books may in some circumstances be quite adequate, whereas in another library a collection of twenty thousand may be entirely inadequate. The sufficiency of books might be partially determined by considering such subquestions as these: How many books are allowed to each borrower? Can one generally find the book he is after? Is there a backlog of requests for certain books? Are there multiple copies of books that are in heavy demand?

Kinds of books represented in collection   Is there a broad representation of kinds of children's books—in subject, type, tone, setting, style? For example, can one find *Freddy the Pig and* White's *Charlotte's Web*? Seuss *and* Yashima? *The Hobbit and* the Oz stories? traditional classics *and* recent things by Schlein, Krauss, and Sendak? stories *and* nonfiction biographies and travel books? In short, are there spread and balance?

Freshness of the collection   How well is the collection kept up? Are recent children's books well represented? Does the collection include good new editions of older works, as well as the older editions? Are battered copies replaced?

Availability of the books   Is the main collection on open shelves to which the children have access? Are there any kinds of children's books which are not generally available? What restrictions exist, and why? Are there provisions which make it fairly easy for advanced readers to make use of the adult as well as children's collections when they are ready? Are the checking-out and book-returning processes fairly easy, without unnecessary red tape that will discourage the borrowing of books? Are the books kept in good order so that they can be easily found? Are library hours convenient?

The librarians themselves   Are the head librarian and her assistant librarians well informed on children's literature in general and on their own collection in particular? Also, are they well informed about children's general interests, their reading interests and problems, and the place of reading activities in the local school system? Even though a librarian may know much about national reading trends, this may not help her if she is unaware how they relate to reading activities (or a lack of them) in the local schools. Are the librarians friendly with children and approachable without being smothery in their helpfulness? And are there *enough* of these librarians to go around, or are there so few that they are run ragged and into inefficiency and ill temper?

The physical surroundings   Is the children's library pleasant and inviting? Are there light but restful colors? cleanness? fresh, informal, unified design in room and furniture? Is the design of room and furnishings truly functional? Is the reading light good? Are the shelves reachable? Is the furniture of appropriate size? Is there enough room to permit free movement and at the same time quiet browsing and reading? Will the acoustics permit some talking without creating bedlam?

The library's program of public information   Are there book displays? Are they both attractive and informative? And do they get changed frequently? regularly? Do they involve more than just book jackets—for instance, objects like tools or coins or costumes that relate to the books being considered? Does the library publish lists of new books and make them easily available? Does it offer selected bibliographies of books on certain themes? Does it have prominently posted instructions on where to find and how to use library materials? And can the librarians supplement these instructions?

Supplementary activities   Is there a vigorous, varied program of activities in support of the book-lending program? Are there story and poetry readings for children? book fairs? talks on books, given either at the library or in schoolrooms? library tours? library-connected programs on radio or television?

One will probably find no library strong in *all* the categories listed above. Also, one may well argue whether some of the above facilities are desirable or undesirable. But the questions that have been presented are all questions that *should* arise in one's appraisal of children's libraries, and others may come to mind, depending on special local needs and conditions.

3 *School libraries*   Most of the criteria that apply to the public library apply to the children's school library as well, and most of the above questions may be asked of it too. The school library, however, has some special conditions of its own.

The school library's main function generally is to meet specific class needs; more often than not, individual recreational and exploratory reading is regarded as a secondary, though still important, function of the school library. So its collection is likely to reflect the instructional emphases of each grade, and also the special tastes of teachers who have influenced acquisitions. Often this breaking-up tendency is carried to a logical conclusion by splitting the library into class libraries, usually housed in the classrooms.

One type of library service existing in some large metropolitan areas, however, moves in the opposite direction toward unification and size. Under such a system the central school system builds up and operates a very large juvenile collection or depository from which individual teachers may borrow books to fill out their classroom collections. This system has the advantage of economy and inclusiveness of ordering, but it has all the weaknesses of centralization and bigness—slowness (the books may come long after the class need for them has gone), teacher delegation of responsibility for reading supplies to this far-off, impersonal source of books, and a related tendency for the decisions on which books will go to which classrooms to be made at "headquarters." Under such a system it is easy for one set of criteria, one point of view, to come to prevail in the selection of books throughout the schools in a given area.

A central factor in determining the nature of school libraries is that they tend to be more group-used than used by individual children for their own particular purposes. The school library book may be read as part of a class assignment (multiple copies may then become necessary), may be part of a teacher-guided emphasis on a certain subject or mood in so-called free reading, or may be the teacher's choice for his own reading and/or showing to the whole class. In any of these instances the selection is mainly class need, not an individual child's personal wish at the moment.

4 *Other Sources of Books*   In this little survey of book sources we have considered three main ones—the bookstore, the public library, and the school library. There are others which occasionally, under certain circumstances, can become quite important and useful to the teacher.

For the teacher who is taking postgraduate or refresher courses at a college, the college library may provide a fresh source of bibliographic information, professional articles, and children's books themselves. The courses too may be new sources; this is one valid reason for a teacher's occasionally taking a summer or night extension course related to children's reading. Single lectures or lecture series about children's books are another way to keep in touch with new developments and sometimes to obtain bibliographic aids. Membership in such professional organizations as the Association for Childhood Education often opens up to the teacher lectures and panel discussions on children's reading and sometimes brings with it periodicals and brochures containing useful information on juvenile books.

And, sometimes more important than any of the foregoing sources, there are one's colleagues in teaching. These people often very usefully suggest books and authors to inquire into, furnish clues to book sources one does not know about, and suggest ways of presenting stories to children. And they provide an excellent forum for one's own guesses, questions, and new certainties. An active exchange of experiences, ideas, articles, and children's books with colleagues is one of the most effective ways for a teacher to keep on top of this rich, constantly changing field.

Finding and Using Children's Literature outside of Books

Thus far in our survey of ways of keeping up with children's literature we have concentrated on sources of children's books and information on books. But it is wise for the adult concerned with children's literature to remain clearly aware that it also exists in other forms. Much literature, as already noted, is available to children through other channels.

1 Children's Magazines Children's magazines should be read by children, although they often are not, and so should be known by adults who have something to do with children's reading. Just as a teacher needs to have some notion of what significant books for children are being published, so he should have a general knowledge of the juvenile-magazine field and an up-to-the-minute knowledge of a few children's magazines that he has settled on as most valuable to him in his work with children. These magazines contain some good reading sometimes, provide a wide assortment of reading material, and nurture the habit of reading current magazines and newspapers (a habit that threatens almost to disappear among adolescents). Also, this is one kind of reading in which a child can very easily feel a kind of personal independence and so personal pride, and reading outside of book covers somehow (quite irrationally, of course) seems less awesome to many young readers than reading books.

There are three general kinds of magazines designed for children, in addition to magazines not intended primarily for them but of interest to many children. There is, first, the magazine definitely patterned for classroom use (generally in the elementary grades) and for use primarily by the teacher; it seeks to give a collection of materials from which the teacher can select readings and activities that fit into the day's classwork. Fantasy is generally a minor element in these magazines; most of the pieces are about historical events or travel in real places, real animal life, or everyday life in American homes and schools. Much of this material lends itself easily (almost too easily) to use by the harried teacher in social studies or other units. The stories and articles tend to relate to national holidays, anniversaries of famous people, the seasons, and steps in the school year. There is usually a good deal of game and cutout or fill-in material—turkeys for Thanksgiving, pumpkins for Halloween. The poems and songs are generally somewhat moralistic or lesson-teaching. Ordinarily, the illustrations are realistic storytelling pictures of a conventional sort. Typical magazines of this kind are *Highlights for Children* and the *Grade Teacher*. The equivalents of this type for older children are the school news magazines and *Scholastic*.

Then there are the magazines designed primarily for the individual child—*Jack and Jill, Humpty Dumpty's Magazine, Child Life, The Golden Magazine, Children's Digest.* These magazines are not aimed so much at the schoolroom as at the elementary school child at home; they are more for individual reading and play than for group activities. Their pedagogic connection is less obvious, or at least less direct. They have some stories and articles on national holidays and heroes, famous scientists and writers, etc., but the tone is often lighter, more playful, and fantasy and nonsense are more common ingredients. The games and cutouts are not so likely to be tied to learning projects. Illustrations are likely to be on the less orthodox, somewhat gayer and more decorative side. Magazines of this sort frequently pride themselves on obtaining contributions from well-known artistic and literary figures.

The equivalents of these magazines for older children are *Boys' Life, Calling All Girls,* and *The American Girl,* and, in England, *The Elizabethan* (obtainable in many public libraries in the United States). Here there is an emphasis on the story for itself—the adventurous tale of sea or warfare or exploration, the girls' story of domestic crises and romantic love, some broad humor, a few idealized biographies. These magazines have considerable variety, for they are trying to meet a large range of interests. This does not mean, though, that they do not fall into certain conventional types or stereotypes; these adolescents' magazines tend to be dominated by oversimplified thinking about what young people are and want. Still, they try to meet the needs of the types as they conceive them.

The third group of juvenile magazines, made up of denominational church-school publications, combines the instructional purposiveness of the first group and the variety entertainment of the second. These magazines (or weekly papers) devote some space to moral lessons, discussions of ethical questions, Biblical passages, and inspirational poems, but they also contain adventure, mystery, and romance stories of the kind found in *Calling All Girls.* Of the three kinds, these magazines are inclined to be the most formularized; in this respect they are like the mass-circulation adult magazines (*Saturday Evening Post,* etc.), for they too are aimed at a very large circulation.

Finally, in considering children's magazine reading, the teacher needs to be aware of those magazines which, although not designed primarily just for children, touch fields of special interest to children and are widely read by them—the nature magazines (*Nature, Audubon*), general- and applied-science magazines (*Popular Science, Scientific American*), mechanics magazines (*Popular Mechanics,* etc.), travel magazines (*National Geographic, Holiday*), and general picture magazines (*Life, Look, Horizon*). Besides having to do with subjects that concern many children, these magazines in thought and style and especially in their wide use of pictorial material are patterned for the general, nontechnical reader and so are easily read by good juvenile readers. Also, magazines of this general sort can easily serve a double function: they furnish all sorts of material easily usable in the classroom and are also well suited to the child's own free reading.

How can the teacher find and keep up with children's material in magazine form? By spending a couple of hours once or twice a year skimming the magazine racks in the public library's children's section or in a good school library. And he may find it useful then to look regularly at one or two children's magazines that he particularly esteems.

2 *Recordings*   Although the usefulness of recordings as a medium for children's literature is obvious, the business of selecting them is sometimes a sad story. For one thing, more than is true of books, the distinction between records of interest to adults and those of interest to children is blurred; for instance, many adult-intended recordings of folk songs are entirely right for children's use, better in fact than many planned solely for juvenile listening. Also, there are a vast number and variety of recordings; there is a great range of kinds of songs and readings and dramatizations, and there are widely different recordings of given selections, varying tremendously in the performer's conception of the piece, the quality of performance, the technical excellence of the recording, and availability. And in this highly competitive field the advertising does not make it any easier to select objectively, to know what is behind the newspaper and magazine blurbs. The past decade's experimentation with various speeds and stereophonic sound has further complicated the job of the teacher who wishes to use the great literary resources available on records. The result is that many teachers, probably the majority, throw up their hands despairingly. They just follow the loudest and most persistent publicity—what's in the air—or let "the audio-visual people" determine what is going to be in the class's record bag for next week. And so they remain unaware of great numbers of records that might be more appropriate to their needs.

Yet it is quite possible to keep abreast of juvenile recorded literature if one knows and regularly uses reliable sources of information, and it can be highly pleasurable.

The sources of such information roughly parallel the kinds of sources we found available in children's books. There we noted that the teacher had at his disposal (1) bibliographic sources, or book lists, (2) reviews, (3) critical and research articles, (4) the bookstores, (5) the public library, and (6) the school library or, sometimes, centralized school collection. In the record field the roughly equivalent sources are (1) catalogs, (2) magazine reviews, (3) critical and research articles, (4) record shops, (5) public record collections at public libraries, universities, and the like, and (6) the school collection and centralized audio-visual offices, city or county.

Catalogs   The lists put out by the record companies are interesting and useful to browse through. A time-saver, though, is the Schwann catalog, which tries to list all records available at present in this country; it is particularly useful in that it includes the recordings of many foreign and rather specialized record makers which one misses if he sticks to a few big-company catalogs—and in the children's field much useful recording is done by little-known groups. There are also the lists of records distributed by record-of-the-month groups. It is good to be on the watch for record lists distributed by libraries, schools, parents' and other organizations, and musical and literary groups; these are especially useful because they generally have a selective focus and are often annotated (e.g., *An Annotated List of Recordings in the Language Arts for Elementary School, Secondary School, College,* published in 1964 by the National Council of Teachers of English).

As with bibliographies, the record list is made much more meaningful by whatever relevant information one already possesses. If one knows how authentic, untrained Southern mountain folk singers sing and if he knows how Lomax collected his Library of Congress versions of "Barbara Allen," he is in a position to infer how the records on the Library of Congress list probably sound—that they are going to be different from Burl Ives's or Jean Ritchie's or Richard Dyer-Bennet's or Joan Baez's, and that they will be suitable for certain uses and not for others. It is wise for a teacher to have listened to a wide variety of folk singers so that he will know what to expect from their recordings; he might well listen to pieces done by Ives, Ritchie, Pete Seeger, Earl Scruggs, Woody Guthrie, Shep Genandes, Carl Sandburg, and Mirais and Miranda.

Magazine reviews and criticism   In a field of such mass production and range of effort, concise, perceptive reviews and critical discussions of developments are especially helpful, for through them one can sift out what may be of real interest and worthy of a personal hearing. During the past decade the reviewing of new recordings has sprung up to meet this need, and children's records have not been altogether neglected. The *Saturday Review's* "Records in Review" from time to time treats the new children's records. Children's recordings are also described in special sections of educational journals, in annual or semiannual special editions of many newspapers, and in music and record magazines.

Record shops   The usual record shop has a collection of children's records, and in larger cities one will occasionally find children's record shops. Here one can play records he is interested in. But to make the best use of this convenience, one needs to have already acquired a pretty clear notion of the general outlines of contemporary recording and also to have focused on certain kinds of records. Once one has established a working relationship with a good record shop, the shop will help one stay informed through catalogs and special notices; often shops make special efforts to help teachers with their record problems.

Public record collections   A teacher should try to find in his area a record collection which contains a section of children's records and which he will be permitted to use. City public libraries often have records and sometimes a group of children's records. Recreation centers also sometimes have them. A teacher may have access to the record collections of colleges and universities close by; their adult collections may contain records he wants to think about in connection with children, and there may be a special juvenile collection in the college or university library or audio-visual office.

School record collections   And finally, there are record collections in the schools. One's own school may have a collection; these vary from being completely inadequate to having more records than anyone could use. And in addition there are often central audio-visual offices and services, for the whole city or county, upon whose large collections one can draw. Here again, as with centralized book collections, there are the advantages of range of selection and the disadvantages of remote control over what one gets to use. The most desirable system, from the individual teacher's viewpoint, is an arrangement whereby the teacher can come to the audio office, test the records he thinks he wants, and borrow them directly. Such a collection should be large and varied enough to meet the borrowing demand, of course.

3   Motion Pictures, Filmstrips and Slides, and Picture Collections   As noted earlier, much literature for children gets retold on film, and a good deal of new literature is constantly being created for children in this medium. This storytelling can be used in its own right by the teacher, or in connection with storytelling in books and magazines and on records; but once again the teacher needs to be able to find his way around in a many-leveled mass of information and to keep up with new work.

Motion pictures related to children's reading may be conveniently classified as (1) films designed as classroom-teaching devices and (2) films intended primarily to interest children, in or out of school. The first type, in which there has been a tremendous increase during recent years, is generally made with particular classroom subjects and situations in mind—a simplified version of a Shakespearean play, a picture about Twain's life, a series of folktales, a little film about a child's first day at school, a biographical sketch of Hamilton. The second type would include Disney fairy-tale retellings or his own story cartoons, the telling of Indian legends (*The Loon's Necklace*), and film-story versions partly for the general public (*Alice in Wonderland, Treasure Island, Peter Pan, Lassie*).

But the splitting of films into films designed primarily for children and those primarily for adults is not an altogether realistic distinction, since so much of film making is slanted toward the young audience which makes up an overwhelming percentage of the total movie-going audience. The simplification of issues and characters, the emphasis on physical action and surface visual appearance, the avoidance of various kinds of adult problems, the happy outcome—these common elements of so much children's literature are common ingredients of the great majority of moving pictures. This means, of course, a great plenitude of pictures adaptable to use in classrooms.

A more realistic distinction might be drawn between (1) films which, seeking to compete for general box-office success, follow accepted, tested formulas for popular taste and (2) films of a more experimental and specialized kind which do not try directly to capture the box office. An example of this might be the difference between Disney's *Bambi* and the Swedish *The Great Adventure*, a story of an otter—or between Disney's *Alice in Wonderland* and John McClaren's whimsical little cartoons on jazz or folk-song themes. A teacher might well keep an eye out for useful films of the latter sort, which may escape one's notice because they do not get a buildup in the press.

Having a general conception of what children's fare is in movies, one's next problem is to know where to look.

The list, annotated if possible, is the logical starting place. The main lists are (1) continuing listings in such magazines as *Parents' Magazine* and the *PTA Magazine*, some of the professional educational journals, the *Saturday Review*, and *Time* and by parent and teacher and library groups, (2) occasional listings by various groups concerned with spreading information on movies and developing public taste, again including parents, teachers, and librarians, (3) lists and catalogs of various audio-visual movie pools, e.g., university extensions, art-film pools, educational-film collections, and (4) distributors' catalogs (*Encyclopaedia Britannica, Coronet*). One can get these lists directly from the source or in libraries or audio-visual pools. For lists to be useful, one needs to know the criteria behind them, what the listers ask. This is the value of full annotation. If such notes are lacking, one may make inferences from the kinds of titles that get on a series of lists and also from what he already knows about the organization sponsoring the list.

A special source of information on children's films is the program announcements of theaters and of organizations sponsoring unusual or noncommercial films—extension programs, libraries, etc. Often one finds in these announcements fine suggestions for children's film fare, even though the programs may be designed mainly for adults.

Then there are school collections of movies from which teachers can draw movies for classroom showing. Individual schools may have their own small collections; large school systems frequently have a centralized collection on which the teachers of the individual schools can draw. Usually in a large school system there is an audio-visual office in charge of the whole operation—responsible for getting out lists of new movies, setting up previews, etc. The preview is a highly desirable although sometimes inconvenient aspect of using motion pictures in classrooms.

Besides school sources of film lists and films, there are important and easily available nonschool pools of films which teachers may use. More and more public libraries are coming to have stocks of films for loan, and many of these are suitable for children. Numerous museums have special film collections which may be borrowed for classroom use, and generally the films are of a kind that offers a welcome break from the conventional diet for children. Such museums often run series of programs for children, usually on weekends; the alert teacher will try to catch these programs and may steer his children there. He will usually find in their catalogs a number of folktales, fantasies, etc., adapted to children.

Probably the simplest way for the busy teacher to learn about the movies for his children is to use the services of an audio-visual center—in his school, school system, or public library or in a nearby college or university. Such a center will usually have a good collection of catalogs and brochures, and its personnel may be able to suggest films and ways of getting them.

The filmstrip and the slide are forms of films which are frequently overlooked by the teacher but which today have much that can supplement children's reading and drama. Many nursery rhymes and folk songs have been put into these forms; dozens of folktales and modern stories for children have been made into filmstrips. And some new imagining has been recorded in this form. Both the filmstrip and the single slide have very real advantages for the teacher who does not wish to become a complete prisoner, as it is easy to become, of film directors and editors. Using the filmstrip, the teacher can slow down or speed up the story as he wishes, and he can contribute to the telling of it. He has more control over either a filmstrip or a set of slides than he has over a motion picture.

Another source of pictorial storytelling and of pictorial supplementing of stories and poems is the picture collection—the collection of photographs, drawings, reproductions, etc., which the teacher can find in almost any good library or museum. He may, for instance, find a series of photographs of a place about which the class has been reading a story—or photographs the class may use to begin its own stories—or enlargements of Tenniel's drawings for *Alice in Wonderland.*

4   Television Programs   And of course there is today the television program, which may be used more or less directly as a source of dramatized literature and related materials. Television contains within a general context of repetitious mediocrity some fine literary moments, but finding and salvaging these for their worth to children involves many problems. Like the productions of the theater, but much more so, its productions are fugitive—they come fast, one after the other, by the thousands, and there are not yet adequate systems for selecting and preserving those things of more than just passing interest. Also, viewing and previewing programs takes much time; and one cannot "read" at his own pace. And the television offerings are so massive, so overwhelming in number and viewer attack, that it is very difficult for a follower of television to preserve and develop real discrimination, to detect in the mass of dullness the glimmers of the real thing.

Still, in answer to this pressing and confused situation, a number of aids have developed that the teacher can use if he wants to expose children to the imaginative literature that television constantly presents. There are, of course, listings, daily and weekly, in newspapers and magazines; these are analogous to bibliographies. And gradually coming into existence are commentators and critics, such as Gilbert Seldes, Hal Humphrey, and Marya Mannes, who can help one think about the welter of television fare. Moreover, many of the most responsible commentators are particularly alert to children's material in television, for they realize that children constitute a very great segment of the total televiewing population.

Choice under Pressures

In his response to recordings, motion pictures, and television as sources of children's literature, the teacher may have a hard time keeping his balance and exercising sound judgment. It is very easy to be so impressed by what a medium has to offer that one accepts and uses it undiscriminatingly, in great chunks, or to be so overwhelmed by its mass that he cannot separate out the valuable parts and so rejects all of it out of hand.

There is the tremendous force of public approval—the simple fact that millions watch and apparently like certain movies and television shows, hear and apparently like certain so-called records of the month or week. And this approval is recorded and stated in so many places so frequently that it may become difficult to hear oneself think and to determine whether one agrees with this mass approval. Also, these approved records, movies, and programs are generally much more easily available than others— usually easier to go to or obtain and often, though not always, less expensive. And in a very real sense, their popularity makes it easier at first for the teacher to introduce them. If there is a choice between a Disney short and *The Loon's Necklace*, many teachers will use the Disney simply because they feel, without admitting it to themselves, that the children already like the picture before even having seen it; they are conditioned to Disney's name and the shapes, colors, and music he has used for many years. Possibly these teachers have come to identify Disney with cinematic storytelling and so to think of him first and most naturally when selecting film stories for little children. Also, the popular thing is likely to be louder, more elaborate, and maybe more sensational than the less well-known, and so it naturally is more easily noticed and less easily overlooked.

In all these ways the conventional popular mass-media offering becomes almost the automatic selection of many teachers. At the same time, some teachers, though not many, automatically reject and steer away from what has general approval. Each response is equally undiscriminating. The sensible, responsible teacher needs to have a general view of popular recordings, movies, and television programs that might be for children, for after all, intermingled with all the tasteless, souped-up, mediocre story-telling and drama one can find fine and appropriate creation. But the teacher needs to be aware of what exists outside of the few channels of temporary mass approval. To do this, he needs to know a few reliable sources of information and judgment, and to know where he can obtain relatively unpopular works when he has decided they may be what he wants. This is not at all impossible, or even difficult. It is simply a matter of first doing a little systematic survey of lists, reviews, and announcements and then using those one finds best adapted to his special needs as a teacher.

Keeping Track

This chapter has suggested many materials to inquire into—children's books, magazines, records, movies, etc.—and has suggested sources of information on each of these forms of children's literature. But such looking around may prove of relatively little value if one either does not have a photographic memory or does not have an adequate system of putting his useful findings into order for future use. Most of us do not have the photographic memory; so we need to develop some method of systematizing and preserving information that promises to be of use to us.

Essential for this purpose is the noting down of information in a uniform way and the indexed keeping of these records in a file. The mechanics of the filing system may vary widely so long as a few simple principles are followed; these principles are needed to make it likely that one will *continue* to keep the record, to assure a fair degree of accuracy, and to make the information as easily accessible as possible.

First, one needs to put down, not *all* sorts of information about the book, story, or poem, but just those kinds of information that will be useful to him as an adult selecting and using children's writings. These are (1) facts and observations which will recall those aspects of the book that will probably be important later, and (2) those facts which will make it easy to find, order, or buy the book later.

One cannot be sure just what one will want later or just how and why he will want it. But he needs to make an educated guess when he is jotting down notes about the book he has in his hand right now. Later he will need to recall whether it was fictional narrative prose, a biography, a nature guide, or what; he thinks he will never forget this, but he will. Then he will want to know what in general the book was about. If it was fiction, he will want to know what the main problem or situation was, and the one or two main characters with their dominant characteristics—in short, a few lines' sketch of the content. If it was biography or history or geography, then he will want to have in a phrase the main person, event, or place treated, and perhaps (here is where one needs to figure ahead) what aspects of the subject were focused on (the exciting action of the event itself? the people in it? the atmosphere? the effects of the event? the boyhood of a famous man or his mature working years or the effects of his work? his happier years or his sadder?). Also, one may want to jot down his present observations about (1) the writer's or illustrator's style (excited? quiet? broad or more sophisticated in humor? everyday or unusual vocabularly?) and (2) possible special uses and limitations of the book (specially suited to certain ages and interests? special information or vocabulary difficulties?). Such information may be jotted down in single words, phrases, or sentences; the important thing is that one record observations that will help him five months or a year or eight years from now in recalling what he *then* needs to remember about the book.

Here are some miscellaneous kinds of information that specific teachers may find important to record, depending on particular conditions: size of book, exterior appearance, substantiality of binding, arrangement of illustrations and printing on page (what proportion of unfilled space? illustrations and printing mixed? an illustration for each poem or for just some?), size and elaborateness or simplicity of print, degree of paper glare, tables of contents and indexes, special tie-ins with other books (sequels? similar subjects? borrowings?). A teacher of primary grades, for instance, would foresee the problem of size of print and book for small children, and so these would be items in his records.

And besides these facts about the *nature* of the book one needs to record facts that will enable him to identify and locate it. Generally, these are (1) the author's and illustrator's names, (2) the name of the piece of writing, (3) the publisher, and (4) the date of publication. Other kinds of data may be desired, too: (1) whether part of a series, and if so, name of the series, (2) what edition, and if revised, any new features, and (3) cost. In children's books the illustrator's name is much more important to know than in most works for adults; and *Alice in Wonderland* illustrated by John Tenniel is a significantly different book from the *Alice in Wonderland* illustrated by Leonard Weisgard.

The primary indexing would be by author's name and by title; that is, there would be for each book two cards, one under the author's name, the other under the name of the book; only one of the cards need contain the descriptive notes, of course. The index maker may, however, foresee uses of his index that would call for further cross filing. He might decide to cross-index by author's name and book title and subject—or by these three plus age levels. He might desire a separate file in which these same cards were grouped according to literary type—fiction, biography, poetry, etc. But in any case it is necessary that a clear plan be worked out at the very beginning and be adhered to rigorously.

Two special types of files prove useful to many teachers working with children's reading materials. One is the file—usually cards, but possibly sheets of paper or large cardboards—of entire poems, sometimes even short stories or sketches. The typed or clipped-out piece is pasted on the card or sheet. For easy reference the author's name and the work's title should always be typed at the top of the card or sheet. A second useful type of file is that of pictures relating to reading—scenes from books or scenes that *suggest* books, pictures of foreign lands which are the subjects of books, pictures of places and events and authors, reproductions of art related to the reading. A regular indexing system and matting uniform in size, placement, etc., are essential to a useful picture file. If one has access to book jackets, these may contribute to such a file or possibly have a file of their own.

One's Own Library

Besides the information on children's reading one can collect from bibliographies, etc., and from one's own reading and looking and listening, a teacher who is working with children's books will find it useful to have a small but good working library on children's books and, if possible, a small library of children's books. These are not essential; with school and public libraries to draw on, the teacher need not be bookless. Still, these libraries are often so heavily used they cannot be relied upon to provide what you want just when you want it, and so a small but flexible, growing collection in the children's book field can be very useful. In this collection one might have one or two reasonably recent general studies of children's literature (e.g., Edna Johnson's [with Evelyn Sickles and Frances Clarke Sayers], May Hill Arbuthnot's, Bess Porter Adams's, Anne Thaxter Eaton's, Nancy Larrick's), a file of the past year's *Horn Book, School Library Journal, Elementary English,* or some other journal containing bibliographies and critical articles, and maybe recent catalogs of children's records and motion pictures. As for children's books, to buy a large number at once is generally too costly to be practical, but one can usually build up a useful, representative little collection gradually. He can pick just those books he thinks he may use more than once in his classes and can try to get a representation of the kinds of books he likes to use, so that whenever he wants to use a book with a certain tone or on a certain subject, he will not be left high and dry upon finding the library copies are all out on loan. One may keep the costs down by using professional discounts when available and by watching for the occasional "remainders" sales in children's book sections; moreover, the paperback has entered the children's field, and Alcott's, Stevenson's, and Twain's books and many other children's books are now available at low prices.

One should be able to accumulate at least the core of a good children's library over a period of about a year for $50 or $60; if one watches carefully, one should be able to obtain twenty to thirty children's books without spending more. This is not enough books, but it is a solid beginning.

Being Aware

The intelligent worker with children's reading will not believe that recent books are necessarily better than earlier books or that current preferences are better than tastes of other periods, but at the same time he will realize that much excellent literature for children is constantly coming out as part of a huge stream; he will know that many fine things appropriate for what he wishes to do have just recently been printed and should at least be considered. But even more important to him may be the feeling of participation—actually, of creation—one gets from looking at recent work that has not yet stood the test of years of judgments. Looking at such work critically and carefully is, in a way, contributing to the establishment of the children's literature of the future, and feeling this can give a special bounce to one's own reading and professional use of books.

What developments might the teacher be alert to in juvenile literature? These depend on his special interests and needs, but they can include some of the following: (1) interesting new authors and illustrators, new works by authors and illustrators one already knows, or new shifts visible in their new works; (2) new publishing houses, new combinations of old firms, or new policies in the juvenile departments of existing publishers; (3) developments of emphasis in certain subject areas or types of juvenile books and new approaches to subject matter; (4) shifts in manner, tone, and purpose in writing and illustrating for children and critical and teacher reaction to these; (5) new methods and problems in the choice and use of children's books in schools, libraries, and homes; (6) new services in libraries, audio-visual centers, and museums; (7) current activities in art, television, motion pictures, radio, and recording that are related in various ways to children's reading; and (8) the continuing debate over the relation of children's reading to other influences on them and to their thought and behavior.

SUGGESTED SOURCES

Newbery Medal Books

1922   **Van Loon, Hendrik Willem:** *The Story of Mankind*, Liveright.

1923   **Lofting, Hugh:** *The Voyages of Doctor Dolittle*, Stokes.

1924   **Hawes, Charles Boardman:** *The Dark Frigate*, Little, Brown.

1925   **Finger, Charles J.:** *Tales from Silver Lands*, Doubleday.

1926   **Chrisman, Arthur:** *Shen of the Sea*, Dutton.

1927   **James, Will:** *Smoky*, Scribner.

1928   **Mukerji, Dhan Gopal:** *Gay-neck*, Dutton.

1929   **Kelly, Eric P.:** *The Trumpeter of Krakow*, Macmillan.

1930   **Field, Rachel:** *Hitty, Her First Hundred Years*, Macmillan.

1931   **Coatsworth, Elizabeth:** *The Cat Who Went to Heaven*, Macmillan.

1932   **Armer, Laura Adams:** *Waterless Mountain*, Longmans.

1933   **Lewis, Elizabeth Foreman:** *Young Fu of the Upper Yangtze*, Winston.

1934   **Meigs, Cornelia:** *Invincible Louisa*, Little, Brown.

1935   **Shannon, Monica:** *Dobry*, Viking.

1936   **Brink, Carol Ryrie:** *Caddie Woodlawn*, Macmillan.

1937   **Sawyer, Ruth:** *Roller Skates*, Viking.

1938   **Seredy, Kate:** *The White Stag*, Viking.

1939   **Enright, Elizabeth:** *Thimble Summer*, Rinehart.

1940   **Daugherty, James:** *Daniel Boone*, Viking.

1941   **Sperry, Armstrong:** *Call It Courage*, Macmillan.

1942   **Edmonds, Walter:** *The Matchlock Gun*, Dodd, Mead.

1943   **Gray, Elizabeth Janet:** *Adam of the Road*, Viking.

1944   **Forbes, Esther:** *Johnny Tremain*, Houghton Mifflin.

1945   **Lawson, Robert:** *Rabbit Hill*, Viking.

1946   **Lenski, Lois:** *Strawberry Girl*, Lippincott.

1947   **Bailey, Carolyn Sherwin:** *Miss Hickory*, Viking.

1948   **Du Bois, William Pène:** *The Twenty-one Balloons*, Viking.

1949   **Henry, Marguerite:** *King of the Wind*, Rand McNally.

1950   **De Angeli, Marguerite:** *The Door in the Wall*, Doubleday.

1951   **Yates, Elizabeth:** *Amos Fortune, Free Man*, Aladdin.

1952   **Estes, Eleanor:** *Ginger Pye*, Harcourt.

1953   **Clark, Ann Nolan:** *Secret of the Andes*, Viking.

1954   **Krumgold, Joseph:** *And Now Miguel*, Crowell.

1955   **DeJong, Meindert:** *The Wheel on the School*, Harper.

1956   **Latham, Jean Lee:** *Carry On, Mr. Bowditch*, Houghton Mifflin.

1957   **Sorensen, Virginia:** *Miracles on Maple Hill*, Harcourt, Brace & World.

1958   **Keith, Harold:** *Rifles for Watie*, Crowell.

1959   **Speare, Elizabeth George:** *The Witch of Blackbird Pond*, Houghton Mifflin.

1960   **Krumgold, Joseph:** *Onion John*, Crowell.

1961   **O'Dell, Scott:** *Island of the Blue Dolphins*, Houghton Mifflin.

1962   **Speare, Elizabeth George:** *The Bronze Bow*, Houghton Mifflin.

1963   **L'Engle, Madeline:** *Wrinkle in Time*, Farrar, Straus & Cudahy.

1964   **Neville, Emily:** *It's like This, Cat*, Harper.

1965   **Wojciechowska, Maia:** *Shadow of a Bull*, Atheneum.

1966   **De Trevino, Elizabeth Borton:** *I, Juan de Pareja*, Farrar, Straus & Cudahy.

Caldecott Medal Books

The illustrator's name is followed by the author's name when the author and illustrator were different persons.

1938 **Lathrop, Dorothy:** *Animals of the Bible*, Stokes.

1939 **Handforth, Thomas:** *Mei Li*, Doubleday.

1940 **D'Aulaire, Ingri and Edgar:** *Abraham Lincoln*, Doubleday.

1941 **Lawson, Robert:** *They Were Strong and Good*, Viking.

1942 **McCloskey, Robert:** *Make Way for Ducklings*, Viking.

1943 **Burton, Virginia Lee:** *The Little House*, Houghton Mifflin.

1944 **Slobodkin, Louis:** James Thurber, *Many Moons*, Harcourt, Brace & World.

1945 **Jones, Elizabeth Orton:** Rachel Field, *Prayer for a Child*, Macmillan.

1946 **Petersham, Maud and Miska:** *The Rooster Crows*, Macmillan.

1947 **Weisgard, Leonard:** Golden MacDonald, *The Little Island*, Doubleday.

1948 **Duvoisin, Roger:** Alvin Tresselt, *White Snow, Bright Snow*, Lothrop.

1949 **Hader, Berta and Elmer:** *The Big Snow*, Macmillan.

1950 **Politi, Leo:** *Song of the Swallows*, Scribner.

1951 **Milhous, Katherine:** *The Egg Tree*, Scribner.

1952 **Mordvinoff, Nicolas:** Will and Nicolas (pseuds. for William Lipkind and Nicolas Mordvinoff), *Finders Keepers*, Harcourt, Brace & World.

1953 **Ward, Lynd:** *The Biggest Bear*, Houghton Mifflin.

1954 **Bemelmans, Ludwig:** *Madeline's Rescue*, Viking.

1955 **Brown, Marcia:** Charles Perrault, *Cinderella*, Scribner.

1956 **Rojankovsky, Feodor:** John Langstaff, *Frog Went a-Courtin'*, Harcourt, Brace & World.

1957 **Simont, Marc:** Janice May Udry, *A Tree Is Nice*, Harper & Row.

1958 **McCloskey, Robert:** *Time of Wonder*, Viking.

1959 **Cooney, Barbara:** *Chanticleer and the Fox*, Crowell.

1960 **Ets, Marie Hall:** *Nine Days to Christmas*, Viking.

1961 **Sidjakov, Nicolas:** Ruth Robbins, *Baboushka and the Three Kings*, Parnassus Press.

1962 **Brown, Marcia:** *Once a Mouse*, Scribner.

1963 **Keats, Ezra Jack:** *The Snowy Day*, Viking.

1964 **Sendak, Maurice:** *Where the Wild Things Are*, Harper & Row.

1965 **Montresor, Beni:** Beatrice Schenk de Regniers, *May I Bring a Friend?* Atheneum.

1966 **Hogrogian, Nonny:** Sorche Nic Leodhas (pseud. for Leclaire Alger), *Always Room for One More*, Holt.

Bibliographies of Children's Literature

The following two lists do not comprise an inclusive listing of bibliographies of children's literature but are a selection intended to *illustrate* the kinds of useful reference sources available to the adult who wishes to keep abreast of children's books and to be able to find specific items of information quickly. List A contains references to the general field; list B contains references to publications of more specialized concern.

A. General Bibliographies

Adams, Bess Porter: *About Books and Children,* Holt, 1953. Large lists of children's books according to age and type—humor, fantasy, animals, etc.

American Library Association: *A Basic Book Collection for Elementary Grades,* 7th ed., 1960.

————: *A Basic Book Collection for High Schools,* 6th ed., 1957.

————: *A Basic Book Collection for Junior High Schools,* 1960.

————: *Let's Read Together: Books for Family Enjoyment,* 2d ed., 1964.

————: *Subject and Title Index to Short Stories for Children,* 1955.

————: *Subject Index to Books for Intermediate Grades,* 3d ed., ed. by Mary K. Eakin, 1963.

————: *Subject Index to Books for Primary Grades,* 2d ed., comp. by Mary K. Eakin and Eleanor Merritt, 1961.

————: *Subject Index to Children's Magazines,* ed. by Meribah Hazen. Monthly except June and July.

————: *Subject Index to Poetry for Children and Young People,* 1957.

————: **Children's Services Division:** *Notable Children's Books.* Annual list.

Arbuthnot, May Hill: *Children and Books,* 3d ed., Scott, Foresman, 1964. Very useful annotated bibliography with each chapter.

Best Books for Children, Bowker, published annually.

Bibliography of Books for Children, Bulletin of Association for Childhood Education International, 1960.

Brewton, John E., and Sara A.: *Index to Children's Poetry,* H. W. Wilson, 1942. Supplement, 1959. Indexed by author, title, subject, and first line.

Bulletin of the Center for Children's Books. The University of Chicago, Graduate Library School. Monthly except August.

Children's Books Too Good to Miss, 3d ed., ed. by May Hill Arbuthnot, Western Reserve University, 1963.

Children's Catalog, H. W. Wilson. New editions every five years, with annual supplements

Crouch, Marcus: *Treasure Seekers and Borrowers: Children's Books in Britain, 1900–1960,* Library Association, London, 1962. Useful annotated lists, mainly of British books.

Cumulative Book Index: A World List of Books in the English Language, H. W. Wilson. Includes juvenile books.

Eakin, Mary K. (compiler and ed.): *Good Books for Children*, rev. ed., The University of Chicago Press (Phoenix Books), 1962. Annotated selection of children's books reviewed in *Bulletin of the Center for Children's Books* from 1948 through 1961.

Eastman, Mary Huse: *Index to Fairy Tales, Myths and Legends*, Faxon, 1926. Supplements, 1937 and 1952.

Eaton, Anne Thaxter: *Treasure for the Taking: A Book List for Boys and Girls*, rev. ed., Viking, 1957. Supplement to *Reading with Children*.

Education Index. Lists articles appearing in a large number of education journals; thus indexes much material on children's literature.

Eyre, Frank: *20th Century Children's Books*, Bentley, 1953. A British selection of contemporary children's books.

Fenner, Phyllis: *The Proof of the Pudding: What Children Read*, John Day, 1957.

Frank, Josette: *Your Child's Reading Today*, Doubleday, 1960.

Growing Up with Books, Library Journal. Annually in August.

Guilfoile, Elizabeth: *Books for Beginning Readers*, ill. by Norma Phillips, National Council of Teachers of English, 1963. More than three hundred books for beginning readers.

Huck, Charlotte S., and Doris A. Young: *Children's Literature in the Elementary School*, Holt, 1961. Annotated listings of adult references on types and aspects of children's books; unannotated lists of children's books; a useful reference work.

Johnson, Edna, et al.: *Anthology of Children's Literature*, 3d ed., Houghton Mifflin, 1959. Contains graded reading list.

Junior Book Awards, Boys' Club of America. Children's selections; subject classification.

Kunitz, Stanley J., and Howard Haycraft (eds.): *The Junior Book of Authors*, 2d ed., H. W Wilson, 1951. Biographies of children's authors, with listings of works. Supplement, *More Junior Authors*, ed. by Muriel Fuller, 1963.

Larrick, Nancy: *A Parent's Guide to Children's Books*, Pocket, 1958.

"Literature for Children," from *World Book Encyclopedia*, Field Enterprises Educational Corp., 1960.

Mahony, Bertha E., and Elinor Whitney Field: *Newbery Medal Books, 1922–1955*, Horn Book, 1955.

Mahony Bertha E., et al.: *Illustrators of Children's Books, 1744–1945*, Horn Book, 1947. Supplement, Ruth Hill Viguers et al., *Illustrators of Children's Books, 1946–1956*, Horn Book, 1958.

National Council of Teachers of English: *Adventuring with Books*. List revised frequently.

"Seven Stories High," comp. by Anne Carroll Moore, reprinted from *Compton's Pictured Encyclopedia*, Compton.

Smith, Irene: *A History of the Newbery and Caldecott Medals*, Viking, 1957.

Tooze, Ruth: *Your Children Want to Read: A Guide for Teachers and Parents*, Prentice-Hall, 1957.

B. Examples of Book Lists with Special Emphases

Barlow, Mildred: *Human Relations in the Primary Grades*, National Conference of Christians and Jews. Also Ray Schmiedlin, *Human Relations in the Intermediate Grades*, and Irene Horney, *Human Relations in the Junior High School.*

Books about Negro Life for Children, ed. by Augusta Baker, New York Public Library, 1961.

Books Are Bridges, American Friends Service Committee and the Anti-Defamation League of B'nai Brith, 1957.

Boylan, Lucile, and Robert Sattler: *A Catalog of Paperbacks for Grades 7 to 12*, Scarecrow Press, 1963.

Children's Books on Alaska, comp. by Ellen Martin Brinsmade, Adler's Book Shop, Fairbanks, Alaska, 1956.

"Children's Literature about Foreign Countries," comp. by Marjorie Scherwitzky, reprinted from *Wilson Library Bulletin*, October, 1957.

"Christmas Materials in General Children's Books," comp. by Hilda K. Limper, reprinted from *Wilson Library Bulletin*, November, 1952.

Good Reading for Poor Readers, comp. by George Spache, Garrard, 1960.

Growing Up with Science Books, comp. by Julius Schwartz and Herman Schneider, *Library Journal.*

Huus, Helen: *Children's Books to Enrich the Social Studies for the Elementary Grades*, National Council for the Social Studies, 1961.

"I Can Read It Myself!": Some Books for Independent Reading in the Primary Grades, ed. by Frieda M. Heller, Ohio State University, Center for School Experimentation, Columbus, Ohio.

Kenworthy, Leonard: *Introducing Children to the World in Elementary and Junior High Schools*, Harper & Row, 1956.

Latin America in Books for Boys and Girls, Child Study Association, Children's Book Committee, 1956.

Light the Candles! comp. by Marcia Dalphin, Horn Book, 1953.

Roos, Jean Carolyn: *Patterns in Reading: An Annotated Book List for Young Adults*, 2d ed., American Library Association, 1961.

Selected Bibliography of Books, Films, Filmslides, Records and Exhibitions about Asia, United States National Commission for UNESCO, GPO, Washington.

The Southwest in Children's Books: A Bibliography, ed. by Mildred P. Harrington, Louisiana State University Press, 1952.

Stories to Tell, ed. by Isabella Jinnette, Enoch Pratt Free Library, Baltimore, 1956.

Strang, Ruth, et al.: *Gateways to Readable Books: An Annotated Graded List of Books in Many Fields for Adolescents Who Find Reading Difficult,* H. W. Wilson, 1958.

Tooze, Ruth, and Beatrice Krone: *Literature and Music as Resources for Social Studies,* Prentice-Hall, 1955

Useful Sources of Bibliographies and Articles Relating to Children's Books

Bulletin of the Center for Children's Books, The University of Chicago, Graduate Library School. Monthly, except August.

Childhood Education, Association for Childhood Education International, monthly, September through May. Contains "Books for Children" and "Books for Adults."

Child Study, Child Study Association of America, Quarterly.

Education. Monthly, except July and August.

Elementary English, National Council of Teachers of English, monthly, October through May. Includes regular section, "Books for Children."

Elementary School Science Bulletin, National Science Teachers Association. Monthly, September to April.

Horn Book. Continuing bibliographies; six times yearly.

London Times Literary Supplement. Special issues in spring and fall devoted to children's books; a good way to keep in touch with British writing for children.

New York Times Book Review. Book Week issue in fall devoted to children's books.

Parents' Magazine. Monthly.

PTA Magazine, monthly, except July and August.

Publishers' Weekly. Annual children's book number.

Saturday Review. Weekly; special issues on children's books.

School Library Journal. Formerly entitled Junior Libraries. Monthly from September to May; articles and continuing bibliographies.

Wilson Library Bulletin, monthly, except July and August. Contains "School and Children's Libraries" section.

Indexes Containing References to Children's Literature

Education Index

Reader's Guide to Periodical Literature

International Guide to Periodical Literature

Juvenile Magazines

The American Girl

Boys' Life

Calling All Girls

Child Life

Children's Digest

The Eizabethan, interesting English publication for children

The Golden Magazine

The Grade Teacher

Highlights for Children

Humpty Dumpty's Magazine

The Instructor

Jack and Jill

Scholastic

Adult Magazines of Special Interest to Children

American Heritage

Arizona

Audubon

Holiday

Horizon

Life

Look

The National Geographic

Nature

Popular Mechanics

Popular Science

Scientific American

SOURCES OF
QUOTED
MATERIALS

Arnold, Matthew: "The Forsaken Merman," from *Poetical Works*, ed. by C. B. Tinker and H. F. Lowry, Oxford University Press, 1950.

Baruch, Dorothy: "Lawn-mower," from *I Like Machinery*, Harper, 1933.

Benét, Stephen Vincent: From "The Ballad of William Sycamore," from *Ballads and Poems: 1915–1930*, by Stephen Vincent Benét. Copyright 1931 by Stephen Vincent Benét. Copyright © 1959 by Rosemary Carr Benét. Reprinted by permission of Holt, Rinehart and Winston, Inc.

Bland, David: *History of Book Illustration*, World Publishing Company, 1958, p. 388.

Brown, Abbie Farwell: "The Fairy Book," from *Songs of Sixpence*, Houghton Mifflin, 1914. By permission of Houghton Mifflin Company.

Bunyan, John: *Pilgrim's Progress*, Holt, Rinehart and Winston, 1961, p. 9.

Burgess, Gelett: "Polite Talk" and "Touching Others' Things," from *New Goops and How to Know Them*. Copyright 1951 by Random House, Inc. Reprinted by permission.

Chaffee, Eleanor: "The Cobbler," *American Junior Red Cross News*, October, 1938. By permission of Eleanor Chaffee.

Coleridge, Samuel Taylor: "Rime of the Ancient Mariner," from *The Portable Coleridge*, ed. by I. A. Richards, Viking, 1961, pp. 80–105.

Colum, Padraic: *The Adventures of Odysseus and the Tale of Troy*, The Macmillan Company, 1918. Copyright 1918 by The Macmillan Company, renewed by Padraic Colum and Willy Pogány, 1946. Reprinted by permission of The Macmillan Company, p. 157.

Conkling, Hilda: "Little Snail," from *Poems by a Little Girl,* by Hilda Conkling. Copyright 1920, 1948 by Hilda Conkling. Published by J. B. Lippincott Company.

Dana, Richard: *Two Years before the Mast,* Doubleday & Company (Dolphin Books), pp. 315, 345.

Day, Thomas: *The History of Sandford & Merton: Moral and Instructive Entertainment for Young People,* James K. Simon, Philadelphia, 1851, pp. 69–75.

Defoe, Daniel: *Robinson Crusoe,* Signet Books, The American Library of World Literature, pp. 62–63.

De la Mare, Walter: From "The Cupboard," from *Collected Poems,* Henry Holt and Company, 1920.

————: "Sleepyhead," from *Poems for Children,* Henry Holt, 1930. By permission of the Literary Trustees of Walter de la Mare and The Society of Authors as their representative.

Dickens, Charles: *David Copperfield,* in *The Works of Charles Dickens,* Chapman and Hall and Charles Scribner's Sons, 1897, vol. 15, pp. 467–470.

Field, Eugene: From "Fairy and Child," from *Poems of Childhood,* Charles Scribner's Sons, 1904. By permission of Charles Scribner's Sons.

————: "Rock-a-By Lady," from *Poems of Childhood,* Charles Scribner's Sons, 1904. By permission of Charles Scribner's Sons.

Field, Rachel: "The Visitor," copyright 1926 by Doubleday & Company, Inc., from the book *Taxis and Toadstools,* by Rachel Field. Reprinted by permission of Doubleday & Company, Inc. Permission also granted by The World's Work Ltd.

Foss, Sam Walter: "House by the Side of the Road," from *Dreams in Homespun,* 1897. Permission granted by Lothrop, Lee & Shepard Co.

Freeman, Mary E. Wilkins: "The Ostrich Is a Silly Bird," in Elizabeth Sechrist, *One Thousand Poems for Children,* Macrae Smith, 1946.

Fyleman, Rose: "Mice," copyright 1932 by Doubleday & Company, Inc., from the book *Fifty-one New Nursery Rhymes,* by Rose Fyleman. Reprinted by permission of Doubleday & Company, Inc. Permission granted outside the United States of America by The Society of Authors as the literary representative of the late Rose Fyleman.

————: From "Yesterday in Oxford Street," copyright 1918, 1920 by George H. Doran Company, from the book *Fairies and Chimneys,* by Rose Fyleman. Reprinted by permission of Doubleday & Company, Inc. Permission granted outside the United States of America by The Society of Authors as the literary representative of the late Rose Fyleman.

Guest, Edgar A.: From "See It Through," from *Collected Verse,* Reilly & Lee Company, 1934, p. 119. Permission granted by Reilly & Lee Company.

Hood, Thomas: From "Ben Battle," from *The Comic Poems*, Moxon, 1876.

Janeway, James: From preface to *A Token for Children: Being an Exact Account of the Conversion, Holy and Exemplary Lives and Joyful Deaths of Several Young Children*, printed for T. Norris and A. Bettesworth, London, 1711(?).

Keach, Benjamin: From *War with the Devil, or the Young Man's Conflict with the Powers of Darkness, in a Dialogue Discovering the Corruption and Vanity of Youth, the Horrible Nature of Sin, and the Deplorable Condition of Fallen Man*, New York, 1707, p. 177.

Kingsley, Charles: "Ballad of Earl Haldan's Daughter," from Charles Kingsley, *Poems*, Macmillan, 1889.

Kipling, Rudyard: From "If," copyright 1910 by Rudyard Kipling, from the book *Rudyard Kipling's Verse: Definitive Edition*. Reprinted by permission of Doubleday & Company, Inc., and Mrs. George Bambridge. Also by permission of Mrs. George Bambridge, The Macmillan Co. of Canada, Limited, and Macmillan & Co., Ltd.

Leaf, Munro: From *Manners Can Be Fun*, rev. ed., J. B. Lippincott, 1936, 1958, pp. 21, 22, 26–27, 29.

Lenki, Lois: "Supermarket," from *The Life I Live: Collected Poems*, Henry Z. Walck Co., 1965. Permission to reprint granted by author.

Longfellow, Henry Wadsworth: From "A Psalm of Life," in *Complete Poetical Works*, Houghton Mifflin, Cambridge ed.

MacLeod, Mary: From *The Book of King Arthur and His Noble Knights*, J. B. Lippincott Company, 1949. Permission to reprint granted by J. B. Lippincott Company, pp. 4–5.

Malory, Sir Thomas: *Le Morte d'Arthur*, Everyman's Library ed., 2 vols., J. M. Dent, 1906, pp. 10–11.

"The Milkman's Horse" (author unknown), from *Read-together Poems*, ed. by Helen A. Brown and Harry J. Heltman, Row, Peterson & Company, 1961.

Moodey, Eleazer: From *The School of Good Manners*, Boston, 1772, pp. 69–70.

Nesbit, E. (pseud. for Edith Bland): From *The Railway Children*, Ernest Benn, Ltd., 1957. Permission to reprint granted by John Farquharson Ltd., pp. 26–27.

Noyes, Alfred: From "The Highwayman," from *Collected Poems*, by Alfred Noyes. Copyright 1906, 1934 by Alfred Noyes. Published by J. B. Lippincott Company. Permission outside the United States of America granted by Hugh Noyes.

Opie, Iona and Peter: From *The Oxford Dictionary of Nursery Rhymes*, Clarendon Press, Oxford, 1952. Permission to reprint granted by The Clarendon Press, Oxford.

Perrault, Charles: "The Fairies," from *Fairy Tales*, Tales for Children from

Many Lands ed., J. M. Dent & Sons, Ltd. Permission to reprint granted by J. M. Dent & Sons, Ltd.

Richards, Laura E.: "Eletelephony," from *Tirra Lirra*, by Laura E. Richards, by permission of Little, Brown and Co. Copyright 1935 by Laura E. Richards.

Rieu, E. V. (trans): From *Homer's Iliad*, Penguin Classics, Penguin Books, Ltd. Permission to reprint granted by Penguin Books, Ltd., Pp. 42, 94, 392.

Rossetti, Christina Georgina: From *Goblin Market*, ill. by Arthur Rackham, Lippincott, 1933.

Scott, Elizabeth Manson: "My Bed," from *Another Here and Now Story Book*, comp. by Lucy Sprague Mitchell. Copyright 1937 by E. P. Dutton & Co., Inc. Renewal © 1965 by Lucy Sprague Mitchell. Reprinted by permission of the publishers.

Sidney, Margaret (pseud. for Harriet Mulford Lothrop): From *Five Little Peppers and How They Grew*, Lothrop, 1881. Permission to reprint granted by Houghton Mifflin Company, pp. 7–8.

Stevenson, Robert Louis: "The Cow," "At the Sea-side," and from "Farewell to the Farm" and "Block City," from *A Child's Garden of Verses*, ill. by Tasha Tudor, Oxford University Press, 1947.

Taylor, Jane (attributed to): "I Like Little Pussy," in *Favorite Poems Old and New*, ed. by Helen Ferris, Doubleday & Company, 1957.

Tennyson, Alfred: "Sweet and Low," from *The Complete Poetical Works of Tennyson*, Cambridge ed., Houghton Mifflin, 1898.

Tippett, James S.: "Fourth Floor!" from *I Live in a City*, by James S. Tippett. Copyright 1927 by Harper & Row, Publishers, Incorporated; renewed 1955 James S. Tippett.

————: "Ferryboats," from *I Go a-Traveling*, by James S. Tippett. Copyright 1929 Harper & Row, Publishers, Incorporated; renewed 1957 James S. Tippett.

Van Dyke, Henry: "Four Things," from *Poems of Henry Van Dyke*, Charles Scribner's Sons, 1930. Permission to reprint granted by Charles Scribner's Sons.

Watts, Isaac: From "The All-seeing Eye," from *Divine Songs, Attempted in an Easy Language for the Use of Children*, Boston, 1774.

————: From "How Doth the Little Busy Bee," from *Divine and Moral Songs for Children*, Religious Tract Society, London, 1869.

"Whisky Frisky" (anonymous), from *Read-together Poems*, ed. by Helen A. Brown and Harry J. Heltman, Row, Peterson & Company, 1961.

INDEX
OF
AUTHORS,
ARTISTS,
AND
TITLES

Note: page numbers in italics refer to bibliographical listings